The
Cornell
School of Hotel Administration
on Hospitality

www.hotelschool.cornell.edu

The Cornell

School of Hotel Administration

on Hospitality

Cutting Edge Thinking and Practice

Edited by
Michael C. Sturman
Jack B. Corgel
Rohit Verma

WILEY

John Wiley & Sons, Inc.

Published by John Wiley & Sons, Inc., Hoboken, New Jersey.
Published simultaneously in Canada.

For general information on our other products and services or for technical support, please contact our
Customer Care Department within the United States at (800) 762-2974, outside the United States at
(317) 572-3993 or fax (317) 572-4002.

Wiley also publishes its books in a variety of electronic formats. Some content that appears in print may
not be available in electronic books. For more information about Wiley products, visit our web site at
www.wiley.com.

Library of Congress Cataloging-in-Publication Data:

The Cornell School of Hotel Administration on hospitality: cutting edge thinking and practice / edited
by Michael C. Sturman, Jack B. Corgel, Rohit Verma.
    p. cm.

  Includes bibliographical references and index.
  ISBN 978-0-470-55499-9 (cloth)
  ISBN 978-1-118-01620-6 (ebk)
  ISBN 978-1-118-01625-1 (ebk)
  ISBN 978-1-118-01626-8 (ebk)
  1. Cornell University. School of Hotel Administration. 2. Hospitality industry—Study and teaching—
New York (State)—Ithaca. 3. Hotel management—Study and teaching—New York (State) 4. Hospitality—
Study and teaching—New York (State) I. Sturman, Michael C. (Michael Craig) II. Corgel, Jack B., 1948-
III. Verma, Rohit. IV. Cornell University. School of Hotel Administration. Career Services Office.
  TX911.5.C585 2011
  647.94071—dc22

                                                                                    2010043313

Printed in the United States of America

10 9 8 7 6 5 4

We are extremely thankful for the support
of the Center for Hospitality Research,
and to Glenn Withiam for all the work he did
and contributions he made
to the creation of this book.

Contents

Foreword   xi
Michael D. Johnson

Chapter 1
Four Paths to Success in the Hospitality Industry   1
Michael C. Sturman, Jack B. Corgel, and Rohit Verma

Chapter 2
The Essence of Hospitality and Service   5
Giuseppe Pezzotti

Part I
SUCCESS IN YOUR HOSPITALITY CAREER

Chapter 3
Preparing for a Successful Career in the Hospitality Industry   21
Kate Walsh, Michael C. Sturman, and Bill Carroll

Chapter 4
The Listening Fast Track   37
Judi Brownell

Chapter 5
Developing and Managing Your Multinational Career   52
Jan Katz

Chapter 6
Becoming a Leader in the Hospitality Industry   65
Timothy Hinkin

PART II
SUCCESS THROUGH OPERATIONS AND SERVICE EXCELLENCE

Chapter 7
Understanding and Predicting Customer Choices   83
   Rohit Verma

Chapter 8
Guiding the Guest Experience   97
   HaeEun Helen Chun

Chapter 9
Harnessing the Power of Your Culture for Outstanding Service   111
   Robert Ford and Michael C. Sturman

Chapter 10
A Scientific Approach to Managing Hospitality Operations   127
   Gary M. Thompson

Chapter 11
Motivating Your Staff to Provide Outstanding Service   142
   Michael C. Sturman and Robert Ford

Chapter 12
How to Build Service Quality into Your Operation   159
   Alex M. Susskind

Chapter 13
Demand Management   174
   Bill Carroll

Chapter 14
Revenue Management for Enhanced Profitability:
   An Introduction for Hotel Owners and Asset Managers   192
   Chris Anderson and Sheryl Kimes

Chapter 15
Competing Successfully with Other Hotels: The Role of Strategy 207
Cathy A. Enz

Chapter 16
Focus on Finance: Aiming for Restaurant Success 227
Alex M. Susskind and Rupert Spies

PART III
SUCCESS AS A REAL ESTATE AND BUSINESS OWNER

Chapter 17
Hospitality Property Ownership: Where You Fit In 247
Jack B. Corgel, Robert Mandelbaum, and R. Mark Woodworth

Chapter 18
Hospitality Properties: How Much to Pay if You're Buying;
How Much to Ask if You're Selling 270
Jack B. Corgel

Chapter 19
Gaining Maximum Benefit from Franchise
Agreements, Management Contracts, and Leases 293
Jan A. deRoos

Chapter 20
Developing and Renovating Hospitality Properties 309
Jack B. Corgel, Jan A. deRoos, and Kevin Fitzpatrick

Chapter 21
Planning and Programming a Hotel 321
Jan A. deRoos

Chapter 22
Measuring Hotel Risk and Financing 333
Peng Liu and Daniel Quan

PART IV
SUCCESS THROUGH MANAGERIAL EXCELLENCE

Chapter 23
Segmenting and Targeting Your Market: Strategies and Limitations   353
  Michael Lynn

Chapter 24
New Media: Connecting with Guests throughout
  the Travel Experience   370
  Lisa Klein Pearo and Bill Carroll

Chapter 25
Building and Managing Your Brand   388
  Robert J. Kwortnik

Chapter 26
Hotel Revenue Management in an Economic Downturn   405
  Sheryl Kimes and Chris Anderson

Chapter 27
Addressing Employee Lawsuits   417
  David Sherwyn and Paul E. Wagner

Chapter 28
Coordinating Information and Controlling Costs   430
  Gordon Potter

Chapter 29
Making the Most of Your Human Capital   444
  J. Bruce Tracey and Sean A. Way

Chapter 30
You Can't Move All Your Hotels to Mexico:
  Unions and the Hospitality Industry   455
  David Sherwyn and Paul E. Wagner

Chapter 31
The Integrity Dividend in Hospitality Leadership   469
Tony Simons

FINAL THOUGHTS

Chapter 32
Afterword: Where Do You Go from Here?   483
Michael C. Sturman, Jack B. Corgel, and Rohit Verma

Index   487

FOREWORD

When John Wiley & Sons, Inc., approached us with this project it immediately brought to mind the great works in this series, works that exemplify the core competencies of the world's best business programs. From *Wharton on Dynamic Competitive Strategy* to *Kellogg on Marketing*, the Wiley "on" series provides a unique platform designed to demonstrate how a collection of highly talented faculty develops a comprehensive and unique body of knowledge that is both academically advanced and business practical. Clearly, our "on" is hospitality. More specifically, the uniqueness that personifies our school, faculty, students, and alumni is hospitality leadership. Unlike traditional general management schools, the Cornell School of Hotel Administration grounds a first-class business education in the practice of a particular industry. We hire the best and brightest business academics, who apply theory to practice to generate new knowledge for the industry. As a result, we hold a singular position as the premier institution for educating future hospitality industry leaders.

Our focus on hospitality leadership underscores the evolution of the hospitality industry. When Dean Howard Bagnall Meek founded the Cornell program back in 1922, hospitality education focused on hotel and restaurant operations and what we would call today unit-level management. The prototype career path of the day was to become a bellboy who, over time, worked his way up to become a hotel or restaurant general manager, in what was, from a gender, cultural, and geographic standpoint, a relatively homogeneous industry. Yet Dean Meek understood how a mom-and-pop industry would both consolidate, through the creation of larger and larger businesses structures, and diversify over time, thus offering business management and business leadership opportunities for a diverse and global population of undergraduates, master students, and executives. Put simply, while yesterday's students could complete on knowing the hospitality business, tomorrow's leaders must master the business of hospitality and how to lead large, complex organizations. Today's hospitality students grow to become the entrepreneurs who change the world, the leaders who deliver operational excellence across global platforms, and the deal makers who shape the industry. As tomorrow's leaders they will oversee a vast spectrum of the global economy, from hotel and restaurant companies to resorts and theme parks to cruise lines, gaming properties, and senior living facilities, and to the retailers and supply chains that serve them all.

Our uniqueness, and the resulting content of this work, is based not just on our hospitality context but on the knowledge that competing in a service business is fundamentally different from competing in a manufacturing economy. While the world is filled with outstanding general management programs, many of their models and frameworks remain holdovers from an economy dominated by manufactured goods, an economy in which business strategy drives company culture. With consumer durables or nondurables, for example, we continue to segment markets, develop innovative product offerings for those segments, and then form teams within our organization to execute on those strategies. In a core service business like hospitality, however, culture drives strategy. A service company's values, which is the core of its culture, directs how its leaders, managers and front-line service employees deliver their value proposition and satisfy customers. Be it the Four Seasons Hotels' "golden rule" or Ritz-Carlton's motto that "We are ladies and gentlemen serving ladies and gentlemen," the strength of a service company's culture dictates where and how well it competes. This collection of research, tools, perspectives, and their implications, exemplifies the peerless quality of our context, hospitality, and the principles for competing in a service business. The insights range from how to develop your service employees' careers to how to manage for operational excellence to how to own and manage your real estate and other physical assets.

This book has benefited tremendously from the input and talents of multiple individuals. On behalf of all of us at Cornell, a very special thank you goes to Richard Narramore, Senior Editor for John Wiley & Sons, Inc., who came to us with this great idea and supported us all along the way. So many talented authors contributed collectively to the richness of this volume, including our lecturers, professors, their colleagues, and our alumni industry leaders. Yet every project needs champions. In this case, the champions at Cornell were clearly the editors, Michael Sturman, Jack B. Corgel, and Rohit Verma, to whom I am deeply grateful. Through their dedication and hard work, *The Cornell School of Hotel Administration on Hospitality: Cutting Edge Thinking and Practice* is the most comprehensive work to date on how to compete in the hospitality industry and beyond.

Michael D. Johnson
Dean and E.M. Statler Professor
Cornell School of Hotel Administration

CHAPTER 1

FOUR PATHS TO SUCCESS IN THE HOSPITALITY INDUSTRY

MICHAEL C. STURMAN, JACK B. CORGEL, and ROHIT VERMA

The book you are about to read distills and shares the expertise of the faculty of the world's preeminent school focusing solely on hospitality industry education. Founded in 1922 at the specific request of the hotel industry, the Cornell University School of Hotel Administration is the oldest school of its kind and the only Hotel School within an Ivy League university. Our mission is to promote hospitality leadership, which we achieve through a combination of teaching, research, and industry collaboration. The 70 faculty members of the school seek to expand the state of knowledge in the industry—whether by creating new knowledge through research, teaching those who are eager to learn, or disseminating knowledge through consulting, writing, and presentations—and help develop the future leaders of the hospitality industry.

This book is another means through which we achieve our mission, and our intent is to give you a comprehensive overview of the hospitality industry. Although we've been sharing research information with our industry from the very beginning, we have never attempted to compile a book such as this one, where we go into detail on the breadth of topics studied at our school. The chapters include the contributions of 28 of our faculty, who have a combination of over 450 years of teaching, 400 years of research, 250 years of hospitality industry experience, and 350 years of consulting with the industry. Selected alumni and friends of the school also made valuable contributions to the book. As we share with you much of what we know about the industry, we hope to provide you with both a broad introduction to topics pertinent to the industry and insights that reflect in-depth state-of-the-art thinking. We combine theory and application, experience and learning, and lessons from the past with visions of the future.

ORGANIZATION OF THE BOOK

We begin the book with the view that business is service. While this book provides insights from a variety of disciplines on a diversity of topics, it is valuable to reflect first on the business we are in. Chapter 2 captures the essence of hospitality and service and the views of service-providers who truly "get it," from famous leaders in the field to dedicated line-level employees. This then sets the stage for the rest of the book.

When we began organizing this book, we sought to organize it around a clear theme. The unwritten subheading for the book became *How to Be Successful in the Hospitality Industry*. The resulting sections of the book align with the following four "paths to success," which reflect the various disciplines studied in the Cornell University School of Hotel Administration:

Section 1: Success in Your Hospitality Career
Section 2: Success through Operations and Service Excellence
Section 3: Success as a Real Estate and Business Owner
Section 4: Success through Managerial Excellence

Each section describes a different way in which you can be successful in the hospitality industry.

The first section considers how you can be a success from the perspective of managing your career. If you are new to the industry, how do you break in? Once in the industry, how do you develop yourself to become a leader in the industry? Jobs in the hospitality industry require you to have certain knowledge, skills, and abilities so you can move up the organizational ladder. The industry also requires the right personal characteristics so that you can love what the job requires and can make a career in the industry a good fit. This section of the book builds on what we have learned about educational and personal development at Cornell's School of Hotel Administration that has worked to create successful careers in the hospitality industry. Chapters in this section include contributions by our faculty in communications, human resources, management, and organizational behavior.

The second section moves from the individual to the business. Any successful hospitality operation—be it a hotel or restaurant, chain or independent, low-cost provider or luxury establishment—requires an effectively performing individual operation. You have to attract the right customers, have the service product, set the right price for your product, and provide the right level of service—all the while managing your employees the right way to achieve your goals. This requires a combination of knowledge from a variety of disciplines, and thus this section includes contributions from our faculty in human resources, management, marketing, operations, and strategy.

The book's third section considers the path to success you may follow as an owner. Ownership of property serves as an important part of the foundation for entire economies, social systems, and individual industries, not the least of which is the hospitality industry. The wealth of hospitality owners increases in accordance with their ability to build and retain their operation's cash flows. In this industry, you can achieve success by owning hotels, restaurants, and other types of hospitality businesses, by owning the real estate underlying these businesses, and by owning both. This section of the book is intended to help you understand the actions available to owners for wealth creation that have been developed and studied at the Cornell University School of Hotel Administration. In many important components of the hospitality industry, control of the business operations has become increasingly separated from ownership of the real estate. The chapters in this section therefore emphasize the profitable actions of hospitality real estate owners who hold the rights to the residual cash flows from their properties. Contributions to this section come from our faculty in finance and real estate, along with prominent school alumni.

The final section of the book takes the perspective of the decision maker in the corporate office—or the person who is responsible for leading a business team at any level. The requirements for managerial excellence when managing a chain of properties or restaurants differ in magnitude from those when managing a single property (although the industry's different levels have many principles in common). At the corporate office, you need to choose the right strategy, manage your brand, coordinate information, control costs, and implement the right systems to achieve success at multiple locations simultaneously. Single-unit operators or those with several units also share many of these strategic responsibilities. Based on our studies of the hospitality industry, this section highlights some of the major areas that require attention to successfully manage a set of hotel properties or restaurants, and provides guidance as to what research and experience has shown can enhance your likelihood of operating a successful multiunit company. Contributions come from a diverse faculty, representing accounting, human resources, law, management, marketing, operations, and organizational behavior.

PATHS TO YOUR SUCCESS

The paths to success described in this book provide you with what we believe is an insightful introduction to content provided at Cornell University's School of Hotel Administration. Our current curriculum exposes our students to each of these paths, providing them with the opportunity to pursue them as they see best. Alumni of the school provide innumerable examples of those who have found success down each of these routes—some have joined the corporate world, others have set up consultancies to assist industry operators, and many have become entrepreneurs in their own right. Importantly, our graduates return to the school and share their learning with the faculty and with current students. The lesson here is that you are not required to pick only one of the four paths we examine in this book. Indeed, the best and the brightest, and the most successful in the industry, have pursued all four at some point during their careers. Whatever career you choose, you need to manage that career, but that career may bring you through managing a single property, owning a property, and then even owning multiple properties and running a chain.

As co-editors of this book, we have combined and organized a wealth of information, from an institution representing one of the best sources of hospitality industry knowledge that exists. While each chapter is based on extensive research and industry experience, we have sought to communicate this information in a clear, straightforward, nonacademic way. We believe that you will find this material interesting, but more importantly, we hope you find it to be useful. That is, we expect that what you learn from this book will change the way you manage your career and your operation. It is by fostering change that the Cornell University School of Hotel Administration succeeds in furthering the state of the art in hospitality, and ultimately in helping forge hospitality leaders. By disseminating knowledge, our goal is to provide insights that help you *do* something differently than you would have without that knowledge. That's why this book doesn't so much present specific data on the industry (although that's in here), as it provides actionable information. At Cornell University's School of Hotel Administration, we aim to bridge the gap between science and practice. By reducing the divide that often exists between the two, we hope to assist current and future leaders of the hospitality industry in knowing how to conduct their business better—for everyone's benefit.

CHAPTER 2

THE ESSENCE OF HOSPITALITY AND SERVICE

GIUSEPPE PEZZOTTI

When you think of the term *hospitality*, many things might come to mind. Perhaps you might think of the famous pineapple, the legendary symbol of hospitality. Some sources trace the pineapple's symbolism to Christopher Columbus, who introduced them to Europe when he returned from the Americas. Another source says the native Caribs used pineapples as a sign of welcome in their villages. Most sources agree that colonial-era sea captains would put out pineapples—a rare fruit at the time—when they returned from voyages, to share with visitors. This practice established the connection between the pineapple and hospitality.

Here at the Cornell School of Hotel Administration, this symbol embodies the concept of hospitality, as we study and teach the many functions that go into our industry. In the spirit of hospitality, we have made every effort in this book to distill what we have learned and what we teach. But before we focus on what research and practical experience tells us regarding the practice of hospitality, let's take a moment to reflect on the fundamental purpose of this industry: providing hospitality.

Let's start this chapter by considering the meaning of hospitality. I want to distinguish hospitality from service, even though they are closely related. Along the way, I also provide quotes showing how many people in our industry—people who know how to provide great hospitality and service— think about these terms. Although I draw a distinction between hospitality and service, I also want to emphasize that the two must go together. To be successful in this industry you must successfully provide both hospitality and service.

THE MEANING OF HOSPITALITY

Hospitality and service are both distinct and interrelated. Hospitality is like strategy, whereas service is its tactics. I believe that they both are integral to every business, and they are fundamental to our industry.

Let's look at hospitality. The Latin words *hospitalitem, hospes,* and *hostis* ("friendliness to guests") mean to welcome with warmth and care. Hospital also comes from that stem, with the concept of caring about human beings who are ill and in need of support, caring, and love. When I talk about hospitality, I talk about guests, and purposely do not use the word *customers.* I believe that the word *customer* is a less welcoming word than *guest,* because customer focuses us on the financial transaction, while guest brings out the full dimensions of hospitality. Hospitality is an essential value in most of the world's cultures. Here in North America, we have formalized the essence of hospitality in the Thanksgiving holiday, which is based on the concept of caring and appreciation.

The word *customer* derives from the word *customary,* and may imply taking the client for granted. In the hospitality industry, however, we need to greet our guests or clients with a warm, genuine welcome. Under this circumstance, we can see that we create an environment that reduces stress and is completely different from the outside world. Here, we expect a warm and hospitable surrounding with a prompt, proper, expedient, and professionally delivered service.

What Is Hospitality?

"To me, hospitality is the art of making someone feel welcomed, appreciated, and important. It's conveyed by words, facial expressions, and body language. During that person's visit, the art of hospitality is continually reinforced. It's not a one-time thing. It's an experience that lasts the entire course of the visit. I mentioned to you that several decades ago, one of the restaurant trade magazines asked their readers why their favorite restaurant was their favorite restaurant. The answers were: hospitality, atmosphere, service, food, and price."

—*Burton "Skip" Sack, chairman and partner,*
Classic Restaurant Concept

"Hospitality: We are in the hospitality business. The first thing I tell people when I define hospitality is that you must be friendly, professional, and be ready to help the guests with whatever it might be."

—*Wolfgang Puck, chef-owner*

"Hospitality is welcoming a person into your environment, such as your hotel or restaurant, your home, or even your office, and making them feel warm and secure and that they will be cared for."
—*John Sharpe, former president and CEO of the Four Seasons Hotels and Resorts*

"Hospitality: To go above and beyond for the guest and be pleasant."
—*Nealy Warfe, waitress (Statler Hotel, Ithaca, New York)*

"Hospitality: Graciousness; the art of making people feel welcomed, comfortable, and at ease, preferably in a seemingly effortless manner."
—*Abigail Charpentier, human resources VP, ARAMARK Sports, Entertainment & Conventions*

"Hospitality: It can be summed up in one word: trust. I trust that you care about me. I trust that I will be welcome at your hotel (or home or restaurant). I trust that my experience will be rich and rewarding. This all leads to me, the guest, being loyal and faithful to you (and your "brand"). This can only be measured in qualitative terms. I "feel" your hospitality and measure it with my heart, not my brain."
—*Jim Joseph, President & Chief Executive Officer, Oneida Ltd.*

"Hospitality: The ability to make people feel comfortable in their surroundings and to connect with them in a genuine and personable manner. Being courteous and smiling are among the hallmarks of hospitality, as is being genuinely concerned for your guest's experience and thinking one step ahead of them at all times."
—*Shane O'Flaherty, president and CEO, Forbes Travel Guide*

"To me, hospitality is to give our guests a sincere and warm welcome; make them feel important, confident, happy, and comfortable; and let them share a privileged moment around the table."
—*Chef Daniel Boulud (New York City)*

"When I think of hospitality, I think of providing warm, caring, genuine service. I think we need to take care of our guests in a thoughtful, caring way as if we were welcoming them into our homes. If ever we come across as aloof, I think we have failed as a hotel."
—*Maria Razumich-Zec, general manager, regional vice president, USA East Coast, The Peninsula (Chicago)*

(continued)

(continued)

"Hospitality: We strive to consistently deliver a Bloomingdale's experience that is both personal and engaging. We want our customers to feel a sense of community, where fashion and style are always made easy to navigate."

— Tony Spring, president and chief operating officer, Bloomingdale's

"Hospitality: Welcoming people, and the customer is always the boss."

—Greg Suresi, manager of Delta Sonic Carwash
(Rochester, New York)

"Hospitality is foremost the application of the golden rule or treating others as you would expect to be treated yourself. While largely universal, every country and culture has its own unique expectations as to how to provide a friendly, welcoming and generous treatment of visitors, which is the essence of hospitality."

—Michael D. Johnson, Dean, E. M. Statler Professor,
Cornell University School of Hotel Administration

"Hospitality: To make someone feel welcome or providing a warm and inviting experience to someone."

— Stephen Weisz, president, Marriott Vacation Club Int'l.

"Hospitality is an extension of the Golden Rule, where you offer whatever is needed for another person, expecting nothing in return."

—Glenn Withiam, executive editor, Cornell Hospitality Quarterly,
Cornell Center for Hospitality Research

"Hospitality is the art and service is the act of giving. Hospitality is a sincere and selfless relationship, connection between a host and a guest. Service is the way the host builds and demonstrates that connection."

—Deniz Omurgonulsen, vice president, membership,
Leading Hotels of the World

"Hospitality is service with heart."

—Staci Chen, assistant director of private dining,
Restaurant Daniel (New York City)

"Hospitality: Try to make the guest to be as comfortable as possible."

—John Hornbrook, dishwasher machine operator
(Statler Hotel, Ithaca, New York)

"Hospitality is the broad concept of making one feel welcome that often includes all or most of the following: a state of mind, a place, actions, environment, expectations including the generation of emotions that are done in concert and is measured both by delivering the intended experience and the level of appreciation by the recipient."

—*Arthur L. Buser, president and CEO, Sunstone Hotel Investors*

"Hospitality: Try to be the best for the people who come to your restaurant hoping they will come back. You always want to leave a good impression so they will never forget your place."

—*Sirio Maccioni, Le Cirque (New York City)*

"When our team, led by the incomparable impresario Joe Baum, opened Windows on the World 35 years ago in 1976, we said that our job was providing legitimate pleasure to people. But in truth it is even more than that; it is making people feel that you really are bringing them into your own home and treating them like family."

—*Dennis J. Sweeney, vice president, operations (1976),*
INHILCO (World Trade Center Restaurants)

THE MEANING OF SERVICE

Now, let's look at service, which has the concepts of being helpful or to be of use, or offering a favor or kindness. The Latin word *servitium,* meaning "act of serving," demonstrates a creative and encompassing function with many nuances and subtleties. The result is attention to details, small and large.

When we analyze the words *hospitality* and *service,* we can see that they are interwoven into each other. Under certain aspects, hospitality is the totality and service is a part of it. Let me share three examples of hospitality, connected with excellent service.

Great Service Means Being Personal

I still vividly remember this encounter. It was August 3, 2009, at 7:30 PM, and I was traveling on the New York Thruway, I-90. I reached the Seneca rest stop, not far from Rochester, New York, and I purchased a package of PB&J sandwich crackers, which cost $1.29. Since I was out of cash, I paid with my credit card. The cashier took my card and without hesitation said, "Good evening, Mr. Pezzotti, and welcome." She then thanked me for my patronage and asked if there was anything else she could help me with. Moreover, she made the point to ask me the spelling of my first name. After such an example of hospitality and service, she gave me the receipt with her name on the top. I made a point of thanking her by name (Judy). What was amazing to watch is that she similarly thanked all patrons using their credit cards, addressing them with their last name, and for the people paying cash, she would address them using Sir or Ma'am. This was quite shocking and special, as I would expect such treatment at the world's finest hotels or restaurants, but not at a thruway stop in the middle of nowhere, for a packet of $1.29 crackers.

Great Service Means Providing Extra Value in Unexpected Ways

A few years ago, I took a group of restaurateurs and hoteliers to visit a number of restaurants in Rochester, New York. At our first stop, a Burger King restaurant, members of our group were pleasantly surprised to find a vase with a bouquet of flowers in the ladies' washroom, and a small plant in the men's room. We had 35 people in our group, but as we ordered our food, the staff remained polite and welcoming, took the food order expediently, and put up the orders promptly, with no mistakes. All of the group members were surprised to see such service and hospitality. Though we never met him, this restaurant owner expressed hospitality and service to us. No corporate policy required plants and flowers in the washrooms. Instead, the independent franchisee personally saw to it that this particular Burger King was memorable.

Great Service Means Having a Personal Touch

In January 1991, I was visiting The Classics Restaurant at the Cleveland Clinic in Ohio. As I was paying the check after having enjoyed an excellent meal, I noticed that the maître d' made a point to call valet parking for my

---

What Is Service?

"Service: The art of catering to the wants and needs of an individual and going so far as anticipating those wants and needs. Excellent service is friendly, helpful, prompt and anticipatory. It exudes warmth and caring and concern. Sometimes, in high-priced restaurants, service is efficacious and professional but lacks warmth and caring. It's more robotic than meaningful. Excellent service happens when the customer's expectations are exceeded by the experience."

—*Skip Sack, chairman and partner, Classic Restaurant Concept*

"Service: Our guests expect great service, which should not be overly formal or stiff. I like when the service staff is friendly, knowledgeable, knows the ins and outs of the menu and wine list, and is not intrusive but always with an eye on the table so that before the customer has a chance to raise his hand, the staff should already be at the table. Anticipation is important."

—*Wolfgang Puck, chef-owner*

"Service is placing yourself at the disposition of others, anticipating their reasonable needs and freely offering the meeting of these needs, with integrity and caring, to the best of your ability."

—*John Sharpe, former president and CEO of the Four Seasons Hotels and Resorts*

"Service: Giving guests what they desire."

—*Nealy Warfe, waitress (Statler Hotel, Ithaca, New York)*

"Service: To take care of another's needs; best when anticipated not asked for."

—*Abigail Charpentier, human resources VP, ARAMARK Sports, Entertainment & Conventions*

"Service: The execution of hospitality. It too can be summed up in one word: time. If I deliver what I say I'm going to deliver with speed and accuracy and ease-of-doing-business, I demonstrate that the guest's time is precious. Service is measured quantitatively (with my brain)."

—*Jim Joseph, president and chief executive officer, Oneida Ltd.*

"Service: The ability to engage with guests in a discreet, professional, and warm manner, to take advantage of each moment one has with a guest, to interact with them as individuals, and to put the guest before all else."

—*Shane O'Flaherty, president and CEO, Forbes Travel Guide*

"When I think of Service, I think of going above and beyond the expectations of our guests."

—*Maria Razumich-Zec, general manager, regional vice president, USA East Coast, The Peninsula (Chicago)*

(continued)

(continued)

"Service: Relationships are the cornerstone of our model. Customers are looking for great merchandise but many times will return because of great service. Our associates are expected to build their business through loyal clients who will reward personalized care."
>—*Tony Spring, president and chief operating officer, Bloomingdale's*

"Service: Making the guest happy and make sure their experience is a memorable one."
>—*John Hornbrook, dishwasher machine operator*
>*(Statler Hotel, Ithaca, New York)*

"Service: The washing of the car and the proper follow-up if the customer is not satisfied with our service."
>—*Greg Suresi, manager of Delta Sonic Carwash*
>*(Rochester, New York)*

"Ultimately, service is the ability to deliver a great customer experience either as a solution to a customer problem or to provide an unmet need. Very few services are new to the world, just new to the company providing them; otherwise, customers would provide the service themselves. An outstanding service provider allows customers to trade off money for time or time for money."
>—*Michael D. Johnson, Dean, E. M. Statler Professor,*
>*Cornell University School of Hotel Administration*

"For if the success of a hotel is dependent upon its kitchens and its table—as it is—the kitchens and the restaurant in their turn are dependent upon the hotel management . . . and what is good food if it is not finely served?"
>—*Cesar Ritz, host to the world*

"Service: Doing something for someone else, providing a good, providing an activity."
>—*Stephen Weisz, president, Marriott Vacation Club Int'l.*

"When it comes to good service, my philosophy is simple: Treat the customer the way you would like to be treated. That means your servers have to understand what it means to be a customer. In our training, we insist that all the servers we hire eat in the restaurant they'll be working in. It's elementary. The success of our hirees is inherent in their personalities. We can train someone until they're blue in the face, but a candidate has to be genuinely sensitive and caring. Perhaps the distillation of hospitality is 'caring.'"
>—*Drew Nieporent, owner, Myriad Restaurant Group*

"There is no 'definition' for service. No customer is the same, and each has their preferences of the type of service they want. For example, a first-time flier appreciates constant attention from our flight attendants. But the frequent flier prefers to be left alone. Korean Air has a high standard of customer service because we train our employees to adapt to each individual rather than become a smiling robot. This is not an easy task because we are not mind readers and the world is our customer. But our belief in Service Excellence and the confidence and professionalism of our employees enables us to touch the hearts of our customers every day."

—Yang Ho Cho, Korean Air chairman and chief
executive officer

"Service: an act of providing a valued need."

—Arthur L. Buser, president and CEO,
Sunstone Hotel Investors

"Service: All you can do is try your best and put the customer first."

—Sirio Maccioni, Le Cirque (New York City)

"Service is anticipation, knowing what a guest needs even before he or she has that thought. Service is not just folding the toilet paper roll into a neat triangle or asking the diner, "Is everything all right?," but it is the sensitive application of attitude and product knowledge being done in a one-on-one setting, that makes a guest feel informed, comfortable, and important at the same time."

—Dennis J. Sweeney, vice president, operations (1976),
INHILCO (World Trade Center Restaurants)

vehicle. As the valet attendant seated me, to my pleasant surprise the car was already warmed up, and—here's the thing—my seat position was as I left it. I still recall that I felt well cared for on that cold winter day. This was an example of hospitality and service that still remains indelible in my memory.

THE INTERSECTION OF HOSPITALITY AND SERVICE

I'm sure that you have had experiences like the ones I just described. Clearly, hospitality and service are not descriptions of a business, so much as they are innate qualities and special attributes that a person possesses. You cannot buy them. You either possess them or you do not. You cannot invent them. Hospitality comes from inside a human being. In each of these three examples, we see that what makes the difference is the person—and it is the person who has the power to deliver hospitality and service.

My own approach to hospitality includes something I have done since I started teaching at Cornell University. I have always tried to learn the names of my students, including their middle name and the city or town they came from. I see this to be an effort that includes hospitality and service because it is an expression of warmth, welcome, caring, and service. I consider learning their names as an expression of this hospitality and service. As human beings, we place high value and importance to our name. So I feel that it is important for students not to have to repeat their names.

In the sidebars accompanying this chapter, I have shared quotes from people at all levels and in diverse segments of the hospitality and service industries. Most are leaders, but some are simply line staff. From them, we can learn a lot about their approach to hospitality and service.

After having read and analyzed all of these quotes from the professionals who were willing and gracious enough to share with me, I think you will see a thread or pattern of words and thoughts. Before you read those quotes, I must tell you that each one said the same thing before they gave their answer about what is hospitality and what is service. Each one said, "Let me think about it." This is important, because hospitality and service are at the heart of our business. Certain words were often repeated with regard to hospitality, including *warmth, friendly, heart, listening, respect, treatment, security, guest, understanding, sensitivity, genuine, memorable,* and *unique*. A different set of words described service, however, including *mechanical, measured, efficacious, technical, delivery, products, scripted, standards,* and *anticipation*.

Looking at those descriptions of hospitality, we see innate qualities that are emotional and that deal more with feelings. Even though I believe the principles of hospitality can be taught, I also believe that it is almost impossible to teach adults to be hospitable if they do not have an internal force or push that they internalized while growing up. So, even though we teach hospitality, it remains abstract because it stems in part from emotions.

If hospitality is heavily qualitative, then service is more quantitative. Service can be scripted and dictated, mechanical and drilled. You can evaluate service more easily than hospitality. Service is repetitive, efficient, consistent, continuous, tailored, customized, and sustainable. Unlike hospitality, service is much easier to perfect through training, drill, exercise, and continuous commitment. With such practice, service can be taken to the highest level of technical perfection. But for true excellence, service and hospitality must combine. One cannot exist without the other.

What Is the Difference Between Hospitality and Service?

"Hospitality is the valued way in which we treat our guests. Hospitality is all about the small details that turn a guest's ordinary visit into an extraordinary stay. Extraordinary service is the vehicle by which we deliver this incomparable experience to the guest."

—Elizabeth Blau, CEO, Blau and Associates

"My view is that service comes from thinking of the head. Hospitality comes from that plus intuition of the gut and emotions from the heart."

—Ted Teng, president and CEO, Leading Hotels of the World

"Hospitality: Graciousness. Service: Respect"

—Randy Morton, president and CEO, Bellagio Resorts/Las Vegas

"I believe that hospitality and service are one and the same . . . both provide an umbrella for treating people first of all with dignity and then giving them an experience that exceeds their expectations. Those expectations vary dependent on the type of product and level of cost, but in all cases if a person gives hospitality and service as they would like to receive, they will understand the correct level to provide to the guest. It is always better to provide a level extra and to provide it in a consistent way."

—David Hanlon, former president and CEO, Rio Casino/Las Vegas

"Hospitality is showing others you are on their side. It builds relationship, has a warm feeling, offers flexibility, understanding and comes from the heart. Service is the technical procedure of doing our work. It is the transaction; has trained/industry knowledge; is systematized, competent, and comes from the intellect. Service defines what we do and hospitality personalizes how we do it. Success results from the integration of Service and Hospitality. Here is the Success Formula:

Integrity = Service ^ (Hospitality)

I = S (to the H degree)

H is exponential thus very powerful!"

—Chick Evans, owner, Maxie's Supper Club and Oyster Bar (Ithaca, New York)

(continued)

(continued)

"Hospitality and Service are two sides of the same coin. One is incomplete without the other. Hospitality and Service can achieve the desired results only when it is done with your heart."
—*Mohan Nair, maitre d'hotel (Statler Hotel, Ithaca, New York)*

"Hospitality is the smell of my food; service is the taste of my food."
—*Hamed Suleiman, street vendor, New York City*

"One can be taught how to provide technical service; however, a hospitable disposition is innate and therefore cannot be taught. Service is the foundational element in each touch point of the guest experience (e.g., order taking and food delivery in a dining environment or guest check-in and check-out in a lodging environment). Service can be conducted in a mechanical manner by a trained service professional, based on procedures established by management . . . this is the level at which many establishments deliver service and that most people experience as acceptable but not memorable—therefore, not necessarily worth a second visit. The guest experience, however, can be enhanced when delivered by a hospitable service professional. Examples include genuinely engaging the guest in a conversation to ascertain his/her general expectation of the service experience, which then enables the service professional to anticipate the guests' needs, add extra touches and make the guest feel welcomed—resulting in a more memorable guest experience and increasing the likelihood of a return visit and positive word-of-mouth endorsements."
—*Elizabeth Ngonzi, president, Amazing Taste*

"Great service can be scripted and measured; true hospitality is innate, unselfish, and forever memorable."
—*Marc Bruno, president, ARAMARK Stadiums,*
Arenas, and Convention Center

"Hospitality: A clean cab, warm in the winter and cool in the summer. Service: To take the passenger to the right place quickly."
—*Mikhail Grigoriev, cab driver, New York City*

"Understanding the distinction between service and hospitality has been at the foundation of our success. Service is the technical delivery of a product—or *how well* you do your job. Hospitality is how the delivery of that product makes its recipient feel—or *who you are* while you do your job. Service is a monologue—we decide how we want to do things and set our own standards for service. Hospitality, on the other hand, is a dialogue.

To be on a guest's side requires listening to that person with every sense, and following up with a thoughtful, gracious, appropriate response. It takes both great service and great hospitality to rise to the top."

—*Danny Meyer, owner, Union Square Hospitality Group*

"Regarding hospitality and service: I have always viewed service as a key element of hospitality. In providing great service to a guest or customer, the customer feels important, comfortable, special, safe. . . . Being hospitable/providing hospitality includes all of those elements, of course, in addition to the physical product (room, food, beverage, etc.). Thus my belief that it is a key subset . . . which can more easily offset deficiencies in the physical product than the other way around. . . ."

—*Ed Evans, senior vice president, chief human*
resources officer, Univar

So, as I have said, hospitality and service are two critical concepts that are unavoidably intertwined. Hospitality and service should work in conjunction and synchronicity, to borrow from the Sting song, so you can provide a total experience for the guest. As an example of how a guest experience fails when either service or hospitality is missing, let's think about a guest going to a restaurant or else checking into a hotel. Say that our guest receives a most hospitable and warm welcome. But then the food takes forever, or the room is not clean. The warm hospitality is for naught, because the service side of the equation is missing. Now let us look at that same guest, but this time the guest receives a poor, careless reception, because the captain or front desk associate is busy or distracted. But the restaurant's food and service are sparkling, and the hotel room is delightful. Even with that superlative service, the experience is still poor because the hospitality side is lacking. Much of what you will read in

Quotes on Hospitality and Service

"Why is service so important to your company's success? The most obvious reason is that services have come to dominate our economies."

—*Michael D. Johnson, Dean, Cornell University School*
of Hotel Administration

(continued)

(continued)

"Every day you can polish or you can tarnish your image."
—John Sharpe, president and CEO, Four Seasons,
addressing the 2002 graduating class of the School
of Hotel Administration

"Sometimes doing your best is not good enough; sometimes you must do what is required."

—Winston Churchill

"They [nurture teamwork] by recruiting people most likely to be team players, by modeling teamwork in senior management, by establishing such high performance standards that attainment requires teamwork, by celebrating group effort and achievement and minimizing any type of [prima donna or individualistic approach]."

—Leonard L. Berry,
Professor, author, and expert on customer service

this book involves perfecting service and operations, but remember that hospitality is the factor underlying it all. This is nothing new; the world's great restaurant and hotel chains are all founded on this principle.

I end this chapter where we began. As expressed in the following quotes, we are all in the business of hospitality and service. It is my sincere view that hospitality is a like a religion, and service is its mantra. You can be selling food or forklifts and you will still need to provide an appropriate level of hospitality and service.

While I use many quotes throughout this chapter, I would like to end with the quote by Ellsworth Statler, the hotel industry leader who was the great benefactor of the School of Hotel Administration. You'll hear this quote many times in the School of Hotel Administration's halls, it is hung in the school's entrance, and you will see it from time to time in this book. "Life is service, the one who progresses is the one who gives his fellow man a little more, a little better, service." To that I would add, "and hospitality."

"Customer service is like taking a bath; you have to keep doing it."
—Fortune Cookie Wisdom

PART I

SUCCESS IN YOUR HOSPITALITY CAREER

CHAPTER 3

PREPARING FOR A SUCCESSFUL CAREER IN THE HOSPITALITY INDUSTRY

KATE WALSH, MICHAEL C. STURMAN, and BILL CARROLL

If you have picked up this book, chances are good that you are either working in the hospitality industry or considering a hospitality position. Great choice! This chapter discusses you as a candidate for employment or advancement in the hospitality industry. Future chapters examine the many aspects of hospitality operations; but, so that you can develop your own competitive advantage, let's start with you. First, we offer a take at what companies are looking for from potential employees. Then, we switch the lens and review the changing nature of careers and what you should look for from a potential employer. We'll also touch on the differences between managing people and leading others—and then you can read more on this topic in Chapter 6. No industry offers better opportunities for you to move up into a leadership role, if you so desire, so we'll also look at leadership opportunities within this industry. Finally, we conclude with advice on what you can and should consider as you move into and up within the world's largest industry.

HOSPITALITY CAREER OPPORTUNITIES

The hospitality industry presents diverse career opportunities, and your prospects for a management position are excellent. Not only can you benefit from industry turnover, but most hotel chains have long-term expansion plans. Although the Great Recession slowed things down a bit, hospitality companies are constantly seeking outstanding talent.[1] The thing you need to do to advance is to make sure that you offer the right "human capital." As explained in greater detail in Chapter 28, human capital refers to your present and future knowledge, skills, and abilities.[2] It is intangible, but it is a critical resource that a company needs to build its competitive advantage. That is, it's the people that make a company profitable, and employees do this by applying their human capital directly and in concert with a company's physical assets—including buildings, equipment, and furnishings—to deliver the company's services. We'll provide an overview of the human capital you need to develop to take advantage of advancement opportunities, and then you can read more specifics about what you need to know in other chapters of this book.

Industry Outlook

By almost any measure, the size of the hospitality labor market is large. Based on traditional economic and business perspectives, the size of the industry is measured by the scope of the hospitality market and the number of individuals employed in its organizations. Globally, the industry is estimated to employ 1 of every 15 workers. In the United States, the restaurant and hotel industries comprise over 328,000 management, business, and financial occupations.[3] As large as the hospitality industry is, we should point out that hospitality industry employment includes not only working in hotels and restaurants, but also jobs in suppliers and other ancillary businesses, such as consulting, technology providers, and construction firms. In addition, you can find employment opportunities in other industries that have human capital requirements similar to hospitality.[4] For example, health care providers have been recruiting hospitality managers to help them enhance their service aspects, and there is a growing interest in the long-term care industry to hire those regularly employed in the hospitality industry. Even grocery stores try to develop a service orientation similar to that of the hospitality industry.[5]

Your employment prospects in the hospitality industry are promising. In the United States alone, the federal Department of Commerce forecasts that the hospitality industry will grow at 5 percent annually through 2018.[6] Growth will be even stronger in Asia, particularly in China and India. So you could definitely consider your opportunities for multinational careers (as discussed in Chapter 5). In short, absent another recession, if you have hospitality-based human capital, you should have excellent prospects, both in the hospitality industry and in its related businesses. Furthermore, the best leaders and companies are always on the lookout for star talent.

Building on Your Current Mix of Skills

So let's look at what you need to do to take charge of your own career and plan for your success. Essentially, you'll have to be your own career coach. While many hospitality organizations plan for management succession and create strong management-training programs—such as Shangri-La Hotels and Resorts, Hilton International, and Fairmont Hotels and Resorts, to name a few—many other hospitality organizations have less organized programs, particularly for new hires. Managers often find they have been forgotten in their operational roles or possibly stalled due to lack of turnover in the upper management ranks. In addition, you could be held back by simply having a boss who fails to promote your human capital to key decision makers or, alternatively, fails to provide you with new learning-oriented challenges, regardless of whether they involve a new job and promotion. While many hospitality companies are working to correct these shortcomings, you would still be wise to take charge of developing your own mix of human capital!

The Power of Past Experience

But before worrying about that big promotion, you first have to get in the door. All companies want to hire people with the right knowledge, skills, and abilities. Often, however, they don't know exactly what this actually looks like in practice and particularly whether you, as an applicant, have the right mix. You'll certainly have an interview, but research shows that interviews are typically unreliable selection devices. From the manager's point of view, interviews often yield little information that can adequately predict an applicant's potential performance. From your point of view as an applicant, it is difficult to demonstrate your abilities in an interview. As a result, many companies rely heavily on past work experience.

The premise behind assessing work experience is simply that past performance is one of the best predictors of future success, particularly for entry-level jobs.[7] Hospitality-based experience signals that you know how to handle crucial customer interactions, a cornerstone of successful service-based companies. Additionally, companies pay more for employees who come from similar businesses, and less for individuals who are switching industries.[8] Thus, your resume acts as a proxy for the "compatibility" of your previous job experience with a potential new job.[9]

Since companies are looking for job experience, you need to show that your background relates well to hospitality. In addition, if you're in the industry and seeking a job with greater responsibilities, you need to demonstrate that your experience has made you ready for this position. Here's how to demonstrate your suitability. If you do not have experience within the hospitality industry, you need to redefine your human capital in terms of the requirements needed for the job in which you are interested. That means that you should determine the knowledge, skills, and abilities that are likely required to perform the job well. Look closely at that job description (or similar ones) for ideas on the specific knowledge, skills, and abilities you need to demonstrate. Then, describe how your work experiences show that you have the necessary human capital. This is true whether or not you've previously worked in the hospitality industry.

Think about the competencies required for the job (or promotion), and match them against the ones you had to develop in your past jobs. The tasks may be different, but the competencies may be similar. Your experience from both inside and outside of the industry may provide you with the requisite experience for a host of positions within the hospitality industry. In short, you need to position your mix of human capital as exactly what a potential employer currently desires.

DEVELOPING YOUR UNIQUE HUMAN CAPITAL

Once you have identified your human capital mix and have found the right industry-related job, you need to convince your potential employer how an investment in you will pay off. But you also need to be thinking about what you will obtain from this job that will help develop your own human capital and enhance your career. What this means is that you should view your job as a "resource-exchange." In essence, in addition to financial compensation, you are trading your knowledge, skills, and abilities in exchange for work experience or opportunities to develop your tool kit of portable human capital. Savvy employees identify learning opportunities within their current jobs that will enhance their human capital and increase marketability within their chosen fields. When the job no longer meets their criteria, they find new opportunities within the company or quite possibly, at competing organizations. They then enter into new exchange relationships. A study of Cornell graduates who had been working in the industry for a number of years revealed the nature of this exchange.[10] As one respondent commented, "[I'm looking for] building transferable skills using cutting-edge methodologies."

Thus, in managing your own career, we suggest you seek out organizations that provide opportunities to perform work that is meaningful to you. This concept is called a "protean career," in reference to the Greek god Proteus, who could alter his shape at will.[11] It is also called a "boundaryless career," suggesting that careers cross over multiple organizations and effectively "zig-zag" rather than proceed in a linear manner within one organization or even job type.[12] Research suggests that those who manage their own careers will likely seek out companies that offer the following: (1) intrinsically challenging work that provides individuals opportunities to learn and grow; (2) learning-oriented relationships with colleagues, supervisors, and clients; and (3) the opportunity to obtain valued extrinsic rewards in exchange for the work performed. The first two job features enable you to develop your human capital mix. The third affords you the opportunity to earn a living and live your desired lifestyle.

Look for Challenging Work

Intrinsically challenging work enables you to acquire and apply new knowledge and skills. You can acquire this form of work in a variety of ways, including participating in special project groups, attending formal and informal training sessions, and accepting opportunities to lead others and direct the department's activities. Those who manage their own careers seek continuously challenging work because this type of work enables them to develop and apply such skills as problem-solving, broad-picture visioning, and long- and short-range planning, as well as refine their interpersonal skills. The Cornell study repeatedly returned to this theme. When asked what they are looking for from their employer, respondents offer such ideas as "constantly being challenged and encouraged to explore beyond boundaries" and "learn new things to make myself a better person professionally and personally." The good news for you is that seeking out intrinsically challenging work makes you a productive organizational member, as well as increases your own marketability. In essence, you become more valuable to your own organization and the industry, as well as on the job market.

Fortunately, the structure of the hospitality industry provides many opportunities to gain experience at various levels and aspects of the industry. From a career perspective, this means that human capital growth opportunities exist at the property, corporate chain, regional chain, and ownership companies, as well as the nonhospitality firms that serve them. In the United States, for example, over 70 percent of the 50,000 larger hotel properties are members of chains. Similarly, while the restaurant industry has many more nonchain properties than the hotel industry, restaurant firms still offer multi-level employment opportunities. In the United States, there are over 33,500 establishments that are part of chains. Furthermore, both independent and chain establishments and both hotels and restaurants are served by other companies, some of which have human capital requirements that are similar to those in the hospitality industry. Thus, you should find numerous opportunities to learn and grow in the hospitality industry.

Develop Learning-Oriented Relationships

Learning-oriented relationships refer to your developing meaningful connections with others at work, such that you capitalize on acquiring new knowledge and skills.[13] You can form connections with other colleagues, superiors, subordinates, and clients. If you create these types of relationships, you likely will learn more from your personal interactions than you would if you were solely focused on your job tasks. These relationships are built on the notion that you learn best through dialogue with others, and they provide you opportunities to broaden your knowledge base, refine your skills, and obtain feedback on your performance. Learning-oriented relationships are characterized by their reciprocity, meaning that both parties in the relationship contribute to the other's learning, as well as remain open to examine the ways in which they, too, can change and grow.[14] Whether it be through creating a trusting relationship with a manager, subordinate, or client, we suggest that if you focus on learning from others in the process of doing your own job (and completing your own work), you will increase your own knowledge and skills and your own job marketability.

In addition, beyond employer-specific relationship-building opportunities, the hospitality industry has a number of professional associations that can assist with your networking and human capital growth. Some examples are American Hotel and Lodging Association, International Hotel and Restaurant Association, and Hotel Sales and Marketing Association International, as well as local associations such as the Greater Philadelphia Hotel Association, the Nevada Hotel and Lodging Association, and the Hotel Association of New York City.

Pay Attention to the Net Return of Extrinsic Rewards

In a reciprocal framework, individuals who manage their careers view their jobs as exchange relationships with their employers. This means that instead of trading job security for loyalty to the organization, they trade their skills for compensation, including salaries and benefits.[15] The mind-set of those who are managing their own careers is a "fair day's work for a fair day's pay,"[16] and these individuals seek out organizations that offer the highest extrinsic net return in exchange for the work they do. Compensation, however, does not refer to just money. It can include job perks, benefits packages, learning opportunities, and even flexible work schedules. Thus, compensation refers to just about any job feature that is important to you.

For example, if you need a flexible work schedule to meet your family needs, part of the exchange framework you create with your employer would include this form of compensation. As one respondent in the Cornell study replied, "It is important that I have my 'Life in Balance.' I never want to look back at my career and feel that it got in the way of my family life and enjoying life in general. My career is a part of my life; it is integrated well into my life."

Smart organizations have figured out ways to make the lifestyles of their employees easier, and keep them on as committed employees. Marriott Corporation, for example, makes a concerted effort to meet the flexible working needs of its employees and even offers them opportunities to develop into franchise owners.[17] Wyndham Hotels offers its female employees support, mentoring, and career advice through its Wyndham on Their Way program for associates.[18] The SAS Institute offers its employees competitive pay and enhances this pay with attractive job features such as on-site health care, workout gyms, a golf course, a community pool, a Montessori school, dry cleaning, and even a post office.[19] These employers want to make the lifestyles and work experiences of their employees as easy and seamless as possible, so that these employees will never want to leave their organization. This is the contemporary careers model in operation: companies determine the job features that induce line staff and managers to enter into and remain in a resource exchange with them.

In this exchange framework, you would view yourself as almost a contingent "in-house temporary worker." Your anticipated time with your company is essentially indefinite (or to be determined).[20] You would continuously weigh the net return or costs and benefits associated with your current job against other potential opportunities. As long as you continue to receive the specific rewards that are valuable to you—in exchange for working hard and well—you will be more likely to remain in your current organization and develop yourself within that company.

YOU AS A LEADER

As you move up the hospitality career ladder, you are increasingly likely to have greater managerial and leadership responsibilities, and these responsibilities begin with your learning how to supervise others. However, having the responsibility for managing others does not ensure that you will be an effective leader. In part, leadership is a human capital capability that has to be learned and practiced, and managing is different from leading. Nonetheless, placing yourself in the position to have such responsibility, directly or through special group assignments, is critical to reaching higher hospitality career levels.

Let's compare the roles of a manager and of a leader. Managers are often required to budget, plan, and solve problems. In other words, a manager's job often involves maintaining the status quo. Successful leaders, however, often must shake up the status quo. Leaders push their team to continuously improve through setting a vision, communicating that vision, and encouraging others by empowering them to act and meeting their motivational needs.[21] The difference is that managers control—and leaders change. Managers enact a plan—and leaders create a new one. So, the natural question is: How can new managers simultaneously be effective leaders and find jobs that will enable them to develop their leadership knowledge and skills?

As you take on various managerial jobs within the industry, look for ways to develop your human capital mix that will strengthen your leadership skills. One thing you will notice is that many of the skills required to be an effective manager are different from the skills required to be a successful leader. As a result, managers can have leadership responsibilities but not perform them well. Alternatively, they can also have no direct supervisory responsibility but exercise leadership every day, for example, as a team leader of a project group. The important point is that, if you wish to advance in the hospitality industry, you need to develop and hone this critical human capital skill. Indeed, it is for this reason that the Cornell School of Hotel Administration's mission is not about hospitality management but, rather, hospitality leadership. Thus, while you will learn more about developing yourself as a leader later in this book (Chapter 6), any discussion of career planning must consider what you need to do to become a future leader.

Leadership skills are crucial to advancement in the hospitality industry. One study that examined competencies required for country club managers identified a list of skills that included budgeting, financial analysis, communication skills, and time management.[22] A second study examined competencies required for hospitality management jobs, whether in rooms or food and beverage. Not surprisingly, both studies found that in the context of managing an operation, leadership skills are paramount.[23] However, these studies also found that certain types of leadership skills are more crucial than others.

Whether you are a brand new hospitality manager or a seasoned executive-level leader, research suggests you'll need a mix of technical know-how, interpersonal savvy or emotional intelligence, and conceptual and analytic skills.[24] If you are a line-level manager, technical skills are paramount. So, if you become the front-desk manager, you'd best know the check-in process; if your new post is at a food and beverage outlet, you should have a good understanding of the ins and outs of the order-placing system (among other functions; see Chapter 16). Rather than rely on your conceptual and analytic skills, you need to be able to pay attention to the operation and spot and correct problems, even before they occur. It's a challenging job.

In contrast to technical knowledge, leaders need conceptual and analytic skills. Leaders need to perform the strategic planning necessary for the company's long-term health. Although leaders usually have technical expertise, that's not their focus. For example, a general manager's job involves applying his or her reasoning, inductive thinking, and planning skills. While it is certainly important that a general manager understands the roles of his or her subordinates, and definitely not be ignorant of their job tasks, it is less critical for the general manager to have specific technical expertise. Even if they are technically skilled in their subordinates' jobs, top managers must be willing to let their subordinates perform their tasks and not micromanage.

Interestingly, interpersonal skills, or emotional intelligence, are equally important at all levels of management. This includes the ability to understand one's strengths and weaknesses, maintain emotional self-control, relate to and convey empathy to others, assess the political layout of any given group, and (especially important) motivate others through developing work relationships.[25]

Certainly, you need to have the technical expertise to perform your job well, but you also must think about ways to strengthen how you interact with your subordinates, bosses, peers, and clients, especially when there are differing opinions. This often involves carefully listening to others (see the next chapter).[26] The good news is that you can work on your emotional intelligence and interpersonal skills at any age.

Specific Skills for Strong Leaders

Looking at the essential conceptual and analytic skills for your human capital leadership mix, we see a growing consensus that successful leaders must do three crucial things in their jobs: sense making, visioning, and being inventive.[27] Sense making refers to the ability to read and understand one's operating environment and map a plan to operate within it. Those strong in sense making have a good handle on the context in which their business operates and are ready to adjust to unexpected outside forces, such as economic pressures, new competition, or a shift in customer needs. These leaders can handle the complexities of multiple operational pressures, and they are strong at mapping out and explaining a plan of action. They also understand that sense making is an iterative process and that the plan needs to be continuously refined. These individuals are also good at listening to and incorporating multiple viewpoints and perspectives into their frameworks. One only has to think of a strong hotel or restaurant general manager who adjusts the plan to shifting price-sensitive markets and a stalling economy to see what this might look like in practice. This type of leader would also be skilled at soliciting and incorporating the input of many individuals as he or she prepares a continuously revised business plan.

J. W. (Bill) Marriott, Cornell Icon of Industry

In recent years, the School of Hotel Administration has presented the Cornell Icon of the Industry Award. The award recognizes the accomplishments of outstanding leaders in the hospitality industry on the basis of lifetime achievements in the hospitality industry and contributions to their community or society. The winner in 2010 was J. W. (Bill) Marriott. He exemplifies leadership in hospitality.

J. W. (Bill) Marriott, Jr., is the chairman and chief executive officer of Marriott International, Inc. He began his hospitality career working for his father's Hot Shoppes restaurant chain during his high school and college years. He joined the company full time in 1956. Just eight months later, Marriott took over the company's hotel operations, shortly after the Twin Bridges Motor Hotel, Marriott's first venture into the lodging industry, opened in Washington, D.C.

Under Marriott's leadership, Marriott International has grown from a family restaurant business to a global lodging company with more than 3,100 properties in 66 countries and territories. Known for its commitment to diversity, social responsibility, and community engagement, the firm is consistently recognized among the most admired companies. Marriott has also worked to compile a family of 18 lodging brands that range from limited-service to full-service luxury hotels. The company manages and franchises hotels and resorts under these brand names: Marriott, JW Marriott, Renaissance, Bulgari, Ritz-Carlton, Courtyard, Residence Inn, SpringHill Suites, TownePlace Suites, and Fairfield Inn. It operates vacation ownership resorts under these flags: Marriott Vacation Club International, Ritz-Carlton Club, and Grand Residences by Marriott. The company also operates Marriott Executive Apartments, provides furnished corporate housing through its Marriott ExecuStay division, operates conference centers, and manages golf courses.

In addition to his work at Marriott International, Marriott serves his country and world as a leader and philanthropist. He is on the board of the J. Willard & Alice S. Marriott (Charitable) Foundation. He is a member of the National Business Council and the Executive Committee of the World Travel & Tourism Council. He also serves as the chairman of the Mayo Clinic Capital Campaign. Marriott recently served as chairman of the President's Export Council and member of the Secure Borders Open Doors Advisory Committee and the U.S. Travel and Tourism Advisory Board.

Visioning refers to the ability to create a captivating future image of the organization. Those who vision well are able to lay out what the organiza tion could and should become, given its purpose and competitive strength. These leaders are able to picture what the future could look like, and they invite others to contribute to and share in this image. Thus, they generate excitement around their ideas and they give people a sense of purpose to their work. They energize a group through identifying a collective set of possibilities. An example of a leader who demonstrates this type of skill is Herb Kelleher at Southwest Airlines. He was able to successfully create and sustain such an energized, customer-focused service culture that the company has earned profits for 37 consecutive years.[28]

Finally, successful leaders are inventive. This means that they are skillful in implementing the vision. This type of skill involves translating broad ideas into a specific action plan. It requires one to think in both abstract terms and concrete details. Mapping out an action plan, though, isn't just about working through detailed steps. It also requires one to think creatively about new ways of working—and organizing the work of others. That is, it can involve reinventing how the business works and the ways in which people carry out the organization's goals. Those strong at inventing are willing to explore alternative and sometimes nontraditional options to reframing work. Human resource executives at Hilton Garden Inn, for example, are using a Playstation-based virtual gaming experience to competitively teach their employees about guest service. They link their training directly to their guest comment system and, in doing so, have redesigned the ways in which they develop their staff.[29]

As you can see, these three analytic skills are related to one another, and woven through them are the crucial interpersonal skills of inspiring, involving, and mobilizing a workforce. Yet, it is also important to remember that no leader can be all things to all people. Successful leaders determine their key strengths in these conceptual areas, and they surround themselves with others who complement their skill sets.[30] Thus, you should not be deterred if these three analytic skills seem daunting to develop and simultaneously enact.

The crucial question to consider at this point is that if sense making, visioning, and inventing—as well as your degree of emotional intelligence— represent a human capital knowledge and skill set central to your success as a hospitality leader, how do you go about finding the managerial jobs that will provide the necessary opportunities to learn these skills? In addition, how do you ensure that while you gain the technical expertise to do your job well, you also learn how to apply leadership skills to enact continuous improvement? After all, as mentioned at the beginning of this chapter, your work experience is reflective of your human capital and central to your ability to meet your career goals. Until you get to that leadership position, you can take advantage of the multiple-layer structure of the hospitality industry to give you leadership opportunities at the property, regional, and corporate (chain) levels. Here's how to manage your career for leadership.

WHAT TO DO TODAY

To begin with, you should search out a job and company that help you add to your leadership tool kit and progress in meeting your career goals. There are subtle, yet important, things to think about in the process. Needless to say, you need to build your credibility by doing your job well. Beyond accomplishing your job tasks, this means being an active self-leader. Research tells us that great leaders (who also make great followers) are self-starters who show their own initiative.[31] They assume responsibility for influencing their own performance and even are willing to do non-motivating work—for a while. Using their emotional intelligence, they are aware of their feelings and attitudes about their work, and they act nondefensively and even welcome developmental feedback and advice. They also seek out their opportunities to learn and grow, using their job as a base from which to work. In addition, they develop solid relationships with their bosses. They regularly keep their bosses updated on their progress—or perhaps even lack thereof on a particular task—and are well aware of how their efforts and results fit into the bigger picture. They are also aware of how others in a team might depend on their performance, and they manage these expectations in positive ways. Finally, future leaders challenge the status quo in a positive manner.

Making Career Decisions—Three Simple Criteria

John Longstreet
President and CEO
Quaker Steak & Lube

To be sure, making a good career decision will have a huge impact on your life, perhaps only second to your choice of a spouse. Studies have shown that one of the top two factors considered in staying with a job is one's supervisor. So should it be the first and foremost consideration in taking a job. Like choosing a mate, your boss must be someone you respect and believe in as a proven leader and, most of all, a person you trust.

Success at work clearly can be attributed to performance, but it is also heavily influenced by your supervisor. Your boss needs to be someone from whom you can learn, who will give you authority, and, most of all, someone who will credit your accomplishments. Think of this person as your representative to upper management. Will they represent you fairly?

So, absolutely the most important consideration in taking a job is your boss. Nearly as essential as selecting your boss is making sure that there is a good fit with the other people with whom you will be working. In the hospitality business, it's all about people. The selection of a company is also all about people.

Another consideration is the economic vitality of the company. Sometimes even the best people cannot overcome a bad balance sheet. And make sure that the company values mirror your own.

Many people make career decisions based on the actual job. This may be the least important of the considerations. For most, especially those who are success oriented, the time spent in a particular job will be relatively short and thus should not be the basis of a career decision. It is important only in that the job must be one where success can be achieved and that provides a step to greater opportunity. And, by the way, when in the job, focus on being successful in that position, do *not* fixate on the next position, or you may never achieve it. Also, do not get hung up by money. If you choose a job in which you can succeed, in a company that is sound, and with a good boss, the money will come.

In summary, determine that the company's financial situation and its values are sound. Make sure the job is one in which you can achieve success and that provides upward mobility. And, most importantly, get to know the people—especially your boss. If the company fails in any one of these three criteria, you should pass.

If you engage in these practices and lead yourself well, you will garner the cachet to manage your career more actively. The next step in this process is to find companies whose executive-team leaders are seeking out, training, and developing new leaders who will one day take over their own jobs. These are leaders who will provide you with the opportunity to enhance your tool kit of interpersonal, conceptual, and analytic skills. Look for executive-team leaders who themselves have the appropriate skills, who will help you develop and take on increasingly challenging tasks, and who actually will let you assume responsibility for those tasks.[32] Ask questions about the path of those who have preceded you and the opportunities these managers were and were not given. Ask your prospective manager to tell you about former subordinates that he or she has developed, and where they went in the industry. If answers are not forthcoming, you probably want to look for a better opportunity. In addition, seek out executive-team members who can communicate well and act as trust-worthy leaders to the managers they supervise. These are the bosses who will provide you with challenge and learning in your work and, as a result, enable you to successfully develop your own unique mix of human capital.

Next, inquire about the specific career paths managers can take within the organization you're considering. Ask potential bosses to outline a possible career path for you, and ask them to commit to regularly revisiting progress. This path could indicate possible jobs, as well as the expected, finite time frame for each position. Map out how these potential jobs enable you to gain important knowledge and develop crucial skills relevant to your career goals. In addition, ask your boss to show you how today's job represents learn-ing opportunities that will prepare you for greater future challenges with increased responsibilities. Also, if relevant, let your boss know whether you are willing to relocate or even make a lateral move to advance your career, while simultaneously contributing to your organization.

The final key to this process is to remain open and flexible. Many opportunities present themselves that were not part of the "original plan." Yet these unexpected jobs may be exactly what you need to develop and strengthen your human capital. So if a job is not ideal (and no job is per-fect), consider whether it can be reframed in ways that meet your needs. If a company is not one you would initially consider, look for opportunities present in the job itself. Alternatively, if both a job and an organization are not exciting to you, consider if you would be working for a strong leader who can provide you with opportunities to grow that go beyond the defined job description. As you consider every opportunity, remember that the goal is to manage your career in ways that will provide you with the human capi-tal mix central to your success—a success that you define.

NOTES

1. C. A. Enz, "What Keeps You Up at Night? Key Issues of Concern for Lodging Managers," *Cornell Hotel and Restaurant Administration Quarterly* 42 (2001): 38–45; and C. A. Enz, "Issues of Concern for Restaurant Owners and Managers," *Cornell Hotel and Restaurant Administration Quarterly* 45 (2004): 315–332.
2. G. S. Becker, "Investment in Human Capital," *Journal of Political Economy* 70 (1962): 9–49; and M. A. Hitt, L. Bierman, K. Shimizu, and R. Kochgar, "Direct and Moderating Effects of Human Capital on Strategy and Performance in Professional Firms: A Resource-Based Perspective. *Academy of Management Journal* 44 (2001): 13–28.
3. U.S. Dept. of Commerce, www.bls.gov/oco/cg/cgs036.htm; www.bls.gov/oco/cg/cgs023.htm.
4. M. C. Sturman and B. Carroll, "The Job Compatibility Index: A New Approach to Defining the Hospitality Labor Market," *Center for Hospitality Report* 9 (2009): 1.
5. T. Hinkin and J. B. Tracey, "What Makes It So Great? An Analysis of Human Resources Practices among *Fortune*'s Best Companies to Work For," *Cornell Hospitality Quarterly* 51(2) (2010): 158–170.
6. U.S. Dept. of Commerce, "Forward Forecast of Employment in Hospitality," www.bls.gov/oco/cg/cgs036.htm#emply.
7. M. C. Sturman, "Searching for the Inverted U-Shaped Relationship between Time and Performance: Meta analyses of the Experience/Performance, Tenure/Performance, and Age/Performance Relationships," *Journal of Management* 29 (2003): 609–640.
8. M. C. Sturman, K. Walsh, and R. A. Cheramie, "The Value of Human Capital Specificity versus Transferability," *Journal of Management* 34 (2008): 290–316.
9. R. E. Ployhart, B. Schneider, and N. Schmitt, *Staffing Organizations*, 3rd ed. (Mahwah, NJ: Erlbaum, 2006).
10. K. Walsh and M. S. Taylor, "Developing In-House Careers and Retaining Management Talent: What Hospitality Professionals Want from Their Jobs," *Cornell Hospitality Quarterly* 48 (2007): 163–182.
11. D. T. Hall, "Protean Careers of the 21st Century," *Academy of Management Executive* 10 (1996): 8–16.
12. M. B. Arthur and D. M. Rousseau, *The Boundaryless Career: A New Employment Principle for a New Organizational Era* (New York: Oxford University Press, 1996).
13. J. K. Fletcher, "A Relational Approach to the Protean Worker. In D. T. Hall, ed. *The Career Is Dead—Long Live the Career* (San Francisco: Jossey-Bass, 1996), 105–131; D. T. Hall, *Careers in and out of Organizations* (Thousand Oaks, CA: Sage, 2002); and K. E. Kram, and D. T. Hall, Mentoring in the Context of Diversity and Turbulence. In E. E. Kossek and S. A. Lobel, eds. *Managing Diversity: Human Resource Strategies for Transforming the Workplace* (Cambridge, MA: Blackwell, 1996), 108–136.
14. Fletcher, 1996.

15. M. A. Cavanaugh and R. A. Noe, "Antecedents and Consequences of Relational Components of the New Psychological Contract," *Journal of Organizational Behavior* 20 (1999): 323–340; S. L. Robinson and D. M. Rousseau, "Violating the Psychological Contract: Not the Exception but the Norm," *Journal of Organizational Behavior* 15 (1994): 245–259; and S. E. Sullivan, "The Changing Nature of Careers: A Research Agenda," *Journal of Management* 25 (1999): 457–484.

16. D. M. Rousseau and K. A. Wade-Benezoni, "Linking Strategy and Human Resource Practices: How Employee and Customer Contracts Are Created," *Human Resource Management* 33 (1994): 463–489.

17. www.Marriott.com.

18. www.wyndham.com.

19. C. A. O'Reilly and J. Pfeffer, *Hidden Value: How Great Companies Achieve Extraordinary Results with Ordinary People* (Boston, MA: Harvard Business School Press, 2000).

20. J. McLean Parks, D. Kidder, and D. G. Gallagher, "Fitting Square Pegs into Round Holes: Mapping the Domain of Contingent Work Arrangements onto the Psychological Contract," *Journal of Organizational Behavior* 19 (1998): 697–730; S. E. Sullivan, W. A. Carden, and D. F. Martin, "Careers in the Next Millennium: Directions for Future Research," *Human Resource Management Review* 8 (1998): 165–185.

21. J. P. Kotter, "What Leaders Really Do," *Harvard Business Review* 68 (1990): 103–111.

22. J. Perdue, R. Woods, and J. Ninemeier, "Competencies Required for Future Club Managers' Success," *Cornell Hospitality Quarterly* 42 (2001): 60–65.

23. C. Kay and J. Russette, "Hospitality-Management Competencies," *Cornell Hospitality Quarterly* 41 (2000): 52–63.

24. Kotter, 1990.

25. D. Goleman, "What Makes a Leader?" *Harvard Business Review* 82 (2004): 1–10.

26. D. Ancona, T. W. Malone, W. J. Orlikowski, and P. M. Senge, "In Praise of the Incomplete Leader," *Harvard Business Review* (February 2007): 1–8.

27. Ibid.

28. Southwest Airlines, 2009 Annual Report.

29. "Hilton Garden Inn Officially Launches Innovative Training Using PSP," *BusinessWire* (January 14, 2009); see also C.A. Enz, K. Walsh, R. Verma, S.E. Kimes, and J. Siguaw, "Cases in Innovative Cases in Hospitality and Related Services, Set 4," Cornell University School of Hotel Administration Center for Hospitality Research Report. (July 2010).

30. Ancona et al., 2007.

31. C. C. Manz and H. P. Sims, "Leading Workers to Lead Themselves: The External Leadership of Self-Managing Work Teams," *Administrative Science Quarterly* 32 (1987): 106–128.

32. Walsh and Taylor, 2007.

CHAPTER 4

THE LISTENING FAST TRACK

JUDI BROWNELL

Listening effectively is one of the key ingredients for success in hospitality management. A study of senior hospitality executives confirmed that listening is the most important communication competency for career development. Listening enables you to build strong relationships with your colleagues and follow your supervisor's priorities so that you can gain resources for key initiatives. Most important, listening is critical to understanding your guests' expectations and delighting them by exceeding those expectations. Career success in hospitality begins with listening—and, as you'll soon discover, the need for effective listening never ends.

You will be far more effective on the job if you train yourself to listen. Although listening skills can be difficult to develop, I think you will find that it's well worth the effort. Listening is what we call a "high-leverage" activity; the time and effort you spend on improving your listening will pay you back in many ways—helping you build your professional success and gain personal respect. Learning to listen takes energy, self-discipline, and focus. As I explain in this chapter, your listening will improve substantially if you simply become more conscious of and knowledgeable about listening-related behaviors. As shown in Figure 4.1, Lyman Steil and Richard Bommelje suggest that the LAW of listening involves a combination of willingness, or motivation, and ability.[1] There's no doubt you can improve your listening effectiveness, and this chapter shows you how.

The skills explained in this chapter are particularly vital to anyone who works in a service environment. Listening will help you to: (1) get things right so that you avoid mistakes and misunderstandings that frustrate your guests, and (2) get along with your coworkers so that you can build the relationships that will promote teamwork and goodwill.[2] Because listening is such a large part of service, listening is particularly critical for anyone in the hospitality

Figure 4.1
The Law of Listening

The LAW of Listening: Listening = Ability + Willingness

Adapted from Steil and Bommelje, 2004.

Figure 4.2
Listening Fast Tracks Your Career

Facilitates Understanding and Reduces Mistakes
- Encourages accurate feedback
- Increases information sharing
- Reduces misunderstandings

Facilitates Relationships and Teamwork
- Increases trust and respect
- Reduces stress
- Increases cohesiveness and morale

Facilitates Quality Service to Customers and Guests
- Increases perceptions of customer care
- Promotes service customization
- Facilitates problem solving

---

business (Figure 4.2). In this chapter, I demonstrate why good service demands good listening—and explain how you can become a great listener.

In short, this chapter tells you how to advance your career by recognizing the importance of effective listening skills and developing key listening competencies. First, we'll examine listening as it relates to working with your colleagues; then, we'll focus on the distinctive requirements of listening to customers and guests. To better illustrate my points, I have created a character named Shana, who is assistant manager of sales at the "Paradise Hotel." By "watching" her deal with clients, you can readily see how important listening competencies are to managerial effectiveness. Sadly, Shana has a hard time with listening, and her situation will demonstrate how important it is that hospitality professionals take control of their listening behavior and not become derailed by common pitfalls. Before we take up Shana's story, though, let's look at the benefits of listening—avoiding mistakes and bringing people together—and talk about how to start practicing your listening skills right inside your own organization.

STOP MAKING MISTAKES

If you don't listen well, mistakes are inevitable. In some cases, you become vividly aware of mistakes right away, but there are other cases where you don't find out about the mistake until some time later (long after service recovery is possible). Imagine the mess caused when the purchasing agent for a cruise ship was not paying attention to the chef's food request. The chef wanted 20 pounds of lobster for Monday and 40 pounds of salmon for Thursday, but the purchasing agent wasn't listening and reversed that order. To be sure, that made the cruise ship's week at sea an interesting time. It's possible that you have made mistakes this week due to a failure to listen that you still don't know about. Not only do mistakes misdirect, frustrate, embarrass, and confuse your guests and coworkers, but they make you look bad and keep you from getting ahead.

BRING EVERYONE TOGETHER—BE A HERO

Being a listener and encouraging listening skills can help bring together the people on your team, in your department, or across your organization. Despite your best efforts, employees do not always automatically work well together. As corporations become more global and the workplace more diverse, differences inevitably arise. While cross-cultural differences are ultimately beneficial, they often make daily interactions more problematic and conflict among employees more frequent.[3] If you are a member of a work team, you have probably noticed that individuals from different cultures have different norms of interaction. While some coworkers have no trouble interrupting a conversation and bluntly stating their ideas and opinions, others may have good ideas but hesitate to offer them. It becomes clear that these cultural patterns of communication also have a significant impact on listening behavior.

Here's where effective listening comes in. By demonstrating basic listening practices, you can begin to bridge cultural differences and align goals. The most powerful and simple step you can take to make colleagues feel valued and to foster teamwork is to make listening to them a priority.

BEGIN BY LISTENING INSIDE YOUR ORGANIZATION

The place to start listening is right where you are. You've probably heard of the term "service within." I'm suggesting that service within begins with effective listening.[4] You can get ahead only if you can make a difference, and one of the simplest ways of having a powerful positive influence on your organization is to begin fostering what we call a "listening environment." All it takes is for you to set the example, to practice the habits of effective listening, and to begin to create a culture where all employees communicate frequently, think big-picture, and come together to accomplish common goals. Listening is the service you provide to your coworkers on the job. It's the foundation for building a productive and supportive organizational culture where serving guests becomes second nature. No matter where you work, your attention to listening lays the piece of track that will get everyone going in the right direction.

Listening *Is* the Fast Track—Follow It

As we'll see in the next section when we're introduced to Shana, listening involves four distinct skill clusters that you need to learn and practice. You can think of these components as stops on your fast track to success. With Shana's help, we'll identify the temptations and poor habits that could derail your progress. By identifying these obstacles and then applying effective listening strategies, you'll be able to reach your destination.

Let me emphasize that no matter what you plan for your career, you'll find that listening is among the critical skills for success. A study of hotel managers found that listening was essential to new employees as they sought to make a positive first impression and to effectively orient themselves to the values and priorities of their supervisor, department, and organization. Those who listened well better understood expectations and more quickly aligned their efforts with their company's goals.

At the other end of the career track, a defining characteristic of successful senior executives also was their ability to listen well. These executives emphasized that listening was key to making good decisions, solving problems, and understanding the perspectives of various constituencies—especially in an increasingly global industry. They reported that, as they advanced in their careers, the scope of their job did not allow them to have firsthand experience with all aspects of a situation. Therefore, they increasingly depended on their listening skill to bring timely and accurate information to bear on the issues at hand. In addition, they believed that their ability to listen to multiple perspectives contributed to effective decision making.[5]

Know Yourself

The key factor that affects your preparation and your listening success is the accuracy of your self-perceptions.[6] To better understand your current listening effectiveness and to determine what direction you need to go, you should make a personal self-assessment, and you should get feedback from those who know you well. Take both assessments into careful consideration. Don't be like the managers in one study who almost always rated themselves as far better listeners than did their coworkers.[7] You might think you're listening, but if no one else agrees, you have some work to do!

LEARN HOW TO GET ON TRACK

Let's look at the four basic skill clusters that you need to master for effective listening. You can think of each skill cluster as a whistle-stop on the fast track to success. The skills are: paying attention, understanding the message, understanding the speaker, and remembering what was said (Figure 4.3). While you can't leave out any of the stops, you may find that you achieve some much more quickly than others.

Now, let's meet Shana, a new assistant manager on the sales staff at the Paradise, an 800-room luxury convention hotel in a large U.S. city. Shana is having a terrible, horrible, no good, very bad day (to borrow the title of a classic children's book).[8] You have the enviable position of learning from her mistakes, and simultaneously assessing your own listening attitudes and skills to keep you firmly on the fast track.

Figure 4.3
The Listening Fast Track

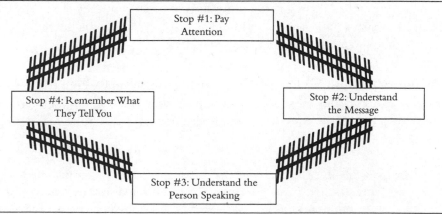

Stop #1: Pay Attention

Stop #4: Remember What They Tell You

Stop #2: Understand the Message

Stop #3: Understand the Person Speaking

FIRST STOP: PAY ATTENTION

Shana's new position as assistant manager of sales was fast-paced and varied—just what she had been looking for when she interviewed several months ago. While she could have stayed in her previous position as sales manager at a smaller property, she was anxious to move up the career ladder and saw the Paradise as a step toward her goal.

At the moment, however, things were a bit too hectic. Shana had just discovered that the largest conference room in the hotel had been double-booked for events taking place that afternoon, and her direct supervisor was not happy. He was certain that he had told Shana how important it was to check the schedule before finalizing a booking. In fact, he called it "unforgivable" and "disappointing," especially given her previous experience. Shana felt that his criticisms were harsh and unfair; after all, just yesterday when she was assisting with an anniversary party she had been the one to notice that the place settings didn't match the decorations and that the flower arrangements were too large for the tables.

Now she was late to her 11 o'clock meeting. As she entered the conference room where the soon-to-be bride and her mother were waiting, Shana felt dizzy and out of breath. The mother of the bride looked at Shana, glanced up at the clock, and immediately began reviewing her menu selections and asking specific questions about options and tasting. "Yes, yes," Shana assured her. Tastings would be no problem and, yes, the entrées she selected could be ready in a day or two. Modifying some of the ingredients would also be possible. Shana hoped she was responding appropriately because it was nearly impossible to hear over the sounds of a birthday party in the next room. The mother of the bride considered herself quite a "foodie" and had very specific ideas about what would be suitable for her daughter's big event. Shana watched the second hand go around on the big clock above the table. She felt completely worn out; all she could think about was that double booking. She wondered if the mother would ever stop talking.

Paying Attention: Causes of Derailment and How to Stay on Track

As you see, Shana has allowed circumstances to distract her and reduce her listening abilities. Here are the three obstacles illustrated in this vignette that Shana will need to address:

1. *Becoming overly emotional and tired.* Shana's anxiety contributed significantly to her poor listening. Keep in mind that whenever you become emotional, your ability to listen decreases dramatically.[9] It

doesn't matter if your emotion is anger, frustration, joy, or excitement. Emotions derail your ability to concentrate and recognize the other person's point of view. Emotional listeners distort messages, miss important details, and become defensive. Learn to catch yourself when you are becoming emotional. Take a moment to breathe and focus. If you can't seem to regroup and become calm enough to listen, you may need to delay the conversation until you are able to get back on track.

Nothing derails listening more than fatigue. Because listening is an active process, it takes work and concentration. When you are tired, you are more likely to feel overwhelmed and unfocused. Rather than approaching problems with a "can do" attitude, fatigue makes you feel depressed and confused. Shana probably cannot address that situation in the short run because the solution is to just be rested. There is no substitute for getting enough sleep.

2. *Letting the voices in your head or the noise in your environment distract you.* Shana was completely distracted by her earlier conversation, which created a form of noise. She needed to be in the moment with her next customers, but she was stuck. A contributing factor in this regard is that your mind can process what you hear nearly twice as fast as a person talks. The great temptation is to use your "bonus time" thinking about other matters. Instead, try to stay in the present. You can do this by becoming actively engaged, whether that means asking questions, taking notes, or repeating the message to yourself (or to the speaker) to make sure you understand the key points. While there are sure to be distractions in your work environment, missing out on something important because you didn't hear what was said is generally a lame excuse. Find ways to eliminate distractions.

3. *Paying attention to the wrong things.* Shana may have heard most of what her supervisor said, but she didn't pick up on the key point of paying close attention to the schedule to avoid double booking a room. Her experience in a smaller hotel didn't prepare her for this type of problem. Her attention during the conversation followed her interests—to flowers and table settings. The familiar Pareto principle, also known as the 80/20 rule, applies here:[10] 20 percent of the things on your "to do" list yield 80 percent of the results. The same is true of listening. If you're not listening to the "right stuff," then much of your effort is wasted.

The way to beat this problem is to focus on the speaker's priorities and meanings, not your own. Recognize the assumptions you may be making that prevent you from hearing the entire message.

SECOND STOP: UNDERSTAND THE MESSAGE

Back at her office, Shana collapsed into her chair. She glanced at her appointment book and realized that she was scheduled for yet another meeting, this time to discuss arrangements for a conference of the International Association of Aerospace Engineers. She was not looking forward to this conversation at all. While she loved making arrangements for weddings and parties, she had no clue what engineers talked about and wondered how much she would have to learn just to carry on a conversation, let alone sell the hotel space. As Shana entered the room, she was relieved to find two Japanese women sitting together at the small conference table. "This will be easier than I expected," she thought to herself. When she looked toward the door, however, she realized that she would be dealing with several more members of the association; five men filed in from the lobby and took seats across from her. From their name tags, it appeared that several of these association members were international as well.

"Good morning," she began. "Welcome to the Paradise." Although she had discovered that greeting generally elicited a smile from her clients, all members of this group remained stone-faced. She paused and then continued, "I'm pleased that you are considering our hotel for your association's conference." There was a long silence, after which one of the men—who spoke with a heavy German accent—began to outline their requirements. He mentioned program titles and the type of equipment needs presenters would have. He used a great deal of terminology with which Shana was totally unfamiliar and that, combined with his accent, left her totally confused. She knew she should be more proactive, that she should be stopping the speaker and asking him to clarify his points, but somehow she just couldn't interrupt. On several occasions there was a hushed discussion among the committee members culminating in a decision that they obviously assumed Shana had been following and understood. She just kept smiling and nodding and said nothing. Looking down at the iPhone in her lap, she began to text message a friend about dinner plans.

Understanding the Message: Causes of Derailment and How to Stay on Track

Three factors combined to interfere with Shana's ability to understand this conversation. Although she attempted to listen, she did not have the tools she needed.

1. *A poor or inadequate vocabulary.* Shana needed to do two things to overcome listening barriers with regard to vocabulary in this discussion.

First, she needed to separate the technical terms relating to aerospace from the information relating to the services to be provided by the hotel—then she needed to clarify terms that she did not understand.

Part of listening is asking appropriate questions. When you are listening to difficult material, or when the speaker doesn't provide enough background information, ask for clarification. You can't always avoid difficult material, so embrace opportunities to learn and to stretch your listening comprehension skills. Active listening by paraphrasing and summarizing key points is particularly useful when you are working with speakers for whom English is a second language.[11]

2. *Information overload.* Shana's listening suffered when she became connected to too many different information sources—notably on her iPhone. We like to believe that we can do two things at once but, contrary to conventional wisdom, multitasking means that one or another task is not being completed effectively. In this case, listening was the casualty because listening requires your full attention, especially when interacting cross-culturally.

3. *Lack of interest in the subject.* Shana had decided before she met with association members that meeting arrangements involving any type of engineering would be boring and complicated, and her listening effectiveness was subsequently diminished. Even if you think you won't be interested in a particular subject, you should make an effort to connect to a speaker if you want to listen effectively. Effective listeners are positive and curious. Why not set a goal of learning about something new every day? You might be surprised to discover how many different things you really do enjoy, and how these ideas contribute, directly or indirectly, to your social networking and ultimate career success.

THIRD STOP: UNDERSTAND THE PERSON SPEAKING

When Shana looked up from texting, the two Japanese women were still indicating nonverbal signs of agreement. Shana thought it was particularly strange since it seemed that the men had differences of opinion on nearly all of the issues being discussed. She was getting frustrated listening to them argue and was anxious to bring the meeting to a close. Apparently, this was the first "international" aerospace conference, and everyone was anxious about the many decisions that needed to be made. Shana wanted to tell them that it was really no big deal, and that most conferences nowadays drew participants from across the globe. She also got the feeling that they weren't taking her advice or suggestions seriously—she wasn't included at all in much of their conversation, and seldom did any of the men look at her. She kept trying to get in a few words, but her efforts were largely ignored.

Since the women seemed so much more agreeable, Shana decided to address her questions directly to them: "So, the three break rooms will be sufficient?" Shana was anxious to move the conversation forward. The women nodded. "And you can take care of your own audiovisual requirements?" Shana continued, thinking this would solve the dilemmas over which the men were still arguing. "Well, I think I have enough information to go on at this point. I want to thank you all for thinking of Paradise for your conference, and I'll be back in touch shortly." Shana gathered her notebook and stood up. Suddenly, all eyes were on her, and silence fell over the room.

Understand the Person Speaking: Causes of Derailment and How to Stay on Track

As you might guess, Shana missed the more subtle communication dynamics in this situation. The following are three issues she could have addressed for better understanding:

1. *Recognize individual differences.* Despite problems arising from unfamiliar vocabulary, second language interference, and speaking rate, understanding content in communication is actually the easy part. Beyond the content of the message, you will find that the greatest challenge is to understand the person speaking. Effective listeners care about the speaker and try to understand what is said from his or her point of view. In contrast to Shana's impatience, a focus on the speaker means that you need to listen to the entire message without interrupting. Effective listeners are patient and nonjudgmental, often paraphrasing what they hear so that they are confident their perceptions and interpretations are accurate.[12]

   A deeper problem in this meeting was that Shana felt that the men ignored her. Even if she were correct, this may have been due to her age or gender. Even in the United States, younger managers often find they must work harder to establish credibility with older colleagues and guests. Numerous variables influence communication, though, and cultural orientation probably influenced her perceptions. Members of some cultures don't hesitate to argue and negotiate, while others are reluctant to disagree or to state their opinions directly.

Figure 4.4
Listen to Nonverbal Communication

Nonverbal Behaviors in the United States That Usually Indicate a Positive Response
- Eye contact
- Smiling
- Head nods
- Forward lean
- Positive facial expression

Nonverbal Behaviors in the United States That Usually Indicate a Negative Response
- Looking down or away
- Nervous habits and fidgeting
- Shaking head negatively
- Frown, squinting
- Staring

---

2. *Pay attention to nonverbal communication.* You are undoubtedly well aware of the importance of nonverbal cues (Figure 4.4), which can carry up to 70 percent of the meaning of a message. However, even as people generate both intentional and unintentional nonverbal clues that accompany their message, you have to be able to tune in to what the speaker is "not saying." Otherwise, like Shana, you can misinterpret the situation. Even silence communicates.

    Most nonverbal behavior is learned,[13] and varies from one culture to the next. To best understand those from other countries or communities, you will have to do some homework. If you have traveled or served international guests, you have certainly noticed that eye contact (or lack of it) and certain gestures don't necessarily mean the same things in all countries. Lack of eye contact may show respect rather than disinterest. Gestures are a particular minefield, since one culture's innocent motion can be highly offensive in another culture.

3. *Don't forget the chairs.* Your ability to listen can be improved if you control the layout of a room. Arrange the environment to facilitate your listening goals. If chairs are too far apart or if they are too uncomfortable, listening is affected. At meetings, where you sit matters, either facilitating or constraining your ability to command attention. Plan your physical environment with the same attention to detail with which you plan your meeting agenda. Instead of letting her guests sit wherever they wanted, Shana might have motioned them to specific seats. That would have required her to know something about the group's interpersonal dynamics. Once she saw the situation, she might have called a break and managed the interactions simply by changing the seating arrangement.

FOURTH STOP: REMEMBER WHAT THEY TELL YOU

When the International Association of Aerospace Engineers' program planning committee left, Shana sighed. Wow! Talk about a challenging situation. The women didn't say much, and when they did, she could hardly hear them because they spoke so softly. Two of the men had such heavy accents that she missed most of what they said, and they were so forceful that she couldn't get in any questions or clarifications. At least this time she had written down a few of her own suggestions. She knew that memory was not her strong suit! While Shana had no idea what most of the requests really meant (who uses oscilloscopes??), she figured she would try to make sense of it all later. Right now she just needed a break.

As Shana thought back about the day, she realized that she had not taken notes regarding the wedding reception. She began to worry about the wedding dinner. While she was pretty sure she made the sale (at least the women had agreed to everything she suggested), there was no way she remembered much about the details of her conversation. Maybe tomorrow she could straighten it all out. What scared her at the moment was that the entire family would be coming the next evening for a tasting, and she had no idea what menu items they were expecting to enjoy—or if the kitchen could get tastings together overnight. She probably should have checked first before making that commitment. It was all Shawn's fault for getting so upset with her about the double booking. It just ruined her entire day.

Remember What You Hear: Causes of Derailment and How to Stay on Track

Finally, based on Shana's experience, let's look at the factors that can interfere with your ability to remember what you have heard. You may find that your guests are not always forgiving if you have forgotten what they said after sitting together in a meeting.

1. *Too much stress.* Shana's day was stressful from the beginning. Stress comes from many sources both on the job and off, but regardless of the source, stress diminishes your ability to listen in a number of ways. Perhaps the most dramatic of these is the impact stress has on your memory.

   There are a variety of ways to reduce (but probably not completely eliminate) stress. Many stress-reducing tactics are simply common sense: give yourself realistic deadlines with sufficient time to accomplish a task, write down what you hear, delegate when possible, and learn and practice simple relaxation techniques.[11]

2. *Assuming memory is automatic.* Shana needed to focus on ways to remember her conversations. Have you seen front-desk attendants who can greet a guest by name, or a server who correctly takes orders without writing them down? Perhaps they were born with a great memory, but more likely they have learned and practiced memory techniques. One effective way you can do this is to "do something" with the information. One key technique is known as mnemonics. You connect or relate a piece of information to something you already know, or you create a simple phrase or key word to remember an item. By linking information together in a way that makes sense, you have created a mnemonic device.[14] For a simple example, if someone is named "Elvis," just think "king of rock and roll" in connection with that person, and you'll remember his name. Pick up a simple book on memory techniques, and soon everyone will be remarking about *your* amazing memory!

3. *Your ego.* Finally, Shana was wrapped up in her own issues. Another problem in remembering names involves mental focus. You can't remember what you don't pay attention to, and generally, when you are introduced to someone, your thoughts are on what you are going to say, how you are coming across, and what the other person is thinking about you. Next time, look right at the person and repeat the name (and create a mnemonic if you need to). Then use it at least twice, and you'll find your ability to recall has improved significantly.

GET ON BOARD: DEVELOP AND PRACTICE YOUR LISTENING SKILLS

You'll discover that the fast track to listening is just the beginning of your travels toward greater personal and professional success. Listening skills are developed over time, so the sooner you get on board, the more opportunities you will have to improve your effectiveness (Figure 4.5).

Essential components of success in the hospitality industry involve getting things right and building relationships. When you listen effectively, you begin a cycle that has a significant positive impact on both your organization and your customers. This effective listening cycle supports an everyday service attitude that makes your colleagues and guests feel valued, welcomed, and understood. In short, listening *is* your business.

You'll soon see that learning to listen is about the journey along the fast track and assessing your progress at each stop along the way. If you set your standards high, the pursuit of listening excellence will help you reach your destination of becoming more effective on the job, delighting guests, and perhaps

Figure 4.5
Quick Stop Listening Facts

Quick Stop 1—Pay Attention: Listening Facts
- Learn what is important to focus on—not everyone notices the same things.
- Identify and control internal and external distractions.
- Use your "bonus time," the gap between the rate of speaking and the rate of listening, to think about the message.
- Not everyone notices the same things.

Quick Stop 2—Understand the Message: Listening Facts
- Improving your vocabulary improves your listening.
- Summarize the main ideas to make sure you have accurately understood.
- Keep an open mind and listen to new information.
- Avoid information overload.

Quick Stop 3—Understand the Person Speaking: Listening Facts
- Try to see things from the speaker's perspective; consider cultural differences when interpreting messages.
- Recognize the variables, like gender and age, that influence listening.
- Incorporate nonverbal communication into the listening process.
- Create a physical environment that is conducive to listening effectiveness.

Quick Stop 4—Remember What You Hear: Listening Facts
- Learn stress-reducing techniques to increase listening effectiveness.
- Understand how listening effectiveness is influenced by your ability to remember.
- Memory is not automatic—learn and practice memory techniques.
- Focus on the person speaking rather than on the impression you are making.

---

earning a promotion. Guests and colleagues will wonder about the secret to your success; tell them the answer is simple—just listen.

NOTES

1. L. Steil and R. Bommelje, *Listening Leaders: The 10 Golden Rules to Listen, Lead, and Succeed* (St. Paul, MN: Beaver's Pond Press, 2004).
2. J. Brownell, *Listening: Attitudes, Principles, and Skills*, 4th ed. (Boston: Allyn & Bacon, 2010).
3. D. Victor, *International Business Communication* (New York: HarperCollins, 1992).
4. J. Brownell, "Fostering Service Excellence through Listening: What Managers Need to Know," *Cornell Hospitality Report* 9(6) (2009), Cornell Center for Hospitality Research, chr.cornell.edu.
5. J. Brownell, "Creating Strong Listening Environments: A Key Hospitality Management Task," *International Journal of Contemporary Hospitality Management*, 6(3) (1994): 3–10; B. Conchie, "Seven Demands of Leadership," *Leadership Excellence* 24(9) (September 2007): 18–21.

6. H. Collingwood, "Leadership's First Commandment: Know Thyself," *Harvard Business Review* (September 2001): 8–13.

7. L. Cooper, "Listening Competency in the Workplace," *Business Communication Quarterly* 60(4) (1997): 75–84.

8. J. Viorst, *Alexander and the Terrible, Horrible, No Good, Very Bad Day* (New York: Atheneum, 1987).

9. J. Brownell, "Managerial Communication: The Critical Link between Knowledge and Practice," *The Cornell Hotel & Restaurant Administration Quarterly* 44(2) (2003): 39–49.

10. W. Pareto, *Manual of Political Economy* (Italian, 1906; French transl. 1909, English transl. 1971).

11. H. Nasution and F. Mavondo, "Customer value in the hotel industry: What managers believe they deliver and what customers experience," *International Journal of Hospitality Management* 27(2) (2007). 204 213.

12. D. Tesone, "Whole Brain Leadership Development for Hospitality Managers," *International Journal of Contemporary Hospitality Management* 16(6) (2004): 363–368.

13. P. C. Earley and S. Ang, *Cultural Intelligence: Individual Interactions Across Cultures* (Stanford, CA: Stanford University Press, 2003).

14. D. Zohar, "Analysis of Job Stress Profile in the Hotel Industry," *International Journal of Hospitality Management* 13(2) (1994): 219–231; R. Brymer, P. Perrewe, and T. Johns, "Managerial Job Stress in the Hotel Industry," *International Journal of Hospitality Management* 10(1) (1991): 47–58.

CHAPTER 5

DEVELOPING AND MANAGING YOUR MULTINATIONAL CAREER

JAN KATZ

Chances are good that you will have an opportunity to work in another country at some point in your career. Having worked abroad and interviewed others who have done that, I can assure you that although international work is challenging, the rewards are substantial, both professionally and personally. The good: You have a chance to develop your observational and communication skills, creativity, and capability to manage up and down the hierarchy, and you will almost certainly have some exciting and enjoyable experiences. The challenge: To get the most out of your global work, you have to maintain a positive attitude and be ready to live in an unfamiliar and possibly difficult place. This chapter outlines some things to think about when you prepare to do that. Even if you never work overseas, the ideas in this chapter may help you work with the many international coworkers in your own operation—and serve international visitors.

LIKE IT OR NOT, HOSPITALITY IS AN INTERNATIONAL INDUSTRY

Let's start with your workplace. Even if you do not intend to have an international career, you still will have to deal with multinational issues. At times, your front-desk staff may be checking in guests from three different countries at once, and guests from many nations may be standing side by side at your restaurant's breakfast buffet. Because of the industry's realities, hospitality employees also have diverse backgrounds. Hotels seek front-of-the-house diversity in language and customs to help respond to global guests, and back-of-the-house diversity arises from the jobs' appeal to immigrants with limited language and workplace skills.

As a result, you probably already have cross-national skills from your daily work. However, if you intend to pursue a multinational career in hospitality, there's much more to consider, as I discuss next.

Preparing for Your International Assignment

Right now, you can begin to prepare for a great international opportunity by learning about your company's international operations, developing your network, honing your global skills, and making sure that any family members who will be joining you are on board with your international aspirations.

Learn the Why behind Corporate Standards You need to become an expert in your corporate standards because when you're abroad, you will be expected to train local employees and ensure that they stay in line with corporate expectations. You will be better at this if you can explain why those rules and behaviors exist, since they may seem peculiar to employees in other nations who operate with different assumptions. Let's take a look at how one general manager dealt with what could have been a troublesome clash between corporate rules and local culture.

This American hotel executive was sent to Hungary to transition a newly acquired property to corporate standards. The first day, he noticed that employees were drinking wine at lunch. He learned that under the previous owner everyone was entitled to two glasses of wine daily. His company's standard barred drinking at work.

Upon reflection, though, he realized that Hungary does not have liability laws like those in the United States, where a lawsuit could be filed if employees were allowed to drink at work and then were injured. Further, responsible wine consumption is not seen as morally suspect in Hungary. The two reasons for barring drinking in the United States therefore didn't exist, and so the general manager talked to executives at headquarters and arranged a variance in the corporate standard.

Grow Your Network Take another look at the end of that anecdote. A key factor that made it possible for the manager in Hungary to negotiate a change in corporate standards was that he knew whom to call. Once you are abroad, you will have substantial autonomy, but you still must be in touch with headquarters and you may need support for problems. If you have a solid network, your associates can help you find solutions. If you have to start figuring out whom to call, how to approach them, and how to gain their trust every time something comes up, you won't have enough hours in the day. When Jim Combs tackled this issue in an article in the *Cornell Hospitality Quarterly,* he concluded that one reason that operations fail abroad is that the local manager is not given sufficient autonomy to adapt as necessary.[1] If you have already developed trust and respect among your colleagues at headquarters, they are more likely to allow you to act as necessary to make your business successful.

So, take some time to create a wide network before you leave home. That means joining internal affinity groups or clubs, helping people in other departments, and taking the initiative to meet people. Especially seek out alumni of your college and share contacts. Building an internal network is a job in itself, and it is difficult to fit that into a busy workday. So consider it as a part of your job and put it in your schedule. Once you are abroad, your network will save you more than the time that you spent building it.

Develop Your International Skills Focus on learning skills that are valuable in any international or multicultural context. Learning why things occur is useful not only in regard to your company, but also in regard to people. The first thing to realize is that people in other cultures behave in ways that you might not initially understand or you might misinterpret. As pointed out by Christopher Earley and Miriam Erez, we think that if people act like us, they are thinking like us.[2] But that is not true. People in the United States often say, "No news is good news," or "Silence means assent." In East Asia, for instance, the opposite is true; silence often means complete disagreement or embarrassment. They simply do not like public conflict and so remain silent when they cannot be supportive.

One thing that will help you avoid communication gaffes is to ***improve your observational skills***. Focus intently on each person who is speaking with you. In the United States or in similar cultures, you probably allow your attention to wander or listen without looking at the speaker because the speaker's expression or the communication context usually doesn't influence your interpretation of the words being said. In many countries, however, body language, the location of the discussion, and personal feelings all matter in interpretation. Central Americans, for example, typically will not question superiors. Say that you ask your Salvadorian head of housekeeping whether she thinks a new product will be useful and she says, "Yes sir." You need to pay attention to other signals to learn whether she really does believe that or she is simply telling you what she thinks you want to hear. If you have learned the signals, you'd know that if the housekeeper flashes a small smile (embarrassment) and quickly looks down, it probably means a problem. Each country has its own signals, but your focus at this point should be on learning how to pick up the signals (and not so much the signals themselves). Once you learn to observe the signals, you can learn what they mean by linking them to the way people ultimately behave. Force yourself to watch body language and facial signals closely; try to figure out the speaker's emotional state; and note the time and place of the discussion. These observation skills should assist you in learning the "silent signals" in any country.

Here's an example of why it's dangerous to jump to a conclusion about why someone is behaving in a particular way:

> In the 1990s, a foreign hotel company faced massive human resource challenges when it took over an established operation in Moscow. A particularly critical problem was that workers were frequently absent when they or their children were ill, even with minor colds. The general manager (GM) thought that this was a holdover from the communist regime, when workers could behave badly without penalty. As a result, he created attendance incentives and severe penalties for absences, but saw little change in workers' behavior. Looking further into the matter, he discovered his error. The workers were worried that colds might develop into a serious illness, including pneumonia. If that occurred, they could not rely on the public health system, which was in disarray. Consequently, staying home and making sure the cold was completely cured was the only safe route. Dropping the penalties, the GM instead helped employees gain access to quality private health services, thereby reducing the absenteeism problem.

As this case demonstrates, you must *learn to postpone conclusions and instead gather information*. You might say that your quick conclusion is based on intuition, but intuition is really based on your experiences, which are very culturally bound. Away from your home context, your intuition is just not helpful.

While you are learning about others, it is useful to learn about yourself. Much of our own behavior has been learned from our own culture. Speaking distance, eye contact, and smiling are just a few of the components of a greeting ritual that we have learned through experience. For Americans, beliefs in egalitarianism, democracy, and individual rights have been taught in school, through the media, and usually at home. Learning about our own culture helps us to avoid unintended effects, such as when we think we are "acting naturally," but we are actually acting in a culture-bound way. Many books are available to help you learn about your home culture and they are generally fun to read.

About Languages Some people think that they should focus on learning a foreign language in advance. It is useful to know a foreign language because it signals an interest and an ability to learn. When it comes to a specific language, however, it often isn't helpful. Your company may be more likely to send you to France if you speak French, but the fact is that you must go where you are most needed, and that may be a place where French is not of much use. So learn some language, but expect to take an intensive course after you are assigned.

Make Sure Your Family Is on Board Years ago, an American company identified the factors that created a successful expatriate manager. The number one issue for American managers was a supportive family, and that was number two for Europeans, behind personal interest in other cultures. An overseas job is difficult enough, but matters are even worse if your family is unhappy.

Dealing with an unfamiliar culture is complicated. In addition to general cultural mores, a trailing spouse also has to learn which over-the-counter medicines correspond to the ones used at home; how children are registered for school; how to get a driver's license (or find a driver if that is the norm); and what you can eat. I once stood in a grocery store with my children trying to buy yogurt, but the flavors and sizes were all unfamiliar—and my children were having none of it. A small example, but these small awkward situations can mount.

The tasks and possibilities for a misstep are endless. The fact that you are the GM of a major hotel may focus employees' attention on your family's actions. Frequently, they must do as the community expects, and not what they want to do. For instance, take the case of a GM for a multinational resort chain who was assigned to Bali.

When the GM moved to Bali with his wife and two children, his wife told him that she wanted to be self-sufficient and create family experiences as she and the children managed the move. So she didn't want servants. This was not to be. A week into the job, the assistant GM, who was Indonesian, told the GM to hire servants. The assistant GM explained that the community was poor and it was critical that all of the top executives be seen as personally helping to improve community members' lives. By hiring servants and paying them a fair wage, the GM would show that commitment to locals. With that information, his understanding wife agreed to hire a driver, two maids, and a gardener.

Lining Up Opportunities

While you are working on building your powers of observation and other international capabilities, you also need to let people know that you are interested in an international assignment. As you develop your network, talk to people who have done stints abroad and mention your interest in a foreign placement. After you have worked with your firm for six months to a year, let executives with whom you interact know that you are interested in serving the company in another country. Don't harp on the topic, so that you don't signal limited commitment to your current position, but do get the word out. You can also talk to former expatriates, to find out how they got their assignments. If your company has an internal job market that lists open positions, find out the criteria they use to select international managers and make sure your profile conforms to the type they select. If the personnel selection process is informal, your network is your asset. Also, pay attention to executive transfers and contact new GMs abroad who might be seeking staff members.

Even if you have a preferred destination in mind, I suggest that you be open to opportunities that come along. Colombia, for example, usually appears in American newspapers in reference to the drug trade or kidnappings, but few Americans realize that Colombia is also the largest supplier of cut flowers to the United States and that Brazil, Ecuador, and Venezuela all have higher kidnapping rates. So your fears about Colombia might be easily overcome. Needless to say, if you know that you strongly favor urban entertainment options and really dislike nature-based activities, then you might want to discourage an assignment to an isolated resort, like those in the Seychelles or Maldives.

The Final Days at Home and the First Days Abroad

Congratulations! You've received your international assignment. As soon as your assignment is clear, you can start to focus your preparation on the destination's specific requirements, including legal requirements, such as proper papers. To give one example, Spain requires an official certificate that states that you have no criminal record in your home country. To get the latest legal requirements for your destination, it is best to contact the local embassy or consulate of your destination country.

It's important to cover each detail specifically, because your life will be even more difficult if you arrive unprepared. Let's take the example of France. Not all apartments there come with kitchen appliances, so if your plan was to immediately start fixing meals at home, you may have a problem. Dining out in Paris may not be the worst problem you could confront, but needing to go out every time you want a hot or chilled beverage can

wear thin quickly. The human resource professionals in the French subsidiary might be helpful, but they also may not realize what information will be
important to you. If they do not know that U.S. homes come with appliances, they will not know to tell you that French ones do not. So you'll want
to speak with other managers that your company has sent to your prospective
destination, check expatriate Web sites, and read books designed for those
who will work abroad. (You may find the *Culture Shock* series particularly
useful, since it is detailed and no-nonsense.)

Your move will go best if you are prepared. If you know that you will be
spending several hours each day during your first 10 days getting through
the bureaucracy, for example, then you will have more realistic expectations about what you can accomplish at work. If you realize that arranging
your life will be difficult (from outfitting your apartment, setting up bank
accounts, learning the transportation system, etc.), then you have the chance
to hire a relocation specialist who can assist you.

Once You Are Abroad

Culture Shock No matter how well you and your family have prepared,
I have found that you will need to brace yourself for an emotional roller
coaster. Typically, the initial weeks or months, called the honeymoon period,
are marked by intense excitement and positive feelings. Everything is new,
there is so much to learn, and the novelty is great. But soon, the novelty
becomes wearing. If you moved to an unfamiliar language zone, the strain
of communication can be substantial. You also may find it tiring to have
to parse every gesture and every word for underlying meaning. Eventually,
most people become exhausted, and as the frustrations pile on, they hit a
period of culture shock. If this occurs with you, you may find yourself sitting at your desk wondering whether you made the right decision coming
abroad. If you are ready for this period, you can get past it, as I explain next.

The first symptom of culture shock will probably be an emotional downturn,
and you also may feel alienated from the local culture. At this point, I urge you
to resist any tendency to withdraw or socialize primarily with other expatriates.
Instead, pull out of culture shock through engagement. Find people who can
help you navigate your way through the new environment and help you become
more comfortable and effective in your new home. Join hobby or social groups
that give you a local friendship group outside of work. Also, a sense of humor
and a sense of perspective are usually keys to recovering quickly from culture
shock. Typically, the problem that leads to the final breakdown is not serious.
Perhaps the employee cafeteria always serves rice and you really miss potatoes; or

maybe back-of-the-house workers won't meet your eye when you talk to them and it is really starting to get to you; or else it's going to the store and finding only grapefruit yogurt. Stepping back and putting these small matters into context, you realize that your problems are actually quite humorous.

Be Modest This is usually important for Americans because we do not generally value modesty. You will need to follow a lifestyle consistent with your position and, in some cases, as with the GM in Bali (noted earlier), the locals will expect you to live in a relatively luxurious style and hire household assistants. If you are an expatriate below a local GM, however, you may be paid more than your superior, but you should avoid living in a larger house or having a fancier car. Modesty also extends to sharing knowledge. In most societies, people appreciate help but are not fond of know-it-alls. Thus, remember to offer information in a supportive way that allows your coworkers to engage and contribute their knowledge. You might say, "I understand that some people have solved this problem by . . . What do you think about that?" In addition, if you can retrieve information needed from someone in your network, offer to do so.

Find an Informant Gathering useful information requires you to learn how to ask questions without being offensive, which is another useful skill for you to learn. You should try to be descriptive rather than judgmental: Rather than ask, "Why are people always late?," you could phrase the question like this: "I notice many people arrive 10 minutes after start time. Do you know why that happens?" Alternatively, you can ask for assistance, "Can you help me to understand why . . ." Most societies place a value on helping others with whom they are in regular contact, so asking a coworker for help usually generates a useful response.

You should quickly try to find a local informant who can provide insights. Your subordinates may be helpful because they probably recognized cross-national differences during their socialization into the corporate culture. They may be worried about offending you with their answers or making their compatriots look bad and therefore may be less than candid. In general, though, when you approach someone and express a genuine interest in getting to know more about their society, they typically will respond positively and you can begin a conversation.

While many informants are locals, an informant could also be another expatriate or former expatriate who worked in your host country. There may be someone in your company who can assist you, or you may meet expatriates professionally or socially. Many countries have specialists who work in relocation services to provide help.

Regardless of the source, beware of anyone who demeans your new location, a habit found in many expatriates. Instead of judgment, what you want is a person who speaks descriptively of the situation to help you to understand how you can respond effectively. Beware of choosing a local informant if that person expects something in return. Many societies have strong reciprocity norms. In Japan, for instance, if someone helps you, you are expected to return the favor. Such an expectation can cause problems if the person is a subordinate. Even in societies with an expected *quid pro quo*, you will probably find people who are generous with their time without expecting a personal return. You can usually quickly identify persons who will expect return favors, because they will typically first ask for small favors. Luckily, in societies with expectations of return favors, you are likely to find the professional informants or consultants.

Keep in Touch with Headquarters In many ways, you're on your own in an international assignment, but do not underestimate the importance of maintaining your ties to headquarters while you are abroad. You need your contacts to get information and resources not only to do your job abroad, but also to help your career. The expression "out of sight, out of mind" definitely applies to the expatriate, and if you do not remind HQ colleagues of your existence, they probably won't consider you when interesting positions open up. To benefit your career, you need to maintain contact.

A good time to touch base at headquarters is during your home leave, the paid trip home found in most international contracts. While you will undoubtedly want to visit family and friends, you should also visit headquarters and renew acquaintances face to face. Also, when you learn something in your new position that you feel might be helpful elsewhere, take the time to contact the relevant people and let them know. Several interesting product and service innovations introduced by U.S.-based firms worldwide have come from their foreign subsidiaries (including McDonald's McCafé, ice cream kiosks, and the no-labor check-in and check-out options offered in many hotels).

Do Not "Go Local" Eventually, you will have learned so much about your new home that you can almost think like a local. You can use this ability in a positive way, as I explain in a moment, but this may also have a negative outcome. No matter how familiar you have become with your destination, you remain a representative of your firm. While it is easy to begin to see everything from the local perspective, that can become a problem when it is time for you to implement a new policy. Remember, your job is to make the new policy work and you must avoid focusing on why the policy won't work in your new context and instead negotiate any amendments necessary to implement the new policy. Otherwise, you have ceased to be a corporate employee and have become a subsidiary employee. Few things annoy headquarters personnel more than an expatriate who has gone local. Only by thinking from both perspectives—local and headquarters—will you be able to manage in a way that helps the company.

Interpret for Headquarters The positive aspect of thinking like a local is that you can analyze directives from headquarters and identify exactly where local implementation problems may arise. Figure out the key goal of the directive, whether it is to provide consistency across operations, to save money, or to raise perceived quality. Once you determine which goals are relevant, you can work with headquarters to determine whether the directive is the best way to achieve that goal in your local environment and work out alternative plans, if need be. For instance, a corporate plan to cut costs on a particular expense had an unexpected outcome for a GM in Peru.

> A call from headquarters informed Rick Ensign, GM of LimaHotel, that a new policy was being implemented globally: The company would no longer support local amateur sports teams. Although he understood that the company wanted to cut costs, he knew that this policy would create a serious problem. His staff particularly valued those teams, which were made up of employees and their children. Dozens of employees attended games to cheer and the "LimaHotel Spirit" not only maintained morale, but also helped recruit better workers. Rick was well aware that there was no such link between employees and the local teams in the United States, where this policy would cause no ripples. After determining that team support cost $3,000 per year, Rick searched for another way to generate the same savings. He calculated that eliminating some beverage options in the staff dining room would cover it. He also knew that this solution would be acceptable because his Peruvian staff did not particularly care about beverage variety (especially compared to U.S. residents). Instead of just telling his boss that the team policy would not work, Rick explained both the problem and his solution, gaining approval to cut his budget in a way that would be acceptable to his employees.

This vignette demonstrates the key position you hold as an expatriate. You are the linchpin between headquarters and the local operation, and you have to realize that your job is to manage up the hierarchy as well as down. To do that, you need to interpret the local environment for the corporation and allow them to understand the challenges you face. Chief among these is human resources, which would have become even more difficult for Rick Ensign if he had been forced to discontinue supporting his employees' teams. Along this line, when Cathy Enz surveyed 243 hotel managers worldwide, she found that executives face different challenges to maintaining an excellent workforce in different regions.[3] She found, for instance, that executives in Latin America had to explain to headquarters that they must invest in training programs because lack of training was the biggest challenge. However, managers in Europe needed to convince headquarters to allow bonuses based on tenure because retention was the biggest challenge.

Not every story works out as well as that of LimaHotel. Sometimes you simply will have to implement a corporate decision, even though it will not sit well locally. Here is the moment to use all that you have learned about your local situation to interpret the corporate perspective for locals and find an implementation process that helps overcome negative outcomes.

Interpreting for Locals Your local knowledge will also allow you to help your employees to understand the corporate perspective, which should help smooth implementation of corporate standards and policies. Interpreting the corporate perspective for your subordinates is also critical to ensuring that those people will have a career path in the company. Many people join the hospitality industry to gain access to the international career opportunities, but to do that they need to become corporate employees rather than local employees. So you can gradually work with them to develop attitudes and behaviors that will help them to be successful in an international career. Be sure to help them understand why, on a global level, the corporate rules and norms make sense even if they are not all locally relevant. This interpretation can help them transition from a local mind-set to a corporate mind-set and ready themselves to move to other subsidiaries.

COMING HOME

Reentry Stress

At some point, you will either return to your home country or pick a country as your "permanent" home. You probably will experience reentry stress, which is similar to culture shock. However, reentry stress can be more difficult because it has no clear end. One source of potential trouble is that you may have unrealistically high expectations for "going home," possibly because you have taken a job that is higher in the corporate hierarchy. First problem: You gain a promotion, but your level of autonomy drops substantially.

Abroad, you were running your own show. Now, your boss is down the hall. Your decisions and actions may have a broader effect, but your choices are usually more constrained by people who share your office floor. You may just decide to accept a demotion and find another expatriate assignment.[4] Many people leave their firms and start consulting practices to regain their autonomy, but if you focus on your new, larger domain, you can often find enough excitement and change to keep you happy.

Your home culture will seem foreign in one or more ways. You may find commonplace things to be annoying. The speed, intensity, and high cost of many American cities often seems like a waste of energy and money to those who have been living in less industrialized countries, for example. Or, to take another instance, expatriates returning to Germany often find the culture's hyperdirect communication to be rude after living in a culture that uses indirect communication approaches. The solution to reentry shock is similar to that of culture shock—namely, resist the urge to withdraw and, instead, engage.

Moving back home may also mean that you lose many of the perks of foreign assignments, including the household help, in many cultures. Many expatriates receive educational subsidies, tax benefits, and travel allowances—you probably will no longer have those when you come home. Needless to say, you'll have to plan for these budget changes.

Finally, you must realize that your domestic colleagues have not worked in other countries because they aren't interested in working in other countries. Thus, they will probably not be interested in your experiences abroad, and perhaps they won't even care about the new ideas you have developed based on what you learned. When you try to communicate your excitement to others who are indifferent, you might feel isolated in your home culture and company. So you could look for other outlets for your experiences. One option is to write down your professional experiences and help your company create a database that can help future expatriates to manage better. Another is to find others with similar experiences who enjoy swapping stories. Some people find guest lecture opportunities at colleges or adult education programs to be a helpful outlet.

In closing, I want to encourage you to think about an assignment overseas. Even with the many potential difficulties that I have outlined in this chapter, I am convinced that you will find the experience to be personally enriching and professionally valuable.

NOTES

1. J. Combs, "Using Cases to Discover Theory: The Case of the Poland-Based Restaurant Operator," *Cornell Hospitality Quarterly* 49(1998): 450–453.

2. P. C. Earley, and M. Erez. *New Perspectives on International Industrial/Organizational Psychology.* (San Francisco, CA: New Lexington Press, 1997).

3. C. A. Enz. "Human Resource Management: A Troubling Issue for the Global Hotel Industry." *Cornell Hospitality Quarterly* 50 (2009): 578–583.

4. N. J. Adler. *International Dimensions of Organizational Behavior,* Third Edition. (Boston, MA: PWS-KENT, 1997).

CHAPTER 6

BECOMING A LEADER IN THE HOSPITALITY INDUSTRY

TIMOTHY HINKIN

Leadership has been defined in many ways, but the essence of leadership involves influencing people toward a desired objective. Leaders do not push followers—they pull them. While management is often concerned about stability, efficiency, and control, leadership is focusing on innovation, adaptation, and employee development. Management focuses on coping with the day to day, while a true leader is looking into the future. A manager can develop a brilliant marketing campaign, create an innovative strategy for growth, and design the most efficient work processes, but if the followers don't engage effectively in the implementation of these initiatives, these efforts will fail. Leadership does not exist in a vacuum but emerges only with the consensus of followers. So, simply being in a leadership position does not automatically make you a leader. Instead, others decide whether you are a leader. In this chapter, I discuss how you can achieve this status.

In truth, we are still learning how leaders develop (see Table 6.1). I like to think of leadership as an evolutionary process, from "little l" to "BIG L." Every individual in any managerial position has a sphere of influence, and within that sphere they can have either a positive or negative impact. The impact may be "little l" if you are the front-desk manager of a small hotel, or "Big L" if you are the CEO of an international restaurant company. Regardless of the size of the sphere of influence, both situations give you the opportunity to be an effective leader. Your success in the position of "little l" may result in the increase of your sphere of influence with the eventual progression to the role of "BIG L."

Table 6.1
Evolution of Leadership Research

Decade	Culture	Leadership
Pre–1950	Hierarchy	Control
1950s	Organization	Supervision
1960s	Systems	Administration
1970s	Strategy	Management
1980s	Innovation	Entrepreneurship
1990s	Diversity	Team Building
Post–2000	Community	Relationships

You may find the answers to the following questions to be revealing with respect to your current leadership effectiveness:

- Are your subordinates willing to give a little extra when needed?
- Have any of their ideas been implemented recently?
- How many of your subordinates have been promoted to other parts of the organization?
- Has there been resistance to your recent efforts to institute change in work processes?
- Do you feel comfortable delegating important tasks to subordinates?
- What happens when you are not there?

You can figure out the correct answers to these questions, but the point of this exercise is to get you thinking about your leadership skills and spark enough interest to read and explore this chapter for yourself.

As I said, we're still learning about leadership and how leaders operate, but we've begun to nail down some basic principles, as I'll discuss in a moment. Table 6.1 shows leaders as being in an era of relationship building. Even if this is just another phase that we're passing through, the fact is that as a leader today, you need to develop relationships, defined as an emotional or other connection with your employees. People follow leaders because the leaders connect with them in some significant way. This model certainly fits the hospitality industry, with its labor-intensive operations and focus on people. Let's look at how one goes about developing these relationships to become an effective leader. The five steps that I offer in this chapter are based on an extensive body of research that examines the phenomenon of leadership in a variety of contexts, including the hospitality industry. They are: (1) be self-aware, (2) understand your organization, (3) establish objectives and provide guidance toward those goals, (4) acknowledge good performance and correct poor performance, and (5) be flexible and willing to adapt.

STEP 1. UNDERSTAND YOURSELF

The importance of self-knowledge may seem obvious, but it is amazing how many managers really don't have a good understanding of their own behavioral patterns and internal motivators. Nor do they see how they come off to other people. They tend to have a single preferred management style, which cannot be appropriate in every situation, and they often don't realize the impact of their actions on others.

To use myself as an example of the importance of self-knowledge, prior to returning to graduate school to pursue my MBA I worked for two major hospitality organizations. I wasn't happy in either one, but I could never figure out why. During my MBA program, I undertook several personality assessments that helped me enormously in understanding myself. I learned that I have an extremely high need for autonomy. That would explain my frustration with the corporate structure with its strict policies, centralized decision making, rigid hierarchies, and top-down management. In another personality assessment, the widely used Myers-Briggs test, I learned that I am what Myers-Briggs calls an ENTP personality type. As an "E" I get my energy from being around people, and this type is described as being theoretical, creative, analytical, and questioning—a good profile for an academic, but perhaps not so great for the structure in the corporate world.[1] I entered my MBA program fully intending on returning to some part of the hospitality industry, but with the insight and introspection I gained in the program, I decided to totally change the direction of my career and consequently my life. Both of the companies I worked for are successful and well regarded—nothing is wrong with them. With self-knowledge, I now know that working there was just wrong for me. This was important information, and it has had a tremendous impact on shaping my career as a professor.

Assessments of this type are not mere parlor games, but can provide powerful insights into your motivations and behavior. In recent years there has been increased research into what has been termed *emotional intelligence*, or EQ, defined by Daniel Goleman as the ability to manage ourselves and our relationships effectively. EQ is characterized by four traits, the first being self-awareness, as we have been discussing here.[2] The second dimension is self-management, demonstrated by self-control and being able to adapt appropriately to a situation. This involves the ability to adjust easily to changing situations without becoming emotionally upset. The third dimension is social awareness, which is empathy for others and an understanding of organizational dynamics. With high social awareness, you are sensitive to the emotions of others and you understand others' perspective on issues. The fourth trait is social skill, which includes effective communication, conflict management, and persuasiveness. With this skill you are able to constructively manage disagreements and influence others. In sum, EQ is an assessment of how well we understand ourselves and how we relate to others.

You might benefit from a brief period of introspection spent asking yourself how you rate on these dimensions. Better yet, getting feedback from trusted colleagues could be even more helpful. Because of the high degree of interpersonal interaction with both employees and guests in the hospitality industry, EQ is especially important to hospitality leaders.

A substantial body of research has shown that executives who possess a higher degree of EQ received more favorable performance reviews and their organizations achieved greater financial success. As an example, in September 2007, Starwood Hotels and Resorts hired Frits van Paasschen as its new CEO. He had held executive positions at Disney, Nike, and Coors, but admitted knowing little about the hotel industry. He was hired for his leadership ability, and the following quote reflects his management style: "What I learned is to work hard, treat everyone well, and listen," he says. "It's more about effort than ability. We all know brilliant people who haven't had a very successful life."[3] His leadership philosophy and career success suggest that he has a high EQ. In July 2010 Starwood's stock price was up over 100 percent from the previous July in a year when many hotel companies were suffering.

Peter Drucker, the noted management scholar, suggests that it is critical to understand your strengths and weaknesses, how you interact with others, and what your values are.[4] In this context, you need to give thought to what is really important to you. Your values are reflected in your behavior. We have learned that subordinates are constantly observing managers to see if their actions match their words. Thus, they soon learn to distrust managers who exhort people to be creative and think out of the box but then are all over them when someone fails, or a manager who prides himself on being open to suggestion but reacts with hostility when his ideas are questioned. As explained further in Chapter 31, studies by my colleague Tony Simons and others have shown that behavioral integrity, the consistency between words and deeds, is related to a number of organizational outcomes including reduced employee turnover and increased profitability. You are a role model, whether you are setting a good example or a bad one.[5]

We all have a preferred way of leading that is influenced by our personality, education, and experience. Clearly, though, your preferred way of leading is not going to fit every situation, and so we need to be aware of when we should behave in a particular way or move away from our preferred leadership style.[6] Goleman discusses the following six leadership styles:

1. **Coercive:** Demands immediate compliance
2. **Authoritative:** Mobilizes people toward a vision
3. **Affiliative:** Creates harmony and builds emotional bonds
4. **Democratic:** Forges consensus through participation
5. **Pacesetting:** Sets high standards for performance
6. **Coaching:** Develops people for the future

Do you see a style on that list that sounds like yourself? Or perhaps a blend of styles? Understanding your preferred leadership style is important because it's a starting point for how you would prefer to lead. The key to leadership is to determine when one style will be effective and when it's time to switch to another. Affiliative leadership might be ineffective in some situations when coercive leadership would be needed. If you are first aware of your behavioral preferences, then you can work on adjusting your style to the situation. A combination of authoritative, democratic, and coaching, for example, is a powerful leadership repertoire. Interestingly, research has shown that coaching is the least used leadership style, yet it can be one of the most beneficial for the long-term success of an organization. Self-awareness and recognizing how you affect others is the first step in becoming a successful leader.

STEP 2. UNDERSTAND YOUR ORGANIZATION

When asked to describe their particular organization, most managers discuss hierarchical reporting relationships and rely on the most recent organizational chart, which might look something like Figure 6.1. These typical organization charts seldom mention customers, either internal or external, or how work actually flows through the organization. To learn about your organization, you need to understand your organization as a system.[7] An organization is much like the human body, with organs serving as functional areas, the skeleton as the structure, and the circulatory and nervous systems providing coordination and communication. If any part of this system is not functioning properly, the whole organism falters. There is a strong sense of interdependence that exists in the human body, and also in and among organizations.

Hospitality organizations exist in a dynamic environment that contains competitors, customers, suppliers, and government—all of which can affect the company. Communicating with these entities is also important,

Figure 6.1
Formal Organization Chart

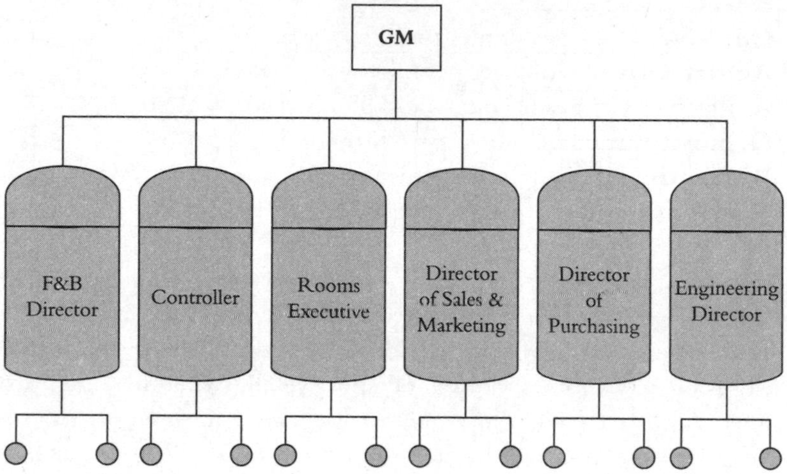

as they provide resources and information necessary for the success of the organization, whether it's Smith Travel Research for its useful hotel benchmarks or the National Restaurant Association, with its educational and lobbying efforts. Sysco Corporation's business model, for instance, is based on forming relationships with its 400,000 customers. In 2009, Sysco was rated number one by *Fortune*'s "World's Most Admired Companies" in the Wholesale Food and Grocery Division.

Every organization has several interdependent key processes that have substantial impact on customers. At the School of Hotel Administration, the three most critical processes are admissions, education, and placement. We also have a number of important ancillary and support functions, such as alumni affairs, development, information technology, and human resources. We must be certain that the key processes are in alignment. The process starts with admissions, which includes activities such as determining where to put our recruiting efforts, and whom to admit, based on our established admissions criteria. Those criteria are driven by our success at placement and by feedback from industry. The education process is informed by our research and supported with classroom technology, and responses from industry also influence the content in the curriculum. Placement has three major processes: industry outreach, on-campus recruiting, and career tracking. The relationships among the key processes are illustrated in Figure 6.2.

Figure 6.2
Systems View—Key Processes

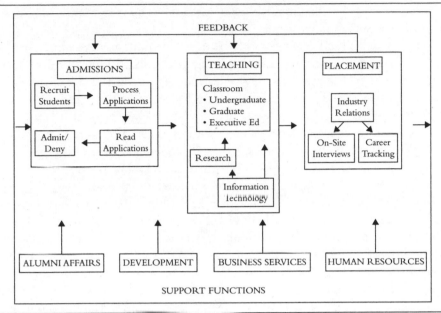

Although I have simplified the model, it illustrates the interdependent relationships that exist among the processes. If we accept the right students and provide the appropriate education, recruiters will hire them. This benefits the hospitality industry and fulfills our mission, which drives the alignment that is designed to "Prepare Leaders for the Hospitality Industry." That means we want to attract a student with a particular profile, provide the education that contains the appropriate content at a level of sufficient rigor, and place graduates in management positions that utilize their intellect and education. Feedback from the industry and recruiters is essential in ensuring that we are attracting the right students and preparing them well. Needless to say, the support functions contribute to our success. If any part of this system fails, the whole system fails. The same is true for any hospitality organization.

Darden Restaurants provides an excellent example of a company where top leadership understands the organization and its operations. They have identified the key interfaces that exist between internal and external customers, managers, and purveyors, and have developed a sophisticated distribution system that allows the firm to meet the needs of all of its constituencies. When they open a new restaurant, the delivery trucks are packed and deliveries timed so the items that are needed first arrive first. As a result, the restaurant can be up and operating within a few days after the first delivery. This does not happen by chance but because the leadership understands the interdependencies involved in opening a restaurant.

To truly understand organizations, however, one must go beyond the formal organization chart. Managers tend to manage vertically and functionally, looking down rather than across their organizations. The danger of this approach is that a manager may not recognize the interdependencies that exist. There are important critical interfaces in every organization such as between housekeeping and the front office or banquets and stewards, where managers often end up taking adversarial positions. Leaders, however, understand their organizations as comprising a number of interdependent processes, and they manage the "white space" on the organizational chart that exists between functional areas.

Informal organizations are "webs of relationships" that transcend the formal organization chart. An analogy would be social media networks, because the informal network may communicate the way friends do on Facebook. That network comprises communication lines and hubs that create a network of relationships that does not show up anywhere on the organization chart, but is enormously powerful.[8] Managers who either ignore or can't see these informal networks are at a distinct disadvantage because research has shown that better understanding of these networks has positive impacts on organizational performance. Leadership is all around you if you pay attention, and informal leaders can be a tremendous asset if their goals are in alignment with those of the organization.

Figure 6.3 presents an example of an informal communication network. You will note that Bill and Fran seem to occupy communication hubs, and that Fran's network is composed exclusively of women, with the exception of her contact with Bill. Don is isolated, while Art and Will seem to rely on Gus, and Tom communicates only with Bill. From this analysis, we can conclude that Bill is influential in the informal organization. Importantly, his position on the formal organization chart might not reveal this influence. Don, however, is so far removed from the action that he is not likely to have a good understanding of what is going on in the organization. That situation might be troublesome if he occupies a prominent position in the formal hierarchy. As a leader, you need to learn about your informal organization and then you can manage it effectively. A perceptive leader may hesitate to promote, say, Art over Bill, even if Art has superior technical expertise because, despite Art's skill and knowledge, he has not developed the relationships with others that would help him be successful. This is a typical example of how your organization goes far beyond what is shown on the organizational chart.

Figure 6.3
Informal Communication Network

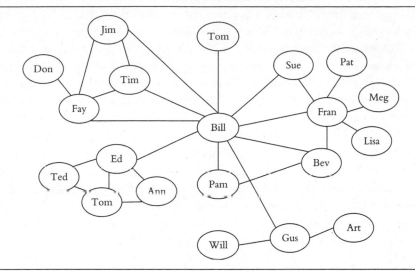

Again, the clearer your understanding of the interdependencies and informal relationships that exist, the more effective you can be.

STEP 3. ESTABLISH OBJECTIVES
AND PROVIDE THE DIRECTION

This step starts by determining the objective of your organization. You need to know what you are *really* trying to achieve. Are you in business to satisfy the guest, for instance, or to maximize profitability—or can you do both? If you are in business to please the guest, your daily decisions will probably be different than if you are attempting to maximize profitability. People at all levels need to understand the overriding objectives of the organization, and these goals need to be aligned with department goals and functional practices as they cascade down through the organization. People can relate to an objective that they understand and accept.

The organization's overall goals should be driving the goals for each manager. Every manager has a sphere of influence, and you should be able to state what are you trying to achieve in your sphere of influence. Beyond that, your subordinates and colleagues also should be able to correctly describe your goals. Leadership at all levels begins with being able to articulate a goal or vision that followers can understand and internalize. That goal for "little l" leaders might be to reduce to five minutes the time it takes to clear and reset a table or to increase market share by 10 percent. For "BIG L" leaders, an objective might be to have 20 hotels open in Asia by 2015. The sum total of these spheres of influence is to design the organization and work processes so that they are aligned with the overall organizational objectives, together with performance management systems that are designed to reinforce the vision.

People need to know what they are doing, why they are doing it, and how it fits into the big picture. For this reason, you need to continually remind people of the organization's goals. Research that examines various ways of influencing others has found that the most effective means of influencing others is by rational explanation. Extending this principle to the hospitality industry, your employees should have been given (and should be able to state) a rational explanation of why they are doing what they do. Much of the front-of-the-house work involves direct interaction with a customer or guest, and I think we can agree that the objectives and outcomes in this area are fairly obvious. The purpose of activities in the back of the house may not always be so clear cut, as some input-output relationships are either not recognized or not acknowledged.

When I visit hospitality organizations, I often ask employees why they are doing whatever task they are involved in. The answer is usually either "I was told to do it this way" or "that is the way we have always done it." As a leader, you need to counteract that type of impression so that all employees understand how their task contributes to the overall guest experience, or who their internal customer is. Not only do you need to explain why the work is important, but you need to make sure employees understand that they are appreciated for doing it. Having clean glassware is more important to most guests than meeting the chef, for instance, yet the steward department may be the hotel's least appreciated and most ignored department. Thus, it's essential that you let people know how their efforts relate to the achievement of the organization's overall objectives.

Bill Marriott's approach provides an excellent example of clearly articulating a vision that reflects the values of an organization. He states that "if we take care of our employees they will take care of our guests."[9] This simple idea so clearly articulated has for decades provided guidance to everyone in the organization about what is important and how individuals treat each other. I don't need to also mention that this has been a successful approach, but I will point out that Marriott has well over 3,000 hotels worldwide with revenues in excess of $12 billion. Not coincidentally, in recent years, it has also been one of only two hotel companies that have been consistently on *Fortune*'s "100 Best Companies to Work For." The other is Four Seasons Hotels and Resorts, founded by another effective leader, Isadore Sharp. He also clearly stated his vision for a hotel that featured superior design, top-quality amenities, and, above all, a deep commitment to service. He recently wrote a book entitled *Four Seasons: The Story of a Business Philosophy* that describes the importance of visionary leadership.

You don't need to write a book to state your organization's purpose, but you do need to be able to state it clearly and make sure that everyone in the organization also has the same goals.

STEP 4. ACKNOWLEDGE GOOD PERFORMANCE AND CORRECT POOR PERFORMANCE

With a clear objective in place, your reward systems must reinforce your organization's objectives and culture. We have all seen companies that fail to reflect their mission statements or codes of conduct in their performance management program. The most successful firms align rewards with objectives. American Express, for instance, has a set of "Blue Box Values." A key such value is: "We value our people, encourage their development, and reward their performance." To reinforce this value, senior leadership is evaluated using a 360-degree performance management process on eight leadership competencies. Four of those competencies focus on quantitative business results, while the other four focus on effectively leading people. The four leadership competencies are: demonstrates personal excellence, communicates effectively, builds and leverages relationships, and creates an environment where cross–team working is effective both internally and externally. Each of these competencies is assessed by specific behaviors such as "actively listens and incorporates input from others" and "shares critical expertise and knowledge to support partners and colleagues."

Similarly, Darden Restaurants separates their performance management systems into two primary categories, "what" a manager does, and "how" he or she does it. The "what" category is composed of four objectives: financial results, impact on the guest, employee development, and process excellence. The weighting for each of these objectives is tailored to the individual based on their responsibilities. The "how" category comprises four leadership competencies: personal leadership, people leadership, business leadership, and results leadership. The fact that so much emphasis in both organizations is placed on leading and developing subordinates sends a message about what is important and reinforces each company's culture and values. As a result, leaders develop leaders, not followers.

Beyond the formal reward systems the day-to-day interaction between a manager and subordinates provides many opportunities to respond to performance. When people perform well, a leader can either respond to that performance, which is termed *contingent reward*, or not, which is termed *reward omission*. The same is true for poor performance, although the choices there are contingent punishment or punishment omission. There is no money involved in these responses; it is simply a matter of responding to subordinates' performance in an appropriate manner.

In the popular series of books based on the *One Minute Manager*, Kenneth Blanchard exhorts you to actively look for opportunities to recognize good performance.[10] Similarly, my own research examining reinforcement behaviors found that what people want is acknowledgment of good performance. We found that use of contingent rewards had strong positive impacts on subordinates' behavior and their attitudes about their manager. We also learned that satisfaction and performance of high performers who do not receive acknowledgment will decline over time, and eventually they may leave. By the same token, counter to intuition, my research also found that people want to know when they are performing poorly, and it is leadership's responsibility to correct the performance deficiency. Again, this is part of acknowledging an employee's actions.

Failure to acknowledge results can be devastating. Not long ago, I received a telephone call from a former student who was chief operating officer for a major restaurant company. In the prior five years, he had doubled the number of restaurants and tripled the company's revenues. Despite that clearly success- ful record, he had just resigned. When I asked him why, he explained that the CEO of the company had never thanked him or acknowledged his efforts. Let me be clear about this: The issue wasn't money; it was acknowledgment. This happens in organizations every day due to poor leadership, and the best people can always leave.

This is far more than a matter of making people feel good, as you will see in Table 6.2. In our study, we asked the regional manager of an upscale casual dining restaurant chain to give us a list of those restaurants whose perform- ance was highest on the dimensions of financial performance, cleanliness and maintenance, and managing people, and also to list those that were lowest on those metrics. We then asked the employees of each restaurant on both lists to describe their manager's reinforcement behaviors, as well as their feeling about a variety of emotions. The results were clear. Managers of both high- performing restaurants and low performers used contingent punishment about equally—an unpleasant but necessary management tool. But we found a real difference in the reinforcement activities by managers in the two types of res- taurants. The managers of the higher-performing restaurants made greater use of contingent rewards, and less use of reward omission than did the managers in the poorly performing restaurants. Those high-performing managers were

Table 6.2
Restaurant-Level Performance Analysis Results

Leader Behaviors	Low Performance	High Performance
Contingent Reward	4.00	**4.37**
Contingent Punishment	4.92	4.84
Reward Omission	**4.36**	3.98
Punishment Omission	3.16	3.10
Subordinate Outcomes		
Behavioral Integrity	3.31	**3.68**
Affective Trust	3.14	**3.40**
Supervisor Effectiveness	3.32	**3.71**
Satisfaction with Supervisor	3.49	**3.77**
Organizational Commitment	3.73	**3.90**

Note: Numbers in bold are statistically significantly different.

also perceived to be higher in behavioral integrity, again demonstrating the importance of that concept. All of the affective responses including satisfaction and commitment were higher in the high-performing stores. Due to the rigorous design of the study, we feel confident that the managers' reinforcement behaviors alone had a substantial impact on store performance.

Providing feedback, both through a formal performance management program and personally in daily interaction, shows your employees that their contribution to the organization is acknowledged. The restaurant managers in our study who used both contingent reward and contingent punishment were evaluated more positively by both the regional manager and their own subordinates. This study demonstrates why leaders must pay attention and respond to subordinates' performance to send a message that they appreciate the effort put forth by their employees and want to help them improve.

STEP 5. BE FLEXIBLE AND WILLING TO ADAPT

The best hospitality managers assemble a team of individuals who have complementary skills and knowledge. A trap that younger managers often fall into is confusing intelligence with knowledge. The employees you are supervising may not have the education you have, but most likely possess institutional knowledge that could be helpful for you if you seek their opinions and truly listen. One cannot, no matter who he or she is, know everything, and relying on others for help does not demonstrate weakness but instead creates a community of distributed leadership where you can capitalize on the knowledge and expertise of others.[11] If you surround yourself with those who view everything the same way, someone is redundant. It's widely acknowledged that the demise of Kodak and General Motors was largely due to intelligent leaders making poor decisions because they either ignored opinions and ideas that were different from their own or never heard any differing views.

At a recent Center for Hospitality Research Roundtable where over 200 industry human resources professionals gathered, we heard one consistent theme. Count on continual change, and the more hats you can wear, the more valuable you will be to your organizations. This may seem to contradict the message in the previous paragraph regarding not being able to do everything, but the message is consistent. Do a few things well and recognize that you cannot be an expert at everything. Focus on your strengths and understand how and where to get the talent and resources you do not possess.

Your understanding of your organization will help you determine who in the organization has the information or expertise that you need to accomplish your goals. Beyond the organization, you can identify vendors who can provide a particular product or service. With the explosion in technology affecting distribution, communication, supply chain management, and even food preparation, it is virtually impossible to keep up with all of the changes. Nonetheless, you need to monitor these changes and evaluate how they may affect your organizations.

In fact, you probably will want to enlist associates to help you determine whether you have all of the information you need to make an important decision. Then you may need help in implementing the decision. You should take advantage of the value of different ideas and knowledge that exist around you. Not only will you get the information you need to make a sound decision, which may be different than had you made it alone, but those involved in the decision will be more willing to assist with the implementation. By including others in the discussion of substantive issues, you send a message that you respect their opinions and ideas, which serves to improve your relationships. This is, in fact, another form of acknowledgment, in which you demonstrate your high regard for others' opinions and expertise and your willingness to adapt as needed.

TOWARD STRONGER LEADERSHIP

The five leadership steps I have offered are based on 25 years of research and teaching on the topic of leadership. Unfortunately, I cannot guarantee that you will become a great leader if you follow them. But I can state with reasonable certainty that if you do not follow these steps, it's unlikely that you will make it as a leader. Understanding yourself and how you prefer to lead gives you the ability to relate well with others and to modify your approach to fit a given situation. Understanding the dynamics within your formal and informal organizations and among other organizations will help you in becoming a more effective leader because you will want to monitor and nurture important interdependent relationships in your organization. Effective leadership requires a clear articulation of a vision of the future because people want to know where they are going, why they should go there, and how their efforts will help get them there. By acknowledging good performance and correcting poor performance, your employees will see that you are focused on improving the work effort. By contrast, not responding in any way will cause your subordinates to doubt your leadership ability. Finally, be willing to adapt to situations as necessary. Recognize that you cannot be an expert at everything, and by understanding yourself, your organization, and your environment, you can know where to get the resources and expertise that you need to complement your strengths. Remember that being the manager does not necessarily make you a leader, but if you apply the principles in this chapter, it is possible to become one.

NOTES

1. I. B. Myers. *Introduction to Type* (Mountain View, CA: CPP, Inc., 1999).
2. D. Goleman. "Leadership That Gets Results" *Harvard Business Review* 78(2): (2000):79–90.
3. usatoday.com/money/companies/management/2008-06-22-starwood-ceo-paasschen_N.htm.
4. P. F. Drucker. *Classic Drucker* (Boston: Harvard Business School Publishing, 2006).
5. G. R. Weaver, L. K. Trevino, and B. Agle. "Somebody I Look Up To: Ethical Role Models in Organizations," *Organizational Dynamics* 34 (2005):313–330.
6. J. P. Kotter. "Leading Change—Why Transformation Efforts Fail," *Harvard Business Review* 85(1): (2007):96–103.
7. G. A. Rummler, and A. P. Brache. *Improving Performance* (San Francisco: Jossey-Bass, 1995).
8. D. Krackhardt, and J. R. Hanson. "Informal Networks: the Company Behind the Chart" *Harvard Business Review* 71(4): (1993):104–111.
9. ABC News *Nightline,* "The Man Behind the Marriott Empire: Bill Marriott," originally broadcast 6/21/07, Films for the Humanities & Sciences.
10. K. Blanchard. *The Heart of a Leader* (Tulsa: Honor Books, 1999).
11. Deborah Ancona, Thomas W. Malone, Wanda J. Orlikowski, and Peter M. Senge. "In Praise of the Incomplete Leader," *Harvard Business Review* 85(2): (2007):1–8.

PART II

Success Through Operations and Service Excellence

CHAPTER 7

UNDERSTANDING AND PREDICTING CUSTOMER CHOICES

ROHIT VERMA

Your customers are confronted with multiple options for where they can dine and where they will stay for the night. The choices they make among the many lodging and dining options are based on criteria that are not always clear—certainly not to you, and often not to them. Your guests may have chosen your hotel because of its favorable room rate, its brand name, its quality rating, its features and amenities, reviews posted by past guests on social media sites, or simply because they were ready to stop for the night and there it was. Similarly, in the case of a restaurant, a customer's choice may be influenced by the cuisine, menu, décor, price, and reputation.

The more you can learn about what factors your guests take into account when they decide whether to book your hotel or a competitor's property, the better you are able to meet those decision criteria and boost occupancy and rate. In this chapter, I explain two ways to find out those criteria: simply ask, or set up discrete choice experiments. The reason for the experiments is that when you simply ask, you might not get an accurate or complete answer. The problem with the experiments is that the procedure can be complicated, even though the information itself is most useful.

ASKING ABOUT DECISION FACTORS

Let's look at a study where we just asked people what web-page factors were most important to them. Table 7.1 shows the results of this survey, in which hotel customers were asked to rate the relative importance of various features

Table 7.1

Relative Importance of Various Hotel Features When Customers Search for Information about Them on Travel-Related Web Sites

	Male	Female	18–24 Yrs	25–34 Yrs	35–44 Yrs	45–54 Yrs	55–64 Yrs	65+Yrs
Photos	392	428	430	428	424	401	388	331
Videos	299	300	311	293	304	308	288	284
Map/location of the hotel	414	428	421	426	424	422	419	389
Reviews by past guests	372	406	406	405	400	382	370	321
Reviews by professional organizations	358	376	365	359	367	373	372	351
Information about common features and amenities available in the hotel	400	435	410	415	425	420	414	382
Information about features and amenities in the room	404	437	410	418	430	422	419	379
Information about promotions and special events	373	405	383	382	397	393	390	347
Information about technology options within the hotel	352	354	372	358	358	352	342	307
Sample size	1592	1321	317	578	641	680	505	174

1 = Least Important; 5 = Most Important.
Source: Survey of Randomly Selected Hotel Customers Located in the United States, May 2010.

of the hotel when they search for hotel information on travel-related Web sites. The results presented here show the different weights assigned to various characteristics of a hotel Web site, and we see that there are considerable differences between subgroups of customers based on age and gender in terms of how they assign weight to various hotel web features.

We can guess that a hotel's features and amenities are important, not only on the web page but in terms of booking the hotels, since those were highly ranked in this survey. But this survey didn't touch on the question of rate, so we must look further.

While it is useful to note the importance of different criteria in this way, your customers are also considering value when they book a stay at your hotel or a meal in your restaurant. They consider all these criteria simultaneously, including different possible values relating to price (e.g., low, medium, or high) and quality (e.g., 2-, 3-, or 4-star rating). Therefore, each option (e.g., hotel) represents one combination, or a bundle, of many different decision variables.

Hotel Decision Criteria

Let's take as an example, the Statler Hotel, which is operated by the School of Hotel Administration as a fully commercial teaching hotel. It's located in Ithaca, New York, right on the beautiful campus of Cornell University. Ithaca is a relatively small market that often sells out on busy weekends (such as homecoming and graduation). If you wanted to reserve a room at the Statler during one of the upcoming busy weekends, you might consider a bundle of benefits such as the one displayed in Figure 7.1. Several fine hotels are located within three miles of the campus, including those shown in Figure 7.2. Thus, assuming the Statler has availabilities, the decision by a customer to stay there will be influenced not only by the Statler's package of benefits, but by those offered by other nearby hotels. Now the customer has to make a choice: she can either choose to stay at one of the three hotels presented so far, or explore additional options.

As I said, Ithaca is a small market, but it has several other hotels (and there are many more in nearby towns). In a major market, the lodging possibilities are nearly endless. Thus, you can see the complexities involved in the customer choice process. This is why simply asking the customer why she booked a hotel doesn't always work. There are too many trade-offs.

In reality, the problem of determining customers' preferences is even more complex than the example we gave because we were considering only one customer. But there are many customers, of course, and the customer

Figure 7.1
Statler Hotel (Ithaca, NY) on Expedia

Expedia Special Rate			
Photos	The Statler Hotel at Cornell University Ithaca, NY | Area: Ithaca View on map Tucked into Cornell University's vibrant campus, overlooking downtown Ithaca and Cayuga... Read more Book online or call ▪ 1-800-391-3613	★★★★☆ 4.9 rating from 11 reviews	$220 avg/night **SEE ROOMS & RATES** ▶

Room type		Sat	Avg per night	
Traditional double Includes: Free High-Speed Internet, Free Airport Shuttle		$220	$220.00	Book it ▶
Superior View King Includes: Free High-Speed Internet, Free Airport Shuttle		$260	$260.00	Book it ▶
Superior View Doubles Includes: Free High-Speed Internet, Free Airport Shuttle		$260	$260.00	Book it ▶

Hide rooms ☆

Figure 7.2
Two Additional Hotel Listings on Expedia for Ithaca, NY

Alternative Hotel #1

Expedia Special Rate			
Photos	Hampton Inn Ithaca Ithaca, NY | Area: Ithaca View on map Centrally located in Ithaca, this hotel is near Ithaca College. Another nearby point of... Read more Hotel Info: ▪ 1-866-276-6393	★★☆☆☆	$118 avg/night **SEE ROOMS & RATES** ▶

Room type	Fri	Sat	Avg per night	
One king bed non smoking-Non Refundable Includes: Free High-Speed Internet	$118	$118	$118.15	Book it ▶
One king study bed-Non Refundable Includes: Free High-Speed Internet	$118	$118	$118.15	Book it ▶
Two quen beds non smoking-Non Refundable Includes: Free High-Speed Internet	$118	$118	$118.15	Book it ▶

Show more rooms ☉

Alternative Hotel #2

Expedia Special Rate			
Photos	Homewood Suites Ithaca Ithaca, NY | Area: Ithaca View on map This Ithaca hotel is located near Cornell Plantations. Another nearby point of interest is... Read more Hotel Info: ▪ 1-866-281-6817	★★★☆☆ 5.0 rating from 21 reviews Insiders' Select™ PAST WINNER	$151 avg/night **SEE ROOMS & RATES** ▶

Room type	Fri	Sat	Avg per night	
Studio suite-No-Refund Includes: Free High-Speed Internet, Breakfast Buffet, Full Kitchen	$151	$151	$151.05	Book it ▶
Studio suite Includes: Free High-Speed Internet, Breakfast Buffet, Full Kitchen	$159	$159	$159.00	Book it ▶
One-bedroom suite-No-Refund Includes: Free High-Speed Internet, Breakfast Buffet, Full Kitchen	$170	$170	$170.05	Book it ▶

Show more rooms ☉

base for hospitality companies is becoming ever more diverse (e.g., business and leisure travelers; customers with different ethnicities and cultures; customers with different views of technology). Therefore, you need to develop a clear understanding of customer choice patterns for each market segment, so that you can properly configure your property's offerings for profitability and success.

Without a clear understanding of customer choices, firms often play "spray and pray" games with their offerings. They send up multiple offers in the hope that at least one will stick! As a result, markets often are flooded with goods and services that have relatively little actual value or significance for customers. Your guests may chow down on your complimentary breakfast, for instance, but do you know for sure that this was a factor that drove their booking decision? Furthermore, firms face complex problems of what to combine when deciding which goods-and-services bundles to offer in the marketplace. Given the many potential combinations of offerings, a simple "gut feel" to decide what might be of interest to customers is not sufficient in a competitive hospitality marketplace. There's no doubt that "informed guessing" might lead to new and innovative ideas; however, it might also lead to "managerial pet projects," causing depleted profits and severe heartaches!

In summary, understanding customer choices is a key to successful management of hospitality businesses. At the same time, predicting customer choices for competitive markets is complex and therefore requires a more scientific approach than simple rules of thumb. As described in the rest of this chapter, an excellent approach for doing this is known as discrete choice analysis (DCA). DCA has been found to be effective in predicting customer choices in a wide range of industries. Chapter 24 explains Marriott's use of DCA in developing the Courtyard brand, for instance. Additional examples of applications of discrete choice analyses in the hospitality industry are presented in Table 7.2. The ideas presented in this chapter will help you in expanding your understanding about how to scientifically predict customer choices.

ASSESSING CUSTOMER CHOICES

The initial ideas for DCA were introduced by Professor Daniel McFadden, Nobel laureate in Economics in 2000. By combining McFadden's framework with experimental methods developed by Professor Jordan Louviere and several other researchers, we can gain valuable insights about how customers choose goods and services in the hospitality industry. DCA comprises the following steps: (1) identify choice criteria, (2) develop choice experiments,

Table 7.2
Articles Based on Customer Choice Modeling Published in *Cornell Hospitality*
Quarterly* and *Cornell Hospitality Report

- R. Verma and G. Thompson, "Basing Service Management on Customer Determinants: The Importance of Hot Pizza," *Cornell Hotel and Restaurant Administration Quarterly* 37 (1995): 18–23.

  This article explains the basics of discrete choice analysis through a study of how customers chose a pizza-delivery company by trading off among several attributes (price, discount, promised delivery time, late-delivery time, variety, temperature, and money-back guarantee). The article further describes how the results of such a discrete-choice analysis can be incorporated into a decision-support system via a computer spreadsheet.

- R. Verma, M. Pullman, and J. Goodale, "Designing and Positioning Food Services for Multicultural Markets" *Cornell Hotel and Restaurant Administration Quarterly* 40 (1999): 76–87.

  A discrete choice analysis based study compares the food-service preferences of individuals from three different language groups (English, Japanese, and Spanish). All three groups of respondents were relatively price insensitive for the four different types of restaurants studied and often were willing to wait either to order or to be served, depending on the food-service concept (e.g., waiting for pizza made sense to them, but waiting for burgers did not). Many respondents liked the idea of pictures of the food on menus to help identify unfamiliar items, but virtually no one wanted menus translated into their native languages. Based on the study, one food-service outlet adopted a new marketing strategy that not only increased its market share but attracted more patrons to the food court.

- R. Verma, G. Plaschka, and J. Louviere, "Understanding Customer Choices: A Key to Successful Management of Hospitality Services," *Cornell Hotel and Restaurant Administration Quarterly* 43 (2002): 15–24.

  This article describes in considerable detail how many different managerial decisions can be derived more effectively by using customer choice modeling techniques. The article describes how the results can be used to identify the preferences of customers in different market segments, calculate market share, identify order winners and qualities; calculate brand equity; calculate switching barrier; and develop implementation guidelines.

- J. Goodale, R. Verma, and M. Pullman, "A Market-utility Approach to Scheduling Employees," *Cornell Hotel and Restaurant Administration Quarterly* 44 (2003): 61–69.

  This article describes how the results of a carefully planned choice experiment can be used to develop effective labor schedules. The paper first discusses the components that make up this approach, which includes methods from customer-preferences modeling, service-capacity planning, and the four tasks of labor scheduling. Next, it is shown how the model applies to balancing queue lengths and operating costs for an airport food-court vendor.

- R. Verma and G. Plaschka, "Customer-Choice Modeling: Reflections, Advances, and Managerial Implications," *Cornell Hotel and Restaurant Administration Quarterly* 44 (2003): 156–165.

  This essay attempts to highlight some of the valuable managerial and methodological insights on customer-choice modeling observed over the course of the past ten years. To make this essay useful to both managers and academic researchers, it discusses thoughts on CCM in the context of methodological advances and managerial applications in service-driven markets. Choice modeling can yield valuable insights for market-driven strategy development by revealing customer clusters, suggesting the potential effects of changing the levels of value drivers, assessing overall brand equity, and identifying customers' switching barriers.

Table 7.2   **(continued)**

- R. Verma, "Unlocking the Secrets of Customers' Choices," *Cornell Hospitality Report* 7(2) (2007).

  This report describes how customer willingness to pay and desirability can be calculated from the results of a customer choice modeling study. The report includes a spreadsheet template that allows readers to manipulate customer choice modeling data and calculate willingness to pay and desirability for a hotel and restaurant context.

- Dixon, Kimes, and R. Verma, "Customer Preferences for Restaurant Technology Innovations" *Cornell Hospitality Report* 9(7) (2009).

  This report presents the results of a national survey on customers' perceptions of eleven restaurant technologies, as well as whether respondents use those technologies and the value they see in them. Using a research technique called best-worst choice analysis, the study found that the technologies used most commonly were pagers and online reservations, while cell-phone payment was used hardly at all. The results show that the perceived value of a specific technology increases after the customers have had the opportunity to use it, and different demographic segments valued the technologies differently.

- Taylor and R. Verma, "Customer Preferences for Restaurant Brands, Cuisine, and Food Court Configurations in Shopping Centers," *Cornell Hospitality Report* 10(3) (2010).

  An analysis of the mall restaurant preferences of a national sample of 1,737 U.S. residents sheds light on how to configure mall food service and demonstrates how local malls can determine what their particular market desires. Using customer choice analysis, this study asked respondents to choose among six mall food-service configurations, including one that had a large food court and one that had no food court at all. The most popular configuration combined a moderate-size food court with several casual and fast-casual restaurants. Least popular was the choice that had only table-service restaurants and no food court.

---

and (3) collect responses and estimate choice models. With those data in hand, you can conduct extensive analyses using decision support systems.

Step 1: Identify Choice Criteria

Before trying to predict future customer choices, one must first understand the list of criteria customers use in their choice processes. As in the relatively simple case of hotels in the Ithaca region, customers consider multiple criteria when making their choices, and you can use DCA to identify them. In Ithaca, the main criterion might be how close you are to the campus, or at least how easy it is to get there. But another criterion might be that customers want to be in walking distance of food and beverage outlets, which argues for the set of hotels that are downtown, or the suburban properties adjacent to the malls.

You can develop a list of these potential criteria by using qualitative market assessment approaches, such as expert interviews, customer focus groups,

Table 7.3
Sample Choice Criteria Considered by the Customers
of Hotels and Restaurants

Hotel Choice Criteria	Restaurant Choice Criteria
Price	Price
Brand name	Cuisine
Star rating	Décor
Past guest reviews	Past guest reviews
Technology and customization options	Reservation options
Room types	. . .
Recreation and leisure options	
Loyalty program	
. . .	

case studies, macro- and microeconomic industry data, and other data-rich information sources (e.g., blogs, social media chatter). From these, you can develop a list of purchase attributes that you believe are influencing customer choices. For a hotel the choice criteria may include type of hotel (e.g., motel, bed-and-breakfast inn, boutique hotel, convention hotel), star rating, average past guest review, price, loyalty program, in-room amenities, or recreation options. Table 7.3 lists some of the potential criteria for selection of a restaurant and a hotel.

Step 2: Develop Choice Experiments

After you identify the criteria that probably influence your customers' choices, you need to develop the possible realistic levels for each of these potential decision factors. For example, you may consider the following options for loyalty program: none; one point per dollar spent; two points per dollar spent; or three points per dollar spent. For in-room amenities, you may consider offering different types of TVs; various levels of bathroom amenities, or the presence or absence of a kitchenette. Similarly, as recreation options within the hotel, you may consider an indoor or outdoor swimming pool; tennis courts; or a golf course.

As you probably have guessed, such lists of hotel choice criteria can become quite lengthy. So before you start surveying consumers, you will have to critically assess the relevance of each criterion in customers' choice processes. For example, you don't have much control over such characteristics as your location or your floor plan. However, you probably do control certain aspects of the property, such as the type of restaurants located on-property, whether you offer a complimentary breakfast, and the extent of room amenities. Therefore, you need to strike a balance between the complexity of choice criteria and the reality of a survey, including its cost and benefit.

After identifying the relevant choice criteria, your next step is to construct several realistic scenarios based on different values of each of the choice criteria identified. A simple example of a hotel choice experiment is presented in Table 7.4. Within the customer choice experiments, respondents are asked to "choose" or "not to choose" among alternatives presented in "choice sets." Each choice set can contain various explicit market offerings based on identified market choice drivers and their value extensions. For a customer choice assessment study in the hospitality industry, you might describe two hotels in a choice set, each with a number of market drivers and specific value extensions for each. So, for a hotel in Ithaca, you might have as a value driver its distance from campus, and the value extensions might be on or walkably adjacent to campus, three miles (or less) from campus, more than three miles from campus. Depending on the objective of the study, you can ask your questions in various formats. One way to do this is to show the respondents lists like those in Table 7.4 and ask, "If these two hotels were your only alternatives, which one would you choose—Hotel 1 or Hotel 2

Table 7.4
Sample Choice Experiment for the Choice of a Hotel

	Hotel 1	Hotel 2
Room Rate	$100	$135
Brand Name	National brand	Independent hotel
Star Rating	2.5-star	3-star
Loyalty Program	1 point/$ spent	None
Recreation options	Indoor swimming pool	Spa and tennis courts
. . .	. . .	. . .

Some options for choice questions:

A. If the above two hotels were your only alternatives, which one will you choose:
    _____ Hotel 1 _____ Hotel 2 _____ Neither

B1. If Hotel 1 was your only option, would you stay there?   _____ yes _____ no

B2. If Hotel 2 was your only option, would you stay there?   _____ yes _____ no

C. List the most attractive and least attractive features of the two hotels:
    Hotel 1 _____ most attractive feature _____ least attractive feature
    Hotel 2 _____ most attractive feature _____ least attractive feature

or neither?" You could also ask: "If Hotel 1 were your only other option, would you go there during your next trip or stay at your previous hotel?" Yet another approach is known as a most-least attractive analysis, based on this question: "What do you consider the *most* and *least* attractive features of each hotel?" These approaches are spelled out in Table 7.4.

Even just a few years ago, a typical choice experiment involved lengthy printed survey forms that used a series of preconfigured, table-like formatted choice scenarios (like the sample in Table 7.4). Although the experiments were solid, the choice sets were presented as static tables with little room for customization to identify the purchase drivers that most interested the respondents. Information technology has made this type of experiment much more effective, because we can use digital imaging and streaming video technologies, almost unlimited computing resources to customize questionnaires, and sophisticated programming languages that allow you to develop realistic and highly customizable choice experiments specific to each respondent. These choice experiments are visually appealing and employ easy-to-use formats, resulting in a high level of respondent involvement.

For example, in our recent studies, we have extensively used web-based technologies to realistically illustrate choice scenarios for our hospitality respondents (with hyperlinked pictures or written illustrations, brand logos, and audio and video files). In one study, we showed professional actors demonstrating several different service scripts in face-to-face customer interactions at a hotel front desk. The video clips of the service scripts along with other features of the service interactions were presented to the customers in the form of a discrete choice experiment to gauge what kind of interaction they preferred at the front desk. In another study, in a retail setting, we showed respondents a series of screens, each with several pictures and detailed descriptions, to depict the customer service, shopping experience, and parking convenience at a futuristic shopping center. Later, when the respondents were presented with the actual discrete choice exercise, the earlier descriptions were available as hyperlinks for ready reference.

When choice experiments require transferring huge amount of data, you can give respondents high-capacity portable storage devices (e.g., USB storage keys) or take along a laptop when you conduct the interview. Although such options have been available for some time, they have only recently become relatively cost effective and easy to implement. Someday, three-dimensional virtual reality technologies will become inexpensively available to create truly realistic choice experiments. Some early indications of the use of such technologies in limited fashion exist (e.g., the launch of a prototype W Hotel in the virtual reality world SecondLife.Com).

Step 3: Collect Responses and Estimate Choice Models

Once you've designed your choice experiments, the next step is to collect responses from a representative sample of customers (or potential customers). To do the study, you show each respondent several choice scenarios and ask each person to register their single choice among the available options (including no choice). As they choose, your respondents gradually build a profile of their decision criteria, including the most desirable, least desirable, and indifferent product features. Usually, you would develop statistical models that predict customer choice for this purpose. These statistical models calculate relative weights that customers explicitly or implicitly assign to different choice criteria. Once the weights are identified, you can select the optimal combination of choice criteria to develop a more profitable and sustainable value proposition.

While the estimation of choice models requires advanced statistical knowledge, you can use a decision support system (DSS) to implement the results. Using a DSS, you can perform various managerial "what if" analyses and predict future customer choices.

MANAGERIAL INSIGHTS FROM DISCRETE CHOICE MODELING

Although you may want to engage professional assistance in developing your DCA experiment, once you have the data, you will be in a position to develop the insights and strategies that are suggested by the resulting information. In a series of articles, my coauthors and I have described a number of managerial insights that have emerged from customer choice modeling studies.[1] Let's look at some of the valuable managerial implications that have arisen from these studies.

As I said, the statistical models developed from customer choice studies can be easily incorporated into decision support systems (Figure 7.3). While design of customer choice experiments and estimation of models requires sophisticated training and skills, implementation of the estimated model(s) can be handled on a DSS spreadsheet. Once the DSS is available, you can input the attributes of your own product and that of your competitors to predict expected market shares. The DSS essentially approximates the dynamic nature of the market, allowing managers to evaluate multiple businesses, operating and marketing strategies, and the effects of changing strategies in the competitive marketplace. In addition, the predictive power of customer choice models can be further improved by market segmentation techniques.

Figure 7.3
Types of Decision Support Models Based on Discrete Choice Analysis

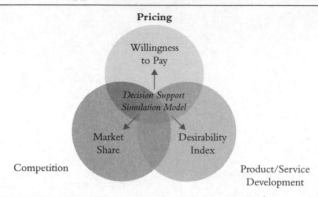

The relative weights of various choice criteria can be used to identify the decision criteria that your customers have in common, and you can assess how these popular product attributes will influence the current and future value of your hotel's offerings. The choice models can also identify key features that drive market share in different customer preference clusters. As I explained in a 2007 article, you can develop clusters of customers based on their preference, and you can even give them fanciful descriptive names.[2] In that article, I labeled different customer preference clusters as Gourmet Buyers, Tough Sells, and Bargain Hunters. Then I could calculate the relative utilities (or value) of various choice drivers for each of those customer clusters (e.g., price, brand name, feature, service). So, for instance, the Gourmet Buyers found relatively high value in the brand name, feature, and service attributes, but not on price. The Tough Sells considered all four of those choice drivers to be relatively equal in importance, whereas the Bargain Hunters seemed to be the most price sensitive (as you might guess). Identifying such preference differences across customer groups can help you develop a more effective marketing campaign for each cluster.

Here's another example of the kind of analysis you can do once you have the DCA information. With my colleague Gary Thompson, I studied the decision factors for a pizza-delivery company.[3] We observed how the customers traded off among various attributes (at least on our selection cards). Those factors were price, discount, promised delivery time, late delivery time, variety, temperature, and money-back guarantee. We discovered that a particular decision point was delivery temperature—in short, people liked their pizza to arrive hot and steaming. Without this kind of analysis, you might be forced to guess what made people choose one company over another—and a wrong guess might cost you money spent on unnecessary product features.

"What If" Analyses The relative importance weights for each decision factor can be used to develop two useful "what-if" analyses for combinations of service offerings, namely customer desirability and willingness-to-pay. The desirability can be presented in the format of a relative index between zero and 100. Calculated this way, a desirability index of zero represents the least desirable service of all possible combinations. Similarly, a desirability index of 100 represents the most desirable service combination. The willingness-to-pay analysis for a specific market offering is just what it sounds like—an index of the price customers are willing to pay for a particular product feature, if they desire it. Generally speaking, if we know a product's relative utilities (i.e., the value assigned to different product attributes), consumers' propensity to choose a particular product, and the desirability of that product, we can calculate willingness to pay. The hotel industry calculations can be confused by the "noise" created by ever-shifting room rates. Nevertheless, it's possible to get a sense of customers' willingness to pay by grouping hotels into price ranges (such as economy, midscale, and upscale). You can download a complete explanation and application of these ideas from the Cornell Center for Hospitality Research (chr.cornell.edu). In these publications, all available at no charge, you will find the report called "Unlocking the Secrets of Customer Choice."[4] Or you can search for my name (Verma) and see a list of several reports that I have written on this topic.

In addition to identifying the overall relative impact of customer preferences, choice modeling results can also be used to assess the relative impact on market share of changing the value of one or more variables. For example, the models can predict how your market share might be affected if one of your competitors makes a change in one or more choice drivers. With this analysis you can focus on a selected few choice criteria as you consider developing new products or services or changing selected features of existing offerings.

Assessment of brand equity (as related to customer choices) is another potentially important analysis that you can conduct once you have the choice modeling results. I also believe that robust and reliable estimates of switching inertia can be easily derived by designing customer choice experiments that ask respondents to choose between "current" and "new" service providers. This kind of analysis will give you a sense of what keeps guests returning to your hotel (switching barriers or inertia) despite the availability of other, "better" offerings. At the same time, it will also give you a sense of what might happen if a new service provider in fact overcomes existing customer inertia by offering a substantially stronger service bundle or by customizing its service bundle to gain dominance in a market.

Customer choice modeling results can also be used for developing effective implementation guidelines or for prioritizing various initiatives so as to maximize the net gain from any chosen strategic plan. By understanding consumer choices, you can effectively develop and position service offerings to better suit your market's needs. In addition, mathematical models representing consumer choice can be linked to several operating decisions (e.g., labor scheduling, special activities planning, service offerings), and optimal service configurations can be identified for further improvement.

In addition to the applications previously described, choice models and associated DSSs also can be used as education and training tools and to help managers better align their decisions with what customers want and are willing to pay for. If you feel that you are too distracted by day-to-day operations, you can get back in touch with your customers' actual needs by examining DCA results. As a test exercise, you might try comparing two choice models: one representing customer choices and another one representing managers' beliefs about customer choices.

While DCA does require some heavy-duty statistical analysis, that is not out of reach. Once you have the data from a well-designed DCA study, you can begin predicting customer choices. For a hospitality firm to be successful, I believe that a sophisticated customer choice approach is essential. If you make DCA an essential component of your managerial decision-making framework, you will have a far more accurate ability to predict market share, your customers' willingness to pay, and how desirable they consider your hospitality services.

NOTES

1. For example, R. Verma, G. Plaschka, and J. Louviere, "Understanding Customer Choices: A Key to Successful Management of Hospitality Services," *Cornell Hotel and Restaurant Administration Quarterly* 43 (2002): 15–24; R. Verma and G. Plaschka, "Customer-Choice Modeling: Reflections, Advances, and Managerial Implications," *Cornell Hotel and Restaurant Administration Quarterly* 44 (2003): 156–165; and R. Verma, "Unlocking the Secrets of Customers' Choices," *Cornell Hospitality Report* 7(2) (2007).
2. Verma, 2007.
3. R. Verma and G. Thompson, "Basing Service Management on Customer Determinants: The Importance of Hot Pizza, *Cornell Hotel and Restaurant Administration Quarterly* 37 (1996): 18–23.
4. Verma, 2007.

CHAPTER 8

GUIDING THE GUEST EXPERIENCE

HAEEUN HELEN CHUN

One of your many jobs as a hospitality manager is to seek ways to improve your guests' experience. You can do this, of course, by making investments to upgrade guest services or provide better products, facilities, and programs, but this is not the only place to invest your money—and it may not even be the best course. As it turns out, guests' perceptions of their experiences can be improved without huge investments. Instead, if you can get your guests to focus on the positive aspects of their experiences, their perceptions of your operation (and their evaluations) will likely improve. The other side of this coin is to avoid calling attention to unpleasant aspects of an experience. In this chapter, I want to discuss ways to encourage your guests to focus on their experience in a positive way (and to minimize attention on unpleasantness). This involves guiding the guest experience.

Guiding the guest experience works like this. Tasting a slice of chocolate cake is pleasurable for most of us, but researchers have found that when people who are eating that slice of cake were also guided to pay attention to their sensations, they felt greater pleasure from the consumption experience compared to people who did not consciously focus on their experience.[1] You can simulate this experiment informally by comparing the difference between wolfing down a slice of cake (or any food) and slowly savoring it. All of us generally experience frequent and intense positive emotions when we are mindfully attentive to the here and now.[2] Even in this simple context of having dessert, people can be attuned to the moment-to-moment taste experience, and thereby boost their enjoyment. You can make this happen by helping your guests pay attention to their specific consumption experience and increasing their awareness of the resulting pleasurable sensations. This can increase their enjoyment of the experience.

In this chapter, I outline ways to enhance your guests' perceived experience by increasing their awareness of the positive aspects of their experience, with a particular focus on enhancing guests' awareness of the experiences as they unfold in the moment. Although we focus on real time, I also explain that you can use this concept for both future and past experiences.

HOW TO INCREASE AWARENESS

We all have had the experience of doing something on "autopilot," when we're not really paying full attention to what we're doing or what's going on around us. In part, we do this in self-defense, to avoid sensory overload. In particular, repetitive actions like eating or commuting often get screened from full awareness. Even enjoyable experiences, like having a piece of cake, can feel dull if we repeat them often. So some of your guests, particularly those for whom a trip or meal out are unusual, will approach your business with excitement and awareness. But many guests, particularly frequent business travelers, are likely to pay little attention to your operation—for them it's just another night in a hotel.

Raising awareness is actually a relatively easy task. It chiefly involves engaging more of your guests' senses and thinking. Helping your guests notice and acknowledge the pleasurable aspects of your hotel can break their habituation and insensibility. Your effort to help your guests become mindful and consciously aware of the pleasures around them can start right at the front desk. Your front-desk associate could point out a facet of your hotel's architectural beauty or even remark to an incoming guest that the weather is beautiful. This type of conversational opening draws your guest into awareness of the moment. The effort by service providers to focus guests' attention becomes more important if you are dealing with extended service encounters such as cruise trips or theme parks, where there is constant opportunity for interaction between consumers and service employees.

The effort to help guests be mindful of the pleasures from their experience can continue as they leave your hotel. One way to do this is to provide cues for awareness. Tour companies, for instance, may hand out photographs or even postcards to tour participants showing activities or locations that they have visited. This way, your guests can relive their travel experience after they return home. Some hotels also hand out a small souvenir to their guests with the same goal in mind.

The cue for mindfulness must be specific. You need to draw your guests' attention to a precise aspect of an experience or of the environment. This is because you want your guests to recognize the value of their stay, and as such, you need to provide cues that move them past a general sense of well-being and into a conscious thinking mode. Making guests more mindful of the positives of their stay increases their emotional connection to that source of pleasure, and their general sense of well-being also rises.

Sources of Pleasure

As depicted in Figure 8.1, we can identify three general types of pleasure: sensory pleasure, aesthetic pleasure, and achievement pleasure.[3]

Your guests can be attuned to the moment-to-moment pleasurable experience in any or all of these types of pleasure. The sensory pleasures derive from an attractive sight, a lovely sound, a pleasant taste or smell, or a touch or kinesthetic experience. Aesthetic pleasure derives from the senses, of course, but it involves appreciation of the beauty of architecture or nature. The pleasure of achievement can involve actions taken, personal growth, or a renewed sense of self. Already, you can see how hospitality operators may tap into all these types of pleasure and find strategic ways to enhance consumer pleasure, especially during service encounters. Having people try to notice and acknowledge pleasurable little things that would otherwise go unnoticed (e.g., flowers, sunshine, or music) boosts overall happiness and enjoyment.[4] As such, enhancing your guests' attention to psychological, physical, or environmental cues will be a key to increasing their enjoyment.

Figure 8.1
Sources of Pleasure

Sensory Pleasure	• **Pleasure derived from positive physical sensations** • Examples: Eating a tasty meal, smelling a delightful aroma, or getting a massage at a spa
Aesthetic Pleasure	• **Pleasure derived from the observation of something that is beautiful, either natural or manmade** • Examples: Enjoying a beautiful painting, landscape, or musical piece
Achievement Pleasure	• **Pleasure derived from attaining something that is desirable or rewarding** • Examples: Finishing a good book, winning a competition, eating in a healthier way, or learning about history

Inkaterra Machu Picchu Pueblo Hotel

Jose Koechlin
Founder and Chairman
Inkaterra

Inkaterra owns and operates boutique eco hotels in Peru. The first property opened in 1975 to lodge the scientists who came to study the rain forest around Machu Picchu. There are currently hotels in Machu Picchu Pueblo, Cusco (La Casona), and the Amazon jungle (Reserva Amazonica). Soon, Inkaterra Cabo Blanco (where Ernest Hemingway fished) will open the first marine conservation area in Peru. Also, three other projects are in the works, at Cusco City, Urubamba Valley, and Tambopata.

Reviving the spirit of a royal Inca retreat, Inkaterra's boutique Machu Picchu hotel invites visitors to find comfort in its stunning whitewashed cottages nestled into the terraced hills at the foot of Machu Picchu. Since the early 1970s, Inkaterra has worked as much to study and discover the history and nature of Peru as it has to expose it to the guests of the hotel. Inkaterra is dedicated to supporting ecological research for conservation and renowned for its natural resource management programs.

We pay special attention to entertain guests' various sensory experiences, ranging from placing a hot water bag on the bed for turndown service to serving organic iced tea grown on site at the hotel lobby. Toiletries are also produced in-house using sublime local natural essences and fragrances. Traditional Peruvian cuisine is served at the restaurant situated against a stunning backdrop of the rushing Vilcanota River. Guests can also enjoy peace and tranquility strolling the organic gardens and smelling fresh mint or green tea leaves. The hotel grounds include more than three miles of ecological paths. Inkaterra has also recorded 192 species of birds (18 hummingbird species); 111 species of butterflies, and numerous ferns, orchids, bromeliads, and medicinal plants. It also grows organic vegetables and has an organic tea plantation. Additionally, its orchid garden houses the world's largest collection of orchid species, including new species discovered on the hotel grounds.

Inkaterra has strived to employ the core principles of tourism not just to please guests, but also to provide them with an opportunity for personal learning and growth. To help guests achieve a sense of achievement, Inkaterra offers multiple daily excursions (both on- and off-property) with trained guides and resident biologists. For example, the complimentary

Twilight Walk tour is designed to encourage guests to connect with the environment on a spiritual level, by learning about the local culture and participating in rituals of paying respect to Mother Nature. Guests are also invited to Tea Garden tours to experience the traditional tea-making process and learn about its many indigenous plants and animals. Fully guided tours outside the property—hiking up the Machu Picchu citadel and archaeological sites—are also offered. Inkaterra has also actively produced educational materials such as CD recordings of indigenous bird songs and films about local culture, and we support the conservation of native communities and cultural preservation. This highly educational process defines Inkaterra's endeavor to cultivate ecotourism.

Focusing Your Guests on Their Experience

Let's look at four ways that you can induce your guests to be aware of their experience and to appreciate their stay in your hotel. These methods are to seize the moment (or stress the brevity of pleasures), evoke imagery, turn guests into observers of their own enjoyment, and label experiences using the narrowest possible categories (and have more categories).

Carpe Diem: *Stress the "Fleetingness"* One of the messages of Stephen Sondheim's musical *Into the Woods* is summarized in this line: "Opportunity is not a lengthy visitor." To help your guests gain more pleasure from their experiences with your operation, you can stress that the experience won't last long—even if it's a multiple-day cruise. When people become aware of the transient nature of positive experiences, they tend to become more appreciative of the experiences and are motivated to enjoy themselves as much as they can.[5] We already do this in reaction to life's major transitional experiences, such as marriage or graduation from college. Although such transitions can evoke both pleasure and sadness (bittersweet experiences), people seek the happiness in these situations by proactively extending the moment by participating in numerous related activities—senior week, for example, or bachelor parties. A vacation or a family trip to a theme park is a perfect context where you can accentuate how fleeting the experience truly is. An imminent return from overseas adventure travel is likely to evoke bittersweet feelings—happy to be back home, but sad that it's ending. Thus, the time remaining on the trip feels more precious to your guests, prompting them to engage in more activities (say, taking more photos, setting up farewell dinners). Realizing that their vacation will eventually end, your guests come to appreciate the positive aspects of their vacation and savor their experience more.

One way you may induce this sense of fleetingness is to frame the remaining time as an ever-shorter interval. For instance, if your customers are in day five of a six-day trip, you may frame the remaining time as "two days left" rather than "Day 5." This frame makes the remaining time seem more precious. Focused on the transience of their vacation, guests would become more aware of their pleasure and enjoyment. Another implication of bittersweet moments is that the last few days of your guests' vacation are likely to seem even more bittersweet and thus generate stronger emotions than the first few days—since good times are about to end and they have to go back to "reality." To increase opportunities for participation, you could offer such indulgences as fancy meals or room upgrades with a nicer view of the ocean, sign-ups for tours to exotic spots, or chances to purchase pricey souvenirs toward the end of their trip or stay.

Evoke Imagery (for an Uncertain Outcome) in Your Promotion Strategy

Imagery can bring your guests' experience to life, but if you add an element of uncertainty, you can engage their imaginations. Here's how that can work. Imagery creates a web of associations that may help your guests become more mindful of the pleasure brought about by positive experiences. One way you can elicit consumers' imagery is by mixing those images with some component of uncertainty. Consumers who win a lucky draw without being informed of the exact prize may be intrigued by the uncertainty as they imagine and visualize the prize.[6] This act of imagining favorable prospects helps guests stay happier for a longer duration. As such, being uncertain about some of the details of a positive service experience can capture guests' attention and prolong their enjoyment of the experience (provided that experience is not disappointingly modest compared to their expectations). Here's how one restaurant incorporated this idea into their marketing strategy and implemented a curiosity-inducing promotional strategy. Cafe 50's, a restaurant in Los Angeles, handed their guests a sealed envelope for a New Year's celebration event. To find out the prize they had won, which included a free dessert or cash prize, the guests had to bring back the envelope—unopened—at a future visit. In this way, Cafe 50's encouraged an increase in awareness of this positive state induced by pleasant uncertainty.

Make Guests Observers of Their Own Enjoyment

When your guests can observe others having a good time and enjoying it, they also enjoy the experience as they share the moment. Not all restaurants want the queue to be visible from the dining room, but if your concept permits, you could design your dining area so that waiting guests get views of diners enjoying their experience, as occurs with customers waiting in line for a ride at the theme park. Interestingly, it turns out that allowing people to watch and experience their own responses to experiences also boosts enjoyment. One interesting device that you may adopt along this line is to put up mirrors so that guests can see themselves as they enjoy an experience.[7] Theme parks use this principle by selling photographs of roller coaster riders as they descend the first huge drop. Guests get to observe their own emotional states (usually positive, sometimes anticipating the drop). Likewise, some restaurants take photos of guests enjoying themselves at a birthday party or other celebration, enabling them to observe their responses and remember the experience.

Finer Labeling Makes Your Guests Less Bored Pleasure or enjoyment tends to decline with greater consumption of a particular type of item. Because customers eventually habituate to or satiate from an experience (even the roller coaster), you need to keep it fresh. One way to do this is to increase the variety of choices, so that your guests can find alternatives to their initial choice. You can achieve your goal without necessarily increasing the number of offerings by paying attention to how you label each offering compared to others.[8] You do this by presenting the offering with a label that fits under specific categories (e.g., finer classification based on flavor, size, texture, color) as opposed to a single general category. Suppose that a confectioner offers two chocolate candies. If the candies are not differentiated, consumers will be satiated (in terms of the tasting experience) with one chocolate, since they seem more or less the same. But when the chocolates are specified under flavor-based categories such as dark chocolate and triple dark chocolate, even though your customers are tasting the exact same set of food items, the finer classification makes them *attend to the details* that differentiate the items.

The same principle works with wines, for instance. If the choice is merely red or white, your guests will pay less attention (and perhaps buy less) than if you are offering a Pinot Noir, a Cabernet Sauvignon, and a Sangiovese — you draw your guests' attention to differences in the wines. Adding vintages or appellations refines this process even further, and you can increase revenues of your existing products and services without necessarily altering or adding to them — it's all in the categorization. In general, this method is more powerful for novice consumers, but novices and experts both will appreciate your finer labeling as enriching their experience.

Minimize Attention to "Unpleasantries" (Dreads)

Certain aspects of travel are unavoidably unpleasant, dreary, or merely repetitive. Business travelers may not look forward to staying at your hotel, and even leisure travelers may approach your hotel with an unfavorable mindset if, for instance, they are visiting less-than-favorite relatives or stuck in an unwanted destination. Even small things can become dreads that can take over our cognitive process and color what should be an overall pleasant experience and have the opposite effect to the heightened awareness of pleasure. They make the experience seem worse than it would seem to be objectively.

Your strategy here is to find ways to reduce the number or duration of unpleasant or boring experiences. For instance, many companies have set up check-in systems that allow premium customers to circumvent lines at the front desk. Airlines use paperless check-in for this reason—e-mail your boarding pass to your smart phone and you don't even need a printer. Other mobile applications are moving toward a similar goal. For example, especially handy for frequent business travelers, apps such as Tripit reduce unpleasant aspects of travel by consolidating information about flight, hotel, and car rental confirmations in all one place, and by updating information about any changes to departure or arrival times and gates. Hotels that offer their signature cookies at the reception desk are also using this strategy of reducing dreary travel experiences.

You should also strive to offer a certain level of stimulation for those who approach hospitality businesses with an unfavorable or routinized mind-set.[9] A novel or creative presentation of a familiar dish could enhance your guests' awareness of the experience. Even for frequent travelers, adding one or two novel components to an otherwise repetitive experience will likely prevent habituation. For example, you could discreetly place workout clothes in your guests' room to raise awareness of your exercise facilities and encourage the guests to use them—thereby adding variety to their stay. If your guest is a frequent visitor, you might have a record of that person's favorite music and have it playing in the guest rooms upon arrival.

IMPROVING THE EXPERIENCE BEFORE THE GUEST ARRIVES

Let's look at ways that you can set the stage for your guests to think consciously about their future experiences. For many guests, looking forward to their upcoming vacation trips or fancy dinners is part of the pleasure of the trip. Thus, you want to make sure your customers take full pleasure in their anticipation.

People who anticipate their future experience and are attentive to their current emotional state not only derive pleasure from anticipation, but they are likely to end up enjoying the event more. Thus, if you find ways to better manage your consumers' pre-event experience, you will probably boost their satisfaction with the service. This can happen when restaurants send out invitations for Valentine's Day or Christmas dinner with a special menu, or when hotels promote special vacation packages with photos of the destination. These two tactics try to tap into consumers' anticipation before the experience occurs.

Manage the Physical Wait to Increase Anticipation

Perhaps the most critical time to influence guests' anticipation of the pleasure of a service is when they are waiting in a queue. No one likes to wait, so hospitality operators have devised many approaches to make waiting more palatable. Disguising the length or configuration of the queue (e.g., a snake line) or giving guests something to distract or divert them while waiting (e.g., music, a television screen, or waiting room magazines) may draw their attention so that they perceive the wait time to be shorter than it actually is. Busch Gardens theme park in Tampa takes this principle one step further by allowing guests waiting for the Congo River Rapids water ride to participate while they wait by aiming water jets at those already on the ride, thereby soaking the riders (who will get wet anyway) and increasing the fun for all. This wait is also a chance for you to invite your guests to consciously think about the upcoming experience and enjoy the good feelings in advance, rather than simply diverting them to reduce their frustration. Such anticipation should highlight the enjoyment of the actual experience and thus make it more memorable.

Here's how you can utilize relatively brief waiting times (such as in a restaurant or at the theme park). As a restaurant manager, you could display dessert samples in an attractive display that will both heighten anticipation and somewhat decrease the boredom of waiting. The Stock-Yard Restaurant in Nashville, for instance, is one of many steakhouses that display the actual cuts of meat in a refrigerator case, and many seafood restaurants have a tank with the lobsters right out front. Both are meant to engage the guests in the upcoming pleasure of their meal, even as they wait for a table. You could also design the waiting area with a view of the kitchen so that they can observe the cooking and experience the aroma of the food in advance. Some restaurants even provide sample bites or wine tastes while the guests are waiting in line.

Addressing Restaurant Wait Times

Mark Censoprano
Chief Marketing Officer
Sbarro, Inc.

In table-service restaurants, one contributing factor to the guest experience is the wait. The wait is one of the first impressions that a guest has of a restaurant, and so it is an important part of their overall dining experience. Initiatives that help reduce the wait or make the wait more enjoyable can help make the difference between excellence and mediocrity. Both approaches address the principle of respecting the guest's time.

The following are initiatives that are designed to reduce the wait, or specifically to reduce idle time in a lobby:

- Call-ahead seating, which gives the guest a target time for arrival and allows guests to determine where they wait
- Online reservations and monitoring of table availability, which can be linked directly to a restaurant's table management system
- Paging systems that ring a guest's cell phone so they can leave the premises to make better use of their time

Beyond tightening the wait time, many restaurants take advantage of this opportunity by meeting the immediate needs of the guest and also implementing initiatives that support their brand positioning. Here are examples of programs that can address the wait wisely and build a brand at the same time:

- Inviting, engaging, sensory pleasing bar areas that serve food or beverage items
- Lobby music specifically designed to improve the productivity and morale of line-level employees and the attitudes and spending behaviors of dining patrons (Muzak is the longest-running such service, and a more recent purveyor is Ambiance Radio™, founded by a graduate of the Cornell Hotel School.)
- "Feature of the Day" menu boards to educate guests and accelerate the ordering process
- Serving samples of a restaurant's most popular food or beverage items, or showcasing new items on the menu
- Wine sampling, which can make wine less intimidating and introduce guests to new varieties or producers

Improving the guest experience through enhancing the wait is predicated on a restaurant's ability to flawlessly execute its initiatives. Hot food samples should be hot; cold beverages samples, cold. Music loud enough to enjoy, but not too loud to distract. Quotes for wait times that aren't too unrealistically short, but not so long that guests leave. Running a restaurant is certainly a complex undertaking, and the more a restaurant company can design their systems and processes to support excellent execution, the better. Managing the dreaded "wait" is no exception.

An example of a practice that cleverly transformed the normally boring physical wait into an enjoyment-boosting device is the Universal Studio's Simpsons Ride, a simulator ride based on the television show. The wait line for this popular ride is designed for guests to watch the preshow clips featuring the Simpsons in multiple steps of waiting rooms, each with a theme designed to introduce guests to the storyline of the ride. The guests are already part of the characters in the storyline even before getting on the actual ride, and the wait line becomes part of the attraction. Once again, the guests get to think about the upcoming ride with excitement during their wait. This strategy goes beyond often-discussed strategies of simply diverting guests' attention away from unpleasant matters to other pleasant environmental cues or soothing their emotions with fun music. In sum, the way to think about this is to design the wait period to be productive and enjoyable with anticipation, in such a way that it supports the enjoyment of the main experience. In many cases, a sense of festivity of an enjoyable service experience can begin in the waiting line if that wait period is incorporated into the entire service experience. These principles also apply if your service involves an experience that may generate anxiety or fear (like waiting in the hospital). You still need to design a waiting area that can reduce stress and that is comfortable and soothing. In this situation, the waiting time can give people an opportunity to cope with the stress and the impending event.[10]

Maximizing Anticipation after Guest Reservations

Let's take a look at how to make use of the longer wait period that occurs after your guests have reserved a trip or a future dining experience. As a hospitality operator, you have the opportunity to make contact with your customers well before consumption occurs, something that other businesses would greatly desire. Once you have the reservation, you know your guests' names and contact information in advance. As with the shorter queue-based wait, you can use that waiting period to improve guests' experience by strategically shaping this wait period to enhance the service experience.

One way to manage your guests' waiting period is to send informative brochures featuring your on-site facilities and nearby attractions. Make sure your Web site is well designed and useful, so that it provides menu descriptions and reviews, if appropriate, or offers a slideshow (or video) of your facility. Beyond that, you can use more sophisticated means to further engage the guests during the wait period. For example, if leisure travelers book a hotel room or a cruise trip weeks ahead of their trip, you can segment the waiting time into a time period when you send your guests relatively general information (usually the earlier period) and then have a time period closer to the arrival date when you send more concrete and specific information, with vivid visual aids.

This approach fits the psychological principle of construal level theory. This theory notes that people tend to think globally and abstractly regarding activities or events that are in the relatively distant future. At this time, they think about such matters as the "why" aspect of actions and the overall desirability of events. By contrast, for the near future situations, your guests tend to think more concretely a level of how, when, and where they'll perform the activity. So, in the context of planning for a vacation, when that vacation is still far away consumers tend to picture it broadly in the context of a bigger goal like having fun, having a quality family time, or engaging in a challenging adventure. However, as the vacation time approaches, the details of the vacation, the context in which the events occur, and possible alternative episodes that might occur during the vacation may become more salient. So it makes sense for you to match the sequence of information you send out with consumers' general tendency to construe situations according to the event's proximity. Also, by sending the information at different points of time, you can engage guests to look forward to the upcoming event throughout the entire waiting period.

Social media and mobile apps are also potentially useful tools to manage consumers' preconsumption experience. One logical thing to do is to tweet guests who have booked their hotel rooms and update them with relevant information over time. This has the effect of inducing excitement and anticipation—as well as providing needed knowledge. Early on, you can send information or simply offer entertaining material (like photos). What matters most is to remind guests of the upcoming event and provide them with the frequent moments of anticipation. Mobile apps can also be designed with

Figure 8.2
How to Guide the Guest Experience Before, During, and After the Visit

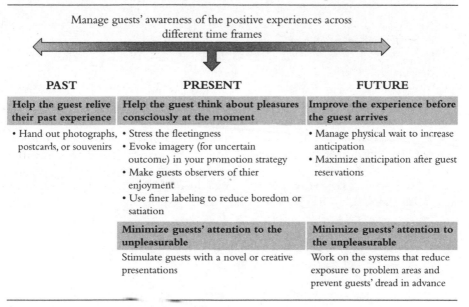

Manage guests' awareness of the positive experiences across different time frames

PAST	PRESENT	FUTURE
Help the guest relive their past experience	**Help the guest think about pleasures consciously at the moment**	**Improve the experience before the guest arrives**
• Hand out photographs, postcards, or souvenirs	• Stress the fleetingness • Evoke imagery (for uncertain outcome) in your promotion strategy • Make guests observers of thier enjoyment • Use finer labeling to reduce boredom or satiation	• Manage physical wait to increase anticipation • Maximize anticipation after guest reservations
	Minimize guests' attention to the unpleasurable	**Minimize guests' attention to the unpleasurable**
	Stimulate guests with a novel or creative presentations	Work on the systems that reduce exposure to problem areas and prevent guests' dread in advance

the same goal in mind. Again, the festivities should begin the moment you have your guests' booking information.

Before I close, it's important to mention what should be a self-evident caveat to the idea of turning your guests' waiting experience into a time of happy anticipation. Your operation must be able to deliver on the expectations that you have created. Thus, the consumer's actual experience must not be drastically different from what is expected. Your effort to keep your promises should be part and parcel with your effort to keep them informed and entertained during the wait.

The ideas presented here (summarized in Figure 8.2.) will help you to constantly improve your guests' experience by heightening their awareness of the pleasurable experiences they will have, are having, and did have in connection with your operation—that is, before, during, and after their visit.

NOTES

1. J. L. Le Bel and L. Dubé, "The Impact of Sensory Knowledge and Attentional Focus on Pleasure and on Behavioral Responses to Hedonic Stimuli," Paper presented at the 13th annual American Psychological Society convention, Toronto, Ontario, Canada, 2001.

2. S. Lyubomirsky, *The How of Happiness: A Scientific Approach to Getting the Life You Want* (New York: Penguin Press, 2008).
3. F. B. Bryant, and J. Veroff, *Savoring: A New Model of Positive Experience* (Mahwah, NJ: Erlbaum, 2007); K. Duncker, "On Pleasure, Emotion, and Striving," *Philosophy and Phenomenological Research* 1 (1941): 391–430.
4. M. E. P. Seligman, T. Rashhid, and A. C. Parks, "Positive Psychotherapy," *American Psychologist* 61(8) (2006): 774–788.
5. J. L. Kurt, "Looking to the Future to Appreciate the Present: The Benefits of Perceived Temporal Scarcity," *Psychological Science* 19(12) (2008): 1238–1241; and Bryant and Veroff, 2007.
6. Y. H. Lee, and C. Qiu, "When Uncertainty Brings Pleasure: The Role of Prospect Imagineability and Mental Imagery," *Journal of Consumer Research* 36 (December 2009): 624–633.
7. J. W. Schooler, D. Ariely, and G. Loewenstein, "The Pursuit and Assessment of Happiness May Be Self-Defeating." In I. Brocas and J. D. Carrilo, eds. *Psychology and Economics, Volume 1: Rationality and Well-Being* (New York: Oxford University Press, 2003), 41–70.
8. J. P. Redden, "Reducing Satiation: The Role of Categorization Level," *Journal of Consumer Research* 34 (February 2008): 624–634.
9. Bryant and Veroff, 2007.
10. See E. G. Miller, B. E. Kahn, and M. F. Luce, "Consumer Wait Management Strategies for Negative Service Events: A Coping Approach," *Journal of Consumer Research* 34 (February 2008): 635–648.

CHAPTER 9

HARNESSING THE POWER OF YOUR CULTURE FOR OUTSTANDING SERVICE

ROBERT FORD and MICHAEL C. STURMAN

Your company's culture can be one of the strongest forces for ensuring excellent customer service and the resulting financial success, or it can stand in the way of your ever achieving your service and financial goals. Company cultures come in all shapes and sizes, but all cultures are assembled from specific parts, such as language, beliefs, and philosophies. In this chapter, we review the elements of corporate culture, give examples of successful corporate cultures, and point out key ways that you can harness your company's culture for outstanding service.

CULTURE DEFINED

Although you undoubtedly have a solid concept of culture, and your firm may even state your culture for all to see, let's start with the following definition. An organization's culture is a way of behaving, thinking, and acting that is learned and shared by the organization's members. So it is the shared philosophies, ideologies, values, assumptions, beliefs, attitudes, and norms that knit a community together. All of these interrelated qualities reveal a group's agreement, implicit or explicit, on how its members should behave, especially when they approach decisions and problems. You might think of culture as "the way we do things around here." Although cultural inertia can be strong, cultures do change, however gradually, due to both outside influences and internal decisions. A culture both influences its members and in turn is influenced by its members.

We've borrowed examples of corporate culture from such diverse firms as Walt Disney World Resort, Southwest Airlines, Nordstrom's, Ritz-Carlton, Gaylord Palms, and Four Seasons Hotels, among others. If you are a member of one of these organizations, you are well aware of the power of culture. If not, these firms present clear examples of how to instill a culture of successful service that creates financial success, regardless of the business concept or niche.

Before we go deeper into the elements of culture, however, we need to underline where you come in as a corporate leader—regardless of your position or formal level. Successful corporate culture depends on leaders—executives, managers, supervisors, and even line employees—to convey and reinforce the culture as a method of ensuring successful service. The sample companies have one thing in common: strong corporate cultures that are driven from the top of the organization and exhibited by all. These cultures were enunciated by a founding visionary and expanded and developed by corporate leaders. Walt Disney began with his vision of "Imagineering"; Herb Kelleher developed a culture for Southwest Airlines that was uncommon for that business; Horst Schultze instilled the concept of "Ladies and gentlemen serving ladies and gentlemen" at Ritz-Carlton; Isadore Sharp created an unrelenting focus on service at Four Seasons; Kemmons Wilson devised a family-oriented culture to match his concept of product consistency for Holiday Inn; and Bill Marriott Sr. and Bill Marriott Jr. developed the customer-oriented culture found at Marriott hotels.

Simply declaring a corporate culture is not enough, of course. You and all other corporate leaders must live that culture. As Isadore Sharp pointed out: "Employees are natural boss watchers. Everything their bosses say and do tells employees their real concerns, their real goals, priorities, and values."[1] In short, you must consistently act within, and, if necessary, enforce your company's culture, if you want your employees to believe in it. Next, let's look at the elements of culture, and then we'll discuss how you can use culture for successful service.

Beliefs, Values, and Norms

We just defined culture in terms of shared philosophies, ideologies, values, assumptions, beliefs, attitudes, and norms.[2] Let's take a look at the key elements of culture, beginning at the end of that definition. As a leader in a culture-driven organization, you seek to define the beliefs, values, and norms of the organization through what you do, say, and write, and whom you reward, recognize, and promote.

Beliefs Beliefs form the ideological core of the culture. A belief is how people in organizations make sense of their relationships with the external world and its influence on the organization. Beliefs define the relationships between causes and effects for the organizational members.

As a simple illustration, if people in an organization believe that the marketplace rewards those organizations that provide good service and punishes those that don't, then the importance of providing good customer service becomes a cultural belief. Culture involves a multitude of beliefs and assumptions about how the environment operates. Most critically, your employees' beliefs reflect how they and your organization will respond to each day's events. The management of an organization that understands the importance of these beliefs will take an active role in defining both the assumptions and the beliefs that those assumptions create.

Values Values are preferences for certain behaviors or certain outcomes over others. Values define for members what is right and wrong, preferred and not preferred, desirable behavior and undesirable behavior. Obviously, your company's stated and implicit values can be a strong influence on employee behavior. If management sends a clear signal to all employees that providing good customer service is an important value, then the employees know they should adopt this value and behave accordingly.

Norms Norms are standards of behavior that define how people are expected to act while part of the organization. Some of your organization's many norms are immediately obvious to both employees and guests, but others require the advice and counsel of veteran employees who have learned these norms over time, especially by what gets rewarded and what doesn't.

Most outstanding hospitality organizations have norms of greeting a guest warmly, smiling, and making eye contact to show interest in the guest. Some use "the 15-foot rule" in which any employee must make positive contact with the guest within this "hospitality zone." Your company might even print service norms like this one on cards and supply them to every employee to serve as the guidelines for service.

Cultural norms in the hospitality industry are strongly defined and shaped by guests who make their expectations plain. Because the hospitality industry's service almost always involves an interaction between employees and guests, guests themselves become potent assistants to the managers in monitoring, reinforcing, and shaping employee behavior. Because guests are involved in "coproduction," your repeat guests are probably aware of your culture. At Disney, for instance, the guest service guidelines are so well established that even the guests often know them. If a ride operator in the Magic Kingdom fails to make eye contact or doesn't smile, a park patron will undoubtedly notice and perhaps remark on the "abnormal" behavior.

Norms of Appearance In addition to the norms of behavior, most hospitality organizations also have norms of appearance, including standards of personal grooming. Your firm may set norms for hair length, jewelry, fingernails, facial hair, and visible tattoos. These appearance norms are included in your culture because appearances are important in hospitality organizations. Ritz-Carlton employees are "ladies and gentlemen." Disney wants a conventional appearance for its cast of characters to create the realistic illusion inherent in its show. Similarly, employees at the Hard Rock Cafe or Hooters must themselves have a particular appearance (far different from what Disney expects).

Folkways and Mores Folkways are the customary, habitual ways in which organizational members act or think, without reflecting upon them. Shaking hands (or not shaking hands); addressing everyone by first name, or by last name with complimentary title; and wearing or not wearing a tie are folkways. In a restaurant, a folkway might be to roll silverware when there is nothing else to do in the quiet times between crowds.

An organization's mores are folkways that go beyond being polite. These are customary behaviors that must be followed to preserve the organization's efficient operation and survival. Mores require certain acts and forbid others. By indicating what is right and wrong, they form the basis of the organization's code of ethics and accepted behaviors.

COMMUNICATING THE CULTURE

While the substance of culture is a set of assumptions that lead to beliefs, values, and norms, other key elements of culture involve how it is communicated to those inside and outside the organization. These communication elements of culture include laws, language, stories, legends, heroes, symbols, and rituals.

Laws

The laws of an organization are its rules, policies, and regulations—the norms that are so important that they are turned into a code of conduct. Two norms are so important to Disney that they are corporate policies—in effect, laws that carry termination as the penalty for violations. A cast member in costume must not walk in an area where the costume is inappropriate. So, for instance, an employee in the futuristic Tomorrowland outfit cannot appear in Frontierland. Another strict policy is that cast members portraying Disney characters must stay completely in character and cannot be seen out of costume or do anything else that might destroy the Disney fantasy. Indeed, a policy forbids transporting any character costume in a public area unless it is in a black bag that completely covers all its parts so no one will see a favorite fantasy character "in pieces."

Language

Each organization develops a language of its own as part of its culture. Elements of this language can be incomprehensible to outsiders, as you are well aware if you know any teenagers. The special language helps create a coherent social group, so it is an important vehicle for both communicating the common cultural elements to which the language refers and in reaffirming your employees' identity with their culture.

Using another example from Disney, this firm uses show business terms for its employees and hiring. *Cast members* are recruited by *casting*. This terminology puts everyone together equally as part of the organization (the production), and it reminds people that they are playing "roles" that help make up the Disney "show." This show concept is reinforced by the use of other terms such as *on stage* to define all situations and areas where cast members are in front of their customers and *back stage* to define areas the customers cannot see. Thus, cast members constantly think of themselves as participants in an ongoing stage production designed to create a magical fantasy experience. So effective is this training in language that Smith and Eisenberg reported that none of the 35 Disneyland Park employees they interviewed used such typical hospitality terms as *uniforms, customers,* or *amusement park;* instead, they referred to *costumes, guests,* and *property.*[3]

Stories, Legends, and Heroes

Stories, legends, and heroes transmit culture by communicating proper behaviors. The Ritz-Carlton is especially noted for the use of many teaching stories. For example, to teach going the extra mile to serve a customer, the story of the *New Gold Standard* reports the following letter from a guest:

My wife accidentally broke a bottle of makeup that she had brought along and left it in pieces on the counter in the bathroom because she wanted to use as much of it as possible. We came back to the room one day to find a note sitting beside the broken makeup bottle from house-keeping offering to replace the broken bottle they didn't even break.[4]

Focusing on its theme of the "power of personal service," Four Seasons tells the story of an employee who overheard a guest telling his wife how embarrassed he was to be the only one without a black tie at a formal function. The employee asked the man to take a seat in his office, and then quickly took off his own tuxedo and rushed it to laundry. Once the tux was clean, this employee called a seamstress to fit the guest. Not only does this story teach the shared Four Seasons values, but the guest turned out to be the chairman and CEO of a leading consulting organization who subsequently directed all of his company's business (worth millions in food and lodging) to the Four Seasons. The man also took every opportunity to give a testimonial for Four Seasons.

Stories like these give you a way to define and teach what your guests find inspiring and what will cause them to give top evaluations. Indeed, many of the examples we offer in this chapter come from the stories used in employee orientation training. Long-established companies, such as Disney, Darden, and The Ritz-Carlton, have a vast repertoire of stories, but what if your firm is relatively new, such as a just-opened hotel? That was the situation facing the Gaylord Palms, a 1,400-room convention hotel located in Orlando. Like the other Gaylord properties (including its flagship, Gaylord Opryland), the property is tightly focused on "extraordinary meetings and conventions" for its guests. To take advantage of the power of stories as a training tool, management created a letter from a fictitious customer to show new employees what the intangible mission of extraordinary meetings means through the customer's eyes. If you haven't already done so, you should encourage your organization to build up its storehouse of stories describing people who did amazing things for your guests, created magical moments, and provided exemplary service.

Symbols

A symbol is a physical object that communicates an unspoken message. At Walt Disney World Resort, Mickey's famous mouse ears are everywhere, including plants grown in mouse-ear shapes, anniversary service pins, and the entrance to Team Disney, which is framed by ears. Mouse ears are subtly hidden everywhere around the property and serve as a constant symbolic reminder of where Disney began and its cultural values.

Rituals

Rituals are symbolic acts that people perform to gain and maintain membership or identity within an organization. Your company's training program has ritualistic significance because everyone goes through the experience upon entry into the company. Additionally, most hospitality organizations develop elaborate ritual celebrations of service excellence. These can range from a simple event like a departmental pizza party to honor all those receiving positive comments on customer comment cards, to very elaborate Employee of the Year award ceremonies that resemble a major gala.

Gaylord's management, which refers to its employees as STARS, gave extra effort to the development of three rituals that would celebrate and reinforce the culture and its commitment to its employees.[5] One ritual was designed for celebrating promotions. The supervisor of promoted STARS pedals the promoted person around the premises on a three-wheeled bicycle. Camera-toting paparazzi wave a sign and make a commotion. As the person is pedaled around the hotel's 10 acres, both front of the house and back, everyone can see and celebrate the event. Guests sometimes even join in the parade. A second ritual is a quarterly "All STARS" rally, which publicly celebrates the successes of individual contributors by selecting STARS in the hotel that best represent the resort's values. In the third ritual, at the end of the year, a corporate-wide process selects the best representative of each value, and that person is flown to Nashville with their family for a corporate-level celebration. The winners have dinner on the stage of the Grand Ole Opry and get $1,500 to give to the charity of their choice.

TEACHING THE VALUES

Although observant guests and employees can infer many elements of your culture, it's still essential to teach your values to new employees and reinforce your values to existing employees. Since everyone brings to a new job the cultural assumptions of past experiences, you must start teaching new cultural values to your employees from day one. Companies known for their strong cultures—like Disney, The Ritz-Carlton, and Four Seasons—earned that reputation by spending considerable time and money on developing their cultures for all entering employees. To socialize its new employees, the Gaylord Palms begins its orientation with two days of training, in which 60 percent of the time is dedicated to teaching culture. Orientation is followed by one to four weeks in the individual departments, where new employees get training in both job skills and more training in the Gaylord culture. This initial orientation is followed by an "orientation reunion" 90 days later to ensure that the employees know their benefits, are comfortable in their job roles, and can see how to apply the flawless service philosophy in their specific departments.

Experiencing Culture

Barbara Talbott
CEO
GlenLarkin Advisors

Building a global brand to support a global hotel organization takes a diverse mix of skills. Some are learned on-property, while others come from farther afield. Despite distances—doing business in more than 30 countries—and despite their different backgrounds and areas of expertise, the Four Seasons marketing team had proved effective. Business results were on track. Trust and collaboration were evident. But everyone believed that more was possible. The solution that the team devised was to spend 24 hours on-property, in Toronto, together with colleagues from the hotel. The goal of this "retreat" was to take effectiveness and teamwork to another level by experiencing the culture in a more meaningful way.

Think of it as a day of circuit training that began with morning meetings and moved on through key functions around the hotel. In the kitchen, the group assembled fresh asparagus bundles for *salades composées*. Later, they quickly turned a meeting room to make way for a private luncheon. Sales shared an update on their key accounts. The concierge coached them on how to give a good restaurant recommendation. There were no lectures and no real handouts. But at each step there was plenty of patience, encouragement, confidence—and quiet urgency.

Housekeeping staff played a major part, demonstrating how many elements must come together to create the comfortable room and "perfect sleep" that guests expect. This group of marketers knew that the bed and bedding were custom manufactured and that great care had been given to how every ingredient was assembled. They knew that, over time, the process had also been refined to reflect guest comments along with learning from hotel management and staff.

The task was to watch, and occasionally help, with the bed-making process. The guide was an experienced housekeeper who, as she worked, also explained how the standards are kept:

"New staff get help from trainers who've been here longer. Then the supervisor inspects some rooms every day. Not just for new staff. Any room might be inspected."

One member of the marketing team then raised her hand.

"How does the supervisor know if the bed's made properly?" she asked. "I understand how the rest can be checked, but the bed is different. Does it have to be unmade, so the supervisor can be certain that it's right?"

"No, that's not necessary," the housekeeper answered. "You see, I would know myself. If the bed wasn't right, then the guest wouldn't sleep as well—and that would not be all right with me."

That night the marketers slept in those well-made beds. The next day, before leaving, the group talked about what they had seen and heard: the many impressions of kindness, skill, and commitment. The woman who'd asked the question shared her story, still deeply impressed by the housekeeper's response.

There are many ways to create and share a service culture. Words are needed but actions convey what words cannot. In the case of this group, actions compressed into a single day accomplished many things. Those who had worked in Four Seasons hotels were reminded how fresh and real the values remained. Those who had never done so gained their own sense of ownership and appreciation for what makes the service possible. Together, they had experienced all of this firsthand, in ways that continue to find expression in their work today.

Subcultures

We must note that an overall culture is usually composed of subcultures, particularly in large organizations. The chief points to note about subcultures are that they exist and that you need to ensure that the subculture's beliefs and norms support your company's main culture. One particular subculture split might be full-time employees and part-time employees. The part-timers in particular may not spend enough in your operation to absorb its culture or care enough about the organization and its members to substitute its values for their own. So be on guard and do what you can to ensure that the subcultures are consistent with the core cultural values even if some specific behaviors, beliefs, and norms do vary somewhat from the desired culture. Here's a place where leadership is critical in promoting your company's culture.

National Cultures

If your company is an international operator, you have seen the effects of cultural differences from one country to another. Disney, for instance, discovered that its EuroDisney (now Disneyland Paris) could not simply transport the entire Disney culture to France and has made necessary adjustments. Seeing this outcome, Four Seasons Hotels took a different approach when it opened its Four Seasons Hotel King George V Paris. It conducted a service quality audit to identify some of the differences between French and North American business culture. Based on these differences, they then altered policy so that it fit with the French culture, rather than assuming the American culture could be forced on employees at the new location.

HARNESSING YOUR COMPANY'S CULTURE

Now that we have examined the many elements of culture, let's return to your role as a manager of culture. You are the person who shares, emphasizes, and embodies your company's culture. Every chance you get, you should reinforce your company's cultural points. Easily said, but challenging in a hospitality environment. Despite the challenge, though, managing your culture is a crucial task, as culture can play an important strategic role in helping you achieve your company's guest service and financial goals.

One goal set by Gaylord Palms, for example, was to get perfect "5s" on its customer satisfaction measures. From its opening in 2002, its general manager strategically defined a path toward top customer satisfaction, starting with creation of a customer-focused mission and values. His leadership team would teach these cultural values and beliefs to all STARS. Gaylord used a variety of communication tools to build trust in and affirm management's commitment to the culture. To emphasize its support of the staff, it uses the term *STARS first*. This message commitment to the staff was backed up by an "employee guarantee," which gives every employee direct access to top management if the promised employment relationship was not being delivered. The guarantee was created to build trust that management really believed in its "STARS" first cultural value.

The customer satisfaction data collected by the Gaylord Palms confirm the success of this approach. Not only did they achieve a strong showing of "5s," but they also gathered every meeting planning award and best place to work award in their market.[6] When this culture was later implemented in other Gaylord properties, it led to the same results in employee and customer satisfaction and financial performance.

STRATEGY AND EMPLOYEE COMMITMENT

Your firm's competitive strategy provides the basis for such critical decisions as how your organization will be structured, what type of service it wants to deliver, what market niche it seeks to fill, what production and service delivery system it will use, who it will hire, and how it will train, reward, promote, and evaluate those people. Since the only way to implement those critical decisions is through employees committed to your mission, you need to use your culture strategically to motivate your employees. We should note here that, as discussed in Chapter 11, money is an important part of this motivation, but many other factors influence hospitality employees' motivation. A strong and focused organizational culture becomes an especially important managerial emphasis in hospitality organizations. The Boulders, a luxury property in Arizona, has the vision statement "Seek opportunities to create memories." This vision is emphasized through the use of coaches, orientation, training, and employee recognition programs.[7] The culture does not spell out specific actions to take, but emphasizes how the employees should look for opportunities to deliver excellent service.

Culture as a Competitive Advantage

Your culture can provide significant competitive advantage if it has value to its members, is unique, and cannot be easily copied by others. If an organization has a strong culture that others cannot readily duplicate, it can use that culture to attract both customers and employees. If you want to benchmark other companies' cultures, look for those that have used culture in this way, to develop competitive advantage.[8] Southwest Airlines is an example of a company that has done this, with its "Living the Southwest Way" culture, which espouses both "displaying a Warrior Spirit" (i.e., work hard, desire to be the best, be courageous, display a sense of urgency, persevere, and innovate), and having a "Servant's Heart" (i.e., follow the golden rule, adhere to the basic principles, treat others with respect, put others first, be egalitarian, demonstrate proactive customer service, and embrace the SWA family).Through all of this, the Southwest culture embraces a "Fun-LUVing Attitude" (i.e., have fun, don't take yourself too seriously, maintain perspective (balance), celebrate successes, enjoy your work, and be a passionate team player).[9] (LUV, of course, is a pun on the Southwest hub, Love Field, and on its stock ticker sign, LUV—a classic example of a cultural in-joke.)

Maintaining Southwest's Culture Southwest also has engaged its employees to reinforce and teach its culture, as do many other outstanding firms. Southwest

Airlines does this with a Culture Committee, whose responsibility was perpetuating the Southwest Spirit. The Culture Committee was created in 1990 "to take the lead in preserving the airline's unique culture."[10] Originally, it was made up of 38 people, most of whom had 10 or so years at Southwest and embraced Southwest's maverick, caring, irreverent way of doing things. It has since expanded to well over 100 individuals, with representatives from each station and part of the airline.[11] Committee members have been known to visit stations with equipment and paint in hand to remodel a break room, or surprised maintenance employees with pizza and ice cream. Still others simply show up periodically at various field locations to lend a helping hand.

Management by Culture!

As you work to strengthen your company's culture, you will discover that your job becomes easier in many ways. A strong, effective culture supplants policies, procedures, and managerial directives by instilling in employees the knowledge of what to do in nearly any situation. Today's thinner hospitality organizations must find ways to delegate more decision-making responsibility and empower their employees, especially their guest-contact employees. Indeed, the more uncertain the task, the more employees must depend on corporate values instead of managerial instructions, formal policies, and established procedures to guide their behavior.[12] In vague and uncertain situations, you can rely on a strong culture to guide your employees to do the right thing.

Leaders Teach the Culture

Although we said that strengthening the culture will simplify your job in some ways, you'll still need to constantly teach the culture to your employees—all the time reinforcing your firm's values, mores, and laws. Ed Schein, one of the earliest researchers on corporate culture, suggests that the only thing of real importance that leaders do is to create and maintain the organization's culture.[13] Perhaps that is a bit of hyperbole, but the fact remains that the best leaders personally model their commitment to the service mission, and they do it visibly. They back up slogans with dramatic, sometimes costly actions. To instill values, they stress two-way communications, opening their doors to all employees and using weekly (sometimes daily) work-group meetings to inform, inspire, and solve service problems. They put values into action by treating employees exactly as they want employees to treat their customers.[14] They use rituals to recognize and reward the behaviors that the culture values, and they praise the heroes whose actions have reflected worthy cultural values in the stories they tell. Other employees can use these hero stories as models for their own actions.

Schein suggests that leaders can use the following five primary mechanisms to define and strengthen the organization's culture: "(1) what leaders pay attention to, measure, and control; (2) leader reactions to critical incidents and organizational crises; (3) deliberate role modeling, teaching, and coaching by leaders; (4) criteria for allocation of rewards and status; (5) criteria for recruitment, selection, promotion, retirement, and excommunication."[15]

Setting the Example   Bill Marriott Jr. provides a good example of how a leader can help to sustain his company's culture. Large as his company is, he is famous for dropping in at a hotel and chatting with everyone he sees. He has been known to get up early in the morning and wander into the Marriott kitchens to make sure the pancakes are being cooked properly. This intense commitment to personal contact with Marriott employees and visible interest in the details of his operations have become so well known in the Marriott organization that his mere presence on any Marriott property serves as a reminder of the Marriott commitment to service quality.[16]

The Role of a Leader

Charles A. Conine
SPHR
Cornell 1973

July 1967. In the midst of a summer lunch rush the restaurant's side door swung open and the CEO strode in confidently, smiling and dressed impeccably. He was accompanied by the restaurant's general manager, intent on fulfilling the big boss's wish to "meet and greet" line employees of the ever-expanding enterprise that bore his name. Meanwhile, a young boy working the cook's line concentrated on a different, more urgent task: filling two fryer baskets with French fries to supply hungry guests at the takeout counter. Just then, at the precise moment the CEO moved toward the boy, his hand outstretched in greeting, the bottom of the case of French fries the boy held gave way—and 30 pounds of sliced spuds spilled out, coming to rest squarely on the CEO's brightly polished shoes. Unfazed, the CEO laughed and shook the kid's hand as the general manager glowered nearby.

Years later, the "kid" found himself employed as a vice president by the same CEO's eponymous, now worldwide hospitality company.

(continued)

(continued)

Once again, it was a chance meeting that brought the CEO and the young man together as they stood in a hallway at company headquarters. Yes, the CEO chuckled, he was certain he remembered the infamous French fry moment two decades earlier, laughingly adding, "We didn't hold it against you, did we?"

Two galvanizing moments had two very different impacts. The first, when the young man was only a child, produced raging fear and motivated the boy to pay closer attention to his work. When a second encounter brought the two men together once more, it caused the younger man to further rededicate himself to the CEO's vision of building profits *and* satisfied employees.

Truly great leaders needn't shout or make splashy headlines to induce motivation; sometimes all that's needed are a few small moments, costing nothing but the leader's time, to galvanize, provoke, and excite an employee's spirit—yielding results that impact both companies and the people who serve them.

By the way, the boy was me. The CEO? J. Willard Marriott Jr.

The vision of deceased leaders also can continue to inform a corporate culture, as in the case of Kimpton Hotels & Restaurants, which maintains a culture based on Bill Kimpton's vision. Although Kimpton died in 2001, the culture he created lives on through the organization's new leadership. According to Niki Leondakis, chief operating officer,

One of the things we do at employee orientation is talk to every one of our employees. Once a year, I and one of our senior executives travel around the country on the Kimpton National Tour and bring together all the employees at each hotel. We talk about the culture of care. It means caring for your co-workers, caring for our guests, caring for the environment, our community, our investors.[17]

The clear commitment to the customer-service culture, demonstrated through the actions of those on the top of the organizational chart, sends a strong message to all employees that everyone is responsible for maintaining a high-quality customer experience. This same modeling behavior can be seen in the many hotel managers who visibly and consistently stop to pick up small scraps of paper and debris on the floors as they walk through their properties. Employees see and emulate this care and attention to detail.

WHAT WE KNOW ABOUT CULTURE

We believe that people will judge your strength as a leader by how well you employ your culture as a mechanism to achieve your company's objectives. By concentrating on using the tools and principles we discussed in this chapter, you can ensure a unified message to employees. They will receive—and perform—according to a consistent set of cultural beliefs, values, and norms. Throughout this chapter, we have emphasized that consistency is important to reinforce the culture. The more consistently you use your cultural mechanisms, the more powerfully reinforced the culture will be. Make your messages intentional and explicit. What you get angry or excited about tells everyone what is important. In particular, if you express outrage over a service failure caused by a careless employee, this sends a strong message to all the employees that good service matters. A story is told of how Bill Marriott Sr. fired an employee on the spot for insulting a guest. When this story got around the organization, there was no question in anyone's mind of the guest orientation that Marriott valued.

In closing, here are some principles about organizational culture that seem to hold generally true. For each principle, there are clear reasons why you should pay careful attention to culture in your organization.

- Leaders define the culture (or redefine it, if necessary), teach it, and sustain it. To create and maintain a service-oriented culture, this may be your biggest responsibility.
- An organizational culture that emphasizes interpersonal relationships is uniformly more attractive to professionals than a culture that focuses on work tasks.[18]
- Strong cultures are worth building; they can provide employee guidance in uncertain situations where company policies or procedures are unavailable or unwritten. There are thus crucial benefits to having a service-oriented culture, and it is worth your while to find ways to be successful in helping create and sustain such a culture.
- Subcultures will form in larger organizations. If you develop and maintain a strong culture, it will increase the likelihood of keeping the subculture consistent with the overall culture values in important areas.

As a final point, sustaining the culture requires constant attention to the means of communicating culture. You must consistently reinforce and teach the organization's beliefs, values, and norms of behavior to all employees.

NOTES

1. I. Sharp, *Four Seasons: The Story of a Business Philosophy* (New York: Penguin Group, 2009): 101.
2. Definitions in this section are indebted to H. M. Trice and J. M. Beyer, *The Cultures of Work Organizations* (Englewood Cliffs, NJ: Prentice-Hall, 1993): 33–34.
3. J. Van Maanen, "The Smile Factory: Work at Disneyland," in P. J. Frost et al., eds. *Reframing Organizational Culture* (Newbury Park, CA: Sage, 1991): 66.
4. J. A. Michelli, *The New Gold Standard: 5 Leadership Principles for Creating a Legendary Customer Experience Courtesy of the Ritz-Carlton Hotel Company* (New York: McGraw-Hill, 2008): 181.
5. T. E. Deal and M. K. Key, *Corporate Celebration* (San Francisco: Berrett-Koehler, 1998).
6. R. C. Ford, C. P. M. Wilderom, and J. Caparella, "Strategically Crafting a Customer-Focused Culture: An Inductive Case Study," *Journal of Strategy and Management* 1 (2008): 143–167.
7. C. A. Enz and J. Siguaw, "Best Practices in Service Quality," *Cornell Hotel and Restaurant Administration Quarterly* 41(5) (2000): 20–29.
8. For further information on adapting the culture ideas of other organizations, see J. A. Chatman and K. A. Jehn, "Assessing the Relationship between Industry Characteristics and Organizational Culture: How Different Can You Be?" *Academy of Management Journal* 37(3) (1994): 522–553.
9. www.southwest.com/careers/culture.html (downloaded 9/4/09).
10. www.southwest.com/about_swa/airborne.html (downloaded 9/7/09).
11. A. McGee-Cooper, D. Trammell, and G. Looper, "The Power of LUV: An Inside Peek at the Innovative Culture Committee of Southwest Airlines," *Reflections: The SoL Journal* 9(1) (2008): 49–55.
12. For more information on this point, see W. H. Davidow and B. Uttal, *Total Customer Service* (New York: Harper, 1989): 96–97.
13. E. Schein. *Organization Culture and Leadership.* (San Francisco: Jossey-Bass, 2004): 2.
14. Davidow and Uttal, 107.
15. Ibid., 224–225.
16. H. B. Gregersen and J. S. Black, "J. W. Marriott, Jr., on Growing the Legacy," *Academy of Management Executive* 16(2) (2002): 33–39.
17. C. Wolff, "What Makes Kimpton Cool," *Lodging Hospitality* 11(8) (2008): 42–43.
18. J. E. Sheridan, "Organizational Culture and Employee Retention," *Academy of Management Journal* 35(5) (1992): 1052.

CHAPTER 10

A Scientific Approach to Managing Hospitality Operations

GARY M. THOMPSON

This chapter illustrates why you and your organization will benefit from taking a scientific approach to managing operations. Does the phrase scientific management give you visions of a person in a white coat with thick glasses and bad hair poring over a clipboard? Well, this chapter is *not* about getting a new wardrobe, new hairstyle, new glasses, or upping your nerd quotient! (You could, however, hire someone who looks like that, I suppose.) Instead, what I discuss here is a thoughtful, careful, analytical way for you to look at operations. The idea is to apply principles of good science to the task of managing operations. You already have many managerial skills, and this chapter seeks to show you how to apply good science to the task of managing operations so that you can make even better decisions.

In this chapter I talk about what I believe is required to take a scientific approach to managing operations. That includes (1) focusing on data, (2) dealing with complexity, and (3) taking actions that are driven by rigorous analysis. To show you how this can work, I give you two fairly detailed examples—one on staffing for seasonal demand variation and the other on optimizing restaurant table mixes. As a word of warning, though, you will see some equations in this chapter! Here we go.

GOOD DATA IS A NECESSITY

Perhaps the most important requirement of applying science to managing operations is the availability of good data. You need accurate data to make sure your decisions are based on solid reality, rather than perceptions. Without data, you'll have to base your decisions on assumptions, but you probably won't have the information you need to fully analyze a situation. Take the time required for a housekeeper to clean a room, for example. Your hotel might be one that uses a standard, say, 30 minutes per room (which amounts to 16 rooms per day). But perhaps the housekeeper doesn't really need 30 minutes; maybe it's really 20, or maybe it's really 40. Without data, you won't really know the real time required, because you don't know if your standard took into account all of the factors that affect the length of time a housekeeper requires. A short list of the factors includes: the number of guests in the room, the nature of the guests (adults or children, for example), whether the guests are staying over or new guests will be occupying the room, the size of the room, the number of beds, and the time of year (which affects guests' activities). So, you could use a fixed standard, but it might make more sense to collect data to determine the complete characteristics of the task. Perhaps the time standard needs to be adjusted by the season or according to the type of room.

In general, the more data you compile, the better, since the analyses that can be performed are limited to the data that are available. I know it costs money to collect data, but let me give you five reasons for why it's worth doing—and might not be as expensive as you think. First, it can often be well worth the cost of hiring some students or having existing employees spend time collecting data. This would not have to done in perpetuity, but rather periodically. Second, you can search for inexpensive ways to collect data as a by-product of the existing operations. Third, employing technology—such as point-of-sale systems—often yields data collection opportunities in addition to operational efficiencies. Fourth, you can consider redesigning your operations to facilitate data collection. Fifth, the benefits of the data often extend beyond their original purpose. For example, the data collected on the factors influencing the time housekeepers require per room could be used for forecasting future labor requirements, rather than simply establishing appropriate standards.

Certainly, not all data are equally good, since data are often inaccurate. Correcting the inaccuracies after the fact can be a challenge. The best way to ensure accurate data, where the data are dependent on employees' actions, is to train employees about the importance of how accurate data leads to operational improvements, and to ensure that the data are used for developmental, rather than punitive, purposes. For example, a fast-food restaurant that uses a timer to measure how long customers wait to receive their meals has the potential to measure the service levels that customers experience. However, if meeting the service standard becomes the primary goal, and employees are chastised for not meeting it, then don't be surprised to see behaviors that result in inaccurate data, such as part of the service happening "off-the-clock."

You'll see an excellent example in Chapter 12 of the value of collecting and using data to correct service issues, rather than to discipline employees.

Dealing with Complexity

The main reason to apply a scientific approach to managing operations is that doing so offers a means of dealing with the complexity of management decisions. Consider, for example, all the constraints and myriad idiosyncrasies related to just one of those decisions—scheduling employees. Even if you're well practiced in setting schedules, I'm sure there are still times when it's a problem to balance all the complications and to predict the outcomes in uncertain environments. Rather than take the many different operational components into account, many managers take shortcuts. Some managers use the "photocopier method" of workforce scheduling, which means that this week's schedule is simply a photocopy of last week's schedule. This saves the trouble of developing a new schedule, but it might not actually match up to the operational needs. You've probably seen the results of such suboptimal decisions when you walk into, say, a quick-service restaurant and find several employees having a wonderful chat, because there's no business.

Actions Driven by Rigorous Analysis

The third component of managing operations scientifically is taking actions based on rigorous analysis. In short, once you have data in hand, you can make powerful decisions that fit well with each situation. Having good data saves you from inadvertently making a decision that is based on a coincidental observation. As an example, where I grew up in eastern Canada, in winter, people would say: "It's always cold when there's a full moon." Well, yes, typically it *is* cold on a Canadian winter night when you can see the full moon. However, the key word in this statement is *see*. It's cold when it's clear, and that's when you can actually see a full moon. When there is a full moon and it's cloudy (and consequently warmer), the moon isn't visible. Thus, people associate full moon and cold, rather than clear and cold. But we know very well that it's not really the moon that causes the cold night. It's the underlying factor—clear or cloudy—that explains what's actually happening. Now, consider a hospitality example. If I were to show you some data that indicate that hospitality companies that have more days of training per employee have lower employee turnover, what would you conclude? Is it the training that leads to reduced turnover, or are they both influenced by a third factor? Well, if you had data only on training hours and turnover, you couldn't actually tell. Driving actions by analysis means that the data have to be extensive and the analysis has to be thorough.

Building Models from Data An implication of driving actions by analysis is the need for model building. Building models has several benefits. First, it forces an organization to be explicit about its assumptions. This means that you can question the assumptions. Second, it allows for knowledge dissemination. Rather than all the decision-affecting factors being locked in someone's head (with the risk of the person being run over by a bus and that knowledge lost forever), explicit models allow other people in the organization to see what factors are being considered. Thus, others can understand the business and better contribute to refining the models. Third, and perhaps most important, models are better able to deal with the complexities of decision making. In the next sections, I'll provide two extended examples of how data analysis and model building can help with complex decisions. In both cases, you'll see some conflict between what we think we see and what actually is happening. The first example involves optimizing the table mixes in a restaurant, and the second considers the problems of seasonal demand variability as managers try to staff a resort.

Before I give you those cases, let me mention one other example of using analysis and a model to guide decision making. This is the Wine Cellar Management Tool that I developed, which is available free from the Cornell Center for Hospitality Research (chr.cornell.edu). The tool, which is spreadsheet based, takes the guesswork out of managing a wine cellar. Essentially, it's a sophisticated inventory management tool, a key feature of which is its ability to consider each wine's "drinkability window," which is the period of time that the wine is at its peak. It's designed to help people avoid one of life's true disappointments—drinking, past its peak, what had been a good, or even great, wine.

EXAMPLE 1—RESTAURANT TABLE MIXES

The first extended example I cover concerns restaurant tables. How many times have you gone into a busy restaurant and seen lots of tables occupied but also many empty seats at those occupied tables? Those empty seats, which occur because the restaurant is not matching its capacity to its demand, represent a missed opportunity for the restaurant. So, if a restaurant manager wanted to go about optimizing the use of the space devoted to seating customers, how would he or she approach the problem? Certainly, one approach would be trial-and-error experimentation: changing the mix a little, observing the results, locking in the change if it yielded an improvement, trying something else if it didn't. Observations could also be helpful: seeing empty seats at occupied 4-tops would suggest that the restaurant should have more 2-tops and fewer 4-tops. Implementing such a trial-and-error approach would almost certainly take a long time and the manager would probably never be confident that the restaurant had the correct mix of capacity.

Now, let's see how that manager could approach this problem scientifically. First, the manager would need some data about customer demand. If the restaurant has a point-of-sale system (a POS), then the manager could extract information on party sizes. If the restaurant does not have a POS, the manager would have to record the data manually. Let's say, for example, that the historical data for a busy period (say, dinner on Friday) was as given in Table 10.1. For the sake of this example, let's also assume that the restaurant seated parties of one and two only at 2-tops and parties of three and four at 4-tops. If the restaurant had 50 seats, how many 2-tops and how many 4-tops should it have?

A common, but incorrect answer is fifteen 2-tops and five 4-tops. The intuition behind the 15-5 answer is that adding the probabilities of parties of one and two gives 59 percent for the 2-tops. Fifty-nine percent of 50 seats is just about 30 seats, which converts to the fifteen 2-tops. Adding the probabilities of the parties of three and four gives 41 percent for the 4-tops. Forty-one percent of 50 seats is just about 20 seats, which converts to the five 4-tops. Now, let's look at why the answer of 15-5 doesn't work.

The answer lies in the fact that a party of three or four seated in a 4-top requires twice as many seats as does a party of one or two seated in a 2-top. The capacity allocation decision needs to consider more than just the likelihoods of the different party sizes—it also needs to consider the capacity required by each party. Doing so, as shown in Figure 10.1, yields eleven 2-tops and seven 4-tops.

Let's think about this for a minute: the first-blush intuition told us to use fifteen 2-tops and five 4-tops, while a more considered approach suggested

Table 10.1
Historical Party-Size
Information for Dinner on Fridays
in a Popular Restaurant

Party Size	Percentage of Total Parties
1	8%
2	51%
3	25%
4	16%

Figure 10.1
Approaching the Table Mix Problem Scientifically

This problem could be approached mathematically (i.e., scientifically). Let x = the number of 2-tops and y = the number of 4-tops. The total number of seats available for allocation would define the restriction:

$$2x + 4y = 50$$

We also know, from the probabilities of the different party sizes, information about the relative commonality of each size table, that there should be about three 2-tops for every two 4-tops:

$$x = 59/41y; \text{ so that}$$
$$x = 1.44y$$

Those of you who remember high school math will recognize that we have two unknowns and two equations, which we can solve by substitution:

$$2(1.44y) + 4y = 50;$$
$$2.88y + 4y = 50;$$
$$6.88y = 50; \text{ so that}$$
$$y = 50/6.88 = 7.27 \text{ tables}$$

Since we can't have a fractional number of tables, we'd round the number of 4-tops to 7, meaning that 28 of our 50 seats were allocated to 4-tops. Once we've set the number of 4-tops, we can then use our total seat restriction to set the number of 2-tops:

$$2x + 4(7) = 50;$$
$$2x + 28 = 50;$$
$$2x = 22; \text{ and so}$$
$$x = 11$$

The correct answer, then, is 11 two-tops and 7 four-tops.

---

eleven 2-tops and seven 4-tops. But that answer seems to move us back toward the problem we noticed in the first place: empty seats in larger-than-necessary tables. Actually, that shouldn't happen, since the 11-7 table mix would give us the best way of matching capacity to demand. It's only as we added even more large tables that we would start to see the empty-seat phenomenon. The extreme case—and I'm sure you can think of restaurants like this—is where all the tables would be 4-tops (a 0-12 mix in our example). If a restaurant has all large tables like that, it seems to me that no one has thought about using the restaurant's capacity effectively. You might argue that it's esthetics that drives the choice of all large tables; I would counter that designers are not necessarily focused on *operations* and consequently are probably costing the restaurant in terms of missed sales opportunities. In any event, a better way of approaching the capacity issue is to provide a designer with some information about the desired mix of tables, with the charge of making it esthetically pleasing.

Greater Complexity Now, the issue of finding the right mix of tables for a restaurant is still not as simple as what I've presented so far. Additional considerations include demand information, differences across parties, table combinability, randomness of real restaurants, rules for selecting parties, and the effects of demand intensity. I'll discuss each in turn.

A common challenge in hospitality businesses is the nature of the information on customer demand that is available. You have information on the number of customers that you actually served. This is referred to as *constrained* demand, but the true, or *unconstrained*, demand includes customers you didn't serve, for whatever reason. Constrained demand refers to the fact that once the business is at full capacity, customers will be turned away, so the demand is constrained by available capacity. For your decision making, the ideal information point is unconstrained demand.[1] Consider the differences in the two types of demand information in the context of determining the best mix of tables in a restaurant. If you use unconstrained demand information, then you'll be attempting to determine the best mix of tables for the restaurant's true customer mix. If, instead, you're using constrained demand, all you'll be doing is finding the best mix of tables for the mix of customers *who were already being served*. These are potentially quite different. Unfortunately, the easy information to obtain is the constrained demand, since that's what's in your POS data. Capturing information on the unconstrained demand can require some imagination: making sure, for example, to track declined reservations, or the number of people who walk away from your restaurant when they're quoted an estimated wait time. Also, it would be important to track the number of people who put their names on the wait list but then leave before being seated. Even with this information, however, you still wouldn't have unconstrained demand information, because you wouldn't have information on customers who took one look at your restaurant and left because it appeared to be too busy. Again, employing some creativity would allow you to try to capture some of that information.

The example I presented earlier was limited to parties no larger than four people. But that's not entirely realistic because you'll always have larger parties. Also, certain characteristics of parties vary by party size. First, dining duration is typically longer for larger parties than for smaller parties. Second, larger parties tend to spend less per person than do smaller parties. Third, the space required to seat large parties can be different, on a per-person basis, than it is for smaller parties. All of these differences mean that the problem of finding the best table mix is more complex than the simple example presented earlier. Yet another consideration is whether tables can or should be combined to seat larger parties, or whether it's better to have a mix of different table sizes in the restaurant. Further, the differences across party sizes typically result in the large parties being worth less on a space-time basis than smaller parties. So, if you find that your unconstrained demand is sufficiently high, your restaurant might consider cherry-picking its more valuable, smaller parties and turning away business from the larger parties.

So, do you have any ideas on how to modify the "back-of-the-envelope"–type calculations (in Figure 10.1) to find the best mix of tables in a restaurant? ("Back-of-the-envelope" calculations can be done by hand or with a calculator.) Certainly, those equations could be modified to take into account differences in party characteristics. However, even with those modifications, the equations would leave out an important characteristic of real business: chance. The only way to deal with chance is to use a model that mimics the chance occurrences. In the restaurant setting, chance—or randomness—exists when parties arrive, the size of the party, the duration of the dining experience, how long customers are willing to wait for a table, and how much they spend. With a model that incorporates chance, we can examine such issues as the rules used to select a party to assign to a newly available table. Should the table be given to the party that's been waiting the longest (regardless of size)? The party that's been waiting the longest that has the "right size" for the table? The largest party that fits in the table (with ties broken by the longest wait)? Or a party selected in some other way? A model that incorporates chance would also allow us to evaluate the accuracy of the back-of-the-envelope calculations. (As an aside, a recent study I conducted found that the back-of-the-envelope calculations can yield table mixes that underperform the ideal mixes by more than 10 percent).

Simulation Models Models that incorporate chance are called *simulation models*, since they simulate the kinds of things that can happen in the real world. The great advantage of using simulation models for operations is that they allow you to simulate different operations scenarios without having to change them in the real business. This means that your customers are not part of "an experiment" to see how to better serve them, with all the risks that entails. Using simulation, you can find those scenarios, configurations, or plans that improve on the status quo. Implementing those plans greatly increases the chance for successful changes to operations. Over the years, I've found simulation to be invaluable, since it allows me to create models that mimic the complexity that exists in real organizations. Simple simulation models can be constructed in spreadsheets such as Excel, though more complex spreadsheet models generally require the use of commercially available simulation software or custom-built software models. (For a more thorough coverage of simulation, see the article I wrote with Professor Rohit Verma entitled "Computer Simulation in Hospitality Teaching, Practice and Research," which is available free of charge from the Cornell Center for Hospitality Research at www.chr.cornell.edu.)

Figure 10.2 shows a screen capture of TableOptimizer, a restaurant simulation tool that I developed and frequently use in research projects. This screen capture was taken at 8:05 PM in the simulation of a real restaurant, and displays the status of the restaurant at that time. The restaurant in question had three 6-tops, while the other 53 tables were 4-tops. Green seats are occupied, while red seats are empty. The table of 8 seats in the bottom center represents two 4-tops combined to seat six people. There are 29 parties waiting for a table, 15 of which have been waiting for more than 50 minutes. To this point, 374 customers have been served, and 77 customers were "lost," having departed because their wait was too long. At the time shown, all of the tables were occupied, but only 122 of the 230 seats were occupied, yielding a 53-percent seat occupancy. In my studies, seat occupancies over 80 percent are achievable if the table mix matches well the customer mix. In fact, after

Figure 10.2
Screen Shot of the TableOptimizer Restaurant Simulator

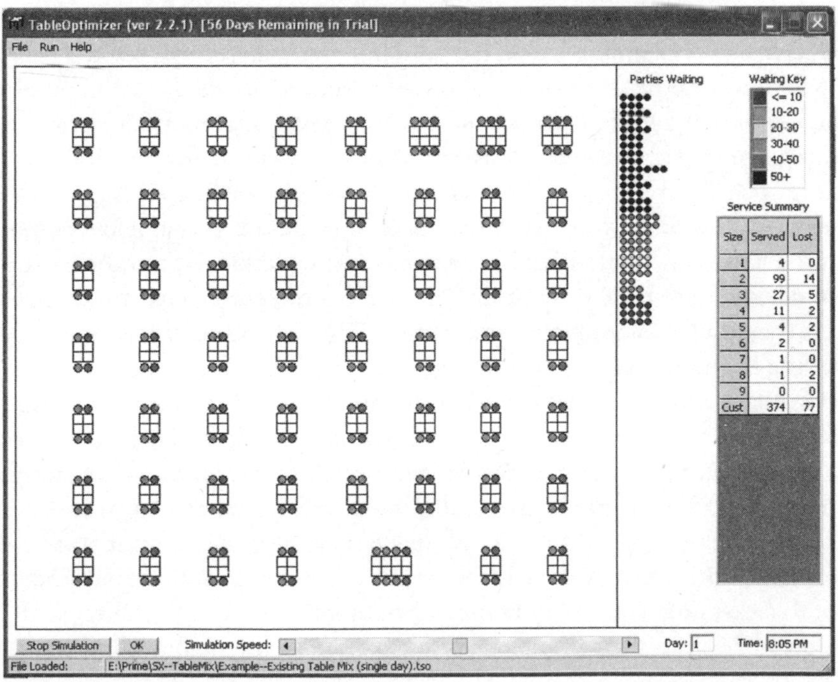

Size	Served	Lost
1	4	0
2	99	14
3	27	5
4	11	2
5	4	2
6	2	0
7	1	0
8	1	2
9	0	0
Cust	374	77

changing its mix of tables, the restaurant in question was able to increase its effective capacity by approximately 30 percent.

EXAMPLE 2—WORKFORCE STAFFING

A challenge common to many hospitality businesses is dealing with the staffing challenges resulting from seasonal demand swings. If your operation is steeply seasonal, perhaps you staff up and staff down as the season changes, but it's worth asking the question of whether you might be better off if you held the staff size constant throughout the year. If you did that, you would have to determine what level would be best. If you do staff up and staff down, you need to determine an appropriate mix between permanent and seasonal staff. Then there's the issue of whether you should contract with outside vendors to supply some of the capacity needed during the peak season. In all of these decisions, the issue becomes how to best meet the demand.

To begin with, a plan to deal with seasonal demand swings should be high-level and deal with groups or types of employees for two reasons. First, the detail required to develop a plan specific to individual employees over an extended period would be impractical. Second, even if the detail could be managed, the random turnover of individual employees would soon make any plan out of date. As such, I'll use the term *employee category* to refer to a particular type of employee, such as full-time, seasonal, or contract.

In addition to the seasonal demand swings, other factors that compound the difficulty of making the staffing decisions are attrition rates, productivity rates, learning curves, labor costs, costs of hiring or terminating employees, and value gained from alternate task assignments—all according to employee categories. Each month, you face similar decisions: how many employees should be hired and how many should be terminated, by employee category. Clearly, these decisions are related, since the number of employees hired in one month affects the number of employees on staff in the next month, which in turn can affect the hiring decision in that month.

If a manager did not take a scientific approach to this problem, using a decision model, then the best he or she would be able to do is to use some rule of thumb that probably would mean being overstaffed at some times, being understaffed at other times, and not delivering the service as cost effectively as possible. Figure 10.3 shows one way that you might approach this problem scientifically. It does involve considerable calculation, but once the formulas are built, you can plug in your numbers.

Optimizing the plan presented in Figure 10.3 would involve finding the values of the decisions that yield the minimum total plan cost. That plan

Figure 10.3
Approaching the Workforce Staffing Problem Scientifically

Let's think about the parameters and decisions in the seasonal staffing context. Let's define:

e = index for employee categories;

m = index for months;

A_e = attrition rate of employees in employee category e, measured as a proportion;

D_m = aggregate level of customer demand that is forecast for month m;

C_e^L = monthly labor cost of an employee in category e;

C_e^H = cost of hiring an employee in category e;

C_e^T = cost of terminating an employee in category e;

P_e = monthly productivity an employee in category e; and

S_{em} = number of employees on-staff in category e at the start of month m.

The decisions to be made are:

H_{em} = number of employees hired in category e at the start of month m; and

T_{em} = number of employees terminated in category e at the end of month m.

There are two types of relationships between the decisions. First, the number of staff on-hand at the start of a month in an employee category is equal to the number of staff on hand at the start of the previous month, less the number lost through attrition in the previous month, less the number of employees terminated at the end of the previous month, plus the number of employees hired in the current month, or:

$$S_{em} = S_{e,m-1} * (1 - A_e) - T_{e,m-1} + H_{em} \text{ (for each employee category } e \text{ and month } m).$$

The second relationship ensures that demand is met every month:

$$\sum P_e * S_{em} * (1 - A_e/2) \geq D_m.$$
sum over employee categories

This relationship sums, across the employee categories, the productivity of the employees on-staff and ensures that it equals or exceeds the demand forecast. The staff on hand at the start of the month is adjusted downward, assuming that attrition occurs evenly over the month, so that the average number of staff available in a month is $S_{em} * (1 - A_e/2)$.

Finally, we have the expression that measures the overall cost of the plan (don't panic, it's not as bad as it looks!):

$$\text{Total Cost} = \sum_{\substack{\text{sum over employee} \\ \text{categories}}} \left(\sum_{\substack{\text{sum} \\ \text{over months}}} (C_e^L * S_{em} * (1 - A_e/2) + C_e^H * H_{em} + C_e^T * T_{em}) \right)$$

In words, the cost of the staffing plan is the sum, across all employee categories and all months, of the labor costs, the hiring costs, and the termination costs. As with the demand relationship, we adjust the number of staff available at the start of a month S_{em} by $(1 - A_e/2)$ to get the average number of people available in a month.

would show the ideal composition of the workforce and how its composition would change over time. For the optimization to be effective, the plan would have to have a planning horizon of at least one seasonal cycle (i.e., at least one year). Having a scope of less than a year would be problematic because the best plan for a partial year would almost always be different from the best plan for an entire cycle.

If the complexity of the staffing model is modest, the plan could probably be created in Excel using its Solver capability (which is limited to 200 decisions). If the complexity increases, or if speed is an issue, commercially available optimization software could be used or a custom-built optimizer created.

This planning process would be ongoing—and you would repeat it every month. The reason for this is that both demand forecasts and the actual status of the workforce at the start of the plan will change. Clearly, there would be up-front effort involved to collect data to populate the model and to construct the model; that effort, however, would pay dividends through better staff planning. You would have the confidence to know that hiring and termination decisions are being made at the right times, for the right numbers of employees, of the right categories, to yield the best overall performance. Moreover, a plan like this would offer a reality check on organization's past decisions about labor staffing.

Once again, I have taken some liberties in presenting this example in a somewhat simplified manner. Ideally, the model would incorporate such other factors as the learning curve of employees and the value of alternative assignments (to be used when capacity exceeds demand). In addition, the plan lumps together all types of demand into something called "aggregate demand," which assumes that all employees can do the work. It may be preferable to separately plan different parts of the business.

As an example of a model for solving a problem like this, I refer you to the "Workforce Staffing Optimizer" tool that I developed, which is available free of charge from the Cornell Center for Hospitality Research. The tool, which uses a sophisticated, custom-build optimizer, allows for up to four categories of employees and a large number of inputs defining each employee category.

Paging Officer Data

To summarize my key points about managing operations scientifically, good data enable analysis, which then can support building and solving decision models. Let's assume you have bought into these ideas, but you are wondering who would have the time to devote to managing operations scientifically, based on all these data requirements. You might also be concerned that you don't have the time, skill, or interest to do all this analysis and model building yourself. Well, it doesn't have to be you! You can find an appropriate employee or vendor and say, as Captain Picard was fond of saying, "Make it so." Managing operations scientifically does require an up-front time commitment to data collection, analysis, and model building. You will see benefits in the form of better decisions, a more robust organization, greater profitability, and personal advancement. Your key role, then, is to be aware of the benefits and to know the extent of what is possible, so that you can either do the requisite work yourself or direct others to do it.

While this chapter has used two primary examples, many more examples can be found at the Cornell Center for Hospitality Research (www.chr .cornell.edu). Figure10.4 lists some of the reports and tools available there, related to scientific management of operations.

Managing operations scientifically does not make managing a business "clinical." Being a good operations manager is still as much art as science. The point is, though, by focusing on the science part of it, you'll be more valuable than ever to your organization.

Figure 10.4
Reports and Tools Available from the
Cornell Center of Hospitality Research That Offer Examples
of Managing Hospitality Operations Scientifically

Cases in Innovative Practices in Hospitality and Related Services: Set 3, 2010, *Cornell Center for Hospitality Research Report*, Vol. 10, No. 10 (Cathy A. Enz, Rohit Verma, Kate Walsh, Sheryl E. Kimes, and Judy Siguaw).

Integrating Self-Service Kiosks in a Customer-service System, 2010, *Cornell Center for Hospitality Research Report*, Vol. 10, No. 6 (Tsz-Wai Lui and Gabriele Piccoli).

Cases in Innovative Practices in Hospitality and Related Services: Set 2, 2010, *Cornell Center for Hospitality Research Report*, Vol. 10, No. 4 (Sheryl E. Kimes, Cathy A. Enz, Judy Siguaw, Rohit Verma, and Kate Walsh).

The Eight-Step Approach to Controlling Food Costs, 2009, *Cornell Center for Hospitality Research Tool* (J. Bruce Tracey).

Revenue Management Forecasting Aggregation Analysis Tool, 2009, *Cornell Center for Hospitality Research Tool* (Gary M. Thompson).

Cases in Innovative Practices in Hospitality and Related Services: Set 1, 2009, *Cornell Center for Hospitality Research Report*, Vol. 9, No. 17 (Judy Siguaw , Cathy A. Enz, Sheryl E. Kimes, Rohit Verma, and Kate Walsh).

(continued)

Figure 10.4
(continued)

How Restaurant Customers View Online Reservations, 2009, *Cornell Center for Hospitality Research Report*, Vol. 9, No. 5 (Sheryl E. Kimes).

Don't Sit So Close to Me: Restaurant Table Characteristics and Guest Satisfaction, 2009, *Cornell Center for Hospitality Research Report*, Vol. 9, No. 2 (Stephani K. A. Robson and Sheryl E. Kimes).

The Wine Cellar Management Tool, 2008, *Cornell Center for Hospitality Research Tool* (Gary M. Thompson).

Service Scripting: A Customer's Perspective of Quality and Performance, 2008, *Cornell Center for Hospitality Research Report*, Vol. 8, No. 20 (Liana Victorino, Rohit Verma, and Don Wardell).

Forecasting Covers in Hotel Food and Beverage Outlets, 2008, *Cornell Center for Hospitality Research Report*, Vol. 8, No. 16 (Gary M. Thompson and Erica D. Killam).

Accurately Estimating Time-Based Restaurant Revenues Using Revenue per Available Seat-Hour, 2008, *Cornell Center for Hospitality Research Report*, Vol. 8, No. 9 (Gary M. Thompson and Heeju Sohn).

Complaint Communication: How Complaint Severity and Service Recovery Influence Guests' Preferences and Attitudes, 2008, *Cornell Center for Hospitality Research Report*, Vol. 8, No. 7 (Alex M. Susskind).

Workforce Staffing Optimizer, 2007, *Cornell Center for Hospitality Research Tool* (Gary M. Thompson).

Customer Satisfaction with Seating Policies in Casual-Dining Restaurants, 2007, *Cornell Center for Hospitality Research Report*, Vol. 7, No. 16 (Sheryl E. Kimes and Jochen Wirtz).

Examining the Effects of Full-Spectrum Lighting in a Restaurant, 2007, *Cornell Center for Hospitality Research Report*, Vol. 7, No. 12 (Stephani K. A. Robson and Sheryl E. Kimes).

The Effects of Organizational Standards and Support Functions on Guest Service and Guest Satisfaction in Restaurants, 2007, *Cornell Center for Hospitality Research Report*, Vol. 7, No. 8 (Alex M. Susskind, Michele K. Kacmar, and Carl P. Borchgrevink).

Restaurant Capacity Effectiveness: Leaving Money on the Tables, 2007, *Cornell Center for Hospitality Research Report*, Vol. 7, No. 7 (Gary M. Thompson).

A New Method for Measuring Housekeeping Performance Consistency, 2006, *Cornell Center for Hospitality Research Report*, Vol. 6, No. 11 (Michael C. Sturman).

Dining Duration and Customer Satisfaction, 2005, *Cornell Center for Hospitality Research Report*, Vol. 5, No. 9 (Sheryl E. Kimes and Breffni Noone).

Perceived Fairness of Restaurant Waitlist-Management Policies, 2005, *Cornell Center for Hospitality Research Report*, Vol. 5, No. 4 (Kelly A. McGuire and Sheryl E. Kimes).

Restaurant Table-Mix Optimizer, 2004, *Cornell Center for Hospitality Research Tool* (Gary M. Thompson).

Workforce Scheduling: A Guide for the Hospitality Industry, 2004, *Cornell Center for Hospitality Research Report*, Vol. 4, No. 6 (Gary M. Thompson).

Figure 10.4
(continued)

Hotel Managers' Perceptions of the Blackout of '03, 2004, *Cornell Center for Hospitality Research Report*, Vol. 4, No. 4 (Robert J. Kwortnik).

Restaurant Revenue Management, 2004, *Cornell Center for Hospitality Research Report*, Vol. 4, No. 2 (Sheryl E. Kimes).

Emergency Preparedness Essentials, 2003, *Cornell Center for Hospitality Research Tool* (Robert J. Kwortnik).

Key Issues of Concern for Food-service Managers, 2003, *Cornell Center for Hospitality Research Report*, Vol. 3, No. 4 (Cathy A. Enz).

Dedicated or Combinable? A Simulation to Determine Optimal Restaurant Table Configuration, 2003, *Cornell Center for Hospitality Research Report*, Vol. 3, No. 2 (Gary M. Thompson).

Multi-Unit Restaurant-Productivity Assessment: A Test of Data Envelopment Analysis, 2002, *Cornell Center for Hospitality Research Report*, Vol. 2, No. 1 (Gary M. Thompson and Dennis Reynolds).

NOTE

1. E. B. Orkin, "Wishful Thinking and Rocket Science; The Essential Matter of Calculating Unconstrained Demand for Revenue Management," *Cornell Hotel and Restaurant Administration Quarterly* 39(4) (August 1998): 15–19.

CHAPTER 11

MOTIVATING YOUR STAFF TO PROVIDE OUTSTANDING SERVICE

MICHAEL C. STURMAN and ROBERT FORD

Your service environment is superb, your operations are efficient, your concept reflects a clear idea of the customers' demands, and your back-of-the-house delivery system is flawless—so far, so good. Now it's up to that front-line employee you've worked so hard to hire and train to deliver the service you've promised, because the guest contact employee usually is the key to having a satisfied guest. Say that there's a problem at the front desk, and a guest's room is out of order or not acceptable. This is the moment of truth. If the front-desk associate is rushed or dealing with a heavy check-in, he or she may not be able to respond to the guest's problem or may be too casual about the problem. Suddenly, all your careful planning is for naught. If the guest feels shabbily treated, the guest will also be angry at your hotel, since the employee represents the hotel. It makes no difference whether the guest's reaction is fair or appropriate. Since quality and value are defined by the guest, the employee who provides the guest experience must be not only well trained but highly motivated to meet the guest's quality and value expectations and to do so consistently. Your role as a manager responsible for providing an exceptional service experience, and specifically for preparing your staff to deliver such service, is vital. In this chapter, we argue that motivating your employees is as critical for excellent service as is training them.

MOTIVATING EMPLOYEES

Let's look at the way in which a motivated front-desk clerk handled an actual room reservation problem. A family was checking in at the Hyatt Grand Cypress on a busy night. The hotel was full, the family's reservation had not been properly handled, and the husband, wife, and three tired children were upset. The front-desk employee assessed the situation and acted promptly. Rather than force the family to hang out in the lobby until things were straightened out, she took some quarters out of the petty cash drawer and gave them to the kids to go and play the video games and gave the parents chits for a drink in the lobby bar. That gave her the necessary time to find a manager to straighten out the problem. The parents were happy, the kids were happy, and the front-desk person had defused a tense situation.

In contrast, you may have heard about the experience of Tom Farmer and Shane Atchison, whose situation eventually went viral on the Internet. They had a confirmed reservation at a hotel, and the room had supposedly been guaranteed by credit card for late arrival. Yet when they arrived a 2:00 AM, they were refused rooms. Tom and Shane publicized their service experience by posting an open complaint to the hotel, called "Yours Is a Very Bad Hotel."[1] They report that "Mike the Night Clerk" was "deeply unapologetic," "had done nothing about finding [them] accommodation elsewhere," and when they suggested that he should have lined up other rooms in advance, Mike the Night Clerk "bristled!" Explaining why the customers were wrong to be upset that their "guaranteed" room was not saved for them, Mike told them, "I have nothing to apologize to you for." After the posting, representatives of the hotel did apologize and reportedly improved their training and overbooking policies, but the damage was done. A Google search in December 2010 on the phrase "Yours Is a Very Bad Hotel" yielded 15,200 results!

Both of the above situations had the same essential cause: a failed reservation. The key here is that the employees' actions brought markedly different results. The Hyatt's desk clerk was motivated to keep the customers satisfied despite a problem that was not of her making, whereas Mike the Night Clerk apparently could not have cared less. As you read this chapter, consider how your employees might respond to a common situation like this one. Your challenge is to discover what motivates your employees not only to do their jobs efficiently and competently but also to go the extra mile for your guests.

In this chapter, we discuss various ideas that will help you motivate your staff. We have divided these ideas into financial approaches and nonfinancial methods—all aimed at helping you motivate your staff to offer the best possible guest experience even when things don't go right. We have all seen that it's impossible to predefine policy and procedures for all guest situations. Something unexpected always comes up. Thus, employees should know that they are encouraged, expected, and trusted to handle all the many and varied situations that come up in the guest service areas for which they are responsible. If they were properly selected and trained in the first place, management must make it possible for them do their jobs with responsibility, skill, enthusiasm, and fun. The purpose of this chapter is to consider the many ways you can accomplish this.

The motivation, the drive, or compelling force that energizes people to do what they do comes from either inside the employees (intrinsic motivation) or from the environment (extrinsic motivation). The best organizations create an environment and policies that enhance both forms of motivation. It's critical to note right at the start that money—important though it may be—is not your employees' only motivating factor. You can motivate employees not only by offering financial rewards, but also providing nonfinancial rewards, or even changing the nature of the job itself. Decades of economic and psychological research have shown that motivation is influenced by numerous factors, including the organization's environment, organizational culture, individual characteristics, comparison across individuals, and the structure and form of existing incentives. Unfortunately, it is impossible for us to offer you simplistic prescriptions on how to increase your employees' motivation, but you do have a wide variety of tools at your disposal to create and sustain an environment where employees want to go the extra mile.

FINANCIAL REWARDS

Let's start with the most common motivator—money. Your employees receive direct compensation (wages or salary). You probably also offer indirect compensation, which puts money in your employees' pockets by giving them services and benefits, such as deferred compensation and health insurance. You may also have at-risk pay, where rewards (if they are given at all) depend on various factors, like individual, team, or organizational performance.

Psychological research is filled with different theories and studies of motivation, many of which are applicable to understanding financial incentives. We won't describe all of these ideas, but let's look at four factors that researchers have identified for why money motivates your workers—or fails to do so. Those factors are individual needs, the power of reinforcement, the expectancy of getting rewards, and the fairness of the rewards.

The Power of Individuals' Needs

To meet employees' living needs, the most obvious inducement is money. Most of your employees are working because they need to earn a living— even if they work in your hotel or restaurant for other, nonmonetary reasons. Motivational speakers like to talk about higher-order needs like social, recognition, or achievement needs, but none of those count if a person is concerned about how they are going to get their next meal, pay their rent, or buy warm clothes in the winter.

You must pay your employees enough to meet their survival needs before they can effectively use incentives or rewards to help satisfy their other needs.[2] While you may not be in the financial position to suddenly increase wages or offer health benefits, you are not powerless either. There are other valued incentives to help them, such as scheduling enough hours, working around child or elder care responsibilities, and helping employees find affordable health care for their families. Listening to employees' needs and preferences (as described in Chapter 4) often reveals simple available solutions. Such an approach can go a long way to satisfy employees' needs.

The Power of Positive Reinforcement

The idea of positive reinforcement is a well-accepted psychological principle. If you reward desired behavior and don't reward undesired behavior, you will get more of the desired behaviors and fewer of the undesired ones. While the idea seems straightforward, successfully using positive reinforcement in the workplace is challenging. Too often, time pressures compel you to focus on the annoying "squeaky wheel" rather than the quietly effective employee. Rewarding the wrong behavior is as big a mistake as not rewarding the right behavior.

Here's an example of how improper reinforcement unintentionally changed the nature of a greeter position for one restaurant. The manager initially told the newly hired employee explicitly that his primary responsibility was to greet and welcome guests. As time went on, however, to keep the employee busy when guests were not entering the restaurant, the manager added responsibilities to the position—such as checking periodically to make sure there were enough trays or making sure that the butter dish was always full. The greeter quickly realized that the manager never complimented him for properly greeting the guests, nor did the manager ever say anything to him when he missed a guest because he was too busy with his other duties. But if he ever let the buffet line run out of trays or butter, he was strongly reprimanded. Therefore, by reinforcing certain employee actions, the manager had redefined the job. The manager made her real priorities clear, the employee adjusted his actions accordingly, and the restaurant no longer reliably offered a greeting to guests.

The Power of Goals and Expectancy

Another key way to motivate employees is by setting challenging yet still attainable goals. Research on goal setting has repeatedly shown that setting specific and challenging goals leads to higher levels of task performance than do easy or vague goals, or telling people to "do their best." If you couple challenging goals with compensation, you have a powerful force to motivate exceptional employee performance. Of course, as shown by the case of the buffet greeter, rewarding the wrong behavior can sabotage motivation. Goals could be too easy or too challenging, may induce unethical behavior or inappropriate risk taking, or may motivate behaviors leading to rewarded tasks at the expense of other, equally important, but unrewarded tasks.[3]

Harrah's casino uses a combination of goal setting and future rewards to motivate both individual and team behavior. Sales staff employed in Las Vegas are rewarded for making sales goals set for the individual person, the hotel, and Harrah's group of hotels in the Las Vegas area. Managers work with the teams to make sure the goals are challenging but attainable. Successful performance is rewarded with both bonus checks and merchandise that the employees can pick out (such as Weber grills and vacation packages). These goals extend beyond simply sales numbers. All employees can achieve bonuses based on a number of critical metrics, including customer service scores. Setting these goals, rewarding them, and using goals that are clearly connected to the company's strategy of excellent customer service allows Harrah's to get highly motivated staff and exceptional performance.

The Power of Equity

Reinforcement, goal setting, and expectancy assume that people make decisions based purely on their own circumstances, but people are social creatures. We see what others do and get, compare ourselves against others, and decide what is fair or unfair, just or unjust. If someone thinks that other employees were given more rewards for similar efforts, this will create feelings of injustice. Feelings of being underpaid have been linked to lower motivation, greater absenteeism, higher turnover, and even increased theft. We hasten to add that employees' feelings of lack of equity involve being comparatively underpaid—few people admit that they are overpaid and feel bad about it.

Individuals will compare against others, both inside and outside of the company. Your employees will compare themselves to their coworkers, to subordinates, and even to the boss, all the time evaluating whether pay differences are (in their eyes) just or unjust. Your employees will also try to figure out what the "market" is paying for their job, talk to friends who are doing similar jobs at other organizations, look at other jobs they might be able to take, or even consider other careers they might pursue. Making this even more confusing, people will often form judgments of fairness based on their perceptions of their own worth or perceptions of others' pay—neither of which may be accurate.[4]

Most know how important fairness is in compensation systems. Indeed, for the process of determining *Fortune*'s "100 Best Companies to Work For" list, compensation fairness is a key criterion

TYPES OF PERFORMANCE-BASED FINANCIAL REWARDS

With those principles in mind, let's look at possible performance-based financial rewards. Your challenge is to discover what employees consider equitable and appropriate and then provide rewards that fit those criteria, while also being fiscally prudent. To make rewarding good performance even harder, employees have changing expectations, moods, and valuations of the employment relationship.

Your first step is to identify the rewards that employees desire. Most employees begin new jobs with energy and enthusiasm. They want to do well. So your motivation program should build on this good start by offering encouragement and help. By giving your employees desired rewards for performance, you can keep people energized, enthusiastic, and working hard. Fortunately, you can choose among many different sorts of financial rewards to do this. We've summarized these rewards in Table 11.1.

Let's look at some of these financial incentives, many of which you may already be using:

- Annual performance bonuses reinforce recognition of individual performance while helping people focus on achieving individual performance goals and recognition.
- Group financial incentives reinforce social needs by rewarding team success and thereby focusing employees on working in a group to achieve common goals.

Table 11.1

Different Ways to Provide Financial Incentives and Rewards

Pay Form	Definition	How Performance Is Assessed	Example
Merit raise	An increase in base pay (i.e., a raise) that is tied to individual performance	Managers review individual performance	Managers give employee a 5 percent annual raise to reward exceptional service
Annual performance bonus	A one-time lump sum payment made to an employee based on a performance evaluation	Managers review individual performance	Managers give employee a lump-sum bonus of $10,000 that year to reward exceptional service
Spot bonus	A one-time payment made to an employee who exhibited great performance through some specific act	Managers observe or customers report a specific incident of exceptional performance	Managers give employee a $100 bonus for handling a difficult guest complaint to the guest's satisfaction
Individual tips	Voluntary payments given to service providers by customers after providers deliver service	Customers observe and judge each service encounter	Customer gives server a 20 percent tip at the end of a service experience
Pooled tips	When all customer tips are put into a common "collection" and are then divided evenly between the servers on duty	Customers assess and reward all instances of server performance on a given night	At the end of a shift, all servers on duty during the shift divide customer tips
Recognition program	A program designed to provide a reward (financial or symbolic) to employees who achieve a notable goal	Managers assess some period of performance (e.g., monthly, annual)	CEO publicly recognizes the rooms agent who takes the most reservations in a year with a ceremony, a plaque, and a check for $5,000.
Group incentive plan	A bonus paid to all employees of a group for successfully meeting a specific goal	Managers assess individual, team, or company-wide performance	Managers pay a $100 bonus to each employee in the group for each month that customer satisfaction ratings exceed a certain level
Compensation through ownership	Enabling employees to own a portion of the company (e.g., common stock or stock options)	Managers assess individual, team, or company-wide performance	Company gives employees the option to purchase 500 shares of stock at $20. If the stock price goes above $20, then the employees will benefit by exercising their option.

- Individual tips can encourage high customer service, while pooled tips can encourage servers to work together.
- Ownership in the company (through stock) helps employees realize how their personal success depends on the company's overall success. This can satisfy social needs (i.e., when the company succeeds, our social group succeeds) and achievement needs (i.e., when the company achieves, I also feel a sense of achievement).

Depending on how a financial reward is presented, it can help satisfy recognition needs as well as financial needs. So different pay methods can focus your employees on achieving high performance. As a caution, though, just as the manager's reinforcement changed the job of the buffet greeter, financial incentives can change behaviors, and so you should be sure that the behaviors you are rewarding are the ones you truly want to see in your employees.

Financial rewards can be a powerful motivator that can reinforce your efforts to build a culture of service excellence. Your employee motivation program can be strengthened even further with nonfinancial rewards, as we explain next.

NONFINANCIAL REWARDS

Many of the reasons why people behave as they do have nothing to do with money (e.g., bringing up children, helping a stranger, volunteering in the community, caring for parents). Consequently, nonfinancial rewards like recognition, praise, personal growth, and an enjoyable working environment (which cost you little or nothing) can produce results that money could never buy. Let's look at the most common nonfinancial rewards.

Recognition Programs

The purpose of a recognition program is to say "thank you" or "well done." Nearly 90 percent of companies offer some form of recognition program. You can recognize your employees for length of service, exceptional performance, sales performance, innovative suggestions, safety, or attendance, as well as celebrating their retirement. The rewards that go along with these recognitions include plaques or certificates, company logo merchandise, gift certificates, jewelry, office accessories, household items, recreational items, and electronics—and even a night or two as a guest of your hotel.[5] These awards are designed to reinforce employee behaviors that support and sustain the company's mission. Awards like these can clearly demonstrate that you desire and appreciate your employees and their work efforts.

A key advantage of these recognitions is that they can create a lasting memorable experience. Not only does the employee have the award itself, but that person has feelings of pride from receiving a plaque, lasting feelings of appreciation or success by having a trophy, or fond memories stirred by photos from a special vacation. Often, the emotional connection of a physical recognition is much stronger than what you'd get from receiving an equivalent amount of money. For example, a trophy that announces an employee's outstanding service may cost only $20, but the emotional impact of receiving a trophy is far greater than that of simply receiving a $20 bill. The trophy presentation can be something that the employee never forgets.

Fairmont Hotels developed a recognition program designed to reinforce their service culture. The program features different award levels, such as "Memory Maker" for an outstanding demonstration of thoughtfulness and creativity, and "Star of the Month" for those who consistently demonstrate superior performance.[6] Employees at all levels are nominated by peers. Thus, the program helps support Fairmont's culture of appreciation and recognition for everyone. Award winners receive gift certificates in small denominations (typically $10 to $50) that can be redeemed with thousands of merchants from around the world. Surveys of Fairmont's employees after the program was implemented revealed that employees felt more recognized for a job well done, felt the best performers were more likely to receive recognition, and felt that they were being recognized in a way that was personally meaningful. Surveys also showed that employees' level of engagement increased significantly since the program's inception.

Making the Job Pleasurable

Sometimes the work itself can be its own reward. Walt Disney said, "You don't work for a dollar—you work to create and have fun."[7] Chili's Norman Brinker said, "If you have fun at what you do, you'll never work a day in your life. Make work like play—and play like hell."[8] Employees who like what they do continue to do it. Not surprisingly, the reverse is also true; dozens of research papers have shown that low employee satisfaction is a strong predictor of employee turnover.[9] The best hotel companies regularly survey their employees to assess their job satisfaction and other attitudes, such as employee relationships with their bosses, their feelings about their pay, and opinions about working conditions.[10] You might consider asking your employees what part of their job holds them back from doing their best, so that you can reconfigure their jobs to focus on the parts that they like best—and therefore perform best. What one employee dislikes, another may find just ideal.

Making the Job Interesting

Obviously, you want to hire people who already want to do the job you hired them to do and are able to perform their job responsibilities. You can make sure of this through an effective recruitment and selection process. But once you have hired qualified people, you want to make sure they remain interested in performing the specifics of their job at the level you need them to. You can make most jobs interesting by using one or more of the following four elements:

1. Give employees the ongoing opportunity to learn and grow, both personally and professionally. People often want to feel a growing sense of professional mastery in their area of interest, but jobs with little to no variation can lead to burnout. Employees may have the ability to perform well, but may have done the same routine task so many times that they simply don't feel like doing the job as well as they can. Job rotation may be effective for some employees in this case, but others want to continue to perform jobs for which they comfortably feel they are qualified. So you might also consider ways to develop new interactions, new tasks, and new challenges.

2. Workers expect to be treated with respect. As employees learn and grow, you may show this by increasing employees' personal responsibility. Increased autonomy can be a sign of organizational respect for their knowledge, skill, and capabilities. In more day-to-day ways, employees need to be treated with integrity (as discussed in Chapter 31). If workers are not treated with respect, the only factor keeping them connected to the company will be their paychecks. If that is the case, once another company provides an equal or better offer, those employees (and all that you invested in them) may walk out your door.

3. Make each job important by making clear its purpose in the organization. If employees think that their job performance really makes a difference in the organization's ability to provide an excellent experience to the customer, then they will feel good about performing their roles well. They will have pride in their job and their organization. Finding ways to show employees that what they do makes a difference to an important operation is a key motivational skill of managers of successful hospitality firms.

4. Arrange to satisfy individuals' social needs as part of the job. Many people want to be part of a good work group, or more generally have relationships with other people where they work. This is particularly

true in the hospitality industry. Well-designed work groups can be helpful in managing employee direction and behavior in the work-place. Indeed, as studies at the Hawthorne Plant of the Western Electric Company showed many years ago, the sense of belonging or not belonging greatly influences what people will or won't do in the workplace.[11] The managerial focus here should be to work in harmony with the group to support each employee's effort to achieve the group goal, which will help achieve your hotel's goal.

Groups may also offer members the opportunity to achieve something greater than themselves by being a part of the group. Membership in organizations with strong corporate cultures and whose purposes are respected by the society as a whole is valuable to both groups and individuals. Asking a group to help accomplish the valued, respected organizational purpose becomes a powerful motivational tool and a primary means for keeping the individual and the group positively involved in your operation.

Motivation and Corporate Social Responsibility

JoAnne Kruse
Founder@www.HC-partners.net

In these challenging economic times, most human resources (HR) organizations are struggling with shrinking budget allocations for services that were historically considered standard, like training, recognition, and incentives. But even in a labor market flush with available talent, the concepts of retention and engagement are of critical importance. At this writing, the unemployment rate hovers around 10 percent in the United States, but how does an employer keep those employees still on-board engaged and motivated to perform without access to the traditional motivators of compensation and career mobility? Adding even more to complicate the equation is the social tone that resists any level of conspicuous consumption. This results in a workplace environment that encourages a low-cost approach to motivation. Together, these dynamics create an ongoing pressure for employers to deliver on true productivity gains while retaining talent when the market does (eventually) pick back up.

Even before the Great Recession, sectors like travel and hospitality were dealing with significant volume declines. Barely able to recover from the impact of 9/11, the travel sector then faced one global crisis after another, including the 2004 tsunami, terrorist bombings in Bali and London, and Severe Acute Respiratory Syndrome (SARS). As the chief HR executive in the travel sector with Travelport Ltd., a travel technology company, I saw the industry enter the millennium dealing with rapid erosion of the top line and a heightened focus on cost containment. At the same time, the employment market was strong, making retention and talent acquisition challenging. Part of our strategy included developing a corporate social responsibility (CSR) strategy to differentiate ourselves with customers and employees. We believed that employee productivity could be improved through higher levels of employee engagement. Applying Corporate Leadership Council research on engagement, we developed a broad array of programs to build employee engagement to drive effort and results. Our CSR initiative was one such program, combining our internal focus on engagement with good business and customer initiatives.

The tragic, deadly Indian Ocean tsunami of 2004 acted as a call to action for Travelport management, and the impetus to develop a broader CSR program that included "voluntourism," charitable giving, and environmentalism. The program had three core goals: engage employees around the world in local volunteer and giving programs; create and deliver against a green strategy for our hundreds of facilities located globally; and align our program investments with our business development and customer interests. The horrific destruction of the tsunami in Thailand provided a critical need, and our initial investment centered on a fund-raising effort to rebuild a destroyed orphanage in the resort area of Phuket. We designed the program with a global logo, Web-based donation site, and ongoing postings of pictures and fund-raising results on the company intranet. The program was successful, raising over $250,000 in a little over three months—with all regions participating, including those where charitable efforts are less culturally common than in the U.S. Employees rallied around the company and the commitment demonstrated to "doing the right thing," providing a bonding moment for local teams and a recommitment to the executive team's leadership. In the midst of significant uncertainty and marketplace challenges, employee satisfaction soared, and feedback from the event continued for years following. The broader CSR program then followed suit, with a commitment to "design globally, apply locally," further reinforcing the company's organizational structure and

(continued)

(continued)

approach to product and service delivery. Further, the opportunity to deliver a positive message to customers proved a much-needed boost for our sales and service teams.

The CSR program became a living example of how the Travelport culture and values were demonstrated—to our employees and customers—around the world. By "walking the talk" we were able to reengage a change-weary employee base and motivate employees and customers around the world by delivering a sense of pride in the company.

THE MOTIVATING CHARACTERISTICS OF THE JOB

Finally, let's look at the interaction of the employee with the job itself. Many people are powerfully motivated intrinsically, or internally. Unattached to specific rewards of any kind, intrinsic motivation is caused by the nature of the person and their environment. One way to take advantage of this is to hire people motivated to perform exceptional service. Another way to foster intrinsic motivation is by structuring the job and work environment to build on employees' personal motivation.

Leadership

It is impossible to overstate the importance of your role as a leader. Leaders must also be able to identify and provide those rewards that the individual employee wants from working in your hotel or restaurant. Effective leadership involves inspiration, challenge, and a strategic vision. Creating a shared purpose among employees can effectively foster motivation.[12] A great leader creates the conditions that promote employee engagement.

Charles A. Conine, SPHR, Cornell 1973

Detroit, Michigan, 1977. The morning sun was reflected in prisms of light off the newly opened, 73-story Detroit Plaza Hotel at the Renaissance Center, the glass centerpiece of and home to what was billed as the Motor City's resurgence. Nearly 2,500 Detroiters had been hired to staff this new Westin hotel. Many, due to Detroit's riots, chronic unemployment, and systemic poverty, had never worked a day in their adult lives before being put on the payroll at the "Ren Cen." My task preopening had been to shepherd 12,000 job applicants, sifting through their midst to identify those whose *attitude* was at least good—not an easy job in a bruised and battered city where "hope" was far from the most common of four-letter words.

Now, with the hotel finally open, as director of personnel, I watched as right away, immovable and opposing forces assembled. On one side were 2,250 union members led by a feisty union business representative. On the other side was Westin's large and as yet unproven management team. "Battles royal" raged for several months, with employees, sometimes at the union's behest, often camping outside my door three deep, hankering to get a crack at convincing me why their boss was guilty of racism and why the employees shouldn't be picked on. Management felt rather picked on, too. I felt engulfed, without a way out.

Finally, in desperation I met with the union business rep, who, to her everlasting credit, suggested we create a shop steward's council, a place for the hotel's departmental union representatives to go and air issues without fear of retribution. We soon found ourselves there, the opposing forces eyeing one another warily before the floodgates opened and out poured dozens of complaints, simmering issues, and stories of mistreatment.

Over the course of three successive steward meetings, however, as issues were heard and, in most cases, quickly addressed, the number and ferocity of complaints gradually subsided. We had turned a corner, discovering what really worked: the knowledge that when management and subordinates care *equally* about respect and working conditions, mutual animus recedes as mutual trust ascends.

Knowing that your concerns will be heard and taken seriously can be a powerful motivator. Indeed, as the nascent truce took hold, its calm spreading as everyone's motivation to work together improved, the "climate" inside the hotel, in that crucible I'll forever recall as simply "the Spring of 1977," became downright balmy.

Empowering Employees

Most hospitality operations function with employee teams, which need to grow and develop just as individuals do. One great asset that a team provides to its members is the opportunity to grow within the group setting. But the

organization must provide additional opportunities for its members to satisfy this important need. The most widely discussed strategy for doing so is
empowerment.

Empowerment is the assignment of appropriate decision-making responsibility to the individual.[13] Empowerment is broader than the traditional
concepts of delegation, decentralization, and participatory management.
Empowerment stretches decision responsibility to include the entire job and
ensures that the performance of that job fits with the organizational mission.
The empowered server can personalize the service experience as it relates to
each guest's expectations and can take whatever steps are necessary to prevent or recover from any service failures.

The danger in empowerment is that some organizations promise employees decision input without giving them any real power or authority.
Employee empowerment must not only ensure that effective decisions are
made by the right employees, but it must provide a mechanism by which
responsibility for job-related decisions is vested in either individuals or
teams.[14] Empowerment also means that management is willing to share relevant information about and control over factors that impinge on effective
job performance. You are not obliged to ratify every employee decision. If
the employees make a decision contrary to your hotel's policies, further discussion is required, but you cannot second-guess every employee decision.

Hyatt Hotels, for example, felt that they should provide better hospitality
to their most loyal customers. So Hyatt began a program that empowered
employees to perform what they called "random acts of generosity." One
member in the loyalty program might suddenly find that his bar tab was paid,
another may receive a complimentary massage, or a member and her family
may discover that the hotel has paid for their breakfast. As you can imagine, there's no way to dictate a set of policies that would tell employees how
to surprise and delight guests. Instead, Hyatt empowered their employees to
see a situation and make the right decision to provide exceptional customer
experiences. The intent of the empowerment is to help fulfill the company's
mission, which they define as making a difference in the lives of the people
they touch—including guests and employees.

PUTTING THE PIECES TOGETHER

Motivation is so complex that no single policy will help you motivate your
employees. While you cannot ignore the reality that financial rewards play a
critical role in motivating hospitality employees, you cannot also ignore the

reality that money isn't everything to everyone. Recognition and feedback can also be effective tools, if you have the leadership and management skills to know when and how to provide these nonfinancial rewards effectively. The work itself can be highly motivating if designed appropriately. Yet a job cannot be designed without considering your hotel's culture, the training employees receive, the types of employees selected, and the way the service product is delivered. Putting all the pieces together in ways that lead every employee to do what they must do for organizational success is the true test of a manager's skill.

For the most part, hospitality employees look for jobs that are fair, fun, interesting, and important. They appreciate leadership by managers who can determine what each person is looking for in the employment relationship and can provide it consistently and fairly. Given what we know about motivation in the hospitality industry, the key to managing and retaining these employees is to create jobs that fulfill your employees' quest for fun, fair, interesting, and important positions; allocate rewards fairly; and provide leadership that takes the time and makes the effort to ensure that employees are appropriately treated, rewarded, respected, and recognized. If you can successfully build these elements into the job situation, employees will be motivated to work hard and follow your leadership. The trick is that everyone's definition of *fair, fun, interesting, important,* and *appropriately managed* is different. Thus, we must conclude by saying that the fundamental key to motivation is to know your employees.

NOTES

1. For example, see www.snopes.com/business/consumer/badhotel.asp.
2. A. H. Maslow, "A Theory of Human Motivation," *Psychological Review* 50(4) (1943): 370–396.
3. G. P. Latham, *Work Motivation: History, Theory, and Practice* (Thousand Oaks, CA: Sage, 2007).
4. C. Albrecht, "Sales Compensation and the Fairness Question," *Workspan* 8(9) (2009): 17–20.
5. World at Work, *A Survey of Members of WorldatWork and the National Association of Employee Recognition (NAER)*, May 2005.
6. M. Smith and D. Irvine, "The Power of Fairmont Hotels and Resorts' Strategic Employee Recognition Program," *Workspan* 52(8) (2009): 28–32.
7. W. Disney, *Famous Quotes* (Anaheim, CA: Walt Disney Theme Parks and Resorts, 1994), 36.
8. N. Brinker and D. T. Phillips, *On the Brink: The Life and Leadership of Norman Brinker* (Arlington, TX: Summit, 1996), 191.

9. N. P. Podsakoff, J. A. LePine, and M. A. LePine, "Differential Challenge Stressor–Hindrance Stressor Relationships with Job Attitudes, Turnover Intentions, Turnover, and Withdrawal Behavior: A Meta-analysis," *Journal of Applied Psychology* 92 (2007): 438–454.

10. J. Barsky, C. Frame, and J. McDougal, "Variety of Strategies Help Improve Employee Satisfaction," *Hotel and Motel Management* 219(21) (2004): 8.

11. E. Mayo, *Hawthorne and the Western Electric Company: The Social Problems of an Industrial Civilisation* (Oxford, UK: Routledge, 1949).

12. J. C. Timmerman, "A Systematic Approach for Making Innovation a Core Competency," *Journal of Quality and Participation* 31(4) (2009): 4–10.

13. Based on R. C. Ford and M. D. Fottler, "Empowerment: A Matter of Degree," *Academy of Management Executive* 9(3) (1995): 21–28.

14. L. C. Plunkett and R. Fournier, *Participative Management: Implementing Empowerment* (New York: Wiley, 1991), 5.

CHAPTER 12

HOW TO BUILD SERVICE QUALITY INTO YOUR OPERATION

ALEX M. SUSSKIND

You've probably heard about or used some kind of quality assurance program in your operation, including total quality management, Six Sigma, lean, quality circle, or Kaizen. These techniques or approaches have been developed to help operators define, create, and execute organizational processes to build and maintain service quality. Regardless of the approach you use, service quality initiatives and processes are widely recognized as critical tools for ensuring guest satisfaction and developing a competitive advantage. Needless to say, creating and delivering a consistent, quality product and service is a key to long-term business success.

Hospitality service-quality initiatives require excellent service processes and consistently effective employees. As a manager, operator, or supervisor, most of your time will be spent working to understand, develop, and modify the behavior of your guests, employees, and owners. A total quality approach to management can help you gain better control over those important people. In this chapter, I present and discuss the foundations of service quality—in particular, what you can do to bring it into your organization.

We start with a general discussion of service quality, look at complaint management, and conclude with a discussion of how to introduce, measure, and monitor your operation's service quality initiatives. Most of my examples are drawn from food-service operations, but the principles are the same in hotels or any other service-based company.

SERVICE QUALITY ASSURANCE

Quality assurance (QA) begins with the definition of what quality means to you and your guests. This definition is specific to your operation—and different from all others.

Quality is typically defined as the conformance to standards to produce and execute a product or service. So quality is achieved based on a set of predetermined standards and desired outcomes, for which you outline standards stating the required levels of performance needed to achieve the desired level of quality. The desired quality varies by operation, of course, but even diverse operations can have similar standards that are realized in different ways.

Smith and Wollensky Steakhouse, Outback Steakhouse, and McDonald's all serve high-quality beef products, but each of these multiunit operators has an explicit definition of what quality means to their operations. As a result, their guests set expectations for the quality level of products and services they receive, based on those explicit definitions. So McDonald's customers expect (and receive) 100 percent beef with no fillers, along with QSCV (quality, service, cleanliness, and value); Smith and Wollensky's guests expect prime beef dry-aged in-house, and Outback will meet a standard of "no rules, just right."

The main premise behind building service quality is to set up reasonable and achievable levels of standards, along with a process to eliminate errors from the service- and product-delivery system.[1] QA processes should be designed to identify areas that need improvement[2] and to maintain current desirable levels of quality. When standards are not met, an error of some sort has occurred in the service or product delivery, meaning that quality was not achieved in that particular instance. As a manager or member of a QA team, your job will be to find and correct the cause of that error.

The principles of service quality and QA apply to any business, be it a hospitality business or a manufacturing business. The only difference is in how the guest uses a product as compared to a service. In both cases, a customer develops a set of expectations and judges the quality of the product or service against those expectations. For a product, its use generally occurs far from the site of its manufacture or sale. Because services are consumed within your operation, your employees and the guest are involved in the service. This is why you need to have quality control and service quality processes in place to continually assess the consistency of your guests' experiences and determine the source of problems when they occur.

One of the early QA planners was W. Edwards Deming, who suggested that you need to take the following four interrelated steps to implement a QA initiative: plan, do, check, and act.[3] In the "plan" stage, you would determine your needs, create standards, and set up the model you will put in place to achieve your goals. In the "do" stage, you will test how the standards worked, and then "check" to ensure that the process you designed is carried out correctly and whether the test yielded the desired results. If your "check" stage yielded the desired results, then you can "act" by instituting the processes into standard operating procedures. This is, however, a continuing process in which you revise the model according to the real-world results. The key behind QA processes is that you need to be able to identify product and service failures (errors) and then develop the fixes for them in such a way that the failures are permanently removed from the system.

TRANSACTION-FOCUSED VERSUS RELATIONSHIP-FOCUSED PROCESS DESIGN

Let's look at two frameworks that demonstrate the importance of having QA processes in place, particularly in service-based settings.[4] The first framework, the transaction-focused approach,[5] presented in Figure 12.1, depicts the process of how a service failure would be detected and remedied. In this model, you have a planned service delivery and you either execute the service delivery properly (which will lead to guest satisfaction) or your planned service delivery results in a service failure (which probably will dissatisfy your guest). To overcome guest dissatisfaction following the service failure, you most likely would offer a remedy to address the failure, with the belief that once the error is remedied, the guest or end user of the product or service will be satisfied.

Figure 12.1
Transaction-Focused Service Recovery

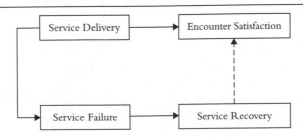

Source: Reproduced by permission from Emerald Group Publishing Limited. Stephen W. Brown, Deborah L. Cowles, and Tracy L. Tuten, "Service Recovery: Its Value and Limitations as a Retail Strategy," *International Journal of Service Industry Management* 7(5) (1996): 32–46.

A classic restaurant service error occurs when a guest orders a steak medium rare and it is overcooked. The guest will probably complain, which would be a common way to uncover this error. (Although no one likes guest complaints, if the guest says nothing and chokes down the overcooked steak, the restaurant will never know why that guest left, never to return.) Once the complaint is lodged, the service provider will need to offer a service recovery, usually by bringing the guest a properly cooked steak, but sometimes with an alternative dish to replace the incorrectly prepared steak or some other form of compensation to redress the problem. The key point here is that in the transaction-focused model, the service failure was corrected, but no other actions are taken to determine what led to the service failure or to prevent a similar problem from reoccurring. The result is a strictly short-term, episodic approach.

Relationship Model Now let's look at what would happen when an overcooked steak is served (or some other service error occurs) in the relationship-focused model (presented in Figure 12.2).[6] As you see, this model addresses both the short-term issue of service recovery and long-term elements of service process

Figure 12.2
Relationship-Focused Service Recovery

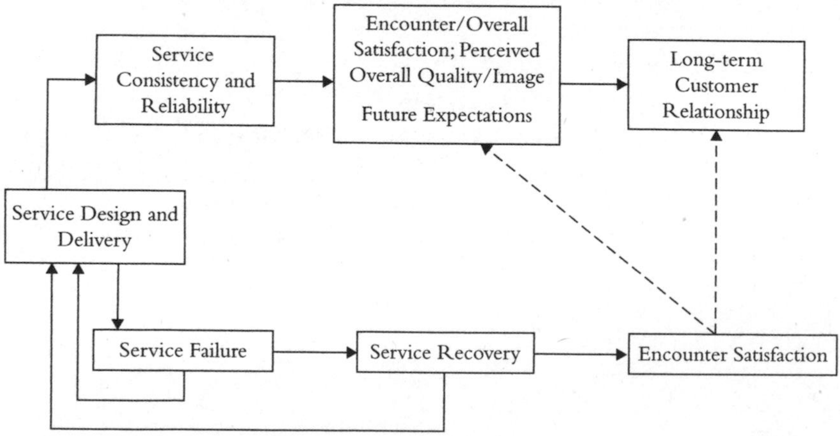

Source: Reproduced by permission from Emerald Group Publishing Limited. Stephen W. Brown, Deborah L. Cowles, and Tracy L. Tuten, "Service Recovery: Its Value and Limitations as a Retail Strategy," *International Journal of Service Industry Management* 7(5) (1996):32–46.

management. In the model, the upper portion begins with service design and delivery, which leads to service consistency and reliability, which will then influence overall guest satisfaction and future expectations, and help build long-term relationships with your guests. The idea here is that delivering a consistent product or service will allow guests to accurately set their expectations and form a relationship with your firm. The second part of the model shows the two parts of the process when a service failure occurs. The first part addresses the immediate need to correct the service failure (like the transactional model), and the second part collects information regarding the service recovery, and feeds that information back into service design and delivery to make improvements to the process (unlike the transactional model). So, when the steak arrives overcooked, the service provider should attempt to correct the problem by determining what remedy will redress the problem to ensure that the guest is satisfied with the corrective action taken. Then, you would need to understand what led to the service failure and what impact the chosen remedy had on the guest and her experience in the restaurant. Figuring out exactly what happened is crucial for solving the problem and preventing it from recurring.

If you're familiar with restaurant operations, you can see many points at which the error could have occurred. The server may have accidentally entered medium well in the point-of-sale (POS) system; the steak could have sat under a heat lamp too long; the cook might have overestimated the cooking time because the cut of meat was thinner than usual; the broiler could have malfunctioned; the cook might simply have overcooked the steak, due to lack of skill or attention; the steak may have been served to the wrong guest; or the guest's idea of medium rare could have been different from the chef's view. To address this service error, the QA team needs to check the process at each point, understand what happened, and use this information to craft a long-term solution. We all know that improperly prepared food and other service failures are inevitable. What separates the strong from the weak is how we learn from our mistakes to prevent them from reoccurring. A QA approach to management is one way to achieve that end.

The Case of the Overcooked Steak

I didn't choose the example of incorrectly cooked steak at random. This was a real problem that occurred in our restaurant, Taverna Banfi, which is operated by the Cornell School of Hotel Administration and open to the public. We noticed that we were getting a large number of steaks returned over a period of about a month. But the complaints were not consistent. Some steaks were being returned as overcooked, others undercooked. A standard

Taverna Banfi operating procedure requires managers to record any guest complaints in a management log. We want to make sure that we have the information regarding the complaint, how it was handled, and the outcome. Our management team reviews this log daily. After seeing the problems with the steaks, we examined the issues presented earlier as we reviewed every step of the process. Through our examination, we found no problems with the equipment, ticket times, servers' POS entries, product consistency, or how the guests interpreted steak doneness. However, we did find two interesting things through our examination: (1) The steaks were being returned during the peak times of the evening meal period, and (2) this occurred when one particular grill cook was working. As it turns out, this grill cook had recently been promoted to his position. We concluded that he needed additional training to be able to handle the grill station during crush time.

I have to emphasize that the purpose of our analysis was not to assign blame or to punish worker errors. Our goal was to improve the process, and we could conclude that we needed to take another look at our training procedures. We were able to quickly resolve the problem because we focused on identifying a solution rather than assigning blame.

Another Case of "Wrong" Steaks Let's look at how Outback Steakhouse dealt with a similar problem and removed an unexpected error from their service delivery system. Because Outback Steakhouse introduced steaks to a much wider audience, they created and produced high-quality steaks that appealed to an audience that was relatively new to steaks. Even though they designed their restaurants, service processes, and staff training to produce these high-quality steaks in a casual environment, they found that their guests had varying perceptions of how steak temperatures worked. As a result, a fair number of guests were unhappy with how their steaks were cooked. To remedy this service failure, Outback assessed the situation and learned that their guests' definitions of steak doneness were different from theirs (as well as being inconsistent). After recognizing the problem, Outback did two things: (1) They printed menu descriptions of what steaks cooked at various temperatures would look like, and (2) they had each server tell the guest what they should expect (inside and out) from a steak ordered to a particular temperature or level of doneness. For example, if you ordered your steak rare, the server would explain that the steak would be served seared on the outside but red and cool in the center. If you ordered your steak well done, the server would explain that the steak would be cooked clear through. By taking these actions, Outback reduced their error rate. Notice also that Outback did not fall into the "expertise trap" of thinking that they were right and the guests were wrong. Instead, they treated guest dissatisfaction as a service failure and sought to resolve it.

With these two examples of what appears to be the same service failure, you see how the application of QA programs and a focus on service excellence will lead you to a competitive advantage. While the specific service failures at Cornell's Taverna Banfi and Outback Steakhouse were based on the same apparent service failure, the reason behind each restaurant's service failure was completely different. Both organizations were able to resolve their problems by taking a service quality approach to management.

Despite the time and expense of implementing and maintaining service quality initiatives, I believe that you'll find that the benefits from QA programs will almost always outweigh their costs. You can check on the value of your QA system by having a sound measurement system in place to collect information on your performance. One mechanism to gauge performance is guest feedback, in the form of both complaints and compliments. Compliments are more fun than complaints, but from a QA perspective, you need both so that you can record elements of your performance from multiple sources. Because complaints are one of the real challenges of hotel and restaurant operation, let's look at complaint management and how to improve performance based on complaints received.

COMPLAINT MANAGEMENT

Before we discuss complaint management, let's set the parameters for how to conceptualize and process service failures and complaints. We have all heard the expression "the customer is always right." The problem with that statement as a way of managing complaints is that you, as an operator, are assigning blame in the process of complaint resolution and management. We have already seen that assigning blame is counterproductive when you are trying to improve your operation. As noted above, when a service failure occurs, you should spend every ounce of energy trying to understand what happened, fixing the problem, and preventing it from reoccurring. Instead, each service failure becomes your responsibility to correct, devoid of blame. Correcting the problem may require you to change your expectations, your guests to change their expectations, or a correction of behavior in how service processes are executed in your operation.

We can define a complaint as a social confrontation that has been initiated to adjust perceptions and outcomes, either in the short term or more preferably in the long term.[7] When a service failure occurs that goes unnoticed by the operator, guests are faced with the choice of communicating a complaint to influence the service delivery process or terminating the service exchange without having their service expectations met in a satisfactory manner.[8] With service-based complaints, the dissatisfying elements of the service experience lead to a number of possible initiating acts on the part of the consumer that begin and frame the social confrontation or the complaint.[9] When operators are trained to identify guests' initiating acts, they can often resolve problems for guests more quickly and more efficiently.

Let's look at five categories of initiating acts, noting that complaint initiation likely occurs through a sequence of negotiated interdependent actions, rather than strictly one initiating act.[10] You've probably noticed these in some of your guests.

1. *Hinting.* In this case, the guest is making a subtle comment or gesture to get the service provider to notice that something is missing from the service experience. It could be as simple as placing the water glass at the edge of the table, or making a scribbling gesture to get the check. At this point, the guest is making the service provider aware of their needs and is awaiting a response or action to take place.
2. *Seeking confirmation.* In this instance, the guest uses a more direct social confrontation to confirm a request that was already initiated. Building on the preceding "hinting" examples, a guest may ask the service provider, "Didn't I ask for the check already?" or "Didn't I ask for a refill of my water?" Frustration is building for the guest, and the remedy should be delivered to further avoid additional conflict.
3. *Blaming or accusing.* At this point, if the guest still perceives a problem, the guest will move to a more confrontational approach. Using the same examples above, the guest might say "I asked you for the check 10 minutes ago. I need to leave," or "I asked you to refill my water 10 minutes ago." In this case, the guest is displeased and the resolution needs to be swift to restore a sense of balance and satisfaction for the guest in the service experience.
4. *Emotional display.* This is more intense than blaming or accusing, and I doubt that an empty water glass would cause an emotional display. However, guests might become emotional if the server fails to close out a check, especially if the guest really wants or needs to leave. Emotional displays may include tears or crying, visible anger, or coldness and sarcasm. At this point, the service failure has clearly gotten the guest upset and a stronger intervention would be required to correct the problem.
5. *Emotional statement.* The most intense reaction is a communication filled with anger or disappointment. Unfortunately, we have all seen this type of behavior at airports, when frustrated passengers pound on the podium,

or you may have had a guest threaten to report you to the Better Business Bureau. Guests in this stage require more care and handling and can also damage the service experience for other guests who witness the outburst.

Even small service errors, such as water refills, cause guest dissatisfaction and may lead to a loss of patronage ("They couldn't even remember to fill my water glass"). To mitigate problems and ensure that guests' complaints are handled appropriately and before they escalate, guest service personnel should be trained to identify escalating failures and features that lead to social confrontations. I also want to point out the effect of a sincere and quick service recovery. I've conducted other research that shows that most guests respond well when you move quickly to take an appropriate recovery action.[11] This is the key in the short term to help you build long term solutions!

Heading Off Failure

Standard operating procedures should include training for guest contact employees to help to recognize potential problems and conflicts before the situation gets to the point of the initiating acts. You cannot hold an employee accountable for an outcome if the employee was not properly prepared to do the job, if the employee is not supported by an effective system, or if the employee is improperly supervised.

When a failure occurs, service personnel should be trained to identify potential problems or concerns, and they should know when they are not properly executing service processes. Going back to the new grill cook at Taverna Banfi, he originally did not know how to perform properly during peak business times, but with additional training and support, as well as attention to detail and service processes, the problem was resolved quickly and appropriately to prevent future problems.

You should encourage your guests to complain when they are not happy. Complaints are direct performance feedback that in most cases will be fully actionable. Your guests should be trained to give you feedback, and you should reward them for doing so by showing them how their comments helped you (or will help you) get better. Take all complaints seriously unless you have information that causes you to act otherwise. Few of the complaints you receive will be disingenuous, and do not forget that a complaint is a social confrontation initiated by one of your guests to correct a problem or error that took place in service delivery!

With the presence of social media and blogs, you'll have to work all the harder to be observant and prevent errors from occurring. You will also have to encourage your guests to tell you their problems, instead of simply posting their complaint. Even so, a guest can have a negative experience in your restaurant, go through the initiating acts described earlier, and still share their experience with others. So prevention is your best strategy. Let's look at how to measure your systems using guest feedback to track and improve service quality.

GUEST MEASUREMENT SYSTEMS

There are four main methods to gather feedback from guests:

1. Direct or indirect communication with management and staff
2. Customer relations call centers
3. Guest satisfaction surveys or other forms of comment cards (including Web, e-mail)
4. Mystery shopping programs

Each of these methods is equally valuable and offers operators direct performance feedback from their guests. In fact, a savvy operator should use as many of these approaches as possible.

Direct or Indirect Communication with Management and Staff

Through the normal course of business, guests, employees, and managers will interact and exchange a lot of information. Guests may pass on their assessment of their service experience in part or in whole (good or bad), or staff or management may prompt them to share their thoughts. It is important to look at both what is said and what is not said. Any comments received from guests should be reported and recorded, if applicable, and acted upon when needed. Be specific in your communication. If you ask generic questions ("How is everything?"), you'll probably get standard responses ("Fine, okay") even if that's not what the guest is really thinking. So make sure your interactions are based on clear, direct goals, and, in addition to appropriate pleasantries, target communication to gather useful information and enhance the guest experience.

Let's go back to the overcooked steak. An observant manager or server looking at the steak should have been able to see that it was not cooked properly. So, instead of a generic question, a server (or a manager) doing a table check should say something like: "Pardon me, but I noticed your steak is not cooked medium rare as you ordered it." That will offer the guest a chance to have the problem corrected without having to engage in a social confrontation (i.e., a complaint). If your staff and management are performing their duties, they are responsible for being in tune with what the guest is experiencing (or not experiencing) and making adjustments as needed. Whether it is a restaurant meal, an airline flight, a hotel stay, or any other hospitality-based experience, management and staff should know what is correct based on the espoused standards of the operation, and they should be able to manage guest experiences to deliver on those standards. The power of observation and the ability to use guest feedback and reactions in service experiences is one easy way to maintain and improve service quality.

Customer Relations Call Centers

Large organizations usually have a call center set up to receive guest feedback and provide guests with needed information. When readily available, call centers can take complaints or compliments, offer directions, take reservations, answer questions, or give information about promotions or organizational features. Call centers allow you to centralize some functions, while providing your guests with an easily accessible platform to communicate with the operation.

Like any communication that transpires among staff, management, and guests, you need to log and review the information to see if any trends are emerging. While a single comment or question is important, being able to track the trends that emerge from guest communication is equally important. Data collected through call centers can add rich layers of information that allow you to improve processes and build service quality.

Guest Satisfaction Surveys

Guest satisfaction surveys (GSSs) allow you to collect specific information from guests, along with open-ended responses when applicable. This type of feedback is useful because it taps into your guests' perceptions of the experience they had in your operation, and it also provides sociodemographic data to help with future decision making. If you do run a GSS system, plan to ask no more than about 30 questions, to avoid respondent fatigue and low response rates. This constraint means that you need to be focused in what questions you ask and how you ask them. While these data can give you an episode-by-episode description of what transpired in your operation, the GSS system's chief purpose is to provide large amounts of data to help extract trends. You also need to keep in mind that because a GSS asks for feedback from your guests, it may require you to make a direct, personal response to a guest's comment. As with all guest interactions, it is important to ensure that all GSS data are closely tracked and monitored for such responses.

Although you can track trends with guest satisfaction surveys, you can also use GSSs to gather data on specific problem areas or processes, using Deming's "plan, do, check, act" framework.[12] For example, a large casual dining chain restaurant used a GSS to measure service quality (measured as servers' attentiveness, knowledge, friendliness, and timeliness), food quality (measured as correct temperature, taste, and value), cleanliness, repeat patronage intentions, and overall satisfaction. The chain's managers noticed that the scores from their carryout guests were significantly and consistently lower than the scores for their dine-in guests. This bit of information prompted the company to institute a separate GSS for their carryout guests. Rather than create a lengthy survey, the organization used a "Six Sigma" approach to measure carryout performance. Six Sigma is an approach to QA that helps operators identify and eliminate errors (defects) in production and service, by effectively reducing the variance in delivery from product to product or, better yet, from guest experience to guest experience. Six Sigma is heavily data driven and focuses on solving problems by creating and building solutions into the culture of the organization, where the goal would be to have zero defects or a standard deviation of zero.[13]

Through the process analysis that was used to develop the survey, the company looked at what makes a carryout experience positive for their guests. The following five questions emerged to capture the essence of a carryout experience for their guests:

1. Were there any items missing from your order?
2. Was the food prepared as ordered?
3. Did the carryout packaging keep the food at the right temperature?
4. Was your food ready when you expected?
5. Compared to other similarly priced restaurants in the same vicinity that offer carryout, would you say your overall experience with the brand was much worse (1), worse (2), about the same (3), better (4), or much better (5).

This new GSS survey accomplished the following three things. First, it checked on whether each restaurant was properly executing carryout processes. Second, it got every manager thinking about their guests' carryout experience and what makes or breaks the experience for them. Finally, it allowed the chain to gauge how its guests felt about their carryout experience compared to their direct competition. The results of the survey over the first quarter helped identify units that were performing well and units that needed improvement.

Mystery Shopping Programs

A mystery shopping program puts a trained observer into the position of a guest who then assesses your operation. As with a GSS program, you need to have clear objectives and be able to identify important elements of the service process that you would like evaluated. Unlike a GSS program, you can ask mystery shoppers to provide a detailed assessment of their experience. You will receive fewer observations tied to a specific service experience, but you can ask for greater detail about each service experience.

Here are four main considerations for setting up a mystery shopper program.

1. *Program timing.* As an operator, you need to determine how many shops per unit will be useful. For some operators, one mystery shopper visit per week is sufficient, while other operations may require more, and others less. The schedule and frequency of the shoppers' visits should be closely tied to operational objectives and outcomes, for example, during slow periods, if that is appropriate, or busy periods, or both. You would also have to determine whether the time of day or day of the week makes a difference. Whatever you determine, you need to closely monitor the shopping schedule to ensure that each mystery shop adds value for all concerned.

2. *Mystery shopper training.* With mystery shoppers you can gather detailed data, but you need to make sure that the people who are mystery shoppers know what they are looking for, and you also need to have a sound organizational structure in place to manage the process. That means that you are selecting the right shoppers and that you have a sound system to record and report shoppers' experiences in a timely manner.

3. *Program design.* As part of making sure that the mystery shoppers give you useful data, you determine what will be measured and why. Your program also should be collected consistently and periodically, to give you an analysis over time. The script that is used for data collection from the shoppers should be inclusive and yield data that can be used for continuous improvement.

4. *Program implementation.* You also have to be clear on how the system works, what it measures, and how you want to use the data. Line-level employees, supervisors, property-level managers, and regional and corporate managers all need to be on the same page to ensure the process is well executed and the data are properly used.

A solid mystery shopping program should yield data that your organization can use directly to assess performance and that offer clear avenues for performance enhancement. Additionally, it should also provide a mechanism to reward employees and managers for their accomplishments. Finally, a well-implemented shopper program provides oversight to managers in a controlled manner and can act as a proxy for a good supervisor, since the output provides management with tools for coaching and developing staff members to achieve QA goals.

Each type of feedback discussed here is an essential part of any QA process. Having multiple mechanisms to collect data will allow you to build continuous improvement into your operation. To get the most benefit from all these efforts, make sure to pass the information to appropriate people at the regional, unit, and line levels. Discussions of specific findings and outcomes can lead to process and output improvements. As a final point, any guest or operational feedback you receive needs to be connected to relevant unit-level and company data (including POS, performance management system [PMS], customer relationship management [CRM], supply chain, and human resources [HR]) to ensure that feedback is used to improve performance.

TOWARD CONSISTENTLY EXCELLENT SERVICE

Understanding how your operation works from the ground up is the best way to ensure that you can consistently deliver quality service to your guests. Your guests will recognize it, be loyal to you for it, and will help you create and maintain a great service-based organization.

Let's review the considerations you should keep in mind for a sound QA program. QA takes time and money to use properly. It won't be useful if you fail to use the data consistently and make sure that the indicated changes are made permanently. Train your staff on how the process works, and make sure they are committed to the process. You need to demonstrate how the process improvements will be good for everyone, and monitor and track performance. You can do this by connecting outcomes of programs to performance for managers and use performance metrics for staff members involved for raises and promotions.

You also need to be consistent and timely with results of the evaluations, process improvements, and outcomes. If too much time elapses between program design, execution, and evaluation, much valuable momentum will be lost.

Finally, after you implement any changes resulting from a QA program, be sure to evaluate the costs and benefits every few months (at a minimum) to ensure that errors remain low and that product and service quality, sales and revenue, and other important metrics remain at the required levels.

NOTES

1. S. S. J. Hall, "The Emergence of Ethics in Quality," in *Ethics in Hospitality Management,* ed. S. S. J. Hall (East Lansing, MI: Educational Institute of the American Hotel and Motel Association, 1992), 9–22.

2. A. J. Lockwood, "Managing Quality in Food and Beverage Operations," in *Food and Beverage Management: A Selection of Readings,* eds. B. Davis and A. Lockwood (Oxford, UK: Butterworth Heinemann, 1994), 172–186.

3. W. E. Deming, *Quality, Productivity, and Competitive Position* (Cambridge, MA: MIT Center for Advanced Engineering Study, 1982).

4. Lockwood, 1994.

5. S. W. Brown, D. L. Cowles, and T. L. Tuten, "Service Recovery: its value and limitations as a retail strategy," *International Journal of Service Industry Management* 7 (1996): 32-46.

6. Ibid.

7. G. Makoul and M. E. Roloff, "The Role of Efficacy and Outcome Expectations in the Decision to Withhold Relational Complaints," *Communication Research* 25 (1998): 5–29; S. E. Newell and R. K. Stutman, "The Social Confrontation Episode," *Communication Monographs* 55 (1988): 266–285; and S. E. Newell and R. K. Stutman, "Negotiating Confrontation: The Problematic Nature of Initiation and Response," *Research on Language and Social Interaction* 23 (1989/1990): 139–162.

8. A. M. Susskind, "Efficacy and Outcome Expectations Related to Customer Complaints about Service Experiences," *Communication Research* 27(3) (2000): 353–378.

9. Newell and Stutman, 1988; Newell and Stutman, 1989/1990.

10. Ibid.; Susskind, 2000.

11. A. M. Susskind, "Guest Service Management and Processes in Restaurants: What Have We Learned in 50 Years?" *Cornell Hospitality Quarterly* 51 (4) (November 2010); and A. M. Susskind and A. E. Viccari, "A Look at the Relationship Between Service Failures, Guest Satisfaction, and Repatronage Intentions of Casual Dining Guests," *Cornell Hospitality Quarterly*, in press.

12. Deming, 1982.

13. M. L. George, *Lean Six Sigma for Service* (McGraw-Hill: New York, 2003).

CHAPTER 13

DEMAND MANAGEMENT

BILL CARROLL

CONGRATULATIONS! YOU NOW ARE A DEMAND MANAGER

More than ever before, you and your operation need expertise in demand management, which involves strategies and tactics to encourage your guests to book your hotel or restaurant by dynamically managing demand to optimize revenue while securing customer relationships for the long term. What that means is that you and your managers must constantly oversee and adjust your operation's use of distribution channels to reach target customer segments; build on and enhance existing customer relationships; and take effective revenue management actions to achieve an objective balance of near-term profitability and long-term viability.

This chapter explains the rapid evolution of demand management in the hospitality industry. I review the many changes in distribution—most of them driven by the rise of the Internet—that have placed the burden of demand management squarely on your shoulders as a chain staff member, regional chain manager, or manager of a local property. At the moment, demand management in most hotels and restaurants is being handled by different positions in different organizations. If you are handling demand management, your title may be marketing manager, revenue manager, or sales manager (or you may have all of those responsibilities with a different title). If more than one person in your operation has demand management responsibility, they may not report to the same boss or even coordinate activities with the same staff group. With the background and strategies presented in this chapter, your firm should move toward a program of integrated demand management, using all distribution and media channels. With an integrated demand management program, you and your managers will make integrated decisions about pricing, promotion, distribution channel management, and customer relationship management (CRM).

At the individual establishment level understanding and applying the principles and organizational considerations of demand management as a hospitality manager or owner can make a difference between profit or loss, a positive or negative return on investment (ROI), and even survival or bankruptcy.

WHY IS HOSPITALITY DEMAND UNIQUE?

Each semester, I tell my freshman economics class at Cornell's School of Hotel Administration that there is no such thing as demand for a hotel stay or a restaurant meal. That's a shock to hear from an economics instructor when parents pay $45,000 a year for their son or daughter to learn how to manage hotel stays and restaurant meals! I am making a deliberate exaggeration to focus on the need by hospitality suppliers to create and then fulfill travelers' demand for a travel experience. To do this, hotels participate either directly or indirectly by combining services, including those of common carriers, destination service suppliers like car rental firms, restaurants, and attractions. The expected value of the experience—and thus the demand—relating to those services is a function of the services themselves and how they are combined for the consumer.

Demand Is for a Travel Experience

The fact that travel involves an experience infinitely complicates your ability to control the way customers experience your firm, particularly how your firm's services fit in with the full travel experience. The amount that a customer is willing to pay for your service might depend on whether you have integrated your operation with other parts of the experience, or it may rest primarily on the value you add. For example, a leisure consumer may be willing to pay a given amount for the segments of a resort trip that involves an economy-class flight with two stops and a stay at a two-star hotel with no airport pickup and no on-site meals. That same consumer will likely be willing to pay much more for a nonstop flight to the same destination with an immediate airport pickup and return plus inclusive on-site meals at a five-star property where activities are coordinated with those of others in the customer's travel party. The difference between these two experiences supports the business of travel agents, tour operators, and online travel agencies (OTAs).

Gauging Market Response

Your most effective tool for developing an integrated approach to demand management is measuring customers' responses to pricing, promotion, and marketing. This task has become increasingly difficult and complex with customers' use of the Internet, social media, and interactive mobile devices.

Let's look first at consumers' hospitality industry purchase behavior. Room sales and restaurant meals are a barometer of consumer sentiment, since they rise and drop in tandem with economic factors such as household income or net worth and corporate profitability. The importance of these factors was dramatically demonstrated in the 2008–2009 "Great Recession." Falling household net worth, rising unemployment levels, and evaporating company profits drove hotel occupancies and average daily rates (ADRs) to historic lows.[1] As the recession gradually abated, consumers expected the same services for the low prices established during the depths of the recession.[2]

How does this fit into a demand management strategy? By cutting rates during the recession, hoteliers and restaurateurs taught consumers that it was possible to obtain hospitality services at much lower prices. For the moment, let's disregard who started the price wars, since everyone says the "other guy" started it.[3] Even after economic recovery, underlying economic forces dampened hospitality demand, starting with a stubborn, high unemployment rate in many places. Also suppressing demand were increases in fuel costs that raised travel costs, reductions in airline lift through mergers, and tacit cooperation and route rationalizations that raised airfares.

If your situation is like that of most hotels and restaurants, you compete aggressively with other operations that you view as your competitive set. These operations produce services of similar quality to yours and perhaps charge similar prices. As a general rule, you probably compare your rates and occupancies or covers with those of your competitive set. However, the consumers' responses to pricing in a competitive set is more complicated than one might expect.

Typically, one expects that when a hotel or restaurant cuts its prices, that operation will gain additional business from customers who are price responsive or price elastic. A study by PricewaterhouseCoopers (PwC) actually measured price elasticity in hotel competitive sets. PwC found that for a given percentage change in price by a single hotel in a competitive set, the occupancy change was a greater percentage. So, for example, an increase in price by 10 percent yielded more than an 11 percent drop in occupancy, provided the other hotels in the competitive set failed to match the price increase.[4] Assuming no variable or marginal cost effects, that suggests that a hotel unilaterally raising its (public) prices will likely experience revenue declines. This is shown in Figure 13.1, Panel A. However, that is only the case if just one hotel acts. By contrast, if all firms in a competitive set match a price increase, revenues will increase for all hotels in a competitive set. This result was also supported by PwC research. To take the example of a 10 percent increase in price by all hotels in the competitive set, room demand might fall by only 3 percent. In this case, revenues for all hotels will increase. This is shown in Figure 13.1, Panel B.

Let's look at hotel price discounting during the 2008–2009 recession. In response to falling occupancies, individual hotels lowered rates (and thus their ADRs) hoping to stabilize occupancy and preserve revenue per available room (RevPARs). Based on PwC's findings, not surprisingly, discounting by one hotel in a competitive set, and likely by more than one, had the effect of forcing others to match in order to preserve their own occupancy levels. Otherwise,

Figure 13.1
Price Response and Revenue

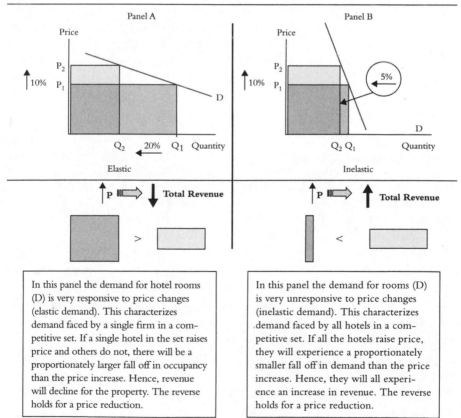

In this panel the demand for hotel rooms (D) is very responsive to price changes (elastic demand). This characterizes demand faced by a single firm in a competitive set. If a single hotel in the set raises price and others do not, there will be a proportionately larger fall off in occupancy than the price increase. Hence, revenue will decline for the property. The reverse holds for a price reduction.

In this panel the demand for rooms (D) is very unresponsive to price changes (inelastic demand). This characterizes demand faced by all hotels in a competitive set. If all the hotels raise price, they will experience a proportionately smaller fall off in demand than the price increase. Hence, they will all experience an increase in revenue. The reverse holds for a price reduction.

the hotel that cut prices would enjoy occupancy gains, albeit at the lower rates. Such price cutting cost hotels revenue and profit. In 2009, U.S. hotel occupancy fell 9 percent, while ADR fell by 10 percent, causing a substantial drop of 19 percent in RevPAR. Using PwC data, if hotels had held their ADRs steady, their RevPAR would have fallen by 9.5 percent.[5] Unfortunately, few hotels could withstand the onslaught of the Great Recession to hold rate, but this situation demonstrates two issues. First, if hoteliers had held their rates in the face of falling occupancy levels, they would have lost revenue from decreased occupancy, but not from lowered rates. By also lowering prices, they lost revenue from undercutting their own rates (effectively, negotiating against themselves) for room-night that they might well have achieved regardless of rate reduction and RevPAR loss not offset by discount-induced additional business.

The point here is that when you change rates unilaterally, consumer room demand response is likely disproportionate to the rate change. Since consumers view a hotel or restaurant as more or less substitutable within a competitive set, you will probably see a higher volume loss (or gain) for a given percentage price change. Yet—and this is the key point—a price change by all members of a competitive set produces proportionately less volume change than the amount of the collective relative price change. As you can see, Figure 13.2 graphically illustrates this "damned if you do and damned if you don't" result. We have been talking here about hotels or restaurants that consumers view as essentially similar. Let's look at how differentiation can help break this competitive-set trap.

Market Segmentation and Pricing

The seemingly iron law of price response within competitive sets illustrated in Figure 13.2 is mitigated when you can differentiate your property's or your restaurant's services from others in your competitive set. (See Chapter 15 for a discussion of differentiation strategies.) You can also become selective in the customer segments served and find ways to communicate value effectively within distribution channels for your services. You can do this through effective marketing, revenue management, and by pricing according to customer segment and distribution channel (as described in the next chapter). Your hotel or restaurant has at least some power to charge price premiums when certain of your customer segments value your services or see them as differentiated from those of your competitors. This is nothing new to the hospitality industry. To take the most obvious example, this is why luxury lodging properties can charge higher prices than economy properties, and upscale restaurants charge higher menu prices than quick-service restaurants.

Figure 13.2
Price Response in Competitive Sets

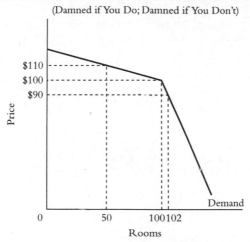

(Damned if You Do; Damned if You Don't)

Situation 1: Price is $100 and occupancy is 100. Revenue is $10,000 per day.

Situation 2: Price is increased by $10 and other firms in the set do not match
in order to steal market share. Revenue is $5,500 per day.

Situation 3: Price is reduced by $10 and other firms in the set match to protect
market share. Revenue is $9,180.

The idea that there is value in service differentiation is nothing new. The challenge you face is assigning a price premium for that differentiation. Firms like Revenue Analytics, SAS, RMS, and JDA have developed a business around the concept of determining price premiums associated with service offerings relative to competitors. Your own revenue management analysis may also help you make this determination.

Customer segmentation adds another layer of complexity and opportunity in attempting to apply this concept. If your hotel property is designed, marketed, and priced to serve business customers, for instance, two issues arise. First, you work to focus on the advantages your property offers its target market. More recently, however, you may also have to examine ways that your property might appeal to different market segments. The idea, of course, is to charge premium prices to target market segments. A classic example of being able to command higher prices is the on-property hotels at Disney World, which offer a distinctive value proposition, as compared to other properties in Kissimmee and Orlando—near immediate park access.

Before we review managing demand in your competitive set and look at the changes in distribution, let's quickly review a key tool in revenue management—rate fences. These should allow your hotel to charge different prices for equivalent services to different customer groups based on their response to price. This concept was illustrated in a 2002 *Cornell Quarterly* article by Richard Hanks, Robert Cross, and Paul Noland.[6] Taking a leaf from the airline industry playbook, they demonstrated that setting prices differently for certain types of customers could dramatically increase both occupancy

Figure 13.3
Effect of Market Segmentation on Revenue

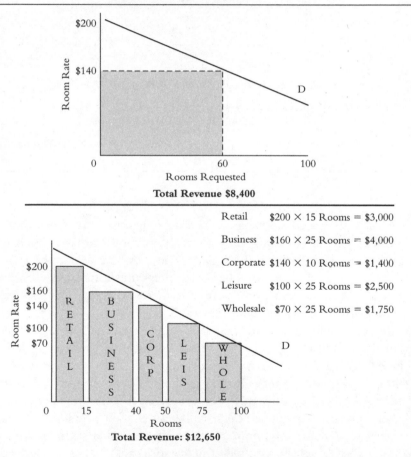

Total Revenue $8,400

Retail	$200 × 15 Rooms = $3,000
Business	$160 × 25 Rooms = $4,000
Corporate	$140 × 10 Rooms = $1,400
Leisure	$100 × 25 Rooms = $2,500
Wholesale	$70 × 25 Rooms = $1,750

Total Revenue: $12,650

Adapted by permission from Richard D. Hanks, Robert G. Cross, and R. Paul Noland, "Discounting in the Hotel Industry: A New Approach," *Cornell Hotel and Restaurant Administration Quarterly*, August 2002, 94–103.

and revenue (see Figure 13.3). Rate fences can be simple (e.g., advance reservation, Saturday night stayover, cancellation penalties) or sophisticated, such as credentialed rate access (e.g., corporate ID, association membership card, loyal club membership). Specific rate fences are discussed in the next chapter. Most hotels place fences on their low rates to preserve higher rates for less price-responsive customers.

MANAGING DEMAND IN YOUR COMPETITIVE SET

Setting your strategic position goes hand in hand with differentiating your property and developing appropriate rate fences. Your hotel may offer the most rooms and the largest event space—giving you a particular strategic position in the market. Likewise, if yours is the only restaurant with a nationally recognized chef, you have a strong strategic position in your competitive set. Your positioning depends on your differentiation—or lack thereof. If your hotel has the advantage of high-quality or excellent facilities, your strategy might well involve premium pricing—and you'll set rates and service levels higher than others in your competitive set. However, if your property is not differentiable, the best strategy may be one of market penetration through price discounting and promotional advertising, where you promote an aggressive price that is set equal to or less than your competitors. More on these strategic issues is presented in Chapter 15.

Regardless of your positioning strategy, you must continually monitor your own and your competitors' pricing and promotional activities. Then, based on your strategic position, you may need to take action as necessary to respond. This should be for each target market segment through distribution channels. While you can certainly do this informally, in many cases it's better to use sophisticated alert and detection monitoring systems that track price positioning, promotional activities, and customer awareness against that of others in your competitive set. Such systems for hotels are offered by firms like TravelCLICK and Rubicon.

Determining your competitive response is complicated by the state of the local economy, seasonality, and marketing activities. In addition, it is based on your long-run strategic objectives versus your short-run goals, not to mention those of your competitors. Again, you can rely on practical experience or use formal modeling and analysis systems. Examples of systems that handle this analysis for hotels include IDeaS, Revenue Analytics, JDA, and PROS. RMS and Avero offer systems for restaurants.

Historical Highlights of Hospitality Distribution

Kathy Misunas
Principal Essential Ideas

Hospitality distribution history is best broken down into preautomation versus postautomation periods. That demarcation point provides valuable insight as to how distribution has changed over time.

Preautomation distribution occurred before the early 1960s when the first electronic hotel reservation systems were being developed. These represented varying degrees of homegrown simple systems deployed mostly at the hotel property level. They were designed to manage the inventory of rooms available versus those sold to particular customer segments at particular rates: group versus transient and contract (business) versus leisure (noncontract). During the 1970s, more sophisticated reservation systems were created by major chains. These were designed to obtain a centralized business view of overall sales and inventory at all of the chain's properties. These capabilities eventually led to enhanced room rate controls and functionality that offered different rates based on room type, time of booking versus arrival date, length of stay, and so forth. Initially, these reservation systems were used internally by the hotel's employees to make bookings for travel agents or consumers via telephone either to the property or through reservation center toll-free phone numbers.

Global distribution systems (GDS)—which today, support travel agents, travelers, and others—were initiated by the airlines. By industry practice, they displayed their own and other airline booking information for themselves and travel agents. From these systems, current GDS evolved, adding information and booking capabilities for other services like hotel and car rentals. Aside from hotels with the same ownership or members of the same chain, hoteliers generally have never sold one another's services. This is an important point for hospitality distribution. Although paper directories existed for the bulk of hotels, there was no electronic compendium or "switch" supporting access to all hotel properties for either the travel agents or travelers.

The first major change in distribution occurred in the late 1970s, when Apollo, Sabre and other airline computerized reservation systems (CRS) were made available to U.S. travel agents for airline booking. Within months of their introduction, there was a desire by travel agents for booking rental cars and hotels as well. In response, the CRSs created databases to allow distribution for car or hotel companies that desired that their products be listed. Because of this, throughout the 1980s, hoteliers, mostly through their chains, were forced to improve their reservation and inventory management capabilities so as to provide the connectivity, quick response time, better accuracy, and richer content required by the CRS users.

Despite having many distribution channels, each channel is comprised of direct or indirect methods. Preautomation, direct sales included those made by the properties and chains themselves using their own reservation capabilities and sales teams. Indirect distribution included sales by travel agents, tour wholesalers, general sales agents, meeting planners, and marketing affiliations or consortia (such as Leading Hotels of the World). These sales were done via phone, fax, or in person.

Throughout the 1980s, the CRSs became global marketers of travel products, enhancing functionality for users and expanding beyond the U.S. travel agent base to agents worldwide. They began referring to themselves as GDSs. This prompted the proliferation of third-party hotel system developers to provide automation solutions to independently owned properties and small chains so they, too, could take advantage of worldwide distribution.

In the 1990s, conditions changed once again as the World Wide Web became functional for consumers. By the mid-1990s, today's well-known online travel agents (OTAs) such as Expedia and Travelocity were launched, followed thereafter by many others who offered or specialized in hospitality products (i.e., Hotels.com). OTAs became even more popular after 2001 as hoteliers turned to them for mass market distribution and consumers gained high-speed connectivity. Once again, hoteliers needed to adapt to a new environment by managing indirect distribution not only through the GDS for travel agents, but also for consumers using OTAs. Building web pages became progressively easier after 2001, and most hotels, inns, lodges, and bed-and-breakfasts introduced their own Web sites as a direct method of reaching potential guests and as a lower-cost (to them) type of distribution.

Today, distribution involves a combination of means for consumers to learn about, compare, and book hospitality services. Over the past 40 years, the means of distribution has multiplied, and there's no reason to believe that changes will cease. Mobile access as a distribution method is increasing. This will require hotels and restaurants to provide access by touch and voice through a myriad of handheld (or earclip) devices. Verbal interaction (with multiple languages required) will become the

(continued)

(continued)

"input" norm. Multi-media images and maps plus social network produced information will be displayed. In addition, the distribution of services will go beyond the traditional planning, shopping, and buying process prior to arrival at the property and include services, reservations, and activities provided while at the property, restaurant, and spa.

THE RISE OF *ELECTRONIC* DEMAND

For the past 10 years, the hotel industry has seen distribution relentlessly shift to the Internet (see Figure 13.4). That shift was initially promoted by online intermediaries such as Travelocity and Expedia,[7] known as online travel agencies (OTAs). These firms initially offered airline services, then

Figure 13.4
Percent of U.S. Hotel Room Revenue Booked Online: 1998–2011

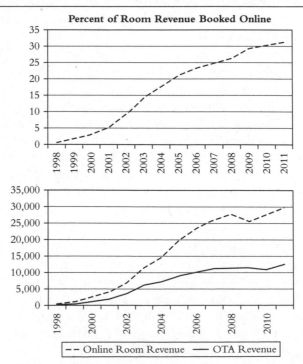

Source: Reproduced by permission from PhoCusWright, Inc.

expanded to lodging, rental cars, and other destination services. Beginning with just *à la carte* sales, the OTAs' travel services have become increasingly sophisticated, offering their own packages, those created by tour operators and dynamically by the customers themselves. It's important to note here that, although distribution has consistently shifted to the Internet and away from traditional channels, those existing channels, such as call centers and the hotels' sales organizations, remain. The 2001 U.S. recession and terrorist attacks opened a period of rate discounting that gave rapid rise to the mass market appeal of OTAs. Recently and to a lesser extent, sites like OpenTable .com and PriceYourMeal.com have made similar inroads into restaurant distribution.

Once hotels launched their own Web sites and other Internet-based strategies to capture *electronic* (realtime interactive) distribution, customers responded favorably. In 2004, the hotel industry's own sites caught up to and surpassed OTAs' room revenue (Figure 13.4). The Great Recession gave a temporary resurgence to OTAs. So your hotel should be involved again with a brand Web site, search-engine strategies, and marketing efforts designed to encourage direct online interactions and bookings (rather than those through an OTA). That said, OTAs should remain a part of your hotel's distribution strategy as a complement (not a substitute) for direct distribution.

Following their success in the leisure market, OTAs have expanded into the business market with sites like Expedia's *Egencia* and Travelocity's *Travelocity Business*. This means that your business customers may increasingly come from electronic and intermediate sources rather than from traditional direct sales or those generated by traditional travel agents and travel management companies like American Express Travel and Carlson Wagonlit Travel. To be sure, American Express and Carlson Wagonlit have launched their own online efforts. These included migrating travel management and travel booking activity online for their largest corporate customers as a means to protect that customer base and as a convenience and cost-saving step. These travel management companies also focused their online service offerings to smaller accounts as a means to grow and protect that customer base.

At this writing, the pace of online migration for hotel sales in the United States has eased somewhat (Figure 13.4). We do not know whether this is a result of the Great Recession, or simply a pause between early adopters and late adopters discovering electronic distribution channels. Expect fundamental changes in the bookings mix among hotel brand sites, traditional travel agents, OTAs, reservation centers, and property-direct channels (see Figure 13.5). Much booking volume has already migrated online and reduced the activity level of chain reservation centers. In response, chains have used their excess call

Figure 13.5
Distribution of Major Chain Revenue by Channel

Channel Shifts in U.S. Hotel Reservations (%), 2008 and 2011

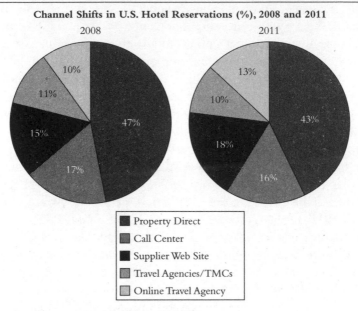

Source: Reproduced by permission from PhoCusWright, Inc.

center capacity to divert calls directed to properties. Group sales and booking activities, particularly for small groups, have moved online and to reservation centers to free up local and regional sales forces to service larger accounts and generate local sales. You may wish to assess the relative strength of your hotel's distribution channels as one means to develop your distribution strategy.

The increased online use of travel-related social media sites like Trip Advisor now requires that you monitor how your hotel or restaurant fares in online review and commentary sites. To the extent possible, you should protect and support your position as it relates to peer-to-peer reviews, Twitter interaction with guests, personalized search, and blogs. While you probably should not be defensive when you see negative ratings or commentaries, you need to be aware of how your customers evaluate your hospitality services, with an eye to amending services that have achieved high levels of disdain and your own position within your competitive set. For more on how to make use of social media, see Chapter 23.

In summary, every opportunity to "touch the customer" through a distribution channel, including social media, is an opportunity to engage that customer, enhance loyalty, and provide service.

Mobile applications are already creating the next major changes in hospitality distribution. Frequent business travelers started this trend,[8] but it's just a matter of time before leisure travelers will be using mobile apps for hotel and restaurant services. The most popular hotel apps facilitate hospitality services such as getting directions, making last-minute reservations changes, and canceling bookings. Your guests may soon expect to be able to employ mobile apps to check-in, get a room assignment, and check out—perhaps even gaining room access without a key. Airlines have already encouraged travelers to use paperless check-in (and pay for checked bags) via their smart phones. More advanced applications might include on-property merchandising.

Restaurant apps involve shopping and searching for dining options in addition to making, canceling, and changing reservations. Initial mobile restaurant apps were centered on getting directions and finding parking for restaurants plus sharing that information with others about food quality and service.

Hospitality mobile applications will have to go beyond simply refitting existing brand web pages, because mobile apps give you yet another chance to make direct contact with your customer by building a preference profile. Unlike Web site visitors, a mobile user's identity, relationship, physical location, and context can be used to refine the information presented; when a loyal guest wants to check in, you can give that person his or her preferred room type or other desired services without any further discussion. Higher-level functions like room check-in or keyless access will require more technological effort and more widespread use of applications by mobile device users. Such applications can give near-term competitive advantages but eventually become "table stakes," like so many other innovations. An exception may be the capacity to promote and merchandise to the guest (perhaps with mobile tweets) while the guest is at or near the property. Here is an opportunity to improve revenue without competitive set response!

THE BRAVE NEW WORLD OF DISTRIBUTION

Changes in distribution have made demand management more complex. Clearly, certain customer segments prefer certain types of distribution channels. At the moment, it is difficult to predict which channel a particular type of customer may use. Some will use more than one channel and for different purposes. I've tried to capture this complexity in Figure 13.6, which illustrates the many segments and channel options.

A particular issue to address is the interaction among pricing, market segment, and distribution channel. Your customers' response to pricing and

Figure 13.6
Customer Segments and Distribution Channels

Segment	Channel						
	Direct	Sales	Chain/ Rep	Travel Agent	Online Inter	Online Direct	CVB/ NTO
Leisure							
Mercenary							
Loyal							
Business							
Corporate							
Less Managed							
Unmanaged							
Wholesale	—				—	—	—
Group							
Large	—		—	—	—	—	—
Small							

promotional marketing can occur differently based on the channel used, their own characteristics, and the nature of the channel. For example, a leisure customer using Priceline's "Name Your Own Price" function will probably have a substantially greater price-elastic response to price differences found on that site than would a brand-loyal corporate customer with a prenegotiated rate calling your reservation center. The Priceline customer has little more than price to go on. The brand-loyal corporate customer is contractually obligated to use the property. Yet another customer may first check one of the OTAs, such as Expedia or Travelocity, and then move to the brand site to confirm the best-price offer. The critical distribution issue is where and how your hotel presents its price offer.

In all of this, your revenue management system will have to be tuned to the steady changes in distribution and the nuances of channel cost variations. This includes marketing and pricing by distribution channel and by customer's segment. You'll need to develop your own answer to what the value is of the top positions in an OTA display, a peer-to-peer review, or a search result. Or you can rely on firms that offer these analysis features, such as IDeaS, SynXis, or TravelCLICK. Experience and analysis will also tell you how your market segments' response changes according to whether they are using a mobile device, a computer, or the telephone. The tools to manage this sort of activity are only now being developed.

DEMAND MANAGEMENT: REGIONAL AND LOCAL FUNCTIONS

We have focused on the role of a particular hotel or restaurant in this discussion because the local operations typically have significant functional responsibility for pricing and demand management. While the regional chain marketing managers still retain considerable responsibility, property and regional managers are the key players in the pricing decision. For many chain hotel and restaurant properties, management and responsibility for pricing, promotion, marketing, sales, and revenue management have been reserved for specific managers. These managers are supported by task-specific systems and processes—yield management for revenue managers, sales force automations for the sales force, and CRM for marketing. Chain central and regional managers may work with local managers in these areas. Yet managing a property's strategic position in a competitive set is essentially a local responsibility. Local management must remain in touch with nuances of local competitor activity and have an intimate understanding of the local market.

This trend toward local and regional responsibility (even if directed centrally) is also being pushed by the evolution of search, social media, and mobile as information media, along with the expanded importance of service personalization. Local management of price and demand management is particularly essential in hotels that are highly differentiated from others in their competitive set and those in distinctive locations. This calls for a greater local application of demand management talent and tools, a concept that is still evolving for hotel chains; albeit chains are providing guidance and tools to help local staffs manage demand.[9]

Successful restaurateurs, particularly independents or those who manage distinctive establishments within chains, are likely to understand the local nature of demand management. The difference today is that managing a restaurant's market position in the face of the evolution of distribution and media has become more challenging. Restaurants have only recently begun to work with revenue management or demand management. That said, restaurants' use of mobile and social media have produced some remarkable results where mobile applications can help customers find the restaurant; review menus; look over reviews; and make or cancel reservations. We can expect restaurants to increasingly rely on applications from Zagat, Foursquare, and OpenTable to project themselves in social media, mobile, and iPad media and to rely on sites like OpenTable to improve revenue management and online reach.

A WORK IN PROGRESS

Effective demand management involves making integrated management decisions about pricing, promotion, and CRM. This means that you will need tools that can guide decision making about everything from the timing and spending on search keyword buys to the impact of peer-to-peer ratings and social media buzz on hotel and restaurant awareness and bookings. For both hotel and restaurant chains, the challenge is to provide tools, direction, training, and support that can promote local and regional demand management, thereby building on brand identity to create local market success and effective brand and network extension. For independent properties, it means finding vendors with tools that can help managers make complicated segment and channel decisions within their competitive sets and marketplaces. Major chains in the restaurant and hotel industry offer proprietary tools for many aspects of demand management. In addition, firms like Revenue Analytics, SAS, JDA, Rainmaker, PROS, EasyRMS, TIG, and Milestone provide tools for independent hotels and chains. Restaurant industry tools are provided by such firms as RMS, SAS, and Avero.

For hotels, responsibility for revenue management, channel management, distribution, and social media marketing is also being redistributed across organizational levels with integrated, shared responsibilities and tools at all levels. The role is being elevated at the property level to a direct reporting relationship with the general manager and at the regional level to a direct reporting relationship to the regional chain vice president.

Strategies and Tactics for Managing Hospitality Demand

To conclude, despite the dramatic changes in hospitality distribution, the key strategies and tactics for demand management still stand. This is despite the shift toward regional and local management of demand.

Demand Management Strategies
1. Have a defined strategic market position within your competitive set(s).
2. Optimize net contribution (total spend less variable cost) by channel and segment.

3. Reward loyalty through distribution channels, with enhanced service delivery and rewards afterward.
4. Support and protect the brand, particularly with evolving social media.
5. Actively manage price, inventory, content, image, and relationships in line with your strategic market position.

Demand Management Tactics

1. As distribution media make price level and structure transparent to customers, price consistently and competitively subject to your differentiated market position.
2. Understand revenue contribution, price response, and promotional effectiveness by segment and channel. Then, use that information to optimize contribution, asset usage, and your overall strategy.
3. Monitor the market for price position, promotion, and awareness versus your competition and your own brand position. Actively promote and protect your brand.
4. Get help from your chain or service providers because decision making is complex and the distribution environment is changing rapidly.

NOTES

1. PricewaterhouseCoopers, Hospitality Directions US Q4, February 2011, Smith Travel Research and PricewaterhouseCoopers U.S. Lodging Forecast, December 2010.
2. Economist Intelligence Unit, *The Austere Traveler* (Amadeus, 2009); and C. Rheem, *Consumer Travel Report,* PhoCusWright (May 2009): Figure 30.
3. See S. Kimes, "Successful Tactics for Surviving an Economic Downturn: Results from an International Study," *Cornell Hospitality Report* 10(7) (April 2010), Cornell Center for Hospitality Research.
4. B. Hanson, "Price Elasticity of Lodging Demand," *Hospitality Directons*, PriceWaterhouseCoopers, September 2005.
5. PricewaterhouseCoopers, *U.S. Lodging Forecast*, November 2010.
6. R. D. Hanks, R. G. Cross, and R. P. Noland, "Discounting in the Hotel Industry: A New Approach," *Cornell Hotel and Restaurant Administration Quarterly* 43(4) (August 2002): 94–103.
7. Actually, the first site was Preview Travel.
8. C. Schetzina, *Consumer Technology Survey,* 3rd ed. (PhoCusWright, December 2009), Part Five.
9. W. Carroll, "U.S. Online Travel Overview," *Lodging,* November 2010.

CHAPTER 14

REVENUE MANAGEMENT FOR ENHANCED PROFITABILITY
AN INTRODUCTION FOR HOTEL OWNERS AND ASSET MANAGERS

CHRIS ANDERSON and SHERYL KIMES

Most hotel managers are familiar with the term *revenue management* (RM), but RM for the hotel industry has evolved considerably from the original practice, which was developed two decades ago by American Airlines. As that company stated in its 1987 Annual Report, RM's goal is to maximize revenues by selling the right seat (or room, in the case of the hotel business) to the right customers and at the right time.[1] While that definition states the essence of RM, as we discuss in this chapter, the hotel industry has refined the concepts of what is the right room, who is the right customer, and when is the right time.

At its most basic level, RM is about a hotel's ability to segment its consumers and price and control room inventory differently across these segments—in essence practicing some form of price discrimination. In many instances, RM used in the hotel industry has been shown to increase revenue by 2 to 5 percent. The high fixed cost and low variable cost typically associated with the hotel industry means that a large portion of this revenue increase flows directly to the bottom line. As an owner or manager, it is important that you understand what RM is, how it works, how it is typically organized, and how you measure its success. In addition, it is essential that you know the right questions to ask to help ensure that your property reaches its revenue potential. In this chapter, we will highlight the ever-changing face of RM and what an owner needs to know about RM. The purpose of this chapter is to provide a broad overview of RM, enabling the reader to be knowledgeable enough to understand the underpinnings of today's RM systems.

REVENUE MANAGEMENT ACTIONS

Selling the right room to the right customers at the right time requires a revenue manager to forecast demand by market segment, understand the price sensitivity of these segments, and then adjust prices and control access to rooms. For the most part, hotel prices are market driven, and most hotels set rates relative to their competition. As a manager, you will have multiple rate classes or price points for each room type, with RM determining which of these rate classes should be available at any particular time. RM systems use existing reservations on hand (ROH) to develop forecasts for future arrivals days. Booking or pace curves are a common way to present ROH as a function of days before arrival (DBA). Figure 14.1a displays a sample booking curve with the solid line representing typical ROH by DBA. The squares represent current ROH for a future arrival date, and the dashed line is the forecasted ROH over the next seven days prior to arrival. Hotels will generate multiple booking curves, one for each segment. Figure 14.1b displays a sample set of booking curves one for regular rate the other for a discounted rate.

Depending on its size and reach, your hotel probably has numerous market segments. Typical ways to segment your customers are the channel they choose to book through, the number of nights they are staying, and the day of week of their arrival. The more distinct segments you can identify and forecast, the more productive your RM system. The key is that the segments need to be distinct and separated by distinctive attributes or restrictions. Common sets of restrictions center around time of purchase, level of refundability, and affiliation with a particular business or organization. As shown in Figure 14.1b, the discount segment tends to book quite early, so you could set a rule that guests who want to qualify for this rate class would have to make their reservations 21 days or more prior to arrival. Other restrictions focus on exchangeability and transferability of the rooms as discounts often come at the expense of flexibility. Focusing on Figure 14.1b helps us understand what an RM system is attempting to do. In that graph, the full-priced product doesn't have much demand prior to three or four days before arrival. If this were your property, you could be selling at the discounted rate up to four days before arrival and not worry much about full-price customers grabbing the discount rate. Then, at three days before arrival, you would need to be cautious with offering the discount rate, as your full-price customers are now in the market.

Figure 14.1
Sample Booking Curves

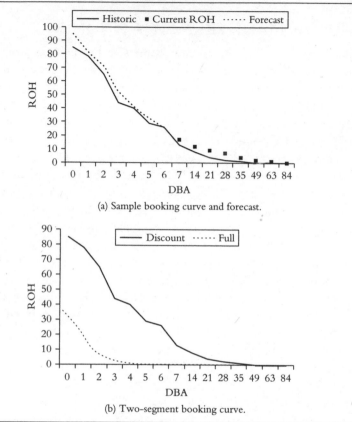

(a) Sample booking curve and forecast.

(b) Two-segment booking curve.

RM has often been motivated by a simple illustration of variable versus fixed pricing. Figure 14.2a shows a sample downward-sloping demand curve and a series of prices that might go with such a curve. The thing to look at here is that the areas trapped in rectangles on the left side of the graph, which represent revenue that your firm has captured, and the areas on the right, with the curved sides right next to the graph, represent forgone revenue. Hotels use a variety of fences or restrictions so that they can sell a certain number of rooms at a discounted price while also being able to sell the remaining rooms at different prices (Table 14.1 summarizes some common rate restrictions). Your hotel or brand undoubtedly uses some of these. For example, in Figure 14.2a, the hotel sells 50 rooms at $175, while simultaneously selling 50 rooms at $100. The rate fences would have to restrict the

Figure 14.2
Variable Pricing and Segmentation

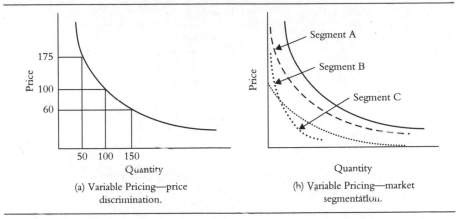

(a) Variable Pricing—price
discrimination.

(b) Variable Pricing—market
segmentation.

50 customers who were willing to pay the $175 room rate from buying the room at the $100 price, or (worse) $60. The rate fences are not failsafe, and some of your customers who are willing to pay the higher rate will be happy to accept a lower price. Figure 14.2b recasts the graph in 14.2a into the marketing view of variable pricing. Think of 14.2a as a price discrimination graph, and 14.2b as a market segmentation approach, where each of the dashed lines presents a segment of the aggregated (total) market represented by the solid line. What you are attempting here is to set a revenue-maximizing price in each distinct market segment versus trying to discriminate across nonsegmented consumers. The point here is that unless your firm can effectively segment consumers (whether by fences or other mechanisms), you probably should not attempt to implement variable pricing.

Variable Pricing and Dynamic Pricing

We've been talking about variable pricing, but let's compare that with a different way to set prices—dynamic pricing. As we just explained, variable pricing involves setting multiple price points for distinct market segments. The key facet is that each price could potentially be offered simultaneously. In contrast, dynamic pricing involves changing prices over time in response to demand uncertainty (usually, you decrease your price in an attempt to stimulate demand, or increase prices in response to strong demand). Be careful with rate reductions because you could lower your rates (and dilute your ADR) without improving occupancy. When contemplating a rate change, you need to first assess the demand response that would be required to make the

Table 14.1
Common Rate Fences

Type	Rate Fences	Examples
Room-Related	• Basic product	• Room type
		• Room location or view
	• Amenities	• Free breakfast, airport pickup, etc.
		• Valet parking
	• Service level	• Priority check-in
		• Dedicated service hotlines
		• Personal butler
Transaction Characteristics	• Time of booking or reservation	• Discounts for advance purchase
	• Location of booking or reservation	• Guests booking rooms from different countries are charged different prices
		• Customers making their reservation online are charged a lower price than those making a reservation by phone
	• Flexibility of reservation	• Fees/penalties for canceling or changing a reservation
		• Nonrefundable reservations fees
Consumption-Related	• Time or duration of use	• Minimum length of stay
		• Saturday night stay
	• Location of consumption	• Price depends on departure location, especially in international travel
Guest-Related	• Frequency or volume of consumption	• Member of certain loyalty-tier get priority pricing, discounts, or loyalty benefits
	• Group membership	• Child, student, senior citizen discounts
		• Affiliation with certain groups
		• Corporate rates
		• Group discounts based on size of group
	• Geographic location	• Local customers are charged lower rates than tourists
		• Customers from certain countries are charged higher prices than those from other countries

contribution from the price change positive. For example, consider a hotel that is contemplating decreasing its room rate from $100 to $90. Say that the hotel would have sold 90 rooms at $100 (for revenue of $9,000). To break even at the $90 room rate, the hotel would need to sell at least 100 rooms. If we further assume that the hotel has a variable cost of $20 per room, the contribution at the $100 rate would be ($100 − $20) × 90 rooms = $7,200. To break even at the $90 rate, taking contribution into account, the hotel would need to be able to sell 103 rooms (contributing $70 each) to hit $7,200.

We suggest being careful with rate reductions for the following reason: Not all segments respond to rate changes with more demand; that is, they are not price elastic. As you consider your breakeven analysis, you need to take into account two possible actions, depending on whether a particular market segment is price elastic (and responds to rate changes) or price inelastic. You can:

- Decrease prices (by either doing it alone or following a competitor's rate reduction) in price sensitive (elastic) segments, or
- Raise prices (or follow a competitor's price increase) in non-price sensitive (inelastic) segments.

The key term here is *segments*, which are the groups of guests who have certain booking attributes in common. Using the rate fences, you can target price changes at specific market segments, as only targeted price changes will generate enough incremental demand to compensate for rate dilution, which occurs when you give a relatively low rate to guests who would have willingly paid more.

Hotels need to differentiate between variable and dynamic pricing. Restrictions and rate fences can be effective at setting variable prices but are less effective at controlling availability.

While firms can use time-based segmentation, they generally use some form of fencing to segment consumers. Your hotel can segment consumers (charge different prices) across room and bed type. Looking again at Table 14.1, you can see that other common types of rate fence include transaction characteristics, consumption characteristics, and customer characteristics.

Because most hotel rates are posted online, customers can compare rates both for different hotels and for various distribution channels. Your hotel undoubtedly maintains price parity on various distribution channels. So your strategy here is to have a series of private rates. We discuss these private rates in more detail in Chapter 26, which addresses strategies for dealing with difficult markets. Private (or opaque) discounts allow you to offer special prices to price-sensitive customers while maintaining higher prices on regular posted price channels. Many hotels offer their private discounts on opaque online travel agents, like Priceline's "Name Your Own Price" channel[2] or on Hotwire.com.[3] Both Hotwire and Priceline hide the name of the property until after the purchase, allowing the service provider to reach price-sensitive customers (who are not brand loyal), while simultaneously maintaining their higher price for brand-loyal customers. Another method of offering private discounts is to package your room with other hotel services (e.g., spa, food, and beverages). The package price is lower than the sum of all the individual prices, but no one can determine how you have apportioned them. Finally, today's online advertising world offers numerous ways to market to individual customers whether via your customer relationship marketing (CRM) system with e-mail offers (where you are using your database of past customers and their travel patterns to create specific offers) or through search engine marketing (e.g., using Google, Yahoo!, or Bing), where you can pay for specific exposure of your ads with links to special reduced prices. Again, we discuss these tactics in greater detail in Chapter 26. With dynamic pricing you run the risk of turning your hotel room into a commodity that is simply purchased on price, as has largely occurred with airline seats, where customers switch airlines to save only a few dollars.

In both recent economic downturns, we have seen many hotels using online travel agents (OTAs) as a means of reaching price-sensitive consumers. This has potential benefits, in addition to the risks. A recent study by Continental Airlines illustrates that while average fares have dropped as consumers moved online to shop and purchase travel, consumers have responded to the airlines' rate fences by choosing to purchase in off-peak periods to obtain lower prices, thereby smoothing out demand.[4] One could conclude that prices are not decreasing, but rather that these online channels are reaching price-sensitive consumers who may not have otherwise purchased a flight. In a related experimental study, chapter coauthor Anderson showed that not only do OTAs generate incremental reservations at the OTA itself, but they also significantly increase reservation volume at non-OTA channels (such as the hotel's own Web site, call center, or traditional travel agent).[5] That study found an approximate lift of 20 percent in reservations was obtained by listing on OTAs like Expedia, Orbitz, or Travelocity. Together, these two studies illustrate the strategic role of OTAs in generating reservations. Again, a note of caution: Use these OTAs strategically and rely on these channels only at times when price-sensitive customers are shopping. More to the point, you need to make sure that you remove these deals when your full-price segments are starting to book. Think of the OTA as a marketing expense, marketing toward price-sensitive consumers. So you use the OTA if you think it's the most efficient use of your marketing dollars.

Like the search engines, OTAs also allow you to purchase Web page positions and advertising. Figure 14.3 shows two types of sample offers at an OTA. The first listing is a sponsored listing where the property has paid to be prominently displayed at the top of the hotel list. You can also use strategies that involve "deals" for the consumer (often as part of engaging the OTAs' services). The listing just below the sponsored listing uses strikethrough pricing (regular price is crossed out with discounted price listed) to

Figure 14.3
OTA Placement and Advertising

(a) Sample Offers at OTA

Sponsored Listing **The Florida Hotel and Conference Center** Orlando, FL   ★★★☆☆

15 min from Champs and Capital Bowl
Connected to Florida Mall and minutes from the theme parks, deluxe hotel, flat screen TVs, pillow top beds and pool.250 stores

SEE DETAILS ▶

Expedia Special Rate   ★★★☆☆   Sale! Save 35% on this Stay.

Lake Buena Vista Resort Village & Spa, a Sky Hotel & Resort   4.4   ~~$245~~ **$159**
avg/night

Orlando, FL | Area: Downtown Disney® area/Lake
Photos / Tours Buena Vista View on map

SEE ROOMS & RATES ▶

rating from
734 reviews

Adjacent to the Lake Buena Vista Factory Outlet Mall, Lake Buena Vista Resort is 2 miles... Read more

Hotel Info: 1-866-264-5744

 Insiders' Select™ MULTI-YEAR WINNER

VIP ACCESS ROOM UPGRADES & MORE

Room type	Sat	Avg per night	
Two bedroom Antigua resort suite-Sleeps up to 6 **Includes: Full Kitchen**	~~$245~~ $159	~~$245.00~~ $159.00	Book it ▶
Two bedroom Antigua resort suite-non-refundable rate **Includes: Full Kitchen**	~~$245~~ $159	~~$245.00~~ $159.00	Book it ▶
Three Bedroom Barbados resort suite-Sleeps up to 8 **Includes: Full Kitchen**	~~$275~~ $179	~~$275.00~~ $179.00	Book it ▶

Show more rooms ⌄

(b) Banner ad

demonstrate savings and to create a sense of urgency in an effort to increase conversion rates. Figure 14.4 shows a sample banner ad typically displayed down the left-hand side of the OTA listing. Most OTAs also offer *Deal* or *Special Offer* sections where hotels can provide special offers and packages. Generally speaking, OTAs are relatively consistent in the products and services they offer consumers; what differentiates each is their ability to market to consumers and drive traffic to the specific OTA. Figure 14.5 summarizes average monthly visitors during the 2008–2009 recession to the four largest North American OTAs.

Most North American OTAs operate on the merchant model. That is, they are the merchant of record in which the OTA sells an agreed-upon number of rooms at an agreed-upon price, which represents the amount you will receive after the OTA marks the price up and sells the rooms. Outside of North America, many OTAs operate on a retail model in which they receive a commission for each sale. Some of these retail OTAs allow hotels to pay higher commissions in exchange for prominent display at the top of their Web pages.

Figure 14.4
Sample Menu Bar Showing Deals at Expedia.com

Figure 14.5
Unique Monthly Visitors (Millions)

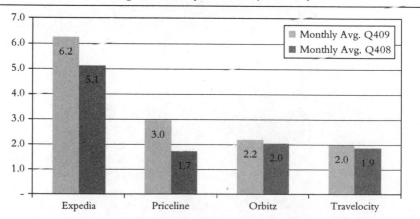

Source: www.compete.com.

Although we go into greater detail in Chapter 26, we need to mention search engine marketing (SEM) and search engine optimization (SEO) in connection with this discussion. You can use the search engines as marketing vehicles, especially since many consumers start with a search engine to research travel opportunities before they go on to other travel sites (e.g., OTAs). Ensuring that your hotel has prime placement on the search engine will undoubtedly drive more demand further down the search funnel. Figure 14.6, a display of a Google search on *hotels in red wing,* illustrates the SEM and SEO principles. This search stems from a project with the St. James Hotel in Red Wing, Minnesota.[6] As you can see, the hotel's URL (www.st-james-hotel.com) is high on the list. They have used SEM to purchase a pay-per-click (PPC) ad, which is fifth down the list of ads on the right-hand side. They may have also optimized their Web site with appropriate search terms so that when someone types in "hotels in red wing," their property comes up near the top of the (unpaid) list. When looking at this first-page result, we see both direct competitors to the St. James being listed (e.g., American Inn), as well as the OTAs, which are also using PPC. SEM will increasingly become an important aspect of all RM activities at a property, as it provides as easy to implement a targeted approach to generating demand. Again, see Chapter 26 for tactics that will benefit your hotel in using this strategy.

Figure 14.6
SEO and SEM at the St. James Hotel

PERFORMANCE MEASUREMENT

To determine which of the many price discrimination tactics are working best for you, you'll probably want to use the typical hotel financial ratios, especially revenue per available room (RevPAR), although some properties also keep track of gross operating profit (GOP). The typical RevPAR calculation is to multiply the occupancy percentage by your ADR, but you can also divide your total rooms revenue by the number of rooms available. RevPAR has a direct effect on the capitalization (cap) rate, cash flow, and net operating income. A small percentage increase in RevPAR can yield a substantial percentage gain in cap rate. Further details on capitalization rates are found in Chapter 18 by John Corgel.

Most likely, you will compare your hotel's performance with that of its competitive set. Because of the hotel industry's cost structure, the focus of RM is typically on guest room sales and particularly on room revenue. RevPAR clearly matters, but you probably want to look at how your hotel is doing compared to the market. After all, a 10 percent increase in RevPAR during a strong economy may not be particularly good if the market is up by 20 percent. Most North American hotels and many hotels in other parts of the world subscribe to services that compare their performance with that of their competitive set. The most commonly used source for this information is Smith Travel Research (STR) but other organizations provide similar data. Let's take a look at how to work with STR data (often referred to as STAR reports).

Depending on the subscription level, hotels share with STR their performance data (occupancy and ADR) each month or each day. In that report, you would also specify the composition of your competitive set (at least three or four other similar hotels, usually located close by). You could have several comp sets—say, one comp set that consists of nearby hotels and another comp set that looks at similar hotels that may be located a bit farther away. Owners need to watch to make sure that the comp set is appropriately chosen, because a poorly chosen comp set can misrepresent a hotel's relative performance.

STR uses submitted data to develop occupancy, ADR, and RevPAR information for both the individual hotel and for the competitive set. Data for the competitive set are aggregated because of government regulations, so that you do not directly know who reported which results.

STR then develops indices for occupancy, ADR, and RevPAR that compare your individual hotel's performance with that of its competitive set. The indices are calculated by dividing the hotel's performance by that of its competitive set. Indices above 100 indicate that the hotel is outperforming its competitive set; those below 100 mean that the hotel is underperforming its competitive set. For example, if your hotel has occupancy of 77 percent and its competitive set has occupancy of 70 percent, you have an occupancy index of 110 (77/70).

The indices conveniently show how well a hotel is performing regardless of the economic situation. The index that commands the most attention is the RevPAR index. If your hotel does not have a RevPAR index of above 100, you should ask why and investigate ways in which to improve it. Obviously, to have a RevPAR index above 100, one of the occupancy and ADR indices must also be above 100 (or ideally both).

During a down market, some hotels and owners may try to raise RevPAR by dropping rate in an attempt to raise occupancy. While such a tactic is tempting, you need to be careful that the ADR index does not fall below that of its competitive set. Research has shown that hotels that have an ADR index of less than 100 have a lower RevPAR index than hotels that have a higher ADR index. Various chapters in this book touch on this research, but the most complete discussion is in the next chapter, on management strategy. The short of it is that dropping rates has implications for the long-term success of the hotel.[7]

The important thing to remember with ADR is that it is an average of multiple rates. Think of revenue coming into the hotel as a pipe with multiple inlets. The inlets represent different market segments and distribution channels with different demand levels and price sensitivities. By adjusting the flow of the different demand inputs, you can better manage revenue flow. For example, during slow periods, you might want to increase the flow of business from certain market segments and distribution channels, but you may choose to restrict this demand during busier time. Your RM system will indicate how and when to adjust the flow levels of the different demand sources.

Organization of the RM Function

If your hotel has not integrated revenue management as a total strategy throughout your hotel, we urge you to start now. Hotel RM began as a function of the local property's reservations department—focused only on room sales. That's still important, but over the past 15 years, RM has taken on a more strategic and marketing function. RM is typically located either in the sales and marketing department or is sometimes placed in a separate department that reports directly to the hotel's general manager. Given the importance of RM in generating a steady cash flow for the hotel, we suggest that the revenue manager should be part of your hotel's executive team.

Brands have taken note of the importance of revenue management, and a number of chains have adopted a relatively centralized approach in which RM is handled at the city or regional level. With this approach, one revenue manager might have responsibility for 10 to 20 hotels. An alternative approach often seen at more moderately priced hotel chains is to completely centralize RM and to have all revenue managed from the corporate office.

If you own a hotel that is part of a chain, you may need to decide whether you will opt in to that chain's RM system. In most cases, this is probably a good idea, but before making the decision, be sure to ask to see the performance data of their system.

RM for Other Parts of the Hotel

Revenue management can be applied to numerous revenue streams in your hotel including function space,[8] restaurants,[9] spas,[10] and golf courses.[11] Any part of the hotel that sells space (whether it be a guest room, meeting space, or a restaurant seat) for a given length of time for a variety of prices has the opportunity to apply RM principles. Essentially, RM can be applied to maximize the revenue per available square foot of the entire hotel.

Key Questions to Ask

Often, one of the major hurdles in understanding or implementing RM is not knowing the right questions to ask of the stakeholders involved in using the system as well as those looking to you to use their system. Following are some key questions you might use to gather further insight into what your RM system (or your potential system) is doing and how well it is doing it.

1. What sort of RM system are you using?
   The answers to this will vary from "We're using the corporate system" to "We're using a manual system." Here's how to respond to the three most common responses:
   - "We're using the corporate system." This is probably good since most major chains have relatively strong RM systems. Key questions to follow up with include:
     o Who is responsible for using the system?
     o What sort of training has the person gone through?
     o How are the results from the system used to make decisions?

- "We're using a purchased system." Again, this is probably good since there are a number of good commercial RM systems, but some are better than others. Key questions to follow up with include:
  - o What other hotels use this system? What sort of success have they had?
  - o Why did you choose this system?
  - o Who is responsible for using the system?
  - o What sort of training has the person gone through?
  - o How are the results from the system used to make decisions?
- "We're using a manual system." This means either that they are not doing much of anything or that they're using a series of Excel spreadsheets to make decisions. This approach can work, but its success is largely dependent on the caliber of the person who is responsible for making the RM decisions. Key follow-up questions include:
  - o Why are you using this approach rather than using a purchased system?
  - o Who is responsible for using the system?
  - o What sort of training has the person gone through?
  - o How are the results from the system used to make decisions?

2. How are you using online travel agents? Are you a preferred partner, merchant model, or are you just using the retail model?

3. Are you using any opaque distribution channels such as Priceline.com? If so, how do you use it and what results have you had? If not, why not?

4. How do you make pricing decisions? How frequently do you change rates? How do you decide if a price move is required? How do you evaluate price changes (i.e., what sort of after the fact performance measurements are you making)?

5. How frequently do you have yield meetings? Who attends? Who is in charge? What sorts of things are discussed? What sorts of reports are generated?

6. How do you use STR reports and other competitive data to make decisions? How frequently do you "shop" the competition? Do you shop manually or do you use a service? If you use a service, which one do you use?

7. Tell me more about the revenue manager. What department is he/she located in? What sort of background does the person have? What sort of training does the person have?

8. Where do your reservations come from? What percentage come from the hotel's Web site, OTAs, call centers etc.?

9. What did you do to survive the last recession? What worked? What didn't work?

Summary

Revenue management in the hotel industry continues to evolve. The recession of 2008–2009 particularly caused hotels to reevaluate and to adjust to situations of surplus capacity—instead of surplus demand. The strategic importance of RM became particularly apparent when demand plunged. Hotels needed to carefully consider their tactics for attracting price-sensitive demand. As we see it, RM is evolving into demand management, a practice that is integrated with sales and marketing. RM will be an exciting place over the next few years as firms further integrate their online efforts as well as embrace mobile technology. Today, it is critical for ownership to be cognizant of how their property is embracing the opportunities created by RM. It will be the firms with targeted marketing and discounting programs that are integrated with RM that lead rates up as the economy improves.

NOTES

1. American Airlines, "The Art of Managing Yield," *Annual Report* (1987): 22–25.
2. C. K. Anderson, "Setting Prices on Priceline," *Interfaces* 39(4) (2009): 307–315.
3. C. K. Anderson and X. Xie, "A Choice-Based Dynamic Programming Approach for Setting Opaque Prices." Cornell University, School of Hotel Administration, Working Paper, 2009.
4. W. G. Brunger, "The Impact of the Internet on Airline Fares: The Internet Price Effect," *Journal of Revenue Management and Pricing* 9(2) (2009): 66–93.
5. C. K. Anderson, "The Billboard Effect: Online Travel Agent Impact on Non-OTA Reservation Volume," *Cornell Center for Hospitality Research Report* 9(16) (2009).
6. C. K. Anderson, G. Bodenlos, V. Bogert, D. Gordon, and C Hearne, "SEO/SEM Best Practices: The St. James Hotel," Cornell University School of Hotel Administration, Working Paper, 2010.
7. C. Enz, L. Canina, and M. Lomanno, "Competitive Pricing Decisions in Uncertain Times," *Cornell Hospitality Quarterly* 50(3) (2009): 325–341.
8. S. E. Kimes and K. A. McGuire, "Function Space Revenue Management: A Case Study from Singapore," *Cornell Hotel and Restaurant Administration Quarterly* 42(6) (2001): 33–46; and S. Hormby, J. Morrison, P. Dave, M. Meyers, and T. Tenca, "Marriott International Increases Revenue by Implementing a Group Pricing Optimizer," *Interfaces* 40(1) (2010): 47–57.
9. S. E. Kimes, R. B. Chase, S. Choi, E. N. Ngonzi, and P. Y. Lee, "Restaurant Revenue Management," *Cornell Hotel and Restaurant Administration Quarterly* 40(3) (1998): 40–45; D. Bertsimas and R. Shioda, "Restaurant Revenue Management, *Operations Research* 51(3) (2003): 472–486.
10. S. E. Kimes and S. Singh, "Spa Revenue Management," *Cornell Hospitality Quarterly* 50(1) (2009): 82–95.
11. S. E. Kimes,. "Revenue Management on the Links: Applying Yield Management to the Golf-Course Industry," *Cornell Hotel and Restaurant Administration Quarterly* 41(1) (2000): 120–127.

CHAPTER 15

COMPETING SUCCESSFULLY WITH OTHER HOTELS
THE ROLE OF STRATEGY

CATHY A. ENZ

Strategy may be one of the most misunderstood business concepts, but it's essential for people at all levels of the organization to understand what strategy is and how it affects their jobs. Regardless of your position in your organization, your company's strategy is a critical element of your job. Even if your job mostly involves tactical decisions, such as daily rate setting, you are still enmeshed in the company's strategy. Not only that, but as I explain the nature of hospitality strategy in this chapter, you will see how your everyday actions contribute to the business strategy. In fact, if you think strategically, you will experience a deeper understanding of your operation and your firm's external environment, so that you'll have an integrated perspective for the operation.

Whether you are currently a manager in a hospitality firm or hoping to redirect your efforts to become one, understanding the strategic management process is important to achieving performance. Hospitality firms' performance is linked to the thoroughness, sophistication, participation, and formality of strategic planning processes.[1] In fact, a study of leadership competencies found that strategic positioning was viewed by senior industry leaders as more important for future leaders than was industry knowledge.[2]

This chapter explores the major strategic responsibilities that you must assume when serving as a business unit manager. After reading this chapter, you will be able to evaluate and develop an overall direction for your organization, deploy strategic tools to conduct an ongoing analysis of the changing business situation, select a competitive strategy, and understand the resource capabilities needed to build a competitive advantage. Let's start by defining strategy so that you can see the difference between strategies and operational plans.

WHAT IS STRATEGY?

Strategy focuses on the long-term direction of your company. The foundation of a strategy is the development of a strategic orientation, which is akin to developing a perspective or a way of coming to envision future business decisions and discerning present actions. Your strategy provides guidance for the preparation of short-term plans and integrates functional plans into an overall scheme for the organization. In contrast to the long-term focus of strategy, tactical thinking is short term and should be based on the business strategy.

People often confuse short-term budgets and functional area plans with strategies, and the term *strategy* is used loosely to mean almost any document or action involving the overall business. Strategy is not a response to short-term fluctuations in operations or the environment—that involves tactical thinking. Similarly, strategy is not a set of numbers that merely project out three to five years into the future, nor is it a functional plan—even a long-run plan—such as a five-year marketing plan or a seven-year capital budget. Those, too, should flow from your overall strategy and not the other way around.

Building a Strategy

Engaging in the strategy-development process involves proactive analysis and learning about your competitive environment and your internal operation. You establish a strategic direction, create strategies that are intended to move the firm in that direction, and implement those strategies, all in an effort to satisfy key stakeholders. The process begins with an analysis of your firm's organizational strengths, weaknesses, opportunities, and threats (known as *SWOT analysis*). SWOT analysis is intended to help you select strategies that (1) take advantage of organizational strengths and environmental opportunities or (2) neutralize or overcome organizational weaknesses and environmental threats.[3] Strengths are resources and capabilities that can lead to a competitive advantage, like a great location or extraordinary service delivery. Weaknesses are resources and capabilities that your firm does not possess, and their absence puts the company at a disadvantage. Opportunities are positive conditions in the broad and operating environments, such as favorable tax incentives. Threats are conditions in the broad and operating environments that may stand in the way of competitiveness such as a shift in consumer preferences.

After strategies are formulated, plans for implementing them are established and carried out, as shown in Figure 15.1.[4] To become a successful manager in the hospitality industry, you need strategy to help chart a course, coordinate others, and conserve energy. Without a long-term strategic direction, your

Figure 15.1
Strategic Management

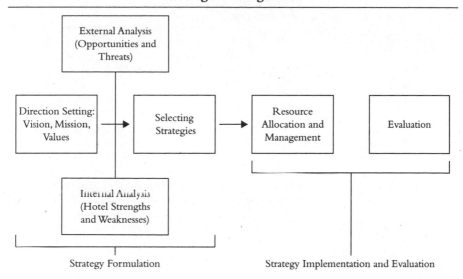

Source: C. Enz, *Hospitality Strategic Management: Concepts and Cases*, 2nd ed. (Hoboken, NJ: Wiley, 2010).

operation will drift and your management team will make inconsistent decisions, thereby wasting both energy and resources.

As a hotel property manager, your major strategic management responsibilities include establishing the overall direction of the business unit, ongoing analysis of the changing business situation, selecting a competitive strategy and the specific tactics needed to carry it out (strategic posture), and managing resources to produce a sustainable competitive advantage (see Table 15.1).

SET A DIRECTION

Your company's strategy begins with a clear understanding of the business, including who is being satisfied, what is being satisfied, and how customer needs are satisfied. Strategic direction, including values and principles, forms the foundation on which plans of action are developed. Hotel Indigo, a brand of InterContinental Hotel Group (IHG), for example, defines itself as a lifestyle boutique hotel designed to appeal to the middle-market, style-savvy guest who desires affordable luxury, genuine service, and an alternative to traditional "beige" hotels without sacrificing any of the business amenities guests expect.[5] In defining who they are, Indigo's managers pinpoint the middle-market, style-savvy guest who is trading up to higher levels of quality

Table 15.1
Management's Strategic Responsibilities

Major Responsibilities	Key Activities
Set a Direction	• Create and share the mission, vision, principles, and long-term goals of the hotel • Create and communicate shorter-term goals and objectives
Analyze the Business Situation	• Perform a SWOT analysis • Examine your competitors and the broad environment • Assess the hotel's internal resources
Choose a Competitive Strategy	• Select a generic approach to competition—low cost, differentiation, focus, or best value • Develop specific strategies to carry out the business strategy
Deploy Key Resources	• Acquire and deploy the resources and capabilities to assure competitive advantage • Develop functional strategies (e.g., HR and marketing) • Use performance metrics to ensure the strategies produce results

Source: C. Enz, *Hospitality Strategic Management: Concepts and Cases,* 2nd ed. (Hoboken, NJ: Wiley, 2010).

and taste but still seeks value. What is being satisfied is the traveler's desire to experience affordable luxury and style instead of the "beige" hotel. Finally, the how is accomplished through a retail service model in which changes are made throughout the year to keep the hotel fresh, similar to the way retailers change their window displays.

One of the most common ways you can communicate your hotel's strategic direction is to write a mission statement, which is a brief statement of the hotel's purpose that defines the scope of the operation. Mission statements often include information on markets served, customers, products, services, employees, location, and strategic features. To give you an example of a thorough mission statement, Adare Manor Hotel & Golf Resort, in Limerick, Ireland, communicates its ideals and direction in the mission statement shown in Table 15.2. This luxury castle hotel rests amid 840 acres of formal gardens and features a Robert Trent Jones–designed golf course and several fine restaurants. Adare has devised a mission statement that communicates its ideals and a sense of direction to both internal stakeholders (such as employees), and external stakeholders (notably, customers).[6]

As you see, a mission statement is more than just what your hotel does. Instead, to begin setting a clear direction, you should think in terms of the

Table 15.2
The Mission Statement of Adare Manor Hotel & Golf Resort

Adare Manor Hotel & Golf Resort Mission Statement

We are built on tradition . . .

We are committed to providing our guests with standards of excellence that surpass their expectations.

We take seriously our responsibility to map out the future development and continuous improvement of our product.

We encourage our employees to learn and teach, creating an environment that is pleasant, safe, and happy.

We will fulfill our commitment to the community and environment at all levels to ensure harmony.

We welcome feedback in all forms. Guest comments provide us with an invaluable tool assisting us in our strides to progression and the enhancement of the guest experience.

We cherish our reputation as one of the finest five-star establishments in Europe providing a welcome and service to rival all competition.

As a family-run hotel, our hospitality is not the product of a corporate mission statement but of a well-built tradition that we are proud to call our home.

Source: Adare Manor Hotel & Golf Resort Web site.

resources the hotel owns and the knowledge people hold. The following are guidelines for preparing mission statements:

- Use terms that are understandable to employees.
- Word your mission to inspire the human spirit. A person should read the statement and feel good about working for the hotel.
- Catchy (but not cliché) slogans can help people remember the mission.
- Keep the mission statement as short as possible.
- Widely distribute the mission.
- Communicate the mission to employees regularly.

While often confused with a mission statement, a vision is an ideal and unique description of the future for your hotel. The forward-looking statements of a vision convey a sense of what might be. A well-understood vision can help your managers and employees see that their actions have meaning. To enhance your ability to communicate a vision you should ask, "How do I passionately convey our dramatic difference to our customers?" Be sure that the housekeepers, wait staff, desk clerks, reservationists, and others buy into the vision.

ANALYZE THE BUSINESS SITUATION

As a strategic thinker, you need to become a trend watcher so that you can continually analyze your business situation and ensure that your strategy is still effective. One element of analyzing the situation is to look at the most important forces in the broad external environment and how your company and competitors will respond to these forces. The external environment includes groups, individuals, and forces that affect the hotel from outside the organization. Key external influences can be grouped under the acronym PEST, as follows:

- Political—governmental laws, regulations, and policies
- Economic—overall economic activity, including inflation, trade deficits, exchange rates, and interest rates
- Sociocultural—population size and content, as well as consumers' attitudes
- Technological—equipment innovations, and new products or processes

As with SWOT analysis, opportunities and threats are conditions in the broad environment that help or hinder a firm's efforts to achieve competitiveness.[7] Key opportunities and threats may come from unlikely sources, and often can be viewed as two sides of the same coin, meaning that an opportunity that competitors exploit can become a threat. Using the PEST rubric, you can analyze trends in the broad environment. Table 15.3 depicts a PEST analysis. On the left, you can describe the nature of each trend. The columns in the middle can be used to identify each trend as an opportunity, a threat, or as neutral to your hotel. The last column should list possible actions you could take to respond to the opportunities and threats.

The internal organization includes all of the stakeholders, resources, knowledge, and processes that exist within the boundaries of the hotel. You also need to examine your hotel's resources and capabilities and match these strengths to emerging opportunities in the broad environment. This analysis is the basis of strategy formulation.

Your hotel enjoys a competitive advantage when it has a long-lasting business advantage compared to rival firms that offers it a significant edge over the competition. Usually, this means that the hotel can do something competitors can't do or has something competitors lack. While it is extremely difficult to sustain a competitive advantage, hotels work to create advantages through the development of resources and capabilities. For example, Starwood has identified several capabilities that they believe lead to a competitive advantage, as stated in Table 15.4.[8]

You can begin your internal analysis by listing your hotel's resources and capabilities. Include on your list both tangible resources (such as the physical property or financial assets) and intangible resources (such as brand or

Table 15.3
Evaluating the Environment—PEST Analysis

Trend	Opportunity	Threat	Neutral	Your Response, If Any
Political Influences				
• New laws				
• New regulations				
• Current government policies				
• Government stability				
• International pacts/treaties				
Economic Influences				
• Economic growth				
• Unemployment				
• Interest rates				
• Inflation				
• Foreign-exchange rates				
Sociocultural Influences				
• Attitude changes				
• Demographic shifts				
• New fads in food/culture				
• Public opinion about travel/ entertainment				
Technological Influences				
• New products				
• New processes				
• Scientific discoveries				

Source: C. Enz, *Hospitality Strategic Management: Concepts and Cases*, 2nd ed. (Hoboken, NJ: Wiley, 2010).

organizational culture, and human, innovation, and reputation resources). Focus on the things your hotel can do that its competitors can't or something your organization has that its competitors lack. What you are developing is a list of resources that together create a competitive advantage; by itself, a single resource is not sufficient for this purpose.

Taken together, these resources and capabilities are the source of your hotel's core competencies, which form the basis of your competitive advantage. Here are two examples of how that works. The core competencies that Ryanair assembled to accomplish its business strategy of being a low-cost carrier included acquiring a fleet of easy-to-maintain aircraft, flying into regional airports, controlling customer service costs, and selling primarily through an online distribution channel.

As an example from the hostels segment of the industry, Chic & Basic, a Barcelona-based hotel company, created a competitive advantage for its

Table 15.4
Starwood's Key Capabilities

Six capabilities provide a foundation for Starwood's strategy:

1. *Brand strength.* Our superior global distribution, coupled with strong brands and brand recognition.
2. *Frequent guest program.* Our loyalty program, Starwood Preferred Guest® (SPG).
3. *Significant presence in top markets.* Our hotel and resort assets are primarily located in major cities in which the supply of sites suitable for hotel development has been limited and in which development of such sites is relatively expensive.
4. *Premier and distinctive properties.* We control a distinguished and diversified group of hotel properties throughout the world.
5. *Scale.* As one of the largest hotel and leisure companies focusing on the luxury and upscale full-service lodging market, we have the scale to support our core marketing and reservation functions. We also believe that our scale will contribute to lower our cost of operations through purchasing economies in areas such as insurance, energy, telecommunications, technology, employee benefits, food and beverage, furniture, fixtures and equipment, and operating supplies.
6. *Diversification of cash flow and assets.* The diversity of our brands, market segments served, revenue sources, and geographic locations provide a broad base from which to enhance revenue and profits and to strengthen our global brands. This diversity limits our exposure to any particular lodging or vacation ownership asset, brand, or geographic region.

Source: C. Enz, *Hospitality Strategic Management: Concepts and Cases*, 2nd ed. (Hoboken, NJ: Wiley, 2010).

business by offering a differentiated product.[9] Breaking with tradition, the company developed a broad definition of the "hostel customer" and incorporated a modern and hip design along with special amenities. The bundle of complementary resources included carefully chosen low-cost locations, a distinctive physical space, efficient staffing, and amenities not commonly found in hostels. Figure 15.2 depicts the way Chic & Basic built its differentiation strategy (i.e., a designer look at a low price) on four core competencies that are, in turn, composed of a bundle of distinctive resources.

CHOOSE A COMPETITIVE STRATEGY

Your choice of strategy is based on the analysis of your competitive situation, strengths, and weaknesses, and opportunities as they relate to those of competitors. Although no two business strategies are exactly alike, we can classify them into just a few generic types to identify common strategic characteristics. The classic strategy taxonomy was developed by Michael

Figure 15.2
Chic & Basic's Bundle of Resources and Capabilities

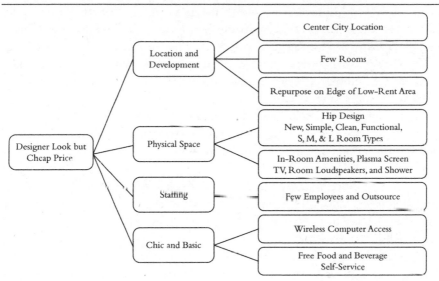

Source; C. Enz, *Hospitality Strategic Management: Concepts and Cases*, 2nd ed. (Hoboken, NJ: Wiley, 2010).

Porter in 1980.[10] Porter advanced the idea that a sustainable competitive advantage is related to the amount of value a firm creates for its customers. According to Porter, firms create superior value for customers either by offering them a preferred product or service at a somewhat higher price (where the additional value received exceeds the additional cost of obtaining it) or by offering them a basic product or service that is produced at the lowest possible cost. He suggested the following strategy types: differentiation, low-cost leadership, and focus, which he divided into differentiation focus and low-cost focus. Finally, he proposed that a company that is following none of those generic strategies is "stuck in the middle."[11] According to Porter, these uncommitted firms should have lower performance than committed firms should because they lack a consistent basis for creating superior value.

The first option, referred to as differentiation, requires the company to distinguish its products or services on the basis of an attribute such as technology embodied in design, location, or the skill and experience of employees. The second option, called low-cost leadership, is based on efficient cost production. For example, a restaurant that is trying to achieve a competitive advantage by producing at the lowest cost will seek some combination of efficiency, low levels of overhead, and high volume. Porter's third strategic option, called focus, involves targeting a narrow segment of the market through either low-cost leadership or differentiation. JetBlue Airlines pursues a strategy of low-cost leadership for a broad market, for example, while Four Seasons Hotels and Resorts relies on a strategy of differentiation. An example of a differentiation focus strategy would be the gay and lesbian hotels developed by Milagro Properties. Some hotel firms have succeeded at melding cost leadership with differentiation. I'll discuss this strategic hybrid, called best value, in a moment, after we cover Porter's classic strategies.

Although each brand should be associated with a particular strategy, a hotel company that operates several brands can pursue several business-level strategies simultaneously through its different brands or business units. InterContinental Hotel Group is one company that owns many brands that pursue a wide variety of strategies. The company's prestige brand, InterContinental Hotels and Resorts, uses a differentiation strategy by offering outstanding facilities and superior service within unique local contexts and cultures. At a different price point, the Holiday Inn brand offers full-service comfort and value to a broad market, while Candlewood Suites offers a focused strategy in a hotel experience created for stays of a week or longer. As I described earlier, Hotel Indigo is another focused brand, while Crowne Plaza puts its attention on the convention and meetings business. The strategy of Holiday Inn Express is probably best described as low-cost leadership because of its broad appeal to the mass market and emphasis on limited service, cleanliness, timelessness, and cost efficiency. I should emphasize that low-cost leadership does not mean low quality. So, in one company, we have brands that illustrate Porter's archetypal strategies. Let's look at each of those strategies.

Creating a Differentiation Strategy

A differentiation strategy focuses on offering products or services that customers perceive to be different and better than the offerings of the competition. This strategy is popular in the hospitality industry, primarily because hospitality services are complex and satisfy self-identity and social affiliation needs, thus creating tremendous opportunities for differentiation. However, while the potential for differentiation is great in service businesses, the ease of imitation can make it likely that several brands will attempt similar strategies, a situation known as competitive convergence. Despite each chain's effort to differentiate, many brands become enough alike that consumers cannot truly distinguish them from each other.

Differentiation is a strategic choice, not a feature of the market, and as such needs to be based on creating a bundle of resource capabilities. Service experiences that complement consumers' lifestyles, and brands that communicate their aspirations may allow the firm that creates these products and services to set itself apart sufficiently that it can charge a premium price. The higher price is necessary to cover the extra costs incurred in offering the unique experience.

To understand and profit from a differentiation strategy it is important to understand customer lifestyles and aspirations, so that the hotel's distinctive offerings are valued by customers. Differentiation can be achieved in an almost unlimited number of ways, including:

- Product features
- Complementary services
- Technology embodied in design
- Location
- Service innovations
- Superior service
- Creative advertising
- Better supplier relationships leading to better services

Certain resources are more effective as a source of sustainable differentiation than others. Reputations and brands are difficult to imitate, for example, whereas particular service features may be easy to imitate. In general, intangible resources such as a high-performance organizational culture are hard to imitate and are a stronger basis of competitive advantage, whereas a tangible resource such as the fixtures and furnishings in a hotel are easy to imitate. So creating value extends beyond just the product, as Four Seasons has illustrated with its fostering of a service culture.[12] Among other distinctive resources, Four Seasons has built its strategy of providing genuine and innovative service on a careful employee selection process and the development of flexible standards to deliver personal service to guests.

The key to success when deploying a differentiation strategy is that customers must be willing to pay more for the service than it cost your hotel to create it. Therefore, a critical aspect of the differentiation strategy is to keep costs low in the areas that are not directly related to the sources of differentiation. Chic & Basic, for example, differentiated on design while keeping staffing costs low. Many large hotel companies avoid investing in real estate so that they can focus their efforts on brand and franchise differentiation. This "asset-light" strategy is common throughout the hotel industry.

Creating a Low-Cost Strategy

Firms pursuing cost leadership set out to become the lowest-cost providers of a good or service. For instance, both Etap and Motel 6 are pursuing low-cost strategies and do not offer significantly more than the basics: simply furnished rooms with a bed, shower, and toilet. Ryanair and JetBlue provide no-frills flights at the lowest prices possible. Burger King and Taco Bell work on value pricing to deliver food quickly to those who want convenience and low price. Management in these companies is good at minimizing costs so that they can keep prices low and attract a wide segment of the market interested in an inexpensive product or service offering.

Theoretically, hotels that are able to achieve the lowest cost do not have to charge the lowest price. In other words, a cost leader does not have to be a price leader. If a hotel is able to achieve the lowest cost but charge a price that is the same as competitors charge, then it will enjoy higher profits. As a practical matter, however, there are few barriers to switching. If the low-cost leader's price is the same as or higher than the price others charge, customers seeking low prices will be just as likely to switch to a competitor. Consequently, many low-cost leaders try to underprice competitors slightly in order to give customers an incentive to buy from them and to keep their volumes high enough to support their low-cost strategy.

Let's examine the tactics typically used by companies pursuing a low-cost strategy. As you will see, these tactics are applicable for any strategy, but are particularly designed to drive down costs. They are as follows:[13]

- High capacity utilization (occupancy management)
- Economies of scale
- Benefits from learning-curve effects
- Technological advances
- Outsourcing

High Capacity Utilization Effective capacity utilization is particularly important in the hotel industry because fixed costs represent a large percentage of total costs. This is the reason that many hotels focus so tightly on maintaining high occupancy levels, using better demand forecasting in the revenue management process, expanding capacity conservatively, or pricing aggressively. Hotels that maintain high occupancy will be better able to maintain a lower cost structure than a competitor of equal size and capability but with lower occupancy.

The potential problem with the industry's focus on occupancy is that hotels often sacrifice rate to maintain occupancy. As you have read in other chapters, research has demonstrated that massive price cutting in the face of falling demand does not stimulate sufficient sales to make up for the loss in average rate. I've been involved with several studies that have revealed that customer demand does not appear to be easily stimulated by price reductions.[14] Take a study that I did with Linda Canina, of Cornell, and Mark Lomanno, of STR, that compared one hotel's rate and occupancy results with those of its competitors. Figure 15.3 shows how customer demand (occupancy levels) remains constant (flat) for hotels in Europe even when the hotels price below their competitors. The figure also shows that revenue per available room (RevPAR) rises when hotels price higher than their competitors do and falls when hotels price below their direct competition.[15] We also found this to be true in U.S. hotels, again during both good times and bad. Careful revenue management can help you maximize revenue by knowing when to raise or lower prices according to occupancy levels. In short, while hotel demand (occupancy levels) cannot be stimulated easily, you can engage in dynamic pricing to effectively manage inventory.[16]

Economies of Scale Many of the largest hotel companies view their scale of operations (as distinct from capacity utilization) as a key competitive

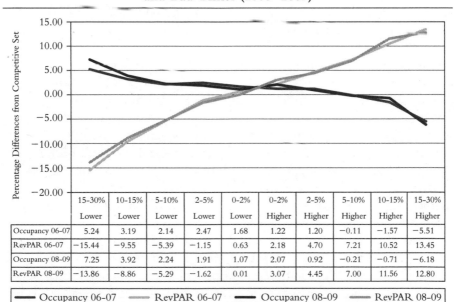

Figure 15.3
European Hotel Pricing Dynamics in Good Times (2006–2007)
and Bad Times (2008–2009)

	15-30% Lower	10-15% Lower	5-10% Lower	2-5% Lower	0-2% Lower	0-2% Higher	2-5% Higher	5-10% Higher	10-15% Higher	15-30% Higher
Occupancy 06-07	5.24	3.19	2.14	2.47	1.68	1.22	1.20	−0.11	−1.57	−5.51
RevPAR 06-07	−15.44	−9.55	−5.39	−1.15	0.63	2.18	4.70	7.21	10.52	13.45
Occupancy 08-09	7.25	3.92	2.24	1.91	1.07	2.07	0.92	−0.21	−0.71	−6.18
RevPAR 08-09	−13.86	−8.86	−5.29	−1.62	0.01	3.07	4.45	7.00	11.56	12.80

━━ Occupancy 06-07   ▪▪▪ RevPAR 06-07   ━━ Occupancy 08-09   ▪▪▪ RevPAR 08-09

ADR Percentage Differences from Competitive Set

Source: C. Enz, L. Canina, and M. Lomanno, "Strategic Pricing in European Hotels, 2006–2009," *Center for Hospitality Research Report* 10, no. 5 (2010).

strength. This is the basis for the industry consolidation that has been led by several firms. Starwood Hotels and Resorts Worldwide, for example, states in its corporate overview that its scale contributes to lower costs of operations through purchasing economies.[17] The central principle of economies of scale is that costs per unit are less when a hotel expands its scale or size of operation, whether at the chain level or the property level. At the property level, the cost of constructing a 200-room hotel will probably not be twice the cost of building a 100-room hotel, so the initial fixed cost per unit of capacity will be lower, and it will not cost twice as much to operate.

Large hotel brands take advantage of economies of scale through frequent traveler programs, reservations systems, and global sales and marketing programs. The large brand can spread its marketing costs over a greater range of properties. Additionally, owners and franchisees of large hotel companies can enjoy advantages from economies of scale. Owners and developers who select a well-regarded brand may find that they can obtain lower interest charges and have access to a greater range of financial instruments because of the size of the brand. Owners will also benefit from managerial specialization of the brand company in hotel development and renovation projects. Support in the areas of architectural and interior design, project and construction management, and procurement related services can reduce the long-run average cost of running an individual hotel.

Learning-Curve Effects Creating systems that are as simple as possible allows low-cost providers to benefit from the learning-curve effect. A simple system does not require as much repetition in the learning process. However, hotels with complex systems can overcome a steep learning curve by offering strong training programs. In either case, you help employees along the learning curve by creating an environment that is favorable to both learning and change and then rewarding employees for their productivity improvements.

Technological Advances Investments in cost-saving technologies are often viewed as a trade-off between increasing fixed costs for a reduction in variable costs. If technological improvements result in lower total-unit costs, then hotels have achieved a cost advantage from their investments, referred to as *economies of technology*.[18] The reservation systems maintained by the major lodging companies represent investments in technology that reduce overall costs and provide information control. For example Mariott's reservation network and demand management tool (MARSHA) was integrated with the company's Internet technology platform and other inventory applications and marketing programs to provide the necessary technology infrastructure to provide a competitive advantage.

Outsourcing—Make versus Buy Purchasing value-creating activities through outsourcing can increase a firm's flexibility while reducing risk and costs. However, it does require effective coordination, and you have to select the "right" activities to outsource. Increasingly, hotel companies are realizing that sometimes another company can more efficiently handle a service than they can. When thinking about outsourcing, you should keep in mind that hotels have begun to subcontract a wide variety of activities, including accounting, reservations, information systems, and even hotel management. Individual hotels have also effectively outsourced food and beverage, janitorial, airport shuttle, valet, human resource, and even housekeeping services. The key to success is whether the outsourced service delivers on both the cost savings you hoped for and the level of performance you require.

Best Value: Seeking the Blue Ocean

In reading about Porter's classic competitive strategies, you might be thinking that your firm is drawing elements from each one. Probably so, and that approach of combining strategic elements from both differentiation and low cost is known as a best value strategy. Best value is about making sure that the things that provide the most perceived value to a customer are done very well, while at the same time you are looking for ways to keep costs low through technology, economies of scale, learning, or reducing waste.

The best value strategy also involves seeking the least crowded competitive position, an approach popularly known as the *blue ocean strategy*. It's hard to believe that there are open niches in the hotel industry, but innovative hoteliers have found them, including Marriott with Courtyard and Starwood with W. The rest of that metaphor is to avoid a red ocean, or a crowded competitive position. While a red ocean is crowded and competition turns the ocean bloody red, a blue ocean is undiscovered, vast, and deep.[19] So think of the blue ocean strategy to seize growth opportunities, while you apply a best value strategy in which you create a new value proposition for the customer.

Chic & Basic is an example of a blue ocean or best-value strategy. It borrowed from the traditional hotel concept and offered a low-cost hostel concept in which design elements were created that had never been offered in this segment, along with such amenities as personal showers and private rooms—almost unheard of in the hostel segment. Figure 15.4 provides a summary of the four factors identified in a blue ocean strategy to increase value as they apply to Chic & Basic. This concept demonstrates the principle of creating high value by enhancing some items and controlling costs by reducing or eliminating other elements. To simultaneously compete on price, quality, service, and innovation, you must strip out costs permanently, eliminate what doesn't add value, and focus on what does.

Figure 15.4
Eliminate-Reduce-Raise-Create Blue Ocean Framework
for Chic & Basic

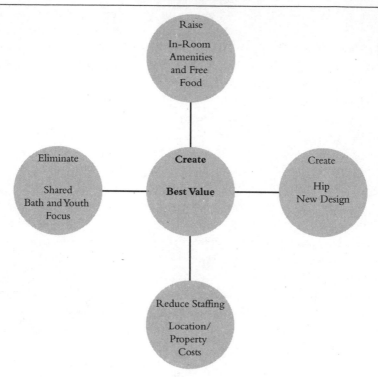

Source: C. Enz, *Hospitality Strategic Management: Concepts and Cases*, 2nd ed. (Hoboken, NJ: Wiley, 2010).

DEPLOYING KEY RESOURCES

One of your most important roles is to acquire, develop, manage, and discard resources. Your business strategy will guide you in making those determinations. Your goal is to make sure your hotel has "superior resources" that confer competitive advantage.[20] Superior resources are valued by customers, possessed by only a small number of hotels, and are not easy to substitute. If a particular resource is also costly or impossible to imitate, then the competitive advantage may be sustainable—at least for a period of time. Unfortunately, most hospitality innovations are easy to imitate, and this type of competitive advantage is fleeting. Westin responded to an unspoken customer need with its "heavenly bed," but eventually competitors copied the concept and reduced that competitive advantage.

Building Your Competitive Advantage

A successful hotel manager is able to build a sustainable competitive advantage by capitalizing on the resources of the hotel. Over a long period of time, a sustainable competitive advantage may lead to higher-than-average hotel performance.[21] To determine whether your hotel has resources and capabilities that yield a sustainable competitive advantage you should ask yourself the following six questions:

1. **Does the resource or capability have value in the market?**
   Valued resources allow you to exploit opportunities and/or neutralize threats.
2. **Is the resource or capability unique?**
   If your hotel is one of very few with a particular resource or capability, then it may be a source of competitive advantage. The uniqueness dimension also implies that a resource or capability is not easily transferable or readily available in the market for purchase.
3. **Is there a readily available substitute for the resource or capability?**
   If a competing hotel has easy access to another resource or capabilities that will help them accomplish the same results, the resource has substitutes.
4. **Do organizational systems exist that allow the realization of potential?**
   For potential to be realized, your hotel must also be organized to take advantage of it.
5. **Is the organization aware of and realizing the advantages?**
   You must be able to identify sources of competitive advantage and take positive actions for potential to be realized.
6. **Is the resource or capability difficult or costly to imitate?**
   The more difficult or costly a resource or capability is, the more valuable it is in producing a sustainable competitive advantage.

Positive answers to the first two questions and a negative answer to the third question means that a resource or capability has the potential to lead to a competitive advantage for your hotel. However, that potential is not realized unless questions four and five are also answered in the affirmative. At this point, your hotel is using its systems and knowledge to take advantage of a unique and valuable resource or capability. However, resource advantages may not be sustainable. The final question regarding imitation determines the long-term value of a resource or capability.

GOING FORWARD WITH STRATEGIC THINKING

The nature of the hotel operation often runs counter to the need to be a strategic thinker. Since hotels are always open, it's easy to focus on daily operation and tactics. Moreover, hotel managers are frequently rewarded for putting out fires. Reacting to problems crowds out time that might otherwise be available for thinking and devising strategies. You can break free of this reactive style by following a strategic management process, as outlined in this chapter. First, create a new mission statement for your hotel. Analyze the environment and list both opportunities and threats that are facing your property. Identify your hotel's resources and capabilities. Give thought to ways of both differentiating and also cutting costs—seek out that blue ocean. Finally, devise your own unique property level strategy and then deploy your resources to accomplish the ongoing task of implementing your strategy.

It's possible that your strategy will be adopted by your entire firm. This is what happened at the Willard InterContinental, when its then–general manager Hervé Houdré devised a sustainability strategy to set his hotel apart from the many hotels in Washington, D.C.[22] His sustainability program was so powerful that IHG has adopted many elements of the Willard's strategy.

Begin now to think about your operation. What is your company really good at? How do you compare to your competition? Who are your most important customers? When you carve out time for reflection, you begin the process of seeing your hotel differently. Taking time to reflect creates an opportunity for insight, and with insights shared with your staff, you can begin to change your own habits and actions and those of others. Now is the time to become a strategic thinker. Blame nobody, take ownership, and create a great future!

NOTES

1. Study results for hotels in the United Kingdom support this linkage; see P. A. Phillips, "Strategic Planning and Business Performance in the Quoted U.K. Hotel Sector: Results of an Exploratory Study," *International Journal of Hospitality Management* 14 (1996): 347–362.

2. See B. G. Chung-Herrera, C. A. Enz, and M. J. Lankau, "Grooming Future Hospitality Leaders: A Competencies Model," *Cornell Hotel and Restaurant Administration Quarterly* 44(3) (2003): 17–25.

3. M. D. Olsen and A. Roper, "Research in Strategic Management in the Hospitality Industry," *Hospitality Management* 17 (1998): 111–124.

4. Adapted from C. Enz, *Hospitality Strategic Management: Concepts and Cases*, 2nd ed. (Hoboken, NJ: Wiley, 2010).

5. InterContinental Hotel Group, www.ichotelsgroup.com/h/d/6c/1/en/c/2/dec/6c/1/en/ob.html, May 28, 2010.

6. Adare Manor Hotel & Golf Resort, Mission Statement. www.adaremanor.com/mission-statement, May 25, 2010.

7. Enz, 2010.

8. Enz, 2007.

9. For a detailed discussion, see C. Enz, R. Verma, K. Walsh, J. Siguaw, and S. Kimes, "Cases in Innovative Practices in Hospitality and Related Services: Set 3," *Center for Hospitality Research Report* 10(10) (2010).

10. M. E. Porter, *Competitive Strategy: Techniques for Analyzing Industries and Competitors* (New York: Free Press, 1980).

11. Ibid.

12. B. Talbott, "The Power of Personal Service," *Center for Hospitality Research White Paper* (2006): 1.

13. This discussion of factors leading to cost savings is based, in part, on material found in Enz, 2010, and derived from M. E. Porter, *Competitive Advantage: Creating and Sustaining Superior Performance* (New York: Free Press, 1985) and R. W. Schmenner, "Before You Build a Big Factory," *Harvard Business Review*, 54 (July/August 1976), 100–104.

14. For a detailed discussion see C. Enz and L. Canina, "Competitive Pricing in European Hotels," *Advances in Hospitality and Leisure* 6 (2010); C. Enz, L. Canina, and M. Lomanno, "Competitive Pricing in Uncertain Times," *Cornell Hospitality Quarterly* 50(3) (2009): 325–341; C. Enz, L. Canina, and M. Lomanno, "Why Discounting Doesn't Work: The Dynamics of Rising Occupancy and Falling Revenue among Competitors," *Center for Hospitality Research Report* 4(7) (2004); and L. Canina and C. Enz, "Why Discounting Still Doesn't Work: A Hotel Pricing Update," *Center for Hospitality Research Report* 6(2) (2006).

15. C. Enz, L. Canina, and M. Lomanno, "Strategic Pricing in European Hotels, 2006–2009," *Center for Hospitality Research Report,* 10 (5) (2010).

16. L. Canina, and C. Enz, "Revenue Management in U.S. Hotels: 2001–2005," *Center for Hospitality Research Report* 6(8) (2006).

17. Starwood Hotels, Company overview. Starwood Hotels and Resorts Web site, http://www.starwoodhotels.com/corporate/company_info.html. (accessed February 1, 2011).

18. Schmenner, 1976.

19. W. C. Kim and R. Mauborgune, "Blue Ocean Strategy: From Theory to Practice," *California Management Review* 47(3) (2005): 105–121.

20. B. Wernerfelt, "A Resource-Based View of the Firm," *Strategic Management Journal* 5 (1984): 171–180; and J. B. Barney, "Firm Resources and Sustained Competitive Advantage," *Journal of Management* 17 (1991): 99–120.

21. J. B. Barney and A. M. Arikan, "The Resource-Based View: Origins and Implications." In M. A. Hitt, R. E. Freeman, and J. S. Harrison, eds. *The Blackwell Handbook of Strategic Management* (Oxford, UK: Blackwell, 2001), 124–188.

22. See H. Houdré, "Sustainable Hospitality: Sustainable Development in the Hotel Industry," *Cornell Hospitality Industry Perspective* 2 (July 2008), Cornell Center for Hospitality Research.

CHAPTER 16

FOCUS ON FINANCE
AIMING FOR RESTAURANT SUCCESS

ALEX M. SUSSKIND and RUPERT SPIES

We all know that the most important thing about a restaurant—the thing that stands out and shapes a guest's experience—is the food. Not only that, but we can name other elements that are crucial to the guest's restaurant experience, including staff, service, location, ambience and décor, menu, and overall execution. But restaurants can survive weaknesses in all those areas and still remain in business. We've all seen those places. What a restaurant cannot survive is failure of financial management, including focusing on revenue, profit, expenses, debt, and appropriate staffing levels. It's true that restaurants fail due to market factors or even due to a lack of expertise,[1] but as we see it, the financial side of the restaurant business doesn't get the attention it deserves. For this reason, in this chapter we explain the specific connection between the elements of food-service management and the income statement and balance sheet. Our goal is to focus on restaurant success factors by discussing these two important documents, and the many operational elements that go into them. Let's start with the income statement.

INCOME STATEMENT

The income statement is a periodic measurement of your business's performance and provides you with important information about four main constituents of any food-service business, namely, the guests, employees, management, and ownership. Most income statements are processed and reported monthly, but, depending on their business cycle, some operators use a 28-day period to provide an equal distribution of days across the year. If you own a franchise, the format will probably be specified by your franchisor; otherwise, you should use a format that meets your operation's needs and provides sufficient operational performance data to assist you in running the business.

Most balance sheets start with the *Uniform Systems of Accounts for Restaurants (USAR),* published by the National Restaurant Association, which details the basics of financial statements, how they are structured, and how line items are annotated and interpreted.[2] The format and definitions in the *USAR* are universally accepted and are used industry-wide. While you're really required only to report finances according to the laws set forth by various levels of government, the *USAR* can provide great guidance on how you can structure and report your financial statements.

Following is an introduction and description of how each line item on the income statement relates to guests, employees, management, and ownership.

Sales

The top line of your income statement is sales or revenue, the money you collect from your guests for the food and beverage you serve, and this is essentially all you have to support the operation of your business. You probably want to break down your sales on a per-guest or per-cover basis. A simple average makes a good starting point. If you record $1 million of sales in a quarter with 50,000 guests, your average check (or cover) would be $20. You probably would want to be more precise, though, and calculate your average check per daypart, for example, or for the drive-through or take-out business. This calculation will give you an idea of your guests' spending behavior in each meal period, and you can get a sense of your guests and the market you serve. It can also help you gauge your performance relative to your competition. Knowing what guests are spending in your competitors' restaurants will help you understand where revenue enhancement opportunities lie.

Breaking down that $20 average check even further, you can determine what percentage of your sales comes from food sales and what is from beverage sales. Casual dining restaurants typically record around 12 to 15 percent of sales from beverage alcohol. So, if you are in the casual dining segment and only have 10 percent of sales attributed to alcohol, you might wish to investigate further. Perhaps you have an area for improvement, or it may tell you something about your guests. You might want to focus on how alcoholic beverages enhance your guests' overall meal experience, and put that in the context of how all beverages relate to the meal. You typically would record nonalcoholic beverage sales under the food category (for sales and the cost of goods sold), but you still need to pay attention to the role that nonalcoholic beverages play in the experience for your guests, even more so than alcohol. Together, all these beverages enhance your guests' experience with their meal and offer you the chance to boost check averages.

For this purpose, your service staff should understand how the food and beverage offerings work together. You can train your staff, without being pushy, to help guests select food and beverage products that pair well together and enhance your average check. Many higher-end restaurants, for instance, maintain well-designed programs that allow guests to choose a bottled water to go along with their meal. This supplants tap water, which has zero revenue and 100 percent cost. Additionally, you can train your servers to suggest cocktails and other beverages, often as specials, before your guests order their food. Likewise, at the end of the meal, you can set up options for coffee, coffee drinks, and other dessert beverages. When properly marketed and offered by service staff, these additional items simultaneously enhance the average check and the guests' experience. Once again, you do have to use caution in upselling to ensure that your guests are receptive to these products and do not feel pressured or pestered.

All types of restaurants use upselling, of course, just as hoteliers do at the front desk and airlines when you check in. Truthfully, you wouldn't be doing your job if you didn't give your guests the opportunity to increase their pleasure. Our point is that value meals, "super sizes," and the famous "would you like some fries with that" are all elements that allow operators to boost their guests' spending, but they also deliver notable add-on value. If you know what your guests are purchasing and why, you can identify ways to enhance your average check, while creating a positive experience for your guests.

Forecasting To ensure that you can meet your guests' demands, you need to be able to forecast those demands. For existing operators, forecasting involves a close examination of historical data and an analysis of market factors—such as market trends, competition, and sociodemographics. All of this should help you uncover guests' behavior and preferences. New businesses that don't have solid historical data can forecast based on an analysis of market trends, competition in the marketplace, and an examination of market demographics and predicted consumption patterns.

Forecasting requires meticulous collection and analysis of data that will allow you to accurately predict how many guests might frequent the restaurant, what food and beverage they will choose (menu mix), and, as a consequence, what ingredients you will need to order and how many staff members you'll need to hire and schedule.

Cost of Sales

Although sales levels are important, you also need to take into account the costs of the products you sell, because your net revenue is what's left after you pay the bills. The best pricing, forecasting, and revenue management strategies will fall flat if costs are not managed appropriately.

Restaurant guests are generally price sensitive, so you have to manage costs carefully to keep your prices as reasonable as possible. The fact that restaurant guests pay for the meal after it has been consumed makes price maneuvering more difficult for restaurant operators.

Three key factors influence an operator's cost of goods: (1) supply chain management (i.e., purchasing, procurement, receiving, storage), (2) recipe management, and (3) product execution.

Supply Chain Management Supply chain management is a set of complex, interrelated tasks that allow operators to select, procure, purchase, receive, store, and issue the products that are needed to serve their guests. *Selection* is defined as choosing among alternative forms and preparations of a particular food item. *Procurement* is the orderly systematic exchange between a seller (or supplier) and a buyer. Procurement involves locating a supplier and determining purchase amounts, purchase sizes, timing, and quality assurance to ensure adequate food supplies. Selection and procurement should be built on requisite product knowledge, including a clear understanding of product quality, standards of identity, and any regulations (e.g., health and legal) that govern the sale and use of these products.

Before you can begin the selection and procurement process, you need a clear understanding of the products you serve and the precise specifications for those products. Some products are easier to "spec" than others, but it is important to identify how the product will be used.

A product specification comprises the following seven elements that need to be considered in concert to ensure that the products you require can be secured for your operation.[3]

1. The spec should offer an accurate quality description. Quality distinctions influence cost, selling price, preparation, storage, and guest perceptions.
2. The spec should have observable features, such as how the food item appears and how it is packed.
3. The spec should be realistic and practical, to ensure that the products and product features fit into your operation, including storage, preparation, and guest demand.

4. The spec should be clear, simple, and direct. The specification is a communication among you, your staff, your suppliers, and your guests. Specs must be aligned with all four.
5. The spec should be based on readily available products that take into account market supply and demand. Although you can get fresh berries year round, you might get different (and inappropriate) quality some times of the year, or the price may be too high for your concept.
6. The products specified should be available from multiple sources if possible.
7. The spec should allow some level of flexibility. For each product, you should specify a range of acceptance. For example, you may require USDA Choice whole beef tenderloins, but may accept products in both the C and D size ranges. In some instances, you may have zero flexibility with the products you require, but those might cost you more.

In essence, the selection and procurement process should provide you with the ability to maintain continuous supply at a minimum cost while maintaining desired quality levels. Above all, your purchasing activities should help you maintain your restaurant's competitive position in the marketplace.

Receiving and Storage Receiving procedures are the other side of the specification coin. After you have properly identified and procured the products you need, you must maintain effective controls in how products are received and stored by your operation. The following are the six key elements of the receiving process:

1. Ensure that product quality, quantity, condition, and price are correct and as specified.
2. Expedite products into storage or move them to production.
3. Aid the purchasing department in evaluating a supplier's performance.
4. Check the performance of the purchasing department.
5. Serve as an accounting checkpoint.
6. Inform purchasing and production of shortages and returns.

Based on those six points, here is a specific approach to receiving. The receiving personnel should:

1. Verify the quantities of the items delivered. This involves reconciling your purchase order against the supplier's invoice, and against the products that are actually delivered.

2. Verify the quality and specifications of the items delivered to make sure that they match your product specifications. You'll generally want to reject products that don't meet specs.

3. Verify the price charged against the quoted price. Your vendors should deliver at the agreed upon price and that amount should appear on all paperwork, along with all discounts, specials, and returns or credits.

4. Initiate the processing of the invoice. Once you receive the products and ensure that you received what you ordered, submit the invoices for prompt payment, based on the terms and arrangements set up with your suppliers.

5. Inform production of any shortages. Whether the vendor doesn't have all the desired product or whether your receiving staff has rejected some foodstuffs, you'll need to make sure that the production team knows about shortages and can adjust production accordingly.

6. Transfer all product to appropriate locations. Once products are received, you need to ensure they are appropriately stored or put into production.

Storage Your storage areas allow you to maintain a sufficient supply of food-stuffs, so that you have a buffer between purchasing and production. But the storage facilities must be appropriately secure, climate controlled, and large enough to meet your operation's needs. This particularly includes controlling both temperature and humidity for perishable products. At a minimum, your storage facilities should maintain the products in the proper condition until needed for production. Managing your inventory to prevent waste and spoilage is a key factor, even for products that improve in storage (e.g., wines and produce that need to ripen, such as avocados and bananas).

The purchasing process should take into account par stocks, of course, along with the short-term and long-term needs of production. Your storage facilities must act as a staging area in the sense that everything can be easily found and retrieved. Products should be inventoried, labeled, and dated. Generally, you'll use the oldest stock each time, but there may be times when newer stock must be used. You need to use the ripest avocados, for instance, no matter when each case was delivered. As that example illustrates, you need to keep track of the quality and condition of all products in storage, with the goal of converting all your purchased items into revenue. We discuss this matter of ordering and storing foods in greater detail later in this chapter, in the context of inventory management.

Recipe Management To ensure that your guests receive consistent products and that your costs are accurately reflected, you need to use well-tested, standardized recipes. Your tested, quantity recipes provide both a method (instructions for making a food dish) and the list of necessary ingredients, specified as the foods are found in inventory. But we want you to think of a recipe as more than a food-chemistry formula. Think of recipes as management tools. Properly developed recipes allow management to employ materials (ingredients), labor, and facilities and equipment in the most effective and efficient manner. A standardized recipe should contain:

- A summary of ingredients, listed in order of use
- The required quantities of each ingredient
- Specific procedures for measurement (weight or volume)
- Portion size
- Yield (anticipated number of portions)
- Equipment needed for portioning, preparing, holding, and serving
- Any garnishing or finishing details
- Storing and serving instructions

A good recipe will provide consistency. If the recipe is properly designed, it can be executed at any time by anyone who has sufficient skill. If you have numerous cooks on different shifts and days of the week, your recipe should control for individual differences among the employees, produce a consistent taste and appearance, and produce the same cost and yield each time it is used.

Although good recipes cut down on the need for direct management supervision, they do not alleviate managers' responsibility to supervise and check production and service quality throughout the process. Recipes are really only the first step to ensure product consistency and quality and cost containment.

Product and Service Execution By controlling product and service execution, your goal is to deliver consistent, quality products and service. This cannot be done without an understanding of your cost structure, supply chain, and production and service processes. All the elements discussed previously regarding cost of sales become meaningless without the necessary attention to detail to ensure that products are made and served correctly and consistently.

Gross Margin

So you bought the raw materials, cooked and served the dishes, and brought in revenue. If you subtract your cost of goods sold (COGS) from sales revenue, you'll have a figure called gross margin. From this, you still must cover your other prime cost of doing business—labor costs. In restaurants, the term *prime cost* is used to refer to the COGS (food and beverage) plus the cost of labor and benefits. Successful restaurants typically have prime costs in the range of 50 to 70 percent, leaving between 30 and 50 percent to cover all other operational expenses and profit. Those other expenses are controllable expenses, occupation expenses, and other ownership-related costs. The way these expenses are handled is a strong indication of how effectively a manager is running the business.

Controllable Expenses Controllable expenses are those under management's direct control. Expenses can be classified as either fixed or variable. Fixed expenses show the same dollar amount for each period or sales volume. Common fixed expenses are rent, license fees, and administrative and general expenses. A variable expense tracks the volume of business, including cost of goods sold and direct operating expenses. Some expenses contain both a fixed and a variable component. Rent, for instance, may be a fixed dollar amount, plus a percentage of sales. Let's look at your controllable costs, starting with a big one—labor.

Labor The management of the labor function will make or break a restaurant. Most restaurants have two types of positions: managerial and supervisory (known in the United States as *exempt employees* under federal labor law), and line-level employees (known as *nonexempt employees*). Managers or supervisors, who are paid salaries and cannot earn overtime, are responsible for the overall functioning of the operation, while line-level employees, who are paid by the hour, are on the line doing the cooking, serving, and support functions related to guest service.

Scheduling is the key to controlling labor costs, and this is a challenging and complex job. Managers must schedule the right number of employees (managers and line-level) with the right skill level to match the level of business for the right amount of time or time period. (The complications of scheduling a seasonal ski operation, discussed in Chapter 10, are similar for restaurants.) A well-planned production schedule for kitchen staff and service schedule for the front of the house is crucial to optimizing your labor. To do this, you'll need a clear understanding of the business demands (i.e., forecast) so that you can adjust staffing by day parts, or days of the week depending on expected business levels. Labor is generally considered a fixed expense, since a particular level of staffing can cover a wide range in the number of meals served, and a certain level of staffing is needed just to open the doors.

Benefits In addition to wages, you must pay for benefits, both mandated ones (Social Security, Medicare, unemployment, and disability insurance) and those given by your choice (medical and other insurance, meal allowance, uniform costs or a uniform allowance, day care or dependent care, and paid vacation or sick time). If you find yourself in a competitive labor market, a well-constructed benefits package may give you a hiring advantage.

Direct Operating Expenses There are many variable expenses directly associated with delivering service to guests, such as uniforms, laundry, china, glassware, menus, cleaning supplies, decorations, and kitchen fuel. Other typical expenses include the following:

- *Music and entertainment*: recorded or live music, licensing, or subscription fees;
- *Administrative and general*: usually fixed, consisting of items needed for the operation of the business, but not directly connected to serving guests, such as office supplies, postage, phone, and data processing costs;
- *Marketing and advertising*: the costs of promoting your restaurant, usually variable, such as mailers, coupons, comped meals, and any advertising;
- *Repairs and maintenance*: regular upkeep and repair;
- *Utilities*: costs of fuel, water, waste removal, etc.;
- *Franchise fees or corporate overhead*: fees paid to a home office or franchisor;
- *Occupation expenses*: Expenses like rent, liquor licenses, property and liability insurance, and any payments for equipment rentals. A lease allows a restaurant operator to keep start-up costs low. In most cases a long-term lease [five years or longer] is beneficial for both parties to help control variation in revenue for the property owner and occupation expenses for the restaurant operator. However, some restaurant operators prefer to own the building and the land, to have greater control of their facility. In this case, the restaurant owner is responsible for all of the mortgage payments, and property taxes and fees associated with the building and land, instead of a rent payment. Occasionally, a restaurant operator will own the building but not the real estate. In this case, the owner of the building will pay rent for the land, and property taxes and fees for the value of the building;
- *Depreciation*: Operators are permitted to depreciate the assets they own over time, as a noncash expense against revenue, for tax purposes. The schedule of depreciation applied depends on the type of asset, but it generally reflects the concept that the value of certain already purchased assets diminishes over time;

- *Interest*: payments on debt or lines of credit;
- *Other income or expenses*: income and expenses related to the sale of auxiliary products, such as clothing, equipment, or package goods;
- *Earnings before income tax (EBIT)*: After you subtract all the expenses described here from, your revenue what remains is your profit before income tax.

All of these revenues and expenses show how a restaurant functions.[4] Let's now look at how you compile these figures (and other numbers) into a balance sheet, which is a critical management tool.

BALANCE SHEET

The balance sheet addresses what you own, what you owe, and who you are in business with—at a given time. A balance sheet consists of assets, liabilities, and equity. By definition, your assets are equal to your liabilities plus equity. Let's look at the relationship of these three categories.

Assets

Your assets will consist of both current and long-term holdings. Your current assets will consist of:

- *Cash on hand*. This is the money you have in the bank. You need sufficient cash to cover operating expenses. This can be a struggle for newer restaurants, which require greater amounts of cash to cover operations until they have sufficient cash flow. This often takes up to a year to establish. Your operations should generate a certain amount of cash, and under normal circumstances you should realize a steady, reliable cash flow from operations so that you don't have to rely on outside cash, such as a line of credit.
- *Investment instruments*. Good as it is to have, cash is a nonproductive asset. Thus, you can use short-term, liquid savings instruments (e.g., certificates of deposit, money market) to ensure that your cash is not idle, but is readily available. (We know interest rates are low, but it's still better than stuffing your cash in a mattress.)
- *Accounts receivable*. This money is owed to you in the normal course of business. The trick is to keep receivables as current as possible, ensuring that guests, vendors, or other partners pay promptly. These accounts are short term and should turn over quickly.
- *Inventory*. This describes the products that you have purchased, but have not yet placed in production. As products are transferred into production from

inventory, the cost of the asset moves from the balance sheet inventory line to the cost of goods sold area on the income statement. The balance sheet provides a good reminder that excessive inventory is an unneeded expense that can lead to waste and pilferage, if not properly managed.

In that regard, inventory turnover is an important indicator as to how well your restaurant is using its resources. Inventory turnover rate is calculated by dividing total inventory (per year) by the average inventory. Generally, the higher the inventory turnover rate, the better, although the actual rate depends on your concept. A quick service restaurant's inventory turnover rate, for instance, can be as high as 100 (turned over every 3.65 days), but a table-service restaurant will have much lower inventory turnover rates. Other assets you hold are considered long term and do not turn over often, if at all. We take a more detailed look at inventory management in the accompanying sidebar.

EOQ: A Scientific Approach to Inventory Management

Few tasks are more important than making sure the inventory is managed correctly, because inventory means dollars invested in goods, some of them highly perishable. Keeping track of inventory requires taking a regular physical inventory (at least monthly or quarterly). Too often, this is left to a junior staff member. Although you always need sufficient, high-quality stock, the less money tied up in inventory, the lower your operating costs. Because of the importance of inventory management, we suggest an approach called economic order quantity (EOQ).

Let's take a look at how much money can be tied up in inventory. The turnover rate is total inventory (per year) divided by the average inventory, which is calculated by adding inventory at the beginning of the period (say, the first of the month) and the inventory at the end, and dividing it by two [(Beginning Inventory + Ending Inventory) / 2]. Thus, if your restaurant generates $3 million in annual revenue, and you have a COGS of 28 percent, you're buying about $840,000 worth of goods each year. If you have a table-service restaurant with an inventory turnover rate of 35, you have about $24,000 tied up in inventory at all times.

(continued)

(continued)

Increasing your inventory turnover rate not only reduces money tied up in your operations, but also decreases the space you need for storage and the chance that products will spoil or be pilfered. If a restaurant fails to forecast its anticipated business volume, managers will be forced to do a lot of expensive last minute ordering. Or, worse, the restaurant runs out of inventory, resulting in lost sales opportunities and disappointed guests.

Economic Order Quantity

One effective purchasing approach is to use EOQ to strike an appropriate balance between order frequency and the cost of keeping inventory on hand. Say that you are operating a pizza restaurant that uses large quantities of tomato sauce. Each time you place an order for a shipment of this sauce, your restaurant incurs the usual expenses connected with ordering and receiving. Placing fewer orders lowers those expenses, but a large order will increase your inventory costs. So, here's how to strike the balance between too few or too many orders.

A simple calculation and table will help you determine the optimum number of cases to order. Let's use the numbers given below, as an example.

Annual Usage (U) = 500 cases (to be ordered in increments of 10 cases)

Case Cost (C) = $96

Acquisition Cost (A) = $25

Annual Inventory Carrying Costs (I) = 12%

Inventory Carrying Costs (ICC) = $\dfrac{10 \times \$96 \times 0.12}{2}$ = $57.60

Acquisition Cost = 50 × $25 = $1,250

Total Cost: $1,250 + $57.60 = $1,307.60

As you can see from the "total cost" cells in Table 16.1, the optimal, or EOQ, lies between 40 and 60 cases. Below 40 and above 60, the total costs increase rapidly. Instead of calculating acquisition cost and inventory carrying cost for each increment, you can use the following

Table 16.1
Hypothetical Cost of Ordering and Inventory
for Tomato Sauce

Order Quantity	Acquisition Cost	ICC	Total Cost
10	$1,250.00	$57.60	$1,307.60
20	$625.00	$115.20	$740.20
30	$416.67	$172.80	$589.47
40	$312.50	$230.40	$542.90
50	$250.00	$288.00	$538.00
60	$208.33	$345.60	$553.93
70	$178.57	$403.20	$581.77
80	$156.25	$460.80	$617.05
90	$138.89	$518.40	$657.29
100	$125.00	$576.00	$701.00

formula for EOQ. Note: In Table 16.1 to calculate the ICC, you use 2 in the denominator to approximate the average inventory which would be beginning inventory less ending inventory divided by 2.

The sample EOQ graph in Figure 16.1 shows the decrease in ordering cost as the order size increases and, at the same time, shows how inventory carrying costs increase as order size increases.

Figure 16.1
Sample EOQ Graph

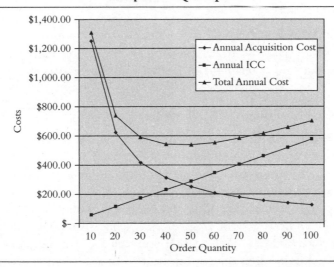

(continued)

(continued)

Although this EOQ example demonstrates the financial effects of inventory and ordering management, we must note that the EOQ approach has its limitations. For example, we assume that ordered items are shelf stable and that demand is relatively level. Furthermore, we assume little or no price fluctuation, sufficient storage space, and enough capital to buy in large quantities. The EOQ concept demonstrates the delicate balance between the cost of too much inventory and the expense of ordering too frequently.

- *Investments in subsidiary companies.* Sometimes operators own shares in other businesses or subsidiaries. The book value of these shares is treated as an asset, for which gains are realized only when sold.
- *Building and equipment.* Finally, any equipment, furniture and fixtures, owned buildings and land, and leased assets are recorded on the balance sheet at book value. Some assets are depreciated, which will affect their value upon replacement.

Liabilities

Your liabilities will consist of both current and long-term debt. Your current liabilities will consist of:

- *Accounts payable*: obligations to the people with whom you do business.
- *Notes payable and other credit*: formal debt obligation that you have undertaken, like a short-term line or credit, a mortgage, or a lease.

A Final Note on Financial Statements

We've presented detailed discussions about the income statement and balance sheet to show how the functioning of a restaurant is documented and recorded. The balance sheet also has an equity section that outlines the ownership characteristics of a business.

Creating and serving great food and beverages is the start to a successful business, but without a solid grasp of the financial implications of all elements in a restaurant, it is unlikely that you will succeed. Let's examine how to use your understanding of your business to be a viable competitor in your market.

A Restaurant Dream

Say that you just received a call from a commercial real estate agent offering you a site that might bring you closer to your dream of opening a restaurant. But you have to work out the finances. The rent alone is $24,000 per month. You will also have to pay for insurance, taxes, and trash removal, amounting to another $ 3,000 per month. Approximately 3,500 square feet of the space can be used for food production (the kitchen and back of the house), the seating area, and the take-out window. Another 1,000 square feet can be dedicated to storage, office space, and other support functions.

So, let's do a quick estimation to help you to assess the feasibility of your restaurant dream. Industry standards suggest that prime restaurant locations dedicate approximately 12 percent of total sales revenues toward rent (including property taxes, insurance, and trash removal). Good locations require about 10 percent of revenue, and standard locations about 8 percent.

You judge that your potential restaurant site is good but not prime, because it's at a busy intersection in a college town. Thus, you assume that dedicating 10 percent of total revenue toward rent seems justified. On that basis, you know that you need to generate about $3,250,000 per year in total revenue to make your restaurant economically feasible (i.e., to cover all of your expenses and still make some fair profit).

Scanning the current competition, a rough calculation puts the average check (lunch and dinner combined) at $12. For ease of calculation you are assuming daily operating hours are from 11:00 AM to 11:00 PM. This means that you need to sell 270,000 meals per year, or about 740 per day. This would require a steady stream of 61 patrons per hour, or about one per minute, on average. You now have to decide if this is realistic.

Although hungry students like to eat out a lot, you must factor in semester breaks. In a true college town, summer business drops off significantly and dies entirely during the winter break. When all those students leave town, you are mostly depending on college professors (a notoriously thrifty bunch) and university staff (not highly paid). This means that you have roughly nine months of the year—perhaps 40 weeks at most—to generate all the revenue to make this restaurant successful. Based on these serious doubts, you wisely tell your real

(continued)

(continued)

estate agent you are putting your restaurant dream on ice until you find a less expensive location.

Just as a closing note, this scenario is not entirely invented. Sadly, we have seen would-be restaurateurs take this plunge without doing the math. The result has been the failure of numerous delightful restaurant concepts.

How Is My Operation Doing?

Now that you have looked at a restaurant's financial aspects, let's look at the key question of how your operation is doing. The first response to this question is: "Compared to what?"

So, you understand how your business operates, you have the data properly recorded, and you understand what it means. The next step is to compare your performance over time, from day to day, week to week, month to month, and year to year. But that is not enough. You also need to be able to benchmark your performance against both direct and indirect competitors. Direct competitors are restaurants similar to yours, say, Applebee's, TGI Friday's, and Chili's, if you're running a midrange casual-dining restaurant. Although each has a distinct concept, many guests might consider them to be interchangeable, since their price points are similar. Likewise, customers might view quick-service operators Wendy's, McDonald's, and Burger King as relatively interchangeable. Even fine-dining steakhouses have direct competitors who are similar. Direct competition is relatively straightforward, and operators actively compete for market share with their direct competition. Operators who do a better job delivering on the food, service, and environment will reap the rewards of a loyal, growing guest base.

Indirect competition is any business that provides consumers with an alternative to dining at your restaurant. The basic premise of indirect competition is that if you are not eating in my restaurant, you are eating somewhere else. Thus, determining competitors is complicated. For mid-scale casual operators, that "somewhere" could be a grocery store that offers prepared foods or an eating area, a fine dining or upscale casual restaurant, or a quick service or fast casual restaurant. Those are just the alternatives for food away from home, since your potential guests could decide to fire up the grill and eat at home. Since you can't do much about indirect competition, your best plan is to be the best among your direct competitors and hope that your offerings are special enough to grab meals from your indirect competition occasionally.

In conclusion, to succeed you need to understand your operation, your guests, and your marketplace. In addition to being in tune with your immediate surroundings, you should also take advantage of industry data that are available to you. Each year the National Restaurant Association, in conjunction with consulting firm Deloitte, publishes the annual *Restaurant Industry Operations Report*. This report contains data that summarize the state of the restaurant industry and provides an analysis of restaurants in the limited and full-service domains separated by check average. This benchmark data offers additional insight to help you better understand how you are doing. Note carefully that the focus is on the numbers.

NOTES

1. H. G. Parsa, J. T. Self, D. Njite, and T. King, "Why Restaurants Fail," *Cornell Hotel and Restaurant Administration Quarterly* 46(3) (2005): 304–322.
2. National Restaurant Association and Deloitte & Touche, *Uniform Systems of Accounts,* 7th revised ed. (Washington, DC: National Restaurant Association, 1996).
3. Adapted from J. Ninemeier, *Planning and Control for Food and Beverage Operations*, 3rd ed. (East Lansing, MI: Educational Institute of the American Hotel and Motel Association, 1995), 132.
4. See National Restaurant Association and Deloitte, "Restaurant Industry Operations Report: 2010 Edition," http://www.restaurant.org/esdpdf/OpsReport2010.pdf. (accessed February 7, 2011).

PART III

SUCCESS AS A REAL ESTATE AND BUSINESS OWNER

CHAPTER 17

HOSPITALITY PROPERTY OWNERSHIP
WHERE YOU FIT IN

JACK B. CORGEL, ROBERT MANDELBAUM, and
R. MARK WOODWORTH

Hotel or restaurant properties, often measured by the number of rooms or seats therein, are the foundation of the hospitality industry. Owners often do not operate hotel properties, as management companies have become nearly essential for large and upscale assets. Restaurant owners are more likely to operate their own properties, although many owners have become franchisees of large organizations. If you participate as a professional in the hospitality industry, you need to be knowledgeable about who owns hotels and restaurants and become familiar with the overall industry structure. In this chapter we discuss ownership structures and what it means to be an owner, and we provide you with a detailed look at the relationships between owners, managers, and franchisors.

Sizing Up the Hospitality Industry

In other chapters, you have read that the hospitality industry is large. Let's take a look at how large is large, in terms of the number of properties. According to the 2009 American Hotel and Lodging Association (AH&LA) Lodging Industry Profile, as of December 31, 2008, there were 49,505 hotels

Note: The authors appreciate the work of Andrew Bekkevold, a student at the Cornell School of Hotel Administration, who provided invaluable research assistance for this chapter.

Figure 17.1
Sizing Up the U.S. Hotel Industry

Properties by Location

By Location	Property	Rooms
Urban	4,804	741,942
Suburban	17,312	1,726,349
Airport	2,189	302,740
Interstate	7,303	493,831
Resort	3,790	595,263
Small Metro/Town	15,402	901,970

Properties by Average Daily Rate

By Rate	Property	Rooms
Under $30	832	56,008
$30–$44.99	7,032	430,790
$45–$59.99	15,276	952,019
$60–$85	13,965	1,195,277
Over $85	13,695	2,128,051

Properties by Room Count

By Size	Property	Rooms
Under 75 rooms	28,224	1,213,907
75–149 rooms	16,545	1,742,398
150–299 rooms	4,385	878,066
300–500 rooms	1,119	417,510
Over 500 rooms	527	510,214

Source: Reproduced by permission from American Hotel & Lodging Association, 2010 Lodging Industry Profile (2009 data).

in the United States offering 4,626,348 guest rooms.[1] Figure 17.1 presents the distribution of these hotels and rooms by location, average daily room rates, and size (room count) categories.

According to the 2010 *Restaurant Industry Overview* published by the National Restaurant Association, total sales in the United States are forecast to be $580 billion in 2010.[2] In total, there are 945,000 restaurants in the United States that employ 12.7 million people. See Figure 17.2 for a summary of the restaurant industry's segments. Forty-nine percent of the dollars spent by Americans to purchase food and beverages are spent in restaurants.

Figure 17.2
Sizing Up the U.S. Restaurant Industry

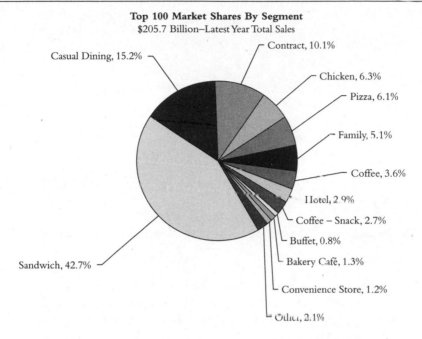

Top 100 Market Shares By Segment
$205.7 Billion–Latest Year Total Sales

Contract, 10.1%

Casual Dining, 15.2%

Chicken, 6.3%

Pizza, 6.1%

Family, 5.1%

Coffee, 3.6%

Hotel, 2.9%

Coffee – Snack, 2.7%

Buffet, 0.8%

Bakery Café, 1.3%

Sandwich, 42.7%

Convenience Store, 1.2%

Other, 2.1%

Source: Reproduced by permission from Nation's Restaurant News, 2010 Top 100 Report.

WHAT IT MEANS TO BE AN OWNER

Ownership means you have the rights to personal and real property, usually called real estate. You have both rights to the physical property itself and legal rights that usually give you control over the space associated with your property—at the surface, above it, and below it, as shown in Figure 17.3. Air rights extend upward until the public "fly-over" space is reached at approximately 1,000 feet. Subsurface and mineral rights vary by legal jurisdiction, but generally run to the center of the earth in a wedge shape. In practice, owners of these rights often subdivide and separately sell the parts to realize more value from their property. Innovators constantly find creative ways to subdivide physical property rights. Several decades ago, for instance, owners began subdividing and selling separate time periods during which individual owners could control physical property rights. Through this concept, known as time-share or interval ownership, many people own a piece of a hotel or resort property.

Figure 17.3
Physical Property Rights of Real Estate Owners

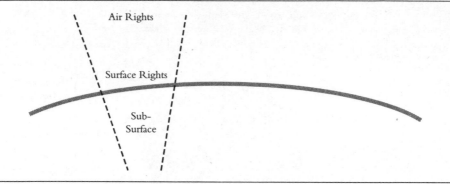

The legal property rights of owners come in the following three basic forms:

1. *Exclusive possession and control.* As holder of the property, you have the right to admit or exclude others and collect damage for trespassing (subject to local laws), and you may use the property as collateral for borrowing.
2. *Quiet enjoyment.* When the title to your property is registered, you do not have to defend yourself from claims of unregistered parties. So your rent and sale proceeds cannot be claimed by other parties.
3. *Rights of disposition.* Owners can freely transfer their property or carve out ownership interests (subject to laws against discrimination and laws regulating foreign ownership).

WHY YOU WOULD WANT TO OWN A HOTEL

There are many reasons why you may want to own property. In this chapter, we assume that you own or are considering owning a hospitality business and related real estate for their cash flow potential. We use the term *cash flows* (instead of *profits*), which are funds you realize while you hold the real estate, and when you sell the hospitality business and real estate. In this context, growing the business means increasing operating cash flows, because these enhance the value of both your business and real estate. Also, we differentiate between cash flows from business operations and rent, which comes from use of the real estate by other parties.

Forms of Ownership

If you'd like to become a hotel property owner, your first decision is the form of ownership. This involves weighing a variety of financial and nonfinancial considerations, including control over the assets, liability for claims against the assets, flexibility of engaging in activities, ease of transferability of the assets, privacy, and taxes. As we examine the common forms of hospitality ownership used in the United States, we discuss the advantages and disadvantages of each. As shown in Figure 17.4, the forms are sole proprietorship, partnership, limited liability companies, and corporations.

- *Proprietorship.* In a sole (or individual) proprietorship one person owns the real estate, runs the business, or both. A chief advantage of this structure in the United States is that the business can generate cash flows for the owner, but generate losses for tax purposes due to the

Figure 17.4
Analysis of Ownership Forms

	Ownership Form Comparison Summary						
Investor Objective	Sole Ownership	C-Corporation	S-Corporation	General Partnership	Limited Partnership	REIT	Limited Liability Company
Avoid double taxation	High	Low	High	High	High	High	High
Pass-through tax losses	High	Low	Medium	High	High	Low	High
Limited Liability	Low	High	High	Low	High	High	High
Avoidance of management responsibility	Low	High	High	Low	High	High	High
Ease of transfer of interest	High	High	High	Low	Low	High	Medium
Flexibility in allocating tax losses	Low	Low	Low	Low	High	Low	Low
Flexibility of Activities	High	High	High	High	High	Low	High
Control by Owners	High	Low	High	High	Low	Low	High
Ability to Diversify	Low	High	Medium	Low	Medium	High	Medium
Privacy	High	Low	Medium	Medium	Low	Low	Medium

Note: High means favorable to owners.

deduction of noncash depreciation. Sole proprietors in many instances can apply tax losses incurred by their business to offset taxes on certain other streams of income (e.g., dividends from stock investments). You also have full rein to operate your business, and your business affairs are private from others. Sole proprietorship, however, carries the substantial disadvantage of full responsibility for all of the business's liabilities. This means that assets not involved in the business may be at risk in connection with the business's liabilities. Sole proprietorships also may encounter difficulty in raising capital from lenders, since banks are usually careful about financing small business owners. As a sole proprietor you may find yourself relying on personal savings, loans from family and friends, and home equity loans for financing.

- *Partnerships.* A partnership involves more than one individual collectively owning and managing a business or real estate. The most common forms of partnership are general partnerships and limited partnerships. General partnerships have many of the same characteristics as sole proprietorships, and thus can be thought of as combinations of sole proprietors, although they have the distinct advantage of greater potential for raising capital.
  - ○ Limited partnerships usually have a single general partner who operates the business or real estate and any number of limited partners who, according to the law, cannot become involved in management. Instead they invest money and remain passive. This arrangement is depicted in Figure 17.5. The general partner also bears all responsibility for

Figure 17.5
Limited Partnership Ownership Structure

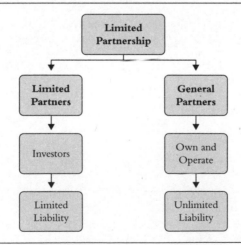

partnership liabilities, while the limited partners are not liable for partnership debts and other liabilities (beyond their investment). Although partnerships file a tax return in the United States, the partnership itself pays no tax. Instead, like sole proprietors, all profits and losses flow through to each individual partner according to their ownership stake. Consequently, partnership provides the opportunity to use tax losses against other income, as discussed previously.

- *Limited Liability Companies (LLCs).* – Now the most popular U.S. business structure, LLCs first became available to U.S. owners in 1977. By fusing partnership and corporate structures, the LLC captures the benefits of each. Overall, LLCs offer the most advantageous tax features for owners of any legal structure. Owners receive the same protection against liability that a corporation provides, but the LLC still does not pay taxes. Like partnerships, profits and losses transfer to the owners in LLCs, and owners list profits and losses on their personal tax returns. LLCs may have an unlimited number of shareholders, all of whom have the opportunity to fully partake in management.

- *Corporations.* Corporations in the United States typically are organized either as C corporations or S corporations. Both entities can operate in perpetuity. Shareholders usually remain independent from the corporation management in both forms, and thus carry no liability beyond the value of their ownership stake. The largest corporations are C corporations. Because of the ease with which ownership shares may be transferred, C corporations are readily able to raise capital, often through public sale of common and preferred stock. One substantial disadvantage for C corporations is that both the corporate profits and the dividends received by shareholders are taxed.

  o The much smaller S corporations are limited to no more than 75 stockholders. In this structure, unlike the C corporation, taxes are due only on dividends paid to shareholders (and not on corporate income). Shareholders retain the advantage of using losses from the business to offset income from other sources. Because of their small size, S corporations often struggle to raise capital. Due to complicated rules, S corporations are not favorable for real estate ownership.

OWNERSHIP IN THE HOSPITALITY INDUSTRY

Tracking ownership in an industry dominated by private businesses can be a formidable task, especially given the industry's many different ownership arrangements. A typical arrangement for restaurants is for one company to own the business and rent the real estate from another. In contrast, few hotels in the

United States are leased, as occurs with fairly high frequency in Europe and other parts of the world. Instead, if the real estate owners do not also operate the hotel, that company will contract with a management firm to operate the business. These contractual arrangements have evolved to maximize the potential returns for both parties' lodging investments. We talk more about management contracts later, but first let's look at who owns lodging and restaurant properties.

Hotel Ownership

As shown in Figure 17.6, individuals, partnerships, and LLCs own the overwhelming majority of the full-service and limited-service hotels in the United States. Only about 10 percent of these properties are owned by

Figure 17.6
U.S. Hotel Ownership Profiles

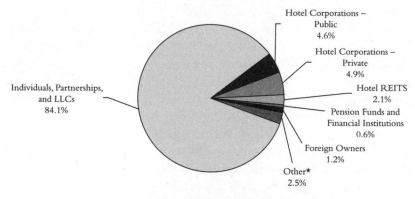

Panel A: Ownership of Full-Service Properties

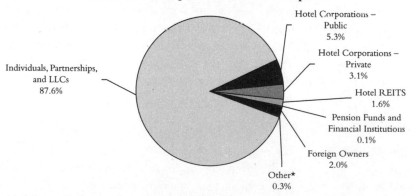

Panel B: Ownership of Limited-Service Properties

* Includes non-hotel corporations, universities, and government.
Source: Reproduced by permission from PKF Hospitality Research.

corporate entities. Among well-known hotel corporations, such as Marriott and Choice, ownership ranges from none at all (i.e., Choice) to 100 percent (i.e., Extended Stay America). While some companies specialize in either management or franchising, many of the large publicly traded companies do both.

Hotel Ownership Outside the United States Ownership structures found in other countries are generally comparable to those found in the United States. The factors that dictate the appeal or popularity of one ownership type over another include maturity of the industry in that country, land availability, legal and tax structures, political environment, and level of governmental regulation.

China, for example, only began to open its borders to substantial international development in late 2001. By 2005, more than half of all hotel properties in the country were still owned and operated by a government entity. This percentage will continue to decline as greater levels of foreign investment, most notably among the global hotel companies, finds its way into the market.

Restaurant Ownership

The National Restaurant Association (NRA) estimates that approximately 45 percent of all restaurants are either sole proprietorships or partnerships, and that three of four restaurants are single-unit operations. Of the approximately 945,000 restaurants in the United States in 2009, 46.7 percent were chain affiliated. Of these chains, McDonald's Corporation is the single largest restaurant firm with approximately 14,000 restaurants in the United States (88.7 percent franchised) and a total of 32,000 restaurants serving more than 60 million people per day in 117 countries around the world.

Similar to the lodging industry, most large restaurant companies both own and franchise restaurants. An exception is Darden Corporation, the world's largest full-service restaurant company with annual sales in 2009 of more than $7 billion. Through subsidiaries, Darden owns and operates (but does not franchise) 1,800 Red Lobster, Olive Garden, LongHorn Steakhouse, The Capital Grille, Bahama Breeze, and Seasons 52 restaurants in North America, employs approximately 180,000 people, and serves 400 million meals annually.

Non-U.S. Restaurant Ownership Restaurant ownership structures found outside the United States are generally comparable to those found in the United States. Chain restaurants have a much smaller presence in international markets than in the United States. The factors that dictate the appeal or popularity of one ownership type over another are the same as for hotels.

WHAT TO CONSIDER IF YOU WANT TO BECOME AN OWNER

Before you become a hotel or restaurant owner, you need to determine what type of property you desire. As we discuss in the rest of this chapter, the baseline criteria you'll want to establish for hotel and restaurant projects are as follows:

- Type of facility
- Location
- Operating structure
- Investment required
- Source(s) of capital

The sections that follow describe facility type, location differences, and common operating structures.

Start-ups in hospitality often find their initial capital from personal funds, or investments from friends and family and small groups of high-net-worth individuals. Because you need a track record to attract debt financing and equity to a hospitality opportunity, becoming an owner frequently necessitates that the project sponsor have hands on experience, or has contractually secured the services of someone who does (notably, a hotel management firm).

Facility Types—How Hotels Are Classified

Unlike other countries, which have government-defined classification systems, the U.S. hotel industry has no uniform method for segmenting hotels. Different analysts apply different classifications, depending upon the analyst's needs. Let's look at these classification systems together with examples of hotels in each category, whenever possible.

Location You can organize hotels by location to compare and contrast performance differences based on a geographical business model (see Figure 17.7). Significant events that affect travel within the country, such as air capacity constraints and rapid rises in gas prices, influence hotel performance depending on location.

Figure 17.7
Hotel Industry Classification by Location

Airport	Hotels adjacent to or nearby an airport. Some hotels are attached to the terminal. Hotel typically provides complimentary transportation to the terminal. Properties cater to airline crews, passengers on layover, and travelers entering or leaving the market on early or late flights.
City center	Hotels located in the central business district of the nation's major metropolitan areas, not those in suburban areas or small cities. Typically, high-rise structures. Commercial and convention oriented.
Resort	Hotels located in destinations that typically attract leisure travelers. Hotels can be resort facilities, but also could be all suite, full service, or limited service.
Suburban	Hotels located in suburban areas of metropolitan area. Frequently found near business parks. Typically accommodate business travelers and friends or relatives visiting local residents.
Highway	Hotels located along interstate or major U.S. highways. Characterized by short stays. Oriented toward either leisure or commercial travelers in midtrip. Dominated by limited-service hotels.
Rural	Hotels located in remote, low-density, nonresort areas. Dominated by small, limited-service hotels.

Source: Reproduced by permission from PKF Hospitality Research.

Figure 17.8
Hotel Industry Classification by Market Orientation

Classification	Description
Commercial	Hotels oriented toward business travelers. Typically a full-service hotel that offers business support services (i.e., fax, Internet access).
Leisure	Hotels oriented toward individuals or families visiting friends and relatives, tourists, seniors, and tour groups. The limited and full-service hotels in this category tend to be economically priced. Upscale and midscale resorts also fall into this category.
Convention	Larger hotels that typically contain several hundred rooms and significant meeting space. Conference centers are also included in this category and accommodate smaller-sized meetings.
Residential	Nontransient hotels that accommodate permanent residents.

Source: Reproduced by permission from PKF Hospitality Research.

Market Orientation Another way to classify hotels is by the primary type of guest staying at the property (Figure 17.8). This classification is useful because each demand segment exhibits different seasonal and pricing characteristics, as well as response to varying economic environments. Guest orientation will also dictate the facilities and services offered at a property.

Property Operations Your hotel's mix of facilities and services influences both operating expenses and revenue streams. Accordingly, hotels can be classified by the facilities and services they offer to guests (Figure 17.9). This classification is most frequently used by owners and operators when making financial performance comparisons.

Figure 17.9
Hotel Industry Classification by Facilities and Services

Classification	Description	Chain-Affiliated Property Examples
Full-Service	Hotels that provide a wide variety of facilities and amenities, including food and beverage outlets, meeting rooms, and recreational facilities.	Hilton Hotels Marriott Holiday Inn
Limited-Service	Hotels that provide only some of the facilities and amenities of a full-service property. No food and beverage service for sale. Complimentary food and beverages may be provided to guests.	Hampton Inn Motel 6 Fairfield Inn
Resort	Hotels, typically located in a rural or isolated location, with special and extensive recreational facilities.	Westin Innisbrook Resort Hilton Waikoloa Village Hyatt Regency at Gainey Ranch
Convention	A hotel which provides facilities and services geared to meet the needs of large group and association meetings and trade shows. Maybe contain their own proprietary meeting/banquet space, or be attached to a convention center.	Marriott Marquis Hilton Anatole Hotel Hyatt Regency McCormick Place
Conference Center	A hotel where 60 percent or more of total occupancy is generated by conferences. Package pricing typically includes guest room, meeting rooms, food, beverage, and convention services.	Wyndham Peachtree Conference Center Marriott Hickory Ridge Conference Center Doubletree Hotel and Executive Meeting Center
All-Suite	A hotel in which all rooms have separate, but not necessarily physically divided sleeping and living areas.	Embassy Suites SpringHill Suites Comfort Suites
Extended-Stay	Hotels oriented toward guest stays of five nights or more. Guest rooms contain more residential equipment and amenities than standard hotels. Pricing is offered on a weekly basis.	Residence Inn Studio Plus Candlewood Hotels
Boutique	Typically small to mid-sized hotels located in historical structures in urban areas. Characterized by highly stylized or themed furniture, fixtures, service, and F&B outlets.	W Hotel Kimpton aLoft

Source: Reproduced by permission from PKF Hospitality Research.

Price Tier Hotels are often classified according to their average daily room rate (ADR) relative to competitors (Figure 17.10). Because room rates vary across markets, this segmentation follows a strict percentage distribution in each market. For example, a Holiday Inn may be classified as an upscale hotel in a moderate-priced market, but as a midpriced property in a more expensive market. Consumers often rely on price when choosing lodging, and price tier segmentation can serve as a proxy for the quality of a hotel's facilities, services, and amenities relative to other hotels in the market.

Chain Scale and Affiliation A hotel's brand affiliation usually indicates a certain quality level, so Smith Travel Research (STR) developed a classification system for chain-affiliated hotels that places all of a brand's properties in a particular chain scale (or market segment). While this system does lead to some discrepancies, it is the most frequently used classification system for analyzing hotel performance (Figure 17.11). One complication is that

Figure 17.10
Hotel Industry Classification by Price Tiers

Classification	Description	Chain Examples
Budget	The lowest 20% of properties in each market by average room rate. Mostly populated by limited-service hotels.	Motel 6 (all locations) EconoLodge (all locations) Thriftlodge (all locations)
Economy	The next 20% of properties in a market by average room rate. Mostly populated with limited-service hotels.	Quality Inn (Manhattan) Super 8 (most locations) Travelodge (most locations)
Mid-Price	The middle 30% of properties in each market by average room rate. Populated with both limited- and full-service hotels.	Quality Inn (Louisville) Doubletree (Buckhead, Atlanta) Courtyard by Marriott (Chicago)
Upscale	The next 15% of properties in each market by average room rate. Populated with full-service hotels.	Marriott Marquis (Manhattan) Hilton Lincoln Center (Dallas) Courtyard by Marriott (Little Rock)
Luxury	The top 15% of properties in each market by average room rate.	Ritz-Carlton (all locations) Four Seasons (all locations) Marriott Convention Center (Memphis)

Source: Reproduced by permission from STR, PKF Hospitality Research.

Figure 17.11
Hotel Industry Classification by Chain Scale

Classification	Description	Chain-Affiliated Property Examples
Luxury	The highest quality of services, amenities, furniture, and fixtures. Multiple food and beverage outlets. 24-hour room service. Concierge service. Typically oriented toward high-end leisure and executive commercial travelers.	Four Seasons Fairmont Ritz-Carlton
Upper-Upscale	A very high quality of services, amenities, furniture, and fixtures. Multiple food and beverage outlets. May have 24-hour room service and concierge service. Typically oriented toward commercial and convention travelers.	Hilton Hyatt Marriott
Upscale	A high quality of services, amenities, furniture, and fixtures. May offer extensive, or limited, food and beverage outlets and concierge service. Typically oriented toward commercial, leisure, and convention travelers.	Doubletree Residence Inns Courtyard by Marriott
Midscale with F&B	Average quality of services, amenities, furniture, and fixtures. Usually offers one restaurant and only lounge. May offer room service. Oriented toward commercial and leisure travelers.	Best Western Ramada Holiday Inn
Midscale without F&B	Average quality of services, amenities, furniture, and fixtures. Does not offer food and beverage service for sale. Typically oriented toward commercial and leisure travelers.	Comfort Inn LaQuinta Hampton Inn
Economy	Lowest quality of furniture and fixtures. Does not offer food and beverage service for sale. Typically oriented toward rate-sensitive commercial and leisure travelers.	EconoLodge Days Inn Extended-Stay America

Source: Reproduced by permission from STR, PKF Hospitality Research.

some brands are not exactly chains. Best Western, for instance, is a membership affiliate group. STR classifies Best Western as "midscale with food and beverage," but not all Best Western hotels offer food and beverage service. Certain organizations, notably, Forbes and AAA, have developed objective consumer-oriented hotel and restaurant rating systems. Online booking sites also rate hotels based on their quality, but those ratings can be subjective.

Restaurant Classifications

Like hotel classification systems, those used to segment restaurants often depend on the analyst's purposes. Here is a description of the various restaurant classification approaches.

Average Check The average check (calculated by dividing sales revenue by number of diners) can be used as an indicator of management's desire to position the restaurant in the marketplace. In general, the higher the average check, the greater the level of service and food quality.[3]

Affiliation The NRA divides U.S. restaurants into single-unit (independent) and multiple-unit operations, and the multiunit firms are further divided into company operated and franchised restaurants. As we said, some franchisors also own and operate some of their restaurants. Franchise companies typically provide owners with operating manuals, national and regional marketing support, and preferred vendor pricing. In return, franchisees are expected to adhere to brand standards for appearance and service.

Ownership U.S. restaurants can be segmented according to whether they are owned by individuals, partnerships, or corporations, and those corporations may be public or private.

Location Type A restaurant's location influences the types of patron, menu offerings, levels of service, and pricing. The NRA applies four location categories: hotel, shopping center or mall, sole occupant (stand-alone), and other.

Size You can measure the size of U.S. restaurants by the number of seats or square footage of the operation.[4] The number of patrons the restaurant can serve depends on the number of seats, and the square footage dictates such expenses as utility and cleaning costs, plus the initial development costs. You can divide the number of covers served or revenue by either the number of seats or square footage to determine utilization efficiency.

Menu Themes Consumers often differentiate restaurants according to their menu theme or primary orientation. A particular menu theme says little about quality and pricing, so operators need to be careful when comparing their operations to others in what seems to be the same segment. Figure 17.12 shows the menu themes listed by the NRA.

Figure 17.12
Restaurant Industry Classification by Menu Theme

Restaurant Classifications by Menu Theme
Hamburger
Steak/Seafood
Chicken
Pizza
Sandwiches/Subs/Deli
American (varied)
Mexican
Italian
Asian
Other

Figure 17.13
Service Level and Menu Classifications of Standard and Poor's

Full-Service	Example
Casual Dining	Applebee's, Chili's, Olive Garden, Red Lobster, Outback
Family Restaurants	IHOP, Denny's, Cracker Barrel
Grill/Buffet Restaurants	Golden Corral, Ryan's
Fast Food	
Sandwich	McDonald's, Subway, Burger King, Taco Bell
Pizza	Pizza Hut, Domino's, Papa John's, Little Caesar's
Chicken	Chick-fil-A, Popeye's, Church's
Other Specialty	Starbucks, Dunkin' Donuts, Baskin-Robbins, Krispy Kreme

Service Level Standard and Poor's has developed the segmentation scheme shown in Figure 17.13 to evaluate publicly owned restaurant companies. This approach combines service level and menu theme.

OWNERSHIP STRUCTURE OF THE HOSPITALITY INDUSTRY

We've mentioned the mixed ownership arrangements in the hotel and restaurant industry. In some cases, a single firm owns and operates all aspects of its business. But in many other cases, the owner contracts with one or more entities to manage the operations, manage the brand, and even manage the value of the asset itself. In the remainder of this chapter, we examine these structures in detail. The following four types of entities constitute the ownership and operating structure for most hospitality properties.

- *Owner.* The entity that holds legal title to the real estate.
- *Lender.* The entity that provides debt capital to finance the acquisition of and improvements to the property. To gain this financing the owner signs a mortgage contract that makes the real estate collateral for loans.
- *Operator or Manager.* The management firm is charged with day-to-day oversight of the lodging and related business conducted at the property, under a management contract. An asset manager also may be involved as an agent of the owner with responsibilities such as hiring and monitoring the operator and managing property renovations.
- *Franchisor.* While many hotel and restaurant properties are independent, an increasing number are affiliated with a chain or brand, usually through a national or regional franchise. Through a franchise contract, an independent businessperson agrees to operate a hotel or restaurant according to the policies and regulations established by the franchisor. In exchange, that business can use the brand's name and trade press.

Let's look at the economic interests of each of these partners:

- *Owner.* As owner, you would receive cash flow from your property, net of all fixed and operating expenses, including management fees, affiliation fees, and mortgage payments. When you sell the property, you would receive the proceeds of that sale, net of all debts (assuming the asset has appreciated in value). You might also share some of that appreciation with your management firm, depending on the terms of your management contract. You can read more about the typical terms of these contracts in Chapter 19.
- *Lender.* The lender receives a regular payment from the owner as outlined in the mortgage contract. The mortgage payment, which could be fixed or variable, includes interest and principal, according to the terms of the loan.
- *Operator or Manager.* Although management contracts have many provisions, the operator typically receives a base management fee plus an incentive fee tied to the operation's profitability. The economic interest of the operator terminates at the end of the management contract period, at other times under the contract provisions, or sometimes upon sale of the asset.
- *Franchisor.* In consideration for the owners' use of the brand name and operating system, the franchisor typically receives a percentage of sales, reservation fees for hotels, and reimbursement for other services provided after the owner pays a one-time initiation fee.

Hotel and Restaurant Ownership Structures

Next, let's look at the five ownership and operating structures that have become common in the hotel industry and the four similar structures in the restaurant business. First, we list the structures and then we discuss their benefits and drawbacks. We note that most lenders require hotel owners to have a chain affiliation in order to qualify for a loan. So hotels are heavily represented by chains. In contrast, independent ownership continues to be the most common structure in the restaurant industry. As with hotels, lenders view restaurants with a brand affiliation as a better risk, and chain affiliation increases the chances that a would-be restaurateur will get a loan. Keeping in mind that lenders influence properties' operating structures, the common ownership and operating structures of the U.S. hospitality industry are as follows:

Structure 1 (Figure 17.14): Owner also is the hotel or restaurant manager, but contracts with a franchise company for an affiliation.

Structure 2 (Figure17.15): Owner contracts with a management firm that has its own brand name and so signs two contracts with one entity for the two business services. Hotel examples include Marriott, Hyatt, and Hilton; for restaurants, this might be Myriad Restaurant Group.

Structure 3 (Figure 17.16): Owner is the manager and has its own affiliation (i.e., company owned, managed, affiliated property).

Structure 4 (Figure 17.17): The owner remains independent and manages the property. Hotels sometimes hire an independent management company, but independent restaurant owners rarely do so.

Structure 5 (Figure17.18): In an arrangement used by hotels but not restaurants, the owner contracts with a management company to operate

Figure 17.14
Structure 1 among Owners, Managers, Brands, and Capital Sources

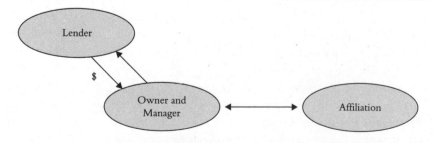

Source: Reproduced by permission from PKF Hospitality Research.

Figure 17.15
Structure 2 among Owner, Manager, Brands and Capital Source

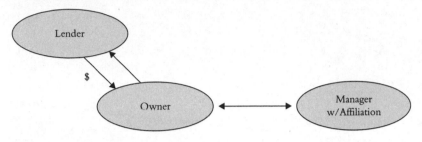

Source: Reproduced by permission from PKF Hospitality Research.

Figure 17.16
Structure 3 among Owners, Managers, Brands, and Capital Sources

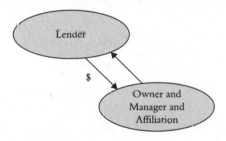

Source: Reproduced by permission from PKF Hospitality Research.

Figure 17.17
Structure 4 among Owners, Managers, and Capital Sources

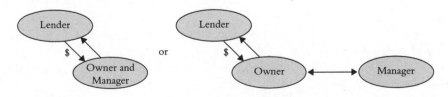

Source: Reproduced by permission from PKF Hospitality Research.

Figure 17.18
Structure 5 among Owners, Managers, Brands, and Capital Sources

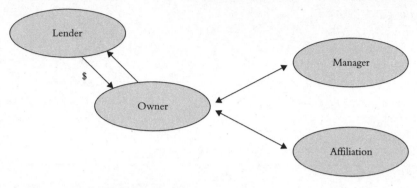

Source: Reproduced by permission from PKF Hospitality Research.

the hotel, and contracts separately with a franchise company for the affiliation. The money partner may also require an asset manager.

ANALYSIS OF STRUCTURES

Structure 1—Owner as Manager, with Franchisor

Positive Attributes

1. The owner-manager is motivated to maximize cash flow and asset appreciation.
2. Management expenses do not include contract fees, and therefore are typically less than if an outside party is engaged.
3. The owner as manager can select the best available affiliation for the asset, given the situation's attributes.
4. Subject to contractual obligations, the affiliation can be changed independent of management if conditions warrant such a repositioning of the asset.

Negative Attributes

1. The cost of securing a recognized affiliation is higher under this structure than under other structures.
2. The owner may not be the most effective entity to manage the property, as compared with professional management firms.

Structure 2—Owner Contracts with One Firm for Both Management and Franchise

Positive Attributes

1. The combined cost of securing both management and an affiliation is typically lower than engaging two separate firms.
2. Since the manager and the brand are one and the same, the manager theoretically will be able to maximize the value of the marketing and sales capabilities associated with the system (usually for hotels).
3. Subject to contractual loan and management constraints, the owner can change the manager and affiliation if desired performance levels are not met.

Negative Attributes

1. Operators that possess their own nationally recognized brand names are inherently large systems, and may not provide maximum focus on the owner's individual asset.
2. If the manager is underperforming and a change is necessary, the brand name affiliation will also most likely have to change. The cost of changing management and brand at the same time can be significant.
3. The manager and owner may have different profit motivations, since the manager may want to maximize its fees, but the owner may want to maximize cash flow and asset appreciation.

Structure 3—Company-Owned, -Managed, and -Affiliated Property

Positive Attributes

1. The costs of management and affiliation are lowest under this structure.
2. The motivation of the manager and affiliation to maximize profits is identical to that of the owner.
3. Since the manager and the brand are one and the same, the manager theoretically will be able to maximize the value of the marketing and sales capabilities associated with the brand system.

Negative Attributes

1. The brand in question may not be the ideal fit for the market in which the asset is located.
2. Similarly, the management team may not be ideally suited to meet the needs of the particular asset.
3. If the owner defaults, the manager and brand will most likely need to be changed.

Structure 4—Independent Operation

Positive Attributes

1. The cost of management is extremely low, since the owner is the manager.
2. The motivation to maximize profits is great.
3. The owner, as the manager, can reposition or market the property to explicitly fit the needs of a particular market without constraints from affiliation requirements.

Negative Attributes

1. Without a recognized name, the property (lacking other attributes such as a unique design or well-established reputation in the market) may not have widespread marketing power.
2. The management team may not be ideally suited to meet the needs of the particular asset.
3. An ownership default, probably closes the hotel or restaurant, but in any event the management will change.

Structure 5—Owner, Management Firm, and Franchisor

Positive Attributes

1. Owner has the ability to optimize the management and brand fit, given the attributes of a particular location, property type, and situation.
2. Subject to management and lender contractual constraints, owner can change manager or affiliation if either is underperforming.

Negative Attributes

1. This structure typically has the highest costs, given the substantial fees paid both to the manager and the franchisor. These fees can be 10 percent or more of revenue in some cases.
2. The lack of an ownership interest in the underlying asset suggests the possibility that the management firm could have less than optimal levels of profit motivation, as in Structure 2.

Industry Structure around the World

As is the case with hotels, restaurant industry structure in other countries is generally comparable to that found in the United States. Chain restaurants are less common in international markets, although Hard Rock Cafe can be found in many international gateway cities, and McDonald's seems ubiquitous around the globe. Like hotels, the factors that dictate the appeal and popularity of one ownership structure over another include maturity of the industry in that country, land availability, legal and tax consequences, political environment, and level of governmental regulation.

Summary

The ownership profile of the hospitality industry is varied across the globe: Large international firms such as Accor, Marriott, and Hilton are top-of-mind organizations. Yet the small, closely held enterprise remains the dominant ownership form of the early twenty-first century. The entrepreneurial character found throughout the world of hotels and restaurants heightens the appeal of the industry to managers and owners alike.

As a hospitality owner, your wealth would increase in accordance with your ability to understand and manage the industry's risks. The management intensive character of the business presents particular challenges. If you can successfully identify and address those characteristics that make hospitality different from most other businesses, the rewards can be significant.

NOTES

1. American Hotel and Lodging Association, *Lodging Industry Profile,* 2009.
2. National Restaurant Association, *Restaurant Industry Overview,* 2010.
3. National Restaurant Association, *Restaurant Industry Operations Report,* 2010a.
4. Ibid.

CHAPTER 18

HOSPITALITY PROPERTIES
HOW MUCH TO PAY IF YOU'RE BUYING; HOW MUCH TO ASK IF YOU'RE SELLING

JACK B. CORGEL

In the previous chapter, we looked at the advantages and disadvantages of different hospitality ownership structures. If you've decided to go forward as a hospitality property and business owner, you will be putting your money into the hospitality industry. You certainly can make money, but those funds are at risk (as discussed in Chapter 22). As we said in the last chapter, as an owner you receive returns in the form of whatever money remains from operations after payment of all expenses, usually called *after-tax cash flow* (ATCF), also known as the *residual claims*.

When your holding period ends (when you sell the property), you have rights (i.e., residual claims) to whatever remains after payment of expenses when you sell a property, usually called *after-tax reversions* (ATRs). In the United States and a growing number of countries, the economic life of hospitality assets typically exceeds the holding period, so hospitality businesses and the properties that support them may have a series of several owners.[1]

So if you buy a property, at some point you probably will also want to sell it. Your decision on what price to pay (or what price to ask) rests heavily on your forecast of ATCFs and ATRs. Most investment decisions no longer rely simply on rough approximations of future cash flow and rules of thumb for figuring out an asset's price. Instead, investment decisions rely on financial economics and can become quite analytically sophisticated.

This chapter's plan is to present the methodology for modern hospitality investment decision making in a useful and understandable form. I address the concepts underlying the following questions:

- How can I estimate the market value?
- How can I forecast future cash flows?
- How much should I bid for a hospitality business or property?
- When is the best time to buy and sell?
- What information and services are needed to complete transactions to own hospitality assets?

The concepts presented in this chapter are intended to help you make money (and not lose money) as an owner of hospitality real estate.

The Difference between Investment and Financing Decisions

As a hospitality investor, you have two separate but related questions about a possible real estate deal—namely, what is the price, and how do you finance the deal? Once you have a price, working out the financing can be so complex that we have devoted several chapters to ownership structures and financing decisions—and the related risk—in the context of the hospitality industry. In this chapter, I discuss your investment considerations and then go into the complex matter of how to place a value on a hospitality property.

FACTORS TO CONSIDER WHEN MAKING INVESTMENT DECISIONS

You don't necessarily have to know how to run a hotel or restaurant when you invest in a hospitality asset, but you do need to adopt a rational approach to investing. The elements of this approach, your investment strategy, comprise your investment philosophy, investment objectives, and investment policies.

Hospitality investing involves the following three types of management:

1. Investment management involves a broad set of activities for evaluating the returns and risks associated with a portfolio of investments taken together.
2. Asset management ensures that the physical property remains in good condition and the operator of the business performs as expected.
3. Business management (or operation) involves generating revenue and controlling expenses to generate necessary cash flows.

Figure 18.1
Continuum of Investment Philosophy

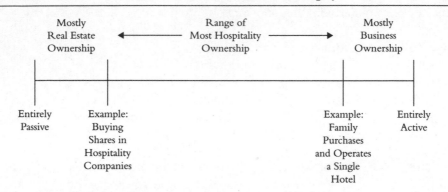

Investment Philosophy

You should start the hospitality ownership process by determining your degree of involvement in operating the assets, ranging from passive ownership at one extreme to entirely active (i.e., day-to-day involvement) at the other extreme (see Figure 18.1). These extreme cases I just mentioned are hypothetical because ownership usually involves some management but rarely means total management responsibility.

The best examples of passive owners are individual U.S. investors who purchase shares in hospitality operating companies, such as Marriott International (NYSE: MAR) and Yum! Brands (NYSE: YUM), and real estate investment trusts (REITs) that own hospitality real estate, such as Host Hotels and Resorts (NYSE: HST) and National Retail Properties (NYSE: NNN). Host owns hotels operated by other firms, and NNN owns restaurant properties that it leases to business operators.[2] These passive owners spend some time in investment management by following companies' businesses and stock prices. The best example of active ownership is a family that purchases a hotel with the plan that each family member assists in the operation of the business. In this case, some management responsibility usually will be undertaken by professionals outside the family (e.g., accounting and tax work).

Investment Objectives

Chances are that you have a particular objective for your hospitality investment. Some owners simply want to make money and earn a predetermined rate of return, essentially wealth maximization. Chances are, though, you have other, personal financial considerations, such as one or more of the following:

- *Preservation of capital.* A hospitality asset investment may be viewed as having a lower risk of loss than alternatives.
- *Tax shelter.* Property and business ownership provide deductions not available from alternatives.
- *One-time capital event.* Investments in developing and constructing new hospitality assets and investing to renovate and refinance later can generate large one-time cash flows, but have higher risk profiles.

I cannot continue this discussion without recognizing nonfinancial motives, including personal ego, but I am focused here on your financial goals. If you can determine your investment objectives, you are one step closer to developing guidelines for the selection of the "right" hospitality assets.

Investment Policies

Based on your objectives, you should specify profiles of your desired ownership interests, such as whether you want to be a passive or active investor. Specify a geographic area, and pick a property type and business, such as select-service hotels, or a quick-service restaurant.

While it's true that some people are simply searching for a place to invest their money, most people have at least subconsciously worked out an investment philosophy and objectives. Certainly, private equity firms, hospitality companies, and other institutional investors take meticulous care to develop investment strategies before engaging in a search for real estate and businesses. If nothing else, constructing a formal investment strategy may help you avoid making a financial mistake.

KNOW HOW YOU WILL GET OUT BEFORE YOU GET IN!

Believe it or not, you need an exit strategy from your real estate before you ever get in. Here's why. If you want to be successful, you first need to give careful thought to this question: To whom will I sell this property in 10 years? The truth is, few owners hold their hotels or restaurants forever. However, hotels are notoriously illiquid, so you probably won't be able to sell your assets quickly. It's unlikely that the remarkable liquidity for hospitality assets (or any real estate) that existed in the bubble of 2005 through 2008 will ever return. At this writing, liquidity has literally dried up. So, you should contemplate your expected holding period, what the market may look like at the end of that period, and who might be the next owner of the property or business. I'm not expecting clairvoyance, just a solid business plan.

Analysis Tools for Simple and Complex Decisions

Next, you need to collect both financial and nonfinancial information relating to particular opportunities. For the nonfinancial considerations, you could just make a list of pros and cons. Financial factors of greatest importance either can be incorporated into the forecast of cash flows during the holding period or become part of the process of adjusting the cash flows for risk (see Chapter 22).

Even if you are an inexperienced individual investor you have access to the same complex tools of financial analysis used by financial services corporations, in the financial functions of Microsoft Excel. These tools include calculating net present values (NPVs) and internal rates of return (IRRs). NPV and IRR allow for an integrated analysis over a multiple-year holding period, explicitly account for the time value of money, and include rules that provide specific recommendations about investing and not investing. Whatever mechanism you use, make sure that you thoroughly consider all factors.

VALUE IS EVERYTHING! MARKET VALUE AND INVESTMENT VALUE

It goes without saying that you want to make money from your investment. To do that, you have to know how to determine asset values—how much to offer and how much to ask. The two most important valuations are market value and investment value. Market values represent the consensus estimates of an asset's purchase price in a competitive market (as determined by all potential buyers and sellers).

Investment values are not consensus estimates, but instead include personalized factors, such as debt financing costs and tax liabilities. Prospective owners need to know investment values to determine their bids on purchase and their listing price on sale. Along the way, investors and lenders have a keen interest in tracking market values because distress may require forced sales or because opportunities arise to sell during expansion periods for extraordinary profit. So value may not be "everything," although it is pretty darn important!

Market Value: Value = Price = Cost

Let's take a quick look at the economic theory of value because it will help with our later discussion. Economist Alfred Marshall assembled the key analysis that satisfaction (i.e., demand or utility) and relative scarcity (i.e., supply) interact in a market to determine prices.[3] So, at equilibrium, an asset valuation should look like this:

$$\text{Value (V)} = \text{Price (P)} = \text{Cost (C)} \tag{1}$$

This concept is shown in Figure 18.2, which is a classic demand and supply graph. The intersection of buyers on the demand side of the market and sellers on the supply side produce agreements on P. From Equation (1), P should not deviate from C, and V will equal P if valuation models do a good job of predicting P. We can observe price and cost, but we must estimate value. Now, let's take this one step further, to a point that is critical for hotels. No buyer will care what your hotel cost to build, and you cannot set a price on that basis, although your buyers may consider replacement cost, as I discuss later. Instead potential buyers are mostly going to look at a factor identified by economist Irving Fisher. He realized that buyers and sellers set asset prices largely according to the income that assets will generate in the future and the risk of collecting these incomes. Hence, the following functional relationship was born:

$$V = f \text{ (future income, subject to risk)} \tag{2}$$

Figure 18.2
Perfectly Competitive Markets

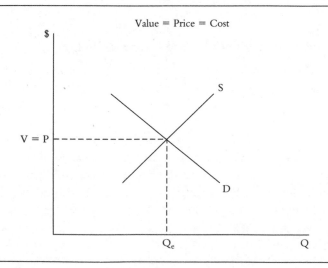

A Formal Definition of Market Value

I return to the discussion of valuation in a moment, but first we must distinguish between a valuation and an appraisal. Anyone can perform a valuation by estimating the worth of assets and businesses using any approach they desire. By contrast, an appraisal is performed by a licensed professional, who follows a set process and uses standard methods. Appraisers' consistency gives rise to the demand for appraisals from clients such as developers, lenders, government, and owners. While many (many!) books have been written on appraisal, *The Appraisal of Real Estate*, published by the Appraisal Institute, will tell you what you need to know.[4]

Three Valuation Methods

Whenever possible, appraisers attempt to apply three different valuation approaches for estimating the most probably sale price of properties. They combine the three estimates in a reconciliation to arrive at the estimate of market value. Based on the economic theories I just mentioned, particularly $V = P = C$, the three approaches are:

1. *Income approach.* The property is worth the present value of expected future incomes.
2. *Sales-comparison approach.* The property is worth the same as prices identical properties sold for in the market.
3. *Cost approach.* The property is worth the cost to replace the property (not the original construction cost).

Income Generation: How Income Becomes Value

Let's start with the income approach to value, sometimes referred to as the income capitalization approach. The idea is to convert the estimates of future income into a one-time monetary representation of those incomes today. This one-time amount is the present value of those incomes and represents the price investors would logically pay for the rights to the future incomes. To predict prices appraisers must estimate the incomes to come in future years as correctly as possible and get the present-value conversion right.

The general term for this conversion of future incomes to value is *capitalization,* which comes from the process of converting flows to capital stocks—that is, capitalizing the flows. Figure 18.3 provides a graphical representation of this idea, based on Irving Fisher's idea that capitalization

Figure 18.3
The Capitalization Process to Estimate Value

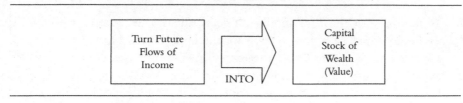

occurs by dividing the incomes by an interest rate that accounts for the risk.[5] So capitalization is not only a conversion process, but it accomplishes the task of adjusting the future incomes for their risk of not being realized as estimated.

As you can guess, this is not necessarily a simple matter, and there are many approaches to this capitalization process. Simple valuation models come with simple assumptions and the risk of inaccuracy. The simplest income capitalization model uses the assumption that all the incomes in future periods will be at the same level and the incomes will continue indefinitely. With these assumptions, the following equation applies for valuation using direct capitalization shown below:

$$V = I / R \qquad (3a)$$

where I represents net income and R the interest rate known as the capitalization (or cap) rate. As an example, if a prospective owner estimates the average future net income of a hotel as $750,000 per year for the 50-year life of the property and the cap rate equals 10 percent, then the estimate of value is $7,500,000 shown in Equation 3b.

$$\$7,500,000 = \$750,000 / 0.10 \qquad (3b)$$

More complicated models incorporate the realistic assumption that incomes go up and down freely in future periods. The conversion process in these models is called discounting and the interest rate is a discount rate. The discounted cash flow (DCF) model, which is commonly used by institutional investors, relies on many complex assumptions about the ups and downs of future incomes and is an advanced version of a discounting-style model. I've included a DCF illustration in the accompanying sidebar.

Hotel Valuation Using the DCF Approach

To demonstrate the discounted cash flow valuation approach for hotels, we begin with a cash flow analysis for the hypothetical Hotel Galactica, as presented in Figure 18.4. A statement of this type that contains estimates of future cash flows is known in business as a *pro forma*. The Hotel Galactica, located in a major U.S. city, has 200 rooms, and before the full impact of the financial crisis was felt in 2009, the hotel ran an occupancy rate of 75 percent with an average daily rate (ADR) of $205. As shown along the top rows of the figure, both occupancy and ADR fell in 2009. Performance numbers beyond 2009 are forecasts made by management and the owner based on an expected recovery. These forecasts extend only five years into the future for demonstration purposes, although owners' holding periods are usually longer than that. The cash flow statement follows a standard construction that aligns with the Uniform System of Accounts for the Lodging Industry.[6] The USALI organizes hotel revenues and expenses by departments, and then includes two categories of expenses that cannot easily be allocated to departments—namely, undistributed expenses and fixed charges. Note that a cash flow statement does not include noncash expenses such as depreciation. The bottom line—the net operating incomes (NOIs)—are the numbers needed to perform the valuation.

The next step in the valuation requires the development of a discount rate, r, to convert the NOIs forecast for future periods into a single present value stated in today's dollars. The relationship between the discount rate and the capitalization rate is:

$$r = R + g \qquad (4a)$$

where g is the assumed growth rate of NOI in the future. The Hotel Galactica NOIs increase at a rate of 6 to 7 percent beyond 2011. Thus, a 16 percent discount rate applies when assuming a 10 percent capitalization rate from the example above and g = 6 percent, as follows:

$$16 = 0.10 + 0.06 \qquad (4b)$$

Next, an estimate of the cash flows to the owner of Hotel Galactica must be derived at the time of sale in 2014. This calculation requires

Figure 18.4
Hotel Galactica Pro Forma Statement, 2010–2014

	2008 Actual		2009 Actual		**Pro Forma** 2010 Forecast		2011 Forecast		2012 Forecast	
Available Rooms	200		200		200		200		200	
Occupancy	75.0%		62.2%		65.0%		70.0%		73.5%	
ADR	$ 205.66		$ 165.50		$ 170.00		$ 193.89		$ 197.23	
	Amount	Percent	Amount	Percent	Amount	Percent	Amount	Percent	Amount	Percent
Departmental Revenues										
Rooms	$ 11,259,885	67.1%	$ 7,514,693	67.1%	$ 8,066,500	67.1%	$ 9,907,779	67.1%	$ 10,582,376	67.1%
Food & Beverage	$ 4,665,049	27.8%	$ 3,113,390	27.8%	$ 3,342,007	27.8%	$ 4,104,862	27.8%	$ 4,384,352	27.8%
Minor Operated Departments	$ 520,203	3.1%	$ 347,177	3.1%	$ 372,670	3.1%	$ 457,736	3.1%	$ 488,903	3.1%
Rentals & Other Income	$ 335,615	2.0%	$ 223,985	2.0%	$ 240,432	2.0%	$ 295,314	2.0%	$ 315,421	2.0%
Total Revenues	$ 16,780,753	100%	$ 11,199,244	100.0%	$ 12,021,610	100.0%	$ 14,765,692	100.0%	$ 15,771,052	100.0%
Departmental Expenses*										
Rooms	$ 2,848,751	25.3%	$ 2,705,289	36.0%	$ 2,823,275	35.0%	$ 2,506,668	25.3%	$ 2,677,341	25.3%
Food & Beverage	$ 3,363,500	72.1%	$ 2,587,227	83.1%	$ 2,770,524	82.9%	$ 2,959,606	72.1%	$ 3,161,118	72.1%
Minor Operated Departments	$ 370,905	71.3%	$ 277,394	79.9%	$ 292,546	78.5%	$ 326,366	71.3%	$ 348,588	71.3%
Rentals & Other Income	$ –	0.0%	$ –	0.0%	$ –	0.0%	$ –	0.0%	$ –	0.0%
Total Departmental Expenses	$ 6,583,156	39.2%	$ 5,569,911	49.7%	$ 5,886,345	49.0%	$ 5,792,640	39.2% $	6,187,047	39.2%
Departmental Profit	$ 10,197,596	60.8%	$ 5,629,334	50.3%	$ 6,135,264	51.0%	$ 8,973,052	60.8%	$ 9,584,005	60.8%

(continued)

Figure 18.4
(continued)

		2008 Actual		2009 Actual		Pro Forma 2010 Forecast		2011 Forecast		2012 Forecast	
Undistributed Operating Expenses											
Administrative & General	$	1,443,145	8.6%	1,679,887	15.0%	1,695,047	14.1%	1,269,849	8.6%	1,356,310	8.6%
Franchise Fees	$	–	0.0%	–	0.0%	–	0.0%	–	0.0%	–	0.0%
Sales & Marketing	$	1,275,337	7.6%	1,366,308	12.2%	1,442,593	12.0%	1,122,193	7.6%	1,198,600	7.6%
Property Operations & Maintenance	$	805,476	4.8%	1,063,928	9.5%	1,081,945	9.0%	708,753	4.8%	757,010	4.8%
Energy Costs	$	654,449	3.9%	940,737	8.4%	961,729	8.0%	575,862	3.9%	615,071	3.9%
Total Undistributed Operating Expenses	$	4178,407	24.9%	5,050,859	45.1%	5,181,314	43.1%	3,676,657	24.9%	3,926,992	24.9%
Income Before Fixed Changes	$	6,019,189	35.9%	578,475	5.2%	953,951	7.9%	5,296,394	35.9%	5,657,013	35.9%
Fixed Changes											
Insurance	$	234,931	1.4%	156,789	1.4%	168,303	1.4%	206,720	1.4%	220,795	1.4%
Property Taxes	$	553,765	3.3%	369,575	3.3%	396,713	3.3%	487,268	3.3%	520,445	3.3%
Management Fee	$	553,765	3.3%	369,575	3.3%	396,713	3.3%	487,268	3.3%	520,445	3.3%
Total Fixed Charges	$	1,342,460	8.0%	895,940	8.0%	961,729	8.0%	1,181,255	8.0%	1,261,684	8.0%

three inputs. First, we need an estimate of the NOI in 2015, given on the assumption that the next owner will pay a price based on future NOIs after 2014. By applying a 6 percent growth rate to 2014 NOI, we obtain $5,326,660. Second, a 10-percent future or terminal capitalization rate is assumed. Third, selling expenses will be 5 percent. The result of combining these inputs is as follows:

Selling Price in 2014 ($5,326,193 / 0.10)	$53,261,953
Less: 5 Percent Selling Expenses	2,663,096
Equals: Cash Flow from Sale	$50,598,856

The estimated value of Hotel Galactica in 2010 becomes the present value of the estimated NOIs plus the present value of the cash flow from sale, both using the 16 percent discount rate. As a reminder, adjusting future cash flows to current dollars includes assumptions about future inflation and the time value of money. These calculations are presented in Figure 18.5.

The value of Hotel Galactica using the DCF modeling approach is $34,933,035.

Figure 18.5
DCF Valuation of Hotel Galactica

Cash Flow	Present Value Factor	Present Value of Cash Flow
2010 NOI ($7,778)	0.8621	$ (6,705)
2011 NOI $4,115,139	0.7432	$ 3,058,371
2012 NOI $4,395,329	0.6407	$ 2,816,087
2013 NOI $4,676,512	0.5523	$ 2,582,837
2014 NOI $5,024,711	0.4761	$ 2,392,330
Cash Flow from Sale (2014) $50,598,856	0.4761	$ 24,090,115
Sum = Value		$ 34,933,035

Restaurant Income, Expenses, and Valuation

Restaurant valuations offer additional complications, compared with hotel valuation, because ownership of the operations and the real estate often reside with different individuals and companies. Those ownership arrangements were outlined in Chapter 17 and are detailed in Chapter 19. Briefly, here are four of the possible ownership scenarios:

1. *Owners control both the business and the entire property.* The profit–motivated combination of restaurant business and the real estate is referred to as the going concern, which produces goodwill, and its value is based on a combination of the two.
2. *Owners only control the assets of the business, and they lease the building and land.* The valuation focuses on how much the business is worth. Lease payments for land and buildings become expenses in the valuation.
3. *Owners control the assets of the business plus the building, but they lease the land.* The valuation focuses on how much the business and building are worth. Lease payments for land become expenses in these types of valuation.
4. *Owners control the land or building but have no ownership interest in the restaurant business assets.* The focus of these valuations centers on the real estate components.

Care must be taken to identify the components of ownership positions involved for particular types of investments. Among the four main components of the going concern one must be certain of which are owned and which are leased (that is, goodwill; furniture, fixtures, and equipment; buildings; and land).

Step-by-Step Restaurant Valuation Method

To demonstrate the valuation of a restaurant, let's look at a step-by-step approach for the hypothetical Restaurant Superior, a small independently owned and operated casual dining establishment. The business operates in a converted historic home with a limited parking area.

- **Step 1.** Create Restaurant Superior's cash *pro forma* by estimating revenues and expenses for the next year and projecting both until some future year when they become stabilized. Panel A of Figure 18.6 displays a restaurant income and expense statement showing two years of historical performance and a stabilized year, one year into the future. Note that food and beverage revenues are separate, and the cost of sales for each is summed for gross profit. The calculation separates expenses into controllable and occupation costs. The "bottom–line" number—the NOI—equals before-tax cash flow (BTCF) when debt is not considered in the income estimate.

Figure 18.6
Superior Restaurant's Statements of Income and Expenses

Panel A: Business Owners' Statement

	Actual 2008		Actual 2009		Projected Maintainable (Stabilized Earnings)	
Sales						
Food	$ 408,867	75.0%	$ 432,925	72.2%	$ 432,902	72.2%
Beverage	$ 136,289	25.0%	$ 166,662	27.8%	$ 166,685	27.8%
Total Sales	$ 545,156	100.0%	$ 599,587	100.0%	$ 599,587	100.0%
Cost of Sales						
Food	$ 145,681	35.6%	$ 170,175	39.3%	$ 147,187	34.0%
Beverage	$ 64,056	47.0%	$ 112,261	67.4%	$ 53,339	32.0%
Total Cost of Sales	$ 209,737	38.5%	$ 282,436	47.1%	$ 200,526	33.4%
Gross Profit	$ 335,419	61.5%	$ 317,151	59.9%	$ 399,061	66.6%
Controllable Expenses						
Payroll	$ 210,998	38.7%	$ 199,004	33.2%	$ 171,880	28.7%
Benefits	–	0.0%	$ 11,747	2.0%	$ 17,188	2.9%
Direct Operating	$ 45,576	8.4%	$ 10,896	1.8%	$ 25,981	4.3%
Advertising	$ 24,062	4.4%	$ 16,699	2.8%	$ 16,189	2.7%
Utilities	$ 17,291	3.2%	$ 5,712	1.0%	$ 17,069	2.8%
Entertainment	$ 12,503	2.3%	$ 10,072	1.8%	$ 6,000	1.0%
Administration, gen'l	$ 32,438	6.0%	$ 10,072	1.8%	$ 17,988	3.0%
Business Tax	$ 1,567	0.3%	$ 1,645	0.3%	$ 1,728	0.3%
Repairs, Maintenance	$ 6,362	1.2%	$ 6,222	1.0%	$ 6,648	1.1%
Total Controllable Expenses	$ 350,797	64.3%	$ 272,069	45.4%	$ 280,671	46.8%
Occupation Costs						

(continued)

Figure 18.6
(continued)

Panel A: Business Owners' Statement

	Actual 2008		Actual 2009		Projected Maintainable (Stabilized Earnings)	
Rent	$ 32,068	5.9%	$ 35,975	6.0%	$ 35,975	6.0%
Common-area Rent	$ 11,180	2.0%	$ 11,180	1.9%	$ 11,180	1.9%
Total Occupation Costs	$ 43,248	7.9%	$ 47,155	7.9%	$ 47,155	7.9%
Net Income Before Taxes, Depreciation, and Debt Service (NOI=BTCF)	$ (58,626)	−10.8%	$ (2,073)	−0.3%	$ 71,235	11.9%

Includes reoccurring replacements and capital expenditures within the restaurant space.
Includes rent for land and buildings.

Source: Adapted from Douglas P. Fisher. 1919. "Restaurant Valuation: A Financial approach." *Cornell Hospitality Quarterly* (February): 89–92.

Panel B: Real Estate Owner's Statement

	Actual 2008	Actual 2009	Projected Maintainable (Stabilized NOI)
Income			
Rent	$ 32,068	$ 35,975	$ 35,975
Common-Area Rent	$ 11,180	$ 11,180	$ 11,180
Total Income	$ 43,248	$ 47,155	$ 47,155
Expenses			
Property Tax	$ 12,000	$ 12,000	$ 12,000
Insurance-Property and Casualty	$ 7,000	$ 7,000	$ 7,000
Common-Area Repairs and Maintenance	$ 11,180	$ 11,180	$ 11,180
Total Expenses	$ 30,180	$ 30,180	$ 30,180
Owners' NOI=BTCF	$ 13,068	$ 16,975	$ 16,975

- **Step 2.** Estimate occupation costs—in this case, rent for the land, which typically ranges from 2 to 3 percent of restaurant gross revenues. If the value of the land is already known, then the land rent may be 1 to 4 percent of the land value. For land and building together, the rent may be 6 to 7 percent of restaurant gross revenues. You could also estimate 4 to 6 percent of food gross revenue, plus 8 to 12 percent of beverage gross revenue. Most restaurant leases include net lease provisions. A net lease means the restaurant business owners pay for one or more of three property expenses—property taxes, property insurance, and common area maintenance (CAM). (If they pay all three, that's a triple-net lease.) The CAM charges, which involve expenses such as snow removal and parking lot repair, appear as a rent payment, but in truth they simply reimburse the landlords for property expenses. The Restaurant Superior has a single-net lease arrangement in which the tenant only reimburses the landlord for CAM expenses, but not property tax or insurance.
- **Step 3.** Estimate real estate owners' NOI as shown in Panel B of Figure 18.6. Note that the common area rent exactly equals common area repairs and maintenance.
- **Step 4.** Establish land and building cap rates. Land capitalization may range from 5 to 10 percent, while land and building capitalization rates may be 8 to 13 percent.
- **Step 5.** Compute land and building value by direct capitalization (see Equations 3a and 3b) after subtracting the expenses of the real estate owner from the rent.
- **Step 6.** Estimate the restaurant operators' income—the NOI or BTCF in the stabilized year. As shown in Figure 18.6, this number comes from finding income before occupation costs and then subtracting rents.
- **Step 7.** Estimate a capitalization rate for the restaurant business. The following guidelines apply: new restaurants, 18 to 25 percent; average operating restaurants, 20 to 33 percent; and older, poor quality operating restaurants, 33 percent or greater. These cap rates exceed those for the real estate because of the higher risk of restaurant failure relative to the sustainability of rents on land and buildings.
- **Step 8.** Compute the restaurant business value by direct capitalization. Note that in this valuation no attempt is made to separate goodwill and furniture, fixtures, and equipment—the values of both become imbedded into the NOI and capitalization rate.

Additional Considerations for Restaurant Valuation Certain restaurant characteristics complicate the process of forecasting future cash flows and assigning either discount or capitalization rates, notably, the presence of personalities, such as a well-known owner or chef. Part of this problem is that personalities come and go. Having a restaurant chain affiliation, however, reduces real estate cap rates by 2 to 3 percent compared to an independent restaurant (i.e., leading to a higher valuation) and reduces business component capitalization rates by 3 to 10 percent due to the income stability that chain affiliation brings.

Numerical Example of Restaurant Valuation Let's do the value calculations for the Restaurant Superior business and real estate. The valuation is as follows.

Restaurant Business NOI / Capitalization Rate

$$\$71,235 / 0.20 = \$356,175$$

Real Estate NOI / Capitalization Rate

$$\$16,975 / 0.08 = \$212,187$$
$$\text{Total Value} = \$356,175 + \$212,187 = \$568,362$$

Price Discovery by Examining Comparable Sales

As I said earlier, sales of comparable properties (comps) are also used to value properties. It makes sense to estimate the most probable sale price for a business by examining comparable businesses or properties that have already sold—but they must be truly comparable. Usually, three or four such comps are sufficient. Several characteristics and conditions become important in searches for comparable sales. First, the transaction should be fairly recent—no more than two years previous. The acceptability of historical sales as comparables is directly related to how much economic change occurred between the time the comp sold and the current market. Second, comparability increases with geographic proximity. Third, comparable properties should have similar physical characteristics and business objectives to the asset under consideration. Fortunately, appraisers and owners can make adjustments for differences in some of these characteristics, as shown in the following example.

The sales comparison approach provides useful ranges of values for commercial property, typically expressed as value per room (hotels), value per seat or value per ft^2/m^2 (restaurants).

The following steps will lead to a valuation according to the sales comparison approach:

1. Research the market to find recent transactions of similar businesses or properties and determine accurate data on the assets, market conditions, and transactions at time of sale.
2. Reject sales that may not be good value indicators for the subject (e.g., related-party transactions).
3. Align comparable properties with your property regarding physical characteristics, location, date of sale, conditions of sale, and financing.
4. Where your property and comparables differ, adjust comparables' selling prices according to the market pricing differences.
5. Determine a value estimate for the subject property from the adjusted sale prices of comparables.

Hotel Sales Comparison Let's see how the sales comparison approach would work for the Hotel Galactica (Figure 18.7). Instead of the income approach

Figure 18.7
Comparable Sales Analysis for Galactica Hotel Valuation

Panel A: Comparable Sales and Characteristics			
	Sale 1	Sale 2	Sale 3
Sale Price (Last 18 mos.)	$ 39,110,000	$28,936,130	$33,671,650
Property Size (rooms)	220	148	190
Sales Price Per Room	$177,773	$195,514	$177,219
Occupancy★	58%	60%	65%
Average Rate★	$107.03	$108.88	$111.22
NOI★	$107.03	$108.88	$111.22
	$3,715,450	$2,604,252	$3,367,165
Comments:	NOI below Potential	Deferred maintenance, but well run	Market leader, Superior location and condition
★*Trailing 12 months*			

Panel B: Adjustments to Comparable Sales			
Sale No.	Summary of Adjustments	Adjusted Sale Price Per Room	Indicated Value of the Subject
1	−3%	$172,440 × 220	**$37,967,000**
2	+2%	$199,424 × 148	**$29,514,793**
3	−5%	$168,358 × 190	**$31,988,029**
Avarage			**$33,156,607**

found in the sidebar, this time we'll rely on a valuation performed using a sales-comparison approach. Information given to the prospective owner and a property inspection indicates that the property is in excellent condition. The trailing 12 months (TTM) occupancy was 60 percent, and average daily rate (ADR) is $153.00. Panel A presents data collected about three comparables. Panel B provides information about the adjustment of the comparable sales and the results form the comparable sales analysis.

Value estimates range from $29,514,793 to $37,967,000. The average of the adjusted sale prices of $33,156,607 is close to the value derived in the sidebar using the income method ($34,933,035).

Restaurant Sales-Comparison Approach

Restaurant valuations using the sales-comparison approach are most commonly based on value per seat, although value per square foot or meter is preferable for quick-service operations, since they have limited seating. For independent restaurants, the best comparables come from the same city, with matches on the menu or theme. Adjustments are made for market demographics, date of sale, different cities, different menu or theme, physical condition, and conditions of sale. For chain-affiliated restaurants, the perfect comparable would have the same chain identity in a market with identical demographics to your restaurant. Finding comps in the same city is not as important for chain restaurants.

Is Cost Important?

Finally, let's look at the idea of replacement cost. It's true that the cost of producing your hospitality property is an important benchmark for valuing the real estate asset. In fact, the cost method is widely recognized as the third method for valuing real estate, although investors do not rely on it as heavily as the income capitalization or sales-comparison approaches. The cost approach is most useful for relatively new properties. As time passes, this approach becomes more difficult to apply because of the many external influences that change the productivity of the property. These influences include physical deterioration, technological obsolescence (e.g., new features that consumers desire), and location obsolescence (e.g., markets moving away as cities grow). Together, the effects of these three influences may be labeled as depreciation.

The following steps lead to a valuation estimate using the cost approach for a 20-year old hotel:

- **Step 1.** Estimate the cost of replacing the structure today with its improvements, but not the cost of the land. You're estimating the cost of a building of similar utility or usefulness applying currently used materials and building techniques.

- **Step 2.** Estimate depreciation, or the loss in property value over the 20-year period, as the result of physical deterioration, technological obsolescence, and location obsolescence. This is by far the most difficult step.
- **Step 3.** Deduct total depreciation from estimated new cost.
- **Step 4.** Estimate the value of the land as if it were vacant using the sales comparison approach.
- **Step 5.** Add the land value to the depreciated value of the structure and improvements for a total value estimate.

The replacement cost estimate provides a useful upper limit on value, but should not be relied on as the primary method for understanding how much a hospitality property is worth.

BUYING AND SELLING HOSPITALITY PROPERTIES AND BUSINESSES

Say that you've determined that ownership is right for you, and you are ready to make an investment in a hospitality property. Although we discuss developing a new property in Chapter 20, let's assume that you decide to acquire an already operating property. The truth is, building a hotel or restaurant is not for the inexperienced! A successful acquisition requires attention to the following considerations: obtaining information, setting rate of return targets, market timing, and, perhaps most important, interacting with brokers and lenders.

Obtaining Information

Owners and managers operating in the hospitality industry are fortunate to have access to outstanding sources of data from which informed decisions can be made. For hotels, the leading sources of data are STR (Smith Travel Research, www.str.com), PKF Hospitality Research (www.pkfc.com), Hospitality Valuation Services (www.HVS.com), and the American Hotel and Lodging Association (www.ahla.com). For restaurants, the leading data sources include Technomic (www.technomic.com), NPD Group (www.npd.com), Malcolm Knapp (www.malcolmknapp.com), and the National Restaurant Association (www.restaurant.com).

Setting Rate of Return Targets Every investment decision should be made with an expected rate of return in mind. When setting a return requirement you should begin by considering the return on a risk-free security, usually a U.S. Treasury bond. Adjusting the return for risk and illiquidity (i.e., the fact that property cannot be sold quickly) is the challenging step. Sophisticated models may be introduced to derive the risk-adjusted rate, but in the absence of access to these models, guidance can be gained from historical information derived from experience and surveys. One such survey comes from PKF Hospitality Research. Their annual *Hospitality Investment Survey* reports the expected return on typical hotel investments (before debt) that has varied within the narrow range of 13 to 16 percent over the past 15 years. Thus, a reasonable expected return for the typical hotel investment would be 16 percent, which we used as the discount rate in the example of Hotel Galactica in the sidebar.

Timing the Market It's difficult to time any market, let alone the market for real estate. Earning the required return would be easy if you possessed the special talent of market timing. The difference between good periods and bad is more apparent in some markets than others. One thing that seems true is that property markets have a cyclical pattern that has been fairly consistent since the late 1980s. This suggests that historically the best times to buy were the trough years of 1991, 2001, and possibly today, while the best times to sell were the peak years of 1988, 1998, and 2008. Unfortunately, you cannot really rely on past trend data. We do not know how real estate will come out of the recent bust.

Interacting with Brokers and Lenders Because of the size and complications associated with property transactions and due to the difficulty in matching buyers and sellers, you will likely interact with two types of professionals when buying and selling hospitality properties—lenders and brokers. You'll need to consult lenders because these transactions are so large that investors usually borrow some of the money needed. Chapter 20 discusses relationships with lenders in the context of developing properties.

Brokers assist both buyers and sellers in transactions, but the traditional arrangement is for a real estate broker to be hired by sellers to find buyers for properties. Buyers also may hire brokers to find suitable properties, but for many property purchases you can do this yourself by contacting brokers. Many properties appear online, and a simple search will uncover many possible investments. To date, transactions are still done in person, but the day will soon be here when buyers and sellers will complete property transactions over the Internet.

Figure 18.8
The Hotel Market Cycle

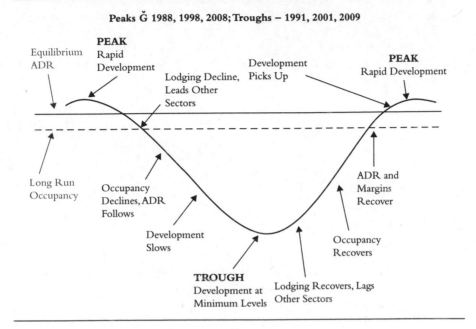

Peaks Ğ 1988, 1998, 2008; Troughs – 1991, 2001, 2009

Equilibrium ADR

PEAK
Rapid Development

Development Picks Up

Lodging Decline, Leads Other Sectors

PEAK
Rapid Development

Long Run Occupancy

Occupancy Declines, ADR Follows

ADR and Margins Recover

Development Slows

Occupancy Recovers

TROUGH
Development at Minimum Levels

Lodging Recovers, Lags Other Sectors

Final Thoughts

With the exception of cruise lines and caterers, hospitality businesses rely on a fixed location. Choose the right location and your business should thrive. In contrast, the best management in the world will have great difficulty defeating the monster of a poor location! You can become successful by managing hospitality businesses at their fixed locations even if you don't own the "locations." Some successful people in the hospitality industry, however, have discovered that one well-executed transaction involving either owner-ship change or financing the ownership position can generate as much profit as an entire career of management.

NOTES

1. For a discussion of hotel property depreciation, see J. B. Corgel, "New Beats Old Nearly Every Day: The Countervailing Effects of Renovations and Obsolescence on Hotel Prices," *Cornell Hospitality Report* 8(13) (2007), Cornell Center for Hospitality Research.

2. For an excellent discussion of REITs and investment in REIT shares, see R. L. Block, *Investing in REITs* (Princeton, NJ: Bloomberg, 2002).

3. A. Marshall, *Principles of Economics,* Vol. 1 (London: Macmillan, 1890).

4. Appraisal Institute, *The Appraisal of Real Estate* (Chicago: Appraisal Institute, 2008).

5. I. Fisher, *The Theory of Interest* (New York: Macmillan, 1930).

6. American Hotel and Lodging Association, *Uniform System of Accounts for the Lodging Industry*, 10th ed. (2006).

CHAPTER 19

GAINING MAXIMUM BENEFIT FROM FRANCHISE AGREEMENTS, MANAGEMENT CONTRACTS, AND LEASES

JAN A. DEROOS

$\mathbf{A}$s the owner of a hospitality property, you can be your own manager, as discussed in Chapter 17. But that chapter also outlined common ownership structures that are intended to maximize the value of your investment by involving various partners. I view these structures as a web of relationships that create and enhance value to all stakeholders.

Hotel and restaurant investors have long recognized that separating the real estate from the brand and from management of a hotel can create value. In fact, today it is difficult to find publicly listed firms that do all three. Firms like Host Hotels and Resorts (NYSE: HST) or Hospitality Properties Trust (NYSE: HPT) are hotel owners that contract with other companies, such as Marriott International (NYSE: MAR) and Accor (PA: AC), which provide brand and management services.[1] In the discussion in Chapter 17, you read about ownership structures that included management contracts, leases, and franchise agreements. In this chapter, I discuss how these contracts provide you with a set of ownership, brand, and management services to help you achieve your investment and ownership objectives. As a start, let's build on the outline of structures in Chapter 17. The examples I give here provide a context for this discussion of contracts and leases.

Let's start with the structure where the owner of the hotel, the franchise, and the hotel management are separate entities (number 5 in Chapter 17). In this case you own the hotel, another firm owns the franchise brand, and a

Figure 19.1
Property Rights in Hospitality

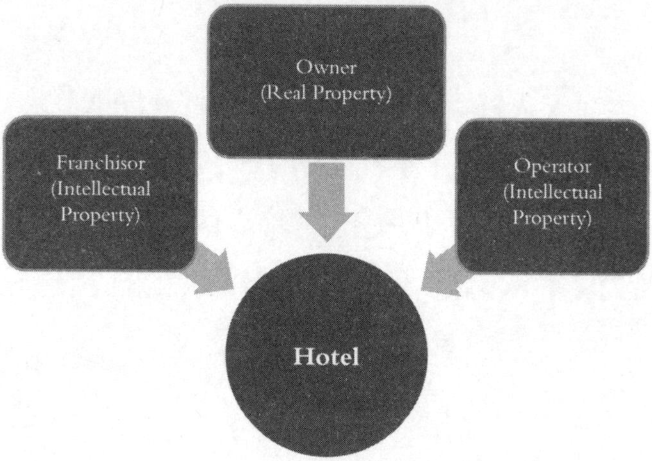

third firm manages the hotel (see Figure 19.1). So if you're a developer with a great site but limited hotel experience, you should see investment returns maximized when specialized management and brand services are used.

You might be able to operate a hotel yourself, especially if it's a relatively small property. If you're an experienced operator, you might purchase a franchise so that your property operates under an established brand. Some hotels and many restaurant operators do this. While the independent owner-operator is common throughout the world, the franchise model is common in the United States.

Many of the largest or best-quality hotels are owned by an institutional owner or real estate fund. Those owners generally sign an agreement with a branded operator, such as Four Seasons, Westin, or Hyatt. These branded operators will not separate their brand from their management services. In some cases, hotel owners lease their properties to the branded hotel operators. In this case, the lease is the only agreement between the two. This is common around the world but not so much in the United States.

As you read in Chapter 17, the restaurant industry uses leases far more than management contracts. Tenants take a similar role to that of operators under a management contract, but they also take on significantly more business risk (see Figure 19.2).

One scenario that we didn't discuss in Chapter 17 was one in which the brand owns the restaurant and then signs both a lease and a franchise agreement

Figure 19.2
Property Rights in Restaurants

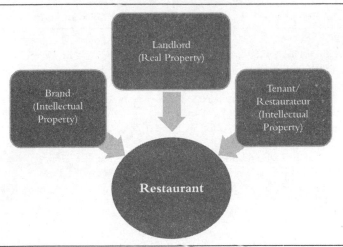

with a local operator. As an operator, the reason that you might sign such an agreement is that you are set up in a location selected by a successful national brand, and you have a proven operating system with the franchise. McDonald's uses this approach for its local franchisees, for instance. As the local operator, you earn your return by operating the restaurant efficiently so that there is excess cash flow after paying both rent and franchise fees.

However, if you own a site, you might work with a company like Buffalo Wild Wings. This firm owns its brand, operates its restaurants, and signs leases with property owners, becoming tenants in community shopping centers or neighborhood centers. As tenant, they keep all of the restaurant's cash flow after paying the rent.

Let's examine the contractual tools mentioned in these examples: franchises, license agreements, leases, and management contracts. These contractual obligations shape property rights in the hospitality industry, and if you understand how to price and how to use property rights, you are at a competitive advantage.

FRANCHISE AND LICENSE AGREEMENTS

The United States Federal Trade Commission defines a franchise using the following three elements. The franchisor must: (1) promise to provide a trademark or other commercial symbol; (2) promise to exercise significant

Figure 19.3
Top 10 Hotel and Restaurant Franchisors

Top 10 Hotel Franchisors	Top 10 Restaurant Franchisors
1. Marriott	1. McDonald's
2. Hilton (Hilton Hotels Corp.)	2. KFC (Yum Brands, Inc.)
3. Holiday Inn (InterContinental Hotels Group)	3. Subway
4. Sheraton	4. Burger King
5. Holiday Inn Express (InterContinental Hotels Group)	5. Pizza Hut (Yum Brands, Inc.)
6. Hampton Inn (Hilton Hotels Corp.)	6. Wendy's (Wendy's/Arby's Group)
7. Courtyard (Marriott International)	7. Taco Bell (Yum Brands, Inc.)
8. Comfort Inn (Choice Hotels International)	8. Dunkin' Donuts
9. Radisson (Carlson Hotels Worldwide)	9. Domino's Pizza
10. Crowne Plaza (InterContinental Hotels Group)	10. Applebee's (DineEquity, Inc.)

Source: Franchise Times, "Top 200 Franchise Chains by Worldwide Sales," October 2009.

control or provide significant assistance in the operation of the business; and (3) require a minimum payment of at least $500 during the first six months of operations."[2] To prevent deception and abuses of franchisees, the U.S. government requires all franchisors to provide prepurchase disclosures in a 23-item Franchise Disclosure Document.[3] As a franchisee you purchase the right to use a concept created by the franchisor, and for your royalty fees, you are granted a license to use the franchisor's trademarks and other trade dress. Figure 19.3 lists the leading hotel and restaurant franchise systems.

Although you're using the franchisor's system, as franchisee you supply the management acumen for the franchised unit. Meanwhile, the franchisor manages the brand image, marketing, and product design. As franchisee you have the right to sell goods using the franchisor's trade name, brand identity, methods of preparation and quality standards, markcting efforts, and distribution systems. Ideally, you would match your business site to the choice of franchise system and promote the local business.

One reason that companies use franchising to grow their system is the financing available from working with many other business operators. While this is undoubtedly true for firms in their initial growth phase, it doesn't explain why mature firms with a low cost of capital such as Choice Hotels or Burger King continue to franchise, and why many franchisors evolve to become capital providers to their franchisees. Instead, franchising offers the following two incentives—better operating results, and efficiency and cost savings.

- *Better results.* Franchising heads off such potential problems as uncaring managers and excessive management risk taking. It also reduces what otherwise would be high monitoring costs for a far-flung network. By franchising units, the incentives of owner and operator of a given hotel or restaurant are aligned because they are one and the same, the franchisee. Franchisors do have to deal with the problem of badly behaving franchisees, but monitoring costs for franchisees are lower than in a regional management hierarchy.

- *Efficiency and cost savings.* The division of labor between the franchisor and franchisee makes for operating efficiencies. Successful franchisees excel at site selection and unit-level management, while franchisors provide efficient distribution and marketing for the brand by combining the purchasing power of the entire network.

While the most common franchise offering is a single franchise, where the franchisee obtains the right to use the franchisor's intellectual property for a single location, some firms use multiunit franchises. In these arrangements, the franchisee is granted a development territory and commits to open new units on a specific schedule. In a master franchise, usually used internationally, the franchisor licenses to the franchisee the right to subfranchise over a large geographic region. One example is the relationship between the Carlson Companies and Rezidor, which holds a master franchise to Carlson's brands in most of Europe, the Middle East, and Africa.

Services Offered by Franchisors to Franchisees

The many services offered to franchisees by franchisors are all geared to increasing franchisee's success and profitability, although franchises do have some disadvantages (see Figure 19.4). Franchisors may offer the following assistance: determining the best available location using sophisticated geo-tagged marketing data; prototype plans and specifications that facilitate unit level efficiencies; a standard operating system; and training assistance and materials at preopening and during subsequent operation. They may sometimes provide financing assistance.

Franchise Fees and Major Terms in Lodging

Most hotel franchise costs are structured as follows. An initial fee to obtain the franchise rights, paid at the signing of the franchise agreement, may be a set fee or a per-room charge. Per-room fees range from $200 to $500 per room, and minimum payments are typically around $25,000. Then, the franchisee pays a royalty fee, usually 4 to 5 percent of gross revenues, for use of trade

Figure 19.4
Benefits and Disadvantages of Franchises

Benefits and Disadvantages for the Franchisee	Benefits and Disadvantages for the Franchisor
Benefits	Benefits
• Reduced Risk of Failure—franchisee receives rights a pre-tested and potentially profitable business format. • Franchisor has designed and fine-tuned the system to maximize profits. • Protected Trade Name—franchisors vigorously protect their trade names and the value of the franchise • Instant market presence and shortened stabilization period	• Receive royalty fees with little capital at stake • Franchises provide a distributional system for good concepts
Disadvantages	Disadvantages
• No guarantee of success • Non-transferable agreement, in general. • Short term of the agreements, generally limited to 20 years or less • Benefits depend on scale of chain • Little control over chain quality and image • Committed to chain-wide initiatives	• Potential loss of operating control • Fees based on revenues; do not participate in cash flows from operations • Franchisees often want independence from franchisor • Must develop strategies to deal with disputes, such as non-conforming franchisees

name, service marks, goodwill, and other franchise services. Other fees include a marketing contribution fee, a reservation fee, a loyalty programs fee, charges for hardware and software, travel agent commissions, training fees, data and communications fees, and the costs of attending the annual conference. These fees and charges are equivalent to 3 percent to 6 percent of gross revenues.

Franchise agreements generally run for 20 years, although I've seen a clear trend to shorter terms. One major franchisor offers a 10-year term. Territorial protection is negotiated on a deal-by-deal basis; some franchisors have a policy of not granting any protections.

Franchise Fees and Major Terms in Restaurants

Restaurant franchisors' fees are similar in many ways to those of hotels. The initial fee averages $25,000 to $50,000, and the royalty fee generally runs from 4 percent to 8 percent of gross revenues. The marketing contribution fee is often combined with the royalty, but in any event is paid as a percentage of gross revenues.

Like hotels, restaurant franchise terms have generally run 20 years, but I've seen an increasing use of the 10/10 contract, which involves a 10-year initial term with a 10-year renewal (contingent on both parties agreeing to the renewal). While few franchisors grant territorial protection, some do give the first development rights for new locations to existing franchisees.

MANAGEMENT CONTRACTS VERSUS LEASES

As a property owner, assuming you have a choice between a management contract or a lease, your decision may rest on your assessment of the allocation of financial risk and control between owner and operator. Leases generally would provide you with relatively predictable returns from your real estate, but once you sign the lease you have little control over how your lessee treats your building during the term of the lease. In contrast, a management contract gives you greater financial potential on both the upside and the downside. Also, with a management contract you have greater control of your property through contractual asset-management provisions. Beyond that, the decision rests on matters of lease accounting, the legal status of tenants, and local custom. Let's take a closer look at management contracts.

Hotel Management Contract Negotiation Strategy

You should not undertake signing a management contract lightly, because it can define a property's identity for up to 60 years. If you've never seen a management contract, you might be surprised by the obligations it imposes on both owners and operators.[4]

As an owner, here are some of the important objectives you might be trying to achieve. Note that some of the goals you have as owner can be at odds with the operator's objectives, and the contract must reconcile those competing agendas. Your chief goals are to achieve a cash flow from your property and make sure that its asset value is preserved. To that end, you might want to insist that the operator bear some financial risk for the success or failure of the operation. This generally occurs through incentive fee mechanisms. You should try to preserve at least some operational influence and control over the hotel by requiring the operator to exhibit appropriate, prudent flexibility in difficult times and not insist on blind adherence to brand standards. You also need transparent systems for monitoring and evaluating your hotel's performance.

For the operator's part, it will seek the exclusive right to manage the hotel without undue ownership interference; the assumption by the owner of most if not all financial risk; indemnification for actions except for gross negligence or fraud; and procedures that require you to provide all funds needed to operate the hotel and to comply with brand standards.

The starting point for discussions over all these points is an agreement between you and your prospective operator regarding the hotel's operating projections. This can take a brief time, but sometimes takes up to a year. If you and the operator cannot even agree on the anticipated financial performance, there's not much point in proceeding with contract negotiations. Your operator may assist you in this process by suggesting ways to optimize the building for minimum costs and maximum revenue.

Once you and the operator have a mutually agreeable set of financial projections, your next step is to negotiate a letter of intent or "deal sheet" that outlines the major areas of agreement without negotiating the legal language in detail. This letter, which runs five to 10 pages, is not an exercise in drafting a legal document. Instead, the purpose is for the parties to identify any "walk-away" items and to memorialize the results of the negotiations regarding the specific hotel being considered. One key point might be what happens if you sell the property. While the operator may not want you to terminate the management agreement if you sell the hotel, it might accept termination if you agree to a significant termination fee or other financial benefits.

Here are some of the other points that go into a letter of intent, all of which outline your fundamental agreement:

- The relationship between the parties (principal-agent or personal services).
- The operator's financial commitment to the project.
- Contract length, including renewals.
- Circumstances for contract termination.
- The management fee structure, including operator services that the owner must pay for outside of the management fee structure.
- Territorial restrictions on the operator's right to operate competing properties near your hotel.
- Dispute handling (arbitration or litigation).
- The lender's rights and obligations in the management contract if you cannot make debt service and the lender must foreclose.

Once you have the deal outlined in the letter of intent, the rest of the negotiations involve converting those understandings into a legal document. This is the province of legal teams, but both you and the operator need to keep tabs on these negotiations.

Important Management Contract Points

Let's discuss the detailed points that go into a management contract.

Agency versus Personal Service This is a contentious matter, because under common law a principal may dismiss an agent at any time, which means an owner can terminate an operator, despite contract language prohibiting such a termination. Yet operators seek (and arguably need) a stable contract term. Court cases supporting agency have changed the playing field and given considerable power to owners. Owners are no longer bound by contract provisions prohibiting termination if they can show that the agency relationship has been violated. In response, you may find that your operator insists that the contract provisions be governed under the terms of Maryland state law. This is because the state of Maryland passed a law in 2003 that requires courts to interpret contracts under contract law instead of agency law, when the two conflict. This means that the termination provisions of the contract will trump the common law of agency. This potential conflict is the reason that you and your operator must consider your relative negotiating power and positions prior to agreement or rejection of an agency relationship.

Operator's Financial Commitment Many owners ask operators to co-invest in the project or otherwise make a financial commitment. As you may guess, this serves as an indication of the operator's commitment to the project, and it provides you with needed capital. I've found such financial commitments in less than half of contracts that I have reviewed. To begin with, the amount of capital involved is relatively small, generally less than 10 percent of the capital needed to acquire or build a hotel. The commitments take one of the four following forms (from the most desirable for the owner to the least desirable):

1. *Key money.* An up-front rebate of management fees provided as a cash payment to the owner. The operator usually demands a rebate of the key money if the contract does not run full term or if the owner sells the hotel within a specified, short period.
2. *Loan.* Generally structured as a mezzanine loan. This type of loan is subordinated to the main mortgage and is not secured by the real estate.
3. *Operating guarantee or cash flow guarantee.* An operator guarantee of a certain level of hotel cash flow in the project's initial years. If the hotel does not produce the guaranteed cash flow, the operator must "cure" the deficiency (make up the difference). This payment is usually subject to a

claw-back mechanism that repays funds advanced under a guarantee out of future cash flows. The cash flow guarantee provides the lender with the assurance that the operator will provide sufficient funds to operate the hotel and cover debt service during the opening years of a hotel project.

4. *Equity.* A partnership arrangement in which the operator contributes funds to the venture. Most owners wish to avoid this, because they don't like the idea of the operator as partner. If your operator is an equity partner you can't terminate the contract, because one cannot terminate one's partners, and the relationship between the owner and operator becomes significantly more complex.

Contract Term and Renewals In general, chain operators are able to obtain terms significantly longer than independent operators as a result of their greater negotiating power. The average term for a chain operator is a 10-year initial term with two 5-year renewal terms at the operator's option. Leading chains obtain substantially longer terms. For independent operators, the initial term is five years with one 3-year renewal term, again at the operator's option. Independent operators are able to significantly extend their initial terms and renewals if they provide key money or another financial contribution.

Contract Termination Assuming that agency is not provided in the contract, owners usually have the right to terminate the contract if the operator consistently underperforms, based on a two-pronged test. First, the hotel must have financial performance that is below the budgeted performance (typically, less than 90 percent of budget) and, second, the poor results must not be the result of poor economic conditions that affect all hotels in the market (often referred to as *force majeure*).

You probably won't be able to obtain the right to terminate the contract without cause, but even if you do you'd have to pay a termination fee in the range of two to five times the most recent annual management fees. The termination fee would decline as a contract approaches maturity.

Chances are that you will be able to negotiate the right to terminate the contract if you sell the hotel, but that probably will be subject to a termination fee. Chain operators often obtain the right of first offer to purchase the hotel if you do plan to sell. In the event that you cannot cover debt service, the typical contract gives the lender the right to terminate the management contract in the event of foreclosure, again subject to a termination fee.

Fee Structure The dominant fee structure in the industry is that the operator earns a base fee based on total revenue, plus an incentive fee based on hotel profitability (see Figure 19.5). Over the past 20 years, contracts have increased the emphasis on incentive fees, which is seen by owners as aligning the interests of the owner and operator. As you see in Figure 19.5, three incentive fee structures are common. Historically, the incentive fee was based on a profit measure called income before fixed charges (IBFC); sometimes a sliding scale is used, with higher payments based on increasing the operating margin. This incentive fee structure remains common in Europe and Asian contracts. A more recent provision is an incentive fee based on cash flow after an owner's priority (or preferred) return. This provision pays the operator a bigger percentage, but it's based on a figure that is more volatile than IBFC. This incentive fee structure is common in North American contracts. In distressed hotel situations, the incentive fee may be based on the improvement in IBFC;

Figure 19.5
Hotel Management Fees

	Basic Fee★			Incentive Fee★★		
	Low	Median	High	Fee Base	Ranges	Relative Use
	% Gross Revenues				% Base	
Chain Operators:						
				IBFC	6−10%	Common
				CFADS	8−20%	Seldom Used
Full-Service	2.0%	2.75%	3.5%	CFAOP	10−30%	Common
				Improved IBFC	10−20%	Seldom Used
				IBFC	8−12%	Common
Limited-Service	2.5%	2.75%	3.0%	CFAOP	10−30%	Common
Independent Operators:						
				IBFC	5−10%	Common
				CFADS	8−15%	Seldom Used
Full-Service	1.5%	4.0%	6.0%	CFAOP	10−20%	Common
				Improved IBFC	10−15%	Seldom Used
				IBFC	8−12%	Common
Limited-Service	2.5%	2.75%	3.0%	CFAOP	10−30%	Common

IBFC = Income Before Fixed Charges (also known as GOP = Gross Operating Profit)
CFADS = Cash Flow After Debt Service
CFAOP = Cash Flow After Owner's Priority (the Owner's Priority is a return on total property investment, generally in the range of a 8−12% return)

★Basic fee sometimes a guaranteed minimum dollar amount.
★★Payment of incentive fee usually subordinated to a negotiated amount; subordinated fees are usually waived, not deferred; if deferred, usually without interest.

Source: Eyster and J. deRoos, "The Negotiation and Administration of Hotel Management Contracts" (Ithaca, NY: Pearson Custom Publishing, 2009).

the operator is rewarded for improving the situation even if the IBFC remains negative. As I said before, in addition to the basic and incentive fees outlined, a contemporary management contract provides for payment for a variety of operator provided services, known as system reimbursable charges.

Other Terms: Protected Territory, Dispute Resolution, and Lender's Rights If you're new to the hotel business you might be surprised to find that your operator would want to open a competing hotel down the street, but most operators seek expansion with multiple brands. The negotiations here must balance your wish to have some territorial protection for your hotel against the operator's wish to have some freedom to expand operations in growing markets. This expansion comes in two potential forms. The operator will want to add brands that do not compete directly with your property, and if you're in a growing market, the operator will want to add competing properties. Your agreement should specify the following: the definition of the restricted area, which brands are excluded from the restricted area, the time period of any restriction, and conditions for adding properties within the restricted area.

With any luck you and your operator will not have major disagreements, but you must decide in advance what dispute resolution mechanisms you will use. In particular, you may want to provide for formal alternatives to litigation. You might use an owner-operator committee with mandated mediation to handle disputes prior to bringing them to arbitration. Then, any arbitration clause should state clearly whether all contract provisions should be subject to arbitration or whether arbitration should be limited to specific disputes such as budget matters, management-fee calculations, operator system-reimbursable expense allocations, determination of unfavorable economic conditions for operator-performance provisions, and disputes about repair and maintenance, reserve for replacement, and capital improvement allocations.

Finally, your contract will have provisions regarding the lender's rights should you default on your loan. The lender wants to be able to terminate existing obligations when taking over a property in foreclosure. That would remove from the lender all of the rights and obligations of the (now departed) owner. However, recent contracts have given rise to the subordination, nondisturbance, and attornment agreement (SNDA), a form of nondisturbance agreement that has the effect of removing the lender's right to terminate under the existing management contract after a foreclosure. Lenders will be increasingly reluctant to grant an SNDA in the future as a result of lessons learned in the 2008–2010 downturn.

HOTEL LEASES

Most hotel brand operators prefer management contracts to leases, because accounting rules require that fixed lease payments be disclosed as a debtlike operator liability and capitalized. No such balance sheet effect exists for management contracts, because the contract creates no debtlike liability.

A lease innovation that makes disclosure moot is an agreement in which the lease payments are 100 percent variable, based on room revenues, as there are no fixed debtlike obligations. This innovation has brought about a change in attitude toward leases on the part of operators, who now see leases as a risk sharing device. The absence of a fixed lease payment makes the owner and operator both at risk for the business's success.

Freed of the accounting requirement, variable leases offer advantages for both you and your tenant. Operators can generally obtain higher "fees" under a lease than a management contract in many situations because they can keep all proceeds beyond the cost of doing business and the rent (even if that is based on revenues). As a landlord, your rent payments would be more bondlike, since they are based on revenues, not profits. Both are variable, but profits are considerably more volatile.

Most leases provide for guaranteed minimum rents that are typically capped. Without that provision, there is an incentive for the operator to walk away in tough economic times. While good operators create leasehold value at the beginning of the term, this benefit diminishes rapidly over the term of the lease.

Important Hotel Lease Points

Although hotel leases are far less complicated than hotel management contracts, they still have important negotiating issues. Legal counsel is essential in helping craft these provisions.

Rent If the rent is fixed, does it have a mechanism to index rent to inflation? If the rent is variable, is it based on a percentage of revenues or a percentage of profits? A recent publication estimates that roughly one-third of current contracts feature fixed rents, more than one-third have fixed plus variable rents, 1 in 10 have variable rents, and the remainder are unknown.[5]

Term Initial terms are split into three roughly even groups: over 20 years, 10 to 20 years, and less than 10 years. Most leases have two renewal options of five years. Long lease terms benefit the tenant, rather than the landlord.

FF&E Ownership and Repair (Personal Property) Generally, the tenant owns and has complete responsibility for replacement and repair of furniture, fixtures, and equipment (FF&E—personal property), but major items such as laundry equipment and kitchen equipment are often negotiated.

Major Repairs The owner often takes responsibility for the upkeep and replacement of repair and replacement of the building structure, heating, ventilation, and air-conditioning (HVAC) systems, roof, and other major systems.

Other Items You must negotiate the size of any security deposit, insurance requirements, whether the lease is assignable, standards for record keeping, reports to the owner, owner audit, and what portions of the lease are subject to arbitration.[6]

Restaurant Leases

Restaurant leases are substantially different from hotel leases, primarily because of the difference in bargaining power between the landlord and the tenant. In restaurant leases, tenants have greatly diminished bargaining power. Whether you're the tenant-operator or the owner, you are effectively in a partnership that is based on the lease provisions. Make sure that you have the advice of legal counsel.

Rent Landlords generally treat restaurants just as they do other retailers, in terms of the rent formula. Retail leases are structured with a fixed minimum rent and an overage rent that is based on sales. So a restaurant with $3 million in annual sales might have a minimum rent of $150,000 per year plus an overage of 6 percent of sales over $2.5 million (or another $30,000). Thus, the landlord has the comfort of the minimum rent, but shares with the tenant when sales are over the threshold (see Figure 19.6 for customary restaurant lease provisions).

In addition to paying rent for the use of the space, tenants also pay common area charges, which are the tenants' fair share of the operating expenses of the shopping center or building.

Term Initial terms for restaurant leases are generally less than 10 years, and many include a 5-year renewal option. One key provision that protects both the restaurateur and the landlord is a cancellation clause. This terminates the lease should revenues fall below a negotiated level.

Figure 19.6
Restaurant Rents

	Rent as % Sales	Total Charges % Sales
Super Regional Malls		
Restaurants	4–7%	9.5–11%
Food Court	6–8%	12–16%
Regional Malls		
Restaurants	5–6%	8–10%
Food Court	6–8%	10–15%
Community Centers		
Restaurants	5–6%	8–10%
Fast Food	5–6%	8–9%
Neighborhood Centers		
Restaurants	5–6%	10–12%
Fast Food	5–6%	8–10%

Source: Urban Land Institute, "Dollars and Cents of Shopping Centers."

Other Items Whether you're the landlord or tenant, you must negotiate language regarding the specific use of the premises. Tenants should expect the landlord to exclude many uses not related to the restaurant business. You'll also need to negotiate security deposit and insurance requirements.

Closing

As we have seen, separating the real property from the intellectual property in the hospitality industry has created many different opportunities for success. Those who are new to the hospitality industry can enhance their success by understanding the value proposition of various combinations of property rights. Whether you enter the industry as an operator or a real estate owner, well-constructed agreements with other property rights holders creates a wide variety of strategies for success.

NOTES

1. For example, see Accor, "Investor Day 2008: Hotel Development Strategy and Financial Targets," www.accor.fr, 2008.
2. United States Federal Trade Commission, "Franchise Rule," 16 *C.F.R. Part* 436, *Compliance Guide*, May 2008.

3. United States Federal Trade Commission, 15445 *Federal Register, Rules and Regulations* 72(61) (March 30, 2007).
4. For an extended treatment of management contracts, see J. Eyster and J. deRoos, *The Negotiation and Administration of Hotel Management Contracts*, 4th ed. (Ithaca, NY: Pearson Custom Publishing, 2009).
5. See Jones Lang LaSalle Hotels and Baker & McKenzie, "Global Lease Agreements," *Hotel Management Contracts,* joneslanglasalle.com, 2008.
6. J. Eyster and J. deRoos, *The negotiation and Administration of Hotel Manegement Contracts* (Ithaca, NY: Pearson Custom Publishing, 2009).

CHAPTER 20

DEVELOPING AND RENOVATING HOSPITALITY PROPERTIES

JACK B. CORGEL, JAN A. DEROOS, and KEVIN FITZPATRICK

Land development includes acquisition of land, securing zoning changes from local governments, installation of infrastructure improvements to land such as streets and utilities, and constructing buildings to generate revenue. In this chapter, we discuss those processes as they relate to developing hospitality properties—a process far more complex than that associated with other commercial real estate.

FORMATION OF DEVELOPMENT TEAMS

From a business perspective, developers function both as entrepreneurs, who commit time and money for uncertain returns, and managers, who assemble and administer the resources necessary to ensure project success. Figure 20.1 shows various business relationships involving a developer and others. These relationships fall into two categories: those who supply services, materials, and labor directly toward the creation of the physical real estate, and those who supply financial capital.

Suppliers of Financial Capital

Development and construction projects, like companies, have a financial capital structure usually comprising debt and equity. Chapters 17 and 19 presented some of the structures of equity investment that help finance real estate, including development projects. One form not mentioned earlier is joint-venture arrangements structured as partnerships. In equity joint ventures, money partners supply most of the funds necessary to advance projects, while developers mainly supply ideas and the managerial skills to complete the projects.

Figure 20.1
Development Team Relationships

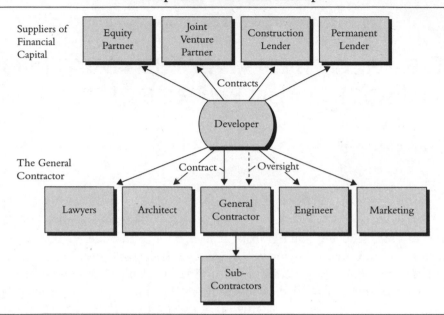

THE DEVELOPMENT PROCESS

Regardless of the ownership structure, the economic viability of a project will depend on several factors, beginning with your goals. The development process is shown in Figure 20.2. As you look at a particular site to determine the highest and best use for that site, you might consider numerous possible investments including hospitality, residential, commercial, or possibly a mixed-use development. An important component of that analysis will include such matters as current zoning and the local planning department's desires for the site, as well as access and proximity to demand generators. One possibility is that you have a mixed-use site that requires a hospitality component due to zoning or as a value-added element to the overall development.

Regardless of the reason, if you are determining the feasibility of a new hotel, you must consider existing and proposed competition, the demand drivers for the product, the seasonality of the business, and any business segments not being served by existing hotels (e.g., corporate traveler, meeting and groups, or leisure travelers). When reviewing the viability of a local hotel, it is critical that you understand the local hotel room demand generators. If a portion of your business is generated by a local business or tourist attraction,

Figure 20.2
Stages in the Development Process

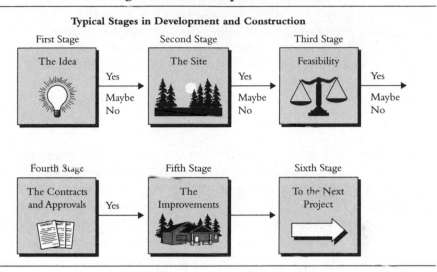

Typical Stages in Development and Construction

it is important to check the economic viability of that demand generator, including its ability to change location. Niagara Falls isn't going anywhere, but a tenant in a multiuse development can easily relocate. You can start by meeting with managers of existing hotels to determine the level of business, and with government officials to determine what revenue information the local hotels file that is part of the public record, including tax assessments.

Given the benefits that hotels provide to the local community (including jobs and tax revenues), you should contact local government leaders to determine all forms of support that they can provide for your proposed development, including improvements to access and utilities, tax credits for training and real estate tax abatements, and financing guarantees. The amount of support for a particular hotel can vary greatly from one location to another.

Determining occupancy rates is critical for your financial *pro forma*. Hotels that cater to business travelers are often busy during the week but suffer on weekends. Such hotels appear to be successful because they operate at or near capacity for four nights per week, but they face low occupancy for the three weekend nights. That pattern does not maximize the use of the property. So you need to determine what other market segments your hotel might serve, to ease this peak and valley occupancy. The most successful hotels are those that have a business mix, which allows them to successfully maximize revenue from a number of market segments. Low-rate business in slow periods adds revenue when demand for high-rate business does not exist. The best measure of revenue is revenue per available room (RevPAR), which combines average daily rate (ADR) with average occupancy. Hotels with a high RevPAR are generally successful. They usually do this by offering a portfolio of rates for different market segments, based on time of booking and time of arrival, as explained in Chapter 26. The process of setting room rates based on demand is called revenue management (RM), which has become a core strategy of most hotels. Most likely, your hotel would maintain high rates for those weekday business travelers, but offer promotional rates for the weekend traffic.

Early in the process, you must determine which hotels are truly competition for the product you intend to build. This is your competitive set. If you misjudge which hotels are truly competitive, your competitive analysis will be inaccurate. For this reason, you would do well to hire a well-qualified, independent appraisal company to complete a market analysis and review of the project's feasibility. We discuss feasibility studies in a moment.

If the site review is favorable and you have identified a product concept, you need to consider your brand positioning. You can choose among a major chain brand, a small chain brand, or an independent operation. As discussed in Chapter 17, part of this decision involves assessing who will manage the property. You can retain a manager and manage it yourself, contract with an independent management company, or contract with the branded management firm. If you want a franchise brand, you must obtain a franchise and execute a separate management agreement with a hotel management company. As discussed in Chapter 19, franchise agreements allow you to use the brand's name, trade dress, reservation systems, and management techniques. You must operate the hotel according to the franchisor's brand standards or lose the right to use the brand. Even if you manage the hotel yourself, for legal and tax purposes you would normally create a separate management company and execute a management agreement between your ownership group and your management company.

One place to look when you are evaluating brands is the major brand's Web sites. Hotel companies' Web sites usually define the products they offer, the markets their products are designed for, and the process you'd follow to obtain approval for a franchise and to build a property. Many hotel company development Web sites will give you such specific requirements as room size, room mix, total building gross area, and even parking. It is important to recognize that these design details are for prototypes only and the ultimate design characteristics need to be refined for the site in question. The hotel company will help you analyze whether and how one of their products may be successful for your site. Some brands won't be available due to prior commitments, but most hotel companies can recommend a particular prototype and provide general cost estimates for construction and project completion.

As you evaluate brands, consider competing brand products in the area, guest loyalty programs, franchise fees, your management company's familiarity with the brand, support from the franchisor, and how the product serves the needs of the market.

If you're planning to purchase an existing hotel, you have a different set of considerations. First, you must determine whether to keep the existing brand or to rebrand the hotel. Your decision may be driven by whether you are buying a successful hotel or one that has been struggling. Rebranding can be a difficult task since you will have to address cancellation rights and costs with the current brand, the cost of modifying the current hotel to meet your new brand's design standards, and what hotels will compete with your newly branded hotel.

While you could retain a firm to perform the initial concept review, it is important that you be knowledgeable and comfortable with the market environment since your money is at risk. In addition, the work of this initial due diligence phase is virtually worthless if the project does not move forward. Costs incurred for projects that are not built are called *dead deal costs,* while costs incurred for projects that are built are included as a project cost. Successful developers make it a point of keeping dead deal costs to a minimum.

Feasibility Study

Once you are comfortable with your market investigation, the next step is to commission a feasibility study. The consultant can either evaluate a particular product for your site or work with you to identify the best prototype for the site. To formulate their recommendation, the feasibility company will use such inputs as interviews with area hotel managers and government officials, local demand generators, and market information gained from other work they have done in the area. When selecting a hotel consultant, seek out one that has extensive hospitality knowledge as well as knowledge of the planned prototype. In addition, the consultant should have access to several years of industry data for your market (usually, STAR reports from Smith Travel Research). The feasibility study will examine the project, the market, and competitors; expected mix of corporate, individual, and leisure travelers; average rate and occupancy; and departmental revenues and expenses, overhead expenses, and reserves. It will also forecast the first five or 10 years of the property's expected financial performance. Since the consultant does not know the capital structure, feasibility projections may not include debt service coverage or return to the owner. That said, you may want to leave the capital structure out of the report, as you consider alternative financing structures.

Often, the consultant also will indicate the value of the hotel. Hotels need time to become fully operational, gain full market recognition and acceptance, and become stabilized in terms of revenue. The feasibility study can provide a value at completion and a value at stabilization. It is important that the stabilized value be higher than the cost of construction, or there's no point in proceeding. This spread between cost and value is known as the *developer profit,* which is your compensation for the risk and expense of building a hotel. You determine the amount of development profit that is "adequate," based on the reason for the hotel's construction. For example, if the hotel is part of a mixed-use project, the contribution the hotel component adds to the overall complex should be taken into consideration.

Financing Review

Feasibility study in hand, you go to a lender or finance broker to determine the amount of construction debt and permanent financing available for the project. The result will be an indicative term sheet that identifies the loan amount, rate, security for the loan, basic loan covenants, and repayment terms. From this, you can summarize the full cost of construction on a spreadsheet, using the information provided by the consultant together with the information prepared by the loan broker or lender. Your estimate will include debt service, the amount of equity required, return to your equity, and your ultimate profit. Make note of any guarantees the lenders are requiring, and realize that the proposed terms are only initial terms that may vary substantially prior to closing the loan. There is still some time before you will be prepared to submit a loan package to the lender, and changes in the market environment will affect the capital package of debt and equity. In the interim, you might see changes in interest rate, the economic situation, and the lender's appetite for real estate loans and hotel loans in particular.

You'll probably be involved with two loans, one for construction and the other for permanent financing. Construction financing can include assistance with land assemblage and includes all construction costs. It extends for a period after opening to allow the property to stabilize. The construction lender is often a commercial bank, which may require that the owner's equity be funded first and require personal guarantees along with other requirements to ensure repayment of the loan. The interest rate for construction financing is generally a floating, or adjustable rate, which changes according to an index such as the prime rate. Once your property is stabilized, permanent lenders provide financing based on the property's performance. The level of debt is determined by many factors including the loan-to-value ratio (i.e., loan amount divided by the property value), the debt service coverage rate (annual property cash flow available for debt service divided by the annual debt service), the operating history of the property, and the management company's expertise. The interest rate for permanent financing is generally fixed for the term of the loan, and often the security for the loan is limited to the hotel. Any personal liability you might have is restricted to representations made to the lender. An experienced mortgage broker familiar with market terms and the requirements of particular lenders can be a great asset to canvass the market for available lenders.

Overall Program

The mix of guest rooms, meeting space, back-of-house space, and food and beverage space is called the program, which is covered in detail in Chapter 21. The program will have a large hand in driving the hotel's design. It is critical to assemble a team of experienced professionals who can properly allocate space within the property so the hotel can both operate efficiently and provide an appropriate level of guest satisfaction. The design team must include professionals capable of determining the project's impact on adjoining sites, including traffic, noise, and water runoff. The team members must also know how to evaluate different design elements to make the property cost effective from an energy standpoint and evaluate whether the property will meet the Leadership in Energy and Environmental Design (LEED) standards established by the United States Green Building Council.

Economic Feasibility of a Select Service Hotel

In this chapter, we examined how you as a hotel developer evaluate projects to determine whether they will receive their desired returns. Let's look at how this works out in a real-world situation, with the investment possibility in Grandville, USA, for Alexandra Brown and her firm, Big Red Development (BRD).

The Investment and Financing Decision

BRD has submitted a loan application for the project to the Local Commercial Bank (LCB), based on the following summary data: BRD's development department has estimated the cost to develop as $21 million.

(continued)

(continued)

The construction costs have been verified by a general contractor, and the furniture, fixtures, and equipment (FF&E) costs are based on a similar hotel that opened recently. The bank's appraiser prepared a forecast of hotel operations, and used that to generate an estimate of market value of $22.5 million. The full investment analysis assumptions are shown in Figure 20.3. Brown feels that the Grandville economy is much stronger than indicated in the appraiser's market study and opinion of market value. She has performed extensive market research to forecast occupancy and average rates, and has worked closely with her operations team to create a realistic set of financial projections using results from the three company-operated properties as benchmarks. Based on this research, she is convinced that property performance will be stronger than the bank's appraisal *pro forma* indicates. However, LCB insists on using the appraisal report's estimate of market value in their evaluation. The bank's conservative approach is evident in the size of the loan they are willing to extend, which is 67 percent of the costs of development, not 67 percent of the appraised value. This means that BRD must invest $7 million of equity (33 percent of the project cost).

Last week, Brown submitted her LCB loan application. LCB responded favorably, indicating that the project would be considered for a loan given the success of BRD's two recently completed projects. The senior loan officer provided a term sheet with the following loan terms:

Development Cost	$21 million
Loan Size	$14 million
Interest Rate on Mortgage	7.5 percent
Amortization Term	25-year term, monthly payments

BRD has a long relationship with LCB and feels that continuing to shop the loan would not be productive. To support the investment decision, Brown must calculate the returns on the investment, using the current loan terms from LCB. For this purpose, she will need to answer two key questions:

- Is the net present value (NPV) of the overall investment decision, not considering borrowing, positive? If yes, the project is economically viable.
- Is the NPV of the equity investment decision (after deducting borrowing costs) positive? This will be considered both before and after the impact of income taxes. If the NPV is positive, this indicates that the decision to invest equity is supported.

Figure 20.3
Investment Analysis

Select Service Hotel, Research Triangle Area, USA
Investment Analysis Assumptions – Select Service Hotel

Overall Property Investment Decision	Year 0	Year 1	Year 2	Year 3	Year 4	Year 5	Year 6	Year 7	Year 8	Year 9	Year 10
Initial Investment	($21,000)										
Hotel Cash Flows from Operations		$1,121	$1,852	$2,278	$2,366	$2,444	$2,514	$2,587	$2,640	$2,694	$2,750
Net Sales Proceeds											$30,238
Total Cash Flows to the Property	($21,000)	$1,121	$1,852	$2,278	$2,366	$2,444	$2,514	$2,587	$2,640	$2,694	$32,988
Cash Flow Dividend		5.34%	8.82%	10.85%	11.27%	11.64%	11.97%	12.32%	12.57%	12.83%	13.10%
NPV @ 11% $2,594.32											
IRR 12.79%											

Equity Investment Decision – After-Tax	Year 0	Year 1	Year 2	Year 3	Year 4	Year 5	Year 6	Year 7	Year 8	Year 9	Year 10
Initial Investment	($7,000)										
Before-Tax Cash Flows to Equity		($121)	$610	$1,036	$1,124	$1,202	$1,272	$1,345	$1,398	$1,452	$1,508
Before-Tax Sales Proceeds											$19,077
Total Before-Tax Cash Flows to Equity	($7,000)	($121)	$610	$1,036	$1,112	$1,202	$1,272	$1,345	$1,398	$1,452	$20,586
Cash Flow Dividend		-1.72%	8.72%	14.81%	16.06%	17.18%	18.18%	19.22%	19.98%	20.75%	21.55%
NPV @ 16% $1,680.80											
IRR 19.27											

Equity Investment Decision – After-Tax	Year 0	Year 1	Year 2	Year 3	Year 4	Year 5	Year 6	Year 7	Year 8	Year 9	Year 10
Initial Investment	($7,000)										
After Cash Flows to Equity		$74	$510	$769	$830	$886	$936	$988	$1,014	$1,039	$1,062
After Sales Proceeds											$15,685
Total After-Tax Cash Flows to Equity	($7,000)	$74	$510	$769	$830	$886	$936	$988	$1,014	$1,039	$16,746
Cash Flow Dividend		1.05%	7.29%	10.99%	11.86%	12.65%	13.37%	14.11%	14.49%	14.84%	15.17%
NPV @ 13% $1,518.31											
IRR 15.85%											

(continued)

Brown performs an analysis that assumes a 12-year holding period, 2 years preopening, and 10 years of operation. She estimates the selling price of the hotel at the end of the 10-year operating period and performs a discounted cash flow analysis to provide an estimate of holding period NPV and the yields (internal rate of return, or IRR). The firm feels that Select Service Hotels should provide a minimum 11 percent overall yield. The firm has a minimum equity return requirement of 16 percent on a before-tax basis and 13 percent on an after-tax basis. Based on Brown's analysis, the project's numbers are as follows:

	Cost	Value	NPV	IRR
Overall Project	$21.0 million	$23.6 million	$2.6 million	12.79%
Equity—before Tax	$7.0 million	$8.66 million	$1.66 million	19.27%
Equity—after Tax	$7.0 million	$8.51 million	$1.51 million	15.85%

Every indicator points to a positive investment decision; the values are greater than the cost, the NPV is positive, and the IRR is above the required rate of return in every case. In addition, the project is eligible for two tax incentive programs; the first is a 50 percent rebate of real estate taxes in the first five years of operation to offset offsite improvements made to develop the hotel; the second is an employee job training tax credit of $350 per employee. The combined value of these programs adds $1 million to the project and equity NPV. Thus, Brown thinks the project is worth approximately $24.6 million when it is developed. For these reasons, the project is a go, and the Grandville Select Service Hotel will be constructed.

Construction and Property Opening

Chapter 17 urged you to seek legal counsel in structuring your ownership, and you received similar advice in Chapter 19, regarding contracts and leases. Again, the importance of a sound legal team cannot be underestimated. The legal team must not only be able to help with purchasing land to assemble the site and with construction, but they must also be able to assist with the negotiations with the franchisor and management company. Coordination of the contracts among varying parties early on is critical to the ease of operation and will hopefully prevent subsequent costly conflicts.

You'll also need an experienced and diligent architectural team. This team not only needs experience with hotels generally, but also with the specific type of hotel that you're building. For franchise hotels, it is important that the architects be comfortable with working in a situation where they must conform to brand standards, leaving little room for creativity. At the same time, no two sites are the same and the plans must be adjusted to local conditions and local construction codes. The architect will retain a mechanical and electrical engineer, a structural engineer, a soils engineer, local code compliance experts, and a traffic engineer, if needed. In addition, you will likely need to retain an environmental engineer that conducts the preliminary site environmental review.

Construction contracts take one of three forms. In a fixed-price or lump-sum arrangement the contractor will build the project for a fixed price; in a guaranteed-maximum-price contract, the contractor agrees to a maximum price for construction and you and the contractor share any savings below that maximum price; and in a construction-management contract the contractor takes bids from various subcontractors, but you are at risk for the ultimate price. Even if the contract is a maximum-price contract or a stipulated-sum contract, you remain liable for any unforeseen site conditions.

As work proceeds, the contractor will issue monthly requests for payment, which you, the construction consultant, architect, and construction lender all review. If there are change orders, you must obtain quick pricing for any such changes. The construction lender will generally require the owner to ensure the work is lien free, which means the contractors must be paid. In addition, the construction loan must be kept in balance so that costs of completion are covered by equity and the construction loan. Any cost increases due to change orders or delayed construction must be funded by additional equity if reserves are insufficient.

Before you even start construction, you must secure financing, obtain all construction approvals, and have a franchise approval, if applicable. Further, it is critical for you to fully understand the local requirements for property inspection during construction, and to receive a certificate of occupancy to open the hotel. This information must be coordinated with the requirements of the construction lender and the franchisor.

Construction costs are often divided into land, hard costs, soft costs, FF&E, and preopening and working capital. A contingency for unexpected items can be added as a separate category or included in each subcategory. Land includes the actual cost of the land and cost related to the acquisition. Hard costs are the actual costs of constructing the building, for example, the construction contract. Soft costs include all consultants and advisors, including the architect, legal, accounting, brokerage, and franchise fees, and testing during construction. The FF&E outfit your hotel for operation. Preopening and working capital are the costs of retaining staff and training personnel and marketing prior to opening, money for the hotel to acquire food and beverages prior to opening, and the estimated initial losses until the hotel achieves breakeven.

Property Opening A hotel opening is a complex matter, since the hotel itself must be ready to open, and you also need to retain staff, market the property, and train the staff prior to opening. Often, the first person retained for a new hotel is the marketing manager, who conducts detailed due diligence on potential clients and establishes a presence in the market. You or your management firm will hire the general manager and other department heads months prior to the hotel's opening. Among other things, this permits them to resign from their current assignment and relocate their families if necessary.

The senior staff will begin to review training and operating manuals prepared by the franchisor or the management company, and adjust them for the needs of the particular property. Staff selection is critical to the success of the property, and managers often work with outside consultants to attract a large pool of potential applicants and select those best suited for the property. Based on the construction completion date, the management team will schedule training periods and begin to take over portions of the property to allow the employees access to the work areas, begin to train in the actual space, stock the work rooms, and operate the kitchen equipment.

The manager will increase the number of employees on the payroll as the opening date approaches. In addition, the sales team will be booking business anticipating the hotel opening (preopening sales). Any delay in construction can be costly at this point, since not only are you paying additional construction interest, but you are also paying for the preopening staff along with potential costs for relocating business that was booked into the hotel. The actual hotel opening requires the approval of the local authorities, including the building department and the fire department, as well as the hotel franchisor, and the management company (if there is one). This period can be stressful especially if the team is not familiar with the process.

For properties that operate in a seasonal business, it is critical that you select a competent contractor that can complete the property on time and not miss the high-rate seasonal business. Many professional meeting planners will not book your hotel until it is actually open to ensure the meeting can be accommodated and the staff is properly trained.

If you successfully make your way through this process, congratulations. Your hotel will probably open quietly (soft opening) to get operations going until the grand or hard opening. From this point, you and your managers will be focusing on the information found in later chapters, such as building your brand, setting appropriate prices through revenue management, and addressing market segmentation.

CHAPTER 21

PLANNING AND PROGRAMMING A HOTEL

JAN A. DEROOS

$\mathbf{I}$f you are planning a hotel you must balance functional, layout, and aesthetic issues to develop a property that simultaneously meets the needs of the guests, the staff, and the owner. In general, five-star properties have public areas that are heavily design oriented, with the functional aspects carefully integrated to enhance, yet not dominate the space. However, budget properties tend to favor function and layout over design, for maximum utility. Regardless of how the spaces are configured, the developer must consider and balance many conflicting needs before a design is ready for the contractor's hand. The best examples provide properties that inspire; are safe, efficient, and cost effective; and that maintain their utility and charm through time.

Programming is the process of defining the activities that will be conducted within a hotel, allocating the requisite space, and establishing relationships between the spaces. This is one of the first steps in the development process. While the developer may work with an architect in developing the program, the developer is responsible for creating the program and for ensuring that the building is designed to accomplish the goals set out in the program. In addition to detailing the activities, space allocations, and relationships within the building, a successful program helps to establish the way the building or buildings are situated on a site, the onsite automobile and pedestrian flows, and connections to the external world. In almost all cases, the activities are the starting point. Once the activities are defined, relationships among them are established. Early in the programming process, you can use schematic bubble diagrams to convey both activities and relationships. Figure 21.1 shows a schematic bubble diagram for a hotel with the basic functional relationships.

Figure 21.1
Basic Schematic Relationships

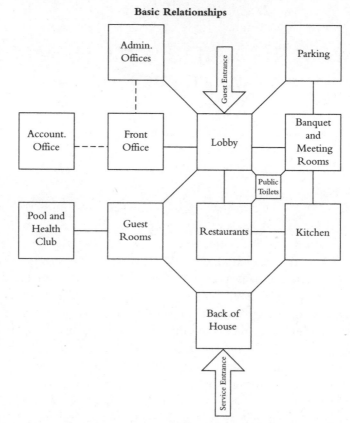

Note the role of the lobby as a central gathering point serving both the public areas and the back-of-house areas. Once the activities and relationships are established, you can allocate appropriate space to the activity, both direct activity space and space needed to support the activity. For example, a hotel needs space not only for its guestrooms, but also for infrastructure such as the plumbing, mechanical systems (heat and air-conditioning), vertical transportation (stairs and elevators), horizontal circulation (corridors), and service areas for housekeeping. The summary of all the activities, relationships, and space allocations in a hotel is called a *building program* or *design brief*. The building program is typically broken down as indicated in Figure 21.2.

You'll find that the program and its preparation are a collaborative endeavor. While the developer drives the process, input is sought from the

Figure 21.2
Contents of a Typical Building Program

- Overall design philosophy including the look and feel of the property
- Site layout and site planning
- Public circulation and lobby
- Guestrooms
- Food and beverage areas
- Meeting space and circulation
- Recreational amenities
- Back-of-house areas

Figure 21.3
Overall Hotel Program

	Guestroom Area (ft²)		Total Hotel
	Net	**Gross**	**Gross Area (ft²)**
Motel, economy hotel	300	380	420
All-Suite hotel	430	590	750
Urban Business hotel	340	480	650
Resort	390	540	780
Convention hotel	340	480	750

Note: Figures are floor area in square feet per guestroom. Guestroom net area is the usable area including bathroom and vestibule. Guestroom gross area includes walls, elevators, stairways, corridors, storage, and mechanical areas on the guestroom floors. Total hotel gross area is the entire hotel, excluding parking.

design team, the franchisor, the hotel operator, and other consultants. The process is iterative, starting with a rather coarse document containing a provisional list of spaces and a rough outline of space requirements. This is used to establish a preliminary construction and development budget. As the project moves through the feasibility process, the program becomes increasingly refined and becomes the basis for the schematic design prepared by the architectural team.

Figures 21.3 and 21.4 give you a preliminary perspective for a hotel building program. Figure 21.3 provides a useful starting point.[1] While an economy hotel may have only 420 square feet (39 square meters) of gross hotel area per guestroom, a resort hotel may have almost double the area or 780 square feet (72 square meters). The reason for the size difference is twofold. First, the resort's guestrooms themselves are 30 percent bigger (390 net square feet vs. 300 net square feet). Second, the resort has a much larger percentage of the overall program devoted to public areas and back-of-house

Figure 21.4
Hotel Space Allocation

	Number of Guestrooms	Percentage of Total Hotel Area		
		Guestrooms	Public Areas	Back-of-House
Motel, economy hotel	<100	90	5	5
All-suite hotel	100–200	80	12	8
Urban business hotel	100–300+	75	14	11
Resort	100–500	70	16	14
Convention hotel	300–1,000+	65	20	15

Note: The number of guestrooms/hotel depends on local market conditions and shows a large variation from country to country. The space allocations (percentages) remain largely the same worldwide.

areas (10 percent of total hotel gross area for an economy hotel versus 30 percent for a resort hotel). Figure 21.4 shows you how the space allocation varies depending on the type of hotel.[2]

If you're involved in developing a chain hotel, the programming work is greatly simplified. Whether the property is franchised or managed by the chain, the brand will have a set of brand standards and prototype designs that go a long way toward defining the activities, relationships, and space allocations. The developer needs to adapt the prototype to the market and the site, but much of the work has been done by the brand. On the other hand, the developer of a five-star independent resort must start from scratch and think clearly about the program; although a significant amount of information comes from the feasibility process, the final program requires careful thinking about the short- and long-term business plan for the hotel.

PROGRAMMING GUESTROOMS

The most fundamental planning for a hotel involves the guestrooms—not only do they account for the bulk of space within a hotel, but a large measure of the hotel experience is in the guestroom. Developing an efficient and effective design of these areas is critical for your initial development budget, but this is also a key to long-term guest satisfaction and operating efficiency. While low-rise hotels with one to three stories typically use a design with guestrooms on both sides of a corridor (the "double-loaded" slab), high-rise hotels use this configuration along with a variety of rectangular, triangular, and circular tower designs. The choice of guestroom floor layout is driven by design, site, and cost considerations. Figure 21.5 shows the most

Figure 21.5
Guestroom Floor Analysis

Configuration	Rooms per Floor	Dimensions	Guestrooms (percent)	Corridor ft²(m²) Per Room	Comments
Single-loaded slab 	Varies 12–30+	32 ft. (10 m) × any length	65%	80 ft.² (7.5 m²)	Vertical core usually not affected by room module
Double-loaded slab 	Varies 16–40+	60 ft. (18 m) × any length	70%	45 ft.² (4.2 m²)	Economical; length limited to egress stair placement to meet building code
Offset slab 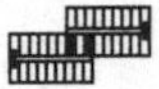	Varies 24–40+	80 ft. (24 m) × any length	72%	50 ft.² (4.6 m²)	Core is buried, creating less perimeter wall per room, more corridor because of elevator lobby
Rectangular tower	16–24	110 × 110 ft. (34 × 34 m)	65%	60 ft. (5.6 m²)	Planning issues focus on access to corner rooms, fewer rooms per floor make core layout difficult
Circular tower	16–24	90–130 ft. diameter (27–40 m)	67%	45–65 ft.² (4.2–6 m²)	High amounts of exterior wall per room, difficult to plan guest bathroom
Triangular tower 	24–30	Varies	64%	65–85 ft.² (6–7.9 m²)	Central core inefficient due to shape; corner rooms easier to plan than with square tower
Atrium 	24+	90 ft. + (27 m)	62%	95 ft.² (8.8 m²)	Open volume creates spectacular space, open corridors, opportunity for glass elevators; requires careful engineering for HVAC and smoke evacuation

325

common guestroom floor types and their overall efficiencies, as indicated by the guestrooms (percent) column.[3] The most efficient are the double-loaded slab and the offset slab, while the least efficient is the atrium-style arrangement. The presence of all types of slabs is a continuing testament to the fact that design, not efficiency drives floor slab design choice.

The most suitable slab design depends on the circumstances, which include the configuration of the site and the desired visual identity. If your hotel is in a dense urban core, land costs drive the decision to use a tower configuration and often the arrangement of the tower on the site itself. In a resort location, though, the desires to maximize views and to minimize the visual impact of the property generally conspire to drive a low-rise guestroom configuration, which might even be single-loaded if there are ocean or other spectacular views. As you can see, developers need to take into account many factors when planning guestrooms. Figure 21.6 provides a summary of things for you to consider.[4]

Figure 21.6
Guestroom Floor Planning Considerations

Siting and Orientation

- Site the guestroom structure to be visible from the road.
- Orient guestrooms to enhance views; "view rooms" command a price premium.
- Where feasible, assess the relative visual impact and construction cost of various guestroom plan configurations.
- Position the guestroom structure to limit its structural impact on the ballroom and other major public spaces.
- Consider solar loads and solar screening, especially for blocks of rooms with east or west exposures.

Floor Layout

- For economy of construction, organize the guestroom tower or wings so that the guestrooms occupy the maximum amount of the gross floor area.
- Develop the corridor plan to facilitate guest and staff circulation.
- Place the elevator lobby in middle third of the structure to minimize walking distances.
- Provide service elevator, linen storage, and vending in a central location on the guestroom floor.
- Plan corridor width at a minimum of 5.0 ft. (1.5 m), 5.5 ft. (1.65 m) optional.
- Significant plumbing economy can result if guest bathrooms are placed back to back.
- Locate handicap-accessible guestrooms on lower floors and near elevators.

Figure 21.7
Guestroom Mix

Type of Hotel	Room type as a percent total guestrooms		
	Double–Double (or Double–Twin)	Single King (or Single Queen)	Suites
Business (downtown)	30%	60%	10%
Boutique or lifestyle hotel	10	80	10
Suburban/airport hotel	50	45	5
Roadside select service hotel	60	40	0
Budget hotel	80	20	0
Resort/family oriented	75	20	5
Resort/couples oriented	20	75	5
Convention hotel	55	35	10
Conference center	30	65	5
All-suite hotel	30	70	0
Super-luxury	20	70	10
Casino hotel	45	40	15+

The planning of individual guestrooms is driven by the locale and the target markets for the property. Almost all hotels include a mix of guestrooms, often composed of rooms with one king (or queen) bed, rooms with two double (or twin) beds, and suites of differing configurations. While the bed mix is an inexact science, Figure 21.7 provides a rough guideline for various types of hotels.[5] Note how the recommended bed mix varies widely depending on the type of hotel. While double-double rooms may make up only 10 percent of a boutique hotel, they could be 75 percent of the beds in a family-oriented resort. It is important that you match the bedroom mix to the market and the marketing plan, as the type of bed configuration has a major impact on guest satisfaction. Single business travelers prefer one bed and like the remaining space devoted to work and lounging space. A family prefers the second bed for their children, although some hotels provide flexibility with a slightly larger room containing a single king (or queen) bed and a sofa that can be converted into a bed.

Once the bed mix is determined, your attention turns to planning the individual room types. Planning guestrooms requires careful consideration of the activities that will happen within the room. Figure 21.8 shows five zones from top to bottom: a lounging or reading zone, a working or dining zone, a sleeping zone, a dressing zone, and a bathroom zone. Good guestroom design anticipates all of these activities, their interrelationships with other

Figure 21.8
Activities to Be Anticipated in Guestroom Design

Programming Public Areas

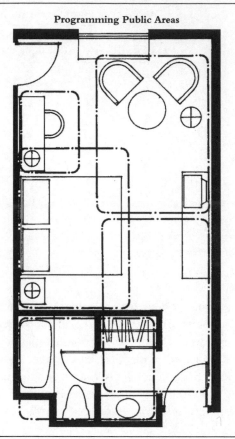

areas of the guestroom, and the space needed for each activity. Experienced developers know that their input is made via the program; communicating the activities, relationships, and space allocations to assist the design team in their work.[6]

Working within the program and with the developer's vision for the property in mind, the design professionals add an appropriate look and feel for the quality level of the hotel—one that is suitable for the locale and surroundings. As an example, it is typical for guestrooms in tropical resort locations to have tile floors throughout the room, with mats or area rugs adding interest, softening the look and feel, and providing comfort. This would be completely inappropriate for an urban hotel in a temperate climate, where some combination of carpet and wood is appropriate, with tile floors

reserved for the bathroom. Another example is that hotels built for vacation-
ers staying more than a few days need much larger closets and storage space
than would an urban hotel with an average stay of one to three days.

PROGRAMMING PUBLIC AREAS

The major public areas that you'll need to program are the lobby and public
flow space, the food and beverage outlets, and the meeting spaces. These
areas are the hotel's "living spaces"; they set the stage for other activities,
frame the image of property, add interest and amenities to the guest experience, and provide space for the formal and informal meetings that take place
in any hotel.

Hotel lobbies have become the most iconic of all hotel spaces. The lobby
must function not only as the hotel's "front office," but also as an important
transition space. The transition from an often hectic and arduous journey to
the security and serenity of the hotel takes place in the lobby. If you think
about it, the best lobbies work so well that guests do not even notice the
attention to program and planning detail. The reception desk is obvious and
inviting, regardless of which entrance the guests use. People circulate effort-
lessly to the other spaces within the hotel, without feeling lost or disori-
ented. Figure 21.9 provides a schematic diagram for a lobby with the major
connections indicated.[7]

In addition, the lobby program should include the following support
functions:

- Clear access to stairs, elevators, or escalators
- Lobby seating, for both individuals and small groups
- Concierge desk and storage, if appropriate
- Front desk administrative areas
- Bell stand and luggage storage
- Public toilets, coatrooms, and house phones

Food and Beverage Programming

The configuration and number of hotel food and beverage (F&B) outlets varies
widely. At one end of the spectrum are the 20 F&B outlets in the Jumeirah Beach
Hotel in Dubai, and at the other end, the coffee shop or quick-service restaurant
that is next to a rooms-only hotel. In addition, standards differ globally. Hotels
in the Middle East and Asia generally have a greater number of F&B outlets than
their European and North American counterparts do.

Figure 21.9
Lobby Schematic Diagram

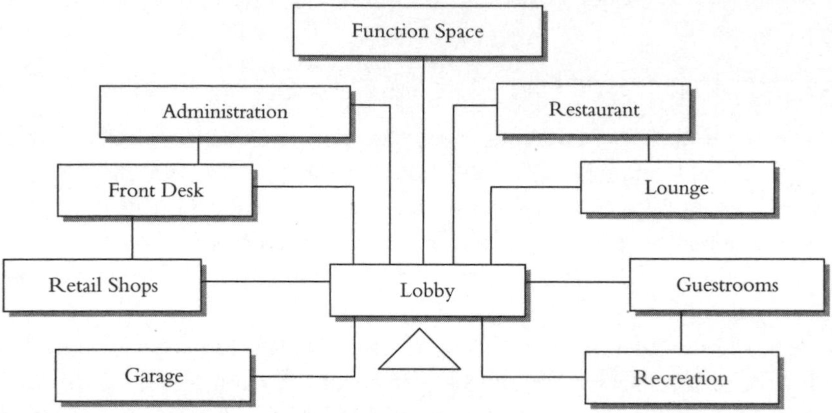

Lobby Schematic

Knowing that hotel F&B outlets are in competition with excellent local rivals, many small and select-service hotels may have only a single, multipurpose space that serves as a combination breakfast room, coffee bar, and sandwich deli in the morning, and transforms into a casual bar and limited-menu dining setting in the evening. The best designs delight guests, while providing a space- and labor-efficient venue.

For larger hotels, especially those that are resort or convention oriented, management creates an overall vision for the F&B operations. The multiple outlets must offer variety, value, and excitement; in general, the program includes fine dining, casual dining, and a set of beverage-oriented outlets with different themes, from quiet lounges to nightclubs. One growing trend you'll find is for hoteliers to partner with celebrity chefs to create signature dining outlets within the hotel (although this arrangement has the potential downside noted in Chapter 18). The celebrity can open a well-located restaurant, and the hotel gets access to customers seeking a unique dining experience, as the restaurant serves both hotel guests and a local clientele.

Programming standards for food and beverage outlets include the following objectives:

- Provide fine-dining venues with direct access to the exterior to maximize street presence and to enhance the restaurant's positioning as a local eatery.
- Locate the hotel's main casual dining restaurant as conveniently as possible in the hotel's main circulation patterns to maximize internal business.

- Conserve back-of-the-house space by sharing kitchens among F&B outlets, except for a kitchen used by a celebrity chef.
- If possible, provide a shared restaurant and banquet kitchen, again for economy of construction and operation.
- Provide satellite bars with an appropriately sized service area for preparation, storage, and backup.
- Design restaurants and bars so that sections can be closed off during slow periods to create more intimate venues.
- If possible, provide separate restrooms for each outlet. This is especially true for high-volume beverage operations.

Function Space Programming

Function space programming, like F&B programming, varies widely across different types of hotels. The largest hotels in any market have at least one distinct ballroom, smaller meeting rooms, boardrooms, conference rooms, exhibition space, and dedicated banquet rooms; a small hotel might have only a single multipurpose room for all events. A convention hotel or a conference center hotel is created specifically for meetings; for these hotels, the size, configuration, and capabilities of the various function spaces are one of the primary design drivers. Commercial-transient hotels add function spaces to provide an amenity and to broaden the hotel's service offerings. Select-service hotels typically have limited meeting facilities, such as boardroom-type venues.

Working with the management company, the developer is responsible for creating the overall meeting space program, consistent with the hotel's location and primary functions. The schematic diagram in Figure 21.10 provides an overview for a moderately large urban or suburban hotel, say 600 rooms, with a variety of meeting spaces.[8]

Figure 21.10
Function Space Schematic Diagram

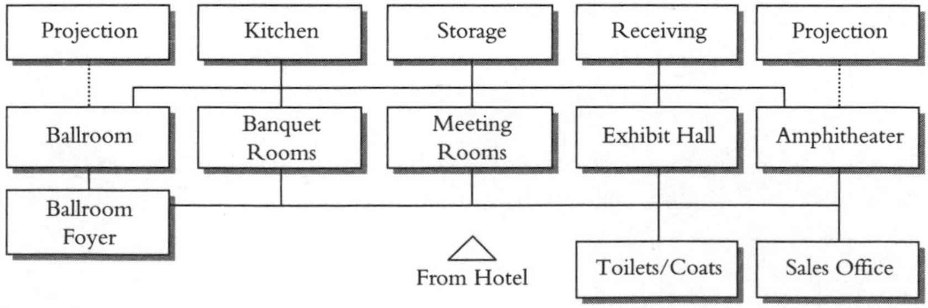

CONCLUSION

Hotel development brings dreams to life when you combine great ideas with financial capital. In this chapter, you have seen how to build a bridge that successfully connects great spaces with healthy financial returns. Though complex, the development process offers rewards for those with the skills and tenacity to orchestrate the mix of design, construction, capital, and brand decisions that create a great hotel.

You will find that planning and programming are important, but difficult, parts of the hotel development process. Programming a hotel involves defining the activities to be conducted within and surrounding the property, establishing relationships among the activity areas, and allocating an appropriate amount of space for the activities. It is the developer's responsibility to prepare a program that is consistent with a property's vision and positioning. Working with the design team and the hotel's management company, the developer takes the program and develops this into a design that achieves the objectives set out in the program.

NOTES

1. Adapted from D. Penner, "Operational planning and relationships," Chapter 10 in J. Ransley and H. Ingram, eds. *Developing Hospitality Properties and Facilities*, 2nd ed. (Oxford, UK: Butterworth-Heinemann, 2004), 195–214.
2. Ibid.
3. Adapted from W. Rutes, R. Penner, and L. Adams, *Hotel Design, Development, and Planning* (New York: Norton, 2001).
4. Ibid.
5. Ibid.
6. Ibid.
7. Ibid.
8. Ibid.

CHAPTER 22

MEASURING HOTEL RISK AND FINANCING

PENG LIU and DANIEL QUAN

The last couple of chapters have discussed your potential for success as the owner of a hospitality business and related real estate. It's true that the possibilities are great, but before you plunge ahead, you should realize that you are considering one of the riskiest forms of commercial real estate investment. Owning a hotel is unlike owning any other form of real estate. As a hotel owner, you face not only the usual risks associated with commercial real estate investments but also hotel-specific risks. Depending on your level of optimism, this can either represent a golden opportunity to obtain a higher rate of investment return or be a signal to consider other property types with lower risks. In either case, your correct decision as to whether to own a hotel will depend on your ability to not only understand the nature of hotel risks, but also to develop strategies to mitigate their effects.

First, let's look at the factors that differentiate a hotel from other real estate investments. A primary difference is the absence of long-term tenant leases, a feature common to most other forms of commercial real estate ownership. Instead of tenants that commit to multiyear lease contracts, your hotel will have "tenants" (hotel guests) who usually stay for just a matter of days. Whereas the lease for a long-term tenant will probably have rent indexation or escalation that provides for increased payments, your new hotel "tenants" will pay prevailing market "rents" or daily rates, which might be higher or lower than what you have projected. These new market rates are influenced by factors that are out of your control, including the condition of the overall economy and the rates charged by your competitors. While hotels can indeed be a highly profitable investment vehicle, it's critical that you understand exactly the nature of the risks you are undertaking.

To turn a profit, hotel property investors or managers must understand and manage hotels' "daily lease" feature. In this chapter, we investigate this source of uncertainty and develop a framework to characterize this effect. Furthermore, we explore methods that you can use to mitigate such risks.

Our approach is based on our consideration of the hotel as a financial asset that generates a cash flow stream, as described in previous chapters. In this context, the lack of tenant commitment corresponds to uncertainty in the cash flow during the time you hold the property. We apply well-developed portfolio allocation tools drawn from the analysis of fixed-income securities to show you how to analyze this problem. In addition, we develop standard portfolio risk measurement tools within the context of hotels when they are viewed as investment vehicles.

HOTEL RISK

As we said, the daily lease feature distinguishes hotels from other real estate investments. To review, you would expect two primary revenue sources to generate financial returns for your real estate investment, namely, changes in the value of the asset and an income stream (after tax cash flow) while you hold the property. Property values in a given neighborhood generally change more or less in concert. For example, if commercial values in Midtown Manhattan appreciate, this increase would likely be felt by all commercial properties. So, that's the appreciation part of the equation.

Hotels still have to account for their variable income streams. The lack of tenant commitment introduces substantial risk for hotel investors, given the variable demand for hotel rooms. We all saw the cancellations of corporate room bookings during the Great Recession. As we write this in the early stages of an economic upswing, bookings are gradually increasing and rates have recovered somewhat. Taken together, changes in rate and occupancy cause hotel income—and your cash flow—to be quite volatile over the course of a business cycle. Therein lies the risk for investors. This problem is further complicated by the nature of hotel cash flows and their dependence on the cost of wages and supplies, as well as the costs of financing. Hotels' volatility, which is a common measure of risk, gives rise to the perception of hotels as a risky type of investment property.

Although an increase in risk does not generally deter investments, it does increase the cost of an investment. Hotel mortgage lenders, for example, routinely price this risk when they underwrite hotel mortgages. A property with a volatile cash flow stream may see periods when there is insufficient cash to make the scheduled mortgage payments, which constitutes a default that would lead to foreclosure. Since default and foreclosure are extremely costly to lenders (and they really don't want to own your hotel), this risk is priced by charging a higher rate, usually referred to as a *risk premium*.

The chart in Figure 22.1 shows the extent of that risk premium, as defined by lenders. The graph shows the spread at the time of loan origination (SATO) for mortgage loans for several property types originated for the securitized commercial mortgage–backed securities market. These spreads, defined as increments to the Treasury bond rate, are essentially the risk premiums charged for different types of real estate loans.

As you can see, among the 10 property types, hotels have the highest spreads over this period—the highest risk premiums. The hotel loan spread peaked after September 11, 2001, at 320 basis points or a 3.2 percent spread over Treasury, and it took about three years for the shock to wear off. Investors were concerned that the events of that day might result in people curtailing their travel, which would, of course, decrease the lodging sector's cash flow and increase the likelihood of default. This didn't really occur, but even for the period before September 11, 2001, it is clear that hotels had the

Figure 22.1
Loan Risk Spread

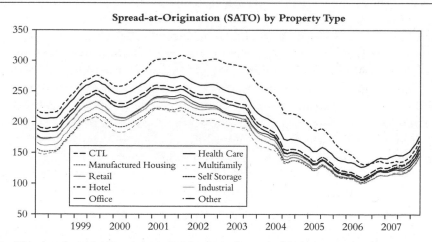

Note: This chart shows the historical trend of the average loan spread (in basis point) over Treasury at origination for each property type. The SATOs are estimated based on loan rates of fixed rate CMBS loans, normalized for loan size and LTV to capture the true difference in SATO by property type. *Data source*: Lehman Brothers.

highest spreads among all property types, again demonstrating the view of hotels as a risky investment.

The immediate consequence of this perception is a higher borrowing cost and the application of conservative underwriting criteria for hotel loans. This increased perception of risks suggests that the required rates of return for hotel investments should also exceed those of other property types since investors will seek additional returns to compensate for these increased costs.

MEASURING HOTEL RISK

Chapter 18 discussed the hotel valuation tool known as the discounted cash flow model. This approach reflects the fact that hotel investors value the stream of future cash flows that ownership affords. A valuation formula is used to determine a property's market value using the hotel's cash flow or its net operating income (NOI). Alternatively, if after-tax cash flow figures are used, this valuation formula determines the investment value or the investors' private valuation of the hotel. The investment analysis typically entails a comparison between these two values, with investments deemed favorable if their value exceeds the property's market value.

Both applications use the discount rate in the model. It is common practice to select a discount rate that reflects the opportunity cost of capital for the investor at the time the decision is made. There is no guarantee, however, that the discount rate—not the investor's opportunity cost—will remain constant throughout the hotel's investment life. In fact, the discount rate will surely change over time, along with the investors' valuation, even if the property cash flows have not changed. As you will see from the following expression, because the discount rate is in the denominator, an increase in this rate will decrease the value of the hotel, and likewise a decrease in the rate increases hotel valuation. It is therefore important to understand and quantify the sensitivity of our hotel valuation to such changes. A powerful tool to measure this sensitivity is called duration.

$$V = \frac{NOI_1}{\left(1 + r_1\right)} + \frac{NOI_2}{\left(1 + r_2\right)^2} + \cdots + \frac{NOI_T}{\left(1 + r_T\right)^T} + \frac{P_T}{\left(1 + r_T\right)^T}$$

In this equation, r_i represents periodic discount rates; NOI_i ($i = 1, 2, \ldots T$) are net operating income streams; and P_T is the projected equity reversion value at time T, which can be estimated using the next period NOI (NOI_{T+1}) divided by terminal capitalization rate (Cap_T).

$$P_T = \frac{NOI_{T+1}}{Cap_T}$$

Duration—An Introduction

Duration is common tool used in the analysis of fixed-income securities, such as bonds.[1] Much like our real estate application in this chapter, a bond's price is the present value of its coupon payments (our property's NOI) and its redemption value at maturity (property reversion value at the end of the holding period). A bond's price, therefore, is influenced by changes in the interest rate or bond yield, and duration determines the percentage change in the bond's price for a given percentage change in yield. A similar thing happens for hotel properties. In our application, we are interested in the change in property value for a given change in the discount rate.

Before developing this tool in the context of our hotel property application, it is important to know under what circumstances the discount rate can change. The discount rate comprises numerous market factors, most notably the expectations regarding currency inflation or deflation, explained next.

Digression—Discount Rate 101

To understand why the discount rate may change, you should consider the underlying factors that influence its movement (see Figure 22.2). The first basic component is the risk-free interest rate. This is largely a conceptual notion since no investments are risk free. Nevertheless, we have a proxy for

Figure 22.2
Factors Driving the Hotel Investment Discount Rate

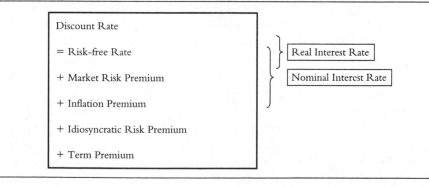

this rate, the U.S. Treasury bill rate, since this instrument is widely viewed as one of the safest investments in the world.

The second component is a market risk premium, meant to reflect the risk of the overall economy, such as when the economy slowed down severely in 2007–2009 after the financial markets collapsed. In such a difficult economic climate, borrowers holding loans that originated during more favorable economic times may experience financial hardship leading to loan delinquency. For lenders to extend a new loan in difficult times, it is reasonable for them to require additional (or higher) payments to compensate for this increased risk. You saw this increased risk premium in Figure 22.1. It is expressed as an increment to the discount rate. An equivalent interpretation of why the discount rate should increase in an uncertain economy is that a given cash flow has less value in the future than it does today because, in an uncertain economy, it is more likely that a borrower will be unable to make a future payment. This makes the value of future payments lower, in light of this increased uncertainty.

The third component is the inflation premium, which is expressed as the inflation rate. If the inflation rate is expected to be 3 percent over the investment period, the inflation premium is likewise 3 percent, which, when added to the risk-free rate, will yield the nominal interest rate.

The nominal interest rate can be understood as the interest rate one observes on the market, such as the widely published prime rate or LIBOR (the London Interbank Offered Rate). Like the prime rate, the nominal interest rate reflects the cost of borrowing for a given loan. Another indicator of the nominal interest rate is the rate paid by the U.S. government on Treasury securities. The purchase of so-called T-bills can be viewed as a buyer extending a loan to the government—in effect lending the government the price of the bond in exchange for receiving a periodic payment by the government in the form of coupon payments.

The rate at which the government borrows varies depending on the loan's term. When we plot these rates for various loan terms, the resulting plot is called the *term structure* of interest rates. The graph in Figure 22.3 shows an example of this term structure on July 27, 2010. Note that as the loan's term gets longer, the rate is generally higher. The simplest explanation for this effect is the increased risk associated with a promise to make loan payments over a longer horizon. A promised long-term loan repayment is generally riskier than a shorter-term loan repayment since more things can go wrong during the course of a lengthy loan. To reflect this increased risk, then, the lending rate should increase to compensate the lender. The difference in this increment between loans made in the short term and loans in the long term is called the *term premium*.

Figure 22.3
U.S. Treasury Rates

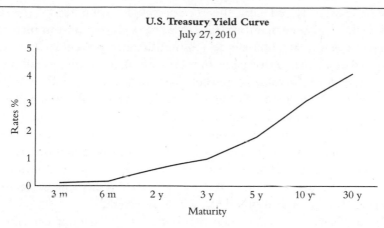

U.S. Treasury Yield Curve
July 27, 2010

Data source: Federal Reserve.

You have perhaps noticed that long-term loans, those with maturities greater than five years, often have higher rates than those made for the short term. Equivalently, the discount rates used for longer term payments should be higher than those for shorter-term payments. Let's point out the inconsistency in the usual hotel valuation formula's use of a single discount rate for all future cash flows. The proper discount rate should be different for each cash flow. Indeed, most other financial applications of the present value model use multiple discount rates, but the real estate industry still adopts the simplifying assumption of a constant discount rate. This also implies that this single discount rate should be some representative "average" value. For hotel investments, you will notice that most investors use a 10- to 20-year planning horizon; thus, the inclusion of a term premium is appropriate.

The fourth and final component of the risk premium is the idiosyncratic risk premium, which is specific to the particular investment. For example, a hotel located in an area where there is a higher risk of not achieving a desired level of revenue will have a higher risk premium than a hotel located in a more desirable area with a stronger cash flow stream.

Duration—A Framework

Because the discount rate includes numerous economic factors, a change in any individual component can lead to a corresponding change in the discount rate. This matter is further complicated by the fact that many of these terms are interrelated. If the U.S. Federal Reserve is working to decrease inflation by reducing the money supply, your inflation premium should decline. At the same time, however, the Fed's action can increase the short-term interest rate, thereby decreasing the term premium. You can see, therefore, that a measure that determines how changes in the overall discount rate may influence the value of a hotel investment can become an important tool not only to investigate the influence of changes in the individual components of the discount rate, but also to indicate how sensitive the value of a hotel is to changes in these components.

Let's look at the mathematics for real estate valuation based on discounted values of all predicted future cash flows. The present value of a hotel corresponds to the sum of its future income adjusted by the time of occurrence and the risk premium discounted for such investment.

Replacing periodic discount rates with an average discount rate, the value (V) of a hotel property is simplified by the following expression:

$$V = \frac{NOI_1}{(1 + r)} + \frac{NOI_2}{(1 + r)^2} + \cdots + \frac{NOI_T + P_T}{(1 + r)^T}$$

As a hotel investor, it is sometimes possible for you to influence a property's cash flow by changing management companies or enacting cost-cutting measures. But you have no control over the discount rate even though changes in the discount rate have substantial influence over your property's valuation. An increase in the discount rate would decrease today's valuation of an otherwise same future NOI, resulting in a decrease in the overall hotel's valuation. Conversely, a decrease in the discount rate would increase the value of the hotel. Because of the importance (and uncertainty) of discount rate movements for hotel valuation, it's important for you to have a measure of the sensitivity of the value of your hotel to changes in the discount rate for a given set of NOIs. This measure, commonly used in the same way for fixed-income securities, is called duration.

More formally, duration, $d,$ is defined as

$$d = -\frac{\partial V}{\partial (1 + r)} \times \frac{(1 + r)}{V}$$

The first term to the right of the equals sign (∂V) is the partial derivative of V with respect to a change in the discount rate, r. This term tells us how

V changes for a unit change in the r. However, because this measure alone does not account for scale, it is often more convenient to express this measure in percentage terms. The last term in the preceding expression normalizes the duration expression in terms of percentage changes. The following can thus be used as another notation for duration:

$$Duration\left(d\right) = -\frac{\%\ \text{change in}\ V}{\%\ \text{change in}\ \left(1 + r\right)} = -\frac{\Delta V\ /\ V}{\Delta\left(1 + r\right)\ /\ \left(1 + r\right)}$$

$$= -\frac{\Delta V}{\Delta\left(1 + r\right)}\frac{\left(1 + r\right)}{V}$$

By applying the first expression to our hotel valuation formula, we see that duration can be calculated as in the following expression:

$$\frac{\partial V}{\partial\left(1 + r\right)} = \frac{-NOI_1}{\left(1 + r\right)^2} + \frac{-2NOI_2}{\left(1 + r\right)^3} + \cdots + \frac{-T(NOI_T + P_T)}{\left(1 + r\right)^{T+1}}$$

Multiplying the right-hand side by $\dfrac{\left(1 + r\right)}{v}$, and simplifying, we get

$$d = -\frac{\partial V}{\partial\left(1 + r\right)}\frac{\left(1 + r\right)}{V} = \frac{1}{V}\frac{NOI_1}{\left(1 + r\right)^1} + \frac{2}{V}\frac{NOI_2}{\left(1 + r\right)^2} + \cdots + \frac{T}{V}\frac{\left(NOI_T + P_T\right)}{\left(1 + r\right)^T}$$

which is the final expression for duration.

Hotel Duration—A Working Example Let's look at how this equation functions. We work from the figures in the representative hotel operating *pro forma* shown in Figure 22.4. Using the NOI numbers from the bottom row of the table, you should be able to determine the duration of the hotel's cash flow stream. Before plugging in the duration expression, you need to calculate two numbers. First calculate the equity reversion value at the terminal year 5, and then the discount rate. Using 6th-year cash flow with a terminal cap rate of 7.5 percent, we can figure the reversion value as follows: $24,856/7.5\% = $331,413 (assuming zero closing costs).

You can determine the average discount rate for your hotel if you know its current value. Let's say that the current value of the hotel is $265,000. The

Figure 22.4
Sample Five-Year Hotel *Pro Forma*

Representative Hotel 5-Year Pro Forma

	2009		2010		2011		2012		2013		2014	
Available hotel rooms	329		329		329		329		329		329	
Available room nights	120,085		120,414		120,085		120,085		120,085		120,414	
Occupied room nights	85,260		87,902		90,064		90,064		90,064		90,311	
Occupancy	71.0%		73.0%		75.0%		75.0%		75.0%		75.0%	
Average daily rate	$386.86		$413.94		$434.64		$447.68		$461.11		$474.94	
RevPAR	$274.67		$302.18		$325.98		$335.76		$345.83		$356.21	
Days open	365		366		365		365		365		366	
	Amount	Ratio	Amount	Ratio	Amount	Ratio	Amount	Ratio	Amount	Ratio	Amount	Ratio
REVENUES												
Rooms	$32,984	39.9%	$36,386	40.9%	$39,145	41.3%	$40,320	41.3%	$41,529	41.3%	$42,892	41.3%
Food & Beverage	$30,507	36.9%	$32,396	36.4%	$34,188	36.1%	$35,214	36.1%	$36,270	36.1%	$37,460	36.1%
Telecommunications	$275	0.3%	$293	0.3%	$309	0.3%	$318	0.3%	$328	0.3%	$338	0.3%
Golf	$8,603	10.4%	$9,135	10.3%	$9,641	10.2%	$9,930	10.2%	$10,228	10.2%	$10,564	10.2%
Spa	$3,885	4.7%	$4,125	4.6%	$4,354	4.6%	$4,484	4.6%	$4,619	4.6%	$4,770	4.6%
Other Departments	$6,321	7.7%	$6,712	7.5%	$7,084	7.5%	$7,296	7.5%	$7,515	7.5%	$7,762	7.5%
Total Revenues	$82,575	100.0%	$89,048	100.0%	$94,720	100.0%	$97,562	100.0%	$100,488	100.0%	$103,787	100.0%
DEPARTMENTAL EXPENSES												
Rooms Expense	$8,906	27.0%	$9,460	26.0%	$9,982	25.5%	$10,282	25.5%	$10,590	25.5%	$10,938	25.5%
Food & Beverage Expense	$23,490	77.0%	$24,297	75.0%	$25,641	75.0%	$26,410	75.0%	$27,202	75.0%	$28,095	75.0%
Telecommunications Expense	$413	150.0%	$439	150.0%	$463	150.0%	$477	150.0%	$491	150.0%	$507	150.0%
Golf Expense	$4,473	52.0%	$4,568	50.0%	$4,820	50.0%	$4,965	50.0%	$5,114	50.0%	$5,282	50.0%
Spa Expense	$2,409	62.0%	$2,475	60.0%	$2,612	60.0%	$2,691	60.0%	$2,771	60.0%	$2,862	60.0%

(continued)

Figure 22.4 (continued)

	NOI$_2$		NOI$_2$		NOI$_3$		NOI$_4$		NOI$_5$		NOI$_6$	
Other Departments Expense	$3,061	48.4%	$3,251	48.4%	$3,430	48.4%	$3,533	48.4%	$3,639	48.4%	$3,759	48.4%
Total Departmental Expenses	$42,752	51.8%	$44,489	50.0%	$46,949	49.6%	$48,357	49.6%	$49,808	49.6%	$51,443	49.6%
Gross Operating Income	$39,823	48.2%	$44,558	50.0%	$47,771	50.4%	$49,204	50.4%	$50,680	50.4%	$52,344	50.4%
UNDISTRIBUTED OPERATING EXPENSES												
Administrative & General	$5,452	6.6%	$5,615	6.3%	$5,784	6.1%	$5,957	6.1%	$6,136	6.1%	$6,320	6.1%
Sales & Marketing	$3,791	4.6%	$3,904	4.4%	$4,021	4.2%	$4,142	4.2%	$4,266	4.2%	$4,394	4.2%
Utilities	$2,334	2.8%	$2,404	2.7%	$2,476	2.6%	$2,550	2.6%	$2,627	2.6%	$2,706	2.6%
Repairs and Maintenance	$3,226	3.9%	$3,323	3.7%	$3,423	3.6%	$3,325	3.6%	$3,631	3.6%	$3,740	3.6%
Total	$14,802	17.9%	$15,246	17.1%	$15,704	16.6%	$16,175	16.6%	$16,660	16.6%	$17,160	16.5%
Gross Operating Profit	$25,020	30.3%	$29,312	32.9%	$32,067	33.9%	$33,029	33.9%	$34,020	33.9%	$35,184	33.9%
FIXED EXPENSES												
Management Fee	$2,477	3.0%	$2,671	3.0%	$2,842	3.0%	$2,927	3.0%	$3,015	3.0%	$3,114	3.0%
Real Estate Taxes	$1,856	2.2%	$1,912	2.1%	$1,969	2.1%	$2,028	2.1%	$2,089	2.1%	$2,152	2.1%
Insurance	$786	1.0%	$809	0.9%	$834	0.9%	$859	0.9%	$885	0.9%	$911	0.9%
Capital Reserves (FF&E)	$3,303	4.0%	$3,562	4.0%	$3,789	4.0%	$3,902	4.0%	$4,020	4.0%	$4,151	4.0%
Total Fixed Expenses	$8,422	10.2%	$8,955	10.1%	$9,433	10.0%	$9,716	10.0%	$10,008	10.0%	$10,328	10.0%
EBITDA	$19,901	24.1%	$23,919	26.9%	$26,423	27.9%	$27,216	27.9%	$28,032	27.9%	$29,008	27.9%
NOI	$16,598	20.1%	$20,357	22.9%	$22,634	23.9%	$23,313	23.9%	$24,013	23.9%	$24,856	23.9%

average discount rate for the five-year holding period can be calculated from the following equation:

$$265,000 = \frac{16,598}{(1 + r)^1} + \frac{20,357}{(1 + r)^2} + \frac{22,634}{(1 + r)^3} + \frac{23,313}{(1 + r)^4} + \frac{24,013 + 331,413}{(1 + r)^5}$$

Thus, the average discount rate (internal rate of return) is 11.871%, and using duration formula, we see that duration is 4.41 years.

$$d = \frac{1}{265,000} \left[\frac{16,598}{(1 + .11871)^1} + \frac{2 \times 20,357}{(1 + .11871)^2} + \frac{3 \times 22,634}{(1 + .11871)^3} \right.$$
$$\left. + \frac{4 \times 23,313}{(1 + .11871)^4} + \frac{5 \times (24,013 + 331,413)}{(1 + .11871)^5} \right] = 4.41$$

The duration of 4.41 seems like a small number, but it represents significant price elasticity compared to the discount rate. Going back to the inverse relationship of the discount rate and your property's value, we see that a 1 percent increase in the discount rate will reduce the valuation of your property by 4.41 percent, translating to an $11,691 decline in asset value.

Hotel Duration—Further Exploration

We still have to account for the special case of hotels' "daily leases." Though the above analysis is correct for most fixed-income instruments with a fixed coupon payment, it is not entirely appropriate in our hotel application. Although often viewed as a negative feature of hotels, in fact the ability to roll over leases on a daily basis allows hotel operators to alter the room rate structure frequently. Thus, hotels have more flexibility than office building owners, who can only renegotiate a new lease on the expiration of an existing lease.

The benefit of frequently changing lease terms is that hotel operators can systematically alter room rates to reflect changing market conditions. These same conditions also may be factors that influence the discount rate. For example, during an inflationary period, room rates can increase to compensate for the lower purchasing power of a hotel's revenue stream. Furthermore, for changes in the nominal interest rate, hotel operators can alter the room rates to reflect changes in their opportunity cost of funds. You can see that when the discount rate changes, you'll probably want to change room rates to compensate for the negative effect.

Consider, for example, changes in the inflation rate. It is reasonable to assume that as operating costs increase due to inflation, hotels will respond by increasing their corresponding room rates (if market forces permit). In our hotel valuation equation, both the numerator and denominator are functions of inflation:

$$V = \sum_{t=1}^{T} \frac{NOI_t(\text{inflation})}{\left(1 + r(\text{inflation})\right)^t}$$

As inflation increases, both the denominator (discount rate) and the numerator (NOI) increase, and the change in one partially offsets the change in the other. Other commercial real estate can't change its NOIs to account for inflation; thus, the effect of an increase in inflation will be much stronger for commercial buildings than for a hotel.

In this situation, the brief duration of a hotel can be an advantage, and the duration of hotel assets has interesting investment implications. In the context of achieving a diversified real estate portfolio investment, hotel ownership can make a strong contribution to portfolio diversity. Another implication is that due to the short duration of hotels, this investment vehicle is desirable if investors are concerned about changes in interest or discount rates.

HOTEL FINANCING—LOAN CHOICE

With that background on the risk involved in hotel investments, let's look at the implications for loans. Most hotel investors finance their hotel acquisitions with mortgage contracts, but you'll face seemingly countless variations on the standard loan terms. Logically, you should seek out the loan with the lowest borrowing costs, but it's also critical that your payments are manageable in both good and bad times.

Because mortgage payments come from often volatile cash flows, a fixed-rate fixed-payment mortgage may not be the most desirable mortgage instrument. Figure 22.5 illustrates how, due to its high volatility, hotel income is more likely to fall under a debt service threshold that is constant over time.

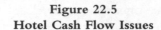

Figure 22.5
Hotel Cash Flow Issues

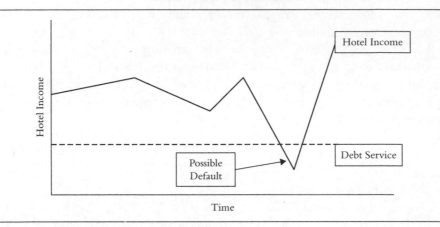

As this example illustrates, a more appropriate mortgage may be one that allows for varying mortgage payments to reflect a hotel's varying income stream. You probably won't find a loan with payments specifically pegged to your hotel's income, but you will find variable payment plans. One such loan is the adjustable-rate mortgage, but even these variable payment loans require a careful analysis to ensure a reasonable match with your hotel's income stream.

Broadly speaking, investors' mortgage choices can be viewed as a problem of matching assets to liability. Hotel revenues are the assets in this case, and debt payments are the liabilities. For investors concerned that their property income may not match their debt obligation as market conditions change, selecting a loan with a duration matching that of their hotel's income stream would be a reasonable approach to this problem. If the durations of both asset and liability are well matched with regard to changes in the discount rate, then both the hotel's income and debt service would move in the same direction by similar amounts. In that situation, you'd be reasonably assured of covering your debt service.

Although this strategy of matching asset and liability durations is used widely in managing interest rate risks for investment portfolios, to the best of our knowledge, the strategy hasn't been applied to hotel income and debt service.

So let's make that match. A common measure of the difference between the durations of two alternatives is the *duration gap,* defined as the difference in duration weighted by the relative size of the two alternatives. Thus, the duration gap is expressed as:

$$\text{Duration Gap} = \text{Duration of Assets} -$$
$$(\text{Total Liabilities} / \text{Total Assets}) \times \text{Duration of Liabilities}$$

Consider the purchase of a $20 million hotel financed by a 20-year, fixed-rate mortgage with 0.8 loan-to-value ratio. Assume the duration of the hotel is five years and that of the loan is nine years. Based on these figures, the duration gap is:

$$\text{Duration Gap} = 5 - (0.8 \times 20{,}000{,}000) / (20{,}000{,}000) \times 9 = -2.2$$

Since the duration of the loan (liability) exceeds that of the hotel (asset), if you held this loan, you would be adversely affected if rates decline. Under this scenario, a decrease in rates will increase the value of the debt by a larger amount than the value of the hotel's income stream. That is, under this scenario, the value of the hotel decreases, while the market value of the debt obligation increases. You'd have to try to refinance this debt, and failing that you might end up with a loan default.

We just showed the situation with a decrease in interest rates and a duration gap in which the hotel's duration was shorter than that of the loan. The reverse case could also be a problem. That is, if the duration of the hotel were significantly longer than the duration of the debt, resulting in a positive duration gap, investors would correspondingly be exposed to an increase in interest rates. Because of its longer hotel duration, the hotel's value would fall by a disproportionately larger amount than the decline in the value of the debt, should rates rise. What you're looking for is a fully hedged position, one in which the duration gap is zero. Next, we discuss how managers and investors using conventional tools can hedge their position. For the example that we gave, the solution involves extending the duration of a hotel asset, reducing that of the debt, or some combination of both. We consider these alternatives and demonstrate how to use the duration gap expression to alleviate this problem.

Duration Hedges

- *Extending a hotel's duration.* One way to increase a hotel's duration is to include tenants who are willing to commit to long-term stays. This is one benefit of mixed-use developments that include residence units integrated into the hotel. Though such practices have often been justified on financial and market-demand grounds, this strategy can be interpreted as an implicit attempt to extend the duration of a hotel. Apartment leases will assure hotel operators of a steady stream of rent payments for the term of the tenant's contract, thereby offsetting some of the volatility of the hotel's income.

- *Shorten the debt's duration.* With adjustable-rate mortgages, the interest rate used to calculate the debt service is based on some benchmark interest rate that will vary over the life of the loan (usually the one-year T-bill rate or the LIBOR rate). This rate is combined with a fixed premium for the mortgage interest rate. As the benchmark rate changes each year, the mortgage payment changes for the following year. Thus, the borrower is assured of a constant fixed payment for the year. Because the benchmark rate is a component of the discount rate, as the benchmark rate changes, the corresponding payments will also change. The durations of such loans are short, perhaps on the order of one or two years. One way to reduce the duration of debt is to consider financing hotels using floating rate loans, which have an even shorter duration.

- *Make use of swaps.* In typical portfolios' interest rate immunization strategies, it is quite common to use interest rate swaps to alter the portfolio's duration. An interest rate swap is a third-party transaction in which a certain investment with a fixed payment at some interest rate is exchanged (swapped) for the same size investment, but with a variable payout determined by some short-term market rate such as LIBOR. This fixed-for-floating swap can be integrated with a portfolio comprising our hotel and the fixed-rate mortgage to result in a matched-duration portfolio. For example, to shorten the duration of the fixed-rate mortgage, investors can simultaneously engage a counterparty in a swap transaction.

Say that a particular investor buys a hotel that pays out a stream of variable net operating incomes. Eighty percent of this purchase might be funded by a fixed-rate mortgage. Let's say that the interest rate for this financing is 6 percent. The hotel investor's cash flow is depicted in Figure 22.6.

This figure shows that the hotel investor has incurred interest rate risk—a duration mismatch—since the (fixed) repayment of mortgage debt service

Figure 22.6
Hotel Cash Flow in a Fixed-Rate Mortgage

could exceed the (floating) hotel net operating income. To ameliorate this risk, the investor can enter into an interest rate swap with a counterparty, the goal being to eliminate the duration gap. As Figure 22.7 illustrates, the hotel receives a fixed-rate payment from a counterparty that matches the fixed-rate mortgage obligation while making a floating-rate payment based on the variable cash flow from the hotel net operating income.

The private agreement that facilitates the exchange of future cash flows between the hotel investor and the counterparty is called a *swap* (as depicted in Figure 22.8). This contract converts part of the hotel's fixed liability into floating liability with reduced duration.

So let's go back to our example, in which the $20 million hotel purchase was financed by a 20-year, 80-percent fixed-rate mortgage with a duration gap of −2.2.

To offset this imbalance in duration, the hotel investor can swap a fixed rate for a floating rate on a portion of the liability portfolio. Say that the duration of the swap is 5; you can then calculate the amount of swap referenced, such that the duration gap equals zero.

$$5 = \frac{0.8 \times 20,000,000 - swap}{20,000,000} \times 9 + \frac{swap}{20,000,000} \times 5$$

The preceding duration matching equation implies that the swap = $11 million. The hedging strategy involves swapping $11 million of the fixed-rate debt for floating debt. The resulting duration gap should be 0.

Figure 22.7
Hotel Cash Flow in an Interest Rate Swap

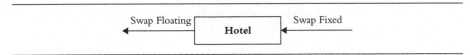

Figure 22.8
Hotel Debt Swap

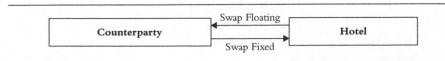

Conclusion

Since the absence of long-term tenant lease contracts imposes an additional risk for hotel owners, it is crucial to understand and manage this unique feature of hotel risk. We hope that this chapter gives you a framework to characterize this effect. Specifically, you have seen how a duration measure is adapted to quantify the sensitivity of hotel valuation to discount rate changes.

Whereas the "daily lease" feature is often viewed as a negative feature of hotels, as a hotel investor, you know that the ability to roll over leases with such frequency allows hotel operators to update the room rate structure to reflect dynamic economic conditions. The ability to align a hotel's revenue stream in the same direction as the discount rate gives hotel owners better control over their investments. Based on this argument, it is reasonable to assume that hotels will in general have a shorter duration than other commercial properties, such as office buildings and retail malls.

If you do have a duration mismatch, you now have strategies to address some of the financing issues that confront hotel investors, particularly the uncertainty arising from the lack of financial commitment from hotel tenants. Because a hotel's often volatile income stream is used to pay the monthly mortgage, this volatility can result in periods in which there is insufficient revenue to make the debt service payments. An adjustable-rate mortgage, therefore, might be a better financing choice than a fixed mortgage. Even with a fixed-rate mortgage, you can use an interest rate swap to help immunize your deal against interest rate risk. Such strategies—aligning a hotel's investment income with debt service—have not been studied closely in the context of hotel asset management but deserve further scrutiny.

Note

1. For formal treatment of duration, see B. Tuckman, *Fixed Income Securities: Tools for Today's Markets,* 2nd ed. (Hoboken, NJ: Wiley, 2002), 98; or R. W. Kopprasch, *Understanding Duration and Volatility* (New York: Salomon Brothers, 1985).

PART IV

SUCCESS THROUGH MANAGERIAL EXCELLENCE

CHAPTER 23

SEGMENTING AND TARGETING YOUR MARKET
STRATEGIES AND LIMITATIONS

MICHAEL LYNN

Almost any marketing textbook will tell you that the key to successful marketing can be summed up by the STP strategy—that is, segmentation, targeting, and positioning.[1] This approach suggests that the mass market consists of some number of relatively homogeneous groups, each with distinct needs and desires. STP marketers attempt to identify those market segments, direct marketing activities at the segments which the marketers believe that their company can satisfy better than their competitors, and position their product offering so as to appeal to the targeted segments. Undoubtedly, your hospitality firm uses some form of this approach.

Critical to this strategic approach is selecting some segments to target and others to ignore. As David Aaker writes, "Positioning usually implies a segmentation commitment—an overt decision to ignore large parts of the market and concentrate only on certain segments."[2] One reason this segmentation commitment is necessary is that the needs of different segments are often conflicting and their satisfaction mutually exclusive. For example, older consumers may prefer a quiet cruise, restaurant, hotel, or resort environment and might be put off by a loud, rock-based show that would appeal to younger consumers. Likewise, amenities and entertainment for families with children might not mesh with those of singles or seniors. Even if those features and amenities are not mutually exclusive, the cost of building a single product with all the features desired by different segments would drive costs to unreasonable levels.

Although STP marketing strategy involves segmentation commitment at the brand level, it does not preclude efforts to capture many different segments at the corporate level. Companies can pursue either a concentrated STP marketing strategy by offering a single brand to only one or two segments or a differentiated STP marketing strategy in which they strive to capture many different segments by targeting a different brand to each segment.[3] Rosewood Hotels & Resorts and Crystal Cruises, both of which are relatively small companies focusing on the luxury-seeking segment, exemplify a concentrated STP marketing strategy. Two firms that apply a differentiated STP marketing strategy are Choice Hotels International, which targets numerous lodging market segments with its many diverse brands (including EconoLodge, Cambria Suites, Clarion, Comfort Inn, and the Ascend Collection), and Carnival Corporation, which likewise targets numerous cruise market segments with its family of brands (including Carnival, Cunard, Holland America, Princess, and Seabourne). Thus, while STP marketing imposes limits on brand strategy, it does not preclude different corporate strategies and ambitions.

Although I discuss the commonly accepted approach to segmenting markets and selecting those segments to target in this chapter, I also want to explain about the limits of market segmentation. In particular, I want to caution you about relying too heavily on the best-known STP marketing strategy—frequent guest programs. Finally, I discuss appropriate strategies to pursue when you've reached the limits of market segmentation and segmentation commitment.

HOW TO SEGMENT MARKETS AND SELECT TARGET SEGMENTS

Let's start with the classic segmentation concepts. To begin with, there is more than one way to segment a market. You may differentiate your customers on the basis of demographic variables (such as age, gender, education, and income), geographic variables (such as nation, state, region, and neighborhood type), psychographic variables (such as attitudes, opinions, interests, and values), and behaviors (such as media habits, purchase frequency, brand loyalty, and channel usage). Segmentation schemes have become quite sophisticated, using advanced statistics and numerous variables. For example, Nielsen Claritas uses geographic, demographic, and behavioral data to divide U.S. households into its different PRIZM segments. Nielsen gives these segments such fanciful names as "Blue Blood Estates," "Country Squires," and "Money & Brains."[4] Nielsen describes the Money & Brains segment, as follows: "The residents of Money & Brains seem to have it all: high incomes, advanced degrees, and sophisticated tastes to match their credentials. Many of these city dwellers, predominantly white with a high concentration of Asian Americans, are married couples with few children who live in fashionable homes on small, manicured lots."[5]

You can identify whatever number of segments makes the most sense for your business. Segmenting the market on the basis of sex results in two segments, of course, but you may need to refine your segment definitions by adding other variables. Continuous variables like age typically give rise to three or more segments, such as young, middle aged, and elderly, and then you can combine these or other variables to create even more segments. The Nielsen Claritas' PRIZM segmentation divides the market into 66 different groups, but your business may not need to define your segments so tightly.[6]

So, which variables should you use to segment the market, and how many segments should you identify? No single answer to these questions applies across the board. Instead, the answer depends on your business, your market, and your customers. Different markets are best segmented using different types of variables and different numbers of segments. Most likely, the pre-existing, generic market segmentations sold by marketing research firms will not be ideal for your situation. For this reason, you should conduct or commission segmentation studies of your own specific market—starting with literally hundreds of different variables, analyzing them, and gradually winnowing the list to see which ones produce segments or groupings of consumers that are most useful.[7]

The key point regarding segments is that to be useful, the segment groupings must contain consumers who are similar to one another and distinct from the consumers in other groups with respect to their responsiveness to your potential marketing offerings and appeals.[8] In addition, the different segments should (1) differ in ways that allow their size and accessibility to be easily measured, (2) be large enough to justify separate targeting efforts, (3) be uniquely reachable via communication media and marketing channels, and (4) be relatively stable and not diminishing in size over time.[9]

Since the best STP approach is to conduct your own study, most market segmentation studies are proprietary and unavailable to the public. However, a good segmentation example of a local restaurant market was described in a 1986 article in the *Cornell Quarterly,* by William Swinyard and Kenneth Struman.[10]

I explain this study in detail so that you can see how a market segmentation study might proceed. However, the process requires considerable expertise and time. As I outline later, you'll probably want to hire someone to conduct a study like this.

Swinyard and Struman first identified a large number of restaurant attributes that might influence consumer choice. Examples of such attributes were:

- A good place for meeting new people
- Consistent food quality from visit to visit
- Friendly service
- Large food portions
- A lively, upbeat environment
- A convenient location
- Attractive waiters and waitresses

Then they asked a sample of consumers to rate the market's restaurants on each attribute, as well as how appealing each attribute would be in an "ideal" restaurant. The respondents also rated the importance of each restaurant attribute, and their agreement with general lifestyle statements (such as, "I never seem to have enough money," "I love to cook," and "I like to meet lots of new people"). Finally, respondents reported on their recent dining-out experiences and provided detailed demographic information about themselves.

Swinyard and Struman analyzed ratings of an ideal restaurant on each attribute using a statistical technique called cluster analysis to identify groups or segments of consumers with relatively similar perceptions of that theoretical ideal restaurant. The authors didn't say this, but I suspect that the cluster analysis was probably performed only on the ratings for those attributes for which performance differed among existing restaurants in the market. I say this for two reasons. First, reasonably large and well-defined clusters typically emerge only when small numbers of variables are used to define the clusters. Second, attributes on which every restaurant performs reasonably well don't cause consumers to choose one restaurant over another, even if those attributes are important. As Swinyard and Struman wrote, "You must select clustering variable measures that describe the reasons a customer would choose your restaurant over another."[11]

After identifying the segments with cluster analysis, the researchers compared different groups or segments on the lifestyle factors, restaurant patronage patterns, and demographic variables. The results of all these analyses are presented in Table 23.1.

Although Swinyard and Struman did not share their detailed statistical results, based on the information they did share, this appears to be a good segmentation of the market because: (1) the segments differ from one another on restaurant patronage behavior and actionable drivers of consumer choice among restaurants, (2) the size of the segments could be estimated from their size in the survey sample, and (3) the segments were substantial enough in terms of share of patrons and dollars to warrant targeting. This segmentation would be even more useful if we knew whether the segments had different media usage

Table 23.1
Restaurant Segmentation Summary (Based on Actual Study Data)

Characteristic	Segment 1 Family Dinners	Segment 2 Romantics	Segment 3 Entertainers
Valued ideal—restaurant factors	Seek food variety and value	Fun and social	Discriminating
	Not interested in entertainment	Food variety and value	Seek quality food and service
		Good drink value	Not interested in food variety or value
		Entertainment	
Key lifestyle factors	Traditionalists	Uninhibited morals	Socially secure
	Restaurant loyalists	Bar drinkers	Not restaurant
	Not bar drinkers	Untraditional	loyalists
	Traditional morality	Not restaurant	Traditional morality
		loyalists	Opinion leaders
Typical restaurant-usage patterns	Dinners, no drinks	Dinners, wine	Lunches and dinners, drinks
Number in party:	3-5 people	2 people	4 people
Consideration choices:	Restaurant A, B, X	Restaurants C, D, E, F	Restaurants F, G, H, I, X
Preference choices:	A	D, F	F, G, H, I
Size of check:	Food $32	Food $19	Food $55
	Drinks $2	Drinks $7	Drinks $20
Occasion of use:	Family dining	Dating	Entertaining
Demographic description			
Sex:	Equally male and female	Predominantly male	Predominantly male
Age:	35 to 50	Under 30	Over 40
Education:	Some college	Some college	Advanced degree
Marital Status:	Married	Single	Married
Income			
Personal:	Over $35,000	Under $20,000	Over $40,000
Family:	Over $45,000		Over $75,000

Source: Reproduced by permission from W. R. Swinyard and K. D. Struman, "Market Segmentation: Finding the Heart of Your Restaurant's Market," Cornell Hotel and Restaurant Administration Quarterly 37 (1) (May 1986): 93.

patterns and geographic dispersions, so that restaurants could more cost-effectively communicate with the target segment and make better site location decisions. But even without this information, the identified differences between the segments are more than adequate to guide marketing decisions.

With this explanation, you can see why segmentation studies like the one reported by Swinyard and Struman usually require you to hire market researchers specializing in such analyses. Even then, the likelihood of identifying segments that are useful for developing a targeting and positioning strategy is low. I explain why when I get to the section on the limitations of the STP strategy.

Once your market segments have been identified, you will need to decide which ones to target and which ones to disregard. Different marketers offer slightly different advice about the criteria you should use in making this decision, but most would agree that attractive targets are those segments that (1) have strong sales and growth potential, (2) are relatively inexpensive to reach with marketing efforts, (3) are currently being served by few or weak competitors, and (4) have needs and desires that your company's resources are well suited to satisfy.[12]

Let's say that you wanted to open a restaurant in the market studied by Swinyard and Struman. If you were entering that market, you would probably find the greatest success targeting the Family Diners segment (Segment 1), because it spends the second most on dining out, has the most restaurant loyalists (which would reduce marketing costs), and has the fewest and weakest competitors.[13] Having said that, I need to state the obvious here, which is that it may make the most sense to choose a concept that fits your own personality and allows you to relate to the people whom you are serving. So your own characteristics and capabilities play a crucial role in selecting target segments. A young, flamboyant, and gay restaurateur, for example, might find more success targeting the Romantics segment (Segment 2), who are less inhibited and more entertainment oriented than the other segments. Similarly, a classically trained chef with years of experience in fine dining might find the most success (not to mention personal happiness) targeting the discriminating Entertainers segment (Segment 3), despite the intense competition for that segment.

As a final consideration about the segments themselves, it's unlikely that any particular segment will be superior to others on all the criteria in question. That is, selecting segments involves a mixed picture, and there is no common metric that would permit you to make comparisons across criteria. This makes the selection of target segments an art as much as a science. You should, however, consider both the size and importance of differences between segments on each criterion when making overall evaluations of segment attractiveness.

THE LIMITS OF STRATEGIC STP MARKETING

The reason that I went into such detail about how to ferret out desirable market segments is that they must be discovered, and cannot be created. This fact is sometimes obscured by a tendency to segment markets by product subcategories (such as all-suite or extended-stay hotels) rather than by consumer characteristics.[14] You can always create a new hotel subcategory, but to be successful it must satisfy the unmet needs and desires of some *existing segment of consumers*. The classic example is Marriott's recognition of a set of business travelers who needed a service and amenities package that differed from that of its existing hotels—an insight that resulted in the Courtyard concept (discussed in greater detail in the context of brand management in Chapter 24). Thus, STP marketing is helpful only if new differences between homogeneous groups of consumers actually exist, if those differences determine the consumers' choices, and if those segments are large or rich enough to justify targeting.

Useful segments should be easy to find in undeveloped markets, as occurred when Kemmons Wilson devised Holiday Inn. At that time, hotel consumers were segmented generally on the basis of desired price point, into economy, standard, and luxury. Over the years, competitors emerged to contest for each segment, and with the product tiers strategy pioneered by Quality International, the industry further subdivided the market and targeted ever narrower segments. Competition is now tight in those narrower segments, too, including such niches as extended-stay and suite hotels. At some point, all the useful segments in a market will have been identified and any further segmentation will produce segments that are insufficiently differentiated in terms of drivers of demand or too small to profitably target.[15] Perhaps this has occurred in the hotel and restaurant industry, but then again, perhaps you can identify a segment that is not being served sufficiently. New brands are continually making their debut.

However, some provocative data suggest to me that most markets can be segmented only broadly. Further, it appears that those segments have already been identified in the markets of the developed world, and that attempts to further subdivide those markets are unlikely to prove useful.

Here's the study that leads me to this conclusion. Using consumer panel data on over 40 different product categories and hundreds of consumer characteristics, Rachel Kennedy and Andrew Ehrenberg compared the demographic, media usage, and psychographic characteristics of individual brand users with those characteristics of the users of all brands in that product category.[16] Specifically, they recorded the percentage of each brand's purchases attributable to customers with distinct characteristics and also the percentage across brands of product category purchases attributable to customers with those characteristics. Then they calculated the differences between these brand and category percentages and averaged the resulting absolute deviations across brands, without regard to whether the deviations were positive or negative. Thus, they calculated mean absolute deviation (MAD) scores for each characteristic (see Table 23.2 for examples from the economy

Table 23.2

Percentage of Stays at Various Economy Hotel Brands Attributable to Customers with Various Demographic Characteristics in the Survey Data Along with Absolute Deviations from the Average Value (in parentheses) and MAD Scores

Segmentation Variable/Level	Hotel A	Hotel B	Hotel C	Hotel D	Hotel E	Hotel F	Hotel G	Hotel H	All Hotels	Mean Absolute Deviation
Respondent Sex/ Male[a]	36.55%	34.10%	33.77%	32.48%	42.465	42.99%	34.66%	33.20%	35.78%	3.17
	(0.77)	(1.68)	(2.01)	(3.30)	(6.68)	(7.21)	(1.12)	(2.58)		
Race of Head of Household/White[a]	89.18%	93.72%	92.9%	93.18%	89.22%	93.28%	94.67%	94.14%	92.86%	1.51
	(3.68)	(0.86)	(0.04)	(0.32)	(3.64)	(0.42)	(1.81)	(1.28)		
Marital Status/										
Married	58.64%	70.27%	64.97%	63.22%	49.00%	57.57%	66.28%	67.35%	63.64%	5.09
	(5.00)	(6.63)	(1.57)	(0.42)	(14.64)	(6.07)	(2.64)	(3.71)		
Never Married	19.49%	12.11%	15.61%	14.04%	21.23%	21.52%	14.55%	15.81%	15.75%	2.72
	(3.74)	(3.64)	(0.14)	(1.71)	(5.48)	(5.77)	(1.20)	(0.06)		
Divorced, Widowed, Separated	21.88%	17.62%	19.42%	22.74%	29.77%	20.91%	19.17%	16.84%	20.61%	2.72
	(1.27)	(2.99)	(1.19)	(2.13)	(9.16)	(0.30)	(0.93)	(3.77)		
Household Size/										
1 Person	26.40%	19.16%	21.93%	24.36%	33.26%	26.47%	22.47%	22.27%	23.47%	3.08
	(2.93)	(4.31)	(1.54)	(.89)	(9.79)	(3.00)	(1.00)	(1.20)		
2 Persons	41.39%	46.27%	41.51%	45.49%	38.01%	45.92%	45.23%	47.27%	43.60%	2.76
	(2.21)	(2.67)	(2.09)	(1.89)	(5.59)	(2.32)	(1.63)	(3.67)		
3+ persons	32.21%	34.57%	36.55%	30.14%	28.73%	27.61%	32.31%	30.46%	32.93%	2.67
	(0.72)	(1.64)	(3.62)	(2.79)	(4.20)	(5.32)	(0.62)	(2.47)		

(continued)

Table 23.2 (continued)

Segmentation Variable/Level	Hotel A	Hotel B	Hotel C	Hotel D	Hotel E	Hotel F	Hotel G	Hotel H	All Hotels	Mean Absolute Deviation
Household Income/										
$0 to $29,999	23.64%	16.52%	21.37%	29.17%	33.71%	24.90%	23.86%	18.94%	22.95%	4.07
	(0.69)	(6.43)	(1.58)	(6.22)	(10.76)	(1.95)	(0.91)	(4.01)		
$30,000 to $49,999	26.91%	23.50%	25.28%	27.56%	26.61%	23.68%	26.61%	27.49%	25.41%	1.49
	(1.50)	(1.91)	(0.13)	(2.15)	(1.20)	(1.73)	(1.20)	(2.08)		
$50,000 to $99,999	37.64%	42.56%	40.57%	33.55%	30.88%	39.02%	38.48%	39.71%	38.74%	2.66
	(1.10)	(3.82)	(1.83)	(5.19)	(7.86)	(0.28)	(0.26)	(0.97)		
$100,000 +	11.82%	17.425	12.79%	9.72%	8.80%	12.40%	11.05%	13.85%	12.90%	2.04
	(1.08)	(4.52)	(0.11)	(3.18)	(4.10)	(.50)	(1.85)	(0.95)		
Respondent's Age/										
20s & 30s	27.27%	24.05%	29.37%	26.1?%	25.48%	28.56%	24.80%	22.81%	26.21%	1.79
	(1.06)	(2.16)	(3.16)	(0.08)	(0.73)	(2.35)	(1.41)	(3.40)		
40s & 50s	45.27%	45.03%	43.40%	43.06%	41.28%	46.44%	44.23%	44.40%	43.95%	1.22
	(1.32)	(1.08)	(0.55)	(0.89)	(2.67)	(2.49)	(0.28)	(0.45)		
60s & older	27.45%	30.92%	27.23%	30.7?%	33.25%	25.00%	30.97%	32.79%	29.84%	2.42
	(2.39)	(1.08)	(2.61)	(0.93)	(3.41)	(4.84)	(1.18)	(2.95)		
Purpose of Trip/ Business[a]	34.91%	41.00%	39.41%	33.55%	42.315	48.68%	40.29%	41.34%	40.48%	3.15
	(5.57)	(0.52)	(1.07)	(6.93)	(1.83)	(8.20)	(0.19)	(0.86)		

Source: Reproduced by permission from M. Lynn, "Brand Segmentation in the Hotel and Cruise Industries: Fact or Fiction?" *Cornell Hospitality Report* 7(4) (2007): 12.

hotel market).[17] What they found was that the typical MAD score was quite small—only 2 to 3 percentage points. Only around 8 percent of the MAD scores were more than 5 percentage points, and only 2 percent of the MAD scores were 10 percentage points or more. Moreover, the rare large MAD scores tended to reflect differences between broad subtypes within a product category (e.g., cereals aimed at kids versus those meant for adults) rather than brand differences within subtypes. I recently replicated these findings in the cruise and hotel industries.[18] Not only that, but other studies have found that demographic and psychographic variables are poor predictors of brand choice—even though many marketers want to rely on those factors.[19] Together, these empirical findings suggest that your customers are pretty much the same as those of your direct competition.

The conclusion that I reach here is that most markets are segmented enough to support broad product subtypes (say, economy hotels versus midscale with food and beverages), but not segmented enough to support more narrow differences between brands within those broad product subtypes (say, any of several economy hotel brands). After decades of competition, most if not all of the viable segments have been identified with numerous competitors vying for each. Those competitors within a product subtype end up competing for the same customers because more refined segments either do not exist or are not profitable. This explanation suggests that efforts to segment most highly competitive, well-developed, and stable markets are unlikely to identify useful new segments or targeting opportunities. The time for new segmentation efforts is when markets are new or have experienced some recent and fundamental change. For example, if social or technological changes in the market provide reason to believe that the underlying drivers of consumer choice have recently changed, then segmentation studies may identify useful new segments and targeting opportunities.

So that is the key limitation of segmentation. It may not prove strategically useful depending on what type of market you are operating in. If you are in a hotly contested and new or fundamentally changed market, then efforts to segment that market and identify a small number of segments to target may prove useful and should be attempted. However, if you are in a fairly stable, mature, competitive market (which describes most markets in the developed world), then refined segmentation and targeting are unlikely to provide the keys to competitive success. In a relatively stable and mature market, success comes not from appealing to a different set of consumers than your competition, but in finding ways to appeal to the same consumers more effectively than your competition does.[20]

TARGETING FREQUENT BUYERS

The tight competition in the hospitality industry has caused many brands to focus on promoting sales from frequent guests. This strategy has become so common in the hospitality industry that it deserves special mention—especially because I believe that it does not necessarily accomplish its intended goal. American Airlines led the industry's use of this strategy in the 1980s when its executives came to believe that they could increase their share of the lucrative but fickle heavy flyer segment by offering rewards tied to repeat patronage. Since then, the world's airlines have created over 70 frequent flyer programs that collectively have over 100 million members and give away 10 million rewards a year. Other travel-related companies were quick to copy this idea, so that frequency or loyalty programs have become commonplace in hotels, car rental firms, and even restaurants.[21]

This strategy seems sound because a small number of heavy users account for a large share of most product category sales and these heavy users tend to switch between several different brands within the product category.[22] The frequent-guest program is designed to give heavy users a reason to be more brand loyal. The concept of setting up cumulative rewards for purchase frequency should provoke a favorable response from heavy users, as compared to light users because earning those rewards requires less change in the behavior of heavy users. Thus, loyalty programs do differentiate between two distinct customer groups. Beyond that, however, reward-based frequency or loyalty programs probably do little to increase repeat patronage because they are easy to copy and heavy users' lack of brand loyalty means that they often join multiple programs and collect rewards as a by-product of purchases made for other reasons.[23] Indeed, several studies have found that reward-based programs increase average purchase frequency only slightly if at all in the long run.[24]

The reward programs do help to identify your heavy users. This is theoretically useful because heavy users are easy to reach and are presumably open to marketing messages because they are already your customers. Thus, the costs of marketing to this segment (outside of the reward program) should be relatively low. The problem is that heavy users are targeted by almost everyone, so competition for their patronage is intense. Furthermore, heavy users are generally more price sensitive and deal prone than are light users, and heavy users are more likely to try new brands and switch brands.[25] As most hospitality marketers have learned, this is a difficult segment in which to induce loyalty and, unless you want to permanently discount your brand, is not an attractive target.

Curious about the possible effects of loyalty programs, I conducted a study in 2008 using consumer panel data on domestic U.S. airline flights. The study was issued by Cornell's Center for Hospitality Research,[26] and the data are presented in Table 23.3. I identify airlines only by a letter because disguising the airline names was a condition for obtaining the data from D. K. Shifflet. There are two things worth noting about these data. First, airlines differ substantially in penetration (the percentage of air travelers patronizing the airline at least once), but only modestly in average purchase frequency of their customers. Penetration varies from 0.3 to 17.2 percent, for an increase from smallest to largest of 5,633 percent, while average purchase frequency varies from 1.1 to 1.5, for an increase of only 36 percent. Sales and market share are a function of the number of customers and how much they buy, so the wide variation in penetration and narrow variation in purchase frequency means that share of category sales is much more dependent on penetration than on purchase frequency. This relationship is shown in Figure 23.1, which depicts an almost perfect correlation between a brand's share of flights and its penetration. The differences in purchase frequency between brands do not add much at all to our understanding of the variation in brands' share of flights. Despite well-established and popular frequency programs in the airlines, differences in airline sales or share of flights are almost exclusively driven by differences in penetration—not purchase frequency.

Even if we thought purchase frequency had an effect, note that brand penetration and buyers' average purchase frequency are positively correlated, although not perfectly so (see Table 23.3). In general, brands with a large market share enjoy not only a penetration advantage but also tend to have a greater average purchase frequency than do brands with small shares. Conversely, small brands suffer not only from small penetration, but also a relatively low average purchase frequency among those who do buy those brands. This pattern of covariation suggests that an airline's average purchase frequency may be dependent on its level of penetration and that substantial increases in the purchase frequency may not be possible without increasing penetration. If that is true (and it seems to be the case), then marketing efforts aimed exclusively at increasing purchase frequency among heavy users are doomed to failure.

By themselves, the data in Table 23.3 speak only to the airline industry. However, the two patterns displayed in those data are so common that they have been identified as the double jeopardy effect. This name comes from the tendency for small share brands to suffer in two ways—from lower penetration and lower average purchase frequency. It also refers to the wider variation in penetration than in purchase frequency as well as to the positive

Table 23.3
Data on 19 Domestic U.S. Airlines

Airline	Number of Customers	Penetration	Purchase Frequency	Market Share	Travel Frequency
A	5,100.00	0.172	1.41	0.156	1.70
B	4,740.00	0.160	1.42	0.147	1.74
C	4,290.00	0.145	1.34	0.125	1.62
D	3,621.00	0.122	1.50	0.119	1.84
E	3,016.00	0.102	1.40	0.092	1.65
F	2,785.00	0.094	1.33	0.081	1.63
G	2,165.00	0.073	1.40	0.066	1.73
H	1,068.00	0.036	1.29	0.030	1.66
I	862.00	0.029	1.32	0.025	1.68
J	643.00	0.022	1.26	0.018	1.62
K	588.00	0.020	1.22	0.016	1.52
L	526.00	0.018	1.33	0.015	1.61
M	307.00	0.010	1.18	0.008	1.59
N	272.00	0.009	1.27	0.008	1.46
O	227.00	0.008	1.30	0.006	1.65
Q	149.00	0.005	1.15	0.004	1.48
S	112.00	0.004	1.14	0.003	1.32
V	79.00	0.003	1.24	0.002	1.61
W	78.00	0.003	1.19	0.002	1.56

Note: Four foreign airlines that primarily serve international travelers and enjoy competitive advantages in serving those markets that the domestic airlines do not have been omitted.
Source: Reproduced by permission from M. Lynn, "Frequency Strategies and Double Jeopardy in Marketing: The Pitfall of Relying on Loyalty Programs," Cornell Hospitality Report 8(2) (2008):10.

correlation between these measures. The double jeopardy effect has been observed in over 50 different common product categories—including breakfast cereals, gasoline, and soap—as well as in retail stores and even television programs. It has also been documented in many markets around the world, including Australia, continental Europe, Japan, the United Kingdom, and the United States. This effect seems to be a universal characteristic of mature, stable markets where competing brands are largely similar and can substitute for one another.[27]

Since most hospitality firms operate in mature, stable markets, the double jeopardy effect suggests that marketing strategies aimed solely at increasing the repeat patronage of heavy users are unlikely to succeed for hotels, airlines, and other such companies. I'm not suggesting that you abandon your loyalty program because you probably need it as a defensive measure to prevent the loss of market share to competitors with similar programs.[28] Instead,

Figure 23.1

Relationship between Share of Flights and Penetration for 19 Domestic Airlines in the United States

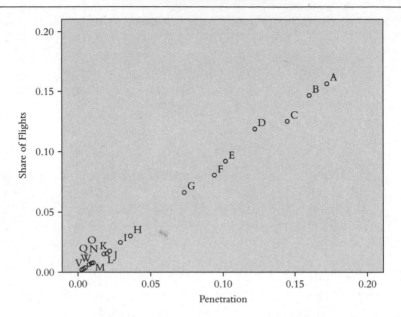

Source: Reproduced by permission from M. Lynn, "Frequency Strategies and Double Jeopardy in Marketing: The Pitfall of Relying on Loyalty Programs," *Cornell Hospitality Report* 8(2) (2008):11.

I'm suggesting that your marketing efforts should focus on increasing the popularity of your brand among all the users in your product category or subcategory—with the idea of boosting your penetration.

SUMMARY

If by chance you are entering a new or underdeveloped market, the STP strategy will offer you a strategic advantage over competitors. You can divide the market into homogeneous groups, identify those groups that your firm is best suited to satisfy, and target those selected groups. This focus will allow you to better and more cost effectively meet the needs of the target segments than can competitors who are going after everyone (or no one in particular). Needless to say, competitive forces mean that any successful strategy will eventually be copied, along with efforts you might make to identify and target even narrower segments. So it is in most geographic markets of the hospitality industry: Mature, stable markets have typically been segmented as much as is practical with several competitors vying for each profitable segment. Despite excellent product development efforts over the years, further segmentation and targeting are rarely helpful in such markets. Even the intuitively appealing division of the market into light and heavy users and the strategy of targeting the heavy-user segment is unlikely to succeed in crowded, mature markets. Instead, you are best advised to target all the users of your product category or subcategory in such markets, with a goal of increasing your penetration. Sales increases will be obtained, if at all, from increasing your brand's relative popularity among all users of the product class.

As a concluding point, given the different strategies best pursued in these two different markets—new or underdeveloped and mature or stable markets— it is important to know which you operate in. Although I believe that the data indicate that most markets are mature and stable, don't assume that you are operating in such a market. Instead, as I suggested previously, you should hire marketing researchers who will collect data on hundreds of variables and use sophisticated statistical procedures to try to segment your market, with a goal of identifying profitable new segments to target. If a plausible argument can be made that such profitable new target segments have been found, then pursue them. If not, you probably are operating in a stable market that has already been segmented as much as it can bear. Certainly, repeated failures by different market research firms to identify profitable new segments to target would be evidence that you are operating in such a market. In that case, try to get to know the users of your product category or subcategory so that you can satisfy their needs better than do your competitors. I believe that adhering to this contingent strategic focus is the path to greater profits in the hospitality industry.

NOTES

1. For example, see P. Kotler, *Marketing Management*, 9th ed. (Upper Saddle River, NJ: Prentice Hall, 1997).
2. D. Aaker, *Managing Brand Equity* (New York: Free Press, 1991), 164.
3. P. Kotler, J. T. Bowen, and J. C. Makens, *Marketing for Hospitality and Tourism*, 4th ed. (Upper Saddle River, NJ: Prentice Hall, 2006), 278–279.
4. http://en-us.nielsen.com/tab/product_families/nielsen_claritas/prizm, March 18, 2010.
5. http://en.wikipedia.org/wiki/Claritas_Prizm, May 10, 2010.
6. Ibid.
7. See K. Clancy and P. Krieg, *Your Gut Is Still Not Smarter than Your Head* (Hoboken, NJ: Wiley, 2007), 59–80.

8. P. R. Dickson and J. L. Ginter, "Market Segmentation, Product Differentiation, and Marketing Strategy," *Journal of Marketing* (April 1987): 1–10.

9. S. Dibb, "Criteria Guiding Segmentation Implementation: Reviewing the Evidence," *Journal of Strategic Marketing* 7 (1999): 107–129.

10. W. R. Swinyard and K. D. Struman, "Market Segmentation: Finding the Heart of Your Restaurant's Market," *Cornell Hotel and Restaurant Administration Quarterly* 37 (1) (May 1986): 88–96.

11. Ibid.

12. Dibb, 1999.

13 Swinyard and Struman, 1986.

14. Dickson and Ginter, 1987.

15. R. Kennedy, and A. Ehrenberg, "There Is No Brand Segmentation," *Marketing Research* (Spring 2001): 4–7.

16. Ibid.

17. Modified from M. Lynn, "Brand Segmentation in the Hotel and Cruise Industries: Fact or Fiction?" *Cornell Hospitality Report* 7(4) (2007): 12.

18. K. Hammond, A. S. C. Ehrenberg, and G. J. Goodhardt, "Market Segmentation for Competitive Brands," *European Journal of Marketing* 30(12) (1996): 39–49; Ibid.

19. Ibid.; J. Dawes, "Interpretation of Brand Penetration Figures that Are Reported by Sub-groups," *Journal of Targeting, Measurement and Analysis for Marketing* 14(2) (2006): 173–183.; and G. Fennel, G. M. Allenby, S. Yang, and Y. Edwards, "The Effectiveness of Demographic and Psychographic Variables for Explaining Brand and Product Category Use," *Quantitative Marketing and Economics* 1 (2003): 223–244.

20. Hammond, Ehrenberg, and Goodhardt, 1996.

21. "History of Loyalty Programs," www.frequentflier.com/ffp-005.htm, February 3, 2008.

22. G. Hallberg, *All Consumers Are Not Created Equal* (New York: Wiley, 1995).

23. B. Berman, "Developing an Effective Customer Loyalty Program," *California Management Review* 49(1) (2006): 123–148.

24. J. Leenheer, H. J. vanHeerde, T. H. A. Bijmolt, and A. Smidts, "Do Loyalty Programs Enhance Behavioral Loyalty? An Empirical Analysis Accounting for Self-Selecting Members," *International Journal of Research in Marketing* 24 (2007): 31–47; L. Meyer-Waarden and C. Benavent, "The Impact of Loyalty Programs on Repeat Purchase Behavior," *Journal of Marketing Management* 22 (2006): 61–88.; and B. Sharp and A. Sharp, "Loyalty Programs and Their Impact on Repeat-Purchase Loyalty Patterns," *International Journal of Research in Marketing* 14 (1997): 473–486.

25. E. C. Hackelman and J. M. Duker, "Deal Proneness and Heavy Usage: Merging Two Market Segmentation Criteria," *Journal of the Academy of Marketing Science* 8(4) (1980): 332–344; Hallberg, 1995; and B. D. Kim and P. E. Rossi, "Purchase Frequency, Sample Selection, and Price Sensitivity: The Heavy

User Bias," *Marketing Letters* 5(1) (1994): 57–67; and J. W. Taylor, "A Striking Characteristic of Innovators," *Journal of Marketing Research* 14 (February 1977): 104–107.

26. M. Lynn, "Frequency Strategies and Double Jeopardy in Marketing: The Pitfall of Relying on Loyalty Programs," *Cornell Hospitality Report* 8(2) (2008).

27. A. A. C. Ehrenberg, G. J. Goodhardt, and T. P. Barwise, "Double Jeopardy Revisited, *Journal of Marketing* 54 (July 1990): 82–91.

28. M. D. Uncles, G. R. Dowling, and K. Hammond, "Customer Loyalty and Customer Loyalty Programs, *Journal of Consumer Marketing* 20(4) (2003): 294–316.

New Media
Connecting with Guests throughout the Travel Experience

LISA KLEIN PEARO and BILL CARROLL

Travel back in time 30 years. You read the paper during breakfast, scanning an ad for a luxurious Caribbean resort with a rate of $450 per week. As you drive to work, you hear an ad on the radio for the same resort. The background music is a Bob Marley reggae jingle that you can't get out of your mind. In the waiting room at work, you spot an ad for that same resort in *Condé Nast Traveler* magazine. What a coincidence! Then, just before bedtime and right after Johnny Carson's monologue, you see an ad appear for that same hotel. That's it! You throw your arms around your partner, whistle Bob Marley's reggae jingle, and promise to call your travel agent in the morning. You both fall asleep dreaming of the romantic getaway to come.

The next morning, your travel agent finds you a better deal at another resort at the same destination. You book it. Months later, you savor your vacation memories. You had a good time despite several issues. Here's a black-and-white photograph taken outside the restaurant that the concierge recommended— a lovely location but not that great a meal. The hotel's plumbing was faulty and the room infested with bedbugs. You tell maybe five or six friends about your experiences and recommend they choose another restaurant and hotel if they go.

The marketing analyst at the resort where you didn't stay wonders why their newly renovated property had not achieved the expected bookings despite media placements on TV, radio, newspapers, and periodicals. The general manager wonders why that dump of a resort two miles away from the beach has such high occupancy versus his. Your travel agent goes to dinner on the 20 percent override commission paid by that dump of a resort.

Fast-forward in time 10 years from today. The video touch screen embedded in your kitchen table serves up your personalized morning news and a permission-granted, vacation-related, peer-group-vetted, rich-media-supported, date prespecified, budget-constrained, personally syndicated offer for a luxurious Caribbean resort for less than $800 per week. You touch the "more details later" button and finish breakfast. On the drive to work, your personalized Sirius car radio program is interrupted with a brief blurb about the resort offer you saw at breakfast and your hands-free car phone crackles with the pleasant voice of Monica Marley (Bob's great-granddaughter) sent to you directly through the resort's app. You prefer a human voice to answer your questions. Monica answers all your questions via the car phone speaker.

During your lunch break, you see a Web video from the same Paradise Luxury resort showing your and your partner's avatars positioned in a resort guest room, dining room, pool, and other common areas. You touch the send button; record a voiceover—"This can be us," and send an instant message with the attachment to your partner.

That night, you and your partner use the remote device for the wall TV and book the hotel, based on glowing recommendations from friends and colleagues; select your room décor; make golf and spa reservations; and choose a restaurant based on reviews from young couples with your dining tastes. You choose entrées from the menu and your favorite wine. Six months later, as you slide into the limo arranged two weeks earlier from your mobile device, that same device chirps with a message from a member of your social travel community: "Get room on higher floor, face SE." You log into the reservation planner and enter your updated room request, along with an order for wine and cheese to be delivered shortly after your arrival. Five minutes later, as the limo driver drops you off, the bellman checks you in to your preferred room with his handheld tablet. Over dinner, your partner gushes, "This is even more wonderful than our avatar portrayed; the menu has our names on it, and they served our favorite wine; let's tell all our friends." You respond, "I posted our picture and a note 10 minutes ago to our friends; all 227 have received it, and so far 23 'like' it."

At the Paradise Luxury resort, the general manager is edified that her focus on quality service and social media management has produced measureable incremental contributions. She is also pleased with the real-time connectivity between her revenue management system and the full-channel marketing and distribution, as well as the large number of guest advocates. Meantime, the restaurant waiter got the biggest tip of the week from guests she never saw before and therefore decided not to accept the job offer from a competitive restaurant across the street.

As the use of social media expands, you must stay abreast of the increasing array of communications media options for how and when to reach your guests. We refer to *new media* as those that extend the boundaries of traditional mass media and direct mail communications. These new media include Internet-based technology platforms that incorporate online banner and search-engine advertising, as well as social media and mobile media. This chapter explains how these new media options have affected your marketing communications.

MEDIA MEASUREMENT AND PLAYERS IN EVOLUTION

Whether you are looking at new media or traditional media, the success measures haven't really changed. They are:

- Additional sales that would not otherwise have occurred (net incremental contribution).
- Expanded market share.
- Increased effectiveness for complementary media.
- Long-term relationships with guests and clients that lead to highly loyal customers and active advocates.

Even if the measurements are essentially the same, the process is in transition. Most of the specific measurements of media activities continue to fall short of directly gauging those success measures. Traditional media measurements could only tally reach, in the form of cost per thousand impressions (CPM) in audience. But what we really wanted all along was a way to record consumer interactions: the number and nature of customer contacts and how they converted to reservations. We could get a sense of this from phone call logs, sales contacts, property visits, and surveys, but this was still inexact.

With Internet and mobile communications devices, we now have better tools for measuring conversions. Companies in all industries have jumped on this opportunity, and independent research firm Forrester Research, Inc. estimates that new media will represent over 50 percent of advertising spending by 2014.[1] As Figure 24.1 shows, the mix in new media spending will change as well by 2014.

Chances are that your hotel or restaurant uses an online travel agency (OTA) for distribution, such as Expedia, Travelocity, or Open Table. Your property or brand probably also has its own Web site for reservations, and many customers use OTAs as a source of information, and then book on a hotel's site, according to PhoCusWright research.[2]

Figure 24.1
U.S. Interactive Marketing Forecast

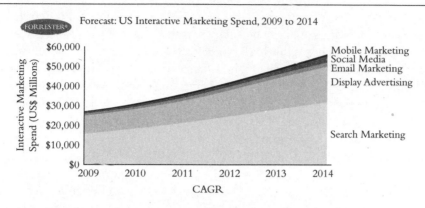

Forecast: US Interactive Marketing Spend, 2009 to 2014

Source: Reproduced by permission from Forrester Research, Inc.

Your Web site's success is measured by the number of unique visitors to your hotel or brand Web site, the percentage of those visitors converted to bookers, and the revenue generated from those bookings. With the growth of social media we are expanding this to include measures of the value of referrals. This is a great step beyond media reach measurements. The Web-based metrics relate costs (of the online effort) with the revenue contribution generated. We still don't know, however, whether some or all of the revenue was incremental or simply a distribution channel shift of existing customers.

Your ability to correlate cost with incremental contribution is even more tenuous with OTAs. It's hard to determine whether the transaction produced by the OTA was incremental and shifted share from your competitor or whether your guest would have booked anyway. If the latter, that booking could cost you 20 to 30 percent of the revenue you would otherwise have received through a regular booking. There is strong indication that the OTAs give you incremental bookings, though. For instance, Cornell research indicates that there may be anywhere from a 7 percent to a 26 percent increase in reservations through your site based on your position on the OTA display.[3] That is, if you're at the top of the display, people see your property and they are more likely to book through your own site. Given this, the average cost of an OTA booking may be closer to 7 or 10 percent, in terms of lost revenue. Although questions remain, that study is based on the principles of search engine marketing and search engine optimization. Both focus on getting your property near the top of any Web search, whether it's an OTA display or a simple search engine query.

Search Engine Marketing

Search engines in all forms have changed the hospitality marketing playing field. An otherwise obscure hotel can have its "name in lights" if it determines what consumers are seeking when they search for hotels in a particular market. Through search engine marketing (SEM) and search engine optimization (SEO), hotels can increase the chances that their property comes up near the top of searches on Google, Bing, and similar sites. SEM involves bidding on keywords that will bring your hotel to the top. The former pits hospitality consultants and programmers against search engine designers to get a hotel's brand message and URL to the top of the search results page, while search engine designers churn out algorithms to provide users only what they want to see.

Choosing the correct keywords to bid on (while minimizing click costs) has created a whole line of business for media advertising agencies like TIG, Milestone, and TravelCLICK. Among other services, these companies analyze search engine mechanics so that their clients design their own Web sites and choose words and phrases that move their Web sites to the top of search engine screens.

Measurement metrics for SEM include the number of search page views containing the brand site URL, the number of click-throughs to the brand site, percentage of click-throughs converted into bookings, and the revenue generated from those bookings. In turn, there are associated pay-per-click and SEO costs. While such metrics are more informative than the cost per impression from traditional media, they still fall short of decisively measuring incremental net revenue contribution. We still don't know whether the keyword purchases or SEO expenditures really generated new business or whether the hotel would have gotten those bookings, anyway. This is a particularly relevant issue when you are bidding for your own brand name. Of course, if you don't bid on it, your competition will, and you may not be found when the consumer is "searching" for you.

One measurement that we still don't have at this writing is the full chain of click-throughs that precede a booking. Search engine analytics provide metrics only for the "last click" from a keyword listing. Measuring only the last click, though, may misrepresent the real net contribution of optimizing keywords or keyword bidding. You can't be sure where the user was in the buying sequence—dreaming, planning, or booking—when the search engine click-through occurred. You also can't know what other sites the user visited before the last click.

Keywords that optimize a search are essential. It is likely that search engines will record a larger relative number of "last clicks" from keywords that contain your brand name because the user is more likely to be searching for a particular brand at the late stage of the search process when she's about to book. Given the search engine algorithms, you want to be certain that your brand comes up when the user is searching for it. At the same time, you may have determined that some generic, destination, or other nonbrand words are influential in capturing searchers. Your hotel's location, descriptors of the destination, and features of your property might be critical to a search. Consumers may start their search by looking for "seaside" or "mountain view," for instance, so your site could include those phrases if they apply. Then, at different points in the buying sequence, other optimizing keywords may come into play.

Search engine analytics can suggest some of these phrases. The analytics also can be informative from a competitive standpoint so that you know whether you are getting your fair share of views and clicks from brand and generic keywords.

SOCIAL MEDIA

So far, we've been discussing the traditional search engines, but in a way they are already old technology. We say this because in 2010, Facebook eclipsed Google as the most visited site on the U.S. Internet.[4] This heralded the entry of social community marketing as a major force in hospitality media marketing. Coincidentally, the potential intersection of online travel community formation with search, shopping, and mobile applications (apps) portends even more changes in future hospitality marketing media approaches.

Social Media: Evolution or Revolution?

Cindy Estis Green
Managing Partner
The Estis Group

The shift by consumers to social media and new media tools began in the late 1990s, but the marketing community took about five more years to start responding. When marketers did engage with the new media channels, they found that the dialogue that occurs in these channels is on a consumer-to-consumer basis, virtually cutting out the brand voice.

The implication for marketing strategy is profound. With the plethora of new channels and a notable shift in consumer behavior, the once

(continued)

(continued)

time-honored approach of aligning product, pricing, promotion, and path no longer applies.

The hospitality consumer's purchase decision process is inexorably altered. Most consumers no longer travel the predictable linear path that represents the process from a premarket need through searching, planning, prevalidating, booking, postvalidating and enjoying a hospitality experience. Through the use of social media, many consumers follow an iterative loop in which they continually interact with friends, family, and even strangers to gather information and verify expectations in parallel with their booking process, and, even more of a change, postexperience. Consumers share stories about their hospitality activities, including photos and video, and make this content available in the public domain.

The variables in a new media marketing plan have expanded by an order of magnitude. Hospitality marketers have to consider reengineering their infrastructure—organizations and budgets—to successfully manage this shift.

Marketing Strategy in a New Media World

Three C's of marketing are emerging: content, context, and conversations. Product decisions have to be infused with a content plan. This is not only brand-made content, but incorporation of consumer-generated content. The context of the product imagery requires a nuanced eye. A brand's products and services can be represented in diverse environments, many of which are not under the control of the marketing team. Whether it is a blog by a travel agent, a Twitter (microblog) feed by a business traveler, a series of YouTube videos posted after a trip by leisure guests, or a meal description by a restaurant guest, this content can have a greater impact on the brand image than anything a brand posts.

The brand's inability to mandate an image through promotional messages means they have to learn to influence these conversations, which often diverge from what the marketing team intended. The residual content amassed by these conversations has opened a new arena for hospitality called *reputation management*. Besides the direct brand message, consumers have unfettered access to each other's commentary, only part of which may be factually accurate, and most of which is purely subjective. In response, the hospitality marketer needs methodology for managing the brand while immersed in this murky and uncontrolled sea of consumer opinion.

The new media world includes booking channels that allow messages and message channels that enable booking. The hospitality marketer must be mindful of the many combinations of sites a consumer will visit. Further, participation in some sites influences success in others. For example, a high level of video, blog posts, and other social media output can improve a brand Web site's ranking in a search engine. The hospitality marketer has to decide the extent to which they will proactively participate in a channel and when they will passively observe the hospitality consumers' booking process. There is a cost associated with each of these channels and finding the optimal mix of channels that deliver the most business at the lowest cost is the marketer's challenge.

Summary
The popularity of social media sites is dynamic and needs to be monitored. Today's Facebook, Twitter, Trip Advisor, Yelp, and YouTube may well be replaced by other sites over time. What won't change is that consumers will continue to interact with each other, they will be skeptical of brand messages, and they will expect full access to a rich and wide array of content. But as hospitality firms gain more expertise in navigating the new media environment, they appear to be taking advantage of three primary applications of social media: (1) managing and burnishing a brand image, (2) engaging customers and prospects by providing higher levels of customer service and more relevant interaction, and (3) conveying tactical sales offers delivered in an appropriate voice and channel.

The first use of social media in connection with hospitality was peer-to-peer reviews of hospitality services (such as consumer comments found on TripAdvisor and Expedia) and instant text messaging among community members. In 2010, PhoCusWright reported that 8 of 10 travelers who had booked online had first read a review of travel-related services.[5] PhoCusWright also reported that unique visitors to peer-to-peer review sites like TripAdvisor and IgoUgo were growing at a rate of 50 percent per year, and TripAdvisor hosted nearly 10 times the number of visitors as its nearest competitor.[6] Remarkably, during 2009, the growth in the number of peer reviews posted to OTA sites was three times greater than peer-to-peer review sites. Since Expedia owns TripAdvisor, and Travelocity is connected with IgoUgo, we can conclude that the OTAs have become a major force in social media marketing. Essentially, OTAs strategically positioned themselves to incorporate social community–based peer-to-peer reviews as part of their service.

Facebook introduced its "I like" and "Social Graph" functions in 2010. We think that consumers will put greater weight on friends' Facebook recommendations than on those of strangers on peer-to-peer sites. Friendship may not be the optimal indicator of shared interests, but until peer-to-peer review sites add greater capability for consumers to identify like-minded reviewers, Facebook may be the most efficient way for consumers to sift through so many opinions. We will also likely see more hospitality marketers offering incentives to users to connect with the brand in order to build an audience and search influence.

Hospitality marketing structured around other social media activities is still coalescing as we write this. We don't know whether the value of Twitter's promotion and information messaging will grow or shrink or whether blogging will remain influential, but it's nearly a sure bet that some form of real-time, consumer-driven messaging will continue to dominate consumer search sources. Most major U.S. chains are still experimenting with these sites to raise awareness regarding their brand at every consumer contact point.

Most critically, you need to work on managing brand reputation in social media by monitoring comments and participating appropriately, in part by responding to posts in blogs and rich media sites. You have to monitor the sites to see if your hotel's name comes up, or rely on software that monitors social media sites and provides formal reports on your competitive position.

As a hotel employee or manager, you should not post on social media unless you are authorized to do so, to protect and support your brand. Carefully managed employee participation at all levels can be beneficial. Your hotel might use tweets to extend service with helpful blast messages to guests who are following your hotel (e.g., as an extension of concierge service) and to produce promotional and merchandising messages.

Measuring Social Media Success

You'll find that social media success metrics are still in the formative stages. They include: (1) measures of attraction that social media communities have with your brand or property; (2) the relative level of "buzz" (online mentions) you're getting; and (3) the relative sentiment of communities, including peer-to-peer reviews. As a manager, you will want to know your customers' position in terms of popularity or "connectedness" (by name, if possible). This includes:

- Those who want to hear from you on a regular or specified basis
- Those who have spoken to their communities about you—positively and negatively
- Those who are active and frequent advocates or critics of your hotel

Companies like TIG Global, Milestone Interactive, and TravelCLICK are active in measuring where you stand against your competitive set in social media. These metrics fall in two areas: awareness and sentiment. You define your competitive set, and the analytics firms give you metrics that include indices of social media awareness about your property compared to competitors, based on the buzz (e.g., mentions in blogs, peer-to-peer reviews, and media posts), and based on the nature of the sentiment being expressed. These firms apply proprietary algorithms that analyze online communications and also compile quantitative scores or rankings. These tools are available to marketing media managers to help you monitor and protect your brand as it appears on social media sites.

The Mobile Revolution and Hospitality Distribution

Norm Rose
President
Travel Tech Consulting, Inc.

Mobile technology will change the guest experience in a way that will likely equal or surpass the Internet's impact. Far from being just an additional touch point, mobile devices constitute a new platform for customer interaction—providing applications and capabilities that were not possible on prior devices. With nearly one-third of the U.S. population owning a smartphone at this writing,[7] the opportunity continues to grow. Seventy-one percent of frequent business travelers use a smartphone for both business and leisure trips.[8] The hospitality industry is particularly well positioned to use mobile technology to enhance the guest experience, promote onsite and local services, and improve operational efficiency. Much in the same way each hotel must have a Web presence, it is essential that every hotel develop a mobile strategy.

(continued)

(continued)

The first step is to reformat your Web site to allow mobile browsing. Even with today's latest smartphones, viewing a standard Web site can be challenging. Many companies can provide you a transcoding service that takes your current Web site and extracts the key elements for viewing on a mobile browser.

The next thing to consider is a downloadable application. Triggered by Apple's iPhone, there has been an explosion of app stores where customers can download applications to their phones. A recent study predicted that mobile app downloads will jump from 7 billion in 2009 to almost 50 billion in 2012 with the market worth $17.5 billion.[9] App stores are now available on every smartphone platform. There are two options in considering a downloadable app. You can create an application for your hotel, or you can partner with an existing provider of location-based services. This choice depends on the number of properties you own or manage, your budget, and your guest profiles. Unfortunately, fragmentation of mobile platforms will continue for the foreseeable future, so you'll need apps written for different devices. Choosing which platform to start with depends on your location and the characteristics of your guests. If you primarily cater to business travelers, a RIM Blackberry app may be best. If you are based outside the United States, you may want to look at Nokia's Symbian operating system as an initial target. Many hoteliers have selected the iPhone to create their application due to its popularity and functionality. Google's Android operating system has emerged as a major force embraced by a variety of device manufacturers and therefore should also be considered.

Your mobile apps should allow booking, check-in, and check-out. Such apps are already available through the mobile Web or branded downloadable apps on the iPhone, Blackberry, or Droid platform. Mobile concierge applications are a natural for the hotel industry, shifting the physical concierge costs to a location-sensitive personalized guide to local restaurants and attractions. Marketing through upgrades, spa reservations, add-ons, and mobile coupons can help hoteliers promote on-property services, restaurants, and local merchants. Ancillary purchases can be facilitated through mobile payment capabilities. Companies such as OpenWays are pioneering electronic room entry via mobile phones.

But this is only the beginning. Smartphones are increasingly acting as sensors that interact with the physical world by providing instantaneous information that influences guest behavior. An example of this is augmented reality applications such as TripWolf that overlay location-based information with destination guides. Annotating the physical world has its challenges, as crowd sourcing will influence guest decisions on restaurants, activities, and merchants.

Since users are storing their personal preferences and information on their smartphones, personal information (with proper opt-in controls) can be used for guest segmentation and more targeted promotions and dynamic rate offers based on guest value. The mobile phone will be used to enhance the conference experience, for instance, allowing you to identify attendees with similar interests and goals. The mobile device will provide personalized alerts to customers based on their preferences, providing them instant destination information based on their location. The smartphone will truly live up to its name by delivering updates of applications and prioritizing the apps most important for your customers' location and situation.

The mobile revolution promises to change hotel distribution as radically as the Internet itself. Innovation will continue, with thousands of third-party developers innovating on smartphone platforms. It is essential that hoteliers embrace this new platform and create applications to improve the guest experience, providing a new platform for guest interaction.

MOBILE MEDIA

Mobile applications are already changing hospitality distribution. Although frequent business travelers are current heavy users, leisure travelers will soon catch up. As examples, travelers can now download their boarding passes on their smartphones, and most major U.S. hotel chains have mobile apps. For the moment, we consider mobile as a subcategory of new media, but we expect that technological advancements will blur these boundaries. The most popular hotel apps empower travelers to get directions, make last-minute reservations changes, and change bookings.[10]

Mobile apps can also create efficiencies for travelers and hotels by allowing mobile device check-in, room assignment, and check-out. More advanced applications include on-property merchandising. So far, companies have extended their Internet-based applications to mobile platforms, but we see these mobile devices as enabling communications, which can be more time and location sensitive.

Similar to hotels, restaurant apps involve shopping and searching, in addition to making, canceling, and changing reservations. Early mobile restaurant applications were centered on getting directions and finding parking for restaurants, plus sharing information with others about food quality and service.

We think you can expect mobile apps to go beyond simply refitting existing brand Web site applications because you can do much more for your customers through the mobile platform. As time goes on, you'll be able to use the mobile user's identity, relationship, physical location, and context to refine the information and services you present to these customers, say, expediting check-in for a loyal guest. Room check-in or keyless access will require more technological effort on the part of hotels and more widespread use of applications by mobile device users. At the moment, these apps might set your property apart, but before long they'll be "table stakes." Your frequent guests will simply expect to walk in and use their phone to open their room.

A particular opportunity for mobile apps is to market to your guests during their stay (and not just before). With mobile apps, you can remain engaged with the consumer and encourage consumer-to-consumer communication during a hotel stay, all with the goal of improving the guest experience, while gaining incremental revenue.

Media: The New and the Newer

Taking a broad, philosophical approach, Figure 24.2 depicts the evolution of media in the hospitality industry from the perspective of media's role in the consumer decision process. In the era of print and television, as we said, media spending and measurement was determined by reach, measured by CPM. The goal was to reach the largest and most targeted audience at the lowest cost. In most cases, these messages reached consumers before they had actively begun to search for specific service providers—in their "dreaming" stage. The eruption of Internet search engines moved the marketing model to pay-per-click analysis and marketing spending, with measurements of immediate response to search results. These messages reached consumers at a late stage, when they were gathering information prior to their actual decision. Consumers had moved from the dreaming stage to seeking information by category, location, or even brand.

With the relatively recent availability of consumer-to-consumer social media, consumers can actively search for opinions, activities, and experiences of those with whom they are connected. This connection is at a fairly late stage of the purchase decision process. Moreover, as indicated by the shading in Figure 24.2, consumers can then use these networks to share their experiences with others who are at the same decision stage. The real innovation, which is enabled by mobile apps, is that people can gather information

Figure 24.2
Consumer Use of Media During Hospitality Purchase and Use Stages

Media Focus	Measurement	Before	During	After
		\textbf{Decision Stage}		
Print/TV	Reach and CPM	X		
Computer: Internet Search	CPC	X		
Computer: Social Media	Followers/Fans/Connections	X	X	X
Mobile	Check-Ins/Location	X	X	X

Note: While the shading used is solid, a better representation might show blendings between stages as decision making occurs repeatedly throughout any hospitality experience as guests choose meals, spa treatments, room service, etc.

Heavy use ▮ Moderate use ▭ Little to no use ▭

during a trip, including getting recommendations on destination activities, restaurants, and transportation. Thus, marketers can use this channel to let their guests know about spas, concierge services, restaurants, and room service, thereby enhancing the guests' on-site experience.

Even more interesting and potentially game changing is the notion that your current guests will interact with other current, future, and past guests during their stay. This means you will be engaging with consumers during their actual experience, and also with other consumers that now have access to the property's (and destination's) information. Consequently, the link between consumers is now completed by connecting those in the midst of their experience with those who are "before" and "after," as shown in Figure 24.3. For this purpose, consumers can use third-party applications such as Foursquare and Gowalla or proprietary applications such as those being developed for specific properties and destinations, such as Disney World. Thus, marketing must focus on enabling and facilitating connections among (the appropriate) consumers at all stages in their travel experience. These connections must tie in tightly with the consumer decision-making process, as highlighted in Figure 24.2.

Figure 24.3
The Flow of Consumer Conversation

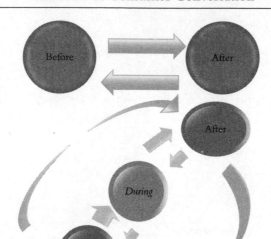

A key point here is that the new media do not replace the old, but instead add value at different stages of the consumer decision process. What now challenges you as a hospitality marketer is to identify when a consumer is ready to move from one stage to the next and to supply the appropriate tools. Identifying how and what information your consumers need at each travel stage will enable you to provide the right links and connections to that consumer. Consumers do indeed have the power to gather information from almost anyone, anywhere now, but you as a marketer also have the power to communicate with anyone, anywhere to give them exactly the information they need. With new media, your constraints involve only access and engagement. You must make it valuable for the consumer to give you access to them and to provide incentive (intrinsic or extrinsic) for them to engage with you and with other consumers.

RESTAURANTS: SO WHAT DO I DO?

As a restaurant manager, you need to view new media primarily as an opportunity to get to know your customers. With new media, including social networks and mobile platforms, you can help consumers make dining decisions by providing them with the right information at the right time and encourage your best customers to help other customers make reservation decisions. The following suggestions can help you move toward these goals:

- *Before the experience.* Monitor and respond to peer-to-peer reviews on the most relevant sites for your restaurant(s). Use premium services to address interested customers on the most valuable sites. Find ways to track your customers' use of these sites to post and read reviews.
- *During the experience.* Use location-based applications such as Four Square to understand repeat purchase patterns and test promotional influences directly. Recognize and reward frequent visitors. Rather than simply assessing how many additional covers or meals a promotion attracts, you can now evaluate which customers they attracted. You can assess whether these were incremental visits by "light users," trial visits by new customers, or loyal customers who merely shifted to a different daypart.
- *After the experience.* Use social media as an opportunity to extend your listening beyond your dining room. Monitor the changes in the volume and tone of these conversations (for you and your competitors). Use microblogging tools, such as Twitter, to join in the conversation.

HOTELS: SO WHAT DO I DO?

For hotel marketing managers, the opportunities are similar but focus less on knowing who the customer is and more on the why and how of the customer's visit. That is, interactions through new media can help you understand the objectives for customer's visit, as well as the information gathering paths for fulfilling them. The following suggestions outline the key strategies:

- *Before the experience.* In the planning stages, continue to use SEO and SEM to target your customers. Focus on optimizing results on Google, Facebook, and Twitter, among others. Once the reservation has been made, use e-mails and mobile apps to engage customers in the specifics of planning their experience before they arrive. Early engagement extends the brand immersion.
- *During the experience.* Onsite mobile apps allow the hotel to serve as the liaison or assistant in customers' spontaneous decisions for incremental services. With the added revenue comes added knowledge about the choices guests make throughout their stay. Encourage the customer to engage with other customers onsite through appropriate networking tools.

- *After the experience.* As with restaurants, continue to monitor peer-to-peer review sites. Enable customers to use your applications to provide specific advice to other guests and to leave direct feedback for you. Provide customers with the incentives to continue the relationship with discussions, photos, and videos through social networks.

As a hotel marketing manager, your goal should be to act as the customer's primary "liaison" to his travel experience before, during, and after his travels. Technology has changed the focus of your interactions at different stages of the experience. Now, with the growth of mobile platforms, you can maintain contact throughout the guest's experience by providing planning tools (before), experiential tools (during), and feedback and sharing tools (after). Beyond that, you can gather information on and make connections with guests of competing hotels. Finally, you can measure your marketing response continuously and implement simple tests of new promotional offers with little cost and low risk.

Conclusion

New media represent opportunities for hotel and restaurant marketers both to acquire and retain customers. You can use new technologies to (1) encourage your loyal customers to recruit new customers through social media, and (2) find new customers directly through the interests they express. To retain guests, you should evaluate new media as channels for listening, monitoring, measuring, and responding throughout the guests' experience. For both acquisition and retention, return-on-investment measurement will help you determine which activities have been successful, even though not all will generate revenue immediately. Some new media activities such as gathering customer feedback, may simply be more effective substitutes to older ways of doing business. In general, you must be part of the changing world of media, integrating the old with the new.

Notes

1. S. V. VanBoskirk, "US Interactive Marketing Forecast, 2009 To 2014, *Forrester Research, Inc.* (July 2009).
2. C. Rheem, *PhoCusWright Consumer Travel Report,* Section 5, 2009.
3. C. Anderson, "The Billboard Effect: Online Travel Agency Impact on Non-OTA Reservation Volume, *Cornell Hospitality Report* 9(16) (2009).
4. Hitwise Industry Report, December 2010 (http://www.hitwise.com/us/press-center/press-releases/facebook-was-the-top-search-term-in-2010-for-sec/).

5. PhoCusWright, *Consumer Technology Survey* (November 2009).
6. PhoCusWright, *Social Media in Travel: Traffic and Activity* (April 2010).
7. NPDGroup, http://paidcontent.org/article/419-deep-discounts-on-smartphones-drive-u.s.-adoption-rates-to-nearly-a-thi/, 2009.
8. PhoCusWright, *Mobile: The Next Platform for Travel,* www.phocuswright.com/research_publications_buy_a_report/585, 2010.
9. Chetan Sharma Consulting, mashable.com/2010/03/17/mobile-app-market-17-5-billion/, 2010.
10. C. Schetzina, *Consumer Technology Survey,* 3rd ed. PhoCusWright (December 2009), Part Five.

CHAPTER 25

BUILDING AND MANAGING YOUR BRAND

ROBERT J. KWORTNIK

Have you eaten at Zoup!, Smashburger, or Big Al's Steaks? Have you stayed at Andaz, Aloft, or Element? If you haven't yet experienced one of these products, let alone heard of them, it's probably because they are brands that are still in the building process. Each of these brands is relatively new in their industry sector, but they may someday be as familiar as Taco Bell or Marriott. From Andaz to Zoup!, these companies were built with a simple but powerful promise to guests that they will receive specific benefits from patronizing that brand. Smashburger's promise, for instance, is to be "THE place for burger lovers . . . Where smash. sizzle. savor. means a dedication to creating the best-tasting 'cooked-to-order' burger."

Building a brand is not a new idea, but the process has become increasingly sophisticated and supported by marketing research. This chapter helps you to think like a brand marketer. Even as an independent operator, you can borrow from the playbook of the established brands and take a strategic approach to brand building and management. If you do work for an established brand—or are thinking about affiliating with one, this chapter helps you to understand the importance of branding in a crowded marketplace. The approach to brand strategy I introduce in this chapter is derived in part from a course on Service Experience Management that I teach at Cornell University's School of Hotel Administration, as well as lessons I've learned while providing brand-strategy consulting to hotel companies, cruise lines, and tourism destinations. The centerpiece of the approach is a Process Framework for Strategic Branding that serves as a guide for diagnosing brand problems and opportunities and for building successful brand experiences.

WHAT IS A BRAND?

A brand identity may include a name, logo, trade character (e.g., Ronald McDonald or a gecko), package design, or trade dress (including a color scheme and look of a building exterior). All of these are used to identify the product's owner and distinguish the product from competitors. Typically, these elements of a brand are legally protected as intellectual property through a trademark, which is registered with a government agency responsible for overseeing property rights (e.g., the U.S. Patent and Trademark Office). Creating a legal brand is important for your business, because the brand identifies you to consumers and protects both parties from product imitators.[1]

For hospitality companies, a strong brand can be one of the most valuable assets—because the brand provides value to customers, primarily by promising a uniform level of quality delivered by the brand.[2] Customers use brands to make inferences about benefits offered based on knowledge about brand attributes (e.g., Ritz-Carlton Hotels and Resorts provide highly personalized service) and about brand associations (e.g., Ritz-Carlton is associated with luxury). Strong brands also possess top-of-the-mind awareness, so that when customers recall brands in a particular category (e.g., a luxury hotel chain) the brand automatically comes to mind (Ritz-Carlton). Such brand awareness is especially important for decisions where consumers may not have ready access to complete information about their available choices. In that case, consumers are likely to choose familiar brands. These are some of the reasons why owners of hospitality services looked to established brands as partners.

THE BRAND-AFFILIATION DECISION

In some sections of the hospitality industry, affiliating with a brand versus going it alone as an independent operator is a pivotal strategic decision. In the lodging industry, it seems that brands are gaining increasing ascendancy, even though independent, single-location properties have long been the norm, as shown in hotel census data from the leading research firm, STR Global (see Table 25.1).[3]

Looking at the numbers, we see that branded hotel companies added nearly 4,700 properties (+10.4 percent) versus the addition of 1,587 independent properties (+2.2 percent). Growth was particularly strong in the Asia-Pacific region, where branded properties increased by 13.2 percent, and in the North American region, where branded properties increased by 14.7 percent. Branded properties now outnumber independent properties

Table 25.1
STR Global Hotel Census Data (2005–2010)

Region/Ownership	Brands			Properties			Rooms		
	2005	2010	% +/−	2005	2010	% +/−	2005	2010	% +/−
Asia-Pacific									
Branded	211	219	+0.5%	4,106	4,647	+13.2%	706,703	845,955	+19.7%
Independent				10,525	11,052	+5.0%	1,234,315	1,315,436	+6.6%
Total				14,631	15,699	+7.3%	1,941,018	2,161,391	+11.4%
% Branded				28.1%	29.6%		36.4%	39.1%	
Europe									
Branded	364	352	−3.2%	13,397	13,488	+0.6%	1,482,027	1,566,106	+5.7%
Independent				31,819	32,926	+3.5%	2,017,847	2,109,928	+4.6%
Total				45,216	46,414	+2.6%	3,499,874	3,676,034	+5.0%
% Branded				29.6%	29.1%		42.3%	42.6%	
North America									
Branded	272	267	−1.8%	27,710	31,776	+14.7%	3,244,780	3,651,979	+12.5%
Independent				28,773	28,726	−0.2%	1,756,927	1,820,606	+3.6%
Total				56,483	60,502	+7.1%	5,001,707	5,472,585	+9.4%
% Branded				49.1%	52.5%		64.9%	66.7%	
Total									
Branded	667	636	−4.6%	45,213	49,911	+10.4%	5,433,510	6,064,040	+11.6%
Independent				71,117	72,704	+2.2%	5,009,089	5,245,970	+4.7%
Total				116,330	122,615	+5.4%	10,442,599	11,310,010	+8.3%
% Branded				38.9%	40.7%		52.0%	53.6%	

Note: Many brands are in multiple regions; each of these brands was counted only once.

Source: Author's analysis of STR Global lodging census data made available to the author May 12, 2010.

Table 25.2
The 10 Largest Hotel Companies in the World

Company	# Brands	# Properties	# Rooms
InterContinental Hotels Group	7	4,389	634,888
Marriott International	18	3,400	595,461
Wyndham Worldwide	11	7,090	593,300
Hilton Hotels	10	3,500	545,000
Accor Group	16	4,111	485,549
Choice Hotels	11	6,032	547,968
Best Western	1	4,032	308,428
Starwood Hotels & Resorts	9	999	298,047
Global Hyatt	8	434	120,031
Carlson (Rezidor Hotel Group)	5	396	84,200

Source: Author's analysis of lodging supply published on company Web sites or obtained from company media and public relations departments.

in North America, where two out of three rooms are managed by branded hotels. The growth in these regions from 2005 to 2010 occurred despite a net decrease in the number of brands due to bankruptcies, mergers, and buy-outs (a drop of 4.6 percent to 636). In the United States, the 10 largest hotel companies now either directly own or franchise more than half of lodging supply (see Table 25.2).[4]

Research indicates that there are financial benefits to brand affiliation. For one thing, brand affiliation increases a hotel property's market valuation.[5] For another, a 2009 study by Ypartnership/Yankelovich found that four out of five leisure travelers prefer a brand-affiliated hotel.[6] Additionally, STR analysis released in April 2009 reported that, in the United States, brand-affiliated hotels have outperformed independent properties for the past 15 years on occupancy, average daily rate (ADR), and revenue per available room (RevPAR).[7] This trend continued through the first half of 2010 (see Table 25.3). The same pattern of results holds for properties in the Asia-Pacific region, with brand affiliated hotels achieving 7.4 percent higher ADR and 7.2 percent higher RevPAR (occupancy differences are negligible). As discussed shortly, though, performance differs for hotels in Europe.

Allying with an established brand brings a number of advantages that contribute to improved financial performance, including access to consumer-tested marketing knowledge and tools, such as the brand Web site and reservation system, marketing communications programs, service standards and training programs, sales and marketing teams, and referral and loyalty programs. Branded hotels also frequently have an advantage in booking

Table 25.3
STR Lodging Performance Metrics, United States and Asia/Pacific

	Occupancy (%)	ADR (US$)	RevPAR (US$)
U.S. brand-affiliated	57.7	98.35	56.80
U.S. independent	53.4	94.30	50.32
Asia brand-affiliated	63.9	128.37	82.04
Asia independent	64.1	118.82	76.16

Source: STR Global Trend Statistics made available to the author on July 20, 2010.

Table 25.4
STR Lodging Performance Metrics, Europe

	Occupancy (%)	ADR (Euro)	RevPAR (Euro)
Europe brand-affiliated	61.2	93.49	57.18
Europe Independent	58.3	118.96	69.35

Source: STR Global Trend Statistics made available to the author on July 20, 2010.

meetings, incentive, conference, and exhibition (MICE) business, which typically involve corporate accounts that are negotiated nationally.[8]

Perhaps the biggest benefit of brand affiliation is access to the customer-based brand equity—the brand awareness, loyalty, perceptions of quality, and beliefs about the brand.[9] Thanks to brand standards and marketing, consumers perceive—and seek out—the consistency and reduced purchase risk that a brand provides. This is why automobile travelers who see the Golden Arches in the distance are apt to choose McDonald's for a meal over a local independent diner, even though the latter may provide better food. Such uncertainty reduction is especially important for the transient market, where hotels make the bulk of their profits.[10]

Despite all those benefits of affiliating with an established brand, for many hotel owners in much of the world, independent operation works well. The STR lodging census also reveals that approximately 70 percent of hotels and 60 percent of rooms in Europe and Asia are *not* brand-chain affiliated. Furthermore, STR metrics covering Europe (as of June 30, 2010) shows that although brand-affiliated hotels achieved higher occupancy rates (4.7%), independent hotels earned much higher ADRs (21.4%) and RevPAR (17.5%); see Table 25.4. This is also true in some parts of the United States, where independent properties outperform brand-affiliated hotels in certain regional or local markets.[11]

One reason that hoteliers operate independently is the expense of brand affiliation. HVS International reported in 2009 that lodging franchise fees are often the second-largest operating expense (after payroll), typically averaging around 9 to 10 percent of total room revenue.[12] In addition to royalties and system expenses, franchisees usually support the costs for upgrades to the brand, such as enhanced room amenities, bedding, and technology. For example, much of the cost of the billion-dollar Holiday Inn brand relaunch, started in 2007 by InterContinental Hotels Group, will be borne by the owners of the 3,300 properties, to cover new signs, marketing, and service and property upgrades.[13] Beyond that, if you chafe at the prospect of being forced to use the brand's management systems and to be held accountable for brand standards, you may prefer independent operation.

Independent operation is also appropriate for hotels that operate in particular markets, for example, where guests desire boutique lodging or where traffic would support a small independent operation. Independent operation is also supported by the growing availability of low-cost Web applications or third-party systems that provide hotel owners with reservations and revenue management systems. With all of these considerations, your decision of whether to affiliate with a brand involves your own business strategy, which requires an analysis of the marketing environment and return on investment. Table 25.5 summarizes the main benefits and drawbacks of brand affiliation and independence.

GOING INDEPENDENT—BUILDING YOUR BRAND

In the rest of this chapter, I assume that you are going independent. While brand building involves creativity, it's primarily an analytic process that depends on data-driven decisions and the alignment of key stakeholders. Fundamental to this alignment is the articulation of a clear brand promise that attracts customers and provides a call to action. The importance of this brand promise cannot be overstated—the promise is the essence of both your value proposition to customers and the motivation for employees to live the brand. Let's examine this process and see examples of hospitality firms that have successfully implemented brand strategies.

As reflected in the Process Framework for Strategic Branding (Figure 25.1), building your brand starts with a research-based audit of customers' purchase motivations, your firm's competencies and systems, and your competitors' activities. As a brand strategist, once you determine how the brand

Table 25.5

Brand Affiliation in the Hospitality Industry: Benefits and Drawbacks

Benefits	• Access to an established brand's equity—customer awareness of the brand, beliefs and knowledge about the brand, familiarity and comfort with the brand, perceptions of brand quality and value, trust in the brand, and loyalty to the brand • Recognizable brand symbols, trade dress, and imagery • Perceived consistency of brand environment, attributes, and service • Market power derived from brand size and networks • Efficiency and strength of one-stop marketing management—brand Web site, sales support, central reservations system, revenue management system, marketing communications programs, and loyalty programs • Established service training programs and standards • Advantage is booking MICE business • Positive effects on financial market valuation of the property • Generally better performance on financial metrics (occupancy, ADR, and RevPAR) depending on market location
Drawbacks	• Costly brand-affiliation (franchise) fees that average 9 to 10% of room revenue, including revenue-based royalty fees, payments for joint advertising, and fees for bookings made through the brand's CRS • Risk of being deflagged and losing franchise fees for failure to uphold brand standards • Strict franchise contracts • Required payment for brand upgrades (e.g., property renovations or new brand signs) • Loss of some financial and operational control to brand franchisor • Reduced ability to be entrepreneurial • Required adherence to management approaches, training, pricing systems, brand standards, and brand symbols • Loss of individual business identity subsumed by the brand • Greater time required for reporting of operational performance to corporate • Uncertain financial returns to brand affiliation depending upon market location

experience addresses customers' needs and wants, you then can determine the core elements of the brand that your firm can efficiently provide; articulating a brand promise that demonstrates value; and selecting brand touch points, which are the tangible and experiential cues used in marketing communications to help consumers develop meanings about the brand.

Figure 25.1
A Process Framework for Strategic Branding

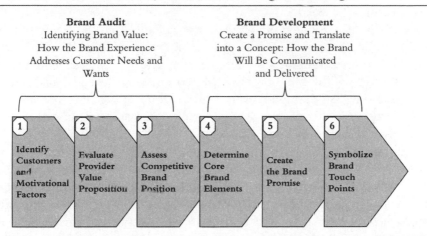

Brand Audit	Brand Development
Identifying Brand Value: How the Brand Experience Addresses Customer Needs and Wants	Create a Promise and Translate into a Concept: How the Brand Will Be Communicated and Delivered

1. Identify Customers and Motivational Factors
2. Evaluate Provider Value Proposition
3. Assess Competitive Brand Position
4. Determine Core Brand Elements
5. Create the Brand Promise
6. Symbolize Brand Touch Points

Step 1: Identify Customers and Their Motivational Factors

Start developing your brand strategy by talking with your existing and (carefully chosen) potential customers. Have a type (or types) of customer in mind as you develop your brand. For example, as part of a destination-branding project, a team of Cornell University graduate students that I supervised used tourism data from a variety of sources to determine current source markets for visitors to the African nation of Zambia. Next, the team performed a demographic and psychographic (lifestyle) analysis to map the types of travelers with the financial means for and personal interest in a Zambia tourism experience. This analysis produced a type of target visitor—relatively affluent, well educated, avid travelers from the United States and the United Kingdom.

Although a good start, the customer picture was incomplete because it lacked a description of purchase motivations—that is, the reasons why one would travel to Zambia. Developing a brand requires a rich understanding of what motivates consumers to buy from certain product categories—to tap into the "Whys for Buys."[14] Direct questions about purchase motivations often yield purely rational explanations—when in fact the decision may be largely emotional or influenced by self-relevant motives.[15] A better approach is to use indirect methods to evoke customers' motivations, such as depth interviews and focus groups, analysis of online forums where consumers talk about their product experiences, and surveys that use indirect questioning and interpretive analysis of consumer responses. So an effective question might be, "Tell me about the best vacation experience you've had recently and what made it special?"[16]

Determining consumers' underlying purchase motivations early in the strategic branding process will yield significant dividends later. This is because you can translate consumers' "whys for buys" into brand elements that are the foundation of the brand promise. Moreover, using a data-driven approach helps to ensure that decision makers hear the voice of the customer and don't impose assumptions and personal preferences on the prospective market.

A classic excellent example of such fact-based brand building is Marriott International's development of the Courtyard by Marriott brand in the early 1980s.[17] The original idea for Courtyard was to create a smaller version of the typical Marriott hotel. However, rather than rely on management assumptions, Marriott hired consultants who used sophisticated statistical approaches to extract a set of hotel features that would provide the most value to the target market of price-sensitive frequent business travelers and occasional leisure travelers. In addition to hotel design and room-amenity preferences, the research revealed that customers sought a hotel with personality that was informal, quiet, relaxing, and charming. These benefits became the foundation of the Courtyard brand when it was launched as "a special little hotel at a very comfortable price."

With Courtyard's success, Marriott kept the customer-listening system attuned to the market and the brand evolved as customer preferences changed. For example, in the early 2000s, Marriott again used a research-based approach to develop a reinvention and renovation program, in part to stave off the fast-growing Hilton Garden Inn brand.[18] The hotel design had to support the brand identity, which had evolved to "exactly the room they need, no more, no less," and which was articulated by the brand slogan, "The Room that Works." Ongoing brand redesign in 2010 focused on a new lobby concept that featured an open-access front desk, casual meeting spaces, flexible work areas, a bistro, and a touch-screen virtual concierge. These brand "touch points" symbolize the new Courtyard brand message, "It's a New Stay." As you can see from Marriott's experience, brand building is a continuous process that demands rigorous analysis of customer markets and a fact-based approach to brand design.

Step 2: Evaluate Your Value Proposition

Although your brand's value resides in the minds of customers, to deliver on your brand promise you must determine the sources of this value with a thorough and objective assessment of how you deliver your guests' desired services. In addition to the information about your target markets' needs, wants, and motivations gleaned from the customer analysis in Step 1, assessment of the value proposition must examine customers' expectations and their perceptions of product performance relative to those expectations.

Comment cards and customer surveys will give you some of this information, but ratings alone are incomplete. Web comments will give you insights—particularly from travel review sites (e.g., TripAdvisor.com) and online discussion forums where consumers describe their expectations, their experiences, and what they think about it. Another source for information about expectations is your firm's marketing communications, such as advertising, sales materials, and Web site, which show your brand promise. Furthermore, you should scan published reports, travel guides, and expert reviews that may also influence consumers' expectations.

Even a good service experience may be perceived poorly if the customers expected something different. For example, with a service operations colleague, I conducted a study of a cruise line's onboard dining experience.[19] A key brand promise for this cruise line was complete freedom of choice for onboard dining, which was compelling to customers who were not attracted to the typical cruise's structured itineraries. Such a promise is particularly unusual for a cruise ship catering to 2,500 or more guests. As you can guess, though, delivering on this promise presented significant operating challenges. Not surprisingly, allowing for freedom of choice meant that queues were common during peak dining times, some restaurants were underutilized early in the cruise, and others were inaccessible to guests later in the cruise. The cruise line attempted several fixes, such as a reservations system (which, arguably, countered the free-choice promise) and guides posted in public areas who showed which restaurants were available and which ones were full or had waits. Still, customer ratings showed that guests too often rated the dining experience negatively. Our analysis indicated, though, that customer dissatisfaction was as much a function of high expectations set by brand marketing as it was of inadequate performance.

Brand management depends on service experience management before, during, and after the actual service. Customer expectations become a part of the service, which is why value is actually co-created by the customer and hospitality provider.[20] Thus, analysis of the value proposition must address both the firm's sources of value (e.g., physical service environment, the service provided by employees, and processes by which service is delivered), and also the customer's input to value co-creation, such as service expectations, price paid for service, and the effort and actions required of customers for service delivery. By evaluating these dimensions, you can help to ensure that brand messaging is consistent with the promised experience.

Step 3: Assess Competitive Brand Positions

Customers are comparing your brand's value to that of competitive brands. To differentiate from your competition, you must ascertain key competitors' value propositions. Points of differentiation between your brand and those of competitors may be specific features or a focus on different experiences. To begin this assessment, you need look no further than competitors' Web sites and marketing communications, which typically highlight what aspects of the brand its marketers feel contribute most to customer value. What you're looking for is competitive weaknesses along dimensions that your customer research shows are important for motivating purchase—what I call positioning points. These positioning points must matter to customers. You need to identify some distinctive aspect of the product, such as a design, technology, service, or a combination of these factors that customers value and that are aligned with the brand.

Returning to the Zambia study, when my students conducted a positioning assessment of African destinations that attracted the same tourism markets as Zambia, they charted the other nation's brand slogans and symbols. They found the following: Botswana: Opportunity and Tranquility; Kenya: The Magic of Africa; South Africa: It's Possible; and Tanzania: Land of Kilimanjaro and Zanzibar. Next, the team analyzed each country's positioning points, such as destination attractions and experiences. The team also analyzed travel Web sites and discussion forums to see what visitors were saying were the must-see and must-do aspects of each destination, as well as the weaknesses (e.g., crime, poverty, poor infrastructure, or high costs).

With this detailed analysis, we gained greater clarity of Zambia's competitive position. A key attraction for Zambia is Victoria Falls, on the border with Zimbabwe. The fact that Zimbabwe has experienced economic and political problems creates an opportunity for Zambia. Zambia also possesses huge national parks that permit unspoiled and relatively uncrowded game viewing, unlike some competitors with busier and more commercialized safari operations. Zambia is English speaking and politically stable, has little crime, and is known for friendly people—attributes that facilitate a close interaction between visitors and the local culture. Aligned with traveler motivations, these positioning points are the core elements for Zambia's customer-based brand strategy.

A useful way to visualize competitive brand positioning is to create a brand hierarchy that summarizes the brand—the promise, elements, and touch points—for each competitor (see Figure 25.2). A brand hierarchy can reveal areas where a brand enjoys a differential advantage and should be actively promoted. Let's look at the specifics of the brand hierarchy as a tool for conceptualizing brand strategy.

Step 4: Develop Core Brand Elements

As discussed in Step 1, the foundation of a brand promise is your customers' needs, wants, and motivations that most influence customer choice. In the Process Framework for Strategic Branding, these motivations are translated into core brand elements, which provide meaning and connect the customer to the brand. Brand elements should speak to why customers select a hospitality service and specific provider, what they seek from the experience, and what the brand promises to deliver. Solid and compelling brand elements are derived from your brand audit and represent the mapping of customer motivations to the services and experiences that you provide.

For example, since the mid-1970s, management of Carnival Cruise Lines has positioned the brand based on the simple promise of a fun ship experience, a contrast to existing cruise lines.[21] Instead of formal, upscale experiences, Carnival offered cruisers a party at sea with late nights, dancing, drinking, and gaming. Even though Carnival has toned down the activity over the years (aiming to attract families), the "fun ships" promise still rests on such brand elements as fun, excitement, and novelty. These are emotional and experiential benefits that motivate Carnival's customers to choose the brand (see Figure 25.2), and Carnival clearly delivers those benefits. From the design of the ships, with their "entertainment architecture," to the messages in online and television ads (including talking towel animals or shrieking adults flying down a water slide), every brand symbol suggests (shouts!)

Figure 25.2
Brand Development Hierarchy

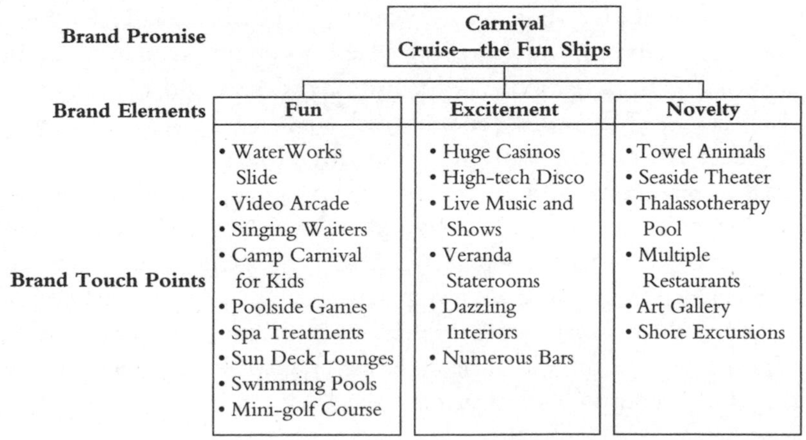

Brand Promise	Carnival Cruise—the Fun Ships		
Brand Elements	Fun	Excitement	Novelty
Brand Touch Points	• WaterWorks Slide • Video Arcade • Singing Waiters • Camp Carnival for Kids • Poolside Games • Spa Treatments • Sun Deck Lounges • Swimming Pools • Mini-golf Course	• Huge Casinos • High-tech Disco • Live Music and Shows • Veranda Staterooms • Dazzling Interiors • Numerous Bars	• Towel Animals • Seaside Theater • Thalassotherapy Pool • Multiple Restaurants • Art Gallery • Shore Excursions

fun. Thus, the customers' motivations are well aligned with the brand's core elements.

If listening systems used in Step 1 of the process are well attuned to the market, brand elements should be readily evident. However, in some cases, you might have to categorize your customers' motivations to reveal brand elements. The reason for this is that brand elements need to be communicated at a level that encompasses enough of a range of related reasons for purchase, but not at such a high level that they lose meaning. Individual motivations for travel are remarkably diverse and nuanced. For instance, some Carnival customers might say they want to meet new people and see new places, whereas others might say they want to escape their ordinary day-to-day routines to experience fantastic environments and wild activities. But that's all still fun.

Here's why you must link motivations to the brand through the brand elements. First, brand elements form the plot points for brand communications—the messages and imagery that create a dialogue with consumers. Second, clarity of brand elements helps to ground the brand promise by focusing it on the customer (i.e., basing it on customer motivations), and ensuring that it is firm specific (i.e., aligned with what your organization can efficiently and effectively provide). So, the Carnival Cruise Lines promise of a "fun ship" experience is based on the customers' desire for fun, excitement, and novelty, and the firm's continuing efforts to produce ships, services, and itineraries that are aligned with these brand elements.

Step 5: Build a Brand Promise

The brand promise, which guides your management of the brand, is developed from the four preceding steps. I want to emphasize that development of the promise is a "bottom-up" process, based on brand elements. The brand promise conveys the experience that a customer desires and a hospitality firm intends to deliver. The promise should spark a positive reaction, which means it must be succinct and compelling. Some brand promises also serve as slogans used in marketing communications, as in the case of the famous slogan developed for the Las Vegas Convention and Visitors Authority. Analyzing Vegas's successful "What happens here stays here" theme, the account director of the agency that created the campaign, said: ". . . if you can't boil down your brand to three words, you're not trying hard enough."[22] For Las Vegas, the brand strategy team boiled the experience down to the concept of adult freedom. The account director further explained:

Your brand is not simply your ad campaign, rather the campaign is the articulation of the brand. [For Las Vegas] we needed something that not only conveyed "adult freedom," but actually encouraged it. Something that gave consumers permission to enjoy themselves in a way they don't do elsewhere. The "What Happens Here" campaign became the means of delivering the brand message and reflecting the Las Vegas experience.

Another notable example of a powerful brand promise comes from the Recreational Boating & Fishing Foundation, which developed a "Take Me Fishing" brand to promote boating and fishing as a means to bring families together and to encourage environmental stewardship of aquatic resources. One print advertisement shows a father and daughter fishing from a boat; the ad's text says, "Take me fishing, because I get the giggles when the boat bounces. Take me fishing, you can think about work later. Take me fishing, and show me that worms really aren't that icky. Take me fishing, because my wedding will be sooner than you think." The message makes the subtle promise that the activity of recreational boating and fishing will create a lasting bond between father and daughter—a self-relevant outcome with a strong emotional appeal to most any parent.

Arriving at an encompassing and memorable brand promise requires more than just a catchy slogan. Many companies struggle to articulate what their brand is—but if it's hard for brand managers to put the promise into words, it will be even more difficult for customers, employees, and other key stakeholders to "get" the brand. Brand ambiguity creates additional problems down the road as brand marketers try to communicate the brand or as product developers have to make decisions about new features or services that are consistent with the brand. So, whatever you do, make sure your brand promise is clear.

The best brand promises work because they resonate with customers and are true to the brand. For example, Costa Rica's "No artificial ingredients" tourism slogan promises an environmentally friendly beach-and-nature vacation experience. Not only is this what travelers to Costa Rica seek, but the country is also well positioned to provide that experience. Royal Caribbean Cruise Line's award winning brand slogan "Get Out There" symbolized the brand's active-adventure cruise experience. Its new slogan, "The Nation of Why Not," continues the same theme, with such touch points as an onboard rock-climbing wall, zip line, and similar extreme-sports activities.

By contrast, if you pick a vague or otherwise ill-considered slogan, you can interfere with your customers' satisfaction, even if your operation is running well. I saw this in a small hotel chain in Europe, which used the brand promise, "A remarkable stay sure to exceed your expectations." Not only was this promise vague, but it also sets the service bar so high that it is nearly impossible to meet.

Step 6: Select Salient Brand Touch Points

Your final step in the process of strategic brand development is to select salient brand touch points that symbolize the brand promise and elements. These are aspects of the brand that your customer can sense or touch to determine the brand's meaning and imagine how a service will deliver a certain experience. I just mentioned the RCI touch points, and Carnival Cruise Lines touch points symbolize fun (including singing waiters and the water slides), excitement (brightly colored interiors and large casinos), and novelty (the towel animals and theme restaurants).

An excellent example of a hotel company that selected bold touch points to symbolize the brand is W Hotels. W's target market is the hip influentials— the trendsetters (or people who like to feel that they are trendsetters). W starts with an edgy brand promise: a "Wow" experience for the "ultimate insider." W's brand marketing intends to evoke impressions of the chic life, though with sensibility. That is, W offers style, but also substance—cutting-edge design combined with the service and amenities expected from an upscale hotel chain. As a lifestyle brand, W offers "contemporary restaurant concepts, glamorous nightlife experiences, stylish retail concepts, and signature spas." Even the W language used in the service promise, "Whatever/Whenever" (with the play on the W letter) serves as a brand touch point in support of the Wow! promise: "Birthday Party at 35,000 Feet? Bathtub of Hot Chocolate? At W Hotels, your wish truly is our command with our Whatever/Whenever service. Whatever you want (as long as it's legal!)."

BRAND TESTING AND MONITORING

Finally, you must test your new brand concept or any changes you are making to your existing brand to ensure that the brand hierarchy is relevant and resonant. For example, my students created brand hierarchies for several potential brand promises for Zambia. These concepts were then tested using presentations to the country's tourism officials and suppliers, allowing plenty of feedback opportunities, and an online survey test with more than 500 past and potential visitors to the country. Data from these tests were used to aid the country's tourism leaders in their determination of the final brand.

Testing a brand concept with employees, intermediaries, management, and customers can help align stakeholders by establishing a transparent, fact-based filtering process. It also can reduce chances of promoting a brand that fails to motivate employees or customers—or worse, that creates a negative image. Our Zambia study found that the nation had inadvertently done this with an earlier slogan, "The Real Africa." The intended promise was that visitors could have an authentic African experience in Zambia. Unfortunately, however, the team's study revealed that the Real Africa brand invoked negative imagery related to warfare, disease, poverty, and crime. So when you choose any slogan, test it carefully for unintended meanings. You can minimize the risk of weak or negative communication by affiliating with an established brand, but you can also use the Process Framework for Strategic Branding to guide you in building brand equity.

Data-driven strategic branding applies not only to building of new brands, but also to relaunching or refreshing existing brands, and to brand reviews. All brands—even highly successful ones—should be put through the process of strategic branding to ensure that the brand still connects with customers. Consumer needs and wants are dynamic. Competitors change and introduce new products to develop new markets, to satisfy unmet needs of existing markets, or to take market share from firms that have a hold on profitable customers. A brand that rests on past successes is likely to go the way of Oldsmobile—a bygone brand emptied of brand equity. Compare that failure to the 2007 brand relaunch of the 60-plus-year-old Holiday Inn brand, for which their brand strategists boast: "We're changing a good deal of things. But we're not changing the fact that we're a good deal." A comparison of prices for rebranded Holiday Inn properties relative to properties that have yet to receive the brand upgrade shows a price premium for the "refreshed" properties—a brand-driven boost to the bottom line that any owner will find similarly refreshing.

NOTES

1. See D. A. Aaker, *Managing Brand Equity* (New York: Free Press, 1991).
2. K. L. Keller and D. R. Lehmann, "How do brands create value?" *Marketing Management* 12(3) (2003): 26–40.
3. STR Global, Hotel Data Set, 2010.
4. A. Kalnins, "Markets: The U.S. Lodging Industry," *Journal of Economic Perspectives* 20 (Fall 2006): 203–218.
5. J. W. O'Neill and Q. Xiao, "The Role of Brand Affiliation in Hotel Market Value," *Cornell Hotel and Restaurant Administration Quarterly* 47(3) (2006): 210–223.

6. Ypartnership/Yankelovich, *National Travel Monitor,* www.hospitalitynet.org/news/4042580.search?query=national+travel+monitor, seen on May 15, 2010.
7. C. Church, "Independent Supply, Demand Growth Closer to Brands after 2001," HotelNewsNow.com, www.hotelnewsnow.com/Articleprint.aspx?ArticleId=953&print=true, seen July 19, 2010.
8. Kalnins, 2006.
9. Aaker, 1991.
10. Kalnins, 2006.
11. Church, 2009.
12. S. Rushmore, K. Fitzpatrick, and T. Lam. *2009 U.S. Hotel Franchise Fee Guide* (Mineola, NY: HVS, 2009).
13. www.hotel-online.com/News/PR2007_4th/Oct07_HIRelaunch.html, seen on May 13, 2010.
14. S. J. Levy, "Symbols for Sale," *Harvard Business Review.* 37(4) (1959): 117–124.
15. See R. J. Kwortnik and W. T. Ross, "The Role of Positive Emotions in Experiential Decisions, *International Journal of Research in Marketing* 24 (December 2007).
16. Compare R. J. Kwortnik, "Clarifying Fuzzy Hospitality-Management Problems with Depth Interviews and Qualitative Analysis," *Cornell Hotel and Restaurant Administration Quarterly* 44 (April 2003): 117–129; and B. Wansink, "Using Laddering to Understand and Leverage a Brand's Equity," *Qualitative Market Research,* 6(3) (2003): 111–118.
17. J. Wind, P. E. Green, D. Shifflet, and M. Scarbrough, "Courtyard by Marriott: Designing a Hotel Facility with Consumer-Based Marketing Models," *Interfaces* 19(1) (1989): 25–47.
18. C. Lambert, Guest lecture at Cornell University, October 3, 2002.
19. R. J. Kwortnik and G. M. Thompson, "Unifying Service Marketing and Operations with Service Experience Management," *Journal of Service Research* 11(4) (2009): 389–406.
20. S. L. Vargo and R. F. Lusch, "Evolving to a New Dominant Logic for Marketing," *Journal of Marketing* 68 (January 2004): 1–17.
21. R. J. Kwortnik, "Carnival Cruise Lines: Burnishing the Brand," *Cornell Hotel and Restaurant Administration Quarterly* 47 (August 2006): 286–300.
22. R. O' Keefe, "What Happens Here Stays Here Story," *Travel Marketing Decisions* 9 (Fall 2007): 4.

CHAPTER 26

HOTEL REVENUE MANAGEMENT IN AN ECONOMIC DOWNTURN

SHERYL KIMES and CHRIS ANDERSON

When people talk about revenue management, they typically talk about good economic times in which demand exceeds supply. Indeed, that was the assumption that supported the discussion of revenue management principles in Chapter 14. But as we pointed out in that chapter, this book was written as the United States and the world were recovering from a remarkably deep recession and credit freeze. Consequently, we thought it would be important to discuss revenue management tactics for times when supply exceeds demand, with the continuing goal of selling the right room at the right price at the right time to the right customer, so as to maximize revenue.

As you may painfully recall, the Great Recession was a particularly difficult time for the hotel industry. Hotels recorded widespread drops in occupancies, average daily rate (ADR), and revenue per available room (RevPAR) in 2009. The trade press was filled with articles discussing the downturn and proposing possible tactics for surviving it.[1] Not surprisingly, hotel owners and hotel operators disagreed on how best to manage rates during that recession as owners tried to maintain sufficient cash flow to cover their costs while operators attempted to maintain service levels and long-term brand equity.[2]

Back in that chapter, we touched on the repeated research, which has shown that hoteliers have to resist the temptation to offer across-the-board price cuts in response to a drop in business. You'll find more about that study in Chapter 15, if you haven't already read that. Instead, you should focus on particular market segments and distribution channels. Even though your rate structure may be relatively transparent because of the Internet, you still can maintain a portfolio of rates, some of them hidden. An ADR is just that, an average, and by managing your rates carefully you should be able to keep your ADR at near or above the average of your competitive set (if that is your strategic goal). As has been mentioned in other chapters, it's hard to increase occupancy enough to make up for having a lower ADR than that of your competitive set. With a relatively lower rate, chances are you will also have an inferior RevPAR performance. This relationship has been shown to hold true across all hotel market levels. Basically, while you may think that you can drive sufficient occupancy by having a lower rate than your competition, the research shows that this doesn't usually work.

The challenge is how to compete when you are faced with a price war. We believe it's possible for hotels to "intelligently" discount.[3] Essentially, there are two ways this can be done: through nonprice methods and through price methods. Nonprice methods include competing on the basis of quality, creating strategic partnerships, focusing on your loyalty program, developing additional revenue sources, and developing additional market segments. Price-based methods consist of offering packages, using opaque distribution channels, and offering discounted rates to selected market segments (as we mentioned in Chapter 14). We are not saying that you shouldn't discount prices, but what we suggest is ways to do so that fit your overall strategy and will not kill your ADR. We'll discuss these rate-setting tactics in a moment, after we look at the overall considerations.

A variety of articles and books have been written on the topic of managing price during an economic downturn.[4] After compiling the findings of this research, we used them in conjunction with the results of a 2010 survey of hoteliers,[5] which studied the effectiveness of the tactics hotels used during the 2009 economic downturn to develop a concrete set of guidelines that can help you navigate through a price war.

CONSIDERATIONS IN A PRICE WAR

When developing a response to a price war, you should assess three factors: (1) your current and potential guests, (2) your hotel and your competitors, and (3) your distribution channels.

1. *Your customers.* Customer issues that need to be assessed are the price sensitivity of certain market segments and the possible emergence of new segments if new rates are offered. To aim discounted rates at specific price-sensitive market segments, you can develop rate fences that prevent less price-sensitive customers from availing themselves of the discounts

as we described in Chapter 14. In addition, you should identify other potential market segments that might be attracted by a selected discount and determine whether it is a market segment that fits in with your hotel's image.

2. *Your hotel and your competition.* In developing your discount program, you'll want to take into account your hotel's cost structure and market positioning, its capabilities, and its strategic positioning. Hotels with a lower cost structure than their competition can more profitably offer discounts since they may be able to withstand the reduced margins. But you may not want to offer discounts just because you're able. Rates are part of an overall brand proposition, so the type of hotel matters. Luxury or upscale properties should exercise great care before discounting because of the potential impact that this could have on the hotel's long-term image. Conversely, budget or economy hotels may not be as affected by a price war because they may benefit from customers "trading down" from more upscale hotels. Their lower prices may appear to offer better value.

   The same analysis should be conducted for your competition so as to gauge their potential response to a price war and to determine their strengths and vulnerabilities.

3. *Your distribution channels.* In addition, you can assess your hotel's distribution channels to determine which ones are most effective at delivering business. Part of that analysis involves whether the volume through that channel would increase if the commission or percentage paid was increased. Opaque channels and distribution channels that offer packages in which your rooms are bundled with other services such as airfare and rental car become even more attractive because they give you an opportunity to obscure your true rate.

What Works and What Doesn't

Let's start with the nonprice methods for competing in a price war without discounting massively and suffering long-term damage.

Nonprice Methods The six types of nonprice methods that we discuss here are the following: (1) reveal your strategic intentions, (2) compete on the basis of quality, (3) create strategic partnerships, (4) take advantage of your loyalty program, (5) develop additional revenue sources, and (6) develop additional market segments.

1. *Reveal your strategic intentions.* Let your competitors know what you're planning on doing and operate from a position of strength. If you have lower operating costs or if you have deeper reserves that will allow you to withstand a prolonged price war, let them know it. The airlines do an excellent job at coordinating their actions, as they typically preannounce major pricing actions (e.g., fuel surcharges, baggage fees, fare increases) prior to their implementation, allowing their competitors time to respond in the popular press.
2. *Compete on quality.* If you are operating in the luxury or upscale segment, you may want to emphasize the quality that your hotel delivers and perhaps even add features (such as personalized stationery, free airport pickup, or fresh flowers) that add additional value to your offerings.

    Another tactic may be to highlight the performance risks associated with low-price hotels. For example, you could mention the lower service levels and reduced amenities that are provided at your less expensive competitors and contrast that to the superior service offering of your hotel.
3. *Create strategic partnerships.* Based on your analysis of distribution channels, you can create strategic relationships with particular channels. If you give certain distribution channels a higher commission (whether travel agents or third-party intermediaries), they may be willing to deflect a higher proportion of their business to you. Your costs would go up, but you would not need to cut rates. For example, Booking .com allows properties to have strategic placement at the online travel agent (OTA) for increased commissions—so the property has more prominent display (and increased conversion rates) without having to discount rates.
4. *Take advantage of your loyalty program.* Reduced demand can also provide your hotel with the capacity needed to reward your loyalty program members. You could, for instance, reduce the number of points needed to redeem a free night's stay for a limited time or make more desirable rewards available. Doing this has two benefits: (1) it brings people into the hotel who may spend money in other outlets, and (2) it keeps loyal guests connected with your hotel. US Airways, for example, offered promotions where travelers could qualify for frequent flyer status with a reduced number of flights. Similarly, certain Hampton Inns offered a "fifth night free" during the winter of 2009–2010.
5. *Develop additional revenue sources.* Full-service hotels have a variety of facilities that can be used to generate much-needed revenue. While some of these facilities (most notably, food and beverage) have lower

profit margins than rooms, they can still provide additional cash, which can help sustain your hotel during low-demand periods. Creative promotions and discounts may bring more local customers into your restaurants and recreation facilities.

6. *Develop additional market segments.* An economic downturn is a good time to carefully examine your marketing plan and determine whether there are other market segments that can be developed for your hotel. While this can bring in additional revenue and customers for your hotel, care must be taken to ensure that the new market segments fit in well with your brand image.

7. *Apply marketing-based approaches.* The Internet gives you numerous approaches for creating demand through marketing. When consumers start researching travel possibilities on the Google, Yahoo!, or Bing search engines, you can be ready with a strategy of search engine optimization (SEO) and search engine marketing (SEM) We touched on these strategies in Chapter 14, but let's explore them in detail here. These strategies involve ensuring that consumers find your Web page. SEO is about designing your hotel's Web page such that it places high on the search page. You can do this through properly tagging the pages on your Web site, as well as its images and photos. Your page should contain optimizing terms and phrases making sure that your Web site descriptions and keywords are the ones that consumers are using to search for hotels. Tools such as SEODigger.com can help with this. Make sure your site is linked to important local attractions and agencies. Your Web page needs a site map so the search engine knows how to navigate it. Have pages be consistent and concise—don't have too much information on one page (e.g., have separate pages for your romance package and your fall season preview package). Rather than force people to retrace their clicks, make sure that every page has a booking mask to allow consumers to book whenever they are ready.

For search engine marketing, you bid on keywords and search terms—basically paying to ensure that your Web page gets prime placement on the search pages. Figure 26.1 shows a sample Google search result. As you see, the search page has three areas: local, organic, and paid. A strong SEO strategy should give you a high free placement in the local and organic areas of the search page, while SEM will display your hotel in the paid area. All the search engines provide great tools and analytics to help you effectively bid on keywords and ensure you are making the best use of your search engine marketing dollars. Ideally you want to capitalize on the free clicks

Figure 26.1
Search Engine Optimization and Search Engine Marketing Sample

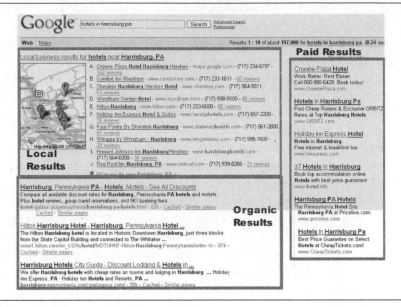

from SEO, but SEM is more immediate and may help you drive volume for specific events and arrival dates.

You also need to be reaching out to consumers directly via e-mail. You can do this directly through internal customer relationship management (CRM) efforts or indirectly through firms like Travelzoo, which have their own databases of consumers. Many of the OTAs also have programs where your property can be featured in e-mail offers they send out to targeted consumers.

Price Methods

The key strategy in price-related discounting is to avoid instituting across the board rate cuts and instead to either camouflage your discounted rates or target those rates at selected market segments or through certain distribution channels. The following are some tactics to execute that strategy:

1. *Bundle.* As we suggested in Chapter 14, bundling allows you to disguise rates. If you can bundle your room rate in with either additional nights

(e.g., stay two nights, get another one free) or with other services at the hotel (e.g., free spa treatment, free Internet), it will help disguise the fact that you are offering lower rates. Restaurants and cruise lines have successfully used this approach for years. Restaurants offer *prix fixe* meals or value meals in which several courses are offered for one price. Cruise lines use bundling effectively by packaging the cruise with airfare and hotel accommodations. Bundling makes it difficult for customers to determine the prices of the individual components. About 40 percent of the hotel executives who responded to the 2010 survey on successful tactics for surviving an economic downturn had used some sort of bundling tactic and gave high ratings to its effectiveness. Respondents said that they were very likely to use bundling during the next economic downturn.[6]

The key to developing an effective bundle is to determine what your customers want and then deliver it in a profitable manner. Most full service hotels have facilities that are not fully used (e.g., a spa, a golf course, restaurants). By including some of the unused capacity in with the room rate, you do not incur a great deal of incremental cost, can more fully use other parts of your hotel, and have the potential to increase business in these other outlets in the future if guests decide to come back.

2. *Unbundle.* Depending on your competitive situation, another approach is to base your rate on only your core room product (i.e., a clean room with a bed and bath) and charge additional amounts for any other services that guests might wish to use. Airlines use this approach with their checked-bag fees, and some discount hotels have also adopted this practice. By unbundling, you can keep your base rates relatively low and allow guests to choose which additional services they would like. Although care must be taken when using this approach because of the potential damage to customer satisfaction, unbundling may be an option for discount hotels.

   Asia-based discount operator Tune Hotels has been using the unbundling approach quite successfully. They charge an additional fee for air-conditioning, for towels, and for Internet use.[7] Even higher-end chains are starting to impose higher fees. Guests are already accustomed to hotels in many product tiers that charge extra for phone calls and Internet access. Surcharges are expected to amount to US$1.7 billion in 2010.[8]

3. *Use opaque distribution channels.* Opaque distribution channels such as priceline.com, hotwire.com, and topsecret hotels (known as Lastminute .com in Europe and Travelocity in North America) represent a way in which you can offer discounts while hiding the discount from the customer. They allow you to sell additional rooms while still protecting

your rate and brand image. About 50 percent of respondents to the 2010 survey had used opaque distribution channels and considered it to be a highly effective tactic that they would use again. Usage was even higher in the Americas generally, and particularly among three- and four-star hotels. Respondents from five-star hotels were not as enamored with opaque distribution channels, and some were concerned about the potential damage that it might do to their brand image.[9]

4. *Offer selected rate cuts*. Discounted rates should be provided only to selected market segments. As discussed in Chapter 14, building effective rate fences requires knowing your customers well and understanding what rate fences will be effective in attracting particular market segments. We noted there the different types of rate fences: room related, transaction related, consumption related, and guest related. Remember also to consider fairness and rate parity issues. Again, common rate fences involve advance purchased restrictions, minimum length of stay restrictions, and more restrictive cancellation fees, thereby limiting the discounts to specific customer segments and also help protect you against potential cannibalization.

Finally, ensure that rate cuts are available at the right time. Given today's ease of comparative shopping most properties have similar prices (for the same arrival dates) posted on all channels. This rate parity means that if posted rates are reduced, all customers get these reduced rates regardless of which channel they use to make their reservation. Since you cannot segment customers by channel, you need to make sure that you segment by time. Most particularly, you need to be sure that you offer your discounted rate at an OTA when price-sensitive customers are shopping (which is many days before arrival, as we noted in Chapter 14). Then you need to remove this limited-time offer a few days before the arrival date, as indicated by your booking curves.

ADVICE FROM THE FRONT LINES

One of the intents of the study of hotel managers that we mentioned earlier in this chapter was to help you develop a plan for how to approach the next economic downturn. While we all would like to think that a recession won't happen again, we know that it will. So let's prepare to respond to a market downturn in an intelligent and strategic fashion.

Several lessons emerge from the survey results and from the insightful comments that responding hotel executives made. The foremost piece of advice was to be prepared and to have a plan on how to respond to a recession (some people even suggested a standard operating procedure manual). As one respondent stated, "It is never too early to be prepared. You should always have a contingency plan that you can implement within minutes."

When you develop your plan, focus on the long-term and consider the impact that your plan will have on customer satisfaction, employee satisfaction, and the long-term image of your hotel or chain. If you lose sight of the long-term, you may end up compromising customer and employee satisfaction and hurting long-term profitability and viability. As one respondent said, "Maintain the brand image, be insistent on the pricing strategy. Focus on your long-term goal and be patient."

Several other lessons emerge from the research:

- *Don't panic!* Respondents talked about the need to stay calm and look for solutions. One respondent said it quite succinctly, "Do not panic. Do not compare downturn periods with previous good periods. Think more in terms of long-term decisions."
- *Be wary of broad-scale discounting.* Of the four basic strategies for approaching a future economic downturn, respondents were least likely to recommend discounting. Time and again, respondents discussed how it would take years for their rates to recover from the discounting that they engaged in during the previous year. As one respondent advised: "Don't drop rate—or let me state it this way: don't drop your public/retail rate. Use the retail rate as the benchmark for discount rate programs and fence these discounts appropriately." Another made a similar comment: "My advice would be to be very careful about playing the rate-reduction game. In 2007 and 2008, we were very aggressive with increasing our corporate pricing and in the space of a few months, all that and more has been undone. We have literally undone three years of solid work in the space of the past eight months. It will take us another three to four years at least to get that back." If you must discount, consider creative packaging and using opaque distribution channels.
- *Don't cut your marketing budget.* Respondents discussed the need to keep current guests and to develop packages and promotions that attracted both current and potential guests. If you cut your marketing budget, this won't be possible. As one respondent suggested, "When the bad times hit again, save the marketing dollars on new initiatives (e.g., acquiring new customers or promoting new hotels) but focus the spending on the existing customer base."
- *Consider marketing approaches.* Respondents felt that the development of smaller, less price-sensitive market segments had been highly successful

during the recession. As one respondent suggested, "Explore new market segments and new ways of promotions. Try not to drop down rates for all market segments; there are some of them that are not so price sensitive. We have to identify these guests and work hard to attract them to our property." Another popular and effective tactic was to develop other new revenue streams (such as food and beverage or spa) within the hotel. One respondent summarized this nicely, "We just have to diversify our business rather than rely too heavily on a particular business and geographic segment. At the same time, more emphasis has to be put on how to optimize revenue conversion from all revenue streams be they major or minor, which will ultimately help to improve bottom line."

Other tactics that were highly rated were pay-per-click advertising and other Web-based marketing approaches. For example, one respondent said that the hotel planned to rebound by, "Capitalizing on e-channels. We have relaunched our Web site, restructured our URLs for better ranking and organic search in the Search Engines."

- *Consider rate-obscuring practices*. Remember that there is a difference between your "public" rate and your "private" rate. Focus on how you can develop packages and bundles that add value to the consumer without costing the hotel too much. Consider the following suggestion: "My advice is maintain rate, continue to look for new markets (such as religious retreats, romantic weekend packages), develop specials which focus on value added extras like spa treatments, be creative in your food and beverage promotions, and watch for prolonged gaps in occupancy that might be filled with Internet promotions or opaque distribution channels which won't later effect your rate strategy so dramatically." Think about what customers want and try to deliver it without "giving away the house." Also, focus in on packages that are hard to imitate—anyone can offer an extra night for free, so try to develop packages that are unique to your hotel.

Respondents were generally pleased with the performance of opaque distribution channels. As one respondent mentioned, "Don't drop rate drastically and use opaque distribution systems when you are forced to do so." Conversely, some respondents were concerned about the possible effect on brand image. As one respondent from a five-star hotel stated, "Opaque channel customers are not desirable. They don't want to pay the premium an upper-upscale or luxury charges on services (parking, food and beverages), but expect the moon in return. In the long run, it doesn't cover your costs and often can drive down your GSI."

- *Maintain service levels.* If you need to cut costs, do so in areas of the hotel that have the least impact on customer service and the hotel image. As one survey respondent said, "Don't reduce standards but add added value; guests are very sensitive to changes. Bad times are not forever, and it could take a longer time to recover if you cut corners to save a buck!" If customer satisfaction and service quality are diminished, it will be more difficult to both maintain your current guests and attract new guests after the recession is over. Consider the following suggestion: "Do not make cost cuts on quality service. It is okay to bring prices down, but set yourself a limit which will not handicap you when you want to bring the ADR up again the following year."

CONCLUSION

Economic downturns create pressure to maintain market share, and many hotels were tempted to reduce rate in an attempt to attract additional customers. It is important to realize the limitations of your traditional RM system and its potential inability to properly manage your inventory when demand is less than supply. During a downturn you need to remember that many guests still value your property and are willing to pay a premium to stay with you. You need to be sure to maintain your rate, as often the incremental demand generated from a price cut is not enough to offset the rate dilution caused by guests who would have stayed with you anyway (at higher rates). The goal in a downturn to is to reduce your ADR and increase your RevPAR. Nonstrategic rate actions simply reduce both your ADR and RevPAR. If you must offer price cuts make sure they are limited time offers, receive predominant display (typically at the OTA—with a price tag or discount highlight), and are enabled only during the shopping window when price-sensitive consumers are online booking deals. Better yet, use private price reductions. Bundling and packages allow you to provide consumers with deals while maintaining posted prices. Opaque OTAs offer steep discounts to brand agnostic consumers and provide an ideal forum to reach price-sensitive consumers without having to worry about rate dilution. Last, marketing focused efforts like SEM and e-mail offers that bring consumers to pages with promo code–enabled rates provide another way for you to offer price reductions to consumers who are out there searching for deals (while simultaneously maintaining your regular posted prices). In summary, revenue management involves analytical thinking to create demand and opportunistically fill in weak spots with targeted price-sensitive consumers.

NOTES

1. For example, see: www.rockcheetah.com/blog/hotel/us-hotel-industry-recession-enters-new-rate-erosion-phase/, http://www.occupancymarketing.com/white-papers/marketing_recession.html, asiaone.com/Travel/News/Story/A1Story20090302-125501.html).

2. travel.nytimes.com/2009/05/26/business/26hotel.html, http://travel-industry.uptake.com/blog/2009/05/26/owners-brand-hotel-operators/.

3. S. E. Kimes, "Hotel Revenue Management in an Economic Downturn: Results from an International Study," *Cornell Hospitality Research Report* 9(12) (2009).

4. For example, see K. B. Monroe, *Pricing: Making Profitable Decisions* (New York: McGraw-Hill, 2003); R. J. Doland and H. Simon, *Power Pricing* (New York: Free Press, 1996); A. R. Rao, M. E. Bergen, and S. Davis, "How to Fight a Price War," *Harvard Business Review* 78(2) (2000): 107–117; and H. J. Van Heerde, E. Gijsbrechts, and K. Pauwels, "Winners and Losers in a Major Price War," *Journal of Marketing Research* 45 (October 2008): 499–518.

5. S. E. Kimes, 2010. "Successful Tactics for Surviving an Economic Downturn: Results from an International Study," *Cornell Hospitality Research Report* 10(7) 2010.

6. Ibid.

7. J. A. Siguaw, C. A. Enz, S. E. Kimes, R. Verma, and K. Walsh, "Cases in Innovative Practices in Hospitality and Related Services, Set 1," *Cornell Hospitality Research Report* 9(17) (2009).

8. J. L. Levere, "With Airlines Showing the Way, Hotels Are Seeing Big Money in Small Fees," *International Herald Tribune* (May 5, 2010): 14.

9. Kimes, 2010.

CHAPTER 27

ADDRESSING EMPLOYEE LAWSUITS

DAVID SHERWYN and PAUL E. WAGNER

For months you tried to save this employee. You gave him numerous second chances, you gave him a performance improvement plan, and you even put him on probation. Finally, after all the warnings, the low productivity, and the time and effort, you have no choice but to let the employee go. You agonized over the decision but knew it was right. Imagine your surprise when you received a letter in the mail today accusing you and your company of disability discrimination! You did not even know the employee was disabled. You are faced with the reality: All managers are, at one time or another, accused of discrimination. The purpose of this chapter is to help you respond to this complaint by: (1) defining the law; (2) explaining how discrimination claims are adjudicated; (3) discussing the Americans with Disabilities Act and sexual harassment; and (4) advising employers in the hospitality industry on how to avoid liability.

WHAT IS THE LAW?

There are four federal law statutes prohibiting discrimination. Title VII of the Civil Rights Act of 1964, as amended by the Civil Rights Act of 1991, covers employers with 15 or more employees and simply states that employers may not discriminate against applicants and employees because of color, race, national origin, religion, or gender. The Age Discrimination in Employment Act of 1967 (ADEA) states that employers with 20 or more employees may not discriminate against those who are over 40 years of age; the American with Disabilities Act of 1992 (ADA) prohibits discrimination by employers with more than 15 employees against those who are disabled, and Section 1981 of the Civil Rights Act of 1866 (1981, which covers all employers), states that black people have the same right to enter into contracts as white people. This statute, which came out of the Reconstruction era, is applied to race cases in employment. We refer to gender, color, religion, national origin, race, religion, age and disability as the "protected classes."

The first three statutes also prohibit retaliation against any person who invokes their protection. The prohibition against sexual harassment is a subset of sexual discrimination under Title VII. Many states, counties, and cities have their own antidiscrimination laws that add additional protected classes (e.g., sexual orientation, family status) and may provide for different damages or adjudication schemes. Because it is impossible to address the laws of all 50 states as well as municipalities, we will focus our analysis on federal law.

Under federal law, your company can be liable for your actions, but you cannot be held personally liable (so, no one can take your house or your car). That's the good news. The bad news is that in some states (New York, for example), you can be held personally liable for discrimination and harassment.

The damages that a plaintiff may recover consist of back pay (what plaintiffs would have earned less what they actually earned), reinstatement, compensatory damages, attorney's fees, and litigation costs. Under Title VII and the ADA, punitive damages are available if the conduct is reckless or malicious. These damages are capped depending on the number of employees, so, for example, punitive damages may not exceed $50,000 for employers with fewer than 100 employees, whereas employers with more than 500 employees may be assessed as much as $300,000. Under the ADEA, there are no punitive damages, but employees can recover double their back pay if the conduct was willful. The Civil Rights Act of 1866 allows for unlimited punitive damages. In addition, some jurisdictions allow for greater damages awards, such as the state of California and the city of New York.

Juries are not informed of damage caps. Thus, when you see a punitive damage award of millions of dollars in a discrimination case, one of three things is going on: (1) a state or local statute allowed greater damages; (2) it's a race case and the plaintiffs' lawyers were smart enough to invoke the Civil Rights Act of 1866; or (3) the damage award is meaningless and will be reduced in accordance with the cap.

The protected classes set forth in Title VII are, for the most part, fairly straightforward. Courts employ the plain meaning of the terms *race, religion,* and *national origin.* Still, there are some anomalies that are not obvious. For example, religion is not limited to established, traditional religions, and requires only that an employee possesses a true belief in the religion, however unusual. Title VII's protection against religious discrimination even extends to the belief in no religion. While the term *sex* as it appears in Title VII means gender, this protected class gets complicated because it includes sexual harassment. The ADEA is very simple—it protects those employees over the age of 40. The ADA is not so simple. The ADA protects those who are disabled as defined by the law, but this definition presents a complex and moving target. In addition to prohibiting discrimination on account of disability, the ADA also requires employers to reasonably accommodate disabled employees. Finally, the fastest-rising discrimination claim is retaliation. Because of their relative complexity and prevalence for today's employers, we address sexual harassment and disability claims in detail in this chapter. While space constraints prevent us from examining retaliation, a full discussion can be found in the 2009 Cornell Center for Hospitality Research law roundtable proceedings.[1] Before we do that, however, we explain the process for filing and defending discrimination claims.

THE ADJUDICATION PROCESS

To file a discrimination lawsuit, an employee must first file a charge of discrimination with either the Equal Employment Opportunity Commission (EEOC) or with a state or local agency authorized to investigate such claims. The agency with which the employee files a charge will investigate the allegation and try to settle the matter by having the employer remunerate or reinstate the employee. If the employer and employee cannot agree on a settlement, the agency determines whether there is cause to believe that discrimination occurred. In most jurisdictions, if the agency finds "no cause," it still issues a "right to sue letter," allowing the employee to file an action in court (at this point, most employees walk away). If the agency finds cause, it may, depending on the agency, (1) issue a right to sue letter; (2) set the case for trial before its own administrative adjudication process; or (3) become the employee's counsel and file an action in federal court on the claimant's behalf.

When a discrimination claim is filed, employers are required to complete a questionnaire and provide the investigating agency with a position statement. If the case is not resolved at the agency level and, instead, is adjudicated in court, the employer's attorneys' fees will almost always be in excess of $50,000 and could exceed $500,000, regardless of the merits of the case. Additional employer costs include the loss of productivity of other employees involved in the case, adverse publicity, and, of course, liability. Because defending discrimination lawsuits in federal court results in substantial costs to employers regardless of guilt, there is a strong incentive for employers to settle a case *regardless of the worthiness of the plaintiff's claim.*

The administrative procedures also provide investigators with incentives to settle cases. From the time they receive the case, investigators, who are often evaluated by the number of cases they resolve regardless of merit, push employers and employees to settle. This system has created a backlog of cases, cynicism about the enforcement of the discrimination laws, and what we refer to as "the discrimination *de facto* severance system." This occurs when employees file baseless discrimination charges because they know that their former employers are willing to pay a sum of money in order to avoid the costs and aggravation of defending the allegation. Smaller companies that do not have in-house counsel or sophisticated human resource departments are especially vulnerable to this practice.

The EEOC, which encourages settlement at all the steps of the process, requires investigators to place each case into one of three categories before they even have discovered any facts. Cases placed in the A or highest-priority classification fall within the national or local enforcement plan, which focus on class actions, systemic discrimination, and new areas of law. In such cases, the EEOC actually becomes the plaintiff in the case.

An example of a B case would be a charge involving only one or two employees who allege that they were not hired or were terminated because of their protected status. It is not a class action, and there are no genuine issues of law present. Instead, the case turns on factual disputes. Such cases will never be labeled an A regardless of the strength of the evidence. B cases are investigated in due time, which means that the EEOC will eventually make a determination. However, these cases will not receive a priority classification and may still take approximately one year before the investigation is complete. Once completed, claimants who do not settle will have to begin the litigation process to adjudicate their claims. Litigation can take anywhere from two to eight years.

Cases placed in the C category are, for all intents and purposes, dead. The EEOC labels a case a C when it determines that the case is either frivolous or the agency lacks jurisdiction. On its face, this seems appropriate because it conserves scarce resources and reduces *de facto* severance by discouraging potential plaintiffs that wish to capitalize on the employer's known incentives to settle.

Statistical Analysis of the EEOC's Case Handling

In 1980, the EEOC found no cause in 28.5 percent of the 49,225 cases it closed, while in 2009, the agency found no cause in 60.9 percent of the 85,980 cases it closed. Employers argued that the increase in the number of no-cause findings reflects an increase in the number of frivolous claims. This may be true. However, there may be another explanation for the increase in the number of no-cause findings. A General Accounting Office (GAO) study explained that the large number of no-cause findings were due to the EEOC's failure to adequately investigate between 40 and 80 percent of the cases.

The EEOC classifies resolved cases into one of two categories: merit resolutions[2] and nonmerit resolutions. Nonmerit resolutions consist of cases being given a no-cause finding or dismissed because of an administrative resolution. In 1997, only 11 percent of the cases were classified as merit resolutions. From 2000 through 2009, however, the percentage of merit resolutions has ranged from a low of 19.5 percent (2003) to a high of 22.2 percent (2004). This means that even in the "best" years, close to 80 percent of all the claims are considered nonmeritorious.

Being classified as a merit resolution does not mean that the case has merit or that it has been resolved. Merit resolutions include cases that will be litigated and frivolous cases settled for nuisance amounts. Likewise, the "merit resolution" classification also encompasses worthy claims that are settled for nuisance amounts. In 2009, 50 percent of the merit resolutions (which is 10 percent of the total cases resolved) were settled. In fact, in 2009 the EEOC found "cause" in only 4.5 percent of the cases resolved.

Two conclusions can be drawn from these statistics. First, it is possible that numerous cases are "slipping through the cracks" at the EEOC and being dismissed without receiving proper attention. This applies to the cases resolved by either a finding of no cause or an administrative closing. The second possible conclusion to be drawn from observing the outrageously small number of meritorious cases is, as employers would argue, that the overwhelming majority of the cases filed are frivolous. Regardless, the fact is that antidiscrimination is a growth industry and all employers will face claims. Employers should therefore understand how courts analyze these cases.

HOW COURTS ANALYZE AND ADJUDICATE DISCRIMINATION CASES

There are two types of discrimination: (1) disparate treatment, and (2) adverse impact. *Disparate treatment* is intentional discrimination, and *adverse impact* is unintentional discrimination. Adverse impact occurs when a company has a policy or practice, which is neutral on its face but has adverse impact on a protected class. For example, a company policy stating that all servers must be women discriminates on its face. Such a policy would be considered disparate treatment against men. Conversely, requiring all employees to be over 6 feet tall does not, on its face, discriminate, but could have an adverse impact against women or certain ethnic groups. Such a policy could lead to an adverse impact claim.

While statistics made available by the EEOC do not provide a breakdown of adverse impact versus disparate cases, interviews with dozens of management lawyers reveal that a very small percentage of cases are adverse impact cases. In fact, most lawyers report that despite defending hundreds of discrimination cases, they have never had an adverse impact case. Still, employers should understand the burdens of proof in adverse impact cases.

Adverse Impact

The best way to describe the burden of proof in adverse impact cases is to examine the lead adverse impact case, *Griggs v. Duke Power Company*. Employer Duke Power required employees who wished to work in any job other than those in the laborers department to have, among other things, a high school diploma. This facially neutral policy, the employees argued, had an adverse impact because, according to the most recent census, only 12 percent of the African-Americans in North Carolina had graduated from high school, while the high school graduation rate for white people was 32 percent. To determine whether this constituted an adverse impact, the Supreme Court established the so-called 80 percent rule. Under the 80 percent rule, the plaintiffs can establish adverse impact if their pass rate is less than 80 percent of the majority's. The test has been made more sophisticated today, but the basic rule applies. Here, 80 percent of 32 percent is 25.60 percent. Because 25.60 percent is greater than 12 percent, the plaintiffs established a *prima facie* case of adverse impact. To avoid liability, the employer had to prove that being a high school graduate was a business necessity—there existed a manifest relationship between the passing of the test and success on the job, and there was no other means to achieve this. Because Duke Power could not satisfy this burden, the plaintiffs prevailed.

For you, adverse impact is an issue to keep in mind when setting neutral policies for hiring, promotion, terminations, and leaves of absence. Polices that are neutral on their face may still result in liability, and thus, before enacting such policies, employers should make sure that no protected class is adversely affected. To illustrate this point, there is a case holding that requiring employees to work one year before taking a leave of absence adversely affected women (several needed a pregnancy leave and no men were ill or injured in the time frame).

Disparate Treatment

The vast majority of discrimination cases are disparate treatment cases. There are two ways to prove disparate treatment. The first, the so-called, "pretext method" was the method used in most cases from 1981 through 2009, but the new motivating factor method may now change the way discrimination cases are litigated. We describe each in this section.

Pretext Method Under the pretext method, the employees must prove the following:

- They are members of a protected class.
- They were minimally qualified for the position in question.
- They suffered an adverse employment action.
- The job remained open or went to someone outside the protected class (in hiring cases), or similarly situated people engaged in similar conduct and were treated differently.

If the employee satisfies each of these elements, the employer must articulate a nondiscriminatory reason for its decision. If the employer fails to satisfy this burden of production, the employee prevails. If the employer does satisfy this burden, the employee must prove that the reason articulated was not worthy of belief (pretext) and that the real reason was discrimination. While the four steps are not onerous, prevailing under the pretext standard is not easy for employees. This is the case because proving discrimination is difficult. Most employers do not blatantly discriminate, and thus employees have a difficult time finding evidence of discrimination. Furthermore, because the burden-shifting procedure is deemed to be too complex by most jurisdictions, the usual jury instruction is simple: Did the employer make its decision because of the employee's protected class?

Motivating Factor The second method for proving discrimination, the motivating factor method, also known as the mixed motive, has a long and complex history. The "new method" arose in 1989 when PriceWaterhouse had both illegitimate (sex) and legitimate reasons (interpersonal skills) for refusing to make Ann Hopkins a partner. The Civil Rights Act of 1991 and subsequent court cases have resulted in making this second method for proving discrimination much easier for plaintiffs to prevail. Under the motivating factor method, juries are asked two questions: (1) Did the protected class motivate the employer? and (2) would the employer have made the same decision regardless of the protected class? If the answer to the first question is no, the case is over. If the answer to the first question is yes, the jury moves to the second question. With regard to the second question, the jury is informed that a yes means no damages and no means damages.

Because of the format, most jurors believe that answering no to the first question is the same as answering yes to both questions, because in neither situation would the jury award damages. In fact, no = no damages and no court costs, but yes/yes = the employee receives litigation costs and attorneys' fees (in many cases, costs and fees greatly exceed damages). Thus, juries who think they are finding for the employer are unknowingly awarding hundreds of thousands of dollars in costs and fees. Because plaintiffs' lawyers are finally learning this fact, there has been an increase in the number of plaintiffs asking for this type of instruction. Currently, the court decides the type of instruction to use.

In 2009, the Supreme Court held that the motivating factor scheme did not apply to age cases. Because courts are split if motivating factor applies to ADA and retaliation cases, it could be that the easier-to-demonstrate motivating factor scheme is limited to Title VII. Pending legislation would not only make the motivating factor scheme open to ADEA, ADA, and retaliation plaintiffs, but it would allow plaintiffs to choose the type of instruction they want. This will increase the costs of settlements as plaintiffs' lawyers will know that in most cases they will be able to satisfy at least the first question.

THE ADA

The ADA is fundamentally different from the other federal antidiscrimination laws, which start with the premise that being a member of a protected class has no detrimental effect on an individual's ability to perform a job. The ADA is premised on the fact that those with disabilities are not equal to those without, and thus employers need to accommodate the disabled if they can perform the job. On a practical level, this difference manifests itself in three different elements of the law: (1) the definition of disability; (2) the question of qualifications; and (3) the obligation on employers to "reasonably accommodate" disabled employees.

A disability under the ADA is a physical or mental condition that substantially limits one or more major life activities, having a record of such, or being regarded as such. Because this definition creates more questions than it resolves, what constitutes a disability remains contentious, and is often determined on a case-by-case basis. For instance, we now know that HIV-positive status is considered a disability, but whether attention deficit disorder and alcoholism constitute a disability is more subjective, depending on the severity of the condition and its effect on major life activities. Homosexuals, transvestites, and transsexuals are not protected. Current drug users are also not protected. Going back to the opening vignette, you cannot be guilty of an ADA violation if you did not know the employee was disabled.

An employer may not discriminate against an applicant or an employee if they can perform the essential functions of the job with or without a reasonable accommodation. What is an essential function is not what the employer or job description says it is. Instead, the court will answer the question.

The obligation to "reasonably accommodate" the employee is another unique feature of the ADA among discrimination laws because it imposes the cost of providing jobs for the disabled on the employer. You have an obligation under the ADA to engage in an interactive process with an employee or potential employee to determine whether you can reasonably accommodate the employee's disability. You may refuse such accommodations, however, if the requested accommodation is either unreasonable or presents an undue hardship.

If you are faced with an employee requesting an accommodation, you need to first determine whether the disability is covered by the law (consult counsel); if not, there is no obligation to accommodate. If so, you must engage in a process where the employee will ask for certain accommodations, and you and your counsel will determine whether they are reasonable—meaning whether the benefits to society outweigh the costs. If the benefits do outweigh the costs, you may still deny the request if you can't afford it (an undue hardship). As part of the interactive process, you need to suggest other, more affordable options. You do not need to accommodate any request, but you need to engage, consult counsel, and make a determination in accordance with the law.

SEXUAL HARASSMENT

Title VII does not specifically address or prohibit "sexual harassment." However, in 1986, the United States Supreme Court in *Meritor v. Vinson* addressed whether employers violated Title VII when a supervisor harassed an employee on the basis of gender but the employee did not suffer any economic consequences.[3] The Court held that "sexual harassment" did, in fact, violate Title VII, regardless of whether there was an economic loss. This case began the evolution of sexual harassment law.

The Supreme Court's *Meritor* decisions held that there were two types of sexual harassment: (1) *quid pro quo*; and (2) hostile environment. *Quid quo pro* harassment is defined as requiring "sexual activity" in exchange for continued employment, promotions, and the like. Hostile environment is more difficult to explain. In *Harris v. Forklift Systems*, the U.S. Supreme Court defined hostile environment as conduct that, from the perspective of both an objective (a reasonable person) and subjective (the plaintiff) observer, was "so severe or pervasive that it created a work environment abusive to employees because of their race, gender, religion, or national origin." The standard from *Harris* is anything but clear, as Justice Scalia lamented, when he wrote that the standard: "does not seem to me a very clear standard. Be that as it may, I know of no alternative to the course the Court today has taken." In defining *hostile environment,* most commentators simply list examples such as staring, sexual references, and touching. Hostile environment is a moving target, and you should always check with counsel before determining whether certain allegations violate the law.

The *Harris* Court's holding was distilled as a two-part test requiring that: (1) the *conduct* is severe or pervasive, and (2) the *motivation* is the plaintiff's sex. In reality, however, it was the conduct and not the motivation that the Court and legal commentators emphasized as important. Motivation was not considered relevant because almost all cases consisted of men harassing women, and thus courts presumed that the conduct was "because of sex." This changed in the early 1990s with the rise of same-sex sexual harassment cases.

After a series of lower court opinions resulted in four different laws in four different jurisdictions, the Supreme Court, in *Oncale v. Sundower* held that motivation was the key issue in all sexual harassment cases (opposite and same-sex). The Court held that plaintiffs could make out a case only if they were harassed "because of sex." As the Court stated, "the plaintiff . . . must always prove that the conduct at issue actually constituted discrimination . . . because of . . . sex."

As one of several examples to illustrate motivation, the Court held that same-sex plaintiffs could make out a case by comparing their treatment to that of the opposite sex: "a same-sex harassment plaintiff may also, of course, offer direct comparative evidence about how the alleged harasser treated members of both sexes in a mixed-sex workplace." At first glance, this method of proof seems both logical and unambiguous. In fact, it created a new, unanticipated defense for employers: the equal opportunity harasser. If disparate treatment among men and women means that motivation is unlawful, then harassing both men and women should mean that motivation is not unlawful. That is exactly what courts in several jurisdictions have held. Thus, employers prevailed in cases where a supervisor ordered both a man and woman to have sex with that supervisor and when men displayed pornography in the workplace. In fact, sexual conduct in the form of pictures or conversations that are not directed at women should no longer be a legal concern for employers.

Oncale purported to open the doors to a whole set of new claims when it, in fact, made it more difficult for sexual harassment claims to succeed by creating a number of new defenses. This is not all good news. First, the fact that employees can display pornography or that a supervisor may lawfully sexually harass men and women does not make such actions good management practices. Moreover, employee rights advocates, plaintiffs' lawyers, and academics are not the only interested parties who are uncomfortable with the changes in the law. There are judges who seemingly do not want to follow *Oncale* and thus might accept ill-conceived arguments or apply tortured reasoning to achieve what they believe to be a just result. A prime example of a case where a panel of judges muddied the law and exasperated employers is *Rene v. Mirage*.

In *Rene*, the plaintiff, a butler at the hotel, alleged that he had been sexually harassed. According to the plaintiff, the harassers' conduct included coworkers calling Rene offensive names, forcing him to look at pictures of naked men having sex, grabbing him in the crotch, and poking their fingers in his anus through his clothing. When asked why the harassers directed such conduct at him, the plaintiff stated that it was because he was gay.

Under *Oncale*, the case should have ended right there. Sexual orientation is not protected under federal law, and thus, harassment based on orientation is not actionable. The United States Court of Appeals for the Ninth Circuit did not, however, apply the law when it was faced with this case where the employee suffered from harassment that was sexual in nature and clearly both severe and pervasive. The conduct more than satisfied the criteria set out in *Harris Forklift*. If the plaintiff were a woman and endured such treatment, any court, applying pre-*Oncale* law, would have focused on conduct alone and clearly found for the plaintiff. After *Oncale*, however, motivation had become an issue. Here, the stated motivation was not unlawful, and thus the court should have dismissed the case, but did not. Instead, the court, in a classic example of results-oriented jurisprudence, misapplied the law in general, and *Oncale* specifically, in order to achieve its desired result.

Rene creates a number of problems for employers. First, because *Rene* is a Court of Appeals decision, the holding is now the law in the Ninth Circuit. Moreover, this is an example of courts trying to make "bad law" right. The majority in *Rene* ignores the law, and a concurring opinion manipulates the facts. Thus, 45 years after the Civil Rights Act and 25 years after *Meritor*, the definition of what constitutes sexual harassment remains unclear.

Still, this story should have had a relatively happy ending for employers. In summer 1998, the Supreme Court articulated new standards for employer liability in sexual harassment cases. In the *Burlington Industries v. Ellerth* and *Faragher v. Boca Raton* opinions, the Court held that employers are liable for actions of supervisors who engage in either *quid pro quo* sexual harassment or hostile environment sexual harassment, regardless of whether they knew, or should have known, of the alleged conduct. Employers can escape liability if the employee did not suffer a "tangible loss" (e.g., terminated, demoted, or not promoted) and if the company satisfies the Court's affirmative defense. To do this, employers must prove that (1) the employer "exercised reasonable care to prevent and promptly correct any sexually harassing behavior" and (2) the plaintiff "unreasonably failed to take advantage of any preventive or corrective opportunities provided by the employer or to otherwise avoid harm." The problem here is that the standard was unclear. We did not know (1) what is reasonable care and (2) when an employee is unreasonable.

In 2001, my colleagues and I studied the 72 motions for summary judgment that employers filed after the *Ellerth* and *Faragher* decisions. In each motion, the companies argued that the employer satisfied, as a matter of law, the affirmative defense. We found that to exercise reasonable care, employers needed only to have a "good sexual harassment policy," defined as being written, disseminated, and providing an opportunity for employees to report to someone other than the harasser. When employers exercised reasonable care and the employee did not report, the court granted the employer's motion every time. When the employee did report harassment to an employer who had exercised reasonable care, the vast majority of courts found for the employer by holding that either (1) the employee was unreasonable because of delay or defect, or (2) the employer's appropriate response absolved it of liability. Thus, there were two key elements to avoiding liability: (1) have a good policy and (2) react properly to a complaint. Because employers could comply with these two prescriptions relatively simply, sexual harassment became less of a minefield for employers. This, however, may not be the case as we move forward.

Today, management attorneys report that judges are not so quick to label non-reporting employees as unreasonable, and are less likely to find fault in employees who do report. Moreover, a number of jurisdictions, including the state of California and New York City, have rejected *Ellerth* and hold that employers may be strictly liable for the harassment of supervisors. Thus, as time passes, the standards for harassment remain amorphous and the affirmative defense is weakening. What this means is that, as an employer, you cannot rely on the defense and must work to prevent harassment from occurring. Indeed, as seen in *Rene* and then evolution of state and city laws, sexual harassment may result in damages regardless of the employer's response or even the law.

HOW TO AVOID DISCRIMINATION

Avoiding discrimination charges is impossible. Avoiding "bad facts" that could lead an investigator or jury to find for the employee is difficult. Avoiding discrimination can be accomplished. Here, we discuss the latter two points.

To avoid "bad facts," the key is document, document, document. Employers who give every employee a positive annual review, don't put discipline in employee files, or don't provide real reasons for decisions are providing plaintiffs' lawyers with all the ammunition they need to prove discrimination. Juries will see a terminated employee who is in a protected class or who engaged in a protected expression, and will believe that the class or the expression at least motivated the employer's action. In such cases, the employer will end up paying its lawyer, the plaintiff's lawyer, and maybe other damages. Employers need to evaluate, discipline, document, and tell the truth.

Furthermore, to avoid bad facts, make sure that your human resource (HR) department approves major decisions. Supervisors should not hire, fire, promote, or demote employees in a vacuum. HR professionals who possess institutional knowledge are able to determine whether a perfectly reasonable decision (e.g., terminating an employee for excessive tardiness) will result in a discrimination charge because another employee, outside the class and in a different department, engaged in similar conduct and was only warned. HR can avoid these bad facts.

Make avoiding discrimination part of your corporate culture—with such conduct never tolerated. Employers need to have published policies, train employees, and discipline violators. Along with teaching employees the company values, such actions will signal to the EEOC, judges, and juries that your company engages in proper behavior.

NOTES

1. D. Sherywn and G. Gilman, "Retaliation: Why an Increase in Claims Does Not Mean the Sky Is Falling," *Cornell Hospitality Roundtable Proceedings* (2009): 2.
2. For definitions of the EEOC terms, see EEOC.gov.
3. *Meritor Savings Bank FSB v. Vinson,* 477 U.S. 57 (1986).

CHAPTER 28

COORDINATING INFORMATION AND CONTROLLING COSTS

GORDON POTTER

I want to cover two essential and related topics in this chapter: determining the extent of decision rights you grant to your employees, and the management reports you provide to these employees to motivate them to effectively utilize resources. I recognize that if you are a sole practitioner, you may handle these all on your own. But if you hire people to manage your property, you should consider the points I discuss here.

ASSIGNING ORGANIZATIONAL UNITS FINANCIAL RESPONSIBILITY

As an owner or operator of a hospitality enterprise, one of your primary objectives is to maximize the value of your organization. To meet this objective, one of the most important resources you will need to develop and motivate is a highly competent property-level management team. Most hospitality firms motivate, control, and evaluate the behavior of their property managers and other key property employees using performance measurement systems. From an owner's perspective, the issue becomes the degree of responsibility and the type of measurable results that you assign to your property-level managers.

Depending on the size of your organization, you need to determine whether decision making should be centralized at your headquarters or decentralized and given to your property managers. Then, once you have assigned a set of decision rights to key property personnel, you need to determine how you will motivate and measure their performance. Assuming that you are not a sole proprietor or a hands-on manager (and even if you are), this chapter discusses the factors that determine the extent of decision-making authority you might want to give to property-level employees. After we discuss management decision making, we illustrate how you can design property-level financial reports to motivate your property-level employees to focus on the dimensions of performance you wish them to attend to. The better you can link your property-level manager's responsibilities to their measured performance, the more likely it is that your organization will succeed in meeting its objectives.

Location of Decision Rights

Your first consideration is how much decision authority you will give to your property managers. The degree of accountability that you will expect evolves from your decision about property managers' responsibilities. Although it might be hard for you to give up direct control, let's look at the many benefits you might realize by having a decentralized firm where you allow property-level general managers and their subordinates to make most of the operating decisions (based on your overall strategy and principles). These benefits may include quick response time to customer requests and unforeseen events, the ability to obtain and use local information, and an empowered workforce whose commitment is escalated because they are given substantial responsibilities. Additional benefits you may realize from decentralization include the conservation of your headquarters' resources (or your own personal time and energy) and the development of future corporate managers.

To the contrary, you probably are thinking of arguments for you to retain decision rights, or to be more centralized. These include the ability to transfer knowledge throughout the organization and therefore adopt best practices, specialization of your workforce, and the benefits that come from economies of scale. An additional benefit for lodging companies with multiple units within a market is the coordination of marketing activities and information for pricing policies. This last point is important, because it has long been recognized that highly decentralized units in the same company can unintentionally compete with each other. For large branded hospitality firms, the push for centralization also comes from the need for a uniform and consistently high-quality product across operating units.

Financial Performance Measures

If you have decided to decentralize your management operations, you will need to develop a well-defined set of responsibilities for managers operating at the property level. The results from these responsibilities are generally measured in financial terms based on a financial control system that is, in turn, based on the decision rights you have given to your unit-level managers. Financial control systems, sometimes referred to as *financial performance measurement systems,* are used for many reasons. Perhaps the most important reason is that profit-seeking organizations expressly state many of their objectives in financial terms. For instance, you may have an explicit goal to maximize the profit or value of each property that you own. Financial measures are also needed to ensure that your organization remains solvent, and in many instances these measures are the basis for distributing the cash flows from your enterprise among the various claimants. Financial numbers also provide a good summary of the overall achievements of the business unit and are reasonably precise and objective. Finally, because lenders and taxing authorities require financial information, developing additional financial information for managers should be relatively costless for your organization.

Although financial measures have drawbacks, virtually all hospitality organizations use control systems based on financial performance measures. Specific concerns with financial measures include that they can be manipulated by managers; they address only past performance; many workers don't know how to influence financial measures, and financial measures may discourage investment because of the time lag between current investment and the future income from the investment.

Consequently, many performance measurement systems also incorporate nonfinancial measures to ensure that managers are focused on the future, have contracting alternatives, and to provide guidance for frontline personnel who have little effect on financial numbers. However, nonfinancial measures also have drawbacks. Workers may lose sight of the enterprise's goal of ensuring future cash flows and value creation. Additionally, not all nonfinancial measures suggest the same action, little is known about the true cost of obtaining high scores on a particular measure, nonfinancial measures are costly to obtain, and in some instances, they are manipulated. Despite these factors, designing performance measurement systems with nonfinancials can lead to improved financial performance.[1]

Since the use of financial measures seems unavoidable, let's consider the responsibility center you should design for your property managers. As an owner, you should consider designing financial responsibility centers that align the incentives of employees with those of your organization. If you are a manager, you certainly want to be assigned financial responsibility only for financial numbers that you can control. That said, as an owner, you may wish to assign certain financial goals to managers that you want them to attend to even if the goals are not controllable by these managers. In lodging companies, for instance, many property-level general managers are evaluated on gross operating profit (GOP), which is a reported profit number before management fees and fixed charges for property tax and insurance. However, if you want general managers to take actions that might, however slightly, drive some other cost, such as property taxes or insurance costs, you might hold general managers accountable for net operating income (NOI) or earnings before interest, taxes, depreciation, and amortization (EBITDA).

You sometimes see alternative financial performance measurement systems that can inform you about the actions of the managers. For example, you or your staff might compare the manager's financial performance to that of a group of comparable hotels, which is called *relative performance evaluation*. In this instance, even though the manager cannot control the performance of the other hotels, a comparison of her performance to a set of similar properties may help your assessment of the manager's ability and effort, by controlling for the uncertain economic environment. Finally, because the payment of managerial rewards requires cash flows, the manager's performance may be assessed more on the property's ability to pay off its obligations than on the items that are controllable by the manager. For instance, proxy statements of Marriott and Starwood revealed that Starwood, but not Marriott, required that EBITDA reach a certain threshold before *any bonus* was paid to top executives.

From the agency perspective, good attributes of measures include the precision with which the measures reflect your employee's activities and the extent to which the measures motivate actions that are consistent (congruent) with your organizations' goals. GOP is a typical measure for property-level managers, so that's the one we'll discuss going forward.

Types of Responsibility Centers

Although hotel managers generally are responsible for profits, let's look at four types of responsibility centers, as shown in Table 28.1. In a *cost center,* your manager's focus is on controlling costs, and performance is controlled and evaluated by comparing actual costs incurred to standard or budgeted costs allowed, given the actual output (actual rooms sold). Examples of cost centers at lodging properties might include maintenance, housekeeping, and human resource departments.[2] In a *revenue center,* your managers' focus is on generating revenue without consideration of costs, with the possible exception of certain minor direct costs. Examples include the room reservation department or banquet sales. A revenue center's performance report compares actual sales with budgeted sales. In a *profit center,* your managers must consider both revenues and costs, and their performance compares actual profit to budgeted profit. Hotel profit centers typically include rooms and food and

Table 28.1
Typical Financial Responsibility Centers

Type of Responsibility Center	Manager Responsibilities	Performance Measurement Report
Cost center	Operating costs.	Actual costs vs. standard cost allowed.
Revenue center	Operating revenues.	Actual revenues vs. budgeted revenues.
Profit center	Operating revenues and costs.	Actual profit vs. budgeted profit.
Investment center	Operating revenues, costs, and investment.	Actual ROI or economic profit vs. budgeted ROI or economic profit.

beverage divisions. Managers of an *investment center* have responsibility for investment, as well as revenues and costs. Managers are often evaluated by comparing return on investment (ROI) or other profit measure to a budgeted amount. While an owner's analyses of a property's economic viability will generally be from an ROI perspective, it is rare that you would evaluate your general managers at the property level as if they operated as an investment center.

Choosing a Type of Responsibility Center

From the owner's perspective, an important issue is whether to assign financial responsibility to your property-level managers, and if so, how much? By following the Uniform System of Accounts for the Lodging Industry (USALI), you will have available a well-defined uniform financial report on property-level operations.[3] In a survey of USALI use, 78 percent of the respondents stated their property used the system, primarily due to corporate demands. Moreover, many studies reported that lodging organizations all reported using budgetary amounts as the main performance indicator, or as one of the few key indicators, when evaluating the property-level management team.[4]

Your choice of financial responsibility center depends on your goals and managers' ability to influence the performance measure. For example, property-level managers have little to no control over the initial financial investment in the property and may only have minor influence over new capital investment. Thus, it is unlikely that you would evaluate your property-level managers based on investment center measurements. It would, however, be possible for you to include certain measures that the managers do influence, such as inventory turnover (or the total inventory amount), accounts receivable turnover, total working capital measures, or perhaps capital expenditure amounts to ensure that managers attend to some aspects of costly investment. It also seems inappropriate that you would judge property managers on a revenue center model. There is no question that property-level managers are seeking to drive revenue, but they also need to ensure that the necessary resources are available and that the appropriate activities are being undertaken to provide a high-quality product or service according to your organization's expectations.

Profit Center versus Cost Center

Let's compare profit center and cost center reporting. The choice hinges on how much you and your corporate staff want property-level managers to focus on revenues and how much control you believe managers have on revenue outcomes. There are clear benefits to having your property-level management team focus on revenues. For one, revenue may be a proxy for the quality of the service at the hotel, as high-quality service should generate increased demand and a price premium. Thus, having the manager focus on revenues may drive her efforts on guest service. This rationale also argues against your choosing a cost center responsibility system. Important as it is to control costs, focusing solely on costs runs the risk of cutting back on resources too much, at the cost of quality. If managers are responsible for profit center reporting, they are also more likely to find new customers or sources of business in the local community and seek other ways to increase net revenues.

Despite the potential pitfalls of cost center performance measurement, you still might want to consider measuring your manager against a cost center report. To begin with, many of the benefits that come from focusing on revenues can be obtained using alternative performance measures, as I mentioned earlier. For instance, customer expectations and service quality can be directly measured using nonfinancial performance measures such as customer satisfaction, customer complaints, quality metrics, and property-level audit reports. You can also obtain measures of new customers and new product growth, as well as employee measures. While the collection of this information is costly, many organizations already accumulate this information for other purposes.

Although managers seek to drive revenue, in many instances they often have little control over rates and revenues. In restaurant chains, for instance, managers have little control over prices, and those with a large transient business also have little control over demand. In the lodging industry, central reservation systems and overall brand image can have significant influence over revenues, leaving little rate leeway for general managers. In addition, changes in economic circumstance, such as 9/11, volcanic and flu activity, and deep economic downturns like the recent severe recession, limit the unit-level manager's ability to influence revenues. In these instances, property-level employees have much more control over costs than they do over revenues. Thus, operating as a cost center induces the manager to focus activities on dimensions where they can truly make a difference even in the face of a huge economic downturn.

As you have seen from this discussion, the issues of decision rights and financial control systems are not necessarily cut and dried. While every owner desires a fair financial return on each property, and properties must yield positive cash flows to remain viable, there may be added benefits to your organization by designing appropriate responsibility centers and rewarding property-level managers according to the financial factors that they can control effectively.

Few hospitality organizations provide information on their performance measurement systems. Those that do typically provide profit center performance reports for their properties. Denton and White describe the design and implementation of a performance measurement system for a company that operated 38 limited service properties.[5] The performance measurement system included one measure for each dimension of the balanced scorecard. The company also used a flow-through measure of profitability that compares actual profit to expected profit given actual output (rooms sold). As such, this latter measure focuses on cost control and thus the performance measurement system provides an example of a form of cost center supplemented with nonfinancial measures.

MEASURING YOUR MANAGER'S FINANCIAL CONTRIBUTION

Numerous studies have reported that all properties use financial amounts as a part of their performance measurement system. Studies have also revealed that these financial budgets are not adjusted for changes in economic circumstances during a period. That is, lodging organizations do not use flexible budgets. For instance, surveys of the budgeting practices of small hotel companies found that the primary perceived benefits of budgets concerned coordination and control issues. Several studies have confirmed that even though budgets suffered from a lack of accuracy that was related to the impact of economic events, virtually no firms used flexible budgeting techniques for performance evaluation. Thus, budgets remained constant over the reporting period; hotels did not adjust budgets during the period as conditions warranted.[6] These studies suggest, therefore, that property-level managers' overall performance, as measured against budget, is highly dependent on the economic environment and that any changes in economic conditions will have a large impact on measured performance.

Typical Performance Report

A depiction of a simplified financial performance report for a limited-service hotel is presented in Table 28.2, ignoring income other than room revenues. Other income is typically a small portion of income for limited-service hotels. Although my example is a limited-service hotel, this model can be extended to a full-service hotel and to a restaurant by assuming a constant product mix. If your manager is held accountable for profit variances from budget, your performance measurement system requires a profit center report similar to the one in the table. Note that the statement stops at the GOP (gross operating profit) line, and therefore the statement does not provide for any management fees and fixed charges that may include insurance, rents, and property taxes. As I said earlier, GOP is a typical number for assessing a general manager's performance. The report reveals that for the period,

Table 28.2
Summary Annual Operating Statement for 120-Room Limited-Service Hotel

	Actual	Budget	Variance
Room Revenue	$2,370,000	$2,531,640	($161,640)
Room Expense	(552,120)	(559,149)	7,029
Departmental Income	1,817,880	1,972,491	(154,611)
Undistributed Operating Expenses			
Administrative and General	(225,480)	(227,330)	1,850
Sales and Marketing	(171,480)	(179,028)	7,548
Property Operations and Maintenance	(122,160)	(122,460)	300
Utilities	(135,600)	(138,690)	3,090
Gross Operating Profit	1,163,160	1,304,983	(141,823)
ADR	83.89	85.00	
Occupancy Rate	64.50%	68.00%	
REVPAR	54.11	57.80	
Rooms Sold	28,251	29,784	
Rooms Available	43,800	43,800	

the property missed its budgeted GOP by $141,823. A review of sales activity also demonstrates that actual average daily rate (ADR) and occupancy were below budget. The report reflects the key aspects of financial reporting of most hotels, as properties tend to operate as profit centers and compare actual results to beginning-of-the-period budgeted amounts.

This report doesn't really tell you how the general manager and other property-level employees managed costly activities and resources in response to the unforeseen changes in demand. For this, you might look at expense per occupied room or expense as a percentage of revenue. These calculations are useful, but an underlying assumption with these metrics is that all operating costs are variable. Alternatively, using a measure such as expense per available room treats the expense per available room as completely fixed. Either way, the performance report doesn't provide the information to ascertain how well the management team has controlled costs in response to a drop in demand. A useful way for you to examine this is by means of a flexible budget that provides for a benchmark cost for any level of activity. Flexible budgets help motivate managers to adapt cost effective strategies as conditions change. These types of budget provide clear benchmarks for identifying and explaining cost variances.

Building a Cost Model

To create a flexible budget your organization needs to estimate how costs will behave with changes in output, in this case, rooms sold. Although lodging companies have some sense of the variable cost of a room-night for their properties, the accuracy of the estimate is ascertained only after the model estimates have been compared to actual realizations. Thus, the largest drawback to constructing a flexible budget is the potential error in cost modeling. A simple approach that your organization could use to estimate a property's fixed and variable costs is through detailed account analysis. For instance, Table 28.3 depicts how a manager could estimate the fixed and variable portions of the rooms department expense. In account analysis, the manager examines each line item, reads any contract related to the costly resource, and classifies each cost as fixed, variable, or mixed, if it includes both fixed and variable components.

In our example in Table 28.3 you begin by examining payroll records and classifying employee pay as salary (fixed) or wages (variable). Payroll-related expenses are apportioned by employee type. The other key expenses, such as laundry, linens, supplies, commissions, and complimentary food are assigned as a variable cost. Finally, other is apportioned equally. Obviously,

Table 28.3
Account Analysis Approach to Cost Behavior Estimation:
Rooms Department Expense

	Estimated Total	Estimated Fixed	Estimated Variable
Salaries and wages	$307,291	$118,000	$189,291
Payroll related expenses	59,458	24,000	35,458
Laundry, linen, and supplies	55,600	0	55,600
Commissions and reservations	45,800	0	45,800
Complimentary food	43,000	0	43,000
Other	48,000	24,000	24,000
Total rooms expense	$559,149	$166,000	$393,149

Estimated variable cost per room night sold = estimated total variable cost/estimated rooms sold

$393,149/29,784

$13.20 per room sold

Table 28.4
Estimated Fixed and Variable Costs by Expense Item

	Estimated Fixed	Estimated Variable per Room Sold
Rooms expense	$166,000	$13.20
Admistrative and general	135,000	3.10
Sales and marketing	45,000	4.50
Property operations and maintenance	48,000	2.50
Utilities	27,000	3.75
Total	$421,000	$27.05

more detailed analysis would be necessary, as there are numerous costs in each summary expense category. Summing up the amounts in our example, the rooms department is estimated to have annual fixed costs of $166,000 and a variable cost per room–night of $13.20.

The cost behavior of the other expenses at the property is provided in Table 28.4. The table reveals the fixed and variable costs for each expense item. It also demonstrates that the annual estimated fixed expenses are $421,000, and the variable cost per room–night is $27.05. Clearly, your estimates are going to be measured with error, but your intuition is the best way to begin the modeling of costs. Eventually, you might want to use more heavy-duty statistical techniques, such as linear regression. Although it's not

Table 28.5
Flexible Budget Performance Report of Summary Annual Operating Statement

	Actual	Flexible Budget	Original Budget	Variance
Room Revenue	$2,370,000	$2,401,335	$2,531,604	($161,640)
Room Expense	(552,120)	(538,913)	(559,149)	7,029
Departmental Income	1,817,880	1,862,422	1,972,491	(154,611)
Undistributed Operating Expenses				
Administrative and General	(225,480)	(222,578)	(227,330)	1,850
Sales and Marketing	(171,480)	(172,130)	(179,028)	7,548
Property Operations and Maintenance	(122,160)	(118,628)	(122,460)	300
Utilities	(135,600)	(132,941)	(138,690)	3,090
Gross Operating Profit	1,163,160	1,216,145	1,304,983	(141,823)
ADR	83.89	85.00	85.00	
Occupancy Rate	64.50%	64.50%	68.00%	
REVPAR	54.11	54.83	57.80	
Rooms Sold	28,251	28,251	29,784	
Rooms Available	43,800	43,800	43,800	

perfect, regression is quick, uses all data points, and uses a well-defined criterion. A good cost model will be intuitively plausible, will have been tested on data, will fit the data, and will do a good job predicting future observations. Moreover, it will be in need of constant refinement and will need to be altered to meet the needs of the organization. During the last deep recession, for instance, your organization might have had the incentive to treat as many costs as possible as variable costs to induce managers to cut back on resource use in the face of the drop in business. While cost estimation is difficult, it should be an integral part of your budgeting process, and therefore it should be available for performance evaluation.

Flexible Budget Report

Let's look at the flexible budget report, as shown in Table 28.5. The total profit variance is the same as that reported in Table 28.2, $–141,823, but the report in Table 28.5 provides a flexible budget column that represents what the revised budget would have been once the actual number of room-nights is known. Thus, the flexible budget uses the actual room-nights sold, 28,251, to create a column that represents what budgeted performance would be if the actual number of rooms sold were known at the time the budget was produced. The flexible budget reveals that your property under review should have earned a gross operating profit of $1,216,145, as compared to the original budget profit forecast of $1,304,983. This profit difference is related to the change in quantity of rooms sold, 28,251 actual rooms sold versus 29,784 planned rooms sold. This profit volume variance of $-88,838 (= $1,216,145 - $1,304,983) is equal to the drop quantity of rooms -1,533 (= 28,251 - 29,784) times the lost contribution per room. In this case, the estimated lost contribution per room is the ADR minus the variable cost, or $57.95 (= $85.00 - $27.05). Therefore, the profit lost is $57.95 × 1,533 rooms = $88,838. Some practitioners compute a flow-through percentage, which is the percent of each extra dollar of revenue that should result in profit. This is the contribution margin divided by revenues, or on a per-unit basis, contribution per unit divided by price. In this instance, it is $57.95/ $85.00 or about 68.18 percent. This is also called the *contribution margin ratio*.

The profit volume variance that we just calculated is due to changes in occupancy, which you may determine the general manager at the property has little control over. The flexible budget also isolates the impact of ADR changes on revenues. This can be ascertained by examining the difference between actual room revenue, $2,370,000, and room revenue under the flexible budget, $2,401,335. This amount is the ADR rate differential, which is $-1.11 times the quantity of rooms sold (rate differential calculated as $-1.11 = $83.89 - $85.00). Thus, this variance is $-31,335 (= $-1.11 × 28,251 rooms, with rounding).

What is most important is the examination of your property's operating costs, which can be seen by comparing actual costs to costs allowed, given the actual output of the flexible budget, as shown in Table 28.6. With the exception of marketing, all of the expenses in Table 28.6 are over the amounts allowed by the flexible budget. Assuming the cost modeling is correct, this suggests that the managers at the property did not reduce costs sufficiently in response to the drop in demand. Note that actual costs are $1,206,840 and budgeted costs allowed given actual room-nights sold are $1,185,190. Thus, there were cost overruns of $21,650. Compare this to the analysis of the typical profit center report presented in Table 28.2. In that table, the cost variances are all favorable, in the sense that costs came in under the original budget, but that was easy to accomplish given the drop in room-nights sold. The flexible budget reveals the cost reductions were insufficient. Therefore,

Table 28.6
Flexible Budget Cost Center Report from Summary Annual Operating Statement

	Actual	Flexible Budget	Variance
Room Expense	($552,120)	($538,913)	($13,207)
Administrative and General	(225, 480)	(222,578)	(2,902)
Sales and Marketing	(171,480)	(172,130)	650
Property Operations and Maintenance	(122, 160)	(118,628)	(3,533)
Utilities	(135,600)	(132,941)	(2,659)
Total costs	($1,206,840)	($1,185,190)	($21,650)
ADR	83.89	85.00	
Occupancy rate	64.50%	64.50%	
REVPAR	54.11	54.83	
Rooms Sold	28,251	28,251	
Rooms Available	43,800	43,800	

your managers at this property probably did not cut back on inputs as much as they might have, given the drop in rooms sold. The important question is, if the manager's performance had been measured against a flexible budget would she have been more likely to cut back on costly unnecessary resources as room demand dropped?

CONCLUSION

Performance measurement systems are a key method for you to motivate, control, and evaluate your managers. This chapter shows you how to determine how well your organization's performance measurement accomplishes its intended task. In addition to looking at the factors that will help you determine the extent of decision-making authority you are going to give to property-level employees, this chapter has offered some alternative ways to think about designing financial control systems to control operating costs and thereby increase your profits. In general, hospitality organizations align property-level managers' incentives with their organization goals by rewarding these managers for meeting or exceeding budgeted profit. However, in environments like that of the recent deep recession, where there is much demand uncertainty, or in organizations where revenue is generated primarily from corporate activities, it may be better for you to use benchmarks that managers can actually control, or at least isolate different components of performance. In this environment, designing property-level performance measures that more closely monitor costly activities may be beneficial. As such, this chapter has presented alternative performance measurement approaches that may help your property-level employees focus on the aspects of performance they best control and in this manner improve your organization's overall performance.

NOTES

1. R. D. Banker, G. Potter, and D. Srinivasan, "Association of Nonfinancial Performance Measures with the Financial Performance of a Lodging Chain," *Cornell Hotel and Restaurant Administration Quarterly* 46(4) (2005): 394–412.
2. American Hotel and Lodging Association, *Uniform System of Accounts for the Lodging Industry, 10th ed.* (Washington, DC: American Hotel and Lodging Association, 2006).
3. F. Kwansa, and R. S. Schmidgall, "The Uniform System of Accounts for the Lodging Industry: Its Importance to and Use by the Hotel Managers." *Cornell Hotel and Restaurant Administration Quarterly* (1999): 40(6): 88–94.
4. T. A. Jones, "Changes in Hotel Industry Budgetary Practice," *International Journal of Contemporary Hospitality Management* 20(4) (2008): 428–444.
5. G. A. Denton and B. White, "Implementing a Balanced-Scorecard Approach to Managing Hotel Operations," *Cornell Hotel and Restaurant Administration Quarterly* 41(1) (2000): 94–107.
6. J. G. Kosturakis and J. J. Eyster, "Operational Budgeting in Small Hotel Companies," *Cornell Hotel and Restaurant Administration Quarterly* 19(4) (1979): 80–84; and R. S. Schmidgall, and A. L. DeFranco, "Budgeting and Forecasting: Current Practice in the Lodging Industry," *Cornell Hotel and Restaurant Administration Quarterly* 39(6) (1998): 45–51.

CHAPTER 29

MAKING THE MOST OF YOUR HUMAN CAPITAL

J. BRUCE TRACEY and SEAN A. WAY

If you ask hospitality executives and managers, "What keeps you up at night?" one of the most common responses is "human resources."[1] Indeed, there's no question that you have to pay close attention to your workforce. We often use the term *human capital* to refer to employees, so when we talk about maximizing human capital, we are simply saying that you should make a focused effort to support and encourage your employees to do their best possible work. Since knowledge of how you and your firm can get the most from your employees has expanded greatly in recent years, we discuss ways to make the most of human capital. It wasn't so long ago that managing human resources (HR) was primarily an administrative function. Today, however, the effective management of human capital requires more complex and sophisticated policies, programs, and systems that have a direct impact on your hospitality firm's performance, effectiveness, and long-term competitive success.

This chapter looks at (1) the importance of effective human capital management in the hospitality industry, (2) the emerging forces in the hospitality industry and their implications for the effective management of hospitality employees, and (3) the "best practices" that you can use to effectively manage your hospitality employees.

THE IMPORTANCE OF HUMAN CAPITAL IN THE HOSPITALITY INDUSTRY

No doubt you are well aware of the value of the employees who constitute your firm's human capital. However, you also can see the factors that make it difficult for employees to do their jobs effectively. These problems stem primarily from the nature of front-line work in the hospitality industry. The hours are long, and many operations are open 24 hours a day, 365 days a year. In addition, customers can be fickle and demanding. Moreover, the nature of work in many front-line hospitality positions is fairly low in complexity, relatively stable, and requires little or no formal education and training.[2] Finally, the labor force is extremely diverse, which poses significant cultural and communication challenges. As such, a well-considered HR strategy is essential, since you must find individuals who are not only able to work in this kind of context, but who also are motivated to excel.

Emerging Forces and Key Implications

In addition to the challenges noted above, there are a number of competitive forces that could impede your efforts to optimize your human capital. One of the most salient factors is globalization. This isn't a new trend, but it has accelerated significantly in recent years. Even though you may not see a direct effect from globalization on your local or regional operation, your brand undoubtedly considers itself in global terms. It's also true that global concerns place significant pressures on how hospitality firms attract, select, and retain quality employees. For example, Zurich-based Mövenpick Hotels & Resorts, which managed about 70 properties in 26 countries in the mid-2000s, sought to increase the number of properties in its portfolio to 100 by the end of 2010. Most of the new properties were to be developed in Asia, the Middle East, and Africa, which means that its property-level leaders must not only fulfill their functional responsibilities, but they must also "carry the flag" and help the firm enhance its identity and overall competitive position. These dynamics require careful consideration of the HR policies, procedures, and systems that are used to attract, select, develop and retain individuals who will support Mövenpick's growth plans. Some of these leaders will undoubtedly be expatriates, with all the complications that entails (see Chapter 6).

The need to maintain efficiency—and often to do more with less—while increasing quality will also play a major role in your human capital management decision making. For example, companies such as Four Seasons Hotels and Resorts, Royal Caribbean International, and Union Square Hospitality Group have included environmental sustainability as a central part of their overarching business plans, in part to reduce their operating costs, but also to enhance their social responsibility. To support these plans, a number of human capital management initiatives have been developed and implemented, including job descriptions that articulate "green" responsibilities, training programs that teach employees how to conserve energy and reduce waste, and incentive programs for meeting sustainability goals. These practices exemplify a purposeful and objective means for supporting the corporate value system, and demonstrate the ways in which human capital management can be linked directly to strategic-level priorities. Moreover, the results from this type of strategic alignment are reflected in the company's financial results and provide a strong basis for creating a balance between efficiency and growth.

Another competitive challenge comes from your customers, who are increasingly demanding that your employees provide more and better service. In response, a number of companies, including ARAMARK, Hillstone Restaurant Group, Loews Hotels and Resorts, and Ritz-Carlton, have structured jobs that give front-line employees significant discretion to accommodate guest needs and requests. This empowerment approach to job design is supported by several human capital management initiatives, such as rigorous selection procedures, comprehensive training programs, and incentive programs that link individual and collective performance to clearly defined performance outcomes.

You certainly have found that advancements in technology give you the potential to expedite and automate routine transactional work so you can focus on value-adding activities that enhance the functionality and effectiveness of your decision making. Starwood, for one, has an extensive information systems platform that provides real-time access to comprehensive information that can be used for a variety of planning and evaluation efforts—including workforce scheduling, performance management, and succession forecasting. Such systems provide the means to respond to, and even anticipate, your company's ongoing human capital needs, and increase the timeliness and quality of all human capital management decision making.

Then again, the pace of technological change means that you and your employees must embrace continuous improvement and engage in behaviors that support experimentation and innovation. So your HR strategy may be caught up in competing demands, muddy information, noisy communication systems, and organizational politics—not to mention external competitive forces. With that background in mind, let's look at the HR strategies that should help your hospitality firm achieve its overall strategic objectives.

HUMAN CAPITAL BEST PRACTICES

Your human capital strategy begins with plans and an infrastructure that addresses your organization's specific needs. From a strategic point of view, the primary focus is to start with your existing strengths—the knowledge, skills, and abilities of current employees—and to figure out how to get more of what you need. So, you identify and retain talent that can support your firm's competitive strategy and contribute to achieving your firm's strategic goals, and then you recruit and hire additional the employees who reinforce and complement this vision. Your employees all must share a commitment to the firm's objectives, and all individuals should demonstrate the ability and willingness to learn and grow. When these conditions are met, the firm becomes more agile and adaptable to the changes it faces. It goes without saying that some employees are more critical to your firm than others. This means that your firm's HR policies, practices, and systems must account for the differences in employee contribution (and ability), while simultaneously providing a means for developing and supporting all employees. This leads to a "best practices" HR system that is able to develop talented, committed employees who are capable of continuous learning and growth. Such an HR system is dynamic and flexible. Not only does it respond to the external and internal forces of change, but it can also help forecast and prepare your firm for future competitive conditions. Let's outline some of the best practices that can help you ensure effective management and promote a long-term competitive advantage.

Strong, People-Focused Culture One of the most fundamental human capital management best practices is the development and reinforcement of a culture that emphasizes the importance of people. This idea sounds fairly obvious and even simplistic, but creating and maintaining a work environment in which your employees know what types of behaviors and outcomes are most valued and needed by your firm can be difficult. In Chapter 9, we dug into the idea that a firm's culture stems primarily from the views expressed by senior management. This is the starting point for making the most of your human capital, by encouraging and supporting your employees to do their best possible work.

Based on the lead of top management, you must be able to articulate clear and compelling statements about what is important to your firm and what types of employee behaviors and outcomes are expected. In addition to "walking the talk," you must communicate the firm's culture and core values using whatever resources and media are at hand. In particular, electronic media, such as e-mail, message boards, and social media, can be used quite effectively for communicating core values and directing employee conduct. For example, Bill Marriott has developed *Bill's Blog*, in which he expresses the importance of Marriott's corporate values to all employees and guests. This provides a foundation for all other human capital management policies, practices, and systems, a guide for tactical decisions, and a yardstick for measuring outcomes.

Flexible Job Design With the diversity and complexity of the workforce—including the many single parents, dual-career couples, and parents with child care needs—it is necessary for hospitality firms to develop flexible jobs and work schedules. Many companies have adopted job-sharing programs that allow employees to share a position. However the job is split, it's a good idea to give the individuals who are sharing the job the opportunity to have a say in creating their own schedules, as that kind of autonomy provides an important source of ownership and motivation for those involved in the process. Depending on employee preferences and your company's needs, the job can be divided so that one employee works Sunday through Wednesday, and another takes Thursday through Saturday. Instead of dividing the job by the day, another common approach is for employees to split a shift between them. Rather than splitting jobs, another flexibility option that is used in many businesses is to offer employees a compressed workweek. The most common approaches allow individuals the opportunity to work four 10-hour days or three 12-hour days. Finally, you can offer flextime. This approach gives employees the opportunity to choose when, and in some cases where they work (e.g., from home), as long as they are able to effectively accomplish their job.

A flexibility approach that was implemented at Le Meridien is the 60/40 job design. This plan gives managers employees who are capable of performing a wide array of multifunctional tasks, duties, and responsibilities. The basic premise is that at least 60 percent of an employee's time will be dedicated to one particular job (e.g., front-desk agent or receptionist), and the remainder of their time will be assigned according to the property's needs as they relate to the employee's interests and skill sets (e.g., previous experience with night audit, desire to take on food and beverage responsibilities). For employees, this kind of flexibility provides an enriched work experience and offers many opportunities for development and growth. At the same time, Le Meridien and other employers who use an approach like this can be more responsive to changing workload demands because their employees are highly skilled, engaged, and have a sense of purpose.

Another example of flexibility is the use of contingent, part-time, or temporary employees. This flexibility tactic may improve an organization's capacity to respond to specific and short-term competitive needs, such as hiring additional banquet servers for an event. This type of practice can provide an efficient means for addressing fluctuating demands and helps maintain a high-quality service environment that promotes customer satisfaction, loyalty, and, ultimately, profitability.

Rigorous Recruitment and Staffing Procedures Your recruiting and hiring procedures can send a strong signal to potential employees about the kind of employer you are and, thus, directly affect the number and kinds of individuals who apply for your open positions. When recruiting employees, one of the most important considerations is the message or image that is conveyed in job advertisements. The standard, boilerplate help wanted ad is probably not where you want to start. You know the one, a short position description, a statement about offering "competitive" compensation and benefits, and an e-mail address where applicants may submit their application or resume. Instead, recruitment ads should present a positive but balanced message that expresses not only what your firm needs, but what it has to offer—beyond a job. This shouldn't be filled with advertising-speak puffery or business jargon. Instead, information about your culture, professional development opportunities, community involvement, and even awards or recognition your company has received—especially if the recognition has anything to do with being a "best place to work" or similar accolade—will have a direct effect on the number and quality of applicants you get.

Another good way to enhance your recruiting efforts is to use video-based, online job previews. A video can give prospective candidates the opportunity to see what the work environment is like instead of having to speculate. For example, Kimpton Hotels produced several "A day in my Kimpton life" video segments that are embedded in the HR section of their corporate Web site. Each segment offers insights from various employees—for example, a newly hired food-and-beverage management trainee, general manager, and executive housekeeper—about working at Kimpton. This kind of promotion helps prospective employees assess their fit for the organization, culture, and the job itself. Thus, the resulting applicant pool includes a higher percentage of individuals who are both qualified *and* interested.

Another way you can enhance the effectiveness of employee recruitment is to implement a referral rewards program, which usually involves a cash bonus when an employee identifies a candidate who takes the job and stays for some stated period of time. One of the key benefits of this practice is that it involves all staff in the recruitment process, and helps increase retention and overall employee morale.

When making hiring decisions, you need to go beyond interviews and background checks to determine the best candidates for your open positions. One of the best predictors of job performance for many jobs is an individual's general mental ability (GMA).[3] This characteristic is similar to intelligence and provides an indication of a person's ability to learn new information quickly. Given the importance of doing things right in guest service, you can easily see the importance of hiring someone who is quick on the uptake. Many GMA assessments are easy to administer and inexpensive—some tests can be completed in about 15 minutes and cost a few dollars per applicant. In addition to GMA, some measures of personality are excellent predictors of job performance. In particular, a person's conscientiousness—the extent to which a person is efficient, punctual, well-organized, and dependable—can be a good indicator of a person's work results. Finally, obtaining objective measures of a candidate's ability to perform critical job functions should be included in the selection process. These assessments must be based on the position's essential tasks, duties, and responsibilities—for example, a drink-mixing test for bartenders, a sales pitch for sales managers, or a cash flow analysis for a controller—and administered in a standardized, consistent manner.

After a careful audit of their selection procedures, for instance, the corporate HR team at Uno Chicago Grill found that the scores from a 12-minute assessment of GMA and several items from a 20-minute personality survey were significant predictors of performance for servers, bartenders, and hosts in their restaurants. After using these tools for several months, management found that they had not only hired more capable, higher-performing employees who generated higher sales, but the recently hired staff also demonstrated higher levels of commitment, which significantly reduced employee turnover.[4] Thus, increasing the rigor of selection procedures improved both top- and bottom-line performance by boosting efficiency and service quality.

Comprehensive Training and Development Training is far more than simply showing someone what to do. Here is where instilling your corporate culture is critical. Once you have hired an individual, her or his experiences during the first few weeks on the job can deeply affect assimilation into your firm and proficiency in performing her or his key responsibilities. Start by getting the tedious and annoying administrative requirements out of the way. Before the first day on the job, ask the person to come in and sign tax and work eligibility forms, enroll in the benefits plan, obtain identification cards, and so on. Also, send new employees such items as the employee handbook, training guides, operating procedures, and related documentation before their first day to help them hit the ground running. If all this can be accomplished, your new employee can focus on more important matters on her or his first day, such as building relationships and learning the job. Although learning from other employees is a valuable training approach, your firm should have a formal employee orientation, with a structured induction or orientation program. Such programs are best designed and implemented using a collaborative approach whereby you, other managers, and coworkers take collective responsibility for ensuring that the new employee learns his or her job requirements, as well as the firm's cultural values and norms. You also should use on-the-job training, and classroom-based and computer-assisted training opportunities throughout, as well as ongoing assessment and feedback so that everyone involved—especially the new employee—knows that he or she is making adequate progress.

Orientation and training should be just the beginning of an employee's continuous learning efforts. Many successful hospitality organizations offer a wide variety of professional development opportunities. In addition to formal programs that are specifically directed toward improving job performance and enhancing career advancement, employees should have access to cross-functional assignments, special projects, and even community service involvement—especially when such efforts are clearly linked to core firm values or strategic priorities. Management involvement, flexible jobs (similar to Le Meridien's 60/40 plan), and accountability and reward systems that reinforce the application of newly acquired knowledge and skills, are also necessary for supporting for these types of learning-focused environments, and promoting a continuous improvement workplace.

One company that offers a wide range of training and development programs for its employees is Taj Hotels and Resorts. Staff members have the opportunity to develop skills in an area of specialization, or pursue broader development opportunities that may prepare them for both domestic and international assignments. Taj offers continuous training that involves both on-the-job and formal classroom development opportunities—including programs on Taj's service culture and courses on food and wine pairing, business writing, and financial management. All programs are evaluated using rigorous assessment methods. Results are tied directly to program improvement efforts, and performance incentives are given to those who effectively use their newly acquired knowledge and skills.

Clear, Comprehensive, and Open-Book Performance Evaluation The final step in ensuring your employees' success—and that of your organization—is to be clear about individual performance requirements and to measure and reward employees based on the stated expectations. Every study that we have seen emphasizes the importance of clear management expectations.[5] These drive excellence in customer service and are critical for financial success. As a side effect, employees who work for employers who cultivate a positive work climate (which is created by clear and consistent management expectations) are generally happier and more productive than those who are not sure about how they will be evaluated. So employees should have a clear understanding of what is required of them, and how decisions based on performance evaluation information are made, such as merit pay adjustments, incentives, recognition programs, and promotions. In addition, collective contributions should also be incorporated in performance evaluation systems. In hospitality contexts, departmental ratings of customer satisfaction provide an excellent means for linking individual efforts and results to a key indicator of firm performance. In fact, customer satisfaction and loyalty have been shown to be leading indicators of financial performance in several hospitality and service firms.[6]

Make sure that your performance evaluation draws from multiple reliable sources. Then you must make sure that you use that information for both evaluative and developmental purposes. In addition to linking evaluations to customer satisfaction, service quality indices, and other strategically important outcomes, assessments of individual performance requirements should be based on self- and supervisor reports—and those of peers and subordinates as applicable. In addition, a substantial proportion of an employee's annual performance assessment should be linked directly to behaviors that support the firm's culture and core values. This portfolio-based approach generates information about how well an employee is performing and contributing to important organizational requirements, as well as developmental information that can be used for identifying training and development needs, developing succession plans, and other types of planning-based decisions. ARAMARK's career management program (CMP), for instance, incorporates multiple sources of performance data that include job-specific requirements (e.g., maintaining compliance with all safety and sanitation requirements), and strategically critical requirements (e.g., helping meet or exceed revenue targets for base business growth). Moreover, the results are tied directly to training and succession plans and merit pay decisions.

Strategically Based and Balanced Incentives Incentives play an important role in attracting, retaining, and motivating employees. An effective incentive system goes beyond "competitive" base compensation (within 10 percent of the market average), although a competitive base pay certainly is necessary. Beyond that, decisions regarding incentives must be just like those involving performance evaluation—that is, based on clearly defined objectives and linked to other HR policies and programs as appropriate. Performance bonuses and profit sharing should be part of all reward and incentive programs, because they provide a strong basis for creating high performance work systems, promoting teamwork, and helping to motivate employees to go beyond their performance expectations.

A good example of a strategically based incentive program comes from Harrah's Entertainment. CEO Gary Loveman and his senior HR leadership team developed a bonus program for all line employees that is based exclusively on customer satisfaction scores from the Targeted Player Survey, which is an assessment tool that captures perceptions about service quality among Harrah's reward players. Employees are awarded credits that they can redeem for a wide array of merchandise, similar to credit card reward points. These awards are allocated every quarter to all employees who work in departments that meet or exceed their specific customer satisfaction standards. One big benefit of this program is that Loveman has first-hand knowledge regarding the firm's customer satisfaction status. Because of the relationship between satisfied customers and financial success, Harrah's customer service reward program is actually a means for driving financial performance. The more satisfied the targeted players, the more likely they will remain loyal and generate predictable increases in revenue for Harrah's. Another key benefit of this incentive program is that it promotes continuous improvement efforts. A focus on meeting and exceeding customer expectations induces people to experiment and search for ways to enhance the quality of service.

Finally, you should ensure that all incentives have personal meaning for your employees. Money is important, but don't overlook the intangibles. Employees need to know they are valued, which you can demonstrate through praise and recognition for achieving work goals, going the extra mile, and being a good organizational citizen. In this regard, you must continuously articulate and communicate the behaviors and performance outcomes that you value. Incentive programs should also include policies that extend beyond work, such as those that help employees maintain a healthy work-life balance. Policies such as flexible job designs and family-friendly and community-focused policies not only provide employees opportunities to effectively manage their personal lives, but they also strengthen your operations. Employees who have time to take care of family members or to attend their children's school-related functions will be more focused on the job. Employees who volunteer their time to charitable organizations help create a better environment in your community. Policies that offer incentives for employees to participate in activities that extend beyond their immediate work settings can have a substantial impact on job satisfaction, organizational commitment, and of course, performance. In addition, these kinds of efforts enhance a firm's image and can strengthen the firm's overall brand.

The Need for Evaluation and Flexibility

We have discussed several human capital management best practices that will help your hospitality firm encourage employees to perform at their best level. Merely adopting these practices without consistent application will not provide the benefits that you might expect. Instead, continuous monitoring and assessment is needed to ensure that all major policies, practices, and systems create value. This means that you and your firm's leaders must clearly understand the evaluation procedures that can be used to examine the impact of all components of your firm's human capital management system—including demonstrating that information gathered during the selection process can predict future job performance, and showing that the various health and welfare benefits are linked to employee morale and retention.

In closing, all human capital, or HR, management policies, procedures, and systems must be flexible and adaptive. For example, when an employee attends training, performance evaluations must be modified to account for the individual's use of the new knowledge and skills. Moreover, employees who effectively use their training on the job should be rewarded for doing so. If such changes are not made, then the time, effort, and money that were invested will be wasted. This is the core principle of strategic resources as we have presented it here: be clear, be consistent, and be fair. Your employees will respond by doing their best to deliver the best possible customer service.

NOTES

1. C. A. Enz, "What Keeps You Up at Night? Key Issues of Concern for Lodging Managers," *Cornell Hotel and Restaurant Administration Quarterly* 42(2) (April 2001): 38–45; and C. A. Enz, "Issues of Concern for Restaurant Owners and Managers," *Cornell Hotel & Restaurant Administration Quarterly* 45(4) (2004): 315–332.
2. J. B. Tracey, M. C. Sturman, and M. J. Tews, "Ability versus Personality: Factors that Predict Employee Job Performance," *Cornell Hotel and Restaurant Administration Quarterly* 48(3) (2007): 313–322.
3. Ibid.
4. J. B. Tracey and T. R. Hinkin, "Contextual Factors and Cost Profiles Associated with Employee Turnover," *Cornell Hotel & Restaurant Administration Quarterly* 49 (2008): 12–27.
5. See, for example, S. A. Way, M. C. Sturman, and C. Raab, "What Matters More? Contrasting the Effects of Job Satisfaction and Service Climate on Hotel Food and Beverage Managers' Job Performance," *Cornell Hospitality Quarterly* 51(3) (August 2010): 379–397.
6. J. L. Heskett, T. O. Jones, G. W. Loveman, W. E. Sasser, and L. A. Schlesinger, "Putting the Service-Profit Chain to Work," *Harvard Business Review* 86 (2008): 118–129; and G. W. Loveman, "Employee Satisfaction, Customer Loyalty, and Financial Performance: An Empirical Examination of the Service Profit Chain in Retail Banking," *Journal of Service Research* 1 (1998): 18–31.

CHAPTER 30

YOU CAN'T MOVE ALL YOUR HOTELS TO MEXICO
UNIONS AND THE HOSPITALITY INDUSTRY

DAVID SHERWYN and PAUL E. WAGNER

For many years, most hotel workers were not a particular focus of the labor movement. Traditionally, hotel employees were not highly paid, often worked for tips, and did not stay in bargaining-unit positions for the duration of their careers. Since union dues are composed of a percentage of employee base pay (excluding tips) and because union members who benefit the most are those who stay at the same job for long periods of time, a hotel was not the model employer on which the union movement would theoretically wish to concentrate its efforts. If you worked in the hospitality industry, this made your life easier, because instead of organizing hotel or restaurant employees, the union movement focused on "heavy labor," the skilled and semiskilled employees of America's factories. This has changed.

With the decline in manufacturing, the relevance of the hospitality industry to organized labor grew. Indeed, part of what makes the industry so appealing is that you can't outsource your jobs or move your hotels overseas. Most of the "great hotels" in large American cities today are organized, including nearly all of New York's large, prestigious hotels. A strong union presence is also found in Boston; Chicago; Los Angeles; San Francisco; Washington, D.C.; Las Vegas; Philadelphia; and Honolulu. Since the jobs are staying put, the hospitality industry is now a priority, if not the holy grail for the future of the labor movement. This chapter explains the state of union-management relations in the hospitality industry. Chances are, if you work or plan to work in the hotel industry, you are going to have to deal with either a union campaign or a unionized workforce, and so you will need to know what you can and cannot do. We begin with a brief overview of the law. We then explain traditional organizing as compared with card check or neutrality agreements and how to identify and deal with them at your hotel or resort. We then provide a description of the 2006 negotiations and the union split that followed. Finally, we provide practical advice for those of you who are living with a union, have experienced union organizing, or simply wish to remain union free.

THE NATIONAL LABOR RELATIONS ACT

The first thing you must realize is that union organizing and activities are protected by law, and the law is evolving. The National Labor Relations Act (NLRA) provides employees with the right to organize and to engage in protected, concerted activity, which means two or more employees acting together. This activity is protected if the issues concern wages, hours, or terms and conditions of employment. Thus, two employees who walk out of a nonunion hotel's kitchen because it is too hot are protected. It is unlawful to interfere with employees' organizing rights. Thus, as an employer, you may not refuse to hire employees, fire, or discipline them because they want to form a union. You are also prohibited from forming company unions (unions that are controlled by or answer to management). Most hotel organizing in the twenty-first century has been the result of efforts by large international unions as opposed to small local or regional groups.

Traditional Organizing Drives

The typical organizing approach under the "old-fashioned" method involves a union targeting a particular company from the outside. In that situation, the union begins by selecting a possible target, assessing employees' interest in organizing, identifying the issues that concern employees, and then contacting the employees to begin the communication process. Other times, employees may start organizing from within and then seek out a union for representation. Regardless, once contact is made between the union and the employees, the union campaign begins in earnest. The contact may come in the form of a "blitz" as the union bombards the employees with information, or a slow buildup of support. In rarer situations, the union may send their members to apply for jobs in a "Trojan horse" technique. The applicants' real reason for applying for work is to gain access to other employees. This method, referred to as *salting,* may strike you as unfair, but it is protected by law. Even if an applicant openly admits to you in his job interview that he is applying for an open position so that he can organize your workforce on behalf of a union, you cannot decline to hire him on that basis.[1] Another method for organizing is to enter your property and hand out authorization cards (referred to as "hand billing") or set up picket lines at the entrances and exits to your property for the same purpose. All of these approaches fit within the traditional method of organizing because they all culminate in a government-monitored election at your hotel or resort.

The NLRA sets forth the laws regulating this traditional form of employee organization, which follows the critical path shown in Figure 30.1.[2] Under those rules, before any labor organization can be certified as the exclusive bargaining representative for any group of your employees, the employees in that group, called a bargaining unit, vote for or against union representation in a secret-ballot election monitored by the National Labor Relations Board (NLRB). In most cases, the NLRB seeks to schedule such an election approximately four weeks after the union initiates the process by filing a representation certification petition, also known as an "RC petition." The time period for election may be extended if you as the employer contest the bargaining unit or if other contested issues must be decided by the NLRB. Regardless, the period between RC petition and election provides the union and you as the employer with an opportunity to present your respective positions to the employees eligible to vote.

Under the NLRB rules, a union needs a minimum of 30 percent of your eligible employees to have signed authorization cards before an RC petition may be filed and a secret ballot election scheduled. As a practical matter, however, most unions will not file an RC petition unless at least 60 percent of the employees have signed cards. To prevail in the election, the union needs a simple majority of those who actually vote, not a majority of those eligible. Thus, if 50 of your employees are in the proposed bargaining unit, but only 21 vote, the union needs only 11 votes to win. The employer wins in the event of a tie.

Both sides are free to campaign prior to the election, and most of the time they do so with vigor. The period between the time the RC petition is filed and the election is held is often referred to as the "campaign period" or

Figure 30.1
Election Timeline

"critical period." During this time, the law prohibits employers from using certain tactics. During the "critical period" you may not threaten, interrogate, make promises to, or engage in surveillance of any of your employees. In addition, you may not solicit grievances from or confer benefits on your employees. If an employer violates these rules, the NLRB may either order the election to be rerun or issue a bargaining order (meaning the union is in even if you won the election). You may, however, attempt to persuade your employees to vote against the union, typically by informing employees of their rights and the consequences of voting for or against the union. Most employers engage in a multiweek campaign where they communicate with employees using e-mails, letters, speeches, videos, group meetings, campaign materials, and one-on-one conversations. In most campaigns, each week has a theme. For example, during the first week, you might explain that union promises of increased pay or benefits are not trustworthy because the company—not the union—pays for wages and other benefits. In this way, you illustrate that the union cannot guarantee anything that it claims it will do. During the second week, you might educate the employees about strikes and emphasize that employees who are on strike receive no pay and no health insurance, and that they may not get their jobs back when the strike ends. In the third week, you may discuss the issue of union dues and how the money is spent. During the final week, employers often explain that the union's claim of enhanced job security is a myth because unions cannot prevent or have any effect on economic layoffs, and further that employers can still terminate employees who violate company polices or rules. In addition, throughout the campaign, you may focus on the union's reputation and other issues specific to the parties and the local area.

Figure 30.2
Staying Lawful During the Critical Period

According to management-side labor lawyers, you should carefully diagnose the reasons your employees may be interested in unionization, and then address the root of the problem in your campaign. According to Arch Stokes, a labor lawyer based in Atlanta, Georgia, "the number one reason for unionization is a perceived lack of leadership. If you want to remain non-union, make sure your managers and supervisor are real leaders of men and women. It's more important than wages and benefits." Well-planned and carefully implemented antiunion campaigns culminating in secret-ballot elections have led to employers succeeding in defeating unions in the majority of elections.

Not surprisingly, many unions are skeptical of the traditional secret-ballot election. Union advocates claim that employers win secret-ballot elections because employers illegally threaten, intimidate, and terminate employees who favor the union. Unions point to the numerous unfair labor practice charges filed against employers as well as anecdotal evidence of unlawful employer behavior.

Card Checks and Neutrality Agreements

Regardless of the reason unions lose more elections than they win, one thing is clear: Many unions including UNITE HERE (the union representing the largest number of hotel employees) no longer wish to organize under the traditional NLRB election rules. In fact, as one organizer stated: "[W]e will never go to an NLRB election again."[3] Instead UNITE HERE's strategy is to organize using card-check and neutrality agreements instead of NLRB-supervised elections. To accomplish this objective, unions need to have some leverage over employers to pressure them into signing card-check and neutrality agreements.

Although neutrality agreements come in several forms, the common denominator for all of them is that employers agree to stay neutral with regard to the union's attempt to organize the workforce in exchange for the union promising labor peace.[4] Some agreements simply state that the employer will remain neutral with no other language, while other agreements contain more specific provisions.[5] For example, UNITE HERE's standard agreements clearly state that employers "will not communicate opposition" to the union's efforts.

Neutrality agreements commonly provide the union with access to employees in the form of a list of their names and addresses (and sometimes telephone numbers), as well as permission to come onto company property during work hours for the purpose of collecting signed authorization cards. This provision diverges from the guidelines set up by the NLRB and the courts, under which an employer has no obligation to provide the union with such sweeping access to its employees, and may actually be prohibited from doing so.

Finally, most neutrality agreements also include a *card-check* provision, which requires the employer to recognize the union if a majority of bargaining-unit employees sign authorization cards. Under a card-check agreement, the employees do not engage in a secret-ballot election. Instead, the employer recognizes the union if it presents the company with a majority of signed authorization cards. From an employer perspective, the obvious problem with card-check and neutrality agreements is that it takes away your ability to campaign against the union.

The Effect of Neutrality Agreements

Neutrality agreements have radically changed the landscape of union organizing. One study conducted in the late 1990s examined 170 private-sector "union campaigns" in which the employer and the union agreed to neutrality with a card-check provision. With the aid of such agreements, the union prevailed in 78.2 percent of those 170 campaigns.[6] In contrast, the unions' success rate in contested NLRB elections during the same time period was 46 percent. While the difference between these two numbers seems substantial, it actually understates the true value of the card-check and neutrality agreement to unions. Given the reality that no union will petition for an election unless they have well over 50 percent support of the prospective bargaining unit, one can infer that when a union loses a secret-ballot election, it initially enjoyed majority support and then lost the majority support by the time of the vote. Under a card check-neutrality agreement, the union would have won these organizing campaigns. Thus, almost every election where the employer won (54 percent) would have resulted in a union victory if there had been a card-check agreement.

What this means for you as an employer is that if you want to avoid becoming unionized, be sure not to sign a card-check or neutrality agreement. As set forth below, however, the decision is not that simple.

To Sign or Not to Sign? That Is the Question

So why would you ever accede to a card-check and neutrality agreement in the first place? The short answer is that you may sign one because it is in your best interests to do so—either to obtain an affirmative benefit, or more likely to protect your company from the union's corporate campaign against you. Observers who believe that unionization is never in the employer's best interest would likely be puzzled by this statement, but signing a neutrality agreement is, in fact, in the employer's best interest in some situations. One example occurs in some municipalities that have instituted labor peace agreements that required neutrality for employers that wish to obtain building permits or even to operate in the particular jurisdiction. As another example, a union may even buy a hotel and make a neutrality agreement a condition for any operator wishing to manage that property. Finally, an employer might sign a neutrality agreement because the union is selling something that the employer wishes to buy.

Perhaps the greatest bargaining chip that unions have to offer an employer in exchange for neutrality is labor peace. To sell peace, though, the union needs the ability to create unrest. At the turn of the century, UNITE HERE forged a strategy that allowed it to create unrest for the hotel industry to afford it the opportunity to peddle peace. The union employed this tactic with tangible results in summer 2006.

Union Summer 2006

Most of the unionized hotels in the major cities in the United States and Canada are part of citywide employers' associations that bargain as a multi-employer groups. The contracts that emerge from these negotiations are referred to as area or industry-wide agreements and cover all the hotel employers in the association. In addition, some properties who are not part of the mul-tiemployer group sign what are referred to as "me-too agreements," which bind the nonassociated by the area agreement. Traditionally, the contracts in the major cities expired in different years because the older hotel union, HERE, did not have the resources to negotiate on several fronts at the same time. Likewise, the hotel companies found it too cumbersome to juggle multiple negotiations for their properties in several cities simultaneously. Thus, both sides were agreeable to having the contracts for each market expire in different years.

For the series of negotiations prior to 2006, the merged union, UNITE HERE, changed its strategy. Specifically, it sought to have all the contracts in a number of large cities expire in the same year. UNITE HERE did not, of course, announce this strategy to employers. In spring 2000 the union and the New York employer's association extended to 2006 their contract, which had been set to expire in 2001. Then, in 2003, the union and the associations in Chicago and Boston signed three-year contracts. Next, by agreeing to short contracts, or no contracts at all, the union made sure that, in addition to New York, Boston, and Chicago, the contracts in Honolulu, Los Angeles, San Francisco, Detroit, and Toronto all expired in 2006.

Having these contracts expire in 2006 was not completely successful, nor was it without a significant amount of rancor. First, the employer association in Washington, D.C., refused to agree to a short contract. The Washington, D.C., contract, signed in 2004, expired in 2007. Similarly, the San Francisco contract expired in 2004 and the employers refused a two-year contract. The union called a strike, and the employers issued a lockout. Even after the work stoppages concluded, the union issued a boycott of certain unionized hotels. Consequently, there was no contract signed until summer 2006. Despite these disruptions, the union was able to align most of its major city contracts to end in 2006.

Having contract negotiations in several cities allowed the union to pursue its twenty-first-century strategy. Instead of focusing on the property or even the city level, UNITE HERE wanted to negotiate and apply pressure at the corporate level. That was the reason it wanted to negotiate in all the major cities at one time and to negotiate neutrality agreements. That is precisely what the union did in 2006.

Since neutrality agreements are merely permissive subjects of bargaining (as opposed to mandatory subjects), UNITE HERE could not insist that the hotels discuss this form of organizing. Instead, the union had to offer something to employers—namely, labor peace. Hotels were faced with a choice; buy peace in exchange for neutrality or go to war. To get hotels to purchase peace, the union had to make realistic its threats of labor unrest.

To embark on that approach, the union first needed to ensure that it had the financial resources and the member support to strike. The union had worked hard to achieve both of these goals. For example, in June 2004, the union's New York leadership proposed that members agree to payroll deductions of $10 per week to create a strike fund. The membership overwhelmingly agreed, and by the time the New York contract expired in 2006 the union had accumulated $26 million. The union also did a masterful job of getting its members to buy into the necessity of the cause. For example, speaking to the Hotel Trades Council's 2006 Contract Convention on June 10, 2004, union head Bruce Raynor told his audience: "You and your members are about to become members of the biggest and baddest union on the planet! . . . You fight one of us, you'll fight all 500,000 of us." John Wilhelm expressed similar sentiments when he told the council: "You don't permit the hotels to divide you by job, by hotel, by race, by age, or by any other factor, and you're not going to let them divide you by city. In fact, in 2006 you are going to divide and conquer them!"

From the time it began its plan to have numerous contracts expire during the same summer, UNITE HERE's strategy was clear: Begin corporate campaigns. Instead of negotiating against one employer association with numerous properties, UNITE HERE set up a system where it negotiated against one operator with hotels throughout the country. The union then set up an "us versus them" strategy. Smaller operators were encouraged to stay out of negotiations with the large operators and invited to sign "me-too" agreements. The November 1, 2005, issue of *Hotel Voice* contained the following quote: "The hotels that sign a "me-too" agreement are the good guys. The hotels that sign the Hotel Association's Mutual Assistance Pact are trying to pick a fight with the union and their employees."

Mutual assistant pacts would require properties to lock out employees if any of their sister properties went out on strike. Signing a mutual assistance agreement put a hotel in line to participate in a prospective war. A me-too agreement, however, meant an employer could stay on the sidelines of the potential war and simply benefit (or suffer) from the agreement negotiated by the association. Most operators decided to sign me-too agreements.

With many small operators on the sidelines, the union focused on major operators. The first major strategic decision was to attempt to split the chains. In this instance, the union exercised its right to exclude Hilton from the industry-wide bargaining agreement, based on accusations regarding Hilton's labor record. Peter Ward, president of the New York Hotel Trade Council, explained: "Our reasons for isolating Hilton are well known. We firmly believe that a separate contract with the Hilton Corporation is necessary because of its record in dealing in bad faith with the union and with its employees." Separating such a large operator from its cohorts caused unrest among the operators and forced Hilton to negotiate on its own. The employers' associations were forced to decide whether to wait to see what would come out of the Hilton negotiations or to try to cut a deal before UNITE HERE's Hilton negotiations got messy. Moreover, regardless of the employers' desires, the union had substantial control over the sequence of negotiations. In other words, the Union could focus on Hilton and ignore the association for a period of time. For example, in New York, the association and the union reached an agreement before Hilton did so, while in Chicago, the opposite occurred.

The Union Pits Owners against Operators

The union's divide and conquer strategy did not stop with operators. The union also used hotels' distinctive ownership structure (discussed in Chapter 17) to its advantage. Since operators rarely own the hotels they manage, the interests of the owner and the operator conflict in many situations. For example, an owner of a unionized hotel has no interest in fighting for the right of new (competing) hotels to be nonunion. Indeed, the unionized owner may want the new operator to agree to a neutrality agreement to level the playing field in the area of labor costs and work rules. Even owners with different goals might not form a united front, as short-term investor-owners would have a different perspective from long-term buy-and-hold owners. Owners soon hired their own counsel and bargained alongside, but not always consistent with their operator agents.

As operators separated from each other and owners separated from operators, the union remained united. By November 2006, the union could call or threaten to call strikes against one operator in all seven cities or even against several operators. The multiple-strike threat was viable because the union had employee support, a well-financed strike fund, and strong communication. The companies knew that the employees possessed the will to strike if a strike was called by the union leadership. A multicity strike was particularly daunting for employers because hotel operators could not bring in members of management from other cities to do strikers' work. More important, the companies knew that the me-too signatories would not support operators who were suffering from a strike. Instead, the me-too signatories would actually take the available hotel and convention business. To complete the "perfect storm" scenario, the hotel industry was in the midst of an upswing and was finally getting over the negative business effects of 9/11. Summer 2006 was, from a financial standpoint, the best summer for hotels since the watershed year of 2000. Simply put, the operators could not let labor unrest prevent the industry from enjoying what looked to be one of its most successful summers ever. With most if not all of its pieces in place, the union's real ability to wage war allowed it to sell peace.

The union did, in fact, sell peace. Except in San Francisco, which had endured the strike, lockout, and boycott of 2004, the summer 2006 negotiations resulted in no strikes, no lockouts, and no labor strife at all. Hilton, once referred to as evil, became the preferred hotel company for UNITE HERE. By the end of the year, New York, Chicago, Los Angeles, San Francisco, Honolulu, and Toronto all signed agreements. Soon after, agreements were reached in Boston and Detroit. The union declared victory; a conclusion with which operators, owners, and management lawyers seemed to agree.

What remains unclear today is what the union really gained in exchange for the peace with regard to neutrality. In New York, the issue of neutrality

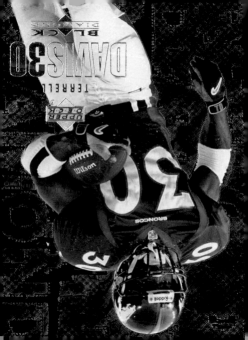

5 STARS

YR	TEAM	ATT	YDS	AVG	LG	TDS	REC	YDS	AVG	LG	TDS
95	BRONCOS	237	1117	4.7	60	7	49	367	7.5	31	1
96	BRONCOS	345	1538	4.5	71	13	36	310	8.6	23	2
97	BRONCOS	369	1750	4.7	59	15	42	287	6.8	25	0
98	BRONCOS	392	2008	5.1	63	21	25	217	8.7	35	2
99	BRONCOS	67	211	3.1	26	2	3	28	8.7	10	0
5-Year Totals		1410	8624	4.7	71	58	155	1207	7.8	35	5

AFC

Even though he missed 12 games with a knee injury last season, Davis has still put up one of the best five-year runs in NFL history, particularly to begin a career. He is set for a huge comeback campaign.

RB

TERRELL

DAVIS 30

BRONCOS

PRO FOOTBALL

NFL DIAMOND

34

was irrelevant because all new properties operated by any member of the association (including me-too signatories) were covered by an existing neutrality agreement. This was not the case in other cities, however, where the union obtained neutrality agreements for new hotels that would be owned or operated in the future by existing employers. While a few traditionally nonunion properties have unionized since 2006, UNITE HERE did not make significant organizing gains through its peace-for-neutrality strategy and thus, the unions are turning to the government for help through proposed legislation.

Labor Law Reform

Unions' organizing hopes revolve around the passage of the Employee Free Choice Act (EFCA). EFCA requires the NLRB to recognize a union if a majority of the employees signed authorization cards, increases the money owed to employees who were disciplined or discharged for trying to organize a union from straight back pay to triple back pay, imposes fines of up to $20,000 for certain unfair labor practices, and requires parties who cannot agree on a contract after 90 days of negotiations to submit their issues to "interest arbitration," a process whereby an arbitrator decides the terms and conditions of employment.

On March 2, 2007, the House of Representatives overwhelmingly passed EFCA. Because President Obama, a sponsor of the bill, was elected with a 60–40 Senate majority, many thought EFCA would pass in the first 100 days. The economic crisis, health care reform, and other legislative initiatives, however, derailed EFCA. Moreover, employers mobilized and argued that free choice and eliminating secret-ballot elections were inconsistent principles. Soon, some prominent Democrats were questioning the bill. After the 2010 mid-term elections, EFCA has left the national debate. However, even if it is not revived, labor reform appears possible.

While the National Labor Relations Act does provide for secret ballot elections, many other aspects of union organizing are the products of NLRB decisions and rulemaking. The NLRB is made up of five members appointed by the president for five-year terms. The general rule is that the party in power will hold a 3–2 majority. Now that the Obama board has a majority, there may be labor law reform without legislation. For example, the NLRB currently attempts to hold elections within approximately 30–40 days of the petition being filed. The NLRB could change this to 20, 10, or even 5 days. Elections occurring within such a short time period would fundamentally change organizing. Currently, employers do not have to allow unions on their properties. The NLRB could change this and require employers to provide access for unions. These are just two examples of what the NLRB could do to shift the balance of power in the labor-management relationships.

Whatever the source—legislative action or NLRB rule-making—labor law reform may be on the horizon. Accordingly, you should expect it to be easier for unions to organize your workforce in the coming years.

How to Address Union Issues for Nonunion and Union Hotels

Union issues are a fundamental component of the hospitality industry. Hotels that are union-free generally want to stay that way. Unionized hotels must learn to live and work with the union.[7]

Nonunionized Hotels Employers seeking to remain nonunion should follow a few simply principles. First, if the city has a strong union presence, you should ensure that you offer compensation and benefits similar to or better than that of the union hotels. Since most employers contend that it is union work rules and not compensation and benefits that makes unionization untenable, matching union wages and benefits should not be daunting. Second (and most important), you must have effective leadership and a positive employment culture. Concerns about leadership and fairness are what drive union organizing campaigns. If your employees believe your managers and supervisors do not act with integrity (see Chapter 31) and are not acting in the employees' best interest, they will go outside your hotel and seek a third party to represent them. However, if your employees believe in your leadership team and the employment culture they have created, your employees will see no need for collective power and no need to pay someone to speak on their behalf.

If you have signed a card check and neutrality agreement, your employment culture is even more vital to a remaining nonunion, for two reasons. First, you cannot actively campaign against the union because you have agreed to remain "neutral." Thus, you must let your strong leadership, employment culture, and integrity as an employer speak for itself. Second, the union might get a majority of eligible employees to sign cards before you even know the union is organizing, at which point you have to recognize the union before you can even react.

In sum, the best way to avoid unionization is to be proactive, not reactive. Anticipate your employees' needs and concerns. Fix problems before they fester. Remove and replace poor or mediocre managers with effective leaders. Union prevention is simply good leadership practiced 24 hours a day, 365 days a year. If you follow these principles and are faced with a union-organizing effort, you will be well-positioned to succeed in your campaign with the help of an experienced professional to guide you through the legal labyrinth.

Unionized Hotels Hotels that are already unionized face a different set of challenges. If your employees are represented by a union, you can choose to have either a cooperative or an adversarial relationship with your employees and their union. Our observation is that establishing a good working relationship with the union is essential to a successful union hotel. A union's business model encourages cooperation and good communication with its members' employer because conflict costs the union more time and money than harmony does. Thus, most union representatives assigned to your hotel (often called "business agents") will seek quick and efficient solutions to problems that could become grievances and ultimately arbitrations. You should encourage frequent communication with these representatives and creatively seek solutions to your disputes. That is not to say, however, that you should roll over every time the union makes a demand or opposes discipline against one of your employees. Essential to the operation of your unionized hotel is an experienced and tough HR professional who knows every detail of the collective bargaining agreement with the union and is prepared to enforce your contractual rights when necessary. That person also needs to be fair and open to creative solutions within the context of your contractual rights and obligations under the collective bargaining agreement. Ideologues who see the world as black and white rarely do well in this position. The most successful union hotels are those that resolve employee conflicts at the lowest possible level.

The cycle of collective bargaining with a union is an especially daunting aspect of a unionized hotel. Most collective bargaining agreements have a term of three years or more. As a collective bargaining agreement nears the end of its term, the union will invariably start to file grievances and make other demands in order to gain leverage at the bargaining table. In other words, the union will often create artificial conflict and then trade resolution of that conflict for some benefit during negotiations. Your managers need to be aware of this dynamic and be extra vigilant during these times to prevent problems before they arise (or before they are manufactured). A strong employment culture and good employee relations will discourage many of your employees from participating in this theatrical exercise.

Finally, collective bargaining itself is usually a long, difficult, and expensive process. Unions in the hotel industry are typically represented at the bargaining table by experienced labor negotiators who have immediate access to competent labor lawyers. Rarely will the union's proposals reflect only the interests of your employees, but will also reveal a regional or even national agenda. You might even be the target of picketing or a strike during negotiations, often as part of the union's larger strategy and not in response to anything you did. For all of these reasons, you should hire an experienced labor professional and carefully prepare for collective bargaining negotiations and all of the contingencies associated with them.

NOTES

1. *N.L.R.B. v. Town & Country Elec. Inc.,* 516 U.S. 85 (1995).
2. For the full text of the NLRA, see: www.nlrb.gov/nlrb/legal/manuals/rules/act.asp.
3. M. Hughlett, "Hotel Worker's Union in St. Paul, Minn., Plans New Tack in Organizing," *Hotel Online,* www.hotel-online.com/neo/news/2001_June_22/k.SPH.993243589.html, June 20, 2001 (quoting Jaye Rykunyk, head of H.E.R.E. Local 17).
4. For a discussion of neutrality agreements, see A. E. Eaton and J. Kriesky, "Union Organizing Under Neutrality and Card Check Agreements," 55 *Industrial and Labor Relations Review* 42(48): 8–9.
5. Ibid., p. 9.
6. Ibid., p. 15.
7. For example, see A. Eaton, T. Kochan, R. McKersie, and P. Adler, *Healing Together: The Labor-Management Partnership at Kaiser Permanente* (Ithaca, NY: Cornell University Press, 2009).

CHAPTER 31

THE INTEGRITY DIVIDEND IN HOSPITALITY LEADERSHIP

TONY SIMONS

Almost any leadership book will mention the need for leaders to walk their talk, and to deliver on their word.[1] These books mention integrity alongside many other tactics and strategies for effective leadership. And it is the same with books about sales. But I have found that integrity is far more than just a leadership skill. It is essential to an effectively functioning hotel.

I have spent the past 13 years as a business scholar tracking what I call the "integrity dividend." This dividend is an actual, bottom-line business return that occurs when people see that you live by your word. This dividend is far bigger than you might guess, and I demonstrate that fact in this chapter, using both numbers and comments from industry leaders.

One reason that I study the integrity dividend and share information about it is that in my many surveys and hundreds of executive interviews, I have come to the conclusion that leaders and salespeople of an impeccable word are, unfortunately, rare. Consequently, these people are prized— mostly due to their ability to bring in financial results. The other reason that I continue this research is that I have learned that the problem here is not one of moral deficiency—I am not making value judgments. Instead, this is a matter of skill and focus. As I explain in this chapter, people need to practice the skill of integrity, in part because many circumstances impede the required focus. Integrity is learnable, like many other skills. Managers, salespeople, teams, and whole companies can increase their individual and collective credibility, and support the integrity of their peers through their language and habits. When you strip away the moralizing from the issue of integrity, it becomes something one can study and learn to improve.

The key point in this chapter is to focus on being good to your word. This is an essential principle in any business relationship, including building and managing a brand. As discussed in Chapter 25, a brand is nothing more or less than a set of promises. The strength of your brand—and the value of your company—is built on your ability to keep those promises.

There is one other element in managing integrity as it is discussed here. Beyond aligning your words and actions, you must ensure that others are able to see this as being so. I know that you will gain payoffs in terms of personal satisfaction and self-esteem from living by your word. But the integrity dividend is most effective when you have a cadre of committed repeat clients and followers who consistently go the extra mile for you. To collect those aspects of the integrity dividend, you have to develop skills and habits of communicating openly and effectively.

THE INTEGRITY DIVIDEND DEMONSTRATED

Before I go any further, let's take a look at the financial implications of the integrity dividend. A few years ago, I conducted employee surveys for a firm that operated 76 Holiday Inn franchises in the U.S. As with most employee climate surveys, I asked how happy employees were with their pay, benefits, and supervision. But then I also asked questions like, "When your boss says something is going to happen, how sure are you that it is going to happen?" "How often does your boss keep promises?" and "How well does your boss conduct himself or herself by the same values he or she talks about?" The survey also asked about employees' trust in their bosses, their commitment to the company, the extent to which they saw their peers going the extra mile for service, and their intention to stay with the company. I received surveys from 6,800 employees, around 80 per hotel, or about two-thirds of the entire staff.

I averaged the employee scores for each hotel, and then lined up each hotel's score against the guest satisfaction scores for each hotel, its actual employee turnover, and its profitability. The results were overwhelming. Hotels with high integrity scores typically reported higher guest satisfaction, lower employee turnover, and higher profitability. So powerful was the overall impact on the bottom line that a difference between two hotels of a mere one-quarter point on a 10-point integrity scale translated into a profit difference of $250,000 per year (on gross revenues around $10 million). Extending that finding, this study suggests that a company that improves its average manager integrity score by a full point stands to improve its profit margins by 10 percent of gross revenues. Thus, developing the skills and practices of maximizing integrity is well worth the investment. Figure 31.1 shows the sequence of events that leads to the integrity dividend.

Figure 31.1
Integrity Dividend Model

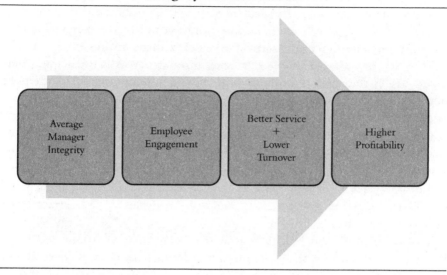

Although we can think of many times when people don't live up to their word, the fact is that most people who seek to build relationships and be solid leaders are reasonably good at living by their word. The hotel management company that hired me to run the surveys knew about the importance of integrity, and most of the managers scored reasonably well. The average hotel scored around 7 on the 10-point scale, and the lowest was just below 6. However, if we recall the financial benefit of a slight increase in this index, the upside potential for shifting from being "pretty good" at living by your word to being impeccable is huge.

How Leaders View Integrity

When I wrote my book on the integrity dividend, I found numerous executives who recognized the importance of integrity. Michael Kay, who was president and CEO of LSG SkyChefs, summed it up:

> It's all about results time. It ain't about feeling good. It ain't about being a nice place to come to work. It's that heightened levels of trust produce heightened levels of results. Because people feel better, work better, *are* better, in a trusting environment than in one where distrust saps their energy.

A key outcome of acting with integrity is trust. Trust entails a certain amount of vulnerability because if you trust a person, you are counting on that person to deliver, and you leave yourself open to disappointment (or worse).[2] If, as a leader, you are asking employees to try something new, to work harder, or to focus on particular values, you are really asking for their trust. This trust must be earned, in part, through integrity (matching word and deed). If your people are uncertain of the power of your word, they will never go that extra mile for you.[3]

Integrity is the beginning of trust, but you have to go beyond that, of course. You also need a certain benevolence, or genuine good intention toward your employees, and you need competence, or an ability to deliver.[4] You also need a sense that you share key values. But you can't even get to those other factors if your word cannot be relied upon. Behavioral integrity is necessary for trust to grow. And trust is necessary for extraordinary employee performance.

I interviewed Lloyd Hill, who was then chairman of Applebee's International, one of the world's largest casual-dining chains, with over 28,000 employees and 3,300 restaurants worldwide. He summarized the role of behavioral integrity in trust this way:

> Genuine leadership incorporates a number of attributes, but none of them works until there is trust. If as a leader—as a leader of a restaurant unit or the leader of a $4.5 billion chain like Applebee's—people can't trust my integrity, in the smallest sense, it creates problems. And I think that goes to an issue so small that if I say, "I'm going to call you at ten o'clock," and I am unprepared to call you at ten o'clock, or if I've had an accident and can't call you, I better have someone call you and say, "Lloyd cannot call you and he wants to reschedule." Or, I better call you at ten o'clock and say, "I don't have the information."
>
> Two or three of those missed appointments erode trust in an organization. Then, if I'm going to ask the organization to go somewhere that it might be frightened to go, if I'm going to ask an individual to step up and take on a job that he or she doesn't feel qualified to take, or I may be asking you to take a family risk, . . . you may see it as a career risk. And if you do not trust me, you will not do it. You just will not.

Here's another look at trust from another of the managers whom I interviewed, Paul Hortobagyi, who is the general manager at a Marriott resort in Santa Monica, California. Paul has consistently outperformed his competition, largely because of the service that he elicits from his employees. He does this in part through a deep well of trust between himself and his employees.

He knows every one of their names and their stories. He considers that his work is building and maintaining relationships. Here is how he says it:

> In my opinion, we are not in the hotel business. We are in the relationship business. A relationship with your front desk agent, a relationship with your bellmen, a relationship with the high roller who comes in and gives hundred-dollar tips to the bellmen, or the road warrior who comes in on a per diem. It doesn't really matter. It should never, ever change. You have to project the same style and the same relationship-building process with all those people. I don't know why, but it's going to come back to you twofold, threefold, a hundredfold. In so many different ways.

Communicating Integrity In addition to trust, the executives whom I interviewed cited the importance of clear communication. When people get confused about what you want from them, they will often feel surprised by your actions, and will often interpret this as hypocrisy or broken promises. Cleaning up communication—deliberately—builds trust.

As a leader, employees look to you for direction, and they interpret everything you do. They are looking for road signs regarding what's important and how things operate, but the road signs work only if you are credible. Frank Guidara, president and CEO of the Uno's Chicago Grill restaurants, explained:

> The laying out of consequences, good and bad, is fundamental to leadership. When, as a leader, you say you're going to do something and you don't do it, it's not going to destroy your leadership status, but each time there will be a little bit more erosion, and a little more, until finally you really can't lead any longer.

When a leader does not deliver a stated consequence—a raise, a promotion, a firing—his credibility drops. The next time he lays out a consequence, his followers consider it a possible consequence, but it is no longer definite. Without follow-through, any pronouncement becomes an empty promise or an empty threat.

Anyone who has raised children recognizes this as a key foundation of good parenting. Consultant Darryl Stickell, a principal for Trust Unlimited, recounted his parent-like experience from early in his career, when he worked for a drop-in center for troubled teens. As you might expect, the center had policies against the kids' bringing in weapons, fighting, intimidating others, drug use, and swearing. The credibility of those policies relied on enforcement, but staff members did not always enforce these policies. Instead of being appropriately firm, they wanted to be liked. Darryl, however, acted with integrity, and thus earned respect. The center was open from noon until 11:00 PM, and so there were two shifts.

> If I came in for the noon shift, as I came in, guys would drop off their weapons with me. If I came in for the late shift, when I came in, there'd be a lineup of guys who would drop off their weapons with me. I'd say, "You guys have been here for hours." They'd say, "Well, yeah. But you weren't here." Folks got so that they knew "if you show up stoned, he's not going to let you in." There was this incredible power to being overwhelmingly consistent, and never making a statement that I didn't intend to follow up on. So, if I would see someone doing something, I would say, "You know you're not allowed to do that. Stop it, or you'll have to leave." And they would stop.

To sum up, for a leader, being seen as living by your word builds follower engagement in two ways:

1. It builds trusting relationships, which means employees can bring the full measure of their passion to work for you.
2. It creates and supports clear direction, which means employees do not have to waste time trying to figure out what you want from them.

Both of those processes help a leader create a team that is dedicated, focused, and high performing. It is far more difficult to create such a team with less than impeccable credibility. Creating an excellent team is key to creating a high performance company. Having your people know you live by your word—especially when it is costly or difficult—is essential to building that team.

Communicating for Accountability

Let's look more closely at the importance of clear communication. As I indicated earlier, one factor that causes people to conclude that you have failed to keep your word is that they misunderstood what you said.[5] We've all had experiences with missed or incomplete communication. The following story captures the essence of failed communication.

> A friend of mine, Ralph, was coaching an ambitious young executive, Jim, who was facing a challenge at work. Jim needed the input

of a colleague (Mike) for a report that Jim had to generate every two weeks. Mike's problem was that, due to office politics, he did not want to seem to be in a deferential position toward Jim. So Mike delivered his numbers through a third party, in this case, a secretary. But this secretary worked part time, and couldn't always deliver the information from Mike to Jim in a timely fashion. As a result, Jim often lacked the input he needed.

Jim complained to Ralph: "I told my boss about the problem and I asked him to talk to Mike about it. Nothing happened—my boss obviously did not follow through; I cannot really trust him." Ralph asked Jim, "What exactly did you ask your boss to do?" "To talk to Mike," Jim answered. On investigation, Ralph discovered that this is exactly what the boss had done. He had gone to Mike and said, "Jim is upset about this." He had not asked Mike to use a different method for delivering the information because Jim hadn't requested that. Jim had failed to ask for exactly what he wanted. There are several lessons here, but the key point is to maintain clear communication.

Practical Tips for Clear Communication

- Avoid automatic or polite promises that can easily be misinterpreted. Consider your commitment carefully before you make a promise (or decline to make one).
- Realize that your subordinates assign great weight to your words, even when you don't.
- Communicate in a way that secures and gives clear and actionable commitments. To avoid fuzzy commitments you can apply the following three steps:
  1. Ask for a commitment, specifying the conditions of fulfillment and the due date.
  2. Wait for a response. Allow yeses and nos. Negotiate if necessary.
  3. Follow up after the fact to remind both parties of the commitment, whether it was fulfilled.

INTEGRITY AS A PERSONAL DISCIPLINE

We manage our integrity with every action and interaction. Bringing an integrity level of 7.5 or 8 up to an impeccable 9.5 or 10 will be difficult because it takes a sustained effort. To that end, here are some key elements of a personal discipline of integrity that emerged from my conversations with executives:

- *Detecting habits of social deceit.* It takes more skill to speak the truth tactfully than to automatically tell people what they want to hear.
- *Delaying gratification.* Be willing to take an occasional short-term hit.
- *Facing fear with courage.* Accept the risk of admitting to an error or to try out new ways of talking to people.
- *Looking within.* You must recognize and anticipate the ambivalences that can drive you to fail in follow-through.
- *Arranging social support.* Create a circle of peers to share the journey.
- *Engaging in a deliberate process when giving your word.* Every promise puts your credibility on the line.
- *Keeping track and following up.*
- *Apologizing and recovering.* Errors are inevitable.

Let's expand on each of those points. It's often easy to tell people what they want to hear. I caught myself once telling my then five-year-old son how important it was to say he loved Grandma's presents—even when 'he didn't really appreciate the clothing and would have greatly preferred toys. Most of us have learned such social niceties, often called "white lies" or "habits of social deceit." They help us get through the complexities of social life, but they can also stand in our way. I'm not saying that you must answer every question with the unvarnished truth, without regard to the emotional context, because that can be cruel. Instead, be aware of what you are saying when you do speak. Then, speak truth, however diplomatically you couch it.

The skill of delaying gratification allows you time to consider your options, without cutting corners. The payoffs to integrity are often in the long time frame of relationships and reputations. To consistently earn the integrity dividend, it is necessary to practice taking the longer view and the larger long-term gain over the immediate one. A Stanford study discussed by Joachim de Posada connects the ability to delay gratification with career success. In his book, *Don't Eat the Marshmallow Yet,*[6] de Posada explains that children in the study were seated individually at a table with a single marshmallow. They were told that if they waited 15 minutes and did not eat the marshmallow, they would be given a second marshmallow and they could then eat both. Ten years later, the researchers found that the children who resisted temptation were significantly more successful in their school and their careers.

Fear often holds people back from telling more truth in their daily lives. That includes not only the fear of how people would react if they found out what we really think, but also the fear of being predictable—as you will be if your word is truly your bond. Aneil Mishra, a scholar and consultant who focuses on trust issues, argues: "You have to be both very humble and very courageous if you're going to be a high integrity person. It takes humility to recognize your faults, the things you do not know. And it takes courage to admit them to others."[7]

Many people fail to keep their word because of their internal ambivalences. If you voice a commitment, but you are really half-hearted about it, your ambivalence will make it hard for you to follow through consistently. You must know yourself and your own mind to act with integrity and credibility.

The last four elements on the list fall more into the realm of concrete skills and habits rather than the deeper internal pursuits suggested by the first four. Social support comes in the form of people who care but do not control your career, and to whom you can speak your truth without fear of repercussions. Create a circle of peers with whom you can meet or conference call every two weeks. Practice a deliberate process for giving your word, so that you *never* do so automatically. Before you give your word, reflect soberly about (1) whether you want to commit, given your other commitments, and (2) whether you can realistically guarantee delivery. If you cannot guarantee delivery on the promise, then think carefully about what you *can* guarantee. When you do commit, realize that the people to whom you voice commitments will tend to hear what they want to hear. Make sure the other person understands your commitment the same way you do. Develop a system for immediately recording and keeping track of all your promises, and keep your commitments recorded in one place. Finally, do not be afraid to apologize when you break a promise. Do it cleanly and without self-abuse. Don't bother with excuses—they do not matter much, anyway. Then make a new promise, and make sure you deliver on it promptly.

Here is one more thing. Most of us are much more careful to keep the promises that we make to others than those we make to ourselves. Our personal conviction of the strength of our own word is important. A colleague of mine once explained that in order to do his job as a trainer he needed to exercise hard at least three times a week. He said he hated to exercise, but he did it, anyway. He said, "Do you know why I do it? Because I said so." His word was his bond *to himself*. Because of that fact, he was an extraordinarily powerful person.

Practical Tips for Building Integrity

- *Develop a single sentence* that sums up your key values and purpose as a leader. Think it through carefully. The phrase should resonate deeply in your heart and may remind you of your life mission beyond the workplace. Improve or modify the sentence as new ideas and insights come to you.

- For several weeks, *contemplate the sentence* for a full minute before every scheduled meeting, every phone call, every substantive e-mail, and every significant task you engage as a leader. Ask yourself how the action you are about to take relates to the values and purpose you describe. Strive to make this reflection an automatic, ongoing habit.
- *At the end of each day,* ask yourself what you have done to enact the values you claim to hold dear. Don't beat yourself up about shortfalls, but strive to be able to say you have done everything you could to support your claimed values. Conduct inventory every day until it becomes second nature.
- *Deal with your backlog* of agreements. Make a single list, in one place, of your outstanding commitments or promises: at work, to friends, to family, to yourself. Put it in a form that you can easily carry around. You might even have to ask people what they are owed. Assign a due date to each agreement.
- *Review your whole list,* daunting though it may be. Think about each item realistically and soberly, and consider whether you can keep the commitment in light of your overall load. Mark each item into one of four categories:
  1. Committed: I will do this, on time.
  2. Renegotiate: Consult whoever I made the promise to—to yield a promise I can commit to, or to release me from the promise.
  3. Ambivalent: I am choosing to remain unclear.
  4. Ignore: Notice that ignoring a promise does not make it go away, and often generates ill will among the people you made the promise to.
- *Revisit the list* often, with the intention of moving every item into the "committed" category or renegotiating in good faith to get released from it. Your goal is to have all the commitments fulfilled or on track to get fulfilled. Clear out the pipeline. Feel the growing power of keeping your word.

My book, *The Integrity Dividend*,[8] goes into much greater depth and includes an extensive series of exercises and a couple of surveys you can use to gather feedback on the impeccability of your promise keeping. Consider it an investment in a more profitable way of doing business, and enjoy the related personal benefits as well.

CONCLUSION

Credibility is the coin of the realm. In leadership or sales, or simply in building a brand—others' view of the strength of your word determines their willingness to follow or to buy or to bond. Few of us intentionally fail to keep our word, but what I suggest here is that your word is your most potent tool—and keeping it powerful needs to be one of the first things you consider. My research supports the suggestion of those leadership books that tell you to "walk your talk" and keep your promises. Those behaviors are fundamental and necessary for effective leadership. It is not always easy to live by your word, and it is more difficult still to communicate clearly enough that others recognize that you live by your word. But it pays off, in the integrity dividend. It pays off for your own success, and it pays off for your company's success.

NOTES

1. For example, see J. Kouzes and B. Posner, *The Leadership Challenge* (Hoboken, NJ: Jossey-Bass, 2008); or J. Collins, *Good to Great: Why Some Companies Make the Leap . . . and Others Don't* (New York: Harper Business, 2001).
2. R. Mayer, J. Davis, and J. Schoorman, "An Integrative Model of Organizational Trust," *Academy of Management Review* 20 (1995): 709–734.
3. T. Simons, "Behavioral Integrity as a Critical Ingredient for Transformational Leadership," *Journal of Organizational Change Management* 12(2) (1999): 89–104.
4. Mayer, Davis, and Schoorman, 1995.
5. R. Lewicki, D. Saunders, and B. Barry, *Essentials of Negotiation*, 5th ed. (New York: McGraw-Hill, 2011).
6. J. Posada and E. Singer, *Don't Eat the Marshmallow Yet: The Secret to Sweet Success in Work and Life* (New York: Berkeley, 2005).
7. A. Mishra and M. Karen, *Trust Is Everything: Become the Leader Others Will Follow* (Lulu [lulu.com], 2009).
8. T. Simons, *The Integrity Dividend: Leading by the Power of Your Word* (Hoboken, NJ: Jossey-Bass, 2008).

FINAL THOUGHTS

CHAPTER 32

AFTERWORD
WHERE DO YOU GO FROM HERE?

MICHAEL C. STURMAN, JACK B. CORGEL, and ROHIT VERMA

"PLEASE SEND ME THE BOOK ON HOW TO SUCCEED IN THE HOSPITALITY INDUSTRY"

From time to time, someone at Cornell's School of Hotel Administration has received a phone call to the effect of, "Hi. I've just bought a hotel. Could you please send me the book on how I should run it?" Unfortunately, there is no simple book to tell you exactly *how* to run a hotel. Even after reading this book, you now have only a broad overview of the intricacies of hotel operations. With this book, though, you can see the Four Paths to Success that you can follow in the hospitality industry. With this overview, you can investigate further the many issues you need to consider in order to be successful in the hospitality industry.

Having read this book, you can see that we did not write for people like Bill Marriott Jr., E. M. Statler, Herb Kelleher, Horst Schultze, Isadore Sharp, or other such legends of the industry. Our picture of you, the reader, is that you may be experienced in the industry and looking to learn something new, or maybe you were just checking up to see what the Cornell Hotel School is up to these days. Even if you're far advanced in this industry, the breadth of this book should make it valuable to you. Perhaps the book helped refresh your perspective on issues you have not thought about for a while. Or it may have helped you recall components of the industry that indirectly affect you but, because of the way they affect your work, you haven't given the topic serious in-depth thought in a while. Or you may be an advocate of continuous learning and you read the book simply to see what various experts in the field have to say.

We also considered people who are not yet in the hospitality industry. If you are considering entering the hotel industry, or perhaps you suddenly found yourself in this industry for whatever reason, we hope this book was useful to you. You may be switching industries to find a more fulfilling career (or simply to find a job at all), you may have worked your way up in an organization and are now managing a property, you may have found a deal too good to pass up and acquired a property, or you may have moved suddenly from the property level to the corporate level and are facing a new world of decision-making issues.

Regardless of your background, experience, investments, and goals, you still may have many questions. Novices and experts alike are faced with similar issues when they seek to make a decision. Do you want to buy a property? If so, how will you finance it? If you own it, will you run it or hire a management company? Will you be an independent property or part of a chain? What will be your strategy? How will you attract the right customers? How will you deliver the desired service product? How will you set the right price? How will you get the right employees? How will you get these employees to behave the right way? How will you develop yourself as you go through this entire process? And what on earth are you going to do to make money with that restaurant?

If you are new to the industry, it may be overwhelming to figure out where to begin. We hope that the sequence of chapters and sections provides a sort of progression. As noted above, we can't tell you *how* to do your job. How you make your decisions will be forged through a combination of experience, analytical skills, and person skills that you will need to combine to make the decisions that need to be made.

If you are a veteran of the industry, you are still faced with many of these questions, but bring to bear an arsenal of experiences and applicable human capital that help you make your choices. Nonetheless, we know from decision-making research that we can often over-rely on the experience and information that is easiest to acquire. The broad perspective of this book should have helped remind you of the types of issues, information, research, and other resources that exist to help you continuously improve within the industry.

WHERE DO YOU GO FROM HERE?

Now that you've read this book, you are better equipped to enter and advance in the hospitality business, but your education should not stop here. There are two reasons you need to continue reading and learning. First, this book provides considerable introductory and intermediate-level material to help you become successful. But success in the hospitality business comes as a result of the most advanced thinking to gain an edge on competitors. Second, growth industries such as the hospitality industry are characterized by rapid technological and environmental changes. Business professionals in the industry must remain current about new theories and practice to ensure continued success.

The Cornell School of Hotel Administration presents a number of avenues for you to continue your hospitality education. Our *Office of Executive Education* offers a variety of programs to keep hospitality professionals abreast of the ever-changing needs and trends of the industry. This includes offerings like short, focused courses (Professional Development Program); a 10-day program focused on strategic property-level issues (General Managers Program); other formal multi-day programs; online learning; and custom programs. The Hotel School provides a wealth of material—including our journal, the *Cornell Hospitality Quarterly*. We also produce research reports, tools, industry perspective white papers, and roundtable programs—through our Center for Hospitality Research, Center for Real Estate Finance, and the Leland C. and Mary M. Pillsbury Institute for Hospitality Entrepreneurship. Most of our reports are available at no charge.

In the past, when we've gotten that strange call looking for *the* book on how to run a hotel, we are often at a sad loss of what to suggest. We may have told such callers to consider heading back to school, hiring a consulting firm, hiring the right kind of people to assist in the situation, or referring them to any number of the resources that the Cornell University School of Hotel Administration offers to further knowledge in the field. But any of those approaches is unsatisfactory, as you still need a foundation to understand what questions you need to ask, and what type of information you need to gather before you figure out *how* to deal with your problem. It is our hope, now, that this book serves as this foundation.

It should be clear from all the chapters in this book that the hospitality industry provides wondrously rich personal, professional, and financial opportunities. The authors of this book share a passion for this industry, for the type of product it provides, and for the role it serves in our society and economy. If you are a veteran of the industry, we hope this book provided you with new insights that broaden your perspective and let you see new opportunities. If you are new to the industry, we hope this book can serve as a resource for understanding the many opportunities our industry has to offer. As a veteran in the industry, we appreciate your continuing efforts. We hope you enjoy your stay.

Table 32.1

Resources to Continue Your Learning from the Cornell School of Hotel Administration

Office of Executive Education

Professional Development Program: www.hotelschool.cornell.edu/industry/executive/pdp/index.html

General Managers Program: www.hotelschool.cornell.edu/industry/executive/gmp/index.html

Online learning: www.hotelschool.cornell.edu/industry/executive/online/index.html

Custom programs: www.hotelschool.cornell.edu/industry/executive/custom/index.html

Resource through the Center for Hospitality Research (www.hotelschool.cornell.edu/research/chr/)

Cornell Hospitality Quarterly: www.hotelschool.cornell.edu/research/chr/pubs/quarterly/

CHR Reports: www.hotelschool.cornell.edu/research/chr/pubs/reports/

CHR Tools: www.hotelschool.cornell.edu/research/chr/pubs/tools/

Industry perspective white papers: www.hotelschool.cornell.edu/research/chr/pubs/perspective/

CHR Roundtables: www.hotelschool.cornell.edu/research/chr/pubs/roundtableproceedings/

Center for Real Estate Finance (www.hotelschool.cornell.edu/industry/centers/cref/)

Leland C. and Mary M. Pillsbury Institute for Hospitality Entrepreneurship (www.hotelschool.cornell.edu/industry/centers/pihe/)

INDEX

Accor, 269, 293
 Etap Hotel, 217–218
 Motel 6, 217–218
Adare Manor Hotel & Golf Resort, 210–211
ADRs (average daily rates):
brand affiliation impacting, 391
 demand management use of, 176, 177–178
 development consideration of, 312
 rate differential, 441
 revenue management use of, 195, 202–203,
  405–406, 415
Affiliation, brand, 259–260, 261, 389–393, 394
Age Discrimination in Employment Act
  (ADEA/1967), 417, 418, 419
Agency, 301
American Airlines, 192, 363
American Express, 75, 185
American Hotel and Lodging Association,
  247, 289
Americans with Disabilities Act (ADA/1992),
  417–418, 419, 424–425
Anticipation, building guests', 104–109
Appearance, personal, 114
Applebee's International, 472
Apple's iPhone, 380
Appraisals, 276
ARAMARK, 446, 452
Assets, on balance sheet, 236–240
Atchison, Shane, 143
Avero, 181, 190
Awareness:
 guests', increasing, 97–98, 98–104
 self-awareness, 40–41, 67–69, 78–79

Balance sheets, 236–240
Behavioral integrity. See Integrity
Beliefs, corporate culture conveying,
  112–113
Benefits, employee. See Compensation
Berry, Leonard L., 18
Best Western, 260
Bing, 198, 374, 409
Blau, Elizabeth, 15

Bonuses:
 employee motivation influenced by, 147–148
 financial responsibility leading to, 433
 human capital incentives using, 452–453
 recruitment offering, 449
Booking.com, 408
Boulders, The, 121
Boulud, Daniel, 7
Brand:
 brand-affiliation, 259–260, 261, 389–393, 394
 brand elements, 399–400
 brand promise, 393, 396–397, 400–402, 470
 brand strategy, 388–403
 brand touch points, 399, 402
 building independent, 393–402
 competitive brand position assessments,
  398–399
 customer analysis for, 395–396
 defined, 389
 development brand evaluation, 312–313
 differentiation strategy by, 215–217,
  354, 362
 discrete choice modeling assessment of brand
  equity, 95–96
 loyalty/frequent buyer programs, 354,
  363–366, 408
 Process Framework for Strategic Branding,
  393–402
 testing and monitoring, 402–403
 value proposition of, 396–397
Brinker, Norman, 150
Brokers, 290
Bruno, Marc, 16
Budgets, flexible, 436–442
Buffalo Wild Wings, 295
Bundling rates, 410–411, 414
Burger King, 10, 218, 296
Burlington Industries v. Ellerth, 428
Busch Gardens, 105
Buser, Arthur L., 9, 13
Business strategy:
 best value/blue ocean strategy,
  221–222

Business strategy *(continued)*
brand strategy, 388–403
business situation analysis influencing, 208, 212–215
competitive, selection of, 215–222
corporate culture influencing, 121–124, 217
defined, 208
demand management, 190–191
development of, 208–209
differentiation strategy, 215–217, 354, 362
direction setting in, 209–211
economic downturn planning, 412–415
key resources for, 214, 222–224
low-cost leadership strategy, 215–216, 217–221
mission statements conveying, 210–211
motivation-related, 156–157
revelation of, to competition, 408
successful competition using, 207–224

Cafe 50's, 102
Call centers, guest relations, 169
Candlewood Suites, 216
Capacity utilization, 218–219
Capital. *See also* Lenders
for development, 309, 314–315, 315–318, 319
human *(see* Human capital)
for ownership, 256, 263, 264–266, 301–302
Capitalization, 276–286
Career preparation:
building on current skills, 23–24
career opportunities, 21–22
developing unique human capital/career management, 24–27
leadership development, 27–32
multinational, 22, 52–63
steps to take, 32–34
Carlson Companies, 297
Carlson Wagonlit Travel, 185
Carnival Corporation, 354
Carnival Cruise Lines, 399–400, 402
Cellular telephones. *See* Mobile devices
Censoprano, Mark, 106
Chains, corporate:
10 largest hotel companies, 391
brand affiliation with, 259–260, 261, 389–393, 394
chain scale and affiliation classification, 259–260, 261
franchises, 261, 263, 264, 266–267, 268, 293–299, 312, 319, 393
management contracts with, 302, 303

number of, 25
ownership of, 255, 261, 263, 264, 266–267, 268
regional and local demand management in, 189–190
revenue management in, 203–204
Charpentier, Abigail, 7, 11
Chen, Stacy, 8
Chic & Basic, 213–215, 217, 221–222
Chili's, 150
China:
hospitality industry in, 22
ownership in, 255
Cho, Yang Ho, 13
Choice Hotels, 255, 296, 354
Churchill, Winston, 18
Civil Rights Act (1866), 418
Civil Rights Act (1964), 417, 418–419, 425
Civil Rights Act (1991), 417, 423
Clients. *See* Guests
Colleagues:
learning-oriented relationships with, 26
listening to, 37–50
networking among, 53–54
teamwork among, 39, 77–78, 79, 147–149, 151–152
Colliers-PKF Hospitality Research, 289, 290
Communication:
clarity of, 41, 44–45, 50, 473–475
of corporate culture, 114–117, 447
guest feedback as, 161–172
integrity-focused, 473–475
international/multinational, 54–56
interpersonal, 29, 32, 37–50, 67–68, 125
listening and, 37–50
nonverbal, 46–47, 54–55
questions as, 45, 59–60, 83–87, 204–205
Comparative sales valuation, 276, 286–288
Compensation:
bonuses as, 147–148, 433, 449, 452–453
career management consideration of, 26–27
contingent rewards/punishment *vs.*, 76–77
employee benefits as, 235
employee motivation using, 144–149, 452–453
equity of, 146–147
financial responsibility impacting, 433
human capital incentives using, 452–453
labor costs related to, 234
nonfinancial rewards and, 75–77, 79, 149–154, 453

performance-based, 147–149

Competition:
business strategy as competitive advantage, 212–214, 215–222, 222–224
competitive brand position assessments, 398–399
competitive business strategy, selection of, 215–222
corporate culture as competitive advantage, 121–122
demand management impacted by, 176–178, 181–184
development analysis of, 312
direct vs. indirect, 242
financial comparison to, 242–243
key resources as competitive advantage, 222–224
market segmentation among (see Market segmentation)
price wars with, 406–412
revelation of business strategy to, 408
revenue performance measurement against, 202

Complaint management:
service quality assurance and, 165–168
transaction- vs. relationship-focused approach to, 161–165

Conine, Charles A., 123–124, 154–155

Continental Airlines, 198

Cornell University School of Hotel Administration:
continuing education through, 485–486
Cornell Icon of the Industry Awards, 30–31
founding and mission of, 1, 4
organizational structure/key processes of, 70–71
Statler Hotel operated by, 85–87
Taverna Banfi operated by, 163–164, 165

Corporate culture. See Culture, corporate

Corporate social responsibility, 152–154

Corporations, ownership via, 253, 254–255

Costa Rica tourism, 401

Costs:
budgets including, 436–442
capacity utilization and, 218–219
controllable, 234
cost centers, 433–434, 435–436
cost models, building, 438–440
direct operating, 235–236
economies of scale and, 219–220
franchise, 297–299, 393
labor, 234
lawsuit-related, 418, 419, 424
learning curve impacting, 220

low-cost leadership strategy, 215–216, 217–221
occupation/lease/rental, 235, 241, 285, 305–307
outsourcing impacting, 221
recipe management impacting, 233
sales-related, 230–233
supply chain management impacting, 230–232
technological advances impacting, 220
valuation consideration of replacement, 275, 276, 288–289

Courtyard, 87, 221, 359, 396

Crowne Plaza, 216

Crystal Cruises, 354

Cultural differences:
corporate culture impacted by, 120
listening and, 39, 46
multinational careers impacted by, 53, 54–56, 58–59

Culture, corporate:
beliefs, values and norms conveyed via, 112–114
business strategy based on, 121–124, 217
communicating, 114–117, 447
defined, 111–114
discrimination avoidance as part of, 429
employee commitment to, 121–124
employee motivation influenced by, 144, 150, 152, 153–154
harnessing power of, 120
human capital-focused, 447
language expressing, 115
leadership role in, 112, 119, 120, 122–125
listening environment in, 39–40
national culture impacting, 120
new media communication of, 447
policies and procedures conveying, 114–115
rituals signifying, 117
service enhanced through, 111–125
stories, legends and heroes of, 115–116
subcultures, 119, 125
symbols of, 116
teaching the values of, 117–120
union membership influenced by, 466–467

Customers. See Guests

Darden Restaurants, 71–72, 75, 255

Data:
financial, 227–243 (see also Financial performance)
measurement of (see Measurement systems)
modeling (see Models)

Data *(continued)*
  operational uses of, 127–130, 134–136,
    138–139
  quality assurance, 161–165, 168–172
Decision-making authority, 122, 155–156,
    430–431, 446
Demand management:
  competition impacting, 176–178, 181–184
  constrained *vs.* unconstrained demand, 133
  electronic demand, rise of, 184–187, 189–190
  historical view of, 182–184
  market segmentation and, 178–181,
    187–189
  overview of, 174–175
  pricing and, 176–181, 187–189, 197, 218–219
  regional and local functions, 189–190
  seasonal demand, 136, 320
  strategies/tactics for, 190–191
  uniqueness of hospitality industry demand,
    175–181
Deming, W. Edwards, 160
Depreciation, 235
Design, hotel. *See* Programming and planning,
    hotel
Detroit Plaza Hotel, 154–155
Development, property:
  capital/financing for, 309, 314–315,
    315–318, 319
  construction phase of, 318–319
  development team formation, 309–310
  feasibility study for, 313–314
  investment decision for, 315–318
  process of, 310–320
  profit from, 314
  program considered during, 315
  programming and planning considered during,
    315, 321–332
  property opening, 320
Differentiation strategy, 215–217, 354, 362
Direct operating costs, 235–236
Discounted cash flow model/discount rate,
    277–281, 336–345
Discrete choice analysis (DCA):
  articles about, 88–89
  choice criteria identification in, 89–90
  choice experiment development in, 90–92
  guest decisionmaking analyzed through, 87–96
  managerial insights from, 93–96
  response collection and choice model estimates
    in, 93
Discrimination, employee, 417–418,
    421–425, 429
Disney, Walt, 112, 150

Disney World. *See* Walt Disney World Resort
Distractions, listening impacted by, 43
Duration, 336–337, 339–345, 346–350

EasyRMS, 190
Economic order quantity (EOQ), 237–240
Economies of scale, 219–220
Economy:
  competition impacted by, 212, 213
  demand impacted by, 176, 177–178, 185
  financial performance evaluation impacted
    by, 436–437
  inflation in, 338, 340, 345
  labor needs impacted by, 21–22
  operator/management contracts and, 302,
    304, 305
  revenue management impacted by, 198, 200,
    202–203, 205, 405–415, 436
  risk influenced by, 333, 334, 338, 339
  strategic plan for economic downturns,
    412–415
Education. *See* Training and education
EEOC (Equal Employment Opportunity
    Commission), 419, 420–421
E-mail marketing, 198, 410
Emotional intelligence, 67–68. *See also*
    Interpersonal skills
Emotions:
  complaint expression using, 166–167
  listening impacted by, 43
  pleasure sources for, 99–101
  positive reinforcement of, 75–77, 79, 145–146
  recognition programs fostering positive, 150
Employee Free Choice Act (EFCA), 465
Employee lawsuits:
  adjudication in, 419–424
  Americans with Disabilities Act (ADA/1992)
    and, 417–418, 419, 424–425
  damages awarded in, 418, 424
  discrimination as basis of, 417–418,
    421–425, 429
  laws governing, 417–419, 424–425
  sexual harassment as basis of, 418, 425–429
Employees/staff:
  appearance of, 114
  careers preparation for, 21–34, 52–63
  colleagues among (*see* Colleagues)
  compensation/reward of (*see* Compensation)
  corporate culture of (*see* Culture, corporate)
  cultural differences among, 39, 46, 53, 54–56,
    58–59, 120
  development leading to hiring, 320
  discrimination against, 417–418, 421–425, 429

empowering, 122, 155–156, 446
families of, 56
flexible job design for, 448, 453
hospitality of, 5, 6–9, 13–18
labor costs of, 234 (*see also* Compensation)
lawsuits by, 417–429
leadership for (*see* Leadership; Management)
learning curve for, 220
mentors of, 26
motivating, 142–157, 452–453
outsourcing work of, 221
performance evaluations of (*see* Performance
    evaluations)
professional associations for, 26
quality assurance programs for, 159–172
recruitment and hiring procedures, 449–450
respect for, 151
scheduling, 136–138, 234
service provided by (*see* Service)
sexual harassment of, 418, 425–429
skills of (*see* Human capital; Skills)
social media posting by, 378
stock options for, 149
teamwork among, 39, 77–78, 79, 147–149,
    151–152
training and education for, 23, 26, 117–119,
    125, 220, 429, 450–451
unions of, 155, 455–468
Ensign, Rick, 61–62
EOQ (economic order quantity), 237–240
Equal Employment Opportunity Commission
    (EEOC), 419, 420–421
Estis Green, Cindy, 375
Etap Hotel, 217–218
Evans, Chick, 15
Evans, Ed, 17
Executives. *See* Management
Exit strategy, 273–274
Expedia, 183, 184–185, 198, 372, 377
Extrinsic rewards. *See* Compensation

Facebook, 375, 378, 385
Fairmont Hotels, 150
Families, careers impacting, 56
Faragher v. Boca Raton, 428
Farmer, Tom, 143
Fatigue, listening impacted by, 43
Feasibility studies, 313–314
Feedback:
    call centers receiving, 169
    complaints as, 161–168
    direct or indirect staff communication as,
        168–169

measurement systems for, 168–172
mystery shopping programs providing, 171–172
satisfaction surveys recording, 169–170
Finances. *See* Compensation; Costs; Financial
    performance; Income; Investment decisions;
    Lenders; Pricing/prices; Profit; Revenue
    management; Valuation
Financial performance:
    financial statements summarizing, 227–243,
        274, 311–312, 440–442
    integrity dividend impacting, 470–471
    measurement of, 201–206, 431–433, 436–442
    responsibility of management for, 430–436
Financial rewards. *See* Compensation
Financial statements:
    analysis/measurement of, 241–243, 274,
        311–312
    balance sheets as, 236–240
    budget reports as, 440–442
    income statements as, 227–236
Financing. *See* Lenders
Fisher, Irving, 275, 276
Flexibility:
    flexible budgets, 436–442
    flexible job design, 448, 453
    human capital management system flexibility,
        454
    leaders' ability for, 77–78, 79
Food and beverage, 329–331. *See also* Restaurants,
    specifically
Four Seasons Hotels and Resorts:
    business strategy of, 216, 217
    corporate culture of, 112, 116, 118–119, 120
    human capital initiatives in, 445
    leadership of, 74–75
    management contracts with, 294
Foursquare, 189, 383, 385
Franchises:
    benefits and disadvantages of, 298
    construction of, 319
    fees and major terms, 297–299, 393
    ownership via, 261, 263, 264, 266–267, 268,
        293–299, 312, 319, 393
Frequent buyer/guest programs, 354, 363–366,
    408
Function space, programming, 331

Gaylord Palms, 112, 116, 117–118, 120
General Motors, 78
Globalization, 445
Goals and objectives:
    employee motivation influenced by, 146
    leaders' role in, 73–75, 79

Google:
  Android, 380
  search engine marketing via, 198, 374, 385,
    409–410
Government, development support from, 311
Gowalla, 383
Griggs v. Duke Power Company, 422
Gross margin, 233–236
Guests:
  anticipation of, 104–109
  brand building analysis of, 395–396
  choices of, 83–96
  complaints of, 161–168
  decision factors of, asking about, 83–87
  demand of (*see* Demand management)
  discrete choice analysis predicting decisions
    of, 87–96
  feedback from, 161–172
  finer labeling influencing, 103
  fleetingness of experience for, 101–102
  frequent guest programs, 354, 363–366, 408
  guest feedback measurement systems,
    168–172
  guest room programming/design, 324–329
  guiding experience/perceptions of, 97–109
  hospitality toward, 5, 6–9, 13–18
  listening to, 37–50
  minimizing attention to unpleasantries of, 104
  observation of others' enjoyment by, 102–103
  pleasure sources for, 99–101
  positive awareness of, increasing, 97–98,
    98–104
  post-reservation contact with, 107–109
  satisfaction surveys by, 169–170
  service for (*see* Service)
  uncertainty mixed with imagery for, 102
  wait times for, 103, 105–107
Guidara, Frank, 473

Hampton Inns, 408
Hanlon, David, 15
Hard Rock Cafe, 268
Harrah's Entertainment, 146, 452–453
Harris v. Forklift Systems, 426
Hill, Lloyd, 472
Hillstone Restaurant Group, 446
Hilton Hotels Corporation:
  Hampton Inns, 208
  Hilton Garden Inn, 31, 396
  ownership in, 264, 269
  union negotiations with, 463, 464
Holiday Inn:
  brand relaunch of, 393, 403

business strategy of, 216
classification of, 259
corporate culture of, 112
integrity dividend in, 470
market segment of, 359
Hornbrook, John, 8, 12
Hortobagyi, Paul, 472–473
Hospitality, 5, 6–9, 13–18
Hospitality industry:
  awards in, 30–31
  brands in (*see* Brand)
  business strategy in (*see* Business strategy)
  careers in (*see* Career preparation)
  chains in (*see* Chains, corporate)
  compensation/rewards in (*see* Compensation)
  competition in (*see* Competition)
  complaint management in, 161–168
  corporate culture of (*see* Culture, corporate)
  corporate social responsibility in, 152–154
  demand management in (*see* Demand
    management)
  finances in (*see* Finances)
  guests in (*see* Guests)
  hospitality in, 5, 6–9, 13–18
  investment in (*see* Investment decisions)
  labor unions in (*see* Unions)
  leadership in (*see* Leadership)
  marketing in (*see* Marketing)
  multinational issues in (*see* Multinational careers;
    Multinational issues)
  operations in (*see* Operations)
  ownership in (*see* Ownership)
  personnel in (*see* Employees/staff; Human
    capital; Management)
  professional association in, 26
  quality assurance in (*see* Quality assurance)
  revenue management in (*see* Revenue
    management)
  service in (*see* Service)
  size of, 22, 247–249
  training and education in, 23, 26, 117–119,
    125, 220, 429, 450–451
Hospitality Properties Trust, 293
Hospitality Valuation Services, 289
Host Hotels and Resorts, 272, 293
Hotel Indigo, 209–210, 216
Hotels, specifically:
  chain scale and affiliation of, 259–260
  classification of, 256–260
  facilities and services of, 258
  food and beverage in, 329–331
  franchises, 297–298
  function/meeting space in, 331

guest decisionmaking about, 83–87, 90–92
guestrooms in, 324–329
industry size, 247–248
leases for, 305–306
loan choices for financing, 345–349
lobbies of, 329, 330
location of, 256–257
market orientation of, 257
new media usage by, 385–386
opening of, 320
ownership of, 250–253, 254–255
planning and programming, 315, 321–332
price tier of, 259
public areas in, 329–331
risk associated with, 333–350
union issues in, 466–468
valuation of, 278–281, 287–288, 314
Hotwire.com, 197, 411
Houdré, Hervé, 224
Human capital. See also Skills
  best practices, 446–454
  building on current, 23–24
  corporate culture supporting, 447
  defined, 22
  developing unique, 24–27
  emerging forces impacting, 445–446
  flexible job design supporting, 448, 453
  importance of, 444–446
  incentives/compensation rewards for,
    452–453
  leadership capabilities, 27–32
  performance evaluations impacting, 451–452
  recruitment and hiring procedures for, 449–450
  training and education developing, 450–451
Hyatt Hotels, 143, 156, 264, 294

IDeaS, 181, 189
IgoUgo, 377–378
Incentive fees, 302–304
Income, valuation consideration of, 276–286.
    See also Compensation
Income statement:
  cost of sales in, 230–233
  financial analysis using, 227–236
  gross margin in, 233–236
  sales/revenue in, 228–229
India, hospitality industry in, 22
Inflation, 338, 340, 345
Inkaterra Machu Picchu Pueblo
    Hotel, 100–101
Integrity:
  communicating, 473–475
  dividend, 469–475

employees treated with, 151
  leaders showing, 68, 77, 466, 469–479
  as personal discipline, 475–478
  tips for building, 477–478
InterContinental Hotel Group, 209, 216, 224, 393
  Candlewood Suites, 216
  Crowne Plaza, 216
  Holiday Inn, 112, 216, 259, 359, 393, 403, 470
  Hotel Indigo, 209–210, 216
Interest rates, 277, 314–315, 337–350
International issues. See Multinational careers;
    Multinational issues
Internet services. See New media
Interpersonal skills:
  corporate culture focus on, 125
  leaders need for, 29, 32, 67–68
  listening as, 37–50
Inventive skills, 31
Inventory, 231–232, 236–240
Investment centers, 434
Investment decisions:
  brokers/lenders impacting, 290
  cost approach to, 276, 288–289
  development-related, 315–318
  exit strategy for, 273–274
  factors to consider in, 271–273
  hospitality industry buying/selling as,
    289–291
  income approach to, 276–286
  investment objectives, 272–273
  investment philosophy, 272
  investment policies, 273
  location influencing, 291
  market timing impacting, 290, 291
  market value impacting, 274–276
  overview of, 270–271
  ownership as (see Ownership)
  rates of return on, 290
  sales-comparison approach to, 276,
    286–288
  valuation techniques for, 274–289

JDA, 179, 181, 190
JetBlue Airlines, 216, 218
Johnson, Michael D., 8, 12, 17
Joseph, Jim, 7, 11
Jumeirah Beach Hotel, 329

Kay, Michael, 471
Kelleher, Herb, 31, 112
Kimpton, Bill, 124
Kimpton Hotels & Restaurants, 124, 449
Kodak, 78

Koechlin, Jose, 100
Kruse, JoAnne, 152

Labor. *See* Employees/staff
Labor costs, 234. *See also* Compensation
Labor unions. *See* Unions
Language:
    corporate culture use of, 115
    foreign language knowledge, 56
Las Vegas Convention and Visitors Authority,
    400–401
Lawsuits. *See* Employee lawsuits
Leadership:
    awards for, 30–31
    corporate culture conveyed/reinforced by, 112,
        119, 120, 122–125
    defined, 65
    effectiveness of, 66
    employee motivation through, 154–155
    evolution of leadership roles, 66
    flexibility and adaptation in, 77–78, 79
    goals and objectives responsibilities of,
        73–75, 79
    integrity of, 68, 77, 466, 469–479
    interpersonal skills of, 29, 32, 67–68
    management *vs.*, 28, 65
    organizational understanding impacting,
        69–73, 79
    performance evaluation and response by,
        75–77, 79
    self-awareness and, 67–69, 78–79
    skill development for, 27–32, 67–78
    sphere of influence of, 65
    styles of, 69
    union strength due to poor, 459, 466–467
Leadership in Energy and Environmental Design
    (LEED) standards, 315
Learning opportunities. *See* Training and
    education
Leases:
    daily, hotel risk from, 333–334, 344–345, 350
    hotel-specific, 305–306
    management contracts *vs.*, 299, 305
    occupation expenses and, 235, 241, 285,
        305–307
    restaurant-specific, 306–307
Le Meridien, 448
Lenders:
    development capital from, 309, 314–315,
        315–318, 319
    hotel loan choices from, 345–349
    interest rates charged by, 277, 314–315,
        337–350

investment decision coordination with, 290
ownership capital supplied by, 256, 263,
    264–266, 301–302
rights of, 304
risk premiums charged by, 334–336, 338,
    339–340
Leondakis, NIki, 124
Limited liability companies (LLCs), 253, 254
Listening skills:
    assessment of current, 40–41
    corporate culture fostering, 39–40
    cultural bridging/teamwork development
        through, 39
    developing/practicing, 49–50
    importance of, 37–38, 40
    memory and, 41, 48–49, 50
    message clarity and, 41, 44–45, 50
    mistake avoidance using, 39
    paying attention and, 41, 42–43, 50
    speaker perceptions and, 41, 45–47, 50
Lobbies, hotel, 329, 330
Location:
    hotel classification by, 256–257
    investment decisions influenced by, 291
    restaurant classification by, 261
Loews Hotels and Resorts, 446
Longstreet, John, 33
Louviere, Jordan, 87
Loveman, Gary, 452–453
Low-cost leadership strategy, 215–216, 217–221

Maccioni, Sirio, 9, 13
Malcolm Knapp, 289
Management:
    business strategy of (*see* Business strategy)
    career preparation for (*see* Career preparation)
    contracts, ownership and, 263, 264–266, 268,
        293–295, 299–304, 312
    corporate culture of (*see* Culture, corporate)
    decisionmaking authority of, 430–431
    demand-related (*see* Demand management)
    employee motivation by (*see* Motivation,
        employee)
    families of, 56
    financial performance measurement of,
        201–206, 431–433, 436–442
    financial responsibility assigned to, 430–436
    guest choice insights from discrete choice
        modeling for, 93–96
    incentive fees for, 302–304
    integrity of, 68, 77, 466, 469–479
    leadership of (*see* Leadership)
    listening skills of, 40

networking among, 53–54
quality assurance program involvement of,
   159–172
regional and local, 189–190
responsibility centers for, 433–436
union relationships with (*see* Unions)
Marketing:
brand promise expressed using, 400–402
e-mail, 198, 410
mobile device, 379–381, 382–384
new media, 198, 200–201, 370–386, 409–410
search engine, 198, 200–201, 374–375, 385,
   409–410
social media, 375–381, 382–383
STP (segmentation, targeting, positioning),
   353–367
Market segmentation:
business classification by, 256–262
demand management and, 178–181, 187–189
differentiation strategy for, 215–217, 354, 362
frequent buyer programs as, 354, 363–366, 408
limits of, 354, 358–362, 366–367
low-cost leadership strategy for, 215–216,
   217–221
market orientation and, 257
methods of, 354–358
pricing and, 178–181, 187–189, 197, 412
revenue management and, 192–195, 203, 409
STP (segmentation, targeting, positioning)
   marketing, 353–367
studies on, 355–358, 367
target selection and, 358
Market share, 95
Market timing, 290, 291
Market value, 274–276. *See also* Valuation
Marriott, J. W. "Bill," Jr.:
award for, 30–31
corporate culture development by, 112, 123,
   124, 447
leadership approach of, 74, 123, 124
Marriott, J. W. "Bill," Sr., 112, 125
Marriott Corporation:
business strategy of, 220, 221
corporate culture of, 112, 123, 124,
   125, 447
Courtyard brand development by, 87, 221,
   359, 396
employee benefits/compensation of, 27
financial responsibility in, 433
integrity dividend in, 472–473
investment in, 272
leadership of, 30–31, 74, 123, 124
management contracts with, 293

ownership in, 255, 264, 269
Ritz-Carlton Hotels, 112, 115–116, 389, 446
Marshall, Alfred, 274–275
McDonald's Corporation, 160, 255, 268, 295
McFadden, Daniel, 87
Measurement systems:
brand testing and monitoring as, 402–403
feasibility study as, 313–314
financial performance, 201–206, 431–433,
   436–442
financial statement, 242–243, 274, 311–312
hiring assessments as, 449–450
hotel risk, 336–345
inventory turnover rate, 237–240
new media, 372–375, 378–379
PEST analysis as, 212–213
revenue management performance, 201–206
service quality assurance, 168–172
SWOT analysis as, 208
Meeting space, programming, 331
Mentors, 26
Meritor v. Vinson, 425–426
Meyer, Danny, 16
Milagro Properties, 215
Milestone, 190, 374, 379
Mission statements, 210–211
Misunas, Kathy, 182
Mobile devices:
application downloads to, 380, 381–382, 385
demand management impacted by, 183–184,
   187, 189–190
marketing strategy using, 379–381, 382–384
Models:
cost, 438–440
discounted cash flow, 277–281
discrete choice analysis, 87–96
income capitalization, 277
operations data, 130, 134–136
simulation, 134–136
Morton, Randy, 15
Motel 6, 217–218
Motivation, employee:
corporate culture influencing, 144, 150, 152,
   153–154
corporate social responsibility and, 152–154
employee empowerment as, 155–156
employee needs impacting, 145
equity of compensation influencing, 146–147
factors influencing, 144
financial rewards as, 144–149, 452–453
goals and expectancy influencing, 146
importance/value of, 142–143
job enjoyment as, 150

Motivation, employee: *(continued)*
 job interest as, 151–152
 leadership influencing, 154–155
 motivating characteristics of job, 154–156
 nonfinancial rewards as, 149–154, 453
 performance-based awards as, 147–149
 positive reinforcement as, 145–146
 recognition programs as, 149–150
 strategy for, 156–157
Mövenpick Hotels & Resorts, 445
Multinational careers:
 adjusting to, 57–59
 career opportunities, 22, 57–62
 corporate standards/policies and, 53, 61–62
 culture shock in, 58–59
 families impacted by, 56
 foreign language knowledge for, 56
 "going local" during, 60–61
 headquarters contact during, 60–62
 informants' helpfulness to, 59–60
 international skill development for, 54–56
 interpretation responsibilities in, 61–62
 modest behavior in, 59
 networking impacting, 53–54
 preparation for international assignments, 53–56
 reentry stress in, 62–63
Multinational issues. *See also* Multinational careers
 cultural differences as, 39, 46, 53, 54–56,
  58–59, 120
 globalization as, 445
 non-U.S. ownership as, 255–256, 268–269
Myriad Restaurant Group, 264
Mystery shopping programs, 171–172

Nair, Mohan, 16
National Labor Relations Act, 456–461,
 465–466
National Restaurant Association, 228, 243, 248,
 255, 261, 289
National Retail Properties, 272
Negative experiences, minimizing guests', 104
New media. *See also* Mobile devices
 corporate culture conveyed via, 447
 demand management impacted by, 183–187,
  189–190
 discrete choice analysis use of, 92
 electronic demand via, 184–187, 189–190
 e-mail marketing via, 198, 410
 guest decisionmaking influenced by, 83–85, 86
 hotel-specific use of, 385–386
 marketing strategy using, 198, 200–201,
  370–386, 409–410
 measurement metrics for, 372–375, 378–379
 minimizing unpleasantries using, 104

online travel agencies via, 183, 184–185,
  197, 198–201, 372–373, 377–378, 408,
  411–412, 414
 overview of, 370–372
 post-reservation guest contact via, 108–109
 private discounts marketed via, 198, 411–412
 restaurant-specific use of, 384–385
 search engine marketing/optimization via, 198,
  200–201, 374–375, 385, 409–410
 social media as, 375–381, 382–383
 Web sites as, 83–85, 183, 185, 312, 372–373,
  379–380
Ngonzi, Elizabeth, 16
Nielsen Claritas' PRIZM segmentation,
 354–355
Nieporent, Drew, 12
Nokia's Symbian, 380
Nonfinancial rewards:
 corporate social responsibility and, 152–154
 human capital incentives using, 453
 job interest as, 151–152
 job pleasure as, 150
 leaders' performance evaluations as, 75–77, 79
 recognition programs as, 149–150
Nonverbal communication, 46–47, 54–55
Nordstrom's, 112
Norms, corporate culture conveying, 112–114
NPD Group, 289

Obama administration, 465
Observational skills:
 international communication impacted by,
  54–55
 listening impacted by, 41, 42–43, 50
 service quality assurance using, 168–169
Occupation expenses, 235, 241, 285, 305–307
O'Flaherty, Shane, 7, 11
Omurgonulsen, Deniz, 8
Oncale v. Sundower, 426–427
Online travel agencies (OTAs):
 demand management via, 183, 184–185
 media metrics of, 372–373
 opaque distribution via, 197, 411–412, 414
 peer reviews via, 377–378
 revenue management impacted by, 197,
  198–201, 408, 411–412, 414
 strategic partnerships with, 408
Opaque distribution channels, 197,
 411–412, 414
OpenTable, 185, 189–190, 372
Operations:
 complexity of, 129, 133–134, 138
 data, accuracy, collection and modeling of,
  127–130, 134–136, 138–139

hotel classification by facilities and services, 258
reports and tools on, 139–141
restaurant table mix example of, 130–136
scientific approach to, 127–141
sense making skills for, 29–30
workforce staffing example of, 136–138
Orbitz, 198
Organizational structure:
  leadership understanding of, 69–73, 79
  ownership-related, 262–269, 282, 293–295, 312
  revenue management in, 203–204
OTAs. See Online travel agencies (OTAs)
Outback Steakhouse, 160, 164–165
Outsourcing, 221
Ownership:
  capital for, 256, 263, 264–266, 301–302
  development/renovation by (see Development, property)
  facility type/classification, 256–262
  forms of, 251–253
  franchise, 261, 263, 264, 266–267, 268, 293–299, 312, 319, 393
  hospitality industry-specific issues with, 253–256
  hospitality industry statistics on, 247–249
  investment decisions related to (see Investment decisions)
  issues to consider with, 256–262
  leases with (see Leases)
  management/operation on behalf of, 263, 264–266, 268, 293–295, 299–304, 312
  meaning of, 249–250
  multinational/non-U.S., 255–256, 268–269
  reasons for, 250–253
  risk associated with, 333–350
  structures of, 262–269, 282, 293–295, 312
  unions and owner/operator conflicts, 463–465

Pareto principle (80/20 rule), 43
Partnerships, 252–253, 254
Performance evaluations:
  financial performance measurements, 201–206, 431–433, 436–442
  human capital benefits from, 451–452
  leaders' responsibility for, 75–77, 79
  performance-based awards on, 147–149
Personnel. See Employees/staff; Management
PEST (political, economic, sociocultural, technological) analysis, 212–213
Pineapple hospitality symbol, 5
Policies and procedures:
  corporate culture communicated via, 114–115

discrimination avoidance using, 429
employee motivation supported in, 144
investment-related, 273
multinational adjustment to/of, 53, 61–62
Porter, Michael, 215–216
Positive reinforcement, 75–77, 79, 145–146
Priceline, 188, 197, 411
Pricewaterhouse Coopers study, 176–178
PriceYourMeal.com, 185
Pricing/prices. See also ADRs; RevPAR
  bundling rates and, 410–411, 414
  demand management and, 176–181, 187–189, 197, 218–219
  market response to, 176–178, 218–219
  market segmentation and, 178–181, 187–189, 197, 412
  market value reflected in, 274–276
  opaque distribution channels and, 197, 411–412, 414
  price tier hotel classification, 259
  price wars, 406–412
  private discounts on, 197–198, 411–412
  rate fences, 180–181, 194–195, 196, 197, 406–407, 412
  revenue management and, 192–201, 203, 406–412, 413–415
  valuation as basis for (see Valuation)
  variable and dynamic, 195–201
Private discounts, 197–198, 411–412
Process Framework for Strategic Branding, 393–402
Professional associations, 26. See also specific associations
Profit:
  centers, 433–434, 435–436
  development, 314
  employee profit sharing, 452
  integrity dividend impacting, 470–471

Programming and planning, hotel:
  development consideration of, 315, 321–332
  guest rooms, 324–329
  overview of, 321–324
  public areas, 329–331
Property. See Real estate
Property development. See Development, property
Property ownership. See Ownership
Proprietorships, 251–252, 254
PROS, 181, 190
Public areas, programming, 329–331
Puck, Wolfgang, 6, 11

Quality assurance:
  complaint management and, 161–168
  defined, 160–161

Quality assurance: *(continued)*
  guest measurement systems, 168–172
  service-oriented, 159–172
  Six Sigma, 170
  transaction- *vs.* relationship-focused process
    design, 161–165
Quality International, 359
Questions:
  active listening by asking, 45
  on guest decision factors, 83–87
  local informants answering, 59–60
  revenue management, 204–205

Rainmaker, 190
Rate fences, 180–181, 194–195, 196, 197,
    406–407, 412
Rates of return, 290. *See also* Interest rates
Raynor, Bruce, 462
Razumich-Zec, Maria, 7, 11
Real estate:
  capital for, 256, 263, 264–266, 301–302
  development/renovation of, 309–320,
    321–332
  franchises and, 261, 263, 264, 266–267, 268,
    293–299, 312, 319, 393
  investment decisions related to, 270–291
  leases, 235, 241, 285, 299, 305–307, 333–334,
    344–345, 350
  location of, 256–257, 261, 291
  management/operation of, 263, 264–266, 268,
    293–295, 299–304, 312
  occupation expenses associated with, 235, 241,
    285, 305–307
  ownership of *(see* Ownership)
  planning and programming space in,
    321–332
Receiving and storage, 231–232
Recipe management, 233
Recognition programs, 149–150
Recreational Boating & Fishing Foundation, 401
Recruitment procedures, 449–450
Rene v. Mirage, 427
Rental agreements. *See* Leases
Reputation management, 376
Respect, employees receiving, 151
Responsibility:
  centers, 433–436
  corporate social, 152–154
  decisionmaking, 122, 155–156, 430–431, 446
  financial, 430–436
  interpretation, 61–62
  leadership *(see* Leadership)
Restaurant Industry Operations Report, 243
Restaurant Industry Overview, 248

Restaurants
  affiliation of, 261
  classification of, 261–262
  finances of, 227–243
  franchises, 298–299
  guest decisionmaking about, 90
  hotel-based, 329–331
  industry size, 248–249
  leases for, 306–307
  location of, 261
  menu themes/classification of, 261–262
  new media usage by, 384–385
  ownership of, 255–256, 282
  recipe management in, 233
  service quality assurance in, 161–165
  size of, 261
  table mixes in, scientific approach to, 130–136
  valuation of, 281–286, 288
  wait times in, 103, 106–107
Revenue Analytics, 179, 181, 190
Revenue centers, 433–434, 435
Revenue management:
  actions impacting, 193–201
  defined, 192
  economy impacting, 198, 200, 202–203, 205,
    405–415, 436
  key questions about, 204–205
  market segmentation and, 192–195, 203, 409
  organizational structure for, 203–204
  performance measurement of, 201–206
  price war considerations in, 406–412
  pricing and, 192–201, 203, 406–412,
    413–415
  responsibility for, 435–436
  strategic planning of, 412–415
  variable and dynamic pricing for,
    195–201
RevPAR (revenue per available room):
  brand affiliation impacting, 391
  demand management use of, 177–178
  development consideration of, 312
  revenue management use of, 201–203,
    405–406, 415
Rewards. *See* Compensation; Nonfinancial
    rewards
Rezidor, 297
RIM Blackberry, 380
Risk, hotel:
  daily lease/variable cash flow as, 333–334,
    344–345, 350
  loan choices and, 345–349
  loan risk premiums, 334–336, 338,
    339–340
  measuring, 336–345

Rituals, corporate culture conveyed through, 117
Ritz, Cesar, 12
Ritz-Carlton, 112, 115–116, 389, 446
RMS, 179, 181, 190
Rose, Norm, 379
Rosewood Hotels & Resorts, 354
Royal Caribbean Cruise Line, 401, 402
Royal Caribbean International, 445
Rubicon, 181
Ryanair, 213, 215, 218

Sack, Burton "Skip," 6, 11
Salaries. *See* Compensation
Sales:
   comparable, valuation based on, 276, 286–288
   cost of, 230–233
   financial statements including, 228–229
   forecasting, 229
SAS, 179, 190
SAS Institute, 27
Satisfaction surveys, 169–170
Schedules, employee, 136–139, 234
Schultze, Horst, 112
Search engine marketing/optimization:
   hotel-specific use of, 385
   measurement metrics for, 374–375
   revenue management and, 198, 200–201,
     409–410
Seasonal demand, 136, 320
Self-awareness/self-perception, 40–41, 67–69,
   78–79
Sense making skills, 29–30
SEODigger.com, 409
Service:
   complaint management, 161–168
   corporate culture enhancing, 111–125
   guest measurement systems on, 168–172
   hospitality intersection with, 13–18
   maintaining quality, in economic
     downturns, 415
   meaning of, 9–13
   motivating staff to provide outstanding,
     142–157
   quality assurance for, 159–172
   service level classification, 262
   transaction- *vs.* relationship-focused, 161–165
Sexual harassment, 418, 425–429
Sharp, Isadore, 75, 112
Sharpe, John, 7, 11, 18
Six Sigma, 170
Skills. *See also* Human capital
   building on current, 23–24
   developing unique, 24–27
   integrity, 469–479

   international, 54–56
   interpersonal, 29, 32, 37–50, 67–68, 125
   inventive, 31
   leadership, 27–32, 67–78
   listening, 37–50
   observational, 41, 42–43, 50, 54–55,
     168–169
   sense making, 29–30
   visioning, 31
Smart phones. *See* Mobile devices
Smashburger, 388
Smith and Wollensky Steakhouse, 160
Smith Travel Research, 202, 259–260, 289
Social media, 375–381, 382–383. *See also* New
   media
Southwest Airlines, 31, 112, 121–122
Space allocation. *See* Programming and planning,
   hotel
Spring, Tony, 8, 12
St. James Hotel, 201
Staff. *See* Employees/staff
Starwood Hotels and Resorts:
   business strategy of, 212, 214, 220, 221
   financial responsibility in, 433
   human capital management by, 446
   leadership of, 68
   Le Meridien, 448
   W Hotels, 221, 402
   Westin, 222–223, 294
Statler, Ellsworth, 18
Statler Hotel, 85–87
Stickell, Darryl, 473–474
Stock options, 149
Stock-Yard Restaurant, 105
Stories, legends and heroes, corporate culture
   conveyed through, 115–116
STP (segmentation, targeting, positioning)
   marketing:
   frequent buyer programs in, 354, 363–366, 408
   limits of, 354, 358–362, 366–367
   market segmentation analysis in, 354–358, 367
   overview of, 353–354
   target selection in, 358
Strategy. *See* Business strategy
Stress, 48, 62–63
Supply chain management, 230–232
Suresi, Greg, 8, 12
Sweeney, Dennis J., 9, 13
SWOT (strengths, weaknesses, opportunities,
   threats) analysis, 208
Symbols, corporate culture conveyed
   through, 116
SynXis, 189
Sysco Corporation, 70

Taco Bell, 218
Taj Hotels and Resorts, 451
Talbott, Barbara, 118
Taverna Banfi, 163–164, 165
Teamwork:
   employee motivation through, 151–152
   group incentive compensation rewarding,
     147–149
   leaders using, 77–78, 79
   listening fostering, 39
Technological advances, 220, 446. *See also* New
   media
Technomic, 289
Teng, Ted, 15
TIG, 190, 374, 379
Training and education:
   availability of, 23
   corporate culture taught through, 117–119, 125
   discrimination avoidance through, 429
   human capital development through, 450–451
   learning curve in, 220
   learning-oriented relationships providing, 26
TravelCLICK, 181, 189, 374, 379
Travelocity, 183, 184–185, 198, 372, 377, 411
Travelport Ltd., 153–154
Trip Advisor, 186, 377
TripWolf, 380
Trust, integrity and, 472–473
Tune Hotels, 411
Twitter, 186, 378, 385

Uniform System of Accounts for Restaurants
   (USAR), 228
Uniform System of Accounts for the Lodging
   Industry (USALI), 278, 434
Unions:
   2006 summer negotiation with, 461–466
   addressing hotel-specific union issues,
     466–468
   card check and neutrality agreements,
     459–461, 462, 464–465, 466
   collective bargaining with, 467–468
   employee motivation influenced by, 155
   hospitality industry status of, 455–456
   labor law reforms impacting, 465–466
   National Labor Relations Act impacting,
     456–461, 465–466
   nonunionized businesses, 466–467
   traditional organizing drives by, 456–459
   UNITE HERE as, 459, 461–465
Union Square Hospitality Group, 445
Universal Studio, 107
Uno Chicago Grill, 450, 473
US Airways, 408

Valuation:
   appraisals of, 276
   cost approach, 276, 288–289
   development calculation of, 314
   discounted cash flow approach to, 277–281,
     336–345
   duration measuring sensitivity of, 336–337,
     339–345, 346–350
   hotels, specifically, 278–281, 287–288, 314
   income approach, 276–286
   investment decisions based on, 274–289
   market value, 274–276
   restaurants, specifically, 281–286, 288
   risk measurement using, 336–345
   sales-comparison approach, 276, 286–288
Value proposition, brand, 396–397
Values:
   corporate culture conveying, 112–113
   integrity/commitments conforming to,
     477–478
van Paasschen, Frits, 68
Vendors, supply chain management of, 230–232
Visioning skills, 31

Wait times, 103, 105–107
Walt Disney World Resort:
   corporate culture of, 112, 113–114, 114–115,
     116, 120
   demand management by, 179
   employee motivation at, 150
   new media usage by, 383
Ward, Peter, 463
Warfe, Nealy, 7, 11
Web sites:
   brand evaluation using, 312
   demand management via, 183, 185
   guest decisionmaking influenced by, 83–85
   media measurements of, 372–373
   mobile device access to, 379–380
Weisz, Stephen, 8, 12
Western Electric Company, 152
Westin, 222–223, 294
W Hotels, 221, 402
Wilhelm, John, 462
Willard InterContinental, 224
Wilson, Kemmons, 112, 359
Witham, Glenn, 8
Wyndham Hotels, 27

Yahoo!, 198, 409
Yum! Brands, 272
   Taco Bell, 218

Zagat, 189